T0202942

Lecture Notes in Artificial Intelligence   13054

Subseries of Lecture Notes in Computer Science

Series Editors

Randy Goebel
   University of Alberta, Edmonton, Canada
Yuzuru Tanaka
   Hokkaido University, Sapporo, Japan
Wolfgang Wahlster
   DFKI and Saarland University, Saarbrücken, Germany

Founding Editor

Jörg Siekmann
   DFKI and Saarland University, Saarbrücken, Germany

More information about this subseries at http://www.springer.com/series/1244

Charles Fox · Junfeng Gao ·
Amir Ghalamzan Esfahani ·
Mini Saaj · Marc Hanheide ·
Simon Parsons (Eds.)

Towards Autonomous Robotic Systems

22nd Annual Conference, TAROS 2021
Lincoln, UK, September 8–10, 2021
Proceedings

 Springer

Editors
Charles Fox 🆔
University of Lincoln
Lincoln, UK

Amir Ghalamzan Esfahani 🆔
University of Lincoln
Lincoln, UK

Marc Hanheide 🆔
University of Lincoln
Lincoln, UK

Junfeng Gao 🆔
University of Lincoln
Lincoln, UK

Mini Saaj 🆔
University of Lincoln
Lincoln, UK

Simon Parsons 🆔
University of Lincoln
Lincoln, UK

ISSN 0302-9743   ISSN 1611-3349   (electronic)
Lecture Notes in Artificial Intelligence
ISBN 978-3-030-89176-3   ISBN 978-3-030-89177-0   (eBook)
https://doi.org/10.1007/978-3-030-89177-0

LNCS Sublibrary: SL7 – Artificial Intelligence

© Springer Nature Switzerland AG 2021
This work is subject to copyright. All rights are reserved by the Publisher, whether the whole or part of the material is concerned, specifically the rights of translation, reprinting, reuse of illustrations, recitation, broadcasting, reproduction on microfilms or in any other physical way, and transmission or information storage and retrieval, electronic adaptation, computer software, or by similar or dissimilar methodology now known or hereafter developed.
The use of general descriptive names, registered names, trademarks, service marks, etc. in this publication does not imply, even in the absence of a specific statement, that such names are exempt from the relevant protective laws and regulations and therefore free for general use.
The publisher, the authors and the editors are safe to assume that the advice and information in this book are believed to be true and accurate at the date of publication. Neither the publisher nor the authors or the editors give a warranty, expressed or implied, with respect to the material contained herein or for any errors or omissions that may have been made. The publisher remains neutral with regard to jurisdictional claims in published maps and institutional affiliations.

This Springer imprint is published by the registered company Springer Nature Switzerland AG
The registered company address is: Gewerbestrasse 11, 6330 Cham, Switzerland

Preface

TAROS is the longest-running UK-hosted international conference on Robotics and Autonomous Systems (RAS), which is aimed at the presentation and discussion of the latest results and methods in autonomous robotics research and applications. TAROS offers a friendly environment for robotics researchers and industry to take stock and plan future progress. It welcomes senior researchers and research students alike and specifically provides opportunities for research students and young research scientists to present their work to the scientific community.

TAROS 2021 received 66 submitted papers, of which 45 were accepted (a 68 per cent acceptance rate) with 19 presented orally and 26 as posters. The number of submissions was lower than for a usual TAROS due to submissions taking place during the COVID-19 pandemic. Each paper was single-blind reviewed by at least three Program Committee members and scored from -3 to +3. TAROS is a UK-based conference but the Program Committee contained international members. TAROS aims to present the state of the art in the UK robotics community and to bring this community together so the Organizing Committee decided to retain a larger conference via a higher acceptance rate rather than reduce the size of the conference, so acceptances were made algorithmically for papers with threshold mean scores of 0 or more.

The main conference spanned two days. The first day focussed on algorithms and computer science, with sessions on reinforcement learning, perception, and co-operation. The second day focussed on systems, hardware and mechatronics, with sessions on robot design, sensing, and actuation. Linking to these themes, the keynotes talks were 'Towards Personal Assistive Robots' by Yannis Demeris (Imperial College London), 'An Uncertain Mission: Decision Making for Autonomous Robots' by Nick Hawes (University of Oxford), which was made public and sponsored by the IET, and 'Ant-inspired Robots' by Barbara Webb (University of Edinburgh). As is traditional, TAROS 2021 featured an extended presentation of the best paper from the UKRAS conference, which is included as 'Predicting Artist Drawing Activity via Multi-camera Inputs for Co-creative Drawing' by Chipp Jansen and Elizabeth Sklar. The conference took place remotely due to the COVID-19 pandemic and was hosted virtually by the University of Lincoln.

September 2021

Charles Fox
Junfeng Gao
Amir Ghalamzan Esfahani
Mini Saaj
Marc Hanheide
Simon Parsons

Organization

Organizing Committee

General Chairs

Simon Parsons   University of Lincoln, UK
Marc Hanheide   University of Lincoln, UK

Program Chair

Charles Fox   University of Lincoln, UK

Deputy Program Chair

Junfeng Gao   University of Lincoln, UK

Industry Chair

Mini Saaj   University of Lincoln, UK

Publicity Team

Amir Ghalamzan Esfahani   University of Lincoln, UK
Marcello Calisti   University of Lincoln, UK
Paul Baxter   University of Lincoln, UK

Program Committee

Farshad Arvin	University of Manchester, UK
Fernando Barbosa	KTH Royal Institute of Technology, Sweden
Nicolas Belanger	Airbus, UK
Nicola Bellotto	University of Lincoln, UK
Achim Buerkle	Loughborough University, UK
Marcello Calisti	University of Lincoln, UK
Fanta Camara	University of Leeds, UK
Yaniel Carreno	Edinburgh Centre for Robotics, UK
Grzegorz Cielniak	University of Lincoln, UK
Heriberto Cuayahuitl	University of Lincoln, UK
Gautham Das	Lincoln Agri-Robotics, UK
Abu Bakar Dawood	Queen Mary University of London, UK
Sumeyra Demir Kanik	KTH Royal Institute of Technology, Sweden
Sanja Dogramadzi	University of the West of England, UK
Xin Dong	University of Nottingham, UK
Fethiye Irmak Dogan	KTH Royal Institute of Technology, Sweden
Venketesh Dubey	Bournemouth University, UK

Khaled Elgeneidy	University of Lincoln, UK
Angelo Ferrando	University of Genova, Italy
Charles Fox	University of Lincoln, UK
Alexander Gabriel	University of Lincoln, UK
Junfeng Gao	University of Lincoln, UK
Thomas George Thuruthel	Scuola Superiore Sant'Anna, Italy
Amir Ghalamzan Esfahani	University of Lincoln, UK
Khaled Goher	University of Lincoln, UK
Roderich Gross	University of Sheffield, UK
Dongbing Gu	University of Essex, UK
Leonardo Guevara	Universidad Tecnica Fenderico Santa Maria, Chile
Marc Hanheide	University of Lincoln, UK
Helen Harman	University of Lincoln, UK
Ian Howard	University of Plymouth, UK
Lorenzo Jamone	Queen Mary University of London, UK
Chad Jenkins	University of Michigan, USA
George Jenkinson	University of Bristol, UK
Muhammad Khalid	University of Lincoln, UK
Mohammad Asif Khan	Aberystwyth University, UK
Quentin Lahondes	University of Sheffield, UK
Zhirong Liao	University of Nottingham, UK
Lupo Manes	University of Liverpool, UK
Alan Millard	University of York, UK
Abdelkhalick Mohammad	Rolls-Royce UTC, UK
Hector A. Montes	Universidad Autonoma del Estado de Mexico, Mexico
Pedro Neto	University of Coimbra, Portugal
Ana Paiva	INESC, Portugal
Simon Parsons	University of Lincoln, UK
Martin Pearson	BRL, UK
Ivan Petrunin	Cranfield University, UK
Riccardo Polvara	University of Lincoln, UK
Athanasios Polydoros	Aalborg University, Denmark
Stefan Poslad	Queen Mary University of London, UK
Mark Post	University of York, UK
Jizhong Xiao	The City College of New York, USA
Nicolas Rojas	Imperial College London, UK
Matthias Rolf	Oxford Brookes University, UK
Alessandra Rossi	University of Hertfordshire, UK
Matteo Russo	University of Nottingham, UK
Mini Saaj	University of Lincoln, UK
Alessandro Saffiotti	Orebro University, Sweden
Adrian Salazar Gomez	University of Lincoln, UK
David Sanderson	University of Nottingham, UK
Elizabeth Sklar	University of Lincoln, UK
Oliver Smith	University of Plymouth, UK
Mingfeng Wang	Rolls-Royce UTC, UK

Guowu Wei   University of Salford, UK
Andrew Weightman   University of Manchester, UK
Rob Worley   University of Sheffield, UK
Chenguang Yang   University of the West of England, UK
Ketao Zhang   Queen Mary University of London, UK
Tsvetan Zhivkov   University of Lincoln, UK
Chengxu Zhou   University of Leeds, UK
Sanne van Waveren   KTH Royal Institute of Technology, Sweden

Contents

Algorithms

Systems

Algorithms

A Study on Dense and Sparse (Visual) Rewards in Robot Policy Learning

Abdalkarim Mohtasib[1]([⊠]), Gerhard Neumann[2], and Heriberto Cuayáhuitl[1]

[1] Lincoln Centre for Autonomous Systems, University of Lincoln, Lincoln, UK
amohtasib@lincoln.ac.uk
[2] Autonomous Learning Robots, Karlsruhe Institute of Technology,
Karlsruhe, Germany

Abstract. Deep Reinforcement Learning (DRL) is a promising app-roach for teaching robots new behaviour. However, one of its main limi-tations is the need for carefully hand-coded reward signals by an expert. We argue that it is crucial to automate the reward learning process so that new skills can be taught to robots by their users. To address such automation, we consider task success classifiers using visual observations to estimate the rewards in terms of task success. In this work, we study the performance of multiple state-of-the-art deep reinforcement learning algorithms under different types of reward: Dense, Sparse, Visual Dense, and Visual Sparse rewards. Our experiments in various simulation tasks (Pendulum, Reacher, Pusher, and Fetch Reach) show that while DRL agents can learn successful behaviours using visual rewards when the goal targets are distinguishable, their performance may decrease if the task goal is not clearly visible. Our results also show that visual dense rewards are more successful than visual sparse rewards and that there is no single best algorithm for all tasks.

Keywords: Deep reinforcement learning · Reward learning · Robot learning

1 Introduction

In Deep Reinforcement Learning, the reward signal is typically carefully designed such that the agent can learn behaviour that achieves a good performance. But hand-coding and engineering rewards requires an expert to design it for each task to be learned, and it is often not easy to design rewards for robotic tasks. This limits the applications of DRL to real robots, especially when the end-user of the robot has to teach the robot new tasks. To address this limitation, it is crucial to find a mechanism that can autonomously and intuitively learn the rewards from a human expert for new tasks.

The problem of autonomous reward generation has been recently investigated in the literature by several researchers. Most previous works have used image-based success classifiers—as illustrated in Fig. 1—to learn the task's reward

© Springer Nature Switzerland AG 2021
C. Fox et al. (Eds.): TAROS 2021, LNAI 13054, pp. 3–13, 2021.
https://doi.org/10.1007/978-3-030-89177-0_1

[12,13,21–23,25–27,30]. [21] attempted to use transfer learning to learn the rewards for new tasks, but with slow prediction times (>0.5 s per interaction) that prevent its practical application. Other approaches used goal images to estimate the reward for each time step based on the difference between the goal and the current image, calculated in different ways [6,7,15,16,18,19]. While these approaches achieved good results in learning the task reward, they have not investigated the effects of different types of rewards on DRL agents. There is no clear study that shows how the different DRL algorithms perform with different types of reward in different tasks.

The reward learning pipeline starts with collecting expert demonstrations for the task at hand. Their images are then labelled as success/no-success. Subsequently, the labelled data is used to train an image-based success classifier that estimates the success probability for each environment state. This success probability is used as a dense or sparse (visual) reward signal, see Sect. 3.2.

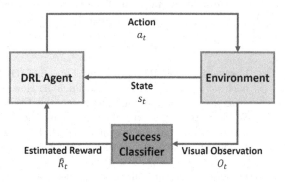

Fig. 1. System overview.

The contribution of this paper is a comparison of different types of rewards (Dense, Sparse, Visual Dense, and Visual Sparse) for learning manipulation tasks. Our study was carried out using four different DRL algorithms (DDPG, TD3, SAC, and PPO) in four different robotic tasks. Our results show that it is indeed possible to learn good policies using visual rewards, where the higher the quality of the success classifier the better the learnt policy. Our results also show that, while a DRL algorithm may perform very well in one task, it may perform poorly in another.

2   Related Work

The literature shows different ways to learn numerical rewards. Some previous works have used Inverse RL to estimate the reward function from demonstrations [1,3,8,9,29]. Here, we consider a setting where the expert labels the visual observations as success/no-success. We use these expert labels to train a success classifier to estimate the reward. This setting differs from the Inverse RL setting (no expert labels). Other approaches use visual representations of the goal state to define the vision-based task [6,7,15,16,18,19]. In these approaches, the goal image has been used in different ways to calculate the rewards: (i) using the latent distance between the current state image and the goal image [7,15,16]; (ii) using the pixel-wise L1 distance to the goal image [19]; or (iii) using the histogram distance to the goal image [6]. The approach of using a goal image to represent the task's success achieved good results. Yet this approach is limited as the goal could have different varieties and shapes. Furthermore, it is not always possible to represent the task goal using one or several images.

Our study focuses on the use of success classifiers to learn visual rewards of the task at hand [12, 13, 21–23, 25–27, 30]. The main neural network architecture that has been used for the task success classification is based on multiple convolutional blocks (convolutional layers followed by a max-pooling layer) followed by a multiple fully-connected layers [13, 22, 23, 26, 27, 30]. Sermanet et al. [21] used transfer learning of the Inception network [24] pre-trained for ImageNet classification [5] to extract the features from the environment's visual states. Subsequently, they used a simple neural network with multiple fully-connected layers to generate rewards from the extracted visual features [21]. However, the interaction of such a large image classifier slows down the execution of the manipulation task.

While some of the previous works have used dense rewards in their experiments [13, 21, 23, 25, 27], some others have only employed sparse rewards [12, 22, 26, 30]. The difference between dense and sparse rewards is important because, in many tasks, the only available reward is a sparse reward and this represents a big challenge for the DRL agent to learn the task's objective. Furthermore, different types of RL algorithms have been used in these works such as DDPG [26], SAC [23], A3C [12, 22], REINFORCE [27], and DQN [25]. While task success classifiers have been used in different ways with different RL algorithms in the literature, there is no ablation study in the literature studying the pros and cons (or effects) of different types of rewards for inducing robot policies. This paper aims to fill that gap. Our ablation study, using different DRL algorithms across multiple tasks, reveals the effects of oracle dense rewards, oracle sparse rewards, visual dense rewards, and visual sparse rewards.

3 Research Methods

3.1 Problem Formulation

We consider environments that can be framed as a Markov Decision Process (MDP) [2], where an agent receives a reward r_t after taking action a_t in the state s_t, then it progresses to the next state s_{t+1}. We focus on the discounted case, where The agent tries to maximise the cumulative discounted reward $G_t = \mathbb{E}_\tau \left[\sum_{t=0}^{T} \gamma^t R_t \right] = \mathbb{E}_\tau \left[\sum_{t=0}^{T} \gamma^t r(s_t, a_t) \right]$, where γ is the discount factor, $\tau = (s_0, a_0, \cdots)$ denotes the whole trajectory, $s_0 \sim p_0(s_0)$, $a_t \sim \pi(a_t|s_t)$, and $s_{t+1} \sim p(s_{t+1}|s_t, a_t)$. We consider a success classifier $\hat{R}_t = f(o_t)$, where o_t is a visual observation of the environment (an image), and $\hat{R}_t \in [0, 1]$ is the probability of having achieved the task in state s_t. We train $f(o_t)$ for a new manipulation task from N demonstrations by updating the parameters of this function to minimize $\sum \mathcal{L}(f(o_i), y_i)$, where $\mathcal{L}$ is the classification loss (cross entropy loss and mean square error in our case) and y_i is the image label. We assume that

Table 1. Rewards for training DRL agents. ϕ is the tilt angle of the pendulum in *radians*, D_R is the distance between the end-effector of the robotic arm and target position in the Reacher task, D_P is the distance between the object and target location in the Pusher task, and D_F is the distance between the gripper of the Fetch arm and target position.

Reward	Pendulum	Reacher	Pusher	Fetch
Dense	$-\|\phi\|$	$-D_R$	$-D_P$	$-D_F$
Sparse	$\begin{cases} 0, & \|\phi\| < 0.15 \\ -1, & \|\phi\| \geq 0.15 \end{cases}$	$\begin{cases} 0, & D_R \geq 0.01m \\ -1, & D_R < 0.01m \end{cases}$	$\begin{cases} 0, & D_P \geq 0.01m \\ -1, & D_P < 0.01m \end{cases}$	$\begin{cases} 0, & D_F \geq 0.01m \\ -1, & D_F < 0.01m \end{cases}$

a demonstrator classifies the ground truth images, which are used by such a probabilistic classifier to learn to generate rewards. The research question that our study aims to answer is: *Can DRL agents learn good policies by using visual rewards derived from task success classifiers?*

3.2   Rewards

For each task, we trained DRL agents using four different types of rewards in order to understand the effects of the different types. The agents were trained using true Dense and Sparse rewards, where they come directly from the physical simulator. The equations of Dense and Sparse rewards are shown in Table 1. In addition, we used Visual Dense and Visual Sparse rewards, which were calculated based on the estimated success probability using our (best) CNN-based success classifiers. While the Visual Dense rewards for all tasks were estimated according to $\hat{R}_t = 2 \times P\left(success = 1|o_t\right) - 1$, the Visual Sparse rewards were estimated according to $\hat{R}_t = \begin{cases} 0, & P\left(success = 1|o_t\right) \geq 0.5 \\ -1, & P\left(success = 1|o_t\right) < 0.5 \end{cases}$ Where $P\left(success = 1|o_t\right)$ is the success probability estimated by the success classifier.

3.3   Task Success Classifiers

We compare two different image classifiers trained using expert demonstrations, and use them to reward the DRL agents. The image classifiers are as follows.

- **CNN Classifier (CNN).** This is a standard CNN-based model that has been used in literature [7,9,13,21,23,25,26,30]. Its inputs are (160 160 3) resized images of the robotic environment, followed by six main convolutional blocks and one convolutional layer, see Fig. 2.
- **Time-Based CNN Classifier (T-CNN).** This architecture extends the CNN one with two pathways and features (shared in between): one is the classification path, the other is a timing path that predicts the proportion of task completion (a regressor), see Fig. 2. The task completion proportion for each image is calculated according to $y_t = \frac{t}{(j-1)}$, where t is a given time step, and j is the total number of time steps in the demonstration at hand. The timing path will add more gradient information and this aims to be helpful in predicting the task success.

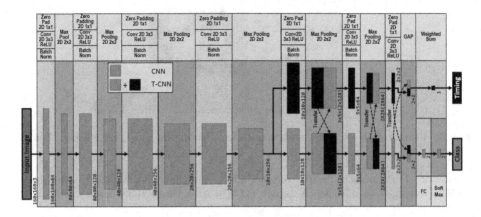

Fig. 2. Model architectures for task success classification with input images of (160 160 3). The Class output is the predicted success probability for both models. On the other hand, the Timing output is associated only with the T-CNN model. This output is the estimated task completion proportion (notation: **GAP** = Global Average Pooling).

3.4 Training Methodology

For each task, we collected a set of 10 successful demonstrations in different tasks (see Sect. 4.1). These demonstrations are used for training the success classifiers in each task. Each image in these demonstrations is labeled as success/no-success. We compare the performance of the classifiers across all tasks and use the best classifier to estimate the success probabilities from visual observations. Thereafter, we train DRL agents using four different learning algorithms[1] (DDPG [14], TD3 [10], SAC [11], and PPO [20]) with dense rewards and sparse rewards across four different tasks. Similarly, another group of DRL agents are trained but using visual dense rewards.

4 Experiments and Results

4.1 Training Tasks

We trained the DRL agents using the following OpenAI Gym Environments [4], see Fig. 3: (1) **Pendulum**. A simple one Degree-Of-Freedom (DOF) task with one continuous action to stabilize the inverted pendulum in the up position. In each episode, the pendulum initial tilt angle is random. (2) **Reacher**: In this task, the end-effector (the green point, see Fig. 3) of the two links robotic arm (2-DOFs) should reach the red target. The position of the red target is initialised randomly in each episode. (3) **Pusher**: The 7-DOFs robotic arm in Fig. 3 pushes the white object to the red target position. The position of the white object is initialised randomly in each episode. (4) **Fetch (Reach)**: The 7-DOFs Fetch

---

[1] We used a PyTorch implementation of the DRL algorithms [17].

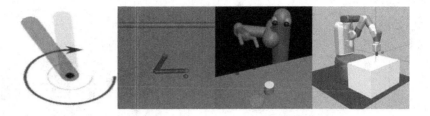

Fig. 3. Visualisation of our simulation tasks: Pendulum, Reacher, Pusher, Fetch (Reach).

Table 2. Performance results of the CNN and T-CNN classifiers (notation: **ACC** = Average Classification Accuracy, **AUC** = Area Under the Curve).

Task	CNN					T-CNN				
	ACC	Precision	Recall	F1 Score	AUC	ACC	Precision	Recall	F1 Score	AUC
Pendulum	1.000	1.000	1.000	1.000	1.000	1.000	1.000	1.000	1.000	1.000
Reacher	0.738	0.970	0.704	0.816	0.962	0.872	0.970	0.872	0.918	0.982
Pusher	0.990	0.992	0.994	0.993	1.000	0.992	0.994	0.994	0.994	1.000
Fetch	0.898	0.908	0.982	0.943	0.976	0.948	0.966	0.975	0.970	0.989
Average	0.907	0.968	0.920	0.938	0.985	**0.953**	**0.990**	**0.960**	**0.971**	**0.993**

robotic arm in Fig. 3 should reach the red target position that is initialised randomly in each episode. This is a realistic robotic task that simulates the real Fetch robot (https://fetchrobotics.com).

4.2   Success Classifiers Results

The CNN (Standard Convolutional Neural Net) and T-CNN (Time-Based CNN) image classifiers in each of the four tasks were trained with a set of 10 demonstration episodes and tested with another set of 10 demonstration episodes. Here, we test the ability of the success classifier to predict the success probability for each observation (image) in the test set. We assess the performance of success classification according to the following metrics: Classification Accuracy, Precision, Recall, F1-score, Area Under the Curve. Table 2 shows the test results of our classifiers, where the T-CNN classifier outperformed the CNN classifier in all classification metrics across all tasks. This suggests that the additional gradient information for predicting the task completion proportion helps in predicting the task success. Thus, the T-CNN model is adopted to estimate the success probabilities for the visual rewards.

4.3   Experimental Results of the DRL Agents

We evaluated different aspects in the performance of our DRL agents. First, we start with the learning curves of the DRL agents under the different settings as shown in Table 3. The most important outcome from these learning curves is that the DRL agents (except for PPO agents) were able to learn good policies

Table 3. Learning curves of DRL agents using different learning algorithms (DDPG, TD3, SAC, PPO) across four tasks when trained using dense, sparse, visual dense, and visual sparse rewards. The agents used five different seeds, 320 learning curves in total.

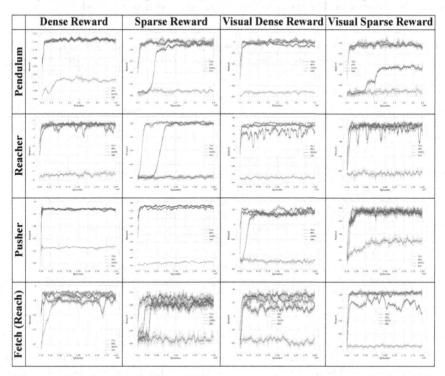

by using only the visual rewards that come from the success classifier. See the following video for example behaviours of the trained DRL agents[2].

It is crucial to test the learned policies to ensure that the visual rewards can be used to learn useful behaviours that lead to the successful execution of the tasks. Table 4 shows the test results of the learned policies. It is clear from these results that the visual rewards are indeed helpful in learning good successful behaviours—as noted by their success rates across tasks. On average, there is a small drop in performance when using visual rewards as the success classifier is error-prone. It can be noted that the drop in performance when using visual rewards is larger in the Reacher and the Fetch (Reach) tasks. With further investigation and experiments, we found that when the target object is behind the robotic arm, the visual images are not reflecting the correct environment's state. Thus, the success classifier fails to predict the correct success probability, and hence the drop in the performance in this task. The ranking of algorithms according to average success rate is as follows: DDPG ($81.4\% \pm 18\%$), SAC ($77.8\% \pm 20\%$), TD3 ($75.7\% \pm 26\%$), and PPO ($12.1\% \pm 21\%$).

---

[2] Video: https://youtu.be/8zOqEQDBleU.

Table 4. Performance of DRL algorithms across tasks. The maximum episode's length is 100 steps. Training and test times of DRL agents: training in HH:MM, and test in seconds. While 2 million steps were used in the **Pendulum** task, 10 million steps were used in the other tasks. The learnt policies were tested with 1000 episodes in each task.

Task	Agent	Dense reward		Sparse reward		Visual dense rew.		Visual sparse rew.	
		Success rate	Average eps. len.	Success rate	Average eps. len.	Success rate	Average eps. len.	Success rate	Average eps. len.
Pendulum	DDPG	98%	62.36	96%	59.68	96%	63.18	87%	53.88
	TD3	100%	62.53	87%	60.56	99%	58.19	87%	63.9
	SAC	95%	66.37	75%	61.76	99%	62.7	38%	61.12
	PPO	1%	60.77	2%	61.19	2%	51.86	4%	61.66
Reacher	DDPG	100%	51.87	97%	53.79	45%	82.16	62%	75.35
	TD3	98%	54.64	8%	97.28	52%	78.34	33%	83.99
	SAC	98%	52.93	97%	56.09	45%	80.38	47%	73.95
	PPO	6%	98.13	8%	95.01	11%	95.12	10%	95.6
Pusher	DDPG	91%	60.44	90%	59.94	80%	60.52	72%	69.38
	TD3	92%	62.8	87%	67.95	83%	66.25	80%	69.89
	SAC	95%	58.17	90%	63.16	87%	67.21	84%	63.1
	PPO	2%	99.46	19%	91.78	4%	98.78	14%	95.27
Fetch	DDPG	91%	52.23	88%	60.95	58%	73.25	51%	74.78
	TD3	94%	53.87	82%	58.07	64%	67.53	65%	68.13
	SAC	81%	58.52	82%	62.5	72%	67.83	59%	75.29
	PPO	90%	52.75	4%	98.11	13%	92.95	4%	97.41
Avg. success		77.00%	62.99	63.25%	69.24	56.88%	72.89	49.81%	73.92
Std. success		37.02%	14.67	38.89%	16.03	34.28%	13.85	29.78%	13.13

A statistical analysis using the Wilcoxon Signed-Rank Test (paired)[28] on the results of Table 4 revealed the following. Comparing Dense Success Vs. Sparse Success, the p-values are: $p = 1e-4$ including PPO, and $p = 6e-7$ excluding PPO. Comparing Visual Dense Success Vs. Visual Sparse Success, the p-values are: $p = 4e-4$ including PPO, and $p=0.016$ excluding PPO. Whilst the first comparison supports our claim that dense rewards are better than sparse ones, the second supports the claim that visual dense rewards are better than visual sparse rewards.

We carried out another statistical analysis using the Wilcoxon Signed-Rank Test (paired)[28] to compare the ranking of algorithms according to average success rate. While comparing DDPG Vs. TD3 gives a p-value of 0.236, comparing DDPG Vs. SAC gives $p = 0.182$. The differences are not significant and more comparisons are needed.

Table 5 reports training and test times of various experimented settings. Considering the training time[3] of agents using visual rewards, their training time is almost twice than non-visual rewards. Although such long training times should be addressed in future work, this cost comes with a large benefit where there is no need to hand-code the reward functions. Similarly and in contrast to agents using non-visual rewards, the test times of agents using visual rewards increase

---

[3] PC: **CPU**: Intel i7-6950 @ 3.00 GHz, 10 cores. **RAM**: 32 GB. **GPU**: NVIDIA TITAN X 12GB.

Table 5. Training and test times of DRL agents: training in HH:MM, and test in seconds. While 2 million steps were used in the **Pendulum** task, 10 million steps were used in the other tasks. The learnt policies were tested with 1000 episodes in each task.

	Task	Dense or Sparse reward				Visual reward			
		DDPG	TD3	SAC	PPO	DDPG	TD3	SAC	PPO
Training	Pendulum	05:45	05:47	09:10	04:12	16:22	16:15	22:27	10:30
	Reacher	27:02	19:18	45:50	12:16	45:24	51:42	77:56	18:40
	Pusher	29:07	27:49	35:01	12:11	47:00	45:59	60:35	29:58
	Fetch (Reach)	29:30	24:33	34:50	14:59	50:20	40:25	62:55	26:34
	Avg.	22:51	19:21	31:12	10:54	39:46	38:35	55:58	21:25
Test	Pendulum	17.03	17.28	16.22	16.75	46.02	33.15	33.90	43.35
	Reacher	16.53	17.42	17.75	17.18	45.60	43.55	47.63	49.03
	Pusher	17.54	17.09	15.84	16.76	44.53	45.17	47.93	46.59
	Fetch (Reach)	16.14	17.56	17.38	17.78	45.72	45.34	45.87	47.13
	Avg.	16.81	17.34	16.80	17.12	45.47	41.80	43.83	46.53

by about 30 ms for every environment step. We calculated the average test time for one environment step across tasks, which resulted in ∼45 ms—acceptable for real robotic tasks.

Furthermore, we investigated the effects of the choice of success classifier by comparing policies using our baseline and proposed success classifiers—CNN and T-CNN, respectively. Results show that while the performance of agents is similar in simple tasks (74% of task success on avg. across algorithms for both classifiers in the Pendulum task), T-CNN-based agents outperform CNN-based agents in more complex tasks (61.7% and 47.8% of an overall average task success across tasks, respectively), suggesting that the higher the performance of success classifiers the better learnt policies.

5 Conclusion and Future Work

This paper shows that it is indeed possible to learn successful policies from visual rewards, though with higher computational cost than non-visual rewards. Our experiments reveal the following. First, dense rewards can achieve higher task success than sparse rewards. Second, the better the success classifier the better the policy. Third, when images do not represent the correct state of the environment, this may lead to learning poor policies. Fourth, while one algorithm might be good in a given task, it may not performs well in another task. DDPG achieved the highest task success across tasks, but the differences in performance against other algorithms were not significant.

Future work will consist of investigating the proposed learned visual rewards on real robotic tasks and multiple robot platforms. Other future works with high potential contribution to the previous work include accelerating the training times of DRL agents, and improving their success rates across tasks.

References

1. Abbeel, P., Ng, A.Y.: Apprenticeship learning via inverse reinforcement learning. In: ICML (2004)
2. Bellman, R.: A Markovian decision process. J. Math. Mech. **6**(5) (1957)
3. Boularias, A., Kober, J., Peters, J.: Relative entropy inverse reinforcement learning. In: AISTATS (2011)
4. Brockman, G., et al.: OpenAI gym (2016)
5. Deng, J., Dong, W., Socher, R., Li, L.J., Li, K., Fei-Fei, L.: ImageNet: a large-scale hierarchical image database. In: CVPR (2009)
6. Edwards, A., Isbell, C., Takanishi, A.: Perceptual reward functions. arXiv preprint arXiv:1608.03824 (2016)
7. Edwards, A.D., Sood, S., Isbell, C.L., Jr.: Cross-domain perceptual reward functions. arXiv preprint arXiv:1705.09045 (2017)
8. Finn, C., Levine, S., Abbeel, P.: Guided cost learning: Deep inverse optimal control via policy optimization. In: ICML (2016)
9. Fu, J., Singh, A., Ghosh, D., Yang, L., Levine, S.: Variational inverse control with events: a general framework for data-driven reward definition. In: NIPS 31 (2018)
10. Fujimoto, S., Hoof, H., Meger, D.: Addressing function approximation error in actor-critic methods. In: ICML (2018)
11. Haarnoja, T., Zhou, A., Abbeel, P., Levine, S.: Soft actor-critic: off-policy maximum entropy deep reinforcement learning with a stochastic actor. In: ICML (2018)
12. Jaderberg, M., et al.: Reinforcement learning with unsupervised auxiliary tasks. arXiv preprint arXiv:1611.05397 (2016)
13. Levine, S., Pastor, P., Krizhevsky, A., Ibarz, J., Quillen, D.: Learning hand-eye coordination for robotic grasping with deep learning and large-scale data collection. IJRR **37**(4–5) (2018)
14. Lillicrap, T.P., et al.: Continuous control with deep reinforcement learning. In: ICLR (2016)
15. Nair, A., Bahl, S., Khazatsky, A., Pong, V., Berseth, G., Levine, S.: Contextual imagined goals for self-supervised robotic learning. In: CoRL (2020)
16. Nair, A.V., Pong, V., Dalal, M., Bahl, S., Lin, S., Levine, S.: Visual reinforcement learning with imagined goals. In: NIPS 31 (2018)
17. Raffin, A., Hill, A., Ernestus, M., Gleave, A., Kanervisto, A., Dormann, N.: Stable baselines3 (2019). https://github.com/DLR-RM/stable-baselines3
18. Sampedro, C., Rodriguez-Ramos, A., Gil, I., Mejias, L., Campoy, P.: Image-based visual servoing controller for multirotor aerial robots using deep reinforcement learning. In: IROS (2018)
19. Schoettler, G., et al.: Deep reinforcement learning for industrial insertion tasks with visual inputs and natural rewards. arXiv preprint arXiv:1906.05841 (2019)
20. Schulman, J., Wolski, F., Dhariwal, P., Radford, A., Klimov, O.: Proximal policy optimization algorithms. arXiv preprint arXiv:1707.06347 (2017)
21. Sermanet, P., Xu, K., Levine, S.: Unsupervised perceptual rewards for imitation learning. arXiv preprint arXiv:1612.06699 (2016)
22. Shelhamer, E., Mahmoudieh, P., Argus, M., Darrell, T.: Loss is its own reward: Self-supervision for reinforcement learning. In: ICLR (2017)

23. Singh, A., Yang, L., Hartikainen, K., Finn, C., Levine, S.: End-to-end robotic reinforcement learning without reward engineering. In: RSS (2019)
24. Szegedy, C., Vanhoucke, V., Ioffe, S., Shlens, J., Wojna, Z.: Rethinking the inception architecture for computer vision. In: CVPR (2016)
25. Tung, H.Y., Harley, A., Huang, L.K., Fragkiadaki, K.: Reward learning from narrated demonstrations. In: CVPR (2018)
26. Vecerik, M., Sushkov, O., Barker, D., Rothörl, T., Hester, T., Scholz, J.: A practical approach to insertion with variable socket position using deep reinforcement learning. In: ICRA (2019)
27. Wang, X., Chen, W., Wang, Y.F., Wang, W.Y.: No metrics are perfect: adversarial reward learning for visual storytelling. In: ACL (2018)
28. Wilcoxon, F.: Individual comparisons by ranking methods. In: Kotz, S., Johnson, N.L. (eds.) Breakthroughs in Statistics, pp. 196–202. Springer, Heidelberg (1992). https://doi.org/10.1007/978-1-4612-4380-9_16
29. Wulfmeier, M., Wang, D.Z., Posner, I.: Watch this: scalable cost-function learning for path planning in urban environments. In: IROS (2016)
30. Xie, A., Singh, A., Levine, S., Finn, C.: Few-shot goal inference for visuomotor learning and planning. In: CoRL (2018)

An Open-Source Multi-goal Reinforcement Learning Environment for Robotic Manipulation with Pybullet

Xintong Yang[1], Ze Ji[1(✉)], Jing Wu[2], and Yu-Kun Lai[2]

[1] Centre for Artificial Intelligence, Robotics and Human-Machine Systems (IROHMS), School of Engineering, Cardiff University, Cardiff, UK
{yangx66,jiz1}@cardiff.ac.uk

[2] School of Computer Science and Informatics, Cardiff University, Cardiff, UK
{wuj11,laiy4}@cardiff.ac.uk

Abstract. This work re-implements the OpenAI Gym multi-goal robotic manipulation environment, originally based on the commercial Mujoco engine, onto the open-source Pybullet engine. By comparing the performances of the Hindsight Experience Replay-aided Deep Deterministic Policy Gradient agent on both environments, we demonstrate our successful re-implementation of the original environment. Besides, we provide users with new APIs to access a joint control mode, image observations and goals with customisable camera and a built-in on-hand camera. We further design a set of multi-step, multi-goal, long-horizon and sparse reward robotic manipulation tasks, aiming to inspire new goal-conditioned reinforcement learning algorithms for such challenges. We use a simple, human-prior-based curriculum learning method to benchmark the multi-step manipulation tasks. Discussions about future research opportunities regarding this kind of tasks are also provided.

Keywords: Deep reinforcement learning · Simulation environment · Pybullet · Robotic manipulation · Multi-goal learning · Continuous control

1 Introduction

Due to the difficulties of reinforcement learning in real-world environments [5], developing simulation environments for robotic manipulation tasks becomes increasingly important. In addition to the requirement of being realistic, such simulation is also required to be efficient in generating synthetic data for training

The authors thank the China Scholarship Council (CSC) for financially supporting Xintong Yang in his PhD programme (No. 201908440400).

Electronic supplementary material The online version of this chapter (https://doi.org/10.1007/978-3-030-89177-0_2) contains supplementary material, which is available to authorized users.

© Springer Nature Switzerland AG 2021
C. Fox et al. (Eds.): TAROS 2021, LNAI 13054, pp. 14–24, 2021.
https://doi.org/10.1007/978-3-030-89177-0_2

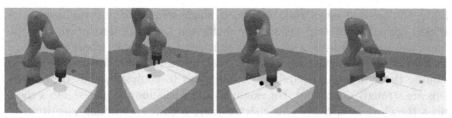

(a) From left to right: KukaReach, KukaPickAndPlace, KukaPush and KukaSlide.

(b) From left to right: BlockRearrange, ChestPush, ChestPickAndPlace, BlockStack

Fig. 1. The robotic arm manipulation tasks. (a) Single-step tasks, reproduced from the original OpenAI Gym multi-goal manipulation tasks [1,8] (described in Sect. 2.1). (b) Multi-step tasks (described in Sect. 2.2).

deep reinforcement learning (DRL) agents. Currently, the most popular physics engines in DRL research are Mujoco [13,16,17] and Pybullet [3,4,15]. Mujoco is known to be more efficient than Pybullet [6], but it is not open-sourced.

The cost of a Mujoco institutional license is at least $3000 per year [9], which is often unaffordable for many small research teams, especially when a long-term project depends on it. To promote wider accessibility to such resource and support DRL research in robot arm manipulations, we introduce an open-source simulation software, **PMG**, **P**ybullet-based, **M**ulti-goal, **G**ym-style [2]. It is written in Python, the most popular language in recent machine learning research[1].

The manipulation tasks proposed by [1,13] focus on goal-condition reinforcement learning (GRL) in sparse reward scenarios. GRL aims to train a policy that behaves differently when given different goals, for example, picking up different objects. While in sparse reward cases, the agent only receives a reward signal when a goal is achieved. This is motivated by the fact that providing task completion information is often easier and less biased than hand-designing a behaviour-specific reward function for most real-world robotic tasks [5].

We implement the four basic tasks (Fig. 1a) proposed in [1] using Pybullet and reproduce the performances achieved by the Deep Deterministic Policy Gradient (DDPG) algorithm with Hindsight Experience Replay (HER) [1,8].

In addition, we further propose a set of new tasks that focus on multi-step manipulations in longer horizon with sparse rewards (Fig. 1b). To improve read-

---

[1] The source codes are available at https://github.com/IanYangChina/pybullet_multigoal_gym.

ability, the original set of tasks is named 'single-step tasks' and the new set of tasks is named 'multi-step tasks'. The multi-step tasks are developed with the aim to inspire new learning algorithms that can handle tasks where the reward signals only appear near the end of the task horizon [5,18]. Beside the delayed rewards, these tasks also require multiple steps to complete, and some of the steps are strongly dependent. For example, a block cannot be placed into a chest unless the chest is opened. This characteristic requires a learning algorithm to reason about the relationships between steps.

To facilitate comparison in future research, we benchmarked the performances on the four multi-step tasks by training the aforementioned DDPG-HER agent [1] with a simple human prior-based curriculum. Potential research directions in this regard are also discussed. To sum up, our contributions in this article are:

- Reproducing the multi-goal robotic arm manipulation tasks [13] using Pybullet, making it freely accessible.
- Reproducing the Hindsight Experience Replay performances [1] on the Pybullet-based environments.
- Proposing a set of new environments for multi-goal multi-step long-horizon sparse reward robotic arm manipulations.
- Benchmarking the multi-step tasks and proposing future research opportunities.

The rest of this paper includes the details of the proposed environments and programming APIs (Sect. 2); the reproduction results of the DDPG-HER agent on the single-step tasks, the benchmark results of the multi-step tasks and discussions of challenges and future research (Sect. 3); and finally the conclusion (Sect. 4).

2   Environment

2.1   Single-Step Tasks

As shown in Fig. 1a, the single-step tasks are:

- KukaReach, where the robot needs to move the gripper tip to a goal location.
- KukaPickAndPlace, where the robot needs to pick up the block and move it to a goal location[2].
- KukaPush, where the robot needs to push the block to a goal location on the table surface.
- KukaSlide, where the robot needs to push the cylinder bulk with a force such that the bulk slides to a goal location that is unreachable by the robot.

---

[2] In training, the PickAndPlace goals are generated either on the table surface or in the air, with even probability, as suggested by [1].

Different from the original environments, which use a Fetch robot, we use a Kuka IIWA 14 LBR robot arm equipped with a simple parallel jaw gripper. This does not affect training as only Cartesian space control (gripper movement and finger width) are used in the original tasks. We plan to support more robot arms in the future.

In addition to the gripper frame control mode, our environments also support joint space control, which results in a 7 dimensional action space for the KukaReach and KukaPush tasks and an 8 dimensional one for the other two tasks (with one extra dimension for controlling the gripper finger width). Such a control mode has been largely ignored in most DRL-based manipulation works, possibly due to its high dimensionality. However, this control mode is important in scenarios that involve collision avoidance. A manipulation policy should not only consider end-effector control, but also learn to control each joint more explicitly when the surroundings are crowded by objects or other agents, e.g., humans. We leave the design of tasks for this specific direction to future work.

The tasks provide two reward functions. The dense reward function uses the negative Euclidean distance between the achieved and desired goals. The sparse reward function gives a reward of 0 when a goal is achieved and -1 everywhere else. We further provide RGB-D images as an optional observation representation. Users can easily define different camera view-points for rendering observations and goals.

Note that, we did not change the design of these four tasks, but reproduce them using a different physics engine. For more details of the task, such as the state and the action spaces, we refer the readers to the original paper [13]. The APIs and programming style are slightly different and are described in Sect. 2.3.

2.2 Multi-step Tasks

Figure 1b visualises the four challenging multi-step tasks developed by the authors, aiming at sparse reward long-horizon manipulations. Briefly, they are:

- BlockRearrange, where the robot needs to push the blocks to random positions. Gripper fingers are blocked in this task.
- ChestPush, where the robot needs to first open the sliding door (in black colour) of the chest and then push the blocks into the chest. Gripper fingers are blocked in this task.
- ChestPickAndPlace, where the robot needs to first open the sliding door (in black colour) of the chest and then pick and drop the blocks into the chest.
- BlockStack, where the robot needs to stack the blocks into a tower in a given order that is randomly chosen.

These tasks require the robot to learn different combinations of behaviours and provide different numbers of step dependencies. For example, the BlockStack task has more dependent steps with the increase of the number of blocks to be stacked. The complexity of these tasks increases with more dependent steps and blocks, as shown in Table 1. Moreover, the number of blocks involved in a task affects its task horizon, and thus its exploration difficulty. Detailed task information is provided in supplementary material Sect. 1.

Table 1. Multi-step tasks summary

Task	Needed behaviours	Step dependency	Num. of blocks
BlockReaarange	pushing	0	2 to 5
ChestPush	pushing	1	1 to 5
ChestPickAndPlace	pushing, picking, dropping	1	1 to 5
BlockStack	pushing, picking, placing	≥ 2	2 to 5

With the challenge of sparse reward in mind, the extreme case of these tasks is that the environment only gives a task completion signal (e.g., a reward of 0) when the ultimate goal (e.g., all the blocks are stacked) is achieved, and provides a reward of -1 everywhere else. In this case, the task is extremely difficult for any naive reinforcement learning algorithm, even the one with hindsight experience replay (see Sect. 3.2). This is because the reinforcement learning agent has an extremely low probability of seeing a meaningful reward value. Compared to the single-step tasks, which only feature the sparse reward problem in a short task horizon, these multi-step tasks can be used to investigate more difficult problems, such as

- How to explore efficiently for multi-step tasks with sparse and delayed rewards?
- How to represent and learn the dependencies among task steps?
- How can ideas such as curriculum learning, option discovery and hierarchical learning help in these tasks?

One possible research direction for these problems is to create a curriculum that provides the learning algorithm with goals starting from easy to difficult [11,12]. In this paper, we design a human-prior based curriculum for the multi-step tasks. It simply generates goals that require increasing time horizons to achieve, e.g., from stacking two blocks to five. However, the results show that such a simple curriculum is not efficient enough for longer horizon tasks (see Sect. 3.2). To tackle these problems, more efficient methods need to be developed. Section 3.3 provides more discussion on future research opportunities.

2.3   APIs and Programming Style

In OpenAI Gym, users create environment instances by specifying a unique task ID pre-registered in the package [2,13]. In contrary, we provide users with an API to make environments more intuitively. As shown in Code 1, the make_env(...) function provides arguments to setup a specific environment instance. Supplementary material Sect. 2 provides a detailed explanation of these arguments. Currently, only eight tasks are prepared, including four single-step tasks and four multi-step tasks.

We provide an argument to activate image observations and goals, while the original Gym environment requires users to rewrite some of the code to

---

Code 1. Create an environment instance

```
# Original OpenAI Gym style
import gym
env = gym.make("FetchReach-v0")
# Our style
import pybullet_multigoal_gym as pmg
env = pmg.make_env(
        # task args
        task='block_rearrange', joint_control=False, num_block=2, render=False,
        binary_reward=True, max_episode_steps=50, distance_threshold=0.05
        # image observation args
        image_observation=False, depth_image=False, goal_image=False,
        visualize_target=True,
        camera_setup=camera_setup, observation_cam_id=0, goal_cam_id=1,
        # curriculum args
        use_curriculum=True, num_goals_to_generate=1e6)

# Interaction loop
obs = env.reset()
while True:
        action = env.action_space.sample()
        obs, reward, done, info = env.step(action)
        if done:
                obs = env.reset()
```

---

achieve this. In addition, users can easily customise cameras for observation or goal images by defining a list of Python dictionaries and passing it to the camera_setup argument. An example is given in Code 2. Intuitively, the setup example defines two cameras, and in Code 1 they are used for capturing observation and goal images respectively, by setting the cam_id arguments to 0 and 1. Alternatively, users can pass −1 to the cam_id arguments, activating an on-hand camera looking at the gripper tip position. Figure 2 shows a scene and three images rendered with the above-mentioned cameras.

Except for the codes that create an environment instance, other user APIs are kept the same as the original multi-goal Gym environment package. In our experiments, the code of training the DDPG-HER agent needs no change from Mujoco to Pybullet, and we successfully reproduce the performances as shown in Sect. 3.1.

3   Benchmark and Discussion

In Sect. 3.1, we reproduced the Hindsight Experience Replay (HER) [1] on the single-step tasks to demonstrate the success of the transfer from the Mujoco-based environments to ours. More specifically, we trained a DDPG agent using the 'future' goal-relabelling strategies, with the same hyperparameters and design

Code 2. A list of camera setup dictionary	Meaning

```
camera_setup = [
    {
        'cameraEyePosition': [-1.0, 0.25, 0.6],        the 3D coordinates of the camera
                                                        frame in the world frame
        'cameraTargetPosition': [-0.6, 0.05, 0.2],     the 3D coordinates which the cam-
                                                        era looks at in the world frame
        'render_width': 128,                            the width of the rendered image
        'render_height': 128                            the height of the rendered image
    },
    {

        'cameraEyePosition': [-1.0, -0.25, 0.6],
        'cameraTargetPosition': [-0.6, -0.05, 0.2],
        'render_width': 128,
        'render_height': 128
    }

]
```

    (a) Scene   (b) Camera 1   (c) Camera 2   (d) On-hand camera

Fig. 2. Images rendered using the two cameras defined in Code 2 and the built-in on-hand camera.

proposed in [1], except that we did not use distributed training. In addition, we also trained the same agent on the single-step tasks with joint control. Section 3.2 shows the results of training the DDPG-HER agent on the multi-step tasks. The results serve as a benchmark for future studies. Section 3.3 provides challenges and future research opportunities.

The Pytorch implementation of the algorithm is available here. The experiment scripts are available here. All experiments were run on Ubuntu 16.04 on a workstation with an Intel i7-8700 CPU and an Nvidia RTX-2080Ti GPU. All performance statistics are averaged from 4 runs with different random seeds.

3.1   Reproducing Hindsight Experience Replay on Single-Step Tasks

For comparison, we ran the same DDPG-HER algorithm [1] with the same hyperparameters on the
Mujoco- and our Pybullet-based environments. As
shown in Fig. 4, the agent achieved almost the same
performances on the both environments[3]. These
results demonstrate our successful transplantation
of the single-step tasks onto the Pybullet engine.
Running an episode of the Reach task in Mujoco
took 0.079 ± 0.007 s, and in PMG, 0.272 ± 0.011 s
(averaged over 100 episodes for 10 random seeds).

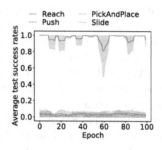

Fig. 3. DDPG-HER performances on Joint space control tasks.

Beside the original tasks, we also ran the experiments with joint space control using the same algorithm. These joint space control tasks differ from
the original gripper frame control tasks in that the robot's actions are now joint
commands, and the state representation further includes the current joint states.
Results show that, in comparison to gripper frame control mode, single-step tasks
under joint space control mode are harder to learn (Fig. 3). Its performance on
the easiest Reach task also shows higher variance.

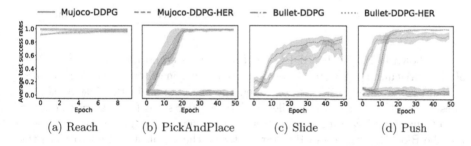

(a) Reach   (b) PickAndPlace   (c) Slide   (d) Push

Fig. 4. Test success rates of the single-step tasks on Mujoco or Pybullet engine.

This is expected as the action space has higher dimensionality. On the other
hand, the gripper is constrained to be pointing top-down under the gripper frame
control mode, but this constraint is released under the joint space control mode.
This makes the tasks harder to learn by increasing the size of its solution space.

For future research, it is valuable to develop reinforcement learning algorithms that can handle such control tasks with higher action dimensionality and
larger solution space, potentially from (depth-) image observations. Investigating harder tasks including collision avoidance and comparing with classic motion
planning methods are interesting directions as well.

---

[3] Note that the Slide task is sensitive to the random seeds in both environments. The
agent was unable to learn anything in some cases. It also exhibited higher variance
than other tasks.

3.2 Benchmarking Multi-step Tasks

This section discusses the performances of the DDPG-HER agent [1] on the multi-step tasks, with and without the use of the proposed simplistic curriculum (supplementary material Sect. 3). We benchmarked the tasks without a chest using 2, 3, 4 blocks, and the tasks with a chest using 1, 2, 3 blocks.

We made one modification to the agent for these tasks. The action values predicted by the critic network are clipped within $[-50, 0]$ in the single-step tasks as suggested by [1], because the lowest value is -50 under sparse reward setting, given that the maximum episode timestep is 50 [13]. For the multi-step tasks, we changed the lower bound of the clipped value range to the negative maximum episode timestep for each task.

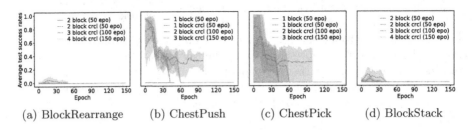

(a) BlockRearrange   (b) ChestPush   (c) ChestPick   (d) BlockStack

Fig. 5. Test success rates of the multi-step tasks. 'crcl' means 'curriculum'.

As shown in Fig. 5, the DDPG-HER agent learned nothing without the help of the curriculum (blue line in each subplot). When aided by the curriculum, it could achieve the easiest steps (open the chest door) in the ChestPush and ChestPickAndPlace tasks, but failed at later harder steps (success rates quickly drop to near 0 as learning proceeds, shown by the orange, green and red lines). For the BlockRearrange and BlockStack tasks, the agent struggled to learn the easiest steps even with the help of the curriculum. This is because exploring to open the chest door is easier than moving a block around. These results indicate that these sparse rewards multi-step tasks are still unsolvable given the current state-of-the-art reinforcement learning algorithms.

3.3 Challenges and Opportunities

This section discusses the challenges and future research opportunities related to the sparse reward multi-step robotic manipulation tasks from two perspectives, including exploration efficiency and representation learning. From each of them, there are several research directions that can be focused on.

Exploration: In sparse reward environments, improving exploration efficiency has long been a research challenge in the field of DRL [14]. However, current research has been restricted within toy problems (e.g., grid world) or the Atari games (e.g., Montezuma's Revenge). These are all 2D tasks with discrete action spaces. Robotic manipulations are tasks in a 3D world, with larger and richer observations and continuous action spaces. It would be valuable to evaluate techniques that work in the 2D tasks on our 3D and continuous action tasks, with the hope to improve them further and transfer to the real-world.

In the multi-goal setting, we have demonstrated the insufficiency of the HER aided by a simplistic goal generation curriculum. It is then potentially fruitful to develop a better curriculum for such tasks. Another interesting direction is to leverage task decomposition for multi-step tasks and make use of hierarchical learning systems [18]. The use of sub-goals is a promising way to tackle the hard exploration problem in such tasks.

Representation Learning: Representation for RL agents, especially in sparse reward tasks, has been increasingly active recently. Different from supervised learning tasks, RL agents rely on the reward signals to learn a representation of the environment and the task altogether. This makes it hard to generate and maintain a good representation in sparse reward tasks, in which the representation learnt can easily collapse. Again, current state-of-the-art in this direction has been largely restricted within 2D tasks or tasks with short horizon [7,10], and our environment is a promising testbed for evaluating and improving them in a 3D world with longer task horizons.

4 Conclusion

We propose an open-source robotic manipulation simulation software implementation for multi-goal multi-step deep reinforcement learning. The implementation of the OpenAI multi-goalstyled environment (based on the Mujoco engine) has been achieved using Pybullet. Performance of the popular DDPG-HER algorithm has been reproduced in our work (Sect. 3.1). Except for the original manipulation tasks, named **single-step tasks**, we designed a set of **multi-step tasks** with sparse rewards in longer task horizons. We benchmarked the performances of the DDPG-HER agent with and without the use of a simplistic goal generation curriculum (Sect. 3.2), demonstrating the inability of the state-of-the-art algorithms to learn in such long horizon and sparse reward environments. Finally, we provided brief discussions of the challenges and future research opportunities, including EXPLORATION and REPRESENTATION LEARNING in sparse reward reinforcement learning. Our future research will focus on developing sub-goal-based solutions to tackle such multi-step sparse reward robotic manipulation tasks.

References

1. Andrychowicz, M., et al.: Hindsight experience replay. In: NIPS, pp. 5048–5058 (2017)
2. Brockman, G., et al.: Openai gym. arXiv preprint arXiv:1606.01540 (2016)
3. Coumans, E., Bai, Y.: Pybullet, a python module for physics simulation for games, robotics and machine learning (2016–2019). http://pybullet.org

4. Delhaisse, B., Rozo, L., Caldwell, D.G.: Pyrobolearn: a python framework for robot learning practitioners. In: Conference on Robot Learning, pp. 1348–1358. PMLR (2020)
5. Dulac-Arnold, G., Mankowitz, D., Hester, T.: Challenges of real-world reinforcement learning. ICML (2019)
6. Erez, T., Tassa, Y., Todorov, E.: Simulation tools for model-based robotics: comparison of bullet, havok, mujoco, ode and physx. In: 2015 IEEE international conference on robotics and automation (ICRA), pp. 4397–4404. IEEE (2015)
7. Laskin, M., Srinivas, A., Abbeel, P.: Curl: contrastive unsupervised representations for reinforcement learning. In: International Conference on Machine Learning, pp. 5639–5650. PMLR (2020)
8. Lillicrap, T.P., et al.: Continuous control with deep reinforcement learning. In: ICLR (2016)
9. LLC, R.: Mujoco: advanced physics simulation (2018). http://www.mujoco.org/
10. Lyle, C., Rowland, M., Ostrovski, G., Dabney, W.: On the effect of auxiliary tasks on representation dynamics. arXiv preprint arXiv:2102.13089 (2021)
11. Manela, B., Biess, A.: Curriculum learning with hindsight experience replay for sequential object manipulation tasks. arXiv preprint arXiv:2008.09377 (2020)
12. Narvekar, S., Peng, B., Leonetti, M., Sinapov, J., Taylor, M.E., Stone, P.: Curriculum learning for reinforcement learning domains: a framework and survey. J. Mach. Learn. Res. 21(181), 1–50 (2020)
13. Plappert, M., et al.: Multi-goal reinforcement learning: challenging robotics environments and request for research. arXiv preprint arXiv:1802.09464 (2018)
14. Rashid, T., Peng, B., Boehmer, W., Whiteson, S.: Optimistic exploration even with a pessimistic initialisation. In: ICLR (2020)
15. Shen, B., et al.: iGibson, a simulation environment for interactive tasks in large realistic scenes. arXiv preprint arXiv:2012.02924 (2020)
16. Tassa, Y., et al.: Deepmind control suite. arXiv preprint arXiv:1801.00690 (2018)
17. Todorov, E., Erez, T., Tassa, Y.: Mujoco: a physics engine for model-based control. In: 2012 IEEE/RSJ International Conference on Intelligent Robots and Systems, pp. 5026–5033. IEEE (2012)
18. Yang, X., et al.: Hierarchical reinforcement learning with universal policies for multistep robotic manipulation. IEEE Trans. Neural Netw. Learn. Syst. (2021)

CPG-ACTOR: Reinforcement Learning for Central Pattern Generators

Luigi Campanaro[✉], Siddhant Gangapurwala, Daniele De Martini,
Wolfgang Merkt, and Ioannis Havoutis

Oxford Robotics Institute, Oxford, UK
{luigi,siddhant,daniele,wolfgang,ioannis}@robots.ox.ac.uk

Abstract. Central Pattern Generators (CPGs) have several properties desirable for locomotion: they generate smooth trajectories, are robust to perturbations and are simple to implement. However, they are notoriously difficult to tune and commonly operate in an open-loop manner. This paper proposes a new methodology that allows tuning CPG controllers through gradient-based optimisation in a Reinforcement Learning (RL) setting. In particular, we show how CPGs can directly be integrated as the Actor in an Actor-Critic formulation. Additionally, we demonstrate how this change permits us to integrate highly non-linear feedback directly from sensory perception to reshape the oscillators' dynamics. Our results on a locomotion task using a single-leg hopper demonstrate that explicitly using the CPG as the Actor rather than as part of the environment results in a significant increase in the reward gained over time (20× more) compared with previous approaches. Finally, we demonstrate how our closed-loop CPG progressively improves the hopping behaviour for longer training epochs relying only on basic reward functions.

Keywords: Central Pattern Generators · Reinforcement Learning · Feedback control · Legged robots

1 Introduction

The increased manoeuvrability associated with legged robots in comparison to wheeled or crawling robots necessitates complex planning and control solutions. The current state-of-the-art for high-performance locomotion are modular, model-based controllers which break down the control problem in different submodules [1]. This rigorous approach is rooted in the knowledge of every portion of the motion, but it is also limited by heuristics handcrafted by engineers at each of the stages.

While the field of legged robot control has been dominated over the last decades by conventional control approaches, recently, data-driven methods demonstrated unprecedented results that outpaced most of the classical approaches in terms of robustness and dynamic behaviours [2]. In particular, controllers trained using deep-RL utilise a Neural Network (NN) policy to map

© Springer Nature Switzerland AG 2021
C. Fox et al. (Eds.): TAROS 2021, LNAI 13054, pp. 25–35, 2021.
https://doi.org/10.1007/978-3-030-89177-0_3

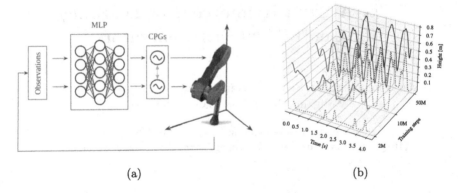

(a)   (b)

Fig. 1. The experiments are carried out on a classic Reinforcement Learning (RL) benchmark – the single-leg hopper based on the ANYmal quadruped robot [3]. It hops along the vertical axis and is controlled by Central Pattern Generators (CPGs). Closed-loop feedback is incorporated using a jointly trained Multilayer Perceptron (MLP) network (a). To demonstrate that the CPG-Actor progressively learns to jump higher peaks of both the hip (solid line) and foot (dotted line) heights (b) are shown.

sensory information to low-level actuation commands. As a result, controllers trained with RL exhibit behaviours that cannot be hand-crafted by engineers and are further robust to events encountered during the interaction with the environment. However, widely-used NN architectures, such as MLP, do not naturally produce the oscillatory behaviour exhibited in natural locomotion gaits and as such require long training procedures to learn to perform smooth oscillations.

A third family of controllers have been used with promising results for robot locomotion: CPGs, a biologically-inspired neural network able to produce rhythmic patterns. However, very few design principles are available, especially for the integration of sensor feedback in such systems [4] and, although conceptually promising, we argue that the full potential of CPGs has so far been limited by insufficient sensory-feedback integration.

The ability of Deep-NNs to discover and model highly non-linear relationships among the observation – the inputs – and control signals – the outputs – makes such approaches appealing for control. In particular, based on Deep-NNs, Deep-RL demonstrated very convincing results in solving complex locomotion tasks [2,5] and it does not require direct supervision (but rather learns through interaction with the task). Hence, we argue that combining Deep-RL with CPGs could improve the latter's comprehension of the surrounding environment. However, optimising Deep-NN architectures in conjunction with CPGs requires adequate methods capable of propagating the gradient from the loss to the parameters, also known as backpropagation.

To address this, this paper introduces a novel way of using Deep-NNs to incorporate feedback into a fully differentiable CPG formulation, and apply Deep-RL to jointly learn the CPG parameters and MLP feedback.

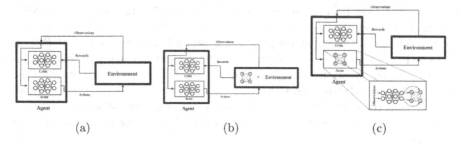

Fig. 2. (a) represents the basic actor-critic Deep-RL method adopted for continuous action space control. (b) illustrates the approach proposed in [10–13], which consists in a classic actor-critic with CPGs embedded in the environment. (c), instead, is the approach proposed in the present work, which includes the CPGs alongside the MLP network in the actor critic architecture.

1.1 Related Work

Our work is related to both the fields of CPG design and RL, in particular to the application of the latter for the optimisation of the former's parameters.

CPGs are very versatile and have been used for different applications including non-contact tasks such as swimmers [6], modular robots [7] and locomotion on small quadrupeds [8]. The trajectories CPGs hereby generate are used as references for each of the actuators during locomotion and a tuning procedure is required to reach coordination. The optimisation of CPG-based controllers usually occurs in simulation through Genetic Algorithms (GA), Particle Swarm Optimisation (PSO) or expert hand-tuning [6,8].

To navigate on rough terrain sensory feedback is crucial (e.g. in order to handle early or late contact), as shown in [9]: here, a hierarchical controller has been designed, where CPGs relied on a state machine which controlled the activation of the feedback.

Similarly to [8,9] also uses feedback, this time based on gyroscope velocities and optical flow from a camera to modify the CPGs output in order to maintain balance. However, in [8] the authors first tune CPGs in an open-loop setting and then train a NN with PSO to provide feedback (at this stage the parameters of the CPGs are kept fixed). We follow the same design philosophy in the sense that we preprocess the sensory feedback through a NN; yet, we propose to tune its parameters in conjunction with the CPG.

Actor-critic methods [14] rely on an explicit representation of the policy independent from the value function Fig. 2a.

Researchers applied RL to optimise CPGs in different scenarios [10]. The common factor among them is the formulation of the actor-critic method; yet, they include the CPG controller in the environment – as depicted in Fig. 2b. In other words, the CPG is part of the (black-box) environment dynamics. According to the authors [13], the motivations for including CPGs in the environment are their intrinsic recurrent nature and the amount of time necessary to train them, since CPGs have been considered Recurrent Neural Networks (RNNs) (which are computationally expensive and slow to train). In [10] during training and inference, the policy outputs a new set of parameters for the CPGs in response to observations from the environment at every time-step. Conversely, in [13] the parameters are fixed and, similarly to [8], CPGs receive inputs from the policy. However, whether the CPGs parameters were new or fixed every time-step, they all considered CPGs as part of the environment rather than making use of their recurrent nature as stateful networks. We exploit this observation in this paper.

1.2   Contributions

In this work, we combine the benefits of CPGs and RL and present a new methodology for designing CPG-based controllers. In particular, and in contrast to prior work, we embed the CPG directly as the actor of an Actor-Critic framework instead of it being part of the environment. The advantage of directly embedding a dynamical system is to directly encode knowledge about the characteristics of the task (e.g., periodicity) without resorting to recurrent approaches. The outcome is CPG-ACTOR, a new architecture that allows end-to-end training of coupled CPGs and a MLP for sensory feedback by means of Deep-RL. In particular, our contributions are:

1. For the first time – to the best of our knowledge – the parameters of the CPGs can be directly trained through state-of-the-art gradient-based optimisation techniques such as Proximal Policy Optimisation (PPO) [15], a powerful RL algorithm). To make this possible, we propose a fully differentiable CPG formulation (Sect. 2.1) along with a novel way for capturing the state of the CPG without unrolling its recurrent state (Sect. 2.1).
2. Exploiting the fully differentiable approach further enables us to incorporate and jointly tune a MLP network in charge of processing feedback in the same pipeline.
3. We demonstrate a roughly twenty times better training performance compared with previous state-of-the-art approaches (Sect. 4).

2   Methodology

As underlying oscillatory equation for our CPG network, we choose to utilise the Hopf oscillator [16] in a tensorial formulation, Eq. (2).

Differently to previous approaches presented in Sect. 1.1, we embed CPGs directly as part of the actor in an actor-critic framework as shown in Fig. 2c. Indeed, the policy NN has been replaced by a combination of an MLP network for sensory pre-processing and CPGs for action computation, while the value function is still approximated by an MLP network.

In practice, in our approach the outputs of the actor are the position commands for the motors. In [10], instead, the actor (MLP-network) outputs the parameters of the CPGs, that are then used by the environment (that includes the CPGs) to compute the motor commands. In this sense, there is a substantial difference in the architectures: in CPG-Actor, both the CPGs' and MLP's parameters are trained, while in [10] only the MLP's parameters are trained and the CPGs' ones are derived at runtime, being the output of the network.

However, a naïve integration of CPGs into the Actor-Critic formulation is error-prone and special care needs to be taken i) to attain differentiability through the CPG actor in order to exploit gradient-based optimisation techniques; ii) not to neglect the hidden state as CPGs are stateful networks.

We are going to analyse these aspects separately in the following sections.

2.1 Differentiable Central Pattern Generators

Since equations in [16] describe a system in continuous time, we need to discretise them for use as a discrete-time robot controller, as in Eq. (1):

$$
\begin{aligned}
\dot{\theta}_i^t &= 2\pi\nu_i(d_i^t) + \zeta_i^t + \xi_i^t \\
\zeta_i^t &= \sum_j r_j^{t-1} w_{ij} \sin(\theta_j^{t-1} - \theta_i^{t-1} - \phi_{ij}) \\
\ddot{r}_i^t &= a_i(\tfrac{a_i}{4}(\rho_i(d_i^t) - r_i^{t-1}) - \dot{r}_i^{t-1}) + \kappa_i^t \\
x_i^t &= r_i^t \cos(\theta_i^t)
\end{aligned}
\tag{1}
$$

where $\cdot^t$ describes the value at the t-th time-step, θ_i and r_i are the scalar state variables representing the phase and the amplitude of oscillator i respectively, ν_i and ρ_i determine its intrinsic frequency and amplitude as function of the input command signals d_i, and a_i is a positive constant governing the amplitude dynamics. The effects of the couplings between oscillators are accounted in ζ_i and the specific coupling between i and j are defined by the weights w_{ij} and phase ϕ_{ij}. The signal x_i represents the burst produced by the oscillatory centre used as position reference by the motors. Finally, ξ_i and κ_i are the feedback components provided by the MLP network.

In order to take advantage of modern technology for parallel computation, e.g. GPUs, there is a strong need to translate the equations in [16] into a tensorial formulation (2) which describes the system in a whole enabling batch computations. Let N be the number of CPGs in the network, then:

$$
\begin{aligned}
\dot{\Theta}^t &= 2\pi C_\nu(V, D^t) + Z^t \mathbf{1} + \Xi^t \\
Z^t &= (WV) * (\Lambda R^{t-1}) * \sin(\Lambda\Theta^{t-1} - \Lambda^\intercal\Theta^{t-1} - \Phi V) \\
\ddot{R}^t &= (AV) * (\tfrac{AV}{4}(P(V, D^t) - R^{t-1}) - \dot{R}^{t-1}) + K^t \\
X^t &= R^t \cos(\Theta^t)
\end{aligned}
\tag{2}
$$

Here, $\Theta \in \mathbb{R}^N$ and $R \in \mathbb{R}^N$ are the vectors containing θ_i and r_i, while $\Xi \in \mathbb{R}^N$ and $K \in \mathbb{R}^N$ contain ξ_i and κ_i respectively. $V \in \mathbb{R}^M$ contains the M, constant parameters to be optimised of the network composed by the N CPGs. This said, $C_\nu : \mathbb{R}^M, \mathbb{R}^d \to \mathbb{R}^N$, $P : \mathbb{R}^M, \mathbb{R}^d \to \mathbb{R}^N$ and $A \in \mathbb{R}^{N \times M}$ are mappings from the set V and the command $D^t \in \mathbb{R}^d$ to the parameters that lead ν_i, ρ_i and a_i respectively. $Z \in \mathbb{R}^{N \times N}$ instead takes into consideration the effects

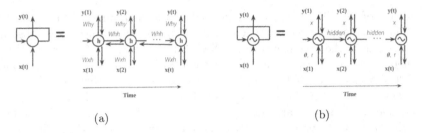

(a)   (b)

Fig. 3. The images above show the difference between back-propagation for classic RNNs (a) and CPGs (b). In particular to train RNNs, the matrices W_{xh}, W_{hy}, W_{hh} have to be tuned, where W_{hh} regulates the evolution between two *hidden states*. Instead, for CPGs only the parameters in $\dot{\theta}_i$ and $\ddot{r}_i$ (Eq. (2)) need tuning, while the evolution of the *hidden state* is determined by an integration operation.

of the couplings of each CPG to each CPG; all the effect to i-th CPG will be then the sum of the i-th row of Z as in $Z\mathbf{1}$, where $\mathbf{1}$ is a vector of N elements with value 1. Within Z, $W \in \mathbb{R}^{N \times N \times M}$ and $\Phi \in \mathbb{R}^{N \times N \times M}$ extrapolate the coupling weights and phases from V, while $\Lambda \in \mathbb{R}^{N \times N \times N}$ encodes the connections among the nodes of the CPG network.

The reader can notice how in (2) only already-differentiable operations have been utilised and that the MLP's output, i.e. the CPG' feedback, is injected as a sum operation, enabling the gradient to backpropagate through the MLP network as well. This further enables us to compute the gradient of each of the parameters in (2) (CPGs and MLP) with respect to the RL policy's loss using the auto differentiation tools provided by PyTorch.

Recurrent state in CPGs. In order to efficiently train CPGs in a RL setting, we need to overcome the limitations highlighted in [13]: In fact, CPGs are considered similar to RNNs (due to their internal state) and consequently they would have taken a significant time to train. In this section, we show how we can reframe CPGs as stateless networks and fully determine the state from our observation without the requirement to unroll the RNN.

RNNs are stateful networks, i.e. the state of the previous time-step is needed to compute the following step output. As a consequence, they are computationally more expensive and require a specific procedure to be trained. RNNs rely on Backpropagation Through Time (BPTT), Fig. 3a, which is a gradient-based technique specifically designed to train stateful networks. BPTT unfolds the RNN in time: the unfolded network contains t inputs and outputs, one for each time-step. Undeniably, CPGs have a recurrent nature and as such require storing the previous hidden state. However, differently from RNNs, the transition between consecutive hidden states, represented by the matrix W_{hh}, in CPGs is determined a priori through simple integration operations without the need of tuning W_{hh}. This observation has two significant consequences: Firstly, CPGs do not have to be unrolled to be trained as the output is fully determined given the previous state and the new input. Secondly, eliminating W_{hh} has the additional benefit of preventing gradient explosion or vanishing during training, Fig. 3b. As a result, CPGs can be framed as a stateless network on condition that the previous state is passed as an input of the system.

3   Evaluation

We evaluate our method on a classic RL benchmark: the hopping leg [17], which due its periodic task is a great fit for the application of CPGs. In fact, a single leg Fig. 1a needs only two joints to hop and this is the minimal configuration required by coupled Hopf-oscillators to express the complete form; less than two would cancel out the coupling terms [16].

We based the environment on a single leg of the ANYmal quadruped robot, which was fixed to a vertical slider. Its mass is 3.42kg, it is actuated by two series-elastic actuators capable of 40N m torque, a maximum joint velocity of $15\,\mathrm{rad\,s^{-1}}$ and controlled at 400Hz. We use PyBullet [18] to simulate the system and use a data-driven method to capture the real system's actuator dynamics.

At every time-step the following observations are captured: the joints' measured positions p_j^m and velocities v_j^m, desired positions p_j^d, the position p_h and the velocity v_h of the hip attached to the rail. While the torques t_j^d and the planar velocity of the foot $v_f^{x,y}$ are instead used in computing the rewards, as described in the following. To train CPG-ACTOR, we formulate a reward function as the sum of five distinct terms, each of which focusing on different aspects of the desired system:

$$r_1 = (1.2 \cdot \max(v_h, 0))^2 \qquad\qquad r_4 = \sum_J -1.e^{-4} \cdot \left(t_j^d\right)^2$$

$$r_2 = \sum_J -0.5e^{-2} \cdot \left(p_j^d - p_j^m\right)^2 \qquad r_5 = -1.e^{-2} \cdot \left\|v_f^{x,y}\right\| \qquad (3)$$

$$r_3 = \sum_J -1.e^{-3} \cdot \left(v_j^m\right)^2$$

where J stands for joints.

In particular, r_1 promotes vertical jumping, r_2 encourage the reduction of the error between the *desired position* and the *measured position*, r_3 and r_4 reduce respectively the *measured velocity* and the *desired torque* of the motors and finally, r_5 discourage the foot from slipping.

3.1   Experimental Setup

CPG-ACTOR is compared against [10] using the same environment. Both approaches resort to an actor-critic formulation, precisely running the same critic network with two hidden layers of 64 units each. Indeed, the main difference is the actor, which is described in detail in Sect. 2 for the CPG-ACTOR case, while [10] relies on a network with two hidden layers of 64 units each.

We trained the approaches for 20M time steps using an Nvidia Quadro M2200 GPU and an Intel(R) Xeon(R) E3-1505M v6 @ 3.00 GHz CPU (8 cores) CPU; the process lasted roughly 2 h.

As Sect. 4 illustrates, an appropriate comparison between CPG-ACTOR and [10] required the latter to be warm-started to generate *desired positions* resulting in visible motions of the leg. Differently from the salamander [16], already tuned parameters are not available for the hopping task, hence a meaningful set from [9] was used as reference. The warm-starting consisted in training the actor network for 100 epochs in a supervised fashion using as target the aforementioned parameters.

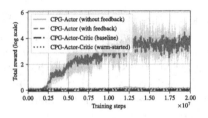

(a) Episode reward over 20M time steps horizon.

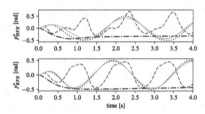

(b) Desired positions generated by CPG-Actor-Critic [10] and CPG-ACTOR.

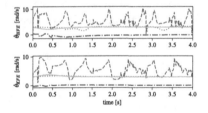

(c) Comparison between $\dot{\theta}$, eq. (2), generated by CPG-Actor-Critic [10] and CPG-ACTOR.

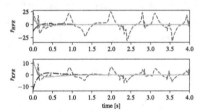

(d) Comparison between $\ddot{r}$, eq. (2), generated by CPG-Actor-Critic [10] and CPG-ACTOR.

Fig. 4. (a) represents how the reward evolves during training, each approaches run five times and averaging the rewards. (b) trajectories generated by the different approaches: [10] warm-start produces an output similar to CPG-ACTOR without feedback. While CPG-ACTOR with feedback presents a heavily reshaped signal. The different contribution of the feedback in the two aforementioned approaches is explained by (c) and (d). The feedback – in CPG-ACTOR case – is interacting with the controller, resulting into visibly reshaped $\dot{\theta}$ and $\ddot{r}$ (green lines).

4 Results

4.1 CPG-ACTOR and Previous Baselines, Comparison

The results of the comparison between CPG-ACTOR ans [10] can be seen in Fig. 1a. Although the warm-starting procedure results in a performance improvement for [10] (red line vs blue line), CPG-ACTOR (green line) achieves roughly a twenty times higher reward after 20 million training time-steps.

We investigated the reason of such different performances and we argue it lies in the way the feedback affects the CPG controller. Figures 4c and 4d represent the evolution over time of the CPGs. Observing $\dot{\theta}$ and $\ddot{r}$ in experiments with [10] it is evident they do not show responsiveness to the environment, since the blue and the red lines remain almost flat during the whole episode. On the other hand, $\dot{\theta}$ and $\ddot{r}$ in CPG-ACTOR experiments (green line) demonstrate substantial and roughly periodic modifications over time. Although [10] relies on feedback information to infer the CPGs dynamics, in practise the effects of the feedback signals on the shape of the output variables are rather weak when compared to CPG-ACTOR, as visible in Fig. 4b: in the case of CPG-ACTOR the original CPG's cosine output is heavily reshaped by the feedback, while [10] presents an almost-sinusoidal behaviour. Hence, to achieve successful hopping strong feedback information is crucial.

To further assess our intuition, we show CPG-ACTOR's open-loop (i.e. without feedback) behaviour (orange line), which shows performances on par with [10] after warm-start. Indeed, albeit explicitly penalised by Eq. (3), both led to policies with the foot sliding on the floor and, as such, with low vertical velocity (yet slightly oscillating as if hopping); this behaviour results in low final rewards even after a large number of training episodes (20 M). It is then evident that the direct propagation of the gradient through a differentiable CPGs allows CPG-ACTOR to learn an effective correction to the open-loop behaviour through the sensor feedback.

4.2 Evaluation of Progressive Task Achievement

The last set of experiments presented assess how CPGs' outputs and the overall behaviour evolve over the course of the learning. The plots in Fig. 1 present the system at 1, 20 and 50 million time-steps of training. Figure 1b, shows the progress of the hopper in learning to jump; indeed, the continuous and dotted lines – respectively indicating the hip and the foot position – start quite low at the beginning of the training, to almost double the height after 50 millions time-steps.

5 Discussion and Future Work

We propose CPG-ACTOR, an effective and novel method to tune CPG controllers through gradient-based optimisation in a RL setting.

In this context, we showed how CPGs can directly be integrated as the Actor in an Actor-Critic formulation and additionally, we demonstrated how this method permits us to include highly non-linear feedback to reshape the oscillators' dynamics.

Our results on a locomotion task using a single-leg hopper demonstrated that explicitly using the CPG as an Actor rather than as part of the environment results in a significant increase in the reward gained over time compared with previous approaches.

Finally, we demonstrated how our closed-loop CPG progressively improves the hopping behaviour relying only on basic reward functions.

In the future, we plan to extend the present approach to the full locomotion task by utilising the same architecture shown in Fig. 1a with a CPG-network made of 12 neurons in order to be able to control a quadruped robot with 12 DOFs.

Acknowledgements. This work was supported by the EPSRC grant 'Robust Legged Locomotion' [EP/S002383/1], the UKRI/EPSRC RAIN [EP/R026084/1] and ORCA [EP/R026173/1] Hubs and the EU H2020 Project MEMMO (780684). The Titan V used for this research was donated by the NVIDIA Corporation. This work was part of the Human-Machine Collaboration Programme, supported by a gift from Amazon Web Services.

References

1. Bellicoso, C.D., Jenelten, F., Gehring, C., Hutter, M.: Dynamic locomotion through online nonlinear motion optimization for quadrupedal robots. IEEE Robot. Autom. Lett. **3**(3), 2261–2268 (2018)
2. Lee, J., Hwangbo, J., Wellhausen, L., Koltun, V., Hutter, M.: Learning quadrupedal locomotion over challenging terrain. Sci. Rob. **5**(47) (2020). https://robotics.sciencemag.org/content/5/47/eabc5986
3. Hutter, M., et al.: Anymal - a highly mobile and dynamic quadrupedal robot. In: Proceedings of the IEEE/RSJ International Conference on Intelligent Robots and Systems (IROS), pp. 38–44 (2016)
4. Righetti, L., Ijspeert, A.J.: Pattern generators with sensory feedback for the control of quadruped locomotion. In: Proceedings of the IEEE International Conference on Robotics and Automation (ICRA), pp. 819–824, May 2008
5. Hwangbo, J., et al.: Learning agile and dynamic motor skills for legged robots. Sci. Rob. **4**(26) (2019). https://robotics.sciencemag.org/content/4/26/eaau5872
6. Ijspeert, A.J.: Central pattern generators for locomotion control in animals and robots: a review. Neural Netw. **21**(4), 642–653 (2008)
7. Bonardi, S., et al.: Automatic generation of reduced CPG control networks for locomotion of arbitrary modular robot structures. In: Proceedings of the Robotics: Science and Systems (RSS) (2014)
8. Gay, S., Santos-Victor, J., Ijspeert, A.: Learning robot gait stability using neural networks as sensory feedback function for central pattern generators. In: Proceedings of the IEEE/RSJ International Conference on Intelligent Robots and Systems (IROS), pp. 194–201 (2013)
9. Ajallooeian, M., Gay, S., Tuleu, A., Spröwitz, A., Ijspeert, A.J.: Modular control of limit cycle locomotion over unperceived rough terrain. In: Proceedings of the IEEE/RSJ International Conference on Intelligent Robots and Systems (IROS), Tokyo, pp. 3390–3397 (2013)
10. Cho, Y., Manzoor, S., Choi, Y.: Adaptation to environmental change using reinforcement learning for robotic salamander. Intell. Serv. Robot. **12**(3), 209–218 (2019). https://doi.org/10.1007/s11370-019-00279-6

11. Ciancio, A.L., Zollo, L., Guglielmelli, E., Caligiore, D., Baldassarre, G.: Hierarchical reinforcement learning and central pattern generators for modeling the development of rhythmic manipulation skills. In: 2011 IEEE International Conference on Development and Learning (ICDL), vol. 2, pp. 1–8 (2011)

12. Nakamura, Y., Mori, T., Sato, M., Ishii, S.: Reinforcement learning for a biped robot based on a CPG-actor-critic method. Neural Netw. **20**(6), 723–735 (2007)

13. Fukunaga, S., Nakamura, Y., Aso, K., Ishii, S.: Reinforcement learning for a snake-like robot controlled by a central pattern generator. In: Proceedings of the IEEE International Conference on Mechatronics and Automation (ICMA), vol. 2, pp. 909–914 (2004)

14. Sutton, R.S., Barto, A.G.: Reinforcement Learning: An Introduction, 2nd edn. The MIT Press (2018). http://incompleteideas.net/book/the-book-2nd.html

15. Schulman, J., Wolski, F., Dhariwal, P., Radford, A., Klimov, O.: Proximal policy optimization algorithms. CoRR, vol. abs/1707.06347 (2017). http://arxiv.org/abs/1707.06347

16. Ijspeert, A.J., Crespi, A., Ryczko, D., Cabelguen, J.-M.: From swimming to walking with a salamander robot driven by a spinal cord model. Science **315**(5817), 1416–1420 (2007)

17. Brockman, G., et al.: OpenAI Gym (2016). http://arxiv.org/abs/1606.01540

18. Coumans, E., Bai, Y.: Pybullet, a python module for physics simulation for games, robotics and machine learning (2016–2020). http://pybullet.org

Deep Semantic Segmentation of 3D Plant Point Clouds

Karoline Heiwolt$^{(\boxtimes)}$, Tom Duckett, and Grzegorz Cielniak$^{(\boxtimes)}$

Lincoln Centre for Autonomous Systems, University of Lincoln, Lincoln, UK
{kheiwolt,gcielniak}@lincoln.ac.uk

Abstract. Plant phenotyping is an essential step in the plant breeding cycle, necessary to ensure food safety for a growing world population. Standard procedures for evaluating three-dimensional plant morphology and extracting relevant phenotypic characteristics are slow, costly, and in need of automation. Previous work towards automatic semantic segmentation of plants relies on explicit prior knowledge about the species and sensor set-up, as well as manually tuned parameters. In this work, we propose to use a supervised machine learning algorithm to predict per-point semantic annotations directly from point cloud data of whole plants and minimise the necessary user input. We train a PointNet++ variant on a fully annotated procedurally generated data set of partial point clouds of tomato plants, and show that the network is capable of distinguishing between the semantic classes of leaves, stems, and soil based on structural data only. We present both quantitative and qualitative evaluation results, and establish a proof of concept, indicating that deep learning is a promising approach towards replacing the current complex, laborious, species-specific, state-of-the-art plant segmentation procedures.

Keywords: 3D perception · Semantic segmentation · Plant phenotyping

1 Introduction

The global agriculture industry currently faces the challenges of adapting to new climates and reducing its environmental impact, while also feeding a fast-growing world population. One essential effort needed to overcome these challenges is the breeding of new high-yielding plant varieties with various resistances to environmental stresses. While recent advances in plant genome research enable quick development of new plant genotypes, *plant phenotyping*, i.e. evaluation of the plant's structure, performance, and physiological and biochemical traits, is a slow and laborious process, which is considered as a bottleneck in the plant breeding cycle. Thus, there is great demand for fully automated high-throughput in-field phenotyping [16]. Importantly, many essential measurements can be extracted directly from the morphology of the plant. The introduction of new 3D sensing technologies and mobile agricultural robots opens up possibilities for in-field data collection and automation of the morphological analysis. Thus, in

© Springer Nature Switzerland AG 2021
C. Fox et al. (Eds.): TAROS 2021, LNAI 13054, pp. 36–45, 2021.
https://doi.org/10.1007/978-3-030-89177-0_4

recent years there have been a number of scientific contributions towards capturing and automatically interpreting three-dimensional (3D) structural models of plants. To extract relevant phenotypic measurements, such as leaf area and inclination angle, semantic segmentation of these representations into individual plant organs is needed. The existing algorithms for plant segmentation in 3D space rely heavily on controlled environments, elaborate calibration procedures, hand-picked features, and manually tuned thresholds. As a result, they do not generalise well to new or changing environmental circumstances or new species.

Instead, we propose to train a supervised deep learning algorithm to predict the point-wise segmentation directly from point cloud data. Deep neural networks are heavily data-driven and typically do not require much explicit prior knowledge about the task, other than a suitably large annotated data set. Besides reducing the need for manual tuning, we anticipate that using a supervised learning approach will also maximise the generalisation potential of the same algorithm for a wide range of crop species and environments, by adjusting the training data accordingly. In this paper we use the PointNet++ network architecture for semantic segmentation [14] to discriminate between three semantic categories (soil, leaves, and stems) based on structural data only. Due to the lack of publicly available labelled agricultural data sets, we train and test the network on a data set collected in simulation from synthesised plants. We evaluate the network's segmentation performance in simulation and provide an indicative qualitative validation of the trained network on a smaller selection of real-world depth data taken from the 4D Plant Registration Dataset [12].

The contributions of this work include (i) a novel fully annotated synthetic data set for 3D plant segmentation, (ii) application of the PointNet++ network architecture to the plant segmentation domain, and (iii) a quantitative and qualitative evaluation of semantic segmentation and generalisation performance.

2   Related Work

2.1   3D Plant Segmentation

Until recently plant segmentation has been focused on classical vision algorithms applied to 2D images. For the purpose of evaluating plant morphology, however, considerable information about 3D configurations and areas obscured by occlusion is lost in 2D projections. There are relatively fewer approaches for semantic segmentation of plants from 3D data.

Several approaches combine clustering techniques with a series of heuristic filters. In [13], a Euclidean clustering procedure is used along with colour and leaf shape heuristics. [18] suggests to apply mean-shift clustering on the depth information of RGB-D images, then classify candidate clusters as vegetation versus background by colour, followed by further instance segmentation based on an active contour model. In [2], individual leaves are segmented in top-down RGB-D images of single plants in a greenhouse environment via blob detection, such that vertically close points are assigned to the same image segments. [10] introduces an elaborate series of filters including removal of statistical outliers, removal of ground points by fixed distance and colour thresholds, followed by 3D equivalents of morphological erosion and subsequent expanding operations. This approach achieves impressive results for a number of greenhouse ornamental plant species, especially in dealing with a complicated occlusion. However, all listed algorithms rely on carefully tuned species-specific parameters and assumptions about plant height, orientation, or colour and lighting conditions. Such tailormade approaches usually do not generalise well to different species or changes in the testing set-up. More recently, in [1,12] binary segmentation into stems and leaves is achieved by using a support vector machine (SVM) classifier with feature vectors containing point coordinates and fast point feature histograms. The SVM classification is later refined by density-based clustering into coherent leave and stem areas, discarding of small clusters, and re-assigning points via k-nearest neighbour classification. This approach requires comparably little annotated training data or manual intervention, but addresses the simpler problem of binary segmentation on very high-resolution point clouds, which were recorded with a precision laser scanner from multiple views, resulting in minimal occlusion and no background interference.

In summary, state-of-the-art methods for semantic segmentation of plants rely on hand-crafted filters or controlled environments. While very effective in specific lab settings, their weaknesses lie in their poor generalisability and need for prior knowledge and manual tuning. Their assumptions do not hold in the field and are often violated due to natural variations in plant morphology.

2.2 Deep Learning for 3D Plant Segmentation

Deep learning algorithms, especially convolutional neural networks (CNNs) are well-established as a standard approach to semantic segmentation for 2D images. CNNs take advantage of the ordered spatial pattern of images by performing convolution operations on the input and extract information about local structures in overlapping receptive fields at different scales. Naturally, there have been attempts to translate their success into 3D space. In [15], a multi-view approach is proposed, which allows the use of a CNN to perform semantic segmentation on 2D images. The 2D projections are then combined into a 3D point-cloud and semantic information from the different views is integrated via a voting strategy. Although much less reliant on manual tuning, this approach also suits lab environments best, as it requires exact camera parameters and positions to be known and assumes that the points are visible from all camera angles.

2.3 PointNet++

Recently, novel deep neural network architectures have been introduced, which are specifically designed to accommodate for the irregular structure of point cloud inputs, without the need for projection or discretisation. Point clouds are unordered sets of points in 3D space and frequently vary in size and point density. Unlike CNNs, the PointNet++ network architecture does not require regular input shapes and can be applied to point clouds, independently of its order or size. In a series of *set abstraction levels*, PointNet++ extracts local shape features from nested subsections of a point cloud and repeatedly aggregates features into higher-level features. Through a corresponding set of *feature propagation levels*, the higher-level features are then interpolated and propagated back into smaller subsections and combined with local features. Eventually, each original input point is described by a feature vector that captures local and global information from all levels of abstraction and can be used for per-point semantic segmentation. This hierarchical architecture has since been applied successfully to tasks such as object detection in indoor scenes [5] and autonomous driving [11], typically focused on rigid, man-made objects and structured environments. There are very few applications to plants, not least because of a lack of training data, but it is also unclear how effectively the network can cope with naturally extreme variations in shape of non-rigid structures.

In [8], PointNet++ is used for a binary segmentation task of detecting strawberry fruit in RGB-D images taken in a real farm. Even though the well-studied 2D CNNs currently still outperform PointNet++, the authors report promising results and suggest further research into using PointNet++ in the agricultural domain, in order to make use of the unique shape information lost in 2D projections. In this work, we aim to apply PointNet++ to the 3D plant segmentation problem using end-to-end deep learning as a possible alternative to the rigid state-of-the-art procedures.

3   Methodology

3.1   Data Set

To provide a suitably large annotated 3D data set for deep learning, we created an artificial set of point clouds captured in simulation from synthesised plant models. First, we defined a general model of a tomato plant, describing its branching structure and relative dimensions, using the random tree generating software Arbaro, an open-source implementation of an algorithm introduced by Weber and Penn [17]. Individual mesh objects were then procedurally generated by randomly varying all descriptors, such that the resulting plants are between 0.15 m and 0.35 m tall, and vary in the number, distribution, scale, and relative dimensions of their branches and leaves. In this way a total of 500 unique tomato plant models were produced. An indicative selection is shown in Fig. 1. Using the open-source 3D modelling software Blender [4], a simulated depth camera captured three depth images of each plant from different angles. A common configuration in agricultural robots features a sensor array aimed at the space below the robot [6]. To emulate the in-field deployment, we chose to capture one top-down view from 1.2 m height and two views at 20° and 40° viewing angles, as shown in Fig. 1.

The depth information was captured by ray-casting in a frustum shape covering a 40° square field of view at a resolution of 480 × 480 rays, yielding 1500 point clouds of 230400 labelled points each. Finally, the data set was shuffled and divided into a training set (1052 examples) and a validation set (224 examples)

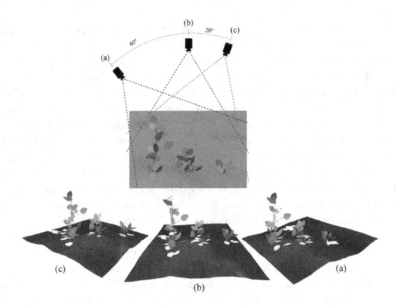

Fig. 1. Schematic diagram of the three partial views captured by simulated depth cameras on a rendered visualisation of three example plant meshes, along with their resulting point clouds.

for training purposes, and a test set (244 examples) which was used for final performance evaluations only.

3.2 Network Architecture

We use the PointNet++ architecture adjusted for point-wise segmentation applications introduced by Qi et al. [14]. The network features four set abstraction levels SA($K, r, [l_1, ..., l_d]$) with K local regions of ball radius r, and using d fully connected layers of width $l_i(i = 1, ..., d)$ within the abstraction level, followed by four corresponding feature propagation levels FP($l_1, ..., l_d$) with d fully connected layers. We also apply a random dropout with a ratio of 0.5 before the final fully connected layer. Following the original paper's notation conventions, the full parameters are: SA(1024,0.1,[32,32,64]) → SA(256,0.2,[64,64,128]) → SA (64,0.4,[128,128,256]) → SA(16,0.8,[256,256,512]) → FP(256,256) → FP(256,256) → FP(256,128) → FP(128,128,128,128,K).

3.3 Performance Metrics

In the following evaluation, we report two standard metrics for multi-class segmentation: Categorical Accuracy and mean Intersection over Union (mIoU). The categorical accuracy, however, is susceptible to distortions by imbalanced class sizes. Our synthetic data set is naturally highly imbalanced, containing larger regions of soil than plant matter. Thus, we monitored the network's learning

Table 1. Confusion matrix for all point-wise semantic class labels in the test set, along with the performance metrics for individual classes

		Predicted labels			κ	IoU
		Soil	Leaf	Stem		
True labels	Soil	50545423	3632	276	0.986	0.999
	Leaf	22758	979967	15497	0.966	0.935
	Stem	2759	26419	12869	0.364	0.223
						MIoU: 0.719

progress throughout training by the mIoU, which is the average across all four semantic classes' individual Intersection over Union (IoU) ratios, computed from the number of true positive (TP), false positive (FP), and false negative (FN) classifications as $IoU = \frac{TP}{TP+FP+FN}$. The mIoU places equal importance on all three semantic classes, and is therefore more appropriate for the data considered here. Finally, we also report Cohen's Kappa (κ) [3] for each semantic class, which also takes into account the scale of imbalance and the expected probability of random correct classifications for each class.

3.4 Network Training

The network was trained on the designated training set for 120 epochs using the categorical cross-entropy loss function, Adam optimiser, and a learning rate of 0.0001. We selected the trained model after 82 epochs, at which point a rolling average of the validation mIoU across 10 epochs reaches its highest value, as the final model used for the remainder of this work.

4   Evaluation

In the following evaluation we report quantitative and qualitative assessments of the per-point semantic annotations produced by the chosen trained network on a test sample of synthetic data, a sample of a more complex growing scenario, and a real plant data sample.

4.1   Quantitative Performance Evaluation

On the remaining test sample (see Sect. 3.1), the network achieved an overall categorical accuracy of 0.999 and a mIoU of 0.712. The sources of error are further broken down in a confusion matrix in Table 1. The matrix displays counts for all point-wise classification cases across the test set. We also report individual IoU and κ metrics for each semantic class. This breakdown suggests that the network produces excellent segmentation results for the soil and leaf classes, and the main sources of error are confusions between leaves and stems. In particular, the network has a tendency to be too conservative in assigning stem labels. The stem class is assigned with high specificity, meaning that 0.999 points from other

Fig. 2. The network's predicted segmentation (left), corresponding ground truth (centre), and highlighted differences (right) for two example test point clouds.

classes are correctly not labelled as stems, and low sensitivity, with only 0.306 true stem points correctly identified as stems. This failing may well be due to insufficient examples depicting the stem class being presented during training. To counteract the effect of class imbalance, we introduced sample weights to the loss function, such that higher importance was placed on examples of the under-represented classes during training. However, the weighted loss did not significantly influence the network's performance.

4.2 Qualitative Performance Evaluation

To contextualise the quantitative results, two segmentation outputs from the test set are pictured in Fig. 2, along with the original ground-truth annotation, and a point cloud visualisation highlighting only misclassified points. As expected, the network prediction appears very similar to the ground truth, and the most common segmentation errors occur where stems are confused with leaf regions. Especially thin stems towards the crown of the plant are often not spotted among the leaves. Occasionally, where only small proportions of a leaf are captured in the point cloud, or stems and leaves overlap closely due to perspective and occlusion, the leaf points are misclassified as stems. In summary, however, we can confirm visually that the segmentation of leaves against soil in particular is sensible, and in most cases the base of the stem can be located too.

Transfer to Complex Growing Scenario. One major weakness of existing plant segmentation algorithms is their poor generalisability. Many procedures discussed in Sect. 2.1 are designed for laboratory settings and can not easily be applied to realistic in-field growing environments with multiple plants, dense foliage, and heavy occlusion patterns. To test how well the concepts our network

Fig. 3. The network's predicted segmentation (left), corresponding ground truth (centre), and highlighted differences (right) for a complex scene of 4 overlapping plants.

learned from single plants translate to more complex scenarios, we generated one example scene with four plants taken from the test set. The result is pictured in Fig. 3. For this point cloud, the network produced slightly more misclassifications, but largely within the same pattern of errors we observed before. The network fails to locate especially thin stems but was able to locate the base and some broader stem regions. We can also observe a few more instances of leaves falsely classified as stems. On the whole, the segmentation works, even though the global shape of this scene was significantly different from any example point cloud presented during training. We conclude that the network did indeed learn to discriminate local shape characteristics and did not over-fit to regularities of the global shape of single plants presented in the training data.

Transfer to Real-World Data. Finally, we tested whether the concepts learned from synthetic data transfer to real-world plants. For a qualitative validation, we selected two scans of tomato plants and one scan of a maize plant from the 4D Plant Registration Dataset [12]. We down-sampled the high-resolution point clouds by ray-casting to reproduce the perspective and resolution of the simulated depth camera as described in Sect. 3.1. Figure 4 shows the segmentation labels predicted by our network for the three resulting point clouds.

The network produces sensible segmentation masks for the two tomato plants, distinguishing well between regions representing soil and plant matter. This experiment serves to demonstrate that knowledge transfer about local shapes to real plants differing from the training data in their acquisition procedure, scale, and natural shape variations, is possible. Finally, the maize plant offers the additional challenge of knowledge transfer to a different species. While similar, the overall morphology and leaf shape differ significantly from our synthetic tomato plants. Still, large regions of all three semantic classes were detected successfully, however, the boundaries between the regions are less precise. Arguably, the semantic separation between stem and leave regions is more ambiguous in this species and previously unseen by the network. Considering these challenging factors, the achieved segmentation demonstrates that the network learned meaningful shape characteristics. It remains to be investigated how well the segmentation algorithm could perform on real data when trained on real

Fig. 4. The network's predicted segmentation for real-world depth data of two tomato plants (left and centre) and one Maize plant (right).

data too. The observed knowledge transfer between the synthetic and real-world data and also across species raises the possibility of pre-training in simulation, reducing the amount of fully annotated real-world training data needed.

5   Conclusions and Future Work

In this work, we successfully applied a supervised machine learning algorithm to the challenge of semantically segmenting plants based on structural data only. On the example of a fully annotated synthetic data set, we demonstrate that the PointNet++ neural network can successfully predict per-point semantic annotations for soil, leaves, and stems directly from point cloud data, and that the learned concepts transfer to new environments and real-world data. Our results serve as a proof of concept, supporting the idea that an understanding of the semantic sub-regions of plants can be learned from data, instead of relying on manually crafted pipelines of classical vision techniques, and that this approach carries potential for increased generalisability compared to current state-of-the-art algorithms. To judge the algorithm's applicability to fully automated in-field phenotyping, more experiments with real-world data are necessary. Our synthetic data set can also be improved by introducing realistic sensor noise and adding models of different crop species to further investigate knowledge transfer and possibilities to learn cross-species concepts for plant organs. To address the network's weakness in segmenting stems, we will trial higher sensor resolutions to improve the sampling density on fine structures and data pre-processing procedures, which augment the training data in such a way as to counter class imbalance without distorting its geometric information (e.g. [7]). Future work should also explore alternative network architectures. Instead of using PointNet++, we are interested in one promising architecture, presented in the context of in-field broccoli head detection [9]. The authors take advantage of the fact that, as a result of the data acquisition technique, point clouds produced by some RGB-D sensors provide an organised structure and allow for the use of a CNN without need for projection.

References

1. Chebrolu, N., Magistri, F., Läbe, T., Stachniss, C.: Registration of spatio-temporal point clouds of plants for phenotyping. PLoS ONE **16**(2), e0247243 (2021)
2. Chéné, Y., et al.: On the use of depth camera for 3d phenotyping of entire plants. Comput. Electron. Agric. **82**, 122–127 (2012)
3. Cohen, J.: A coefficient of agreement for nominal scales. Educ. Psychol. Measur. **20**(1), 37–46 (1960)
4. BO Community: Blender - a 3D modelling and rendering package. Blender Foundation (2018). http://www.blender.org
5. Dai, A., Chang, A.X., Savva, M., Halber, M., Funkhouser, T., Nießner, M.: Scan-Net: richly-annotated 3D reconstructions of indoor scenes. In: Proceedings of the IEEE Conference on Computer Vision and Pattern Recognition, pp. 5828–5839 (2017)
6. Emmi, L., Gonzalez-De-Santos, P.: Mobile robotics in arable lands: current state and future trends. In: 2017 European Conference on Mobile Robots, ECMR 2017 (2017). https://doi.org/10.1109/ECMR.2017.8098694
7. Griffiths, D., Boehm, J.: Weighted point cloud augmentation for neural network training data class-imbalance. arXiv preprint arXiv:1904.04094 (2019)
8. Le Louedec, J., Li, B., Cielniak, G., et al.: Evaluation of 3D vision systems for detection of small objects in agricultural environments. In: Proceedings of the 15th International Joint Conference on Computer Vision, Imaging and Computer Graphics Theory and Applications (2020)
9. Le Louedec, J., Montes, H.A., Duckett, T., Cielniak, G.: Segmentation and detection from organised 3D point clouds: a case study in broccoli head detection. In: Proceedings of the IEEE/CVF Conference on Computer Vision and Pattern Recognition Workshops, pp. 64–65 (2020)
10. Li, D., et al.: An overlapping-free leaf segmentation method for plant point clouds. IEEE Access **7**, 129054–129070 (2019)
11. Ma, X., Wang, Z., Li, H., Zhang, P., Ouyang, W., Fan, X.: Accurate monocular 3D object detection via color-embedded 3D reconstruction for autonomous driving. In: Proceedings of the IEEE International Conference on Computer Vision, pp. 6851–6860 (2019)
12. Magistri, F., Chebrolu, N., Stachniss, C.: Segmentation-based 4D registration of plants point clouds for phenotyping. IROS (2020)
13. Nguyen, T.T., Slaughter, D.C., Max, N., Maloof, J.N., Sinha, N.: Structured light-based 3D reconstruction system for plants. Sensors **15**(8), 18587–18612 (2015)
14. Qi, C.R., Yi, L., Su, H., Guibas, L.J.: PointNet++: deep hierarchical feature learning on point sets in a metric space. In: Advances in Neural Information Processing Systems, pp. 5099–5108 (2017)
15. Shi, W., van de Zedde, R., Jiang, H., Kootstra, G.: Plant-part segmentation using deep learning and multi-view vision. Biosyst. Eng. **187**, 81–95 (2019)
16. Tardieu, F., Cabrera-Bosquet, L., Pridmore, T., Bennett, M.: Plant phenomics, from sensors to knowledge. Curr. Biol. **27**(15), R770–R783 (2017)
17. Weber, J., Penn, J.: Creation and rendering of realistic trees. In: Proceedings of the 22nd Annual Conference on Computer Graphics and Interactive Techniques - SIGGRAPH 1995 (1995). https://doi.org/10.1145/218380.218427
18. Xia, C., Wang, L., Chung, B.K., Lee, J.M.: In situ 3D segmentation of individual plant leaves using a RGB-D camera for agricultural automation. Sensors **15**(8), 20463–20479 (2015)

Discovering Stable Robot Grasps for Unknown Objects in Presence of Uncertainty Using Bayesian Models

Muhammad Sami Siddiqui$^{(\boxtimes)}$ (ID), Claudio Coppola (ID), Gokhan Solak (ID), and Lorenzo Jamone (ID)

ARQ (Advanced Robotics at Queen Mary), School of Electronic Engineering and Computer Science, Queen Mary University of London, London E14NS, UK
{m.s.siddiqui,c.coppola,g.solak,l.jamone}@qmul.ac.uk

Abstract. Autonomous grasping of unknown objects is challenging due to the uncertainty in robotic sensing and action generation. This paper presents a pipeline for predicting a safe grasp in unknown objects using depth and tactile sensing. The main objective of the work is to explore haptically to maximise a given grasp metric, such that the probability of dropping the object after lifting from the surface is minimal. The performance of the uniform grid search method is compared with probabilistic methods (i.e. standard and unscented Bayesian Optimisation) to discover safe points. The results show that unscented Bayesian Optimisation provides better confidence in finding a safe grasp. This is demonstrated by observing optimum points being far from the edges and the exploration converging sooner than other methods in a limited number of exploratory observations.

Keywords: Grasp metric · Dexterous hand · Haptics · Manipulation

1 Introduction

Design solutions for grasping unknown objects often use RGB-D, tactile and proprioceptive sensing modalities. In literature, these modalities are often used separately in different phases of the grasping; however, approaches using multi-modal data are increasing in popularity [1]. Indeed, exploiting the multimodality of data to extract knowledge from different data sources can improve robot intelligence performance. The capability to deal with visual-tactile multimodal information enables robots to acquire more human-like capabilities in several tasks like grasping, object manipulation, and slip detection. While vision plays an essential role in grasp planning, which relies on the global visual features of the scene, it is ineffective to detect the safety of the performed grasp. This ineffectiveness occurs because grasping is dependant on physical contact, forces

Work partially supported by the EPSRC UK through projects NCNR (EP/R02572X/1) and MAN^3 (EP/S00453X/1).

© Springer Nature Switzerland AG 2021
C. Fox et al. (Eds.): TAROS 2021, LNAI 13054, pp. 46–55, 2021.
https://doi.org/10.1007/978-3-030-89177-0_5

exerted by hand, tactile attributes of the object and hand configurations. Vision sensors cannot provide an estimation of these attributes. Thus, incorporating tactile sensing allows enriching the grasping information with features representing the physical contact modalities accessing a safer grasp at the execution stage.

This article describes a model that combines visual and tactile sensory inputs to predict stable grasping points of unknown objects using a grasp metric. The proposed approach can be used to measure the safety of the grasp before lifting the object from the surface. The approach is independent of building an extensive database of 3D objects. Moreover, it does not require the object symmetry assumption or object segmentation for computation. Castanheira et al. [2] proposed the concept of using probabilistic modelling to find a safe grasp in a simulated environment. However, many additional uncertainties are present in a real-world environment (e.g. insensitivity of sensors, disturbance in the position of the object while exploring) that are not present in a controlled simulated environment. This work also validates the practical application of probabilistic modelling in acquiring safer grasp points.

A series of experiments are conducted to compare the performance of probabilistic models with the uniformly distributed model. The experimental results validate the superiority of probabilistic models in finding safer grasp points. Probabilistic models also have a higher probability of convergence during exploration, hence providing confidence in predicting a safe grasp point. The contributions of the paper are threefold:

1. an approach to predict safer grasp of an unknown object from a combination of visual and tactile perception.
2. a model that considers uncertainties of the real world to predict a safer grasp of the object.
3. a series of experiments that demonstrates the proposed system for object grasp prediction.

2   Related Work

Grasping objects of unknown shape is an essential skill for automation in manufacturing industries. Many existing grasping techniques require a 2D or 3D geometrical model, limiting its application in different working environments [3]. On the other hand, acquiring 3D images is an expensive process and mostly simulation-based [4]. Kolycheva et al. [5] introduces a task-specific grasping system for a tridactyl manipulator. The system uses RGB-D vision to estimate for shape and pose of the object. The models for grasp stability are learnt over a set of known objects using Gaussian process regression. The grasp model has iteratively improved through re-planning the grasp around the object and collecting tactile data.

Merzic et al. [6] makes use of deep reinforcement learning technique to grasp partially visible/occluded objects. It does not rely on the dataset of the object models but instead uses tactile sensors to achieve grasp stability on unknown objects in a simulation. Zhao et al. [7] implements probabilistic modelling with a neural network to select a group of grasp points for an unknown object. There is also work on learning object grasping based on visual cues, and the selection of features are often based on human intuitions [8]. However, vision-based accuracy is limited due to its standardization and occlusions. Some details can be overlooked even for known objects, which may cause failure in grasping objects [9].

Tactile sensing is capable of compensating for some of the problems of the vision-only approach. Indeed being able to perceive touch allows the robot to understand when the contact with the object has been made and have a better perception of the occluded areas of the object by making contact with those surfaces of the target object. Techniques are proposed to control slippage and grasp stabilization of the objects using tactile sensors only [10,11]. It is independent of the data of object mass, object centre of mass and forces acting on the object to prevent the object from slipping.

There are seven different kinds of grasp quality metrics to predict how well it performs on the robotic platform and in simulations [12]. Different classifiers are trained on the extensive database, and results are evaluated for each grasp. The human labelled database is used in this work, which requires more accuracy in collecting data using different protocols. To accomplish the autonomous grasping of an unknown object, we aim to predict the grasping stability of the object before lifting the object from the surface. In this paper, we used tactile feedback to predict the safety of the robotic grasp of an unknown object. We present real-time grasp safety prediction by haptic probabilistic modelling exploration with a dexterous robotic hand.

3 Methodology

3.1 Object Extraction from Point Cloud

We define a specific area in an environment as a workspace in which the robot operates safely. The object placed on the workspace is perceived by the robot while the remaining point cloud data is filtered out, as shown in Fig. 1 part A. We are using a non-deterministic iterative algorithm, random sample consensus (RANSAC) [13], for detection of the object. It tries to fit the points from the point cloud into a mathematical model of a dominant plane. RANSAC then identifies the points which do not constitute the dominant plane model. These points that do not fit into the plane model (called outliers) are clustered together to form one object. Dimensions of the object are used to create a 3D bounding box around the object. The midpoint of the object is computed as the difference between the maximum and minimum boundary points in an axis parallel to the plane. This point is then used to reference the robot to move close to the object and initiate tactile exploration. Figure 1 part B shows the robot's planned trajectory, avoiding collision with the environment. Moveit! framework [14] is utilised for the implementation of motion planning.

3.2   Grasp Metric Calculation

The volume of the force wrench space (FWS) [15] is used as a force metric to gauge the stability of the grasp during tactile exploration. FWS is defined as the set of all forces applied to the object with all grasp contacts. It is a three-dimensional grasp matrix consisting of force components from all the four tactile sensors positioned on the tip of the fingers of the robotic hand. This metric is also independent of the coordinates of reference system. Function Q_v for this set of FWS ($\wp$) can be described as:

$$Q_v = Volume(\wp) \tag{1}$$

During the closing state, the robotic hand wraps its fingers around the object. The grasp metric is calculated when a connection is established between the hand and the object. Figure 1 part C displays the Allegro hand position, as observed in one experiment. The size and coordinates of the objects are assumed fixed to limit the size of the exploration space.

3.3   Probabilistic Modelling

Bayesian Optimisation (BO) is a probabilistic model to accomplish the task of exploring global optima [16]. For n number of iterations, the input dataset of query point is $x = \{x_{1:n}\}$ and the resulted outcome is $z = \{z_{1:n}\}$. In general, the algorithm depends on tuning parameters where input $x \in \mathbb{X}$ in some specified domain, where $\mathbb{X} \subseteq \mathbb{R}^D$ The main goal is to find the global optimisation method, which focuses on finding the minimum optimum value for the objective function $f : \mathbb{X} \mapsto \mathbb{R}$, where $\mathbb{X}$ is a compact space. It works on selecting the best grasp points for every iteration geared towards the minimum Consider this process in two basic steps: First, for each grasp point input, a probabilistic model (in our case, the Gaussian process) is built. Second, using an acquisition function α to decide the model to select the next point for exploration. As the method depends on the trial-and-error approach, BO helps optimise the number of steps required for a safe grasp. Grasp metric score is computed as described in Sect. 3. The performance of BO is then compared with the uniform distribution exploration model for different kinds of objects.

Unscented Bayesian Optimisation (UBO) is a method to propagate mean and covariance through nonlinear transformation. The basis of the algorithm is better manageability of an approximate probability distribution than approximate arbitrary nonlinear function [17]. To calculate mean and covariance, a set of sigma points are chosen. These sigma points are deterministically chosen points that depict certain information about mean and covariance. The weighted combination of sigma points is then passed through linear function to compute transformed distribution. The advantage of UBO over classical BO is the ability to consider uncertainty in the input space to find an optimal grasp. For dimension d, it requires $2d + 1$ sigma points that show its computational cost are negligible

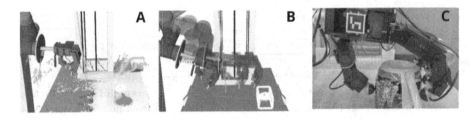

Fig. 1. Methodology for the calculation of force metric. (**A**) Point cloud data of the workspace. (**B**) Path planning towards the bounding box of the object. (**C**) Robotic hand position during metric calculation.

compared to others such as Monte Carlo, which requires more samples or Gaussian function. In UBO, the query is selected based on probability distribution. We choose the best query point considering it as deterministic but also check its surrounding neighbours. Thus, while considering input noise, we will analyze the resulting posterior distribution through the acquisition function. Assuming that our prior distribution is Gaussian distribution where $x \sim \mathcal{N}(\bar{x}, \sum x)$, then the set of $2d + 1$ sigma points of the unscented transform is computed as:

$$x^0 = \bar{x}, x^i_\pm = \bar{x} \pm \left(\sqrt{(d+\kappa) \sum x} \right)_i, \forall i = 1...d \qquad (2)$$

where d is dimensional input space, κ parameter tunes magnitude of sigma points and $\left(\sqrt{(.)} \right)_i$ is the ith row or column of the corresponding matrix square root. Detailed information of UBO is provided in [2]. UBO reduces the chance that the next query point is in an unsafe region where a small change in input results in a bad outcome.

4   Implementation

4.1   Configuration

To achieve our objective of successfully grasping an unknown object, we set up a UR5 robot in the lab. Allegro hand is mounted at the end of the UR5 arm as an end effector. Kinect is fixed at the top of the robot's base, facing perpendicular to the workspace. Optoforce OMD 20-SE-40N is a 3-axis force sensor that measures the forces experienced by the fingers of the Allegro Hand (at a rate of 1 kHz). The workplace is 72 cm from the kinect frame. Any object within the workplace area (a rectangular area of 31 cm by 40 cm) is processed, and the extra points are filtered out. The orientation of the Allegro hand is fixed parallel to the axis of the workspace plane. The setup is shown in Fig. 2.

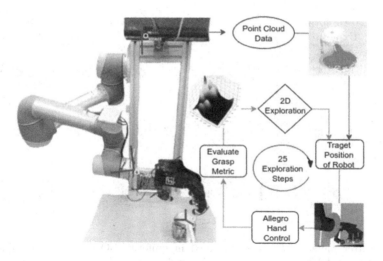

Fig. 2. Overview of the approach to evaluate safe grasps in unknown objects. UR5 robot equipped with an Allegro robotic hand.

4.2 Protocol

To perform the experiments, we apply the following experimental protocol:

1. object detection: unknown object detection using PCL.
2. motion planning: once we have detected the object's pose, the Moveit plans the collision-free movement of the robot to the top of the object.
3. plan execution: after successful planning, the robot navigates itself to the target pose. This is also the starting pose for haptic exploration.
4. gradually gripping the object: when the robotic arm reaches the search point, it starts closing its fingers until contact is detected.
5. applying grasping force: to ensure the gripper applies enough pressure over the object and not just touches it.
6. calculation of grasp metric: evaluate grasp score of the candidate grasp.
7. haptic exploration: open the grip of the robotic hand and move to the next pose directed by the probabilistic model. This process is repeated 25 times.

5   Results

The proposed model is validated by exploring grasp points in the 3D space, but the contact points are searched on two dimensions. Experiments are conducted five times with probabilistic modelling exploration and then compared with the uniformly distributed exploration. BO and UBO models are used for probabilistic modelling exploration. We used the objects from the dataset[1] developed by EU RoMaNs to observe exploration performance. The objects in the dataset are

---

[1] https://sites.google.com/site/romansbirmingham.

Allegro Pose	Uniform Exploration	Bayesian Exploration	Unscented Exploration	Optimal Position

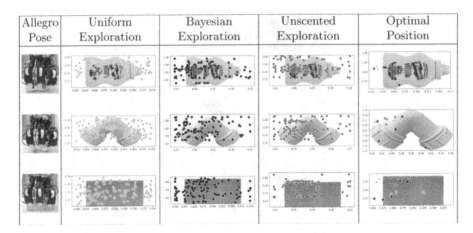

Fig. 3. Scatter plots of all points explored in uniform, BO and UBO for different objects. Pose of Allegro hand at start of experiments is also shown in first column. Final column represents optimum position in 2D from each experiment.

commonly found in nuclear waste and are categorised in different categories such as bottles, cans, pipe joints. We conducted the experiments with different kinds of objects and materials: rectangular-shaped foam (4.6 cm × 15 cm × 6 cm), a complex-shaped c-shaped pipe joint and a complex-shaped mustard plastic bottle. Image of the objects can be seen in the 'objects' column of the Table 1. Objects were slightly fixed to the surface due to the insensitivity of the tactile sensors. Tactile sensors disturb the position of the object during the calculation of the grasp metric.

Scatter Plots: Figure 3 represents the points observed by each exploration method in all the experiments. The point represents the location of the middle finger of the robotic arm. A total of 125 search points (5 experiments with 25 iterations each) are plotted for each exploration method. It can be observed that for probabilistic methods, more observations are recorded at the boundaries of the object. This is due to the concavity of the tactile sensor and its contact with the edges in the objects. The figure also represents the optimal position with the highest metric score for all experiments for each exploration model. There are a total of 15 points represented, five for each approach. The points are the location of the middle finger of the robotic arm.

Optimal Position: The position with optimal grasp score is the distance from the world frame along the horizontal plane of the object. The frames are shown in Fig. 2. Table 1 tabulates the optimal position of the object as observed in each experiment. It also shows the value of grasp metric value in the optimal position. The points are skewed towards one side of the object because of the constraint in the encoders of the thumb, which restricts the movement of the thumb to align with the middle finger. The results indicate that probabilistic models have an optimum position similar to uniform distributed exploration with less standard deviation in position and metric score.

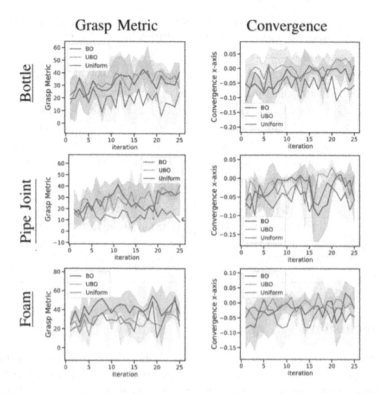

Fig. 4. Mean of grasp metric and convergence of explorations at each observation for all five experiments.

Convergence: Convergence of each exploration to its maximum grasp metric value reflects confidence in a safer grasp. The mean of grasp metric value and convergence to the final optimum position in each iteration for all experiments is shown in Fig. 4. Uniform, BO and UBO are represented by green, blue and orange lines, respectively. A total of five experiments are conducted with twenty-five observations for three different shaped objects. Plots present convergence in the x-axis only because of the confined range of exploration in the y-axis ($<\pm 4$ cm). It can be seen that the probabilistic models have a higher probability of convergence than the uniform-grid search model. The results validate that probabilistic models have a better ability to converge to the optimum position with a higher grasp metric score in fewer iterations than uniformly distributed exploration. The experimental results collected demonstrates:

- the ability of probabilistic methods to provide confidence in predicting a safe grasp in a very limited number of iterations.
- BO and UBO have the advantage of converging sooner than the uniform exploration even with the low amount of observations.
- the potential of UBO to find grasps that are safer. This is evident in the case of the bottle, as the optimum points lie far from the edges.

Table 1. Mean optimal position for respective objects of all experiments from the world frame. Standard deviation of the mean position in x and y axes

Object		Uniform Exploration	Bayesian Exploration	Unscented Exploration
	Optimal Position(cm)	(40.4,114.2)	(41.6,113.7)	(39.4,114.5)
	Standard Deviation[x,y]	3.1,1.1	1.9,1.6	2.1,0.5
	Mean Metric	47.9	51	48.6
	Metric Deviation	6.3	7.4	7.7
	Optimal Position(cm)	(41.2,115.8)	(40.9,115.5)	(41.1,116.6)
	Standard Deviation[x,y]	1.4,0.8	2,1.6	1.1.1.1
	Mean Metric	46.0	52.8	48.6
	Metric Deviation	05.2	9.5	9
	Optimal Position(cm)	(39.9,114.4)	(40.4,113.7)	(38.5,116.6)
	Standard Deviation[x,y]	4.2,1.5	2.9,2	1.6,0.7
	Mean Metric	52.7	56.1	46.2
	Metric Deviation	10.8	10.7	4.2

6   Conclusion

This work validates our approach of using probabilistic modelling for finding safe grasp points for unknown objects in real-time. The approach outperforms the uniform distributed exploration in acquiring a safe grasp configuration with a limited set of exploratory iterations. The approach has application in handling materials in a nuclear environment where the robot can afford the time to find a safe grasp. For future developments, using tactile sensors that are more sensitive [18,19] and distributed over a larger surface [20,21], could allow to: rely on a more delicate haptic exploration; obtain a more reliable estimation of the grasp metric; consider object properties other than geometric, e.g. elasticity, friction coefficient.

References

1. Luo, S., Bimbo, J., Dahiya, R., Liu, H.: Robotic tactile perception of object properties: a review. Mechatronics **48**, 54–67 (2017)
2. Castanheira, J., Vicente, P., Martinez-Cantin, R., Jamone, L., Bernardino, A.: Finding safe 3D robot grasps through efficient haptic exploration with unscented Bayesian optimization and collision penalty. In: 2018 IEEE/RSJ International Conference on Intelligent Robots and Systems (IROS), pp. 1643–1648. IEEE (2018)
3. Ciocarli, M., Allen, P.K.: Hand posture subspaces for dexterous robotic grasping. Int. J. Robot. Res. **28**, 851–867 (2009)
4. Shao, L., et al.: UniGrasp: learning a unified model to grasp with n-fingered robotic hands. arXiv, vol. 5, no. 2, pp. 2286–2293 (2019)
5. Kolycheva née Nikandrova, E., Kyrki, V.: Task-specific grasping of similar objects by probabilistic fusion of vision and tactile measurements. In: 2015 IEEE-RAS 15th International Conference on Humanoid Robots (Humanoids), pp. 704–710 (2015)

6. Merzić, H., Bogdanovic, M., Kappler, D., Righetti, L., Bohg, J.: Leveraging contact forces for learning to grasp. arXiv, pp. 3615–3621 (2018)

7. Zhao, Z., Shang, W., He, H., Li, Z.: Grasp prediction and evaluation of multi-fingered dexterous hands using deep learning. Robot. Auton. Syst. **129**, 103550 (2020)

8. Saxena, A., Driemeyer, J., Ng, A.Y.: Robotic grasping of novel objects using vision. Int. J. Robot. Res. **27**(2), 157–173 (2008)

9. Kiatos, M., Malassiotis, S., Sarantopoulos, I.: A geometric approach for grasping unknown objects with multifingered hands. IEEE Trans. Robot. 1–12 (2020)

10. Shaw-Cortez, W., Oetomo, D., Manzie, C., Choong, P.: Technical note for "tactile-based blind grasping: a discrete-time object manipulation controller for robotic hands". IEEE Rob. Autom. Lett. **5**(2), 3475–3476 (2020)

11. James, J.W., Lepora, N.F.: Slip detection for grasp stabilization with a multifingered tactile robot hand. IEEE Trans. Robot. 1–14 (2020)

12. Rubert, C., Kappler, D., Bohg, J., Morales, A.: Predicting grasp success in the real world-a study of quality metrics and human assessment. Robot. Auton. Syst. **121**, 103274 (2019)

13. Zuliani, C.K.M., Manjunath, B.: The multiransac algorithm and its application to detect planar homographies. In: IEEE International Conference on Image Processing (2005)

14. Coleman, D., Sucan, I., Chitta, S., Correll, N.: Reducing the barrier to entry of complex robotic software: a moveit! case study (2014)

15. Miller, A.T., Allen, P.K.: Examples of 3D grasp quality computations. In: Proceedings of IEEE International Conference on Robotics and Automation-ICRA (1999)

16. Brochu, E., Cora, V.M., de Freitas, N.: A tutorial on Bayesian optimization of expensive cost functions, with application to active user modeling and hierarchical reinforcement learning. CoRR, vol. abs/1012.2599 (2010)

17. Nogueira, J., Martinez-Cantin, R., Bernardino, A., Jamone, L.: Unscented Bayesian optimization for safe robot grasping, pp. 1967–1972, October 2016

18. Jamone, L., Natale, L., Metta, G., Sandini, G.: Highly sensitive soft tactile sensors for an anthropomorphic robotic hand. IEEE Sens. J. **15**(8), 4226–4233 (2015)

19. Paulino, T., et al.: Low-cost 3-axis soft tactile sensors for the human-friendly robot Vizzy, pp. 966–971 (2017)

20. Tomo, T.P., et al.: Covering a robot fingertip with uSkin: a soft electronic skin with distributed 3-axis force sensitive elements for robot hands. IEEE Robot. Autom. Lett. **3**(1), 124–131 (2018)

21. Tomo, T.P., et al.: A new silicone structure for uSkin-a soft, distributed, digital 3-axis skin sensor and its integration on the humanoid robot iCub. IEEE Robot. Autom. Lett. **3**, 2584–2591 (2018)

Improving SLAM in Pipe Networks
by Leveraging Cylindrical Regularity

R. Zhang, M. H. Evans, R. Worley, S. R. Anderson, and L. Mihaylova(✉)

The University of Sheffield, Sheffield, South Yorkshire S10 2TN, UK
{rzhang47,mat.evans,rfworley1,s.anderson,l.s.mihaylova}@sheffield.ac.uk

Abstract. Monocular visual Simultaneous Localisation and Mapping algorithms estimate map points and frame poses simultaneously based on video data. The estimated map point locations do not contain any structural information. Due to the measurement noise, the estimated trajectory is slightly different from the ground truth. This paper improves the estimation accuracy of trajectory in a pipe network by leveraging structural regularity. An optimisation-based method is used to detect a cylinder among map points in the SLAM back-end. When the cylinder is detected, the system enforces cylindrical regularity to the points from the cylindrical pipe surface, which is named cylindrical points. The estimated trajectory and map points will benefit from this structural information. This method is verified and evaluated on both synthetic data and real-world pipe video datasets.

Keywords: SLAM · Structural regularity · Pipe networks inspection · Structure from motion

1 Introduction

Pipe networks play an important role in transporting resources such as water, oil, and natural gas. Due to their low cost and efficiency, pipelines are widely found in cities and industry. However, pipe networks may suffer from defects, such as blockages or leakage, leading to economic losses, environmental contamination, and damage to health [2]. Nondestructive inspection or testing is an essential task, which can provide early detection of defects and avoid undesirable results.

Cameras are low-cost, effective sensors providing detailed appearance in an immersive fashion, and there is an extensive existing literature on *Structure from Motion* (SfM) and visual *Simultaneous Localisation and Mapping* (SLAM) [3]. The majority of vision-based methods focus on SfM [17], which take advantage of the structural information of pipes, but impose strong constraints on the robot motion or cannot perform in real-time. Visual SLAM methods enable an agent equipped with a camera to explore its environment and build a sparse point cloud

---

This work is supported by the UK's Engineering and Physical Sciences Research Council (EPSRC) Programme Grant EP/S016813/1.

© Springer Nature Switzerland AG 2021
C. Fox et al. (Eds.): TAROS 2021, LNAI 13054, pp. 56–65, 2021.
https://doi.org/10.1007/978-3-030-89177-0_6

simultaneously [4,6,16]. These can be divided into feature-based methods, which track features between video frames and estimate frame poses and map points by reducing reprojection error [16], and direct methods, which track informative points and estimate the frame poses by minimizing the photometric error [4].

In the narrow space of the pipe, visual SLAM algorithms suffer from low parallax. The estimated pipe becomes less cylindrical and shapes more like a cone, and the travel distance is underestimated. In order to improve the accuracy in a man-made environment, a natural choice is structure SLAM algorithm which uses structural information such as knowledge of lines or planes. However, previous SLAM algorithms do not consider cylinders, and the SfM methods cannot be used directly for visual SLAM in pipe networks.

In this paper, we propose a new extension to the popular ORB-SLAM2 system [16] to leverage cylindrical regularity in a pipe network. The *main contributions of this work* include: 1) An iterative cylinder detection method based on sparse points, selecting cylindrical points within 95% confidence intervals; 2) In order to leverage the cylindrical information through all related frames, our method estimates the cylinder based on optimised map points, which is different from existing structure SLAM algorithms which detects structural regularities among local map points; 3) The method is verified on synthetic and real-world data. The results demonstrate that the cylindrical regularity improves the accuracy of estimated camera trajectories and sparse points clouds.

The remainder of the paper introduces related work in Sect. 2, and the proposed method is described in Sect. 3. Section 4 introduces how the system detects the cylinder. Section 5 presents the cost function and the cylindrical regularity. Section 6 describes the experiment setups and results. Finally, conclusions and plans for future work are summarised in Sect. 7.

2   Related Work

In man-made environments with many higher-level features and structural regularities, many robots use SLAM algorithms designed to exploit this information to improve localization accuracy. There are two main ways to incorporate structural regularities. The first approach uses the *Manhattan world* [20] which abstracts the man-made environment as a set of blocks. However, many requirements for this approach are not met in the pipe environment, such as lines in orthogonal directions and the vanishing points. The second approach is to add structural regularities to landmarks, including points, edges, and lines, in the optimisation [7,9,13]. These algorithms also optimise the structural parameters in the local optimisation, including other landmarks. However, these specific structural regularities are not present in the buried pipe environment.

A key structural property of pipe environments are their cylindrical shape, and some Structure from Motion (SfM) methods have been designed to exploit this information. Some methods [8,19] estimate the map point location by computing the intersection of the known cylindrical surface and the ray from the camera centre to the observation when the camera moves parallel with the pipe axis. Others methods [8,10] add cylindrical regularity to map points in the bundle adjustment (BA) algorithm to keep the points on the known cylindrical surface. Further, this prior knowledge has been used in local pose optimisation, which can optimise the camera poses and triangulate features iteratively [12].

To date, SfM approaches have typically assumed that the robot moves forward parallel with the pipe axis, where the system benefits most from the cylindrical information [8,12]. In some cases, the pose estimation is simplified by assuming the robot moves in a straight line [3,8,19]. Those assumptions do not typically hold in the SLAM problem. Cone detection among the triangular features has been used to lift restrictions on camera movement [10], which can be done without prior knowledge of the pipe axis, and is less sensitive to camera calibration [14]. This method detects multiple pipe instances with temporary map points incrementally per reconstructed model, which can not perform in real-time.

In summary, although many SfM algorithms exploit cylindrical information, SLAM algorithms cannot implement these methods directly since they incorporate some prior knowledge that is not available in the SLAM problem formulation. Meanwhile, SLAM algorithms have yet to incorporate cylindrical structure information. This paper aims to address this gap.

3   System Overview

The proposed system is derived from ORB-SLAM2 [16] which is a well-known visual SLAM algorithm. ORB-SLAM2 has three threads: tracking, local mapping and loop closing. The conventional ORB-SLAM2 selects frames with much new information as keyframes in the tracking thread. In the local mapping thread, the system triangulates features and optimises keyframe poses and map points in local optimisation. The proposed system applies cylinder-related operations in the second thread. Optimised map points are defined as map points that are optimised in the previous optimisation and excluded from current local optimisation. When enough optimised points are obtained since the beginning of mapping or the end of the last cylinder model, the system estimates a cylinder among optimised map points and select cylindrical points among local map points. The system punishes the distance of the cylindrical points from the cylindrical surface in local BA. Finally, the system culls some map points far outside of the estimated pipe model, considered outliers. Once the ratio of cylindrical points to all local map points is lower than a threshold, the system will stop using cylindrical regularity and prepare to update the cylinder model with new cumulative optimised points.

4   Cylinder Detection

Given a set of 3D map points, the cylinder is detected based on geometric properties. In order to leverage cylindrical regularity in local optimisation, it is essential to estimate the cylinder accurately and distinguish the cylindrical points clearly. This section introduces cylinder representation and cylinder detection.

4.1 Cylinder Representation and Estimation

The cylinder estimation is based on cylinder representation. The cylinder is denoted by $\vec{\pi} = \begin{bmatrix} \vec{L_c}^{\mathrm{T}} & \vec{O_c}^{\mathrm{T}} & r_c \end{bmatrix}^{\mathrm{T}}$, where $\vec{L_c} \in R^3$ is a vector characterising the direction of the cylinder's axis, $\vec{O_c} \in R^3$ represents the 3D coordinates of the intersection point between the pipe axis and the xy plane of the world coordinate, and r_c is the radius of the cylinder. Here $\vec{P_w^i} \in R^3 (0 < i < n)$ represents a cylindrical point. These elements are illustrated in Fig. 1.

The $\vec{L_c}$ vector has three elements but only two degrees of freedom, so one element can be fixed to avoid the singularity. During the initialisation, the coordinate of the first keyframe is regarded as the world coordinate shown in Fig. 1.

The camera will move along the pipe, looking along the pipe axis. Since the z axis of the world coordinate will not be perpendicular to the pipe axis, the pipe axis is likely to intersect the xy plane of the world coordinate. Thus the third element of vector $\vec{L_c}$ would not be zero and is set to a fixed nonzero number to avoid the singularity. The cylinder vector $\vec{L_c} = \begin{bmatrix} a_c & b_c & 1 \end{bmatrix}^{\mathrm{T}}$, where a_c and b_c are the elements of L_c along the x and y axes of the world coordinate, always intersects xy plane of the world coordinate in the point $\vec{O_c} = \begin{bmatrix} x_c & y_c & 0 \end{bmatrix}^{\mathrm{T}}$, at distances x_c and y_c in the x and y axes of the world coordinate. The system therefore uses five numbers to parameterise a cylinder, which is the minimum number of variables, where are estimated in unconstrained optimisation [18]. There are some other line representation methods, such as Plücker coordinates and orthonormal representation [13]. The former has a constraint to their parameters, and it is hard to illustrate the cylindrical regularity with both mathematically. The nonlinear geometry fitting is solved by g2o [1] which is used by ORB-SLAM2.

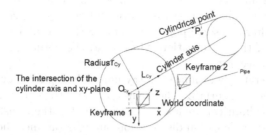

Fig. 1. Cylinder representation, with parameters describing a cylinder in space. Two image frames are shown; the world coordinates are set to those of the first frame.

Theoretically, all cylindrical points are equidistant from the cylinder axis. This property is used to estimate the cylinder and add constraints to the map points in later optimisation. For a cylindrical point P_w^i, as the cross product between two vectors is the area of a parallelogram with the vectors as sides, the following equation holds

$$S = |\vec{L_c} \times (\vec{P_w^i} - \vec{O_c})| = |\vec{L_c}| \cdot r_c \tag{1}$$

where $| \cdot |$ is the magnitude of a vector. According to this cylindrical property, an error function is obtained for a feature i as follows, where $\Delta x = x - x_c$ and $\Delta y = y - y_c$,

$$\begin{aligned}
g(P_w^i) &= |\vec{L_c} \times (\vec{P_w^i} - \vec{O_c})|^2 - |\vec{L_c}|^2 |r_c|^2 \\
&= [b_c z - \Delta y]^2 + [\Delta x - a_c z]^2 + [a_c \Delta y - b_c \Delta x]^2 - r_c^2 (a_c^2 + b_c^2 + 1)
\end{aligned} \tag{2}$$

This is minimized by the Gauss-Newton or Levenberg–Marquardt algorithm [11,15], using the Jacobian $J(\vec{P_w^i})$ of $g(\vec{P_w^i})$ with respect to $\vec{\pi}$

$$J(\vec{P_w^i}) = \frac{\partial g}{\partial \vec{\pi}} = \begin{bmatrix}
2a_c z^2 - 2\Delta x z + 2a_c \Delta y^2 - 2b_c \Delta x \Delta y - 2a_c r_c \\
2b_c z^2 - 2\Delta y z + 2b_c \Delta x^2 - 2a_c \Delta x \Delta y - 2b_c r_c \\
-2\Delta x + 2a_c z - 2b_c^2 \Delta x + 2a_c b_c \Delta y \\
-2\Delta y + 2b_c z - 2a_c^2 \Delta y + 2a_c b_c \Delta x \\
-2r_c(a_c^2 + b_c^2 + 1)
\end{bmatrix}^{\mathrm{T}} \tag{3}$$

4.2 Cylinder Detection

Cylinder detection is to estimate a cylinder among selected 3D points. Noise in the map points can lead to a poorly estimated cylinder, providing incorrect information through cylindrical regularity and causing misclassification in the future selection of cylindrical points. This sensitivity to noise makes cylinder estimation different from other landmarks. For accuracy, this cylinder is estimated from optimised map points instead of local map points observed by the current keyframe and its covisible keyframes. The local map points are noisy before optimisation. The local optimisation not only optimises the local map points but also filter out some points far outside the estimated cylinder as outliers at the end of the optimisation. Since that, the optimised map points are more reliable and accurate.

The system iteratively estimates the cylinder with updated cylindrical points close to the cylindrical surface. The points far from the cylindrical surface are regarded as non-cylindrical points. It is assumed that these distances of cylindrical points satisfy a Gaussian distribution, and the variance should be smaller than an appropriate threshold τ. This system select points whose distances are within 95% confidence intervals as cylindrical points. An alternative to this method could be to use an algorithm such as RANSAC [5], which could improve accuracy with higher computational cost. With a set of map points, the system detects the cylinder with **Algorithm 1**:

Algorithm 1. Cylinder Detection

1: Clean up the set G
2: Add all the map points to set G
3: Initialise the parameters
4: **while** $\sigma >$ threshold σ_t **do**
5:    Fit a cylinder to the map points from set G
6:    Compute the distance of all map points from the cylinder axis
7:    Compute the mean μ and variance σ of the distances $d_j (j \in G)$
8:    Clean up the set G, and add all points close to the mean μ, given by
      $|d_j - \mu| \leq 1.96\sigma$, which is a 95% confidence interval
9: **end while**

After cylinder detection, the estimated cylinder is fixed during the subsequent local bundle adjustment until the low ratio of current cylindrical points to all local map points. The estimated cylinder changes slightly if the system optimises it in every local bundle adjustment due to the measurement noise. This instability will give the system a false impression that the robot moves in a curve pipe, which contradicts reality. With the estimated cylinder, the map points close to the cylindrical surface are classified as cylindrical points, which have a cylindrical regularity in the local bundle adjustment.

5 Bundle Adjustment with Cylindrical Regularity

Formulation. The state of the proposed augmented ORB-SLAM2 system includes local frame poses, local map points, and the estimated cylinder parameters. When the kth keyframe is accepted, the full state set is defined as follows:

$$X = \{T_{wi}, \vec{p_j}, \vec{\pi}\}_{i \in \alpha_k, j \in \beta_k} \tag{4}$$

where the variable α_k denotes the covisible keyframes for the current keyframe k, the set β_k contains the map points observed by frames α_k, and $\vec{\pi}$ is the estimated cylinder. Covisible keyframes share more than a certain number of map points. The following cost function

$$f = \arg\min_X \sum_{i \in \alpha_k} \sum_{j \in \beta_k} \rho(e_v^{ij\,2}{}_{\Sigma_v}) + \sum_{l \in \gamma_k} \rho(|e_c^l|^2_{\Sigma_c}) \tag{5}$$

is optimised via the local bundle adjustment method, with respect to X and with a fixed $\vec{\pi}$, using the g2o solver [1]. Here e_v^{ij} is the reprojection error of feature j observed by the keyframe i, and e_c^l is the cylindrical regularity of cylindrical point l from the set γ_k. The kernel function ρ is used to suppress outliers. Σ_v is the covariance matrix of a feature observation and is set to be an identity matrix; Σ_v is the variance of the point-to-surface constraint.

Reprojection Error. The reprojection error is the distance between the projected map point and observed feature in the image plane, for frame i and feature j, this is given by

$$e_v^{ij} = z_{ij} - \kappa(T_{iw}P_{wj}) \tag{6}$$

where $\kappa(\cdot)$ is used to map a 3D map point P_{ij} to a 2D pixel coordinate f_{ij}, T_{iw} is the transformation matrix between the camera pose and the world coordinate.

Cylindrical Regularity. The cylindrical regularity is same as Eq. (2). Given a cylindrical point P_j and the cylinder parameters L_c, o_c and r_c, the cylindrical regularity is given by

$$e_c^j = |L_c \times (P_w^i - o_c)|^2 - |L_c|^2 r_c^2 \tag{7}$$

In the following experiments, it is assumed that the distances of cylindrical points are within the interval $[-0.05r_c, 0.05r_c]$ from the cylindrical surface. The uncertainty of the regularity is set to $0.00065r_c^2$.

6   Performance Validation and Evaluation

The proposed algorithm is evaluated over different testing scenarios on synthetic and real data. ORB-SLAM2 and ORB-SLAM2 with cylindrical regularity (CRORB) are compared in terms of trajectory accuracy and running time on a computer with Intel Core i7-8700 @ 3.2 GHz, 16 GB memory.

6.1   Synthetic Data

A synthetic environment is shown in Fig. 2. There is a straight 20-meter long pipe with an inner diameter of 1 m. The lower part of the straight pipe is embedded in the ground. The virtual robot moves horizontally in the pipe, and the camera observes the inner pipe surface. To provide features for SLAM, a colourful image covers the inner pipe surface (Fig. 2). Every second, the virtual camera collects 30 images of 1280 × 720 pixels, with added Gaussian noise. The true trajectory of the robot is exported from ROS Kinetic.

6.2   Real Data

The real data is acquired from a small unmanned ground vehicle (UGV) which moved along a long-buried straight pipe. The UGV (Fig. 3) is equipped with a pin-hole camera collecting images of 720 × 576 at 20 FPS (Fig. 3). A length of rope from a rope drum attaches to the UGV. When the robot moves, the rope drum turns and calculates the distance travelled shown on the images. This recorded travel distance is used as a reference instead of frame poses.

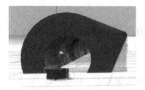 

Fig. 2. Left: The synthetic pipe environment, with a flattened bottom surface to allow easy robot motion, and a cylindrical shape to represent the real pipe environment. The robot is pictured. Right: The pipe's inner surface with a synthetic texture to allow visual SLAM algorithms to detect features.

Fig. 3. Left: The UGV with camera used to collect data. Right: An example image from the pipe environment. The texture on the sides of the pipe can be seen.

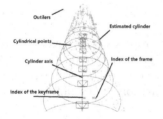 

Fig. 4. The 3D points from actual data and the cylinder fit to them. The *non-cylindrical* points can be seen which are not fit to the cylinder, and the *cylindrical* points which will be fit to the estimated cylinder are seen ahead of the most recent keyframe.

Table 1. Comparison between the two SLAM algorithms

Dataset	Synthetic data		Real data	
Method	ORB-SLAM2	CRORB	ORB-SLAM2	CRORB
rmse	0.026 m	0.007 m	0.378 m	0.285 m
Cylinder detection		0.0158 s		0.0533 s
BA	0.199 s	0.324 s	0.059 s	0.073 s
Local optimisation	0.411 s	0.505 s	0.08 s	0.104 s

6.3 Discussion

The experiments proved that the CRORB is more accurate than the ORB-SLAM2 in a pipe at the cost of additional computation. The Fig. 4 show mapping with actual data, and the cylinder fit to the data points. The error between the ground truth and the estimated trajectory is difficult to visualise. Table 1 compared accuracy and computation between two SLAM algorithms. The root means squared error (RMSE) of the absolute pose error from two estimated trajectories are provided. These numbers indicate the performance of the estimation. Also, the running time of local optimisation, BA and cylinder detection are compared, each of which is the average time over ten runs on the same data. The local optimisation includes cylindrical points classification, optimiser initialisation and BA.

The running time of local optimisation and BA differs significantly between the two algorithms. The difference is because the BA in CRORB has additional cylindrical regularity. Also, the algorithms in actual data cost less computation. In the scale-free map, the robot's speed is faster in the actual data than in synthetic data. The local optimisation in synthetic data involves more covisible keyframes, and they share more common map points, which means a larger optimisation problem with more variables and more constraints. So the running time of synthetic data is longer. The conventional ORB-SLAM2 tends to underestimate the trajectory. The cylindrical regularity cannot solve this problem, but it can slow down this trend.

7 Conclusion

In this paper, a novel SLAM framework is proposed to leverage cylindrical regularity in a straight pipe. The cylindrical regularity can improve the localisation accuracy. In the future, we plan to use a new flexible cylinder representation method and include other structural information from a pipe network.

References

1. Burgard, R.: g2o - General Graph Optimization (2011). https://github.com/RainerKuemmerle/g2o
2. Chuang, T.Y., Sung, C.C.: Learning and SLAM based decision support platform for sewer inspection. Remote Sens. **12**(6) (2020). https://doi.org/10.3390/rs12060968
3. El Kahi, S., Asmar, D., Fakih, A., Nieto, J., Nebot, E.: A vison-based system for mapping the inside of a pipe. In: Proceedings of the 2011 IEEE International Conference on Robotics and Biomimetics (1), pp. 2605–2611 (2011). https://doi.org/10.1109/ROBIO.2011.6181697
4. Engel, J., Schöps, T., Cremers, D.: LSD-SLAM: large-scale direct monocular SLAM. In: Fleet, D., Pajdla, T., Schiele, B., Tuytelaars, T. (eds.) ECCV 2014. LNCS, vol. 8690, pp. 834–849. Springer, Cham (2014). https://doi.org/10.1007/978-3-319-10605-2_54

5. Fischler, M.A., Bolles, R.C.: Random sample consensus: a paradigm for model fitting with applications to image analysis and automated cartography. Commun. ACM **24**(6), 381–395 (1981). https://doi.org/10.1145/358669.358692
6. Forster, C., Pizzoli, M., Scaramuzza, D.: SVO: fast semi-direct monocular visual odometry. In: Proceedings of the IEEE International Conference on Robotics and Automation, no. May, pp. 15–22 (2014). https://doi.org/10.1109/ICRA.2014.6906584
7. Gee, A.P., Chekhlov, D., Calway, A., Mayol-Cuevas, W.: Discovering higher level structure in visual SLAM. IEEE Trans. Rob. **24**(5), 980–990 (2008). https://doi.org/10.1109/TRO.2008.2004641
8. Hansen, P., Alismail, H., Rander, P., Browning, B.: Visual mapping for natural gas pipe inspection. Int. J. Rob. Res. **34**(4–5), 532–538 (2015). https://doi.org/10.1177/0278364914550133
9. He, Y., Zhao, J., Guo, Y., He, W., Yuan, K.: PL-VIO: tightly-coupled monocular visual-inertial odometry using point and line features. Sensors (Switzerland) **18**(4), 1–25 (2018). https://doi.org/10.3390/s18041159
10. Kagami, S., Taira, H., Miyashita, N., Torii, A., Okutomi, M.: 3D Pipe network reconstruction based on structure from motion with incremental conic shape detection and cylindrical constraint. In: Proceeding of the IEEE International Symposium on Industrial Electronics, vol. 2020-June, pp. 1345–1352 (2020). https://doi.org/10.1109/ISIE45063.2020.9152377
11. Levenberg, K.: A method for the solution of certain non-linear problems in least squares. Q. Appl. Math. **2**(2), 164–168 (1944)
12. Künzel, J., Werner, T., Eisert, P., Waschnewski, J., Möller, R., Hilpert, R.: Automatic analysis of sewer pipes based on unrolled monocular fisheye images. In: Proceedings of the 2018 IEEE Winter Conference on Applications of Computer Vision, WACV 2018, vol. 2018-Janua, pp. 2019–2027 (2018). https://doi.org/10.1109/WACV.2018.00223
13. Li, X., He, Y., Lin, J., Liu, X.: Leveraging Planar Regularities for Point Line Visual-Inertial Odometry (2020). http://arxiv.org/abs/2004.11969
14. Lopez-Escogido, D., De La Fraga, L.G.: Automatic extraction of geometric models from 3D point cloud datasets. In: Proceedings of the 2014 11th International Conference on Electrical Engineering, Computing Science and Automatic Control (CCE). IEEE (2014). https://doi.org/10.1109/ICEEE.2014.6978316
15. Marquardt, D.W.: An algorithm for least-squares estimation of nonlinear parameters. J. Soc. Ind. Appl. Math. **11**(2), 431–441 (1963)
16. Mur-Artal, R., Tardos, J.D.: ORB-SLAM2: an open-source SLAM system for monocular, stereo, and RGB-D cameras. IEEE Trans. Rob. **33**(5), 1255–1262 (2017). https://doi.org/10.1109/TRO.2017.2705103
17. Özyeil, O., Voroninski, V., Basri, R., Singer, A.: A survey of structure from motion. Acta Numer. **26**, 305–364 (2017). https://doi.org/10.1017/S096249291700006X
18. Shakarji, C.M.: Least-squares fitting algorithms of the NIST algorithm testing system. J. Res. Nat. Inst. Stand. Technol. **103**(6), 633–641 (1998). https://doi.org/10.6028/jres.103.043
19. Zhang, Y., Hartley, R., Mashford, J., Wang, L., Burn, S.: Pipeline reconstruction from fisheye images. J. WSCG **19**, 49–57 (2011)
20. Zhou, H., Zou, D., Pei, L., Ying, R., Liu, P., Yu, W.: StructSLAM: visual SLAM with building structure lines. IEEE Trans. Veh. Technol. **64**(4), 1364–1375 (2015). https://doi.org/10.1109/TVT.2015.2388780

CRH*: A Deadlock Free Framework for Scalable Prioritised Path Planning in Multi-robot Systems

James R. Heselden$^{(\boxtimes)}$(iD) and Gautham P. Das$^{(\boxtimes)}$(iD)

University of Lincoln, Lincoln, Lincolnshire, UK
{jheselden,gdas}@lincoln.ac.uk

Abstract. Multi-robot system is an ever growing tool which is able to be applied to a wide range of industries to improve productivity and robustness, especially when tasks are distributed in space, time and functionality. Recent works have shown the benefits of multi-robot systems in fields such as warehouse automation, entertainment and agriculture. The work presented in this paper tackles the deadlock problem in multi-robot navigation, in which robots within a common work-space, are caught in situations where they are unable to navigate to their targets, being blocked by one another. This problem can be mitigated by efficient multi-robot path planning. Our work focused around the development of a scalable rescheduling algorithm named Conflict Resolution Heuristic A* (CRH*) (https://github.com/iranaphor/crh_star) for decoupled prioritised planning. Extensive experimental evaluation of CRH* was carried out in discrete event simulations of a fleet of autonomous agricultural robots. The results from these experiments proved that the algorithm was both scalable and deadlock-free. Additionally, novel customisation options were included to test further optimisations in system performance. Continuous Assignment and Dynamic Scoring showed to reduce the make-span of the routing whilst Combinatorial Heuristics showed to reduce the impact of outliers on priority orderings.

Keywords: Multi-robot path planning · Prioritised planning · Decoupled path planning · A* · Reservation tables

1 Introduction

Autonomous mobile robotic technologies have matured over recent decades enabling their uses in many real-world applications. This has resulted in a push towards scaling up systems to large mobile robot fleets to improve operational efficiency, especially when tasks are inherently distributed in space, time or functionality. One of the primary requirements to ensure proper coordination among a fleet of autonomous mobile robots in a shared-workspace, is efficient path planning and allocation. Without effective coordination, interference between robots

© Springer Nature Switzerland AG 2021
C. Fox et al. (Eds.): TAROS 2021, LNAI 13054, pp. 66–75, 2021.
https://doi.org/10.1007/978-3-030-89177-0_7

can have a detrimental effect on the fleet operations. Congestion-free route planning and coordination is needed to address this interference.

In Multi-Robot Path Planning (MRPP), there are four main challenges to overcome: *Completeness*, is the guarantee that a route will be found if one exists; *Optimality*, is the guarantee to find a set of routes minimising some metric such as make-span (time the last robot arrives) or flow-time (sum of all route lengths) [19]; *Deadlocking*, is where a robot will be in a state preventing another from reaching a target [5,8]; and *Scalability*, is the issue of processing resources thinning as the complexity of the joint state-space increases. Among these, optimality and scalability can be considered mutually exclusive, and are tackled well by Coupled and Decoupled approaches respectively.

An example of a scenario where MRPP can be useful is a fleet of agricultural robots deployed in a polytunnel environment to execute a series of in-field logistics tasks [7]. These tasks are dynamic in nature and are dispersed over the environment. This paper addresses the MRPP problem to enable congestion and deadlock-free movement of robots in such a polytunnel environment, by proposing a novel algorithm called Conflict Resolution Heuristic A* (CRH*). By relying on decentralised and decoupled route planning to find sub-optimal solutions, the CRH* algorithm is complete and scalable, as demonstrated by empirical evaluations.

The rest of this paper is organised as follows: Sect. 2 provides an overview of related work in Prioritised Planning; Sect. 3 provides an overview of the implementation; Sect. 4 details the experimental setup, evaluation and results; and Sect. 5 concludes our findings.

2   Related Works

Decentralised and decoupled MRPP approaches are widely preferred to address the high computational complexity and low scalability of centralised approaches. Prioritised Planning (PP) is a decoupled MRPP approach which assigns priorities to each robot and then plans a route for each one sequentially, treating all prior robots as dynamic obstacles.

As the complexity of the joint state-space is proportional to the total configuration of priorities, finding the optimal assignment of priorities is a NP-Hard problem. Thus a full state-space search is unfeasible and smarter approaches must be taken [2]. When routes are unavailable due to blocking from higher priority agents, the robot can be considered to be deadlocked. Rescheduling can be used to optimise priority assignments and replan routes. CRH* tackles the area of rescheduling, making use of enhanced reservation tables and comprehensive replanning in a distributed decision-making topology.

Our approach focuses in the topological domain, in which the map is a finite set of discrete positions (nodes) and connections between them (edges) indicating possible paths from one node to another [10]. It is used as the common discretised environment representation over which all robots plan their routes. Such representations have low planning complexity and can easily detect possible conflicts compared to metric maps.

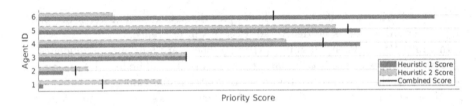

Fig. 1. Example of the potential of combinatorial heuristics, as the combination of two independent heuristics.

2.1 Heuristics

The effective use of heuristics works with the intent to give priority to the robot which needs it the most. In *Static Ordering* (SO) [9] scoring is made using the order the agents were added to the network, and in *Euclidean Distance* (ED) [17] scoring is based on the distance to the target.

These work well in metric maps which are very open and well-connected, however for agricultural environments in the scale of hectares, these are not viable as they are. Polytunnels and fields often include long isolated paths to traverse, which are better managed by approaches such as below, which follow the idea that agents struggle due to environmental constraints. ED can be adapted into Optimal Path Length (OPL) to become viable in these scenarios.

In *Planning Time* (PT) [18], the processing time to find a route is used for scoring, however this falls short in heterogeneous systems where platforms have differing processing hardware. In *Naive & Coupled Surroundings* [6,19] agents are scored based on the cluttering of their workspace by counting the number of local obstacles. Where in Naive Surroundings (NS), obstacles are regarded as distinct and in Coupled Surroundings (CS) they are treated as effective, where effective obstacles are regions the agent is unable to navigate. In *Path Prospects* (PaP) [19] scoring is made based on the number of effective obstacles between the start and target to score on the number of paths available in the homology class of trajectories.

In PP, it is standard to use a single heuristic to assign priorities. We extend on this, exploring the potential of combining multiple heuristics to improve to handling of outliers demonstrated in Fig. 1.

2.2 Rescheduling

Rescheduling works to reduce the impact of deadlocks by modifying the priority schema to optimise generated orderings [9]. In *Random rescheduling* [4] priorities are randomised and replanned whenever a deadlock occurs. The *Hill-Climbing* search [3] extends on this by randomly swapping pairs of priorities. *Continuous Enhancement* [15] allows agents to modify their own score if they are unable to find a route. This is extended by *Deterministic Rescheduling* [1], to award the maximum priority, following the idea that issues are caused by their local environment. *Local Priority Assignment* [14] works by exploring all local priority configurations in proximity to an agent unable to find a route. *Priority Tuning* [13] optimises successful assignments by shuffling priorities between the least optimal agents, repeating until convergence. In our approach, we extend the ideas in Deterministic Rescheduling by integrating the intelligent overriding of higher priorities.

2.3 Path Finding

Path Finding algorithms are a core component within prioritised planning, being used to generate routes once priorities are assigned. As detailed in [11,16], there are many categories of path finding algorithms. Being one of the most fundamental path finding algorithms, *A** [12] works only to identify a route. *Local Repair A** (LRA*) [20], recalculates the remainder of its route when a collision is pre-empted. *Cooperative A** (CA*) [16], uses three dimensional space-time reservation tables to mark off impassable regions. Our approach includes an extension to the reservation tables of CA* to override existing reservations; and an extension to LRA* to optimise replanning from a point of conflict.

3 Design and Development

3.1 Overview

The main architecture of CRH* (Fig. 2), works in three stages, with the final two repeating together till convergence. In the first stage, the robot is assigned a target, plans a route, and informs the coordinator of its reservations. The coordinator, on receiving the route, adds the reservations to the global map, notifying any other robots of overturned reservations in the second stage. The robots each receive their failed reservations (FR) in the third stage, and perform replanning to identify new routes, passing these new routes to the coordinator.

Each message contains a list of reservations, of which each consist of an edge identifier, agent identifier, and a reservation start and end time.

On receiving an FR, the shortest of three replanning methods is returned to the coordinator. These three methods are: *Replanning from Start* where a new route is generated from scratch; *Replanning from Conflict* where the route beyond FR is replanned; and *Replanning with Delay* which adds a time delay (in which the robot will wait to use the FR once it is available) and replans from there.

3.2 A* Adaptations

There were two key modifications to the motion planning algorithm to enable the enhancements for our approach, the first was the reservation override system (CRH Battle), the second was the deadlock management (FAILED List).

The CRH Battle was included within A* where as each edge is initially investigated, a score (referred to as the CRH score) is generated to query against any existing reservations in the time period specified. Only if the robot's CRH

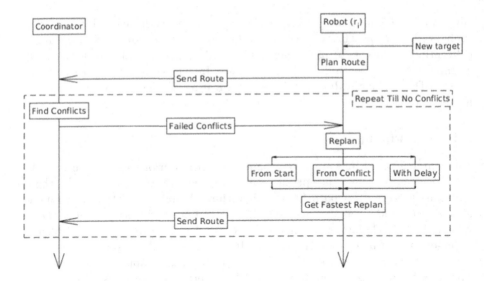

Fig. 2. Visual representation of robot-coordinator communication.

score is greater, will the override work. While this scoring system can utilise any single heuristic such as described in Sect. 2.1, it is also capable of taking the combination of multiple heuristics (e.g. ED, $\sum(ED, OPL)$, or $\prod(PT, NS, CS)$). For our experiments, we utilise a variety of scoring systems as the heuristics themselves are arbitrary to the aim of the research.

The deadlock management is implemented in the form of an additional flag for exploration. A* has two flags, OPEN and CLOSED, which define whether a node is on the frontier for exploration or has already been explored, where if the OPEN list is exhausted, the planning fails. In our approach, when reservation overrides fail, the edge is added to a new FAILED list, which is accessed once the OPEN list is exhausted to obtain the most optimal edge to override, boosting the CRH Score generated.

3.3 Framework Facilities

Continuous Assignment. In PP, the handling of new assignments is done in one of two ways, in *Batch Assignment* replanning will wait till all have completed routes, whilst in *Full Replanning* all agents replan in the current state. In our approach, we propose a third method *Continuous Assignment* as a direct contrast to Batch Assignment in which rescheduling is applied without replanning the entire network, only updating affected agents. This allows for a reduction in make-span as shown in Fig. 3.

Dynamic Scoring. The standard method of score generation is *Static*, in which scores for each agent are assigned before routing. In our approach, we implement the concept of dynamic scoring, where every reservation uses locally relevant information to compute heuristics. As the routing gets closer to a target, each

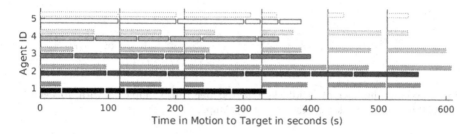

Fig. 3. Example of route times in batch (upper) and continuous (lower) assignment for a series of agents.

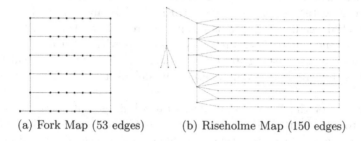

(a) Fork Map (53 edges)   (b) Riseholme Map (150 edges)

Fig. 4. Topological Maps used in the experiments.

edge will be reserved with information relevant to that edge rather then information from the agents current location, for example with ED, each edge will be reserved with its distance to the target rather the distance to the target from the start node as would happen with static scoring.

4   Experiments

Discrete Event Simulation. To ensure a comprehensive evaluation, Discrete Event Simulation (DES) was utilised along with Monte-Carlo simulations, enabled through the deterministic nature of the approach. In this, time jumps to points of interest (POI) rather than evaluating every timestep. In our experiments, these POI consist of any timestep in which a route is completed; time jumps to the next route completion, performs any calculations, and repeats.

Experiment Maps. Experimentation was completed on two topological maps Fork (Fig. 4a) and Riseholme (Fig. 4b), representing a single polytunnel and a pair of polytunnels respectively. The experimentation was completed on the Fork map for the majority of experiments, with the Riseholme map used also for the scalability test.

Heuristics. In the following experiments, used to generate the CRH scores for resolving conflicts are the heuristics of: Optimal Path Length (OPL), Euclidean Distance (ED), Planning Time (PT), and Static Ordering (SO) of which we utilise the Agent's ID.

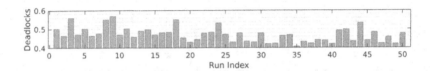

Fig. 5. Average number of deadlocks resolved per run. Completed with 10 agents, across 50 iterations of 1k targets in the Fork Map.

4.1 Evaluation of CRH*

Deadlocks. The FAILED list, is used to handle every deadlock encountered, so by recording the activity of the FAILED list, we are able to identify how often potential deadlock situations occur. Figure 5 shows the average number of deadlocks encountered per target over 50 runs with 1000 targets per run. These results show on average 0.47 deadlocks for each given target, which if not managed as they are here, would cause many delays in navigation.

Scalability. As the approach is decentralised in design, path planning is expected to run distributed, thus does not contribute to scalability concerns. The area of highest concern is thus communication, which consists of one message per replan to the coordinator. So to evaluate scalability, the Replans per Target (RT) is recorded, which accurately measures the load on the coordinator. The results in Fig. 6 show upward trends initially before plateauing, avoiding exponential scaling and thus can be regarded as scalable.

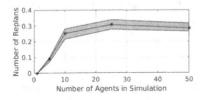

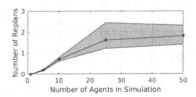

(a) Average Replans in Fork Map   (b) Average Replans in Riseholme Map

Fig. 6. Range-grouped area charts for average RT over five runs of 50 targets

4.2 Evaluation of Optimisation Improvements

Batch vs. Continuous Assignment. Continuous Assignment works to improve make-span by reducing idle time for agents waiting to replan. Figure 7a shows the resulting make-span distributions contrasting Batch and Continuous Assignment. The tests were run five times with 20 targets for each of 5, 10 and 20 agents using OPL as the CRH score to resolve conflicts. The results show Continuous Assignment improves make-span in both small and large simulations. This is evidenced by Fig. 7b showing the same tests run for 1000 targets with make-span reductions of 47%, 38%, and 20% respectively to the number of agents.

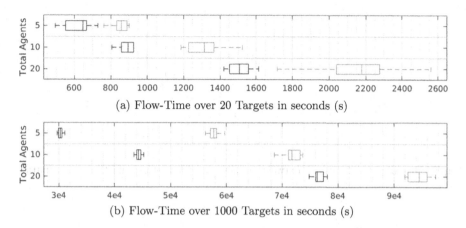

(a) Flow-Time over 20 Targets in seconds (s)

(b) Flow-Time over 1000 Targets in seconds (s)

Fig. 7. Make-Span distribution for Continuous (left) and Batch (right) Assignment with simulations of 5, 10 and 20 agents.

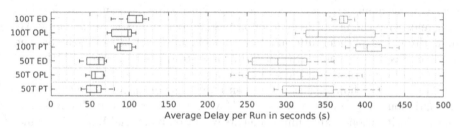

Fig. 8. Distribution of delays contrasting Dynamic (left) and Static (right) Scoring systems with 50 and 100 targets per agent.

Static vs. Dynamic Scoring. To test the efficacy of the optimisation, the decoupled optimal make-span is negated from the CRH* make-span to get the worst-case delay. This delay was recorded across two sets of experiments, the first testing static scoring, and the second with dynamic scoring. This was repeated across six categories using the heuristics of ED, OPL and PT, for each of 50 and 100 targets per agent. The results in Fig. 8 show Dynamic Scoring offers a significant improvement, with the margin between Static and Dynamic Scoring growing larger proportionally to the total targets.

Base vs. Combinatorial Heuristics. To evaluate the efficacy of combinatorial heuristics, 10 tests were performed with 10 agents each, recording the average number of replans per run. Each test consisted of 10 runs with 20 targets, completed for each heuristic independently then combined together. This is repeated three times, the first comparing ED, OPL and PT; the second using SO and OPL; and the third comparing SO and ED. From Fig. 9, the average range of outliers is reduced when using the combination of all heuristics as opposed to purely independent heuristics. In addition, the average number of replans decreases for combined heuristics when using a combination of heuristic and Agent ID.

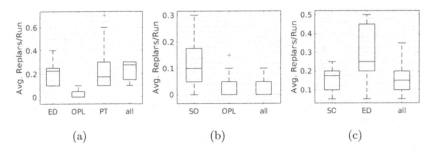

Fig. 9. Distribution of replans between independent heuristics, and their combination (all).

5   Conclusion

In this work, we have proposed the CRH* algorithm, a decentralised and decoupled enhancement to prioritised planning which aimed to improve deadlock avoidance with the use of reservation tables and deterministic rescheduling. We show through experimental evaluation that our approach is both scalable and deadlock-free as the complexity of the joint state-space increases with the size of the topological map and the number of agents.

We have also shown, clear make-span reductions of up to 47% with the use of Continuous Assignment and up to 82% with Dynamic Scoring. We have also shown prioritisation quality improvements with Combinatorial Heuristics reducing the impact of extreme outliers.

Due to the agnostic nature of the approach, the discrete event simulation and specific heuristics chosen are arbitrary to the evaluation of the developed features, however further work will include exploration with a wider sample of heuristics, and performance evaluations beyond discrete event simulation.

References

1. Andreychuk, A., Yakovlev, K.: Two techniques that enhance the performance of multi-robot prioritized path planning. In: Proceedings of International Joint Conference Autonomous agents and multiagent systems, AAMAS, vol. 3, pp. 2177–2179 (2018). ISSN 15582914. arXiv: 1805.01270
2. Azarm, K., Schmidt, G.: Conflict-free motion of multiple mobile robots based on decentralized motion planning and negotiation. In: Proceedings of International Conference on Robotics and Automation, vol. 4, pp. 3526–3533. IEEE (1997)
3. Bennewitz, M., Burgard, W., Thrun, S.: Finding and optimizing solvable priority schemes for decoupled path planning techniques for teams of mobile robots. Rob. Auton. Syst. 41(2–3), 89–99 (2002)
4. Bennewitz, M., Burgard, W., Thrun, S.: Optimizing schedules for prioritized path planning of multi-robot systems. In: IEEE International Conference on Robotics and Automation, vol. 1, pp. 271–276 (2001)

5. Cap, M., et al.: Prioritized planning algorithms for trajectory coordination of multiple mobile robots. IEEE Trans. Autom. Sci. Eng. **12**(3), 835–849 (2015). ISSN: 15455955. arXiv: 1409.2399

6. Clark, C.M., Bretl, T., Rock, S.: Applying kinodynamic randomized motion planning with a dynamic priority system to multi-robot space systems. In: Proceedings, IEEE Aerospace Conference, vol. 7, p. 7. IEEE (2002)

7. Das, G.P., et al.: Discrete event simulations for scalability analysis of robotic in-field logistics in agriculture - a case study. In: ICRA 2018 International Conference on Robotics and Automation, Workshop on Robotic Vision and Action in Agriculture, Brisbane (2018)

8. Dewangan, R.K., Shukla, A., Godfrey, W.W.: Survey on prioritized multi robot path planning. In: 2017 IEEE International Conference on Smart Technologies and Management for Computing, Communication, Controls, Energy And Materials, pp. 423–428. IEEE (2017)

9. Erdmann, M., Lozano-Pérez, T.: On multiple moving objects. Algorithmica **2**(1–4), 477–521 (1987)

10. Fentanes, J.P., et al.: Now or later? Predicting and maximising success of navigation actions from long-term experience. In: Proceedings - IEEE International Conference on Robotics and Automation, June, Seattle, USA, vol. 2015, pp. 1112–1117 (2015)

11. Ferguson, D., Likhachev, M., Stentz, A.: A guide to heuristic-based path planning. In: Proceedings International Workshop on Planning Under Uncertainty for Autonomous Systems, International Conference on Automated Planning and Scheduling, pp. 1–10 (2005)

12. Hart, P.E., Nilsson, N.J., Raphael, B.: A formal basis for the heuristic determination of minimum cost paths. IEEE Trans. Syst. Sci. Cybern. **4**(2), 100–107 (1968)

13. Hu, B., Cao, Z.: Minimizing task completion time of prioritized motion planning in multi-robot systems. In: IEEE International Conference on Systems, Man and Cybernetics, vol. 2019, pp. 1018–1023. IEEE (2019)

14. Ma, H., et al.: Searching with consistent prioritization for multi-agent path finding. In: Proceedings of the AAAI Conference on Artificial Intelligence, vol. 33, pp. 7643–7650 (2019). ISSN: 2159–5399. arXiv: 1812.06356

15. Regele, R., Levi, P.: Cooperative multi-robot path planning by heuristic priority adjustment. In: 2006 IEEE/RSJ International Conference on Intelligent Robots and Systems, pp. 5954–5959. IEEE (2006)

16. Silver, D.: Cooperative Pathfinding. Aiide **1**, 117–122 (2005)

17. Van Den Berg, J.P., Overmars, M.H.: Prioritized motion planning for multiple robots. In: 2005 IEEE/RSJ International Conference on Intelligent Robots and Systems, IROS, pp. 2217–2222 (2005)

18. Velagapudi, P., Sycara, K., Scerri, P.: Decentralized prioritized planning in large multirobot teams. In: IEEE/RSJ 2010 International Conference on Intelligent Robots and Systems, pp. 4603–4609 (2010)

19. Wu, W., Bhattacharya, S., Prorok, A.: Multi-robot path deconfliction through prioritization by path prospects, pp. 22–24 (2019). arXiv: 1908.02361

20. Zelinsky, A.: A mobile robot navigation exploration algorithm. IEEE Trans. Robot. Autom. **8**(6), 707–717 (1992)

Task-Based Ad-hoc Teamwork
with Adversary

Elnaz Shafipour$^{(\boxtimes)}$ and Saber Fallah

University of Surrey, Guildford, UK
{e.shafipour,s.fallah}@surrey.ac.uk

Abstract. Many real-world applications require agents to cooperate
and collaborate to accomplish shared missions; though, there are many
instances where the agents should work together without communication or prior coordination. In the meantime, agents often coordinate
in a decentralised manner to complete tasks that are displaced in an
environment (e.g., foraging, demining, rescue or firefighting). Each agent
in the team is responsible for selecting their own task and completing
it autonomously. However, there is a possibility of an adversary in the
team, who tries to prevent other agents from achieving their goals. In
this study, we assume there is an agent who estimates the model of
other agents in the team to boost the team's performance regardless of
the enemy's attacks. Hence, we present *On-line Estimators for Ad-hoc
Task Allocation with Adversary* (OEATA-A), a novel algorithm to have
better estimations of the teammates' future behaviour, which includes
identifying enemies among friends.

Keywords: Autonomous systems · Adversary agent · Learning agent ·
Multi-agent system · Decentralised task allocation

1 Introduction

The world is moving towards "smart systems", which rely on some form of intelligent agent technology, that can autonomously collect information from their
surrounding environment and act upon it. An example is multiple rovers in
space, which attempt to accomplish their missions cooperatively. These agents
may work collaboratively toward the completion of common tasks that they cannot handle individually. However, there might be differences between the agents
in terms of origin, access to information, and perceptual and actuation capabilities. Therefore, such teamwork might take place without any prior coordination
protocol or even, in some cases, any form of explicit communication. These kinds
of teams are known as ad-hoc teams. Moreover, many domains require agents
to work together to accomplish tasks that are distributed across the system. In
these systems, several tasks need to be accomplished in an uncertain environment
with no centralised mechanism to allocate tasks. Accordingly, the agents in the
team are not managed to perform their tasks, and they autonomously decide

© Springer Nature Switzerland AG 2021
C. Fox et al. (Eds.): TAROS 2021, LNAI 13054, pp. 76–87, 2021.
https://doi.org/10.1007/978-3-030-89177-0_8

which one to complete, without being directly assigned [4]. The *decentralised* allocation is quite natural in ad-hoc teamwork, as we cannot assume that other agents would be programmed to follow a centralised controller. For example, imagine a natural disaster and hazardous situation where autonomous robots (agents) have been dispatched from different countries or different organisations to handle the emergency conditions. Rather than waiting for communication and coordination protocols to develop, these robots need to act immediately to avoid putting lives at risk. In other words, each robot chooses its own strategy for saving as many lives as possible and behaves accordingly.

Nevertheless, there is a possibility of existing potential enemies in the system which are unknown to the rest of the team. The agents of this type display destructive behaviours that prevent their teammates from reaching their targets. This work focused on the tasks-based teams where the team involves multiple agents with a range of cooperative and disruptive behaviours in a decentralised distributed system. As such, we refer to this task-based ad hoc team working with an adversary as *Task-based Ad-hoc Teamwork with Adversary*. Hence, learning and reasoning about the team members are mandatory to improve the team's performance. In our system, there are some learning agents, who are aware of pre-existing standards for coordination and communication, so they can try to learn about their teammates with limited information [3]. Through such intelligent coordination in this ad-hoc team, the shared goals will be achieved more efficiently. However, the sole aim of our team study is not to improve collaboration, and we need to reduce the hostile behaviour of some team members by identifying and examining the enemies correctly. Our solution to this problem is *On-line Estimators for Ad-hoc Task Allocation with Adversary* (OEATA-A), a *novel algorithm* for estimating teammates future behaviours. We show that our algorithm converges to a perfect estimation when the number of tasks to be performed gets larger.

2   Related Works

In the literature, there are many works considering the presence of opponents in the team. In the majority of these studies, the team members know who the adversary agent is. Celli [5] focuses on ex-ante coordination, where team members have an opportunity to discuss and agree on tactics before the game starts, but will be unable to communicate during the game.

Mirchevska [8] presents a domain-independent Multi-Agent Strategy Discovering Algorithm (MASDA), which discovers strategic behaviour patterns of a group of agents under the described conditions. The algorithm represents the observed multi-agent activity as a graph, where graph connections correspond to performed actions and graph nodes correspond to environment states at action starts. Based on such data representation, the algorithm applies hierarchical clustering and rule induction to extract and describe strategic behaviour.

There is another work [9], which is focused on resilience in cooperative MAS and propose an Antagonist-Ratio Training Scheme (ARTS) by reformulating the original target MAS as a mixed cooperative-competitive game between a group of protagonists which represent agents of the target MAS and a group of antagonists which represent failures in the MAS. However, Lin [7] introduces a novel attack where the attacker first trains a policy network with reinforcement learning to find a wrong action it should encourage the victim agent to take. Then, the adversary uses targeted adversarial examples to force the victim to take this action. Uesato [11] addresses the problem of evaluating learning systems in safety-critical domains such as autonomous driving, where failures can have catastrophic consequences. In our work, we assume that we are not aware of which teammate is the adversary agent. However, by observing their behaviour, we show that our method could obtain a better estimation which leads better performance for the team.

3   Methodology

3.1   Ad-Hoc Teamwork with Adversaries

Our ad-hoc team consists of several agents, which do not have enough knowledge about each other. The team's goal is to work together and cooperate to accomplish shared goals. There is, however, a possibility of there being an adversary agent among team members. This agent is attempting to minimise the team's performance in a way the other agents are not aware of.

Three main groups of agents are working together as part of this ad hoc team. The first group is the naive agents ($\omega \in \mathbf{\Omega}$), which attempt to improve the team's achievement. Agents of this type use static algorithms to accomplish their tasks, and they cannot learn from what is happening in their environment. Second are the adversaries, who attempt to defeat the goals of other agents. In our team, we assume there is only one adversary agent, Λ. The last group is the learning agents, and again we consider only one learning agent, ϕ, in our team. The objective of the learning agent is to find the best actions that maximise the performance of the team. The ϕ agent is the only agent in the team which can learn teammates' future actions as it estimates and discovers their models over time.

In this system, there is a set of tasks ($\mathcal{T}$) that team members make an effort to accomplish autonomously, except the adversary group. A task $\tau \in \mathcal{T}$ may require multiple agents, as well as several time steps to finish successfully. For instance, in a foraging problem, a heavy item may require two or more robots to be collected. Furthermore, the robots would need to move towards the task location, taking multiple time steps to move from their initial position.

Model of Naive Agents. All naive agents try to perform their tasks autonomously within the environment. However, choosing and completing each task τ by each ω is dependent on its internal algorithm and capabilities. The algorithm for each ω can be varied in different domains. We assume that all these algorithms have a set of inputs, which we denote as *parameters* of these algorithms. For example, in the foraging domain [10] (explained in detail in Sect. 4.1), there might be multiple boxes in the robot's visible area. Hence, the algorithms in this domain would be the way the robot chooses an item to collect. The algorithm might be selecting the closest box or the lightest box among the visible ones. In addition, the size of the robot's visible cone, as well as its ability to collect the box, are considered its parameters. Like previous works [1,12], we consider the algorithm of choosing targets as the type of naive agents. Furthermore, we suppose the learning agent knows the set of possible types Θ in the system. However, the type of each ω agent is unknown to it. Thus, naive agents' behaviour and actions mirror the type and parameter of the agents, and we define each $\omega \in \Omega$ as a tuple $(\theta, \mathbf{p})$. $\theta \in \Theta$ in this tuple is ω agent's type and $\mathbf{p}$ represents its parameters, which is a vector $\mathbf{p} =< p_1, p_2, ..., p_n >$. Each element p_i in the vector $\mathbf{p}$ is defined in a fixed range $[p_i^{min}, p_i^{max}]$ [1]. Choosing a new task (considered as the agent's "target") happens in the very first state, and whenever ω agent finishes a task. We call these states as *Choose Target State* ($\mathfrak{s}$).

Model of Adversary Agent. The adversary agent has the full observation of the environment, and we define a *Markov Decision Problem* model for it. Although there are multiple agents in the team, we set the model *under the point of view of the agent* Λ. Therefore, we consider a set of states $\mathcal{S}_\Lambda$, a set of actions $\mathcal{A}_\Lambda$, a reward function $\mathcal{R} : \mathcal{S}_\Lambda \times \mathcal{A}_\Lambda \times \mathcal{S}_\Lambda \rightarrow [0, 1]$, and a transition function $\mathcal{T} : \mathcal{S}_\Lambda \times \mathcal{A}_\Lambda \times \mathcal{S}_\Lambda \rightarrow [0, 1]$ for the Λ agent. The actions in the model are only the Λ agent's actions and not any of others. Additionally, the goal of the Λ agent is minimising the reward function. In Λ agent's MDP model, all naive agents and the learning agent are considered as a part of the environment, and they are not directly represented in the MDP model. The Λ agent can only decide its own actions and has no control over the actions of any other agents in the team. However, the Λ agent has not the ability to learn the other teammates' types and parameters. Therefore, it will not be able to estimate the future behaviour of the teammates, and it considers them as obstacles in the environment. The Λ agent employ *UCT-H* [12] for its on-line planning.

Model of the Learning Agent. Like the adversary agent, the learning agent has full observability and its model is defined as a single agent MDP, *under the point of view of the agent* ϕ, as in previous works [1,12]. Like the adversary agent, for the ϕ agent, we consider a set of states $\mathcal{S}_\phi$, a set of actions $\mathcal{A}_\phi$, a reward function $\mathcal{R} : \mathcal{S}_\phi \times \mathcal{A}_\phi \times \mathcal{S}_\phi \rightarrow [0, 1]$, and a transition function $\mathcal{T} : \mathcal{S}_\phi \times \mathcal{A}_\phi \times \mathcal{S}_\phi \rightarrow [0, 1]$, where the actions in the model are only the ϕ agent's actions and not any of others. Similar to the adversary agent, we apply *UCT-H* to solve the MDP model of the learning agent. It is clear that in the *actual* problem, the next state depends on the actions of all agents as they are dynamic in the environment. Whereas, the ϕ agent is unsure about the teammates' next actions. By taking naive agents' into account, given a state s, an agent $\omega \in \Omega$ has an unknown probability distribution (pdf) across a set of actions $\mathcal{A}_\omega$, which is given by ω's internal algorithm $(\theta, \mathbf{p})$. Additionally, as we mentioned earlier, the learning agent has the ability to estimate teammates' future actions. Note that the agents' types and parameters are actually not observable, but in this MDP model that is not directly considered. The estimated types and parameters are used during online planning, affecting the current transition function.

As mentioned earlier, in this task-based ad-hoc team, ϕ agent attempts to help the team to get the highest possible achievement. For this reason, the learning agent needs to find the optimal value function, which maximises the expected sum of discounted rewards $E[\sum_{j=0}^{\infty} \gamma^j r_{t+j}]$, where t is the current time, r_{t+j} is the reward ϕ agent receives at j steps in the future, $\gamma \in (0, 1]$ is a discount factor. Also, we consider that we obtain the rewards by solving the tasks $\tau \in \mathcal{T}$ of the team. That is, we define ϕ agent's reward as $\sum r_\tau$, where r_τ is the reward obtained after the task τ completion. Note that the sum of rewards is not only across the tasks completed by ϕ agent but all tasks are completed by any set of agents in a given state. Furthermore, there might be some tasks in the system that cannot be achieved without cooperation between the agents. Hence, the number of required agents for finishing a task τ depends on each specific task and the set of agents that are jointly trying to complete it.

3.2 On-Line Estimators for Ad-hoc Task Allocation with Adversary

In this paper, we introduce *On-line Estimators for Ad-hoc Task Allocation with Adversary (OEATA-A)*, which is based on the work done by Shafipour [10], called OEATA. In this method, we want to check if all the team members collaborate to finish common tasks. In other words, our goal is to check if there is any adversary agent in the team that has non-collaborative behaviours and wishes to avoid other team members to reach their goals which are called In OEATA-A, when the learning process starts, we assume there is no adversary agent in the team. Additionally, we suppose all non-learning agents will accomplish shared tasks. For this purpose, we record all tasks that each agent accomplishes (except for the learning agent ϕ). The reason for keeping the completed task by each agent is to compare them with the predictions of a set of *estimators*.

All *estimators* are initialised at the beginning of the process and evaluated whenever a task is done. The ones that are not able to make good predictions are removed after several incorrect estimations, and replaced by new *estimators* that can either be created using successful ones or entirely random. Moreover, if the agent is an adversary, then there will not be a recorded task for it.

In OEATA-A as well as OEATA, we have a *set of estimators* to keep the potential parameters $\mathbf{p}$ for a possible type θ, which are applied to predict task selections. Additionally, we have *history of tasks* to keep track of all tasks completed by each non-learning agent. Additionally, in OEATA-A, we have *bags of successful parameters*, which is borrowed from OEATA. However, in OEATA-A, we introduce *suspicious agent* to hold any uncooperative behaviour of the agent. The details of all these fundamentals are described below.

3.3 OEATA-A Fundamentals

3.4 Sets of Estimators

In OEATA-A, there are sets of *estimators* $\mathbf{E}_\delta^\theta$ for each type θ and each non-learning agents ($\delta \in \Delta$), whereas each set $\mathbf{E}_\delta^\theta$ has a fixed number of N *estimators*. Therefore, the total number of sets of *estimators* for all agents are $|\Delta| \times |\Theta|$. An *estimator* e of $\mathbf{E}_\delta^\theta$ is a tuple: $\{\mathbf{p}_e, \mathfrak{s}_e, \tau_e, c_e, f_e\}$, $\mathbf{p}_e$ is the vector of estimated parameters, and each element of the parameter vector is defined in the corresponding element range; $\mathfrak{s}_e$ is the initial state or the last *Choose Target State* , where the non-learning agent δ completed a task and wants to find a new task; τ_e is the task that δ agent would try to complete, assuming type θ and parameters $\mathbf{p}_e$. By having estimated parameters $\mathbf{p}_e$ and type θ, we assume it is easy to predict non-learning agent's target task at $\mathfrak{s}_e$; c_e holds the number of times that e was successful in predicting δ agent's next task; f_e holds the number of failures in predicting correct task.

History of Tasks. As well as OEATA, in OEATA-A, we keep the history of the completed task for all non-learning agents. Therefore, along with the sets of *estimators*, ϕ agent keeps track of the tasks completed by each non-learning agent, as *History of Tasks*. Hence, the *History of Tasks* is defined as $\mathbf{H}_\delta = \{(\mathfrak{s}^0, \tau^0), \ldots, (\mathfrak{s}^n, \tau^n)\}$, where $\mathfrak{s}^i$ is the ith *Choose Target State*, where δ agent plans to find a new target, and τ^i is the actual task that the same agent completes afterwards. As mentioned before, *Choose Target State* is the initial state or the state where δ agent accomplishes a task and wants to choose a new one.

Bags of Successful Parameters. As we mentioned earlier, we assume all non-learning agents as naive agents. Therefore, the same as OEATA, we keep a bag of successful parameters for each δ agent. Hence, if any *estimator* e succeeds in task prediction, for the vector of parameters $\mathbf{p}_e = < p_1, p_2, ..., p_n >$, we keep each element of the parameter vector $\mathbf{p}_e$ in their respective bags of successful parameters.

Suspicious Agent. In OEATA-A, we have a new variable called *Suspicious Agent* ζ_δ. this value increases when the learning agent notices an unusual behaviour from a specific agent.

3.5 Process of Estimation

After presenting the fundamental elements of *OEATA-A*, we will explain how we define the process of estimating the parameters and type for each non-learning agent. The algorithm has five steps: (i) *Initialisation*; (ii) *Evaluation*; (iii) *Generation* and (iv) *Estimation*. Additionally, an (v) *Revision* step is executed for all agents in Δ, any time a task is completed by any agent of the team, including agent ϕ. Notice that the other difference between OEATA and OEATA-A is here in the processing stage. Unlike OEATA, OEATA-A does not have *update* step, and instead, we have *revision* step to find out the adversary agents. These steps are described below:

Initialisation. At the very first step, all *estimators* should be initialised. Therefore, agent ϕ needs to generate N *estimators* for each type $\theta \in \Theta$ and each $\delta \in \Delta$. For every estimator, first, we create a random value per element of the parameter vectors $\mathbf{p}_e$ from the uniform distribution. Generated elements of the parameter vector should be in their defined range. For all *estimators*, in the initialisation phase, the initial state of the environment is set as the *Choose Target State* $\mathfrak{s}_e$. By having the type θ and the parameter vector $\mathbf{p}_e$ of the δ agent, the agent ϕ will be able to estimate its future task τ_e. Lastly, both c_e and f_e are initialised to zero.

Evaluation. The evaluation of all sets of *estimators* $\mathbf{E}_\delta^\theta$ for a certain agent δ starts when it completes a task τ_δ. In this step we check if the τ_e (estimated task by assuming $\mathbf{p}_e$ to be δ's parameters with type θ in state $\mathfrak{s}_e$) is equal to τ_δ. If they are equal, we consider them as successful parameters and save each p_i in the $\mathbf{p}_e$ vector in a respective bag $\mathbf{B}_\delta^{\theta,i}$. If the estimated task τ_e is equal to the real task τ_δ, we set f_e to zero and increase c_e. This penalisation of *estimators* for successive failures aids us in the type estimation. If τ_e is not equal to τ_δ, then we increase f_e and decrease c_e. We do not remove an *estimator* e after a failure since it may still have correct parameters. Hence, we define a *threshold* ξ for it, and if f_e is greater than ξ, we remove e from its belonging set. In this step, after finding successful and failing *estimators*, we update $\mathfrak{s}_e$ and τ_e of all survived *estimators* of the sets $\mathbf{E}_\delta^\theta$. We replace every $\mathfrak{s}_e$ with the current state s_c, and the τ_e with the new predicted task, by considering the current state s_c as the *Choose Target State* and assuming $\mathbf{p}_e$ as δ agent's parameter vector, and θ as its type. Additionally, at the end of this step, as a task has just been completed, we update δ agent's history $\mathbf{H}_\delta$, in order to use it for future evaluations.

Generation. Lets suppose that $\mathbf{E'}_\delta^\theta$ is the new set with only the surviving *estimators* for agent δ and type θ that were not removed in the *Evaluation* step. In this step, the aim is to generate new *estimators*, in order to have the size of the sets $\mathbf{E}_\delta^\theta$ equal to N again. Therefore, $N - |\mathbf{E'}_\delta^\theta|$ new *estimators* should be generated. Unlike the *Initialisation* step, we do not only create random parameters for new *estimators*, but generate a proportion of them using previously successful parameters from the *bags* $\mathbf{B}_\delta^{\theta,i}$. Therefore, we will be able to use a new combination of parameters that had at least one victory in previous steps.

Moreover, as the number of copies of the parameter p_i in the bag $\mathbf{B}_\delta^{\theta,i}$ is equivalent to the number of successes of the same parameter in previous steps, the chance of choosing very successful parameters will increase. The main part of producing new *estimators* is creating a new parameter vector $\mathbf{p}'$, and then updating the other elements of the *estimator* accordingly. Parameters for a portion $(N - |\mathbf{E}'^{\theta}_\delta|) \times \frac{1}{m}$ (where $m > 1$) of the new *estimators* will be randomly sampled from a distribution (e.g., uniform within the parameters range, if there is no domain knowledge). The other portion $(N - |\mathbf{E}'^{\theta}_\delta|) \times (1 - \frac{1}{m})$ will be generated as a new combination from the corresponding bags, which are holding previously victorious parameters. That is, each position p'_i of the parameter vector $\mathbf{p}'$ of the new *estimator* is populated by randomly sampling from the corresponding bag $\mathbf{B}_\delta^{\theta,i}$. If the corresponding bag $\mathbf{B}_\delta^{\theta,i}$ is empty, then that position of the parameter vector will be randomly generated. If all bags are empty, then all parameters will be random. Before creating a new *estimator* e', we check if the newly generated parameter $\mathbf{p}'$ would have at least one success across the history $\mathbf{H}_\delta$ so far. This improves our algorithm since it decreases the likelihood of wasting an *estimator* with a parameter $\mathbf{p}'$ that would not be able to make any correct prediction in the previous steps. As a result, if the output of the function is zero then $\mathbf{p}'$ will be discarded, otherwise, it will be considered as the parameter vector $\mathbf{p}_{e'}$ of the new *estimator* e'.

Estimation. At each iteration after doing *evaluation* and *generation*, it is required to estimate a parameter and type for each $\delta \in \mathbf{\Delta}$ for decision-making. First, based on the current sets of *estimators*, we calculate the probability distribution over the possible types. First of all, we calculate the probability of the agent being adversary. For that, we consider ζ_δ value. If it is bigger than zero we will assume that the agent δ is the adversary. Otherwise, we calculate the probability of agent δ having type θ, $\mathsf{P}(\theta)_\delta$, we use the success rate c_e of all *estimators* of the corresponding type θ. That is, for each $\delta \in \mathbf{\Delta}$, we add up the non-negative success rates c_e of all *estimators* in $\mathbf{E}_\delta^\theta$ of each type θ:$k_\delta^\theta = \sum_{e \in \mathbf{E}_\delta^\theta} \max(0, c_e)$. It means that we want to find out which set of *estimators* is the most successful in estimating correctly the tasks that the corresponding non-learning agent completed. In the next step we normalise the calculated k_δ^θ, to convert it to a probability estimation: $\mathsf{P}(\theta)_\delta = \frac{k_\delta^\theta}{\sum_{\theta' \in \Theta} k_\delta^{\theta'}}$. After calculating the probability distribution over types for each $\delta \in \mathbf{\Delta}$, we use aggregation rules like median, mode, or mean across all parameter vectors $\mathbf{p}_e$ of each set of *estimators* $\mathbf{E}_\delta^\theta$. As a result, we will have one estimated parameter vector $\mathbf{p}$ per $\theta \in \Theta$ for each $\delta \in \mathbf{\Delta}$.

Revision. The *Revision* step triggers when a task τ is completed by any agent in the team. As mentioned earlier, there is a possible issue that might arise in our estimation process when a certain task τ is accomplished by any of the team members (including agent ϕ), and some other non-learning agent was targeting to achieve it. This step has two sub-steps: *Updating Tasks* and *Checking Suspicious Agents.*

- **Updating Tasks:** Consequently, agent δ, would notice in the state s that the task is completed by other agents, and it will try to find a different task at this state. Hence, s would be a new *Choose Target State* for the agent δ. This problem would affect all *estimators* as well. Therefore, once a task τ is completed by any agent in the team, we check every τ_e in all sets $\mathbf{E}_\delta^\theta$, for all non-learning agents ($\delta \in \mathbf{\Delta}$) that *have not* just completed τ, to see if there is any *estimator* e that predicts the same task as τ. If there is any e with the same task, we will consider s as the *Choose Target State* $\mathbf{s}_e$ of e, and will update its target task τ_e accordingly based on the current parameters of the *estimator* $\mathbf{p}_e$ and the type θ of the set.
- **Checking Suspicious Agents:** In this sub-step, we check the sum of all success rates for each agent $\sum_{e \in \mathbf{E}_\delta^\theta} c_e$. If the result is zero then we increase the value of ζ_δ by 1.

4   Experiments

4.1   Level-Based Foraging Domain

We evaluate our approach in level-based foraging, a common problem for evaluating ad-hoc teamwork [1, 2, 10]. In this domain, a set of collaborative agents must collect items (tasks) displaced in the environment and non-collaborative (adversary) agents surround items and prevent other collaborative agents from reaching items. Each item has a certain weight, and each agent has a certain (unknown) *skill-level*. If the sum of the skill levels of the agents (try to collect an item) that surround a target is greater than or equal to the item's weight, it is "loaded" by the team (Fig. 1). Each collaborative agent has 5 possible actions, in a grid-world environment: *North, South, East, West,* and *Load.*

For the *Naive Agents,* the two "leader" types defined in [1]. Additionally, the visibility region of each δ has an angle and a maximum radius, which are unknown. Therefore, there are 3 parameters to be learned for each δ: *Skill-level, Angle* and *Radius.* Based on the agent's type and parameters, the target item (task) will be selected. These two types are $L1$ and $L2$. For $L1$, the target is the furthest visible item that has a lower weight than the agent's skill level. If the agent has the type $L2$, its target will be the visible item with the highest weight below own skill-level, or the item with the highest weight if none are below own level; In both types, the target will be $\varnothing$ if the agent could not find any item that meets the criteria. After choosing the target, the *naive agents* will move towards the target using the A^* algorithm [6].

Each non-collaborative agent has 5 possible actions, in a grid-world environment: *North, South, East, West,* and *Stay*. In our experiments both the adversary agent and the learning agent have full observation of the whole environment.

4.2   Results

For evaluating our novel method, we compare our algorithm *OEATA-A* against using POMCP-based Estimation [10] for finding the existence of an adversary in the team. When using POMCP-based Estimation to find the enemy, we still consider that the agent can see the whole environment. However, agent type and parameters are not observable and hence are estimated using POMCP's particle filter. We use $N \times |\Delta| \times$

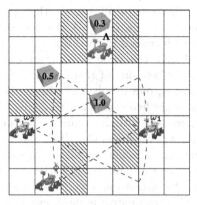

Fig. 1. Level-based foraging domain. There are four agents in three different types in the grid. Boxes are the items that should be collected. Dashed cells in the grid are obstacles.

$|\Theta|$ particles, matching the total number of *estimators* in our approach (since we have N per agent, for each type). We executed 100 runs for each experiment and plotted the average results and the confidence interval ($\rho = 0.01$). When we say that a result is significant, we mean statistically significant considering $\rho \leq 0.01$.

OEATA-A used the following parameters: $N = 100$, $t = 2$, $m = 0.2$. Type and parameters of agents in Δ are chosen uniformly randomly, and the weight of each item is chosen uniformly randomly (between 0 and 1). Each scenario is also randomly generated. Agent ϕ and agent Λ's skill-level are fixed at 1, so every generated instance is solvable. We ran UCT-H, which introduced [12] for 100 iterations per time step, and a maximum depth of 100. We fixed the scenario size as 20×20, and ran experiments for a varying number of items ($|\mathcal{T}|$). We first show how the learning agent ϕ is recognising the adversary agent among six teammates where the number of non-learning agents is 5 ($|\Omega| = 5$). The Fig. 2 illustrates, the mean absolute error for the type, and $1 - P(\theta^*)$ we show here the average error across all types.

As it is shown, the type estimation error of OEATA-A is consistently significantly lower than the other algorithm from the second iteration, and it monotonically decreases as the number of iterations increases. POMCP-estimation, on the other hand, does not show any sign of converging to a low error as the number of iterations increases. We can also see that type estimation of OEATA-A becomes quickly better than POMCP, significantly overcoming them after a few iterations. In Fig. 3(a), we showed how finding the adversary among agents works among six agents with a varying number of items in the grid. In these scenarios, the size of the grid is 20×20. As it is clear, we are significantly better than POMCP-estimation and as the number of items increases the error of finding the enemy decreases.

Figure 3(b) illustrate the performance of the team as the number of items increases in the grid size 20×20, and with the same seven agents in the team where one of them is the learning agent ϕ, one in adversary agent Λ and the other five agents are the naive ones. As we see, with 20 items we are better with a p-value less than 0.05, but as the number of items increases, we can say that we are significantly better. In addition to estimating adversary agents, we

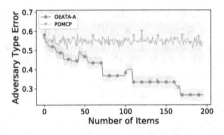

Fig. 2. Error of finding adversary agent when there are 7 agents in the team with $|\Omega| = 5$.

need to estimate the parameters of the ω agents as well and the Fig. 3(c), we proved that results for OEATA-A have an error between 0 and 0.15. Additionally, for all number of items we are better than the other method.

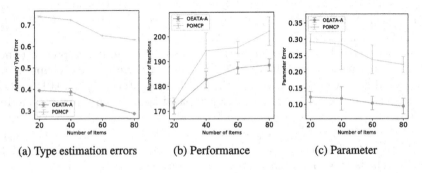

(a) Type estimation errors   (b) Performance   (c) Parameter

Fig. 3. Type estimation errors for a varying number of items in full observability. Error estimating agent parameters when there are 7 agents in the team with $|\Omega| = 5$.

5   Conclusion

We studied ad-hoc teamwork with an adversary for decentralised task allocation. One ad-hoc agent learns its teammates and could distinguish the opponent agent in the team and despite its existence, makes better decisions concerning overall team performance. We proposed a novel algorithm *On-line Estimator for Ad-hoc Task Allocation with adversary*, that obtained better estimations than previous works in ad-hoc teamwork, leading to better performance. OEATA-A converged to zero error, and in our experiments, the error decreased with the number of iterations. We also showed estimations with partial observability for the first time in ad-hoc teamwork, and still outperform previous works. In our future works, we are planning to increase the number of the adversary and learning agents to find out how the results would change.

References

1. Albrecht, S., Stone, P.: Reasoning about hypothetical agent behaviours and their parameters. In: Proceedings of the 16th International Conference on Autonomous Agents and Multiagent Systems, AAMAS'17 (2017)
2. Albrecht, S.V., Ramamoorthy, S.: A game-theoretic model and best-response learning method for ad hoc coordination in multiagent systems. The University of Edinburgh, Technical report (2013)
3. Barrett, S., Rosenfeld, A., Kraus, S., Stone, P.: Making friends on the fly: cooperating with new teammates. Artif. Intell. **242**, 132–171 (2017)
4. Berman, S., Halasz, A., Hsieh, M.A., Kumar, V.: Optimized stochastic policies for task allocation in swarms of robots. IEEE Trans. Robot. **25**(4), 927–937 (2009)
5. Celli, A., Ciccone, M., Bongo, R., Gatti, N.: Coordination in adversarial sequential team games via multi-agent deep reinforcement learning. arXiv preprint arXiv:1912.07712 (2019)
6. Hart, P.E., Nilsson, N.J., Raphael, B.: A formal basis for the heuristic determination of minimum cost paths. IEEE Trans. Syst. Sci. Cybern. **4**(2), 100–107 (1968)
7. Lin, J., Dzeparoska, K., Zhang, S.Q., Leon-Garcia, A., Papernot, N.: On the robustness of cooperative multi-agent reinforcement learning. arXiv preprint arXiv:2003.03722 (2020)
8. Mirchevska, V., Luštrek, M., Bežek, A., Gams, M.: Discovering strategic behaviour of multi-agent systems in adversary settings. Comput. Inform. **33**(1), 79–108 (2014)
9. Phan, T., et al.: Learning and testing resilience in cooperative multi-agent systems. In: Proceedings of the 19th International Conference on Autonomous Agents and MultiAgent Systems, pp. 1055–1063 (2020)
10. Shafipour Yourdshahi, E., Do Carmo Alves, M., Soriano Marcolino, L., Angelov, P.: Decentralised task allocation in the fog: estimators for effective ad-hoc teamwork. In: 11th International Workshop on Optimization and Learning in Multiagent Systems (2020)
11. Uesato, J., et al.: Rigorous agent evaluation: an adversarial approach to uncover catastrophic failures. arXiv preprint arXiv:1812.01647 (2018)
12. Yourdshahi, E.S., Pinder, T., Dhawan, G., Marcolino, L.S., Angelov, P.: Towards large scale ad-hoc teamwork. In: 2018 IEEE International Conference on Agents (ICA), pp. 44–49. IEEE (2018)

Human-Robot Cooperative Lifting Using IMUs and Human Gestures

Gizem Ateş$^{(\boxtimes)}$ (iD) and Erik Kyrkjebø$^{(\boxtimes)}$ (iD)

Department of Computer Science, Electrical Engineering and Mathematical Sciences,
Western Norway University of Applied Sciences, Førde, Norway
{gizem.ates,erik.kyrkjebo}@hvl.no

Abstract. In physical Human-Robot Cooperation (pHRC), humans and robots interact frequently or continuously to manipulate the same object or workpiece. One of the tasks within pHRC that has the highest potential for increased value in the industry is the cooperative lifting (co-lift) task where humans and robots lift long, flexible or heavy objects together. For such tasks, it is important for both safety and control that the human and robot can access motion information of the other to safely and accurately execute tasks together. In this paper, we propose to use Inertial Measurement Units (IMUs) to estimate human motions for pHRC, and also to use the IMU motion data to identify two-arm gestures that can aid in controlling the human-robot cooperation. We show how to use pHRC leader-follower roles to exploit the human cognitive skills to easily locate the object to lift, and robot skills to accurately place the object on a predefined target location. The experimental results presented show how to divide the co-lifting operation into stages: approaching the object while clutching in and out of controlling the robot motions, cooperatively lift and move the object towards a new location, and place the object accurately on a predefined target location. We believe that the results presented in this paper have the potential to further increase the uptake of pHRC in the industry since the proposed approach do not require any pre-installation of a positioning system or features of the object to enable pHRC.

Keywords: Physical human-robot interaction · Cooperative lifting · IMUs

1 Introduction

In physical Human-Robot Cooperation (pHRC), humans and robots work towards a common goal in a shared workspace with physical interaction, and more examples of pHRC such as cooperative lifting and carrying, kinesthetic teaching, coordinated material handling and rehabilitation therapy are seen

---

This work was funded by the Research Council of Norway through grant number 280771.

© Springer Nature Switzerland AG 2021
C. Fox et al. (Eds.): TAROS 2021, LNAI 13054, pp. 88–99, 2021.
https://doi.org/10.1007/978-3-030-89177-0_9

within industry and healthcare [16]. The introduction of collaborative robots (cobots) is particularly important for small and medium-sized enterprises since the configuration of the fully automated production for each design might take as much effort as the conventional production process when the number of product is little. Installation can be done without replanning whole factories or introducing additional safety measures such as fences or cages for the cobots.

The cooperative lifting (co-lift) operation have the potential to enable humans and robots to lift and carry long, flexible, or heavy objects together while exploiting the human cognitive skills and the robot accuracy in different parts of the task. However, to enable safe and accurate pHRC in co-lift tasks, the control system must have access to human motion data to be able to follow human motions. There are several studies on co-lift and manipulation between a human and a robot in the literature. In [11], the authors use haptic data to dynamically allocate human-robot leader roles on a co-lift scenario. A recent study using only haptic data from the robot joints without requiring external sensors is presented in [6] where the authors estimated external forces applied by the human operator during the collaborative assembly of a car engine. In [13], a human operator and a cobot on a mobile platform carry a long aluminium stick between two locations in the work environment. Cartesian impedance control is applied in the co-lift process and the localization in the environment is done by using a laser scanner. Learning algorithms are also quite popular in co-lifting and co-manipulation studies [1,2,12]. In [12], a novel approach using the learning by demonstration for various cooperative tasks is proposed where a demonstrated trajectory is adapted through weighting factors to adjust learning speed and disturbance rejection to collaboratively transport an object. In [2] a table-lifting task performed by a human and a humanoid using programming by demonstration and in [1] the human-robot role change is assessed probabilistically using Gaussian Mixture Regression. While these studies found cover important topics for HRC and co-lift tasks, they generally only address the stages of the cooperation where the human and robot is physically interacting. There is no study found that also address the approach to the co-lift stage of the cooperation as this requires motions sensors able to detect human motions when not in contact with the object or robot directly.

To enable pHRC for a cooperative lifting task where also the approach stage is included, the control system must be able to estimate human motions both to control and to detect gestures that can enable/disable human control over the robot. Studies on human motion tracking and estimation can be categorized based on the type of the motion tracker devices used: visual-based [10,15], and nonvisual-based [3,7,14], and hybrid solutions [8,9]. Each category has its advantages and disadvantages depending on the application area. For example, visual-based solutions are dominant in motion tracking solutions since provide highly accurate human motion tracking but they often fail in industrial usage for pHRC due to occlusion, loss in line-of-sight, intolerant to lightning changes, and lack of mobility etc. IMU-based solutions are stand-alone systems without no permanent installations and can be a good alternative to address the challenges of vision-based systems at a lower cost, but are prone to drift for long term usage. While several solutions to eliminate the drift problem have been proposed [4], there are still few pHRC industrial applications using IMU-based solutions in soft real-time.

The roles in pHRC may change in different stages of a cooperative lifting task [1,5,11]. The human cognitive skills can be exploited in the approach stage of a co-lift task to identify the location of the object to pick up, while the robot accuracy can be used to accurately place the object on a predefined target location. In this scenario, the human takes the leader role in picking and the follower role in placing.

In addition to the active stages, a passive idle stage is also needed for the user to clutch in and out of. This allows the human to disconnect from controlling the robot to re-position. Switching between roles and active/passive stages of the cooperation requires that triggers may be identified in the operation, or that additional control signals are introduced to control the switching.

In this paper, we propose a novel approach for Human-Robot cooperative lifting in Sect. 2, and show how we can estimate human motions using IMUs during the approach and co-lift stage of the cooperation in Sect. 2.1. We also address the different roles of cooperation in Sect. 2.2 by using individual human arm gestures to clutch in and out of active roles. The proposed approach is experimentally tested in Sect. 3, and the results discussed in Sect. 4. Conclusion and outlook is provided in Sect. 5.

2 Human-Robot Cooperative Lifting Using IMUs and Gestures

In this paper, we address the problem of collaborative lifting, carrying and placing an object as a joint operation between a human and a robot to share the load of the object, and also to exploit the accuracy of the robot to place the object at a predefined target location. First, we will show how we estimate human motions and gestures using IMUs. Second, we show how leader-follower roles are defined, and how arm gestures are used to switch between active (approach, co-lift, release) and passive (idle) states.

2.1 Posture and Gesture Estimation

We propose to estimate 13 DoFs upper-body motions (chest, left and right arm) using 5 IMUs placed as shown in Fig. 1. Note that we disregard any wrist motion in this paper.

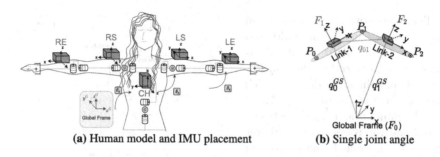

(a) Human model and IMU placement   **(b) Single joint angle**

Fig. 1. Human model, IMU placements and joint angle definitions.

The full upper-body posture and motion estimation is a collection of estimated individual joint angles, and where a joint angle can be found by calculating the rotation between two consecutive links with attached IMUs as shown in figure Fig. 1a. The illustrated body parts in Fig. 1b can be considered as upper and lower arm segments.

The raw orientation data from the IMU sensor is referred as q_i^{GS} where i is the IMU number. Each IMU provides orientation information with respect to global frame F_0. If the link-1's frame of reference is called F_1 and link-2's frame of reference is called F_2, the rotation from the global frame to sensor frames will be q_0^{GS} and q_1^{GS} respectively. We can find the joint angle q^{01} between two links as the rotation from F_1 to F_2 using quaternion multiplication as

$$q_{01} = (q_0^{GS})^* \otimes q_1^{GS} \tag{1}$$

where $\otimes$ denotes the quaternion multiplication and $*$ the complex conjugate of the quaternion. The term q_1^{GS} is the rotation of the IMU attached on link-1 from global to sensor frame. If we apply this process from link-0 (chest to shoulder) to link-2 (elbow to wrist), we obtain the arm posture of a human arm based on estimated IMU orientations. One arm can be modelled as a total of 5 DoFs where 3 DoFs are on the shoulder joint and 2 DoFs are on the elbow joint as shown in Fig. 1a. The kinematic chain for such a human model from the base (chest) to the tip (hand) can be written as:

$$q_c = q_{CH} \qquad q_s = q_c^* \otimes q_{LS} \qquad q_e = q_c^* \otimes q_s^* \otimes q_{LE} \tag{2}$$

where q_c, q_s and q_e are the quaternions representing joint angle rotations, q_{CH}, q_{LS} and q_{LE} are the IMU orientation from global to the sensors frame in Fig. 1a - which are the raw orientation readings from the sensors. The process is identical for the second arm.

2.2 Cooperation Roles and States in Cooperative Lifting

The cooperative lifting scenario can be divided into three active (APPROACH, CO-LIFT, RELEASE) and one passive (IDLE) state of the operation as shown in Fig. 2.

There are two key concepts in
this scenario, one is the **role** and
the other is the **state**. The role is
defined by *who is leading the cooperative task* and the state defines which
stage of the task is running. There
is a dynamic role change between
human and the robot leader-follower
roles based on the human two-arm
gestures and the completion of the
task, and also the state changes are
triggered based on human arm gestures.

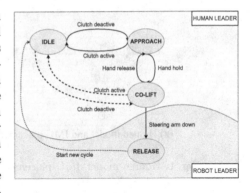

Fig. 2. HRC states and leader roles

Human Leader: This role is where the robot takes actions led by the human
operator based on his/her upper-body motions. The pick position of the object
is not necessarily to be known by the robot. The cognitive skills of the human
can be exploited to approach the object sensibly, identify the object to pick up,
and finally lift and carry it towards a target position. Within a close distance
to the place position, the robot-leader role is activated by a gesture so that a
precise placement is achieved.

In our proposed approach, we track both human arms individually and can
use them for different purposes in human-robot cooperation. We define one arm
as the *motion* arm (left) and the other as the *steering* arm (right). The motion
arm is directly controlling the robot motions in the active stages when the human
is the leader, while the steering arm motions are superimposed on the motion
arm when applied to the robot. In this way, the human can approach and grip
the object on one end using the motion hand – and the robot will mirror this
motion – but also use the steering hand to adjust the robot position to the proper
gripping position on the other end of the object while keeping the motion hand
still. Thus, any misalignment between the starting position of the human and
robot can be corrected. Furthermore, gestures from the steering hand can be used
as triggers or control signals to move from one state to another in cooperation.
There are 3 states in the human-leader role: idle, approach and co-lift.

In **IDLE**, no human motions are mapped into robot motions. The human can
move closer to the pick-up position without moving the robot. This state is also
a *safe* state which the human can switch to from any other state in the human-
leading role, and thus enables the human operator to move freely at any time.
In **APPROACH**, motion and steering arm motions are combined into a *hand*
pose that controls the goal pose of the robot. The individual contribution of the
two arms can be scaled through gains. Human forward/backwards and up/down
motions are identical on the robot, but sideways motions are mirrored by the
robot. In **CO-LIFT**, both the robot and the human is holding the common
object and lifting it towards the desired target position. Only the motion hand
controls the goal pose of the robot. The steering arm is free to move to help

to lift, or to perform gestures. Two gestures of the steering arm are defined as "release down" and "rotate up/down" to trigger state and role changes.

There are two transition gestures and a foot pedal activated transition between states and roles. The "clutch activate/ deactivate" gesture activates and deactivates the human to robot motion mapping. The clutch is triggered by the steering hand rotating to the palm up gesture to switch from IDLE to APPROACH/CO-LIFT, and rotating to palm down gesture to switch from APP-ROACH/ CO-LIFT to IDLE. The "handhold/release" transition is triggered by a foot pedal to close the robot gripper so that the CO-LIFT stage can start. The option to switch from CO-LIFT to IDLE state (dashed lines in Fig. 2) is included for safety reasons in case the human leader need to free the motion hand from the object. Care should be taken to support the load of the lifted object in such a scenario since the load cannot necessarily be supported by the robot alone. The last transition gesture is the "release down" gesture where the human points the steering arm downwards to trigger the role change from human leader to robot leader.

Robot Leader: The trigger gesture "release down" switches from a human leader role strategy to a robot leader strategy where the robot can take over control of the execution to move the object to the target position while the human keeps supporting the load of the object and follows the robot motions. Only one state called RELEASE is proposed in our design, but a sequence of other tasks can be added for more complex tasks. As soon as the robot reaches the desired target position, the gripper is automatically released and the robot moves away from the object and is ready for another cycle.

2.3   Human-Robot Cooperative Lifting of a Table

The cooperation starts in the IDLE state, and is shown in Fig. 3. The robot expects the clutch deactivate signal (see the rotation of the steering hand from Fig. 3a to Fig. 3b). At this stage, the motion hand pose $\hat{P}_{hm}$ and steering hand pose $\hat{P}_{hs}$ are combined into the hand pose $\hat{P}_h$, but the goal pose $\hat{P}_{goal}$ is not sent to the robot in the IDLE state.

When the clutch is released the HRC system switches to an active APP-ROACH state as shown in Fig. 3b. The human operator controls the robot, and as the human approaches to the table with the motion hand, the robot approaches the table with a scaled mimicking motion. If the motion hand reaches and grips the table, the robot can still be controlled using the steering hand to approach the appropriate grip position on the other side. Pose calculations are computed using 4×4 homogeneous transformation matrix (HTM). The robot goal pose is calculated based on the relative position change of the hand pose $\hat{P}_{h,t}$ as shown in Eq. (3).

$$\hat{P}_{h,t}^- = \hat{s} \cdot (\hat{P}_{hm,t=0}^{-1} \times \hat{P}_{hm,t}) + \hat{k} \cdot (\hat{P}_{hs,t=0}^{-1} \times \hat{P}_{hs,t}) \tag{3}$$

where $\hat{P}_{h,t}^-$ is the merged hand pose. To get the approach response from the robot the y-axis in $\hat{P}_{h,t}^-$ is inverted and $\hat{P}_{h,t}$ is obtained to control the approach of the

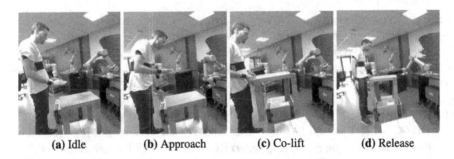

(a) Idle   (b) Approach   (c) Co-lift   (d) Release

Fig. 3. Human and robot poses in co-lift states. (a) shows both the human and the robot initial poses in the IDLE state. The steering hand (right) is palm down. (b) shows both the human and the robot poses in action in the APPROACH state. The steering hand is palm up. (c) shows the CO-LIFT state where both the human and the robot is carrying the table. The steering hand has does not influence motion commands, but is helping the motion hand (left) to lift the object. Finally, (d) shows the RELEASE state triggered by the "release down" of the steering hand, and where the robot takes control of the operation to place the object at the desired target position.

robot. The 4×4 scaling matrix for the motion hand $\hat{s}$ has the last row equal to $[s_x s_y s_z 1]$ with the rest of the elements as 1. The scaling matrix $\hat{k}$ is defined similarly for the steering hand. The robot goal pose based on the combined hand pose is

$$\hat{H}(t) = \hat{P}_{h,t=0}^{-1} \times \hat{P}_{h,t} \qquad \qquad \hat{P}_{r,t} = \hat{P}_{r,t=0} \times \hat{H}(t) \qquad (4)$$

where $\hat{H}(t)$ is the transformation of merged hand pose from initial to the current pose. The goal pose is set to initial orientation of the robot for easier cooperation.

When the system switches to the CO-LIFT state, the contribution of the steering hand is eliminated. The current pose of the motion hand is set to a new initial pose and the robot goal pose is calculated based on only the motion hand's relative position changes as in

$$\hat{P}_{h,t}^- = \hat{s_2} \cdot (\hat{P}_{hm,t=t_{co-lift}}^{-1} \times \hat{P}_{hm,t}) \qquad (5)$$

where $\hat{P}_{hm,t=t_{co-lift}}$ is the new pose measurement of the motion hand in HTM form needed to ensure a smooth transition between states. The $\hat{s_2}$ term is the new scaling factor for the motion hand. Finally, the y-axis measurements of $\hat{P}_{h,t}^-$ are reversed for a mirror the human motions to obtain the new hand pose command $\hat{P}_{h,t}$ in CO-LIFT.

When the steering hand is released down to switch to the RELEASE state, we no longer compute the human hand to robot motion mapping since the robot takes over the leading role in the RELEASE state, and the human follows the robot motions.

3 Experimental Setup and Results

The experimental test was performed as a full human-robot cooperative lifting operation as shown in Fig. 3. We first present the experimental setup and the calibration steps before presenting the resulting data.

3.1 Setup

The human is equipped with 5 Xsens Awinda IMUs to estimate orientations output as filtered orientation raw data in quaternions. The cooperative robot as the Universal Robots UR5e cobot equipped with a Robotiq 2F-85 gripper. The data acquisition is processed in the ROS Melodic environment on two PCs. One PC is running the ROS master and the Universal Robot's ROS driver, and the other PC runs all the other ROS nodes. The UR5e is connected via Ethernet cable to the ROS Master PC, and the URCap software is started after the UR5e ROS driver is started on the ROS Master PC. The data acquisition from the IMUs runs 100 Hz whereas the UR5e controller runs 50 Hz. The inverse kinematic solver node using *ikfast* runs 10 Hz, and scaling factors for the motion and steering hand are set to 1.

3.2 Calibration

The calibration process consists of three steps as following: The first step is to remove any bias on IMU orientation raw data, the second is to initialize human posture and the third is to map the human initial pose to the robot's initial pose.

IMU Orientation Calibration: First, we eliminated the bias and set a relative initial pose of each IMU to make sure the IMUs output zero orientation initially as

$$q_{I,abs} \otimes q_{init-rot} = q_{bias} \qquad\qquad q_{I,rel} = q_{bias}^* \otimes q_{bias}. \qquad (6)$$

where $q_{I,abs}$ is the absolute initial orientation of an IMU, which is a unit quaternion, on a particular 3D orientation where the IMU axes are perfectly aligned with the global frame of reference. The $q_{init-rot}$ is the rotation from the initial orientation to when the data acquisition starts, which is unknown. The q_{bias} is initial raw orientation data from the sensors that changes in every setup. The initial orientation is set based on recording q_{bias} for 2s in a steady T-pose (arms out), and $q_{I,rel}$ is set to the identity quaternion.

Human Body Calibration: The IMU calibration is computed in a the T-pose , and all the joint angles are set to zero, and q_{bias}^* is set to identity quaternion.

Hands to Robot Calibration: This sets the human arm pose to the robot initial pose. The human moves to a desired initial pose and the robot move to its predefined initial pose Fig. 3a. The robot initial pose $\hat{P}_{r,t=0}$ is registered, and the computed hand pose $\hat{P}_{h,t=0}$ is initialized to zero position and zero rotation.

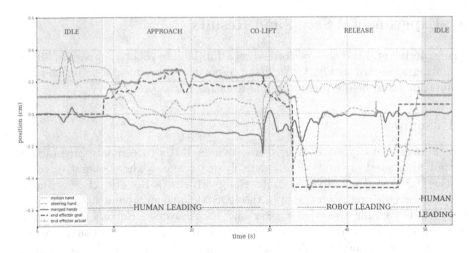

Fig. 4. A full cycle demo of the proposed HRC cooperative lifting scenario. The lines shows the position change on the x-axis of the motion hand (left) in **blue** thin dots, steering hand (right) in **orange** thin dashes, merged hands in **green** thick line, the goal pose to the robot's end-effector in **red** thick dashes and the actual robot pose in **purple** plus signed dashes. The states IDLE, APPROACH, CO-LIFT and RELEASE are indicated as background colours/shades. The roles (human or robot leading) are indicated with blue texts at the bottom of the figure where human-leading role covers IDLE, APPROACH and CO-LIFT and robot-leading role covers only RELEASE.

3.3   Results

The experiment is carried out by an inexperienced user and the data is presented in Fig. 4. As explained in Sect. 3.1, the actual robot data is recorded on the ROS Master PC, and therefore the recorded data clocks are synchronized after recording. In human-leading role states, it can be seen how hand motions affect the goal position of the end-effector of the robot whereas the hand positions are not affecting the goal position in the robot-leading role state. In IDLE, we observe motions of the human arms (blue/orange), but these motions do not affect the robot goal position (red) in this state. The merged hand position (green) at the initial pose shown in Fig. 3a is set to zero. When the clutch is deactivated (t = 8 s), the goal pose is sent to the robot based on the merged hand pose (green), and the robot starts following the same trend as the goal pose (red). Between t = 15–20, the motion hand (blue) is stable (holding the table at one end) and the steering hand (orange) keeps commanding the robot to adjust the robot position to be ready to grip the table. After the human is satisfied with the position on which the robot can grip the table, the handhold signal is sent and the CO-LIFT stage starts. In this state, only the motion hand (blue) is affecting the goal pose (red) - but inverted. The steering hand (orange) helps to lift without affecting the goal pose. After the steering hand is released down as in Fig. 3d, a role changing is triggered and the RELEASE stage starts. No hand motion is sent as the goal pose in this stage. Instead, the goal pose is set to the predefined target position. When the robot reaches the target position at around t = 40 s, it automatically opens the gripper and pulls itself back (t = 40), and waits for input to do another cycle (t = 49 s), where the goal pose is set to the robot initial pose. When the robot reaches the desired position with a small tolerance (the absolute sum of joint angle error is less than 0.001 rad), the system is automatically set to the IDLE and the robot wait for the clutch to deactivate for the new co-lift cycle.

4   Discussion and Future Work

In this study, we demonstrated a human-robot cooperative lifting task scenario based on estimated human motions and gestures using IMUs, and we tested and validated the proposed pHRC states, roles and their transitions using a real robot in experiments.

The proposed method is a novel conceptual design that still requires some tuning based on more extensive user tests. Different learning curves are observed for different users, and also some feedback on preferences are reported which conflict between users:

Motion Mapping: In the current setup, we take the spine-fixed frame as the human motion reference frame. It is reported as *confusing* in the beginning. After a few trials, it is reported to become *more natural*. It is still an open question for real applications and highly depends on the users' learning curve. To develop a training setup is a possibility or more intuitive frame of reference can be analyzed with more user tests - potentially using the motion arm as the frame of reference.

Robot Speed: It is seen Fig. 4 that the actual pose (purple) does not follow the goal pose (red) identically. There is no lagging or real-time during the experiments, but the robot maximum speed is set to be 30% of full speed as a safety measure. If this is increased, the robot becomes more responsive and exceeds the comfort zone of the human operator which then tries to slow the robot down, and thus we can induce harmonic motions around the desired pose. With training, the trust in the robot increases, and the speed limit can be increased.

Contribution of the Two Hands: We set the contribution of the two hands equal in the experiments based on user preferences. However, during tests in the development stage, other users reported that they preferred either the motion or steering hand to be more dominant. Also, the approach direction of the motion hand could be either *mimicked* or *mirrored* based on user preferences. These are open questions.

The pick and place positions are selected close due to the limited workspace of the robot. The `ikfast` module provides a rapid inverse kinematic (IK) solution (on the order of $4\mu s$) but no limitless elbow/wrist configuration can be set. Therefore, we set joint limits in the experiments to make sure the robot works within the configuration space, but this can be extended in future versions, or changed to a recursive IK solver.

The human and robot motions are defined as relative positions with respect to the initial states. Therefore, the parameters of the human model do not play a vital role. An average human model can be used for most users. It should be noted that the behaviours on the other axes are observed; the states and the transitions correspond in all axes yet they are not presented in this paper due to the number of page limitations.

For the proposed method, the initial position of the object and its properties is unknown. The approach is lead by the human, and the release is lead by the robot. Only the target position of the object is necessary. Such a design opens up a wide range of application possibilities such as co-manipulation, co-assembly as well as co-lifting.

The real-time term describes a *soft* real-time behaviour that the human does not *feel* a delay or lagging. We have not assessed quantitatively the real-time capabilities, and we are planning to address this issue in future studies.

The IMUs are prone to drift but the filtered orientation by Xsens Awinda provides relatively stable data. For about 15 min of data collection period without re-calibrating IMUs, no drastic drift issue is reported. However, before testing the system in real industrial applications, a quantitative drift assessment study in various magnetic disturbances should be carried out.

5   Conclusions

In this study, a conceptual design of human-robot cooperative lifting based on human motions and gestures captured using IMU data is presented and validated with a real-world experiment. The proposed system consists of two leading roles as human-leader and robot-leader which dynamically switches based on human gestures. The proposed roles consist of 4 different states and the human-to-robot motion mapping differs according to the system state. This study aims to open up new possibilities in pHRC for industrial applications by using IMUs as cheap, portable, and low-cost measurement systems that do not suffer from occlusion and line-of-sight loss.

References

1. Evrard, P., Gribovskaya, E., Calinon, S., Billard, A., Kheddar, A.: Teaching physical collaborative tasks: object-lifting case study with a humanoid. In: 2009 9th IEEE-RAS International Conference on Humanoid Robots. IEEE (2009). https://doi.org/10.1109/ichr.2009.5379513
2. Gu, Y., Thobbi, A., Sheng, W.: Human-robot collaborative manipulation through imitation and reinforcement learning. In: 2011 IEEE International Conference on Information and Automation. IEEE (2011). https://doi.org/10.1109/icinfa.2011.5948979
3. Kok, M., Hol, J.D., Schön, T.B.: An optimization-based approach to human body motion capture using inertial sensors. IFAC Proc. Vol. (IFAC-PapersOnline) **19**, 79–85 (2014). https://doi.org/10.3182/20140824-6-ZA-1003.02252

4. Kok, M., Hol, J.D., Schön, T.B.: Using inertial sensors for position and orientation estimation (2017). https://doi.org/10.1561/2000000094
5. Kyrkjebo, E., et al.: The potential of physical human-robot cooperation using cobots on AGVs in flexible manufacturing, pp. 1–13 (under review)
6. Liu, S., Wang, L., Wang, X.V.: Sensorless haptic control for human-robot collaborative assembly. CIRP J. Manuf. Sci. Technol. **32**, 132–144 (2021). https://doi.org/10.1016/j.cirpj.2020.11.015
7. Luzheng, B., Guan, C.: A review on EMG-based motor intention prediction of continuous human upper limb motion for human-robot collaboration. Biomed. Signal Process. Control **51**, 113–127 (2019). https://doi.org/10.1016/j.bspc.2019.02.011
8. Malleson, C., Gilbert, A., Trumble, M., Collomosse, J., Hilton, A., Volino, M.: Real-time full-body motion capture from video and IMUs. In: 2017 International Conference on 3D Vision (3DV). IEEE (2017). https://doi.org/10.1109/3dv.2017.00058
9. von Marcard, T., Henschel, R., Black, M.J., Rosenhahn, B., Pons-Moll, G.: Recovering accurate 3D human pose in the wild using IMUs and a moving camera. In: Ferrari, V., Hebert, M., Sminchisescu, C., Weiss, Y. (eds.) ECCV 2018. LNCS, vol. 11214, pp. 614–631. Springer, Cham (2018). https://doi.org/10.1007/978-3-030-01249-6_37
10. Morato, C., Kaipa, K.N., Zhao, B., Gupta, S.K.: Toward safe human robot collaboration by using multiple kinects based real-time human tracking. J. Comput. Inf. Sci. Eng. **14**(1) (2014)
11. Mörtl, A., Lawitzky, M., Kucukyilmaz, A., Sezgin, M., Basdogan, C., Hirche, S.: The role of roles: physical cooperation between humans and robots. Int. J. Robot. Res. **31**(13), 1656–1674 (2012). https://doi.org/10.1177/0278364912455366
12. Nemec, B., Likar, N., Gams, A., Ude, A.: Human robot cooperation with compliance adaptation along the motion trajectory. Auton. Robot. **42**(5), 1023–1035 (2017). https://doi.org/10.1007/s10514-017-9676-3
13. Ramasubramanian, A.K., Papakostas, N.: Operator - mobile robot collaboration for synchronized part movement. Procedia CIRP **97**, 217–223 (2021). https://doi.org/10.1016/j.procir.2020.05.228
14. Roetenberg, D., Luinge, H., Slycke, P.: Xsens MVN: full 6DOF human motion tracking using miniature inertial sensors. Xsens Motion Tech. BV, Tech. Rep. **1**, 1–7 (2009). http://citeseerx.ist.psu.edu/viewdoc/download?doi=10.1.1.569.9604&rep=rep1&type=pdf
15. Sheng, W., Thobbi, A., Gu, Y.: An integrated framework for human–robot collaborative manipulation. IEEE Trans. Cybern. **45**(10), 2030–2041 (2015). https://doi.org/10.1109/tcyb.2014.2363664
16. Haddadin, S., Croft, E.: Physical human–robot interaction. In: Siciliano, B., Khatib, O. (eds.) Springer Handbook of Robotics, pp. 1835–1874. Springer, Cham (2016). https://doi.org/10.1007/978-3-319-32552-1_69

Reinforcement Learning-Based Mapless Navigation with Fail-Safe Localisation

Feiqiang Lin[1], Ze Ji[1(✉)], Changyun Wei[2], and Hanlin Niu[3]

[1] School of Engineering, Cardiff University, Cardiff, UK
{linf6,jiz1}@cardiff.ac.uk
[2] College of Mechanical and Electrical Engineering, Hohai University, Nanjing, China
[3] Department of Electrical and Electronic Engineering, University of Manchester, Manchester, UK
hanlin.niu@manchester.ac.uk

Abstract. Mapless navigation is the capability of a robot to navigate without knowing the map. Previous works assume the availability of accurate self-localisation, which is, however, usually unrealistic. In our work, we deploy simultaneous localisation and mapping (SLAM)-based self-localisation for mapless navigation. SLAM performance is prone to the quality of perceived features of the surroundings. This work presents a Reinforcement Learning (RL)-based mapless navigation algorithm, aiming to improve the robustness of robot localisation by encouraging the robot to learn to be aware of the quality of its surrounding features and avoid feature-poor environment, where localisation is less reliable. Particle filter (PF) is deployed for pose estimation in our work, although, in principle, any localisation algorithm should work with this framework. The aim of the work is two-fold: to train a robot to learn 1) to avoid collisions and also 2) to identify paths that optimise PF-based localisation, such that the robot will be unlikely to fail to localise itself, hence fail-safe SLAM. A simulation environment is tested in this work with different maps and randomised training conditions. The trained policy has demonstrated superior performance compared with standard mapless navigation without this optimised policy.

Keywords: Fail-safe localisation navigation · Mapless navigation · Reinforcement learning

1 Introduction

For robots to navigate in unknown environments without knowing the maps, such as in search and rescue scenarios, reliable decision making for the robot of immediate responses to collisions or efficient path planning towards the goal is critical. We categorise such problems as mapless navigation. Conventional path

The authors thank the China Scholarship Council (CSC) for financially supporting Feiqiang Lin in his PhD programme (201906020170).

© Springer Nature Switzerland AG 2021
C. Fox et al. (Eds.): TAROS 2021, LNAI 13054, pp. 100–111, 2021.
https://doi.org/10.1007/978-3-030-89177-0_10

planning methods have been dominantly applied in most occasions. However, there are known limitations with these algorithms [13]. Usually, hand-crafted heuristic or constraint functions are needed and customised for different conditions. However, too much hand-engineered path planning could limit the generalization capability of mobile robots to be employed in different environments [14].

To address the limitations above, with recent advances in deep learning and reinforcement learning (RL), learning based navigation approaches have continuously attracted increasing attention. Supervised learning that learns from expert demonstrations is one popular approach, which, however, would require a large amount of labelled data for training. An alternative approach is RL that deploys an agent in the environment and lets the agent explore by itself through direct interaction with the environment. By gaining corresponding rewards from environment during exploration, the agent will learn how to navigate gradually. One promising recent work is the RL-based mapless navigation [13] that aims to train an agent, a mobile robot, to navigate in an unknown environment with the capabilities of collision avoidance. This could reduce a considerable amount of time to tailor hand-crafted rules or heuristics for navigation and decision making.

Despite the promising performance from previous works, they all assume that the robots can access their actual poses. However, this assumption is unrealistic, especially for GPS-denied environment. Also, even with GPS localisation, localisation quality along the navigation path should be taken into consideration. SLAM-base localisation will be required in such cases. However, its performance is prone to poor observation of environment features, e.g. navigation in areas with no distinct features, e.g. an open area. Most localisation algorithms, such as PF or Kalman filter, will be negatively impacted by environment ambiguities and, hence, more weights will be given to interoceptive sensors, such as odometers, leading to unreliable localisation. The decoupled nature of robot perception and path planning could lead to catastrophic failures of self-localisation, due to the unpredictable observable features from the surroundings to perform SLAM-based localisation. The unreliable localisation will then in turn result in failures of reaching its goal location. Figure 1 illustrates a real-world scenario, where the grey path is more preferred than the less reliable path in white for drone navigation (assuming GPS localisation is unavailable). In this case, the grey path would allow the drone to observe more local features, hence improving localisation robustness.

This leads to the motivation of this work: how to train a policy for an agent to learn to navigate while also prevent localisation failures during navigation. The aim of our work is, therefore, two-fold: to train a robot that is able to 1) avoid collisions, while also 2) plan its paths that can provide robust localisation. This is different from other mapless navigation agents in previous works, which only consider obstacle avoidance without considering localisation performance.

The remainder of this paper is organised as follows. Section 2 introduces related work. Our method in this work is introduced in Sect. 3, followed by exper-

Fig. 1. A robot navigates from the start location to the destination on the left-hand side. The white trajectory is traversing in a feature-poor area, which is not suitable for SLAM-based localisation. The grey trajectory is a more preferred path, which maximises feature observations for robust SLAM-based localisation.

iments and results in Sect. 4. The conclusion and future research are presented in Sect. 5.

2   Related Work

With the great advances of neural networks, deep learning has been widely utilised to teach mobile robots driving by expert demonstrations by various means. For example, supervised learning techniques, such as Convolutional Neural Networks (CNN), have been deployed to train robots to autonomously make decisions or act directly based on depth images or Lidar data, to learn to navigate [5,9,11]. However, as it would be costly to collect labelled data in the real world, those methods are often trained and evaluated in virtual environments. In recent years, efforts have been paid to focus on transfer the trained networks to work in real world too [2,13].

RL, on the other hand, is more favourable, as it allows an agent to perform autonomous exploration and learning without human intervention. For mapless navigation, one prominent work is introduced in [12], where robots are trained with RL by a two-step method with depth images as inputs. Since then, several variants of related works have been introduced, inheriting the above method to improve the performance of mapless navigation in different aspects [8]. For discretized action space, state-of-the-art Deep Q-Networks (DQN), such as double networks and duel architectures, are integrated together to enhance robot navigation abilities [10].

Further, RL is also used for navigation in continuous action space by deploying the Asynchronous Deep Deterministic Policy Gradient (DDPG) algorithm [13]. RL in continuous action space requires more data than discretized space. To improve its sample efficiency, imitation learning and RL can be combined for improving efficiency [9], where the policy network is first pre-trained with imitation learning, and, then further tuned with the constraint policy optimisation, named as the (CPO)RL algorithm. In [15], a modular architecture is introduced to train robots on the modular basis by dividing a task into local obstacle avoidance and global navigation modules. An action scheduling mechanism is proposed to perform efficient exploration and exploitation. Other improvements have also been made in sampling efficiency [7] and algorithm hyper parameters selection [1]. When visual inputs are used for navigation, a technique called reinforcement learning with auxiliary tasks is applied in order to obtain effective representations from images for navigation tasks [4,6].

Although the works discussed above have achieved relatively promising performance, to the authors' best knowledge, none of these learning-based works have discussed the effect of localisation quality on its final navigation performance. In other words, path planning and robot perception should be considered as tightly coupled problems for decision making. Considerations should be given not only to localisation and mapping, but also optimal path planning or policy to optimise performance of localisation. The agent policy makes decisions to ensure paths are also beneficial to the localisation and mapping performance, such that uncertainty of its localisation and map construction are minimised. This is related to our work.

3 Methodology

3.1 System Description

Figure 2 shows the system overview of this work. First, measurement data of the robot are fed to the localisation algorithm for calculating the current estimated robot pose. The estimated robot pose and the goal position are then used to compute the relative goal pose, represented by the relative distance and relative heading with respect to the robot. Finally, the relative goal pose together with measurement data are provided to the fail-safe localisation reinforcement learning agent to make decision on the next action. This procedure iterates until the robot reaches the designated goal position.

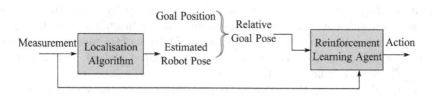

Fig. 2. System overview

As mentioned, most mapless navigation algorithms assume the availability of ground truth poses of the robot and this assumption is highly impractical for real-world applications. On the other hand, robot pose estimation purely based on odometry is unacceptable too, due to unpredictable odometry drifts over time. In our work, it relies on sensors such as Lidar or cameras with a localisation algorithm to estimate robot poses.

3.2   Localisation Algorithm

In this paper, we consider a feature-based PF localisation algorithm, specifically, the Rao-Blackwellized Particle Filter (RBPF) [3], which is probably the most deployed method for robot state estimation. In principle, our focus should not be limited to any particular localisation algorithm. Briefly, according to the RBPF framework, the joint probability of the map m and the robot poses x can be factorised through Rao-Blackwellization, formulated as follows:

$$p(x_{1:t}, m | z_{1:t}, u_{1:t-1}) = p(m | x_{1:t}, z_{1:t}) p(x_{1:t} | z_{1:t}, u_{1:t-1}) \qquad (1)$$

where z and u represent the measurement and the control input respectively. The particle filter maintains a batch of particles, where each particle produces their own pose estimation from control inputs and measurements and then builds a map of their own according to Eq. 1. An importance weight factor is assigned to each particle to evaluate the pose estimation quality of this particle, which is defined by the following equation:

$$w_t^{(i)} \propto w_{t-1}^{(i)} p(z_t | m_{t-1}^{(i)}, x_t^i) \qquad (2)$$

where the weight factor w is updated recursively and i represents the particle identification. The particle filter will do re-sampling based on the importance weight factors. It will recursively select some particles to replace some others. The larger the importance weight factor is, the higher possibility it is of to be selected to replace other particles. After a few iterations, the particles will then converge towards the true pose gradually.

3.3   Reinforcement Learning Agent

An RL agent gains experience from interaction with the environment. At each time step t, it selects an action a from a θ parameterised policy $\pi(a|s; \theta)$ based on its current state s and executes the selected action in the environment. After execution, the state will be updated and the agent will receive a reward r. This process will iterate continuously until a termination condition is met, such as goal state achieved or exceeding the maximum time. The aim of training is to generate a policy, which maximises the accumulated discounted reward, formulated as $R_t = \sum_{k=0}^{\infty} \gamma^k r_{t+k}$, where γ is the discount factor.

As the objective of this work is to illustrate the necessity of considering localisation quality for planning, thus the specific RL algorithm should not affect the final conclusion. Considering DQN is relatively easy to implement and widely deployed, we use DQN in our work for this pilot study.

In DQN, a deep neural network is trained to estimate the action value $Q_\pi(s, a) = E[R_t | s_t = s, a_t]$, which is the expected return for selecting action a at state s following the policy π. The details of the DQN configuration in this work are as follows. The state space of the DQN agent consists of sensor observation measurement o_t and relative goal position g_t, which includes the relative distance d_g and heading β with respective to the robot. As the classic

DQN is designed for handling discrete action space, the action space needs to be discretized. During each time step, the agent selects a linear velocity v_{linear} among a set of values $[v_{l_1}, v_{l_2}...v_{l_i}]$ and an angular velocity among a set of values $[w_1, w_2...w_j]$. i and j can be decided according to different requirements.

In the task, the agent needs to navigate to a designated goal position, while, meanwhile, also avoids obstacles and minimises its localisation uncertainty. Therefore, in this work, the reward function is defined as follows:

$$r = \begin{cases} r_{lost} & \text{if no enough features are observed} \\ r_{collision} & \text{if collision happens} \\ r_{goal} & \text{if } d_g < d_{gmin} \\ f \times (d_{t-1} - d_t) & \text{otherwise} \end{cases} \tag{3}$$

where r_{lost} is negative when the agent observation o_t does not contain enough environmental features for robust localisation; $r_{collision}$ is a negative value to punish the agent when it collides with obstacles; r_{goal} is a positive value and is set when the robot arrives at the goal position within a minimum acceptable distance, defined by d_{gmin}; the term $d_{t-1} - d_t$ is to encourage the agent to make decisions that reduce the relative goal distance; and f is the distance rate factor that can be adjusted.

Previous research works seldom consider the penalty of r_{lost} to regulate agent behaviours. However, this reward is critical to prevent the robot from moving into open space, where no or very sparse features can be observed. According to the description in Sect. 3.2, it is clear that when the robot moves into open space, where has no enough observed features, the second term in Eq. 2 will not be calculated. Hence, the weight factors of the particles will not be updated. Consequently, the PF will not be able to evaluate the quality of the particles and will not perform re-sampling to correctly estimate the robot state using these weight factors. The localisation algorithm will thus fail and depend solely on odometry, which is not accurate.

4   Experiments and Results

4.1   Experiment Setup

We test our work in a 2-dimensional simulation environment using a mobile robot of a 3-dimensional kinematic motion model. As illustrated in Fig. 3a, the grey dots serve as landmarks that may be observed by the robot for localisation. Each landmark also represents an obstacle, in the circular shape with the radius of 1 m (illustrated by the light grey regions in Fig. 3a). The observation of the robot contains relative distances and angles of those landmarks to the robot within the robot maximum observation range, which is 5.0 m with a full 2π coverage. The robot needs to travel to a goal position, denoted by a black star, as shown in Fig. 3a. Those black crosses are the estimated landmarks that are observed during navigation.

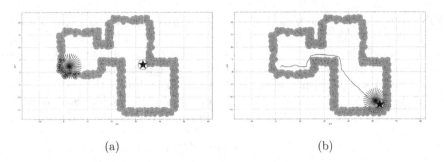

(a)   (b)

Fig. 3. (a) Environment: robot (black dot with laser scan beams) and goal position (star), (b) Robot navigation trajectory with ground truth poses provided

During training, those landmarks and goal positions are generated randomly. We also use randomly generated maps of different shapes. The robot linear velocity is set to be a constant value $v_l = 1.0$ m/s. The angular velocity is a selection from the following set of values $(-2.0, -1.0, 0.0, 1.0, 2.0)$ rad/s. Both linear and angular velocities are added with Gaussian noises during the robot execution to simulate odometry errors. The reward elements r_{lost}, $r_{collision}$ and r_{goal} are -300, -300 and 600 respectively and the distance rate factor f is 10.

For the DQN-based RL framework, measurement data need to be converted into a discrete structure. The observed landmarks are first divided into 36 groups according to relative angles ($10°$ per group). The observation o_t consists of two value lists: $[lmin_1 \cdots lmin_{36}]$, where each element represents the value of the relative distance to the nearest landmark in that angle group and $[number_1 \cdots number_{36}]$, where each element represents the number of observed landmarks in that angle group. Using the restructured observation ($36 + 36$ dimensions) together with the relative goal position (2 dimensions), the agent state would be then represented by a 74-dimension vector. The input data is connected with 2 dense layers (512 nodes each) and the final layer uses a linear activation function, as shown in Fig. 4. Other DQN parameters are shown in Table 1.

Table 1. DQN settings

Parameter	Value
Learning rate	0.00025
Discount factor	0.99
Epsilon decay rate	0.998
Replay buffer	1000000
Target network update rate	Per 10 episodes

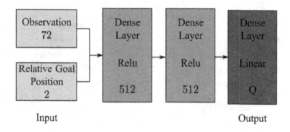

Fig. 4. The Q network structure

4.2   Results

As mentioned before, previous work always assume that the robot ground truth poses are accessible. Figure 3b shows the trajectory, when a robot is provided with true poses and trained without the localisation failure penalty. The robot navigates through an open space diagonally to reach the goal position with a relatively short distance. In the real world, however, it is not always easy to obtain ground truth poses. When PF-based localisation is deployed in the same task, the robot will diverge from the true trajectory, as shown in Fig. 5, where the dash and solid lines are the estimated and ground truth trajectories respectively. During navigation, the divergence is caused by the poor observation of environmental features, as shown in Fig. 5a. In the case of navigation with diverged particles, when new features are observed, particles will be re-sampled to re-localise the robot to re-converge to a new pose estimated with respect to the new observed features. However, the estimated pose could potentially lose its original track and, hence, converge to wrong poses, as illustrated in Fig. 5b. The PF localisation will then fail catastrophically. In certain cases, due to the PF failures, the robot goal position might become unreachable for the robot due to the misaligned obstacles (black crosses at the bottom right corner in Fig. 5b). In this case, the robot will never reach the goal position.

The same experiments are performed with the additional localisation failure penalty r_{lost} introduced in our work. Figure 7 shows the trajectories estimated using the same PF algorithm for localisation. As expected, it can be clearly seen that the estimated trajectories align closely to the true trajectories. It is also worth noting that the new trajectories tend to stay close to landmarks, to ensure high-quality landmark observation for robust localisation. Consequently, the robot can arrive at the goal successfully with only PF-based localisation. As mentioned, the performance improvement is mainly attributed to the new landmark-aware RL-based navigation policy, which encourages the robot to maintain a distance with good observation of features to ensure high localisation confidence.

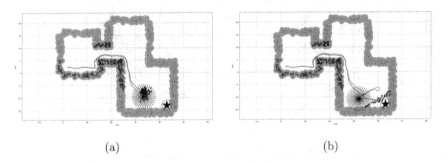

(a)   (b)

Fig. 5. Trajectories without localisation failure penalty (a) PF localisation diverges when no feature is observed, (b) PF localisation re-converges to wrong poses (solid line: ground truth trajectory; dashed line: estimated trajectory)

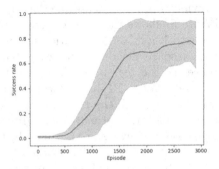

Fig. 6. Success rate

The success rates evaluated at different training episodes are shown in Fig. 6. As can be seen, the success rate rises as the number of training episodes increases and stabilises at about 0.8 after training for 3000 episodes. The network is relatively simple and thus the training takes several hours on a workstation with an Intel i7-8700 CPU and an Nvidia RTX-2080 GPU.

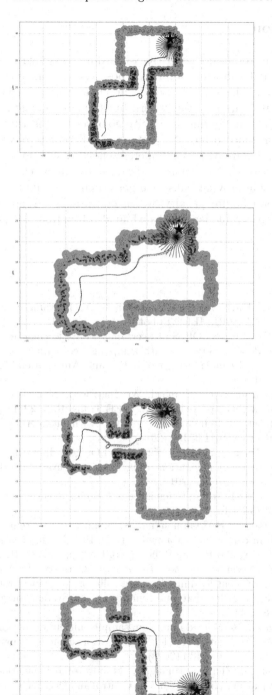

Fig. 7. Example trajectories generated with localisation failure penalty (solid black line: ground truth trajectory; dashed line: estimated trajectory)

5   Conclusion

In this work, we introduced a novel DQN-based mapless navigation method that uses SLAM-based localisation for robot pose estimation, rather than relying on robot ground truth poses as used in previous works. A localisation failure penalty r_{lost} is introduced in the reward function to regulate agent behaviours to prevent robots from entering areas with no observable features, where SLAM-based localisation tend to fail. We performed different tests with and without using localisation failure penalty in different environments for training with randomised robot start/goal locations and maps. It can be clearly seen that our work considerably improves localisation performance attributed to the effectiveness of localisation failure penalty, which encourages a robot to follow paths with consistent observable landmarks while also free from collisions, hence failsafe localisation.

References

1. Chiang, H.T.L., Faust, A., Fiser, M., Francis, A.: Learning navigation behaviors end-to-end with AutoRL. IEEE Robot. Autom. Lett. **4**(2), 2007–2014 (2019)
2. Choi, S., Lee, K., Lim, S., Oh, S.: Uncertainty-aware learning from demonstration using mixture density networks with sampling-free variance modeling. In: 2018 IEEE International Conference on Robotics and Automation (ICRA), pp. 6915–6922. IEEE (2018)
3. Grisetti, G., Stachniss, C., Burgard, W.: Improved techniques for grid mapping with Rao-Blackwellized particle filters. IEEE Trans. Rob. **23**(1), 34–46 (2007)
4. Jaderberg, M., et al.: Reinforcement learning with unsupervised auxiliary tasks. arXiv preprint arXiv:1611.05397 (2016)
5. Kanezaki, A., Nitta, J., Sasaki, Y.: GOSELO: goal-directed obstacle and self-location map for robot navigation using reactive neural networks. IEEE Robot. Autom. Lett. **3**(2), 696–703 (2017)
6. Mirowski, P., et al.: Learning to navigate in complex environments. arXiv preprint arXiv:1611.03673 (2016)
7. Moridian, B., Page, B.R., Mahmoudian, N.: Sample efficient reinforcement learning for navigation in complex environments. In: 2019 IEEE International Symposium on Safety, Security, and Rescue Robotics (SSRR), pp. 15–21. IEEE (2019)
8. Niu, H., Ji, Z., Arvin, F., Lennox, B., Yin, H., Carrasco, J.: Accelerated sim-to-real deep reinforcement learning: learning collision avoidance from human player. In: 2021 IEEE/SICE International Symposium on System Integration (SII), pp. 144–149. IEEE (2021)
9. Pfeiffer, M., et al.: Reinforced imitation: sample efficient deep reinforcement learning for mapless navigation by leveraging prior demonstrations. IEEE Robot. Autom. Lett. **3**(4), 4423–4430 (2018)
10. Ruan, X., Ren, D., Zhu, X., Huang, J.: Mobile robot navigation based on deep reinforcement learning. In: 2019 Chinese Control and Decision Conference (CCDC), pp. 6174–6178. IEEE (2019)
11. Tai, L., Li, S., Liu, M.: A deep-network solution towards model-less obstacle avoidance. In: 2016 IEEE/RSJ International Conference on Intelligent Robots and Systems (IROS), pp. 2759–2764. IEEE (2016)

12. Tai, L., Liu, M.: A robot exploration strategy based on Q-learning network. In: 2016 IEEE International Conference on Real-Time Computing and Robotics (RCAR), pp. 57–62. IEEE (2016)
13. Tai, L., Paolo, G., Liu, M.: Virtual-to-real deep reinforcement learning: continuous control of mobile robots for mapless navigation. In: 2017 IEEE/RSJ International Conference on Intelligent Robots and Systems (IROS), pp. 31–36. IEEE (2017)
14. Wang, C., Wang, J., Zhang, X.: A deep reinforcement learning approach to flocking and navigation of UAVs in large-scale complex environments. In: 2018 IEEE Global Conference on Signal and Information Processing (GlobalSIP), pp. 1228–1232. IEEE (2018)
15. Wang, Y., He, H., Sun, C.: Learning to navigate through complex dynamic environment with modular deep reinforcement learning. IEEE Trans. Games **10**(4), 400–412 (2018)

Collaborative Coverage for a Network of Vacuum Cleaner Robots

Junyan Hu$^{(\boxtimes)}$, Barry Lennox, and Farshad Arvin

University of Manchester, Manchester, UK
{junyan.hu,barry.lennox,farshad.arvin}@manchester.ac.uk

Abstract. Coordination of mobile robot teams has attracted significant attention in the area of robotics research. As one of the most important techniques used in the multi-robot systems, coverage has shown great potential to be applied to many real-world applications. In this paper, we aim to provide a novel path planning method for multi-robot coverage with applications to cooperative autonomous vacuum cleaning. Some preliminary results are presented using an open-source simulator Webots, which lay the foundation for more in-depth theoretical analysis and practical implementation in the subsequent research.

Keywords: Coverage · Navigation · Path planning · Swarm robotics

1 Introduction

Autonomous vacuum cleaning, as one of the most successful applications of mobile service robotics, has received significant attentions since the past decade. Simultaneous localization and mapping techniques are mostly used in the robotic platforms, which lead to reliable coverage performances in small-scale environments. However, with the increasing demand in using robot swarms to collaboratively clean a common large-scale area like hotels, warehouses, office buildings, etc., high-efficiency coordination algorithms for networked cleaner robots are being explored by researchers from both academia and industry.

A team of vacuum cleaner robots can be viewed as a multi-robot system, which shows great potential to be used in real-world applications due to its flexibility, reconfigurability, robustness to faults and cost-effectiveness in solving complex tasks. Some potential applications of multi-robot teams include cooperative transportation [1,2], target monitoring [3], etc. When properly designed, a multi-robot system can provide a more efficient and robust performance compared to a single robot [4]. Various of coordination strategies have been developed by researchers in recent years. Some main research directions include collective decision making, swarm intelligence, multi-robot path planning, formation

This work was supported in part by EPSRC-IAA and TPLC ltd, in part by EPSRC RAIN and RNE projects [EP/R026084/1 and EP/P01366X/1], and in part by the Royal Academy of Engineering [grant number CiET1819].

© Springer Nature Switzerland AG 2021
C. Fox et al. (Eds.): TAROS 2021, LNAI 13054, pp. 112–115, 2021.
https://doi.org/10.1007/978-3-030-89177-0_11

control, etc. Consider the features of the cooperative cleaning tasks, coverage techniques can be utilized to fulfil the objective.

To achieve the goal, robots should be able to communicate with each other to obtain relative position information via a decentralized network. Besides, a control structure should also be designed properly to ensure the robots achieve the pre-specified goal by using the information obtained from the sensors and communication modules. In this paper, we aim to provide a novel coordination solution for multi-robot collaborative cleaning problems.

2   Method

Each vacuum cleaner robot can be viewed as a cyber-physical system. We implement a two-layer control structure for the robot teams, which consists of a cyber layer for the decision making purpose and a physical layer for the target tracking purpose.

In the cyber layer, a frontier-based exploration technique [5] is mainly used to achieve autonomous coverage, where the radius of the frontier point detection should be set the same as the robot's radius to ensure that the robot's footprints fully cover the explored area. To avoid repeated trajectories and overlapping cleaning areas when using multiple robots in the collaborative task, a Voronoi-based path planning technique [6] is also added to improve efficiency. By using the relative position information from the neighbors via the connected communication network, some Voronoi partitions are generated automatically, thus each robot will give a higher priority to the target area in its local Voronoi cell before moving to other robots' working zones. Combine these two decision making processes, a desired set of waypoints can be generated, which are then transmitted to the physical layer for target tracking.

In the physical layer, the assigned waypoint should be tracked precisely by implementing a robust control system based on the robot dynamics. Firstly, the nonlinear robot dynamic model is transformed to a linear system using an input-output feedback linearization controller [7]. Then an adaptive tracking controller which was proposed in [8] can be applied to the robot to achieve position tracking using the state feedback from the onboard sensors.

The proposed coverage strategy will terminate only if there is not new frontier point in the whole environment, which means the working area is fully covered by the robots' footprints.

3   Results

In this section, Webots [9] is selected as the simulation platform, which provides a realistic environment to test the effectiveness of the theoretical results. As a professional robotic platform, Webots has integrated cross-compilation systems allowing users to compile and upload the controllers to real robots with minimum modification, which facilitates the real-robot application of the proposed control architecture.

Fig. 1. Five cleaner robots are used in the simulation case study.

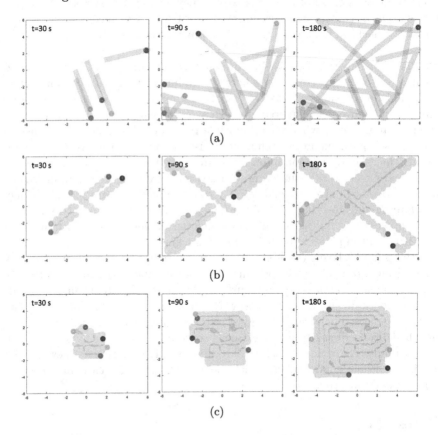

Fig. 2. Trajectories of the vacuum cleaner robots at different time instants. (a) Random movements. (b) Semi-coordinated coverage method. (c) Fully-coordinated coverage method.

In the simulation, the arena's size is set as $6\,\mathrm{m} \times 6\,\mathrm{m}$. We use five vacuum cleaner robots to perform the collaborative cleaning task as shown in Fig. 1. For comparison, three different methods are applied to the robots during the mission.

Firstly, a default control algorithm is directly implemented in the robotic platform, which reflects the random movements commonly observed in the early version of the cleaner robot products. Based on the proposed coverage strategy, a semi-coordinated algorithm is also tested, where the robots are able to cooperate with each other to cover the working area via Voronoi partitions, but the waypoints are randomly selected inside their own Voronoi cells. Finally, a fully-coordinated method is presented, where each robot tends to cover the area closer to its initial position, such that the robots movements are more organized. The trajectories of the robots under different methods during the mission are presented in Fig. 2(a), (b) and (c), respectively. From all these figures, the effectiveness and efficiency of the proposed coverage strategy can be verified.

4   Conclusion

In this paper, we proposed a coverage strategy for networked vacuum cleaner robots. Some preliminary results were obtained to validate the feasibility of the proposed method. For the next step of this research, we will implement the proposed algorithm on real robotic platforms and conduct real-world robotic experiments in large-scale complex environments.

References

1. Hu, J., Bhowmick, P., Lanzon, A.: Group coordinated control of networked mobile robots with applications to object transportation. IEEE Trans. Veh. Technol. (2021)
2. Chen, J., Gauci, M., Li, W., Kolling, A., Groß, R.: Occlusion-based cooperative transport with a swarm of miniature mobile robots. IEEE Trans. Rob. **31**(2), 307–321 (2015)
3. Hu, J., Turgut, A.E., Lennox, B., Arvin, F.: Robust formation coordination of robot swarms with nonlinear dynamics and unknown disturbances: design and experiments. IEEE Trans. Circuits Syst. II: Exp. Briefs (2021)
4. Ban, Z., Hu, J., Lennox, B., Arvin, F.: Self-organised collision-free flocking mechanism in heterogeneous robot swarms. Mobile Netw. Appl. (2021)
5. Keidar, M., Kaminka, G.A.: Efficient frontier detection for robot exploration. Int. J. Robot. Res. **33**(2), 215–236 (2014)
6. Hu, J., Niu, H., Carrasco, J., Lennox, B., Arvin, F.: Voronoi-based multi-robot autonomous exploration in unknown environments via deep reinforcement learning. IEEE Trans. Veh. Technol. **69**(12), 14413–14423 (2020)
7. Ren, W., Sorensen, N.: Distributed coordination architecture for multi-robot formation control. Robot. Auton. Syst. **56**(4), 324–333 (2008)
8. Hu, J., Bhowmick, P., Jang, I., Arvin, F., Lanzon, A.: A decentralized cluster formation containment framework for multirobot systems. IEEE Trans. Robot. (2021)
9. Michel, O.: Cyberbotics Ltd. Webots^{TM}: professional mobile robot simulation. Int. J. Adv. Robot. Syst. **1**(1), 5 (2004)

Network-Aware Genetic Algorithms for the Coordination of MALE UAV Networks

Alexandros Giagkos[1(✉)], Myra S. Wilson[2], and Ben Bancroft[2]

[1] College of Engineering and Physical Sciences, Aston University, Birmingham, UK
a.giagkos@aston.ac.uk
[2] Department of Computer Science, Aberystwyth University, Aberystwyth, UK
mxw@aber.ac.uk, ben@benbancroft.uk

Abstract. Maintaining an ad hoc network infrastructure to cover multiple ground-based users can be achieved by autonomous groups of hydrocarbon powered medium-altitude, long-endurance (MALE) unmanned aerial vehicles (UAVs). This can be seen as an optimisation problem to maximise the number of users supported by a quality network while making efficient use of the available power. We present an architecture that combines genetic algorithms with a network simulator to evolve flying solutions for groups of UAVs. Results indicate that our system generates physical network topologies that are usable and offer consistent network quality. It offers a higher goodput than the non-network-aware equivalent when covering the communication demands of multiple ground-based users. Most importantly, the proposed architecture flies the UAVs at lower altitudes making sure that downstream links remain active throughout the duration of the mission.

Keywords: Genetic algorithms · Wireless communication · Unmanned aerial vehicles · Networks

1 Introduction

It is broadly recognised that area coverage for communication services is a promising application domain for cooperative UAVs [1,2]. Genetic algorithms (GAs) offer significant advances with most of the research concentrated on coordination, route finding, path planning and constraint management in multi-UAV systems [3–5]. In most of these contributions, the communication network between the UAVs is assumed. Exemplar works include Carruthers et al. [6] where the authors proposed a GA-based collision-aware coordination system for UAV missions related to surveillance and searching in unknown areas, with the assumption that the communications are constantly available.

Very few researchers have addressed the quality of network coverage for large-scale missions offered by groups of UAVs. Noticeable examples include Agogino

© Springer Nature Switzerland AG 2021
C. Fox et al. (Eds.): TAROS 2021, LNAI 13054, pp. 116–125, 2021.
https://doi.org/10.1007/978-3-030-89177-0_12

et al., [7] who optimised power levels and antenna orientations using GAs to maximise area coverage for ground-based users.

In this paper, we address the problem of autonomous position coordination for communication UAVs using GAs, by providing and maintaining an efficient airborne network infrastructure capable of supporting the communication needs of users on the ground. Our design includes a network-aware evaluation method for evolving solutions, which incorporates communication links' validation via a network simulator that implements a complete TCP/IP protocol stack. Thus, two objectives are addressed: i) to maximise the number of users being covered based on the available power and ii) to maximise the number of active UAV-to-UAVand UAV-to-users links being provided.

Section 2 introduces the problem with a scenario. The design of the GAs we employ is found in Sect. 3, and in Sect. 4, we discuss the system's architecture along with the network-aware evaluation method. The experimental methodology and results are found in Sects. 5 and 6 respectively. Final remarks and future work are included in Sect. 7.

2   Problem Description

MALE fixed-wing UAVs are equipped with two radio antennae; i) one isotropic for the UAV-to-UAV transmissions, and ii) one horn-shaped able to transfer data to the ground-based users. They have limited power for the communication, denoted as P_{max} with which they have to provide as many communication links as possible. All users, including the UAVs, are equipped with a Global Positioning System (GPS) and periodically broadcast information about their current positions.

Communication links are treated independently. A transmission is considered successful when a UAV's transmitter can feed its antenna with enough power to satisfy the quality requirements. A link is considered of good quality if the ratio of the energy per bit of information E_b to the thermal noise 1 Hz bandwidth N_0 is maintained. Equation 1 expresses the transmitting power P_t required to cover a user at slant range d, as shown in Fig. 1a. For further details on computing slant range values, the reader is encouraged to consult Giagkos et al. [8].

$$P_t = p \times \left(d^2 R_b \frac{E_b}{N_0} \frac{1}{G_r G_t} \left(\frac{4 \pi f}{c} \right)^2 T_{sys} K \right) \tag{1}$$

The higher the UAV flies, the greater its altitude h, the wider its conical footprint on the ground, and thus the greater the area covered. Similarly, the longer the slant range d between the transmitter and the receiver, the higher the signal power required to support the communication. The slant angle α to a user is calculated by applying spherical trigonometry using the available GPS data that each network user is expected to broadcast at regular intervals. A user needs to lie within the footprint of at least one UAV to be part of the network.

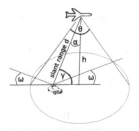 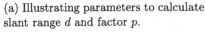 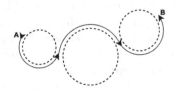

(a) Illustrating parameters to calculate slant range d and factor p.

(b) Three segments of different duration δh_i and bank angles β_i between points A and B.

Fig. 1. (a) A UAV's canonical footprint; (b) The Dubins path flying trajectory.

Noise related to obstacles is represented by the use of the elevation angle γ. A link is achieved when $\gamma \geq \omega$, with $\omega = 10°$. Subsequently, if $\gamma < \omega$ then the factor p in Eq. 1 is set to 0, indicating that no power is dedicated to that specific link, and thus the user is not covered. The link is ultimately considered achievable if and only if P_t is less than or equal to the remaining P_{max}, the maximum power available for communications each cycle.

3   Power-Aware Genetic Algorithms

In our previous work, we describe how genetic algorithms can cooperatively relocate UAVs to maximise coverage [9]. Flying trajectories are described by Dubins paths [10] consisting of 3 segments as depicted in Fig. 1b. We encode a UAV's trajectory as a 8-gene chromosome; three pairs of bank angle β_i and associated duration δt_i for each segment, with $i \in \{1, 2, 3\}$ and $\sum_{n=1}^{3}(\delta t_i)$ equal to the duration a complete trajectory. The final two genes are related to vertical flying with a binary b indicating whether the altitude change (δh) will be applied or the UAV will keep flying at constant altitude.

A single-point cross-over and a mutation operator are designed to evolve groups of N number of flying trajectories for N number of UAVs. A population of $M \times N$ are initiated, with $M = 100$ number of groups. The best previous group is retained unchanged (i.e., elite), whereas all others are combined to form new offspring. Selection is performed using roulette wheel. Every two randomly selected chromosomes among chosen groups are reproduced with a probability of 0.3. Each offspring gene is mutated; we apply a random Gaussian offset (mean 0.0, stdev. 0.1) to all real-valued genes, whereas the binary one is just flipped. The mutation rate is 0.05. Finally, GAs run for 200 generations or until the allowed computation time has elapsed, with $M - 1$ trajectories created at each generation. The time criterion is set to the time necessary to complete the default built-in circle manoeuvre when no solution is available.

The power-aware GAs utilise an evaluation method that measures the fitness of each group collectively. Given that the key objective is to maximise the number of supported users when limited power is available, the fitness score for a solution is calculated by $f = \frac{\sum_{n=1}^{|U|} |C_n|}{|G|}$, with U the set of all UAVs, and C_n the packing array of the nth UAV and G the set of all users on the ground.

Calculating the packing arrays for each UAV plays an important role in the efficiency of the searching algorithm. The packing algorithm that assigns users to appropriate UAVs was initially introduced in Giagkos et al. [9] and thus, its details are omitted. Packing favours those users that are low-maintenance (closer to the centre of the footprint) and, in turn, maximises the total coverage.

4   Network-Aware Genetic Algorithms

We extend our work to form new network-aware GAs that not only consider link budgets but also evaluate each solution by measuring its network topology qualities. We integrate the system with NS3, a discrete-event network simulator capable of providing realistic network phenomena and monitoring network performance metrics [11]. In this section, we describe the integration before documenting the internal mechanisms of the proposed network-aware GAs.

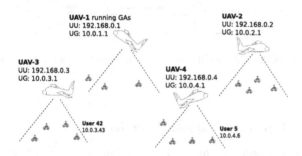

Fig. 2. Illustration of one NS3 network topology depicting a group of 4 UAVs. Each UAV gateway relays packets to and from its own footprint's network.

4.1   Integration with a Network Simulator

NS3's codebase is developed to allow the exchange of information between the GAs and the network simulator, namely the predicted positions of all users at the beginning of the next computational step, and the packing arrays. The built-in functionality to convert geographic to Cartesian coordinates is used, mapping the physical positions of all communicating users to a physical network topology.

All of the users' network interfaces are configured with respect to the packing information associated with each UAV, as seen in Fig. 2. Isotropic antennae's interfaces are given the address $192.168.0.U_n$, with U_n being the UAV's unique identifier (UID). Similarly, the horn-shaped antennae's addressed are set to 10.0.U_n.1 to facilitate footprint networks. Depending on which packing array it belongs to, each user receives an address 10.0.U_n.G_j, with G_j being its UID+1 and U_n the UID of the supporting UAV. For example, user 42 in Fig. 2 uses the gateway address 10.0.3.1 to communicate with the rest of the network.

NS3's wireless PHY and MAC implementations are based on the IEEE 802.11 standards. We increase the request to send/clear to send (RTS/CTS) timeout thresholds, overcoming the failed distributed coordination function pitfall in long-range transmissions. The gain of the horn-shaped antennae transmitters is set according to the manufacturer, i.e., calculated by $G_t = \frac{2\eta}{1-\cos(\frac{\theta}{2})}$, with $\theta = 125°$ corresponding to the half-power beam-width angle of the antenna and $\eta = 0.95$, the efficiency of its transmission. For the isotropic antennae, gain $G_t = 1$.

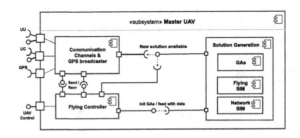

Fig. 3. Network-aware GAs architecture: the master UAV's internal components.

4.2 Network Topology Evaluation Model

The core differences between the power-aware and the network-aware GAs are the integration of the network simulator and its use to evaluate individual solutions by the latter GAs. The new objective is to maximise the fitness of each group of trajectories with respect to whether their resulting network topologies are able to maintain communication.

Figure 3 depicts the internal components of the subsystem installed on the master UAV, which generates and distributes solutions to the rest of the group. The component responsible for the communication sends and receives data using the connected interfaces, including the GPS broadcaster. Data is ported to the flying controller, the component in charge of preparing the next steering parameters (i.e., bank angle and altitude changes). When no trajectory is available or incomplete,[1] the controller initiates the GAs, feeding it at the same time with position related data.

Although the network-aware GAs share both encoding/decoding scheme and genetic operators with the power-aware GAs, the network-aware evaluation method also comprises short network trials (duration of 320 simulated seconds),

---

[1] While the GAs search for solutions, the default UAV manoeuvre is to cruise in circles.

designed to check the validity of all links of a solution's network topology. Link validation is a two-phase process and is performed by using a bespoke network protocol.

For UAV-to-UAV links, the master UAV broadcasts one discovery request packet per second to 192.168.0.255 containing a fresh sequence number (SeqNo). All receiving UAVs save the packet's SeqNo, update their routing tables and broadcast the request further before acknowledging it by sending a unicast ACK packet to the master. Received broadcast packets that contain the same SeqNo are dropped, while unicast ACKs are forwarded using the routing tables. At the end of the trial, the UAV-to-UAV link validation metric is calculated as:

$$N_{uu} = \frac{pkt_{ack}}{pkt_{req} \times (|U| - 1)} \tag{2}$$

where pkt_{ack} is the number ACK packets received and pkt_{req} the discovery requests sent to a topology of $|U|$ UAVs during the course of the trial.

Subsequently, UAV-to-ground links are checked by making use of the footprint networks. Every time a UAV acknowledges a discovery request, it broadcasts a request packet to its own network ($10.0.U_n.255$) with the same SeqNo. Any listening users acknowledge the request by sending ACK unicast packets. At every t of the trial, a UAV-to-ground link validation metric N_{ug}^t is given by:

$$N_{ug}^t = \sum_{n=1}^{|U|} |C_n^{t,ack}|, \quad \text{with } C_n^{t,ack} \subseteq C_n^t \tag{3}$$

where C_n^t is the packing array for U_n at t and $C_n^{t,ack}$ the subset of users from that array that have acknowledged support by U_n. Considering the whole duration T of the trial, N_{ug} is given by:

$$N_{ug} = \frac{\sum_{t=1}^{T} N_{ug}^t}{\sum_{t=1}^{T} |\mathbb{C}^t|}, \quad \text{with } \mathbb{C}^t = \bigcup_{n=1}^{|U|} C_n^t \tag{4}$$

with $\mathbb{C}^t$ the set of packed users at time t. Having calculated both N_{uu} and N_{ug}, the fitness score for the evaluation of a group of $|U|$ flying trajectories is calculated as:

$$f = w_1 \times \frac{\sum_{n=1}^{|U|} |C_n|}{|G|} + w_2 \times N_{uu} + w_3 \times N_{ug} \tag{5}$$

with w_1, w_2 and w_3 equally set to 0.33 for even contribution. Note that C_n of each UAV is not expected to change significantly between every t and $t + 1$. Equation 5 is designed to consider the packing algorithm that regulates the link budget, but also to examine whether the resulting network topology consists of active links for a sufficient period of time.

The fittest solution is decoded and returned to both the flying controller and the communication components, as shown in Fig. 3. At every next trial all routing tables are erased. Note that for the rest of the UAVs, the solution generation component is omitted from the architecture.

5   Experimental Methodology

To compare the power-aware with network-aware GAs groups of 4 UAVs are autonomously controlled to support 50 users uniformly distributed within a $100 \, \mathrm{km}^2$ terrain for 1 h. All users follow a random waypoint mobility model, with varying speeds (5–60 mph) and pausing times of 120 s. The UAVs' speed is 75 knots and flying is constrained by a maximum bank angle of 48° and altitude range of 150 m to 6 km. Other parameters related to link budget are: $P_{max} = 50$ Watts, $\theta = 125°$, $\eta = 0.95$, $R_b = 2$ Mbit/s, $E_b/N_0 = 10$ dB, frequency $f = 5$ GHz and $\omega = 10°$.

The Ad-hoc On-demand Distance Vector (AODV) protocol [12] is used for routing. AODV offers a state-of-the-art reactive mechanism for discovering paths between sources and destinations. To ensure that users can only communicate within the assigned footprint, AODV is disabled outside their $10.0.U_n.0$ networks.

Algorithm 1. Selecting source and destination pairs for communication sessions.

Require: acking arrays C_n of all $n \in U$ and their union $\mathbb{C}$
Ensure: L, a set of source and destination users' pairs

```
 1: L ← ∅
 2: S_used ← ∅, D_used ← ∅                          ▷ sets of used sources and destinations
 3: for each n ∈ U do
 4:     for each n′ ∈ U do
 5:         if n == n′ then
 6:             continue
 7:         S_left ← S_used △ C_n                    ▷ calculate the symmetric difference of two sets
 8:         D_left ← D_used △ C′_n
 9:         if |S_left| − 1 < 0 or |D_left| − 1 < 0 then
10:             continue
11:         S_used ←⁺ S_left(0)                      ▷ append first element of the set
12:         D_used ←⁺ D_left(0)
13:         L ←⁺ < S_left(0), D_left(0) >            ▷ append tuple of source and destination
14: return L
```

A $|U|(|U|-1)$ number of communication sessions are used in each experiment, with the selection of sources and destinations being performed using Algorithm 1. This approach ensures that the airborne backbone is fully utilised by the users on the ground. Constant Bit Rate (CBR) traffic generators are used for the communications between selected pairs, with sources transmitting 512-byte UDP datagrams at a rate of 1 Mbps.

Three performance metrics are used for the comparison of the two systems. Namely, i) coverage as the total number of supported users calculated by the packing algorithm, ii) goodput as the overall CBR throughput of the communication sessions excluding any protocol overhead bytes, and iii) altitude changes as the mean to examine the vertical activity of the group. The metrics highlight coverage capabilities with respect to both the number of users able to participate in the provided networks and the latter's efficiency in supporting communication services. Also, monitoring altitudes is important because it affects the footprint sizes and the slant range distances. As such, it offers useful insights about flying, revealing any emergent specialisation strategy.

Due to the stochastic nature of both systems, we repeat the experiments 30 times using random seeds and aggregate the results.

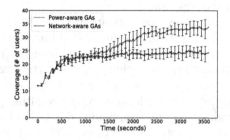

Fig. 4. Coverage results by power-aware and network-aware GAs.

6 Results

Figure 4 shows coverage for both systems. Considering link validation causes a reduced number of supported users for the network-aware GAs. This is an expected result, the magnitude of which highlights the importance of considering network-related qualities. We observe that the network-aware system reaches a plateau while the power-aware exploits several windows of opportunity to improve coverage during the flight. This is due to the less conservative flying of the power-aware GAs, restricted only by the P_{max} values. This is justified by the altitude changes depicted in Fig. 6, where 3 out of 4 UAVs are found to almost reach the maximum altitude of 6 km.

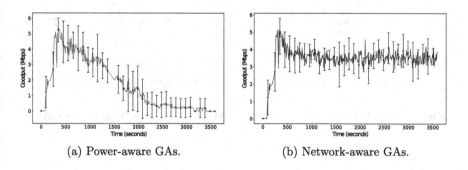

(a) Power-aware GAs.   (b) Network-aware GAs.

Fig. 5. (a) Goodput results for both systems.

In practice, the network topologies generated by the two systems differ significantly in performance. Figure 5 shows the goodput of the multiple CBR traffic generators. The network-aware GAs provide a usable and consistent infrastructure, whereas the links in the power-aware system gradually decline due to the lack of real network awareness of the power-aware GAs. For the latter, the distances between UAVs and their altitudes cause links to fail. Closely looking at the traffic data, we observe that communication is only possible for a single pair of users at the end of the experiment.

Altitude changes caused by the network-aware GAs are found to be less frequent, as shown in Fig. 7. All UAVs fly level (approx. 4 km), ensuring that downstream links remain active. Specialisation in flying emerges less frequently than by the power-aware GAs, as activity in the vertical axis is significantly lower. Although the power-aware GAs seemingly put more effort in increasing coverage by changing their vertical formation, the resulting physical topologies are not efficient throughout the mission, mainly due to the internal mechanisms of the underlying network protocols combined with long-range transmissions. This is addressed by the network-aware GAs using the integrated evaluation method.

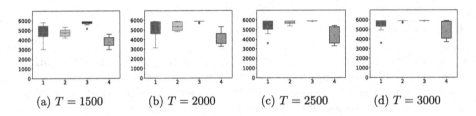

(a) $T = 1500$ (b) $T = 2000$ (c) $T = 2500$ (d) $T = 3000$

Fig. 6. Altitude in metres (y-axes) of 4 UAVs (x-axes) by power-aware GAs.

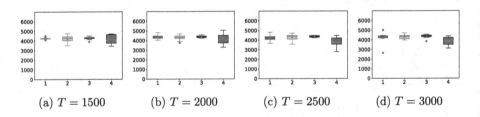

(a) $T = 1500$ (b) $T = 2000$ (c) $T = 2500$ (d) $T = 3000$

Fig. 7. Altitude in metres (y-axes) of 4 UAVs (x-axes) by network-aware GAs.

7   Conclusions

We presented a network-aware coordination system for MALE UAVs, which employs GAs to evolve flying solutions that result in effective physical topology networks. We discussed the integration with NS3 and compared the system's performance with a power-aware alternative that is purely based on link budget calculations. The integrated design offers a usable, consistent airborne infrastructure to support multiple users' communication demands. Considering the network-aware objective in the evaluation mechanism, via NS3, ensures that downstream links remain active throughout the mission and offer higher goodput than the power-aware GAs.

We deem the examination of the network-aware GAs under various scenarios as important future work to identify potential scalability issues. Consequently, we will investigate improvements to the evaluation method, such as considering application-related traffic to improve the performance of the overall network.

References

1. Khan, N.A., Jhanjhi, N.Z., Brohi, S.N., Usmani, R.S.A., Nayyar, A.: Smart traffic monitoring system using unmanned aerial vehicles (UAVs). Comput. Commun. **157**, 434–443 (2020)
2. Zeng, Y., Zhang, R., Lim, T.J.: Wireless communications with unmanned aerial vehicles: opportunities and challenges. IEEE Commun. Mag. **54**(5), 36–42 (2016)
3. Zhang, X., Duan, H.: An improved constrained differential evolution algorithm for unmanned aerial vehicle global route planning. Appl. Soft Comput. **26**, 270–284 (2015)
4. Çakıcı, F., Ergezer, H., Irmak, U., Leblebicioğlu, M.K.: Coordinated guidance for multiple UAVs. Trans. Inst. Meas. Control **38**(5), 593–601 (2016)
5. Rathbun, D., Kragelund, S., Pongpunwattana, A., Capozzi, B.: An evolution based path planning algorithm for autonomous motion of a UAV through uncertain environments. In: 2002 Proceedings of the 21st Digital Avionics Systems Conference, vol. 2, pp. 8D2-1. IEEE (2002)
6. Carruthers, B., McGookin, E.W., Murray-Smith, D.J.: Adaptive evolutionary search algorithm with obstacle avoidance for multiple UAVs. In: Zítek, P. (ed.) Proceedings of 16th IFAC World Congress, 2005, p. 2084. International Federation of Automatic Control (2005)
7. Agogino, A., HolmesParker, C., Tumer, K.: Evolving large scale UAV communication system. In: Proceedings of the Fourteenth International Conference on Genetic and Evolutionary Computation Conference, GECCO 2012, pp. 1023–1030. ACM, New York (2012)
8. Giagkos, A., Tuci, E., Wilson, M.S., Charlesworth, P.B.: Evolutionary coordination system for fixed-wing communications unmanned aerial vehicles: supplementary online materials, May 2021. http://www.aber.ac.uk/en/cs/research/ir/projects/nevocab
9. Giagkos, A., Tuci, E., Wilson, M.S., Charlesworth, P.B.: UAV flight coordination for communication networks: genetic algorithms versus game theory. Soft. Comput. **25**(14), 9483–9503 (2021). https://doi.org/10.1007/s00500-021-05863-6
10. Dubins, L.E.: On plane curves with curvature. Pac. J. Math. **11**(2), 471–481 (1961)
11. Riley, G.F., Henderson, T.R.: The ns-3 network simulator. In: Wehrle, K., Güneş, M., Gross, J. (eds.) Modeling and Tools for Network Simulation, pp. 15–34. Springer, Heidelberg (2010). https://doi.org/10.1007/978-3-642-12331-3_2
12. Perkins, C., Belding-Royer, E., Das, S.: RFC3561: ad hoc on-demand distance vector (AODV) routing (2003)

Self-organised Flocking of Robotic Swarm in Cluttered Environments

Zheyu Liu[1($\boxtimes$)], Ali Emre Turgut[2], Barry Lennox[1], and Farshad Arvin[1]

[1] Swarm and Computational Intelligence Lab (SwaCIL), Department of Electrical and Electronic Engineering, The University of Manchester, Manchester, UK
zheyu.liu@manchester.ac.uk
[2] Mechanical Engineering Department, Middle East Technical University, Ankara, Turkey

Abstract. Self-organised flocking behaviour, an emergent collective motion, appears in various physical and biological systems. It has been widely utilised to guide the swarm robotic system in different applications. In this paper, we developed a self-organised flocking mechanism for the homogeneous robotic swarm, which can achieve the collective motion with obstacle avoidance in a cluttered environment. The proposed mechanism introduces an obstacle avoidance approach to the Active Elastic Sheet model that was previously proposed for self-propelled particles. The proposed mechanism is represented by a nonlinear repulsive force inspired by Lennard-Jones potential function in molecular dynamics. In order to evaluate the flocking performance, three different environmental settings were implemented. Results revealed that the interaction mechanism significantly determines the robustness and stability of the swarm in flocking.

Keywords: Swarm robotics · Flocking · Self-organised · Bio-inspired

1 Introduction

Flocking of social animals is a commonly observed behaviour in many biological systems from tiny bacterial community to social animals such as fish school [9], sheep herds [14] and birds flocking [7]. Flocking, also known as collective motion, has been widely implemented in swarm robotic systems [16] such as exploration in precision agriculture [1] and unmanned aerial vehicles swarm coordination control [21].

The underlying mechanism of flocking behaviour steers a group of individuals to coherently move with an approximately identical speed and direction. Hence, the entire swarm moves together like a super-organism with astounding elegance and flexibility [19]. This large-scale swarm flocking presents the same universal property that, the emergent flocking behaviour only relies on the local interactions between robots without any need for global communication and any central control law. Researchers from physics to biology have proposed different collective motion models [2,4,8,12,20]. These models effectively reveal and describe

© Springer Nature Switzerland AG 2021
C. Fox et al. (Eds.): TAROS 2021, LNAI 13054, pp. 126–135, 2021.
https://doi.org/10.1007/978-3-030-89177-0_13

the collective motion principles in large-scale swarm scenarios. One of the most important models is proposed by Vicsek et al. [20], which was followed by other study like [3]. It is a minimal agent-based model where individuals follow velocity alignment rule. This model establishes a fundamental and explicit interaction principle called the alignment rule. Despite many subsequent complex models were introduced to achieve self-organised flocking in a more precise and natural way [2,3,10], they can be considered as the variants of Vicsek model since they all strongly rely on the velocity-based alignment interaction to perform self-organised collective motion. However, this pioneering model still has limitations to fully depict self-organised flocking motion, especially for swarm robotic applications. Firstly, the velocity-based algorithm not only requires robots to obtain the orientation of neighbouring robots in short communication range, but it also needs their relative positions to determine the neighbouring topology. Hence, the robots must have a strong computational ability and a reliable inter-robot communication to address the issue, e.g. by using local communication methods [11]. Secondly, the swarm achieves collective motion in an infinite and ideal space without any physical boundary restriction, e.g. walls. Therefore, it is not practical for a real-world swarm robotic system where robots encounter obstacles and in a cluttered environment. In addition, velocity-based model assumes that each robot is set up with a fixed speed, and only orientation can be adjusted in each step. It significantly restricts the swarm in terms of flexibility and adaptability in case of the complex environments. Considering the limitations of the velocity alignment, another collective mechanism for flocking was proposed by Ferrante et al. [5,6], which developed a novel position-based decentralised algorithm for achieving a collective motion. They abstracted self-propelled particle swarm in two-dimensional active solids, and introduced the Active Elastic Sheet (AES) model. The individual interaction is based on attractive-repulsive forces. Robot's motion is driven by the combination of linear elastic forces from its fixed neighbouring topology. Therefore, the agent-based model only rely on the exchange information of relative position, rather than including the heading orientation of neighbouring robots, which significantly alleviates the requirement of hardware computation and perception. In addition, in [15,22], both simulated and real robot experiments demonstrated the feasibility of AES model in the real swarm robot applications.

The AES model does not consider the limitations of the real-world environments since it is derived from the collective behaviour of the perfect active crystal. Inevitably, in a real-world scenario, there exists plenty of physical boundaries including obstacles and walls. Therefore, in this work, we developed a new flocking method based on the AES model, that facilitates application of the flocking in real-world scenarios with several obstacles– *cluttered* environments. In this work, we investigated different states of the swarm trajectory when an interaction between the swarm and obstacles happens in a cluttered environment. We modelled a repulsive force for collision avoidance and combined it with the AES model's attraction-repulsion force. In addition, the impact of the proposed model in presence of obstacles with different collective forces was investigated.

2 Flocking Method

2.1 Active Elastic Sheet Model

The agent-based AES model [5] can produce the self-organised collective motion, even in the presence of noise. It can also start from swarm system with random initial orientation and position. Rather than orientation and alignment interaction, each pairwise of robots only exchange the position information, then generate the corresponding elastic force to affect the robot's motion state. Its simplicity contributes to implementing self-organised flocking in swarm robotic applications. As introduced before, in a swarm system including N robots, individual's motion dynamics is determined by the spring-like forces from its fixed neighbouring robot set. The attraction-repulsion forces affect both the linear and angular velocities of the robot during flocking. This continuous-time model can be illustrated mathematically as:

$$\dot{\overrightarrow{x}}_i = v_0 \hat{n}_i + \alpha[(\overrightarrow{F}_i + D_r \hat{\xi}_r) \cdot \hat{n}_i]\hat{n}_i, \tag{1}$$

$$\dot{\theta}_i = \beta[(\overrightarrow{F}_i + D_r \hat{\xi}_r) \cdot \hat{n}_i^\perp] + D_\theta \xi_\theta, \tag{2}$$

where, $\overrightarrow{x}_i$ and θ_i are position and orientation of the ith robot. v_0 is the self-propelled forward biasing speed that is imposed into all robots. $\hat{n}_i$ and $\hat{n}_i^\perp$ are two unit vectors pointing parallel and perpendicular to the heading direction of the ith robot, and two parameters α and β are inverse translation and rotation damping coefficients, respectively. The motion essence of AES model is that the robot adjusts its linear and angular velocities based on the projection of forces in parallel to its heading and perpendicular to its heading.

This model also concentrates on the impact of noise from both measurement and actuation; $D_r \hat{\xi}_r$ is the error from the measured forces and $D_\theta \xi_\theta$ is the fluctuation of the individual motion. $\hat{\xi}_r$ is a randomly generated unit vector for noise strength coefficient D_r. Also, $\hat{\xi}_r$ is a random variable with standard, zero-centred normal probability distribution for noise strength coefficient of D_θ. The total linear elastic force, $\overrightarrow{F}_i$, is originated from those neighbouring robots interacting with the ith robot. It can be calculated as follow:

$$\overrightarrow{F}_i = \sum_{j \in S_i} \frac{-k}{l_{ij}}(|\overrightarrow{r}_{ij}| - l_{ij})\frac{\overrightarrow{r}_{ij}}{|\overrightarrow{r}_{ij}|}, \tag{3}$$

$$\overrightarrow{r}_{ij} = \overrightarrow{x}_j - \overrightarrow{x}_i, \tag{4}$$

where, l_{ij} is the equilibrium distance where the force between ith and jth robot will become zero, and $\frac{k}{l_{ij}}$ is the spring constant. Each neighbouring robot set S_i contains all robots that connect with the focal robot through the "virtual springs" at the beginning of each experiment. This connection would not be broken up regardless of the distance between this pair of the robots. Similar to spring, once the interaction network of neighbouring robots is defined, it will remain fixed throughout the experiment. In addition, according to Eq. (5), the inducing force would become large as the distance to equilibrium position increase. Overall, the total elastic force drives the robot to move toward the equilibrium position.

In order to implement our experiments, we followed experimental setup proposed in [15] and modified the original AES model with adding the goal direction, F_g, which coordinates the swarm to achieve a collective motion with a specific direction. In addition, this modification can also lead to faster convergence of the collective motion. Hence, the goal direction is added to the swarm as a "virtual external force" described as:

$$\overrightarrow{F}_g = \omega_g \widehat{v}_d. \tag{5}$$

The goal force is parallel to the desired velocity unit vector $\widehat{v}_d$ and its magnitude is determined by the weighting coefficient ω_g. The modification steers the swarm system moving towards the region of obstacles by adjusting the desired velocity unit vector.

2.2 Extended AES Model

The robots' interaction with obstacles based on the original AES model purely relies on attraction-repulsion force, which provides a natural benchmark to design obstacle interaction from the point of force. Indeed, the obstacle force can be treated as a repulsive force and its magnitude is also based on the distance between the robot and the obstacle. In contrast to elastic force in AES model, as the robot approaches to obstacle, its magnitude should become significantly large to avoid the collision. It should be close to the infinity when the distance is nearly zero. When a robot detects the existence of an obstacle, the repulsive obstacle force will appear will be imposed into the robot.

Obviously, the previous spring-like force cannot satisfy the requirement. There are some other virtual physical-based models with more complicated relation with distance and are utilised especially for robotic control. One of most widely used virtual physical-based models is the Lennard-Jones (LJ) potential model [17,18], which was proposed to interpret motion of atoms or molecules in molecular dynamics. The obstacle force $\overrightarrow{F}_{obs,i}$ that acts against the ith robot was designed based on the following equation:

$$\overrightarrow{F}_{obs,i} = \sum_{o \in O_i} \epsilon_{obs} [(\frac{\sigma_{obs}}{||\overrightarrow{r}_{io}||})^{2\alpha_{LJ}} - 2(\frac{\sigma_{obs}}{||\overrightarrow{r}_{io}||})^{\alpha_{LJ}}]\overrightarrow{r}_{io} \tag{6}$$

There are some parameters that need to be explained and set for the experiments. Here, $\overrightarrow{r}_{io}$ is the distance vector from an obstacle, o, to ith robot, and obstacle set O_i is the set of all obstacles within the detecting range of ith robot. ϵ_{obs} corresponds to the depth of potential function and α_{LJ} defines the rate of change of the potent versus distance by changing its power. The value of α_{LJ} is set to 2, which contributes to improve the smoothness of collective behaviour. The final important parameter is σ_{obs}, which is related to the equilibrium distance at which the Eq. (6) is equal to zero. According to Eq. (6), by setting the obstacle force to zero and solving it, the proper value for σ_{obs} parameter can be obtained in following relation:

$$\sigma_{obs} = \sqrt{2}d_{0,obs}, \tag{7}$$

where $d_{0,obs}$ represents the equilibrium distance where the obstacle force magnitude is equal to zero. Using the above equation, the σ_{obs} can be tuned automatically and its value can be determined as a function of equilibrium distance $d_{0,obs}$. In order to maintain the repulsion force only, it is necessary to adjust the parameter σ_{obs} in a way that the obstacle exceeds the sensing range of robot before reaching the equilibrium point, i.e. $d_{0,obs} > r_{sens}$, where r_{sens} is the sensing range of the robots. One suggestion is to define $d_{0,obs}$ in a way that the obstacle force turns to zero at the verge of detection zone as follow:

$$\sigma_{obs} = \sqrt{2}d_{0,obs} = \sqrt{2}r_{sens}. \tag{8}$$

In this case, when the robot perceive the obstacle, the repulsive obstacle force would appear and impose on the robot. In addition, as the robot approaches to an obstacle, the magnitude will increase significantly.

Designing all the forces affect the collective behaviour of robots, and consequently the whole swarm system. The motion dynamics of each robot would be redefine to consider the impact from external forces including goal force and obstacle force. The total force in Eq. (1) and Eq. (2) need be substituted by the total force which is simply modelled as the combination of collective force in Eq. (3), goal force in Eq. (5) and obstacle force in Eq. (6). The corresponding equation is illustrated below:

$$\overrightarrow{F}_{tot,i} = \overrightarrow{F}_{c,i} + \overrightarrow{F}_{g} + \overrightarrow{F}_{obs,i}, \tag{9}$$

where, in the new definition, the total force $\overrightarrow{F}_{tot,i}$ replaces the force in original AES motion dynamic, and the $\overrightarrow{F}_i$ in Eq. (3) is viewed as the collective force $\overrightarrow{F}_{c,i}$.

2.3   Metrics

The main aim of flocking behaviour is to achieve a common direction within the swarm members. In addition, the robots should move collectively, which can be characterised by an essential property, so called the *coherency*. The coherency depicts the likelihood of individual remaining in the swarm system. This principle feature can also serve as the performance index of flocking when swarm encounters obstacles in a cluttered environment. In order to evaluate the swarm coherency, a metric was introduced in this work. The metric is the average distance between the swarm individuals. It is also a common method to evaluate the coherency of swarm for collective motion [13]. The coherency is presented as:

$$d_s = \frac{2\sum_{i=1}^{N-1}\sum_{j=1}^{N}||\overrightarrow{r}_{ij}||}{N(N-1)}. \tag{10}$$

Table 1. Setting values of related parameters in the experiments

Parameters	Description	Value/Range
N	Population	15 [robot]
v_0	Forward biasing speed	0.05 [m/sec]
α	Inverse translational damping coefficient	0.01
β	Inverse rotational damping coefficient	0.12
ω_g	Weighting coefficient for goal force	4
$\vec{v}_d$	Desired velocity unit vector	(1,0)
ϵ_{obs}	Depth of potential function	0.01
r_{sens}	Sensing range for robot	2 [m]
r_R	Radius of robot	0.7 [m]
r_{obs}	Radius of circle obstacle	2.7 [m]
L	Length of the swarm arena	35 [m]
l_{ij}	Equilibrium distance	$\{2,3\}$ [m]
k	Magnitude of collective force	$\{0.05, 0.3\}$

This metric describes the mean value of each pair of robot's distance. It should keep unchanged if the swarm maintains a stable motion without an abruption or squeeze deformation.

2.4   Experimental Setup

After defining the obstacle interaction and modifying the AES model, all the prerequisites are fully prepared to implement the simulated experiments. The aim of these experiments is to investigate the performance of self-organised flocking based on AES model in a cluttered environment. We designed three different environmental conditions to implement the experiments, including ideal environment without obstacle, single-obstacle environment and multi-obstacle environment. There are some basic parameters (listed in Table 1) that need to be determined. There are also some critical assumptions needed to be mentioned: i) the simulated experiments do not consider the impact of noise, ii) the network topology of robot swarm is determined prior to flocking and fixed. Each robot establishes a connection within its sensing range, and iii) the equilibrium distance l_{ij} in Eq. (3) is set to the initial distance between robots i and j.

There are essential factors that will affect the flocking behaviour in the cluttered environment such as population size (N), equilibrium distance (l_{ij}) and the magnitude of collective force (k); however, we only considered l_{ij} and k in this work. In order to eliminate the accidental error in observation, repeatability principle need to be considered in these experiments. Therefore, each set of experiments was repeat 10 times.

Experiments without Obstacles: In this set of experiment, swarm moves in a given $L \times L$ square arena with the physical boundaries. Their initial distance between two nearest neighbouring robots is set to equilibrium distance. The initial orientations and positions of the robots were selected randomly and uniformly distributed in the left-hand side of the arena. In this set of experiments, only goal force and collective force are imposed into the individual robots. The set goal force drags the swarm on the x-axis, and the collective force contributes to configure the swarm into a stable structure.

Experiments with a Single Obstacle: This set of experiments simulate a single obstacle environment, where the obstacle was located at a fixed point, where the swarm will encounter. In this experiment, the obstacle avoidance interaction was introduced into the collective motion. Similar with the first set of experiments, the related parameters still remain unchanged.

Experiments with Multiple Obstacles: This set experiments study the self-organised flocking in cluttered environment, with several obstacles which appear in front of robots which they are moving to right-hand side of the arena. There are three obstacles which form a triangle shape to block the motion of the flock. Except for this, other parameters are the same as the previous experiments. Compared with the single obstacle case, the obstacles' force will provide a complex situation. Therefore, the robots will detect more than one obstacle force from different directions at the same time.

3   Results and Discussion

Figure 1 shows examples of the randomly selected flocking trajectories in three different scenarios with $l_{ij} = 3.5$ m and $N = 15$. In the diagrams, the small blue circles represent the robots in a swarm. The red arrows on each robot represent orientation of the robot. The large red circles indicate the obstacles which are nearly 4 times larger than the robots. Obviously, the swarm could achieve a collective motion in an ideal environment without obstacles as shown in Fig. 1(a). In addition, robotic swarm is also capable of avoiding the obstacles in all the scenarios, shown in the rest of Fig. 1. In Fig. 1(b) and (c), the parameter k associated with the collective force is set to 0.05. It can be viewed that the flock will be separated by the obstacle, and it is difficult to recover to the original structure. The swarm was divided into several small clusters by obstacle forces. Figure 1(d) and (e) present the flocking behaviour of the swarm with the same initial conditions (position and orientation). The only difference is to improve the magnitude of the collective force by setting it to $k = 3$. In this case, The flocking performance in the ideal environment does not manifest any significant change. Hence, the swarm still can move collectively like a solid entity with a common direction. However, even if the robots in the swarm were segmented by the obstacles' force, they were able to converge into a single cluster with a stable structure and maintain the self-organised flocking. In addition, this flocking behaviour possesses higher flexibility and robustness. It goes through the obstacles smoothly like a liquid flow in nature.

To analyse the behaviour of swarm in detail, we investigated the average distance of the swarm during flocking. Figure 1(a) shows that the form of the

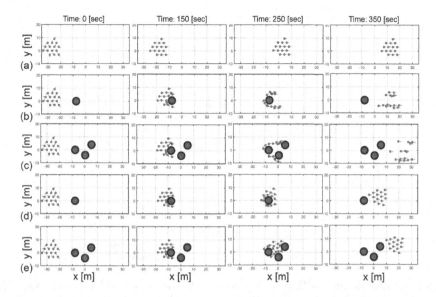

Fig. 1. Flocking behaviour in three environmental cases with $k = 0.05$; (a) without an obstacle, (b) with a single obstacle, and (c) with multi-obstacle. (d) with $k = 3$ and a single obstacle, and (e) with $k = 3$ and multi-obstacle.

swarm do not change during the flocking in the environment without obstacle. Therefore, the results if the average distance for the first case is shown with dashed lines. Figure 2 illustrates the average distance of swarm for two different collective forces, $k \in \{0.05, 3\}$. Figure 2(a) depicts the results for $l_{ij} = 3$ m from single-obstacle flocking motion. It takes approximately $t = 150$ sec to encounter the obstacle and the average distance of swarm becomes bigger while they are crossing the region. This disturbance is recovered and reached the original stable state for large collective force. In contrast, in case of the small collective force, the average distance was increased after the swarm passed the obstacles. The main reason is that the swarm is divided into several clusters that were formed in different positions far from each other. Similarly, this result also appears in multi-obstacle cases shown in Fig. 2(b). In addition, the average distance was much larger than the single-obstacle cases. Figure 2(c) and (d) show the results for $l_{ij} = 3.5$ m. It illustrates that the equilibrium distance has minor impact on the flocking performance in cluttered environments.

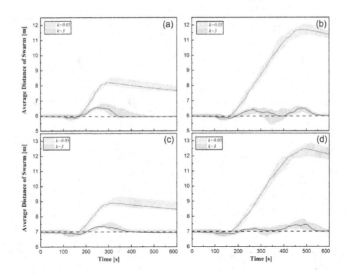

Fig. 2. Average distance with two different collective forces (a) with $l_{ij} = 3$ in a single obstacle, (b) with $l_{ij} = 3$ in multi-obstacle, (c) with $l_{ij} = 3.5$ in a single obstacle, and (d) with $l_{ij} = 3.5$ in multi-obstacle. Line and dashed line indicate the median and shaded area represent the first and third quartiles.

4   Conclusion

This work proposed a self-organised collective motion method based on the AES model. The main aim is to improve the AES collective motion behaviour to make it possible for use in a real-world application. This work designed an appropriate obstacle force and added it into the basic model. The simulation results illustrated the proposed method can achieve the self-organised flocking and obstacle avoidance in the complex environments. In addition, we investigated the flocking performance under the different parameters setting for collective force with a constant obstacle force. The results showed that the relationship between these two essential forces could have a significant impact on the flocking performance. The different equilibrium distances in the AES model were also investigated to illustrate the functionality of the proposed method. Further work will continue to investigate the obstacle interaction mechanisms in AES model using real-robot experiments.

Acknowledgement. This work was supported by EU H2020 Robocoenosis [899520] and the Engineering and Physical Sciences Research Council (EPSRC) RAIN and RNE [EP/R026084/1, EP/P01366X/1].

References

1. Ban, Z., Hu, J., Lennox, B., Arvin, F.: Self-organised collision-free flocking mechanism in heterogeneous robot swarms. Mob. Netw. Appl. (2021)

2. Cavagna, A., Del Castello, L., Giardina, I., Grigera, T., Jelic, A., et al.: Flocking and turning: a new model for self-organized collective motion. J. Stat. Phys. **158**(3), 601–627 (2015)
3. Chaté, H., Ginelli, F., Grégoire, G., Raynaud, F.: Collective motion of self-propelled particles interacting without cohesion. Phys. Rev. E **77**(4), 046113 (2008)
4. Couzin, I.D., Krause, J., James, R., Ruxton, G.D., Franks, N.R.: Collective memory and spatial sorting in animal groups. J. Theor. Biol. **218**(1), 1–11 (2002)
5. Ferrante, E., Turgut, A.E., Dorigo, M., Huepe, C.: Collective motion dynamics of active solids and active crystals. New J. Phys. **15**(9), 095011 (2013)
6. Ferrante, E., Turgut, A.E., Dorigo, M., Huepe, C.: Elasticity-based mechanism for the collective motion of self-propelled particles with springlike interactions: a model system for natural and artificial swarms. Phys. Rev. Lett. **111**(26), 268302 (2013)
7. Flack, A., Nagy, M., Fiedler, W., Couzin, I.D., Wikelski, M.: From local collective behavior to global migratory patterns in white storks. Science **360**(6391), 911–914 (2018)
8. Gautrais, J., et al.: Deciphering interactions in moving animal groups (2012)
9. Hein, A.M., Gil, M.A., Twomey, C.R., Couzin, I.D., Levin, S.A.: Conserved behavioral circuits govern high-speed decision-making in wild fish shoals. Proc. Natl. Acad. Sci. **115**, 12224–12228 (2018)
10. Ihle, T.: Chapman-Enskog expansion for the Vicsek model of self-propelled particles. J. Stat. Mech.: Theory Exp. **2016**(8), 083205 (2016)
11. Liu, Z., West, C., Lennox, B., Arvin, F.: Local bearing estimation for a swarm of low-cost miniature robots. Sensors **20**(11), 3308 (2020)
12. Motsch, S., Tadmor, E.: A new model for self-organized dynamics and its flocking behavior. J. Stat. Phys. **144**, 923–947 (2011)
13. Na, S., et al.: Bio-inspired artificial pheromone system for swarm robotics applications. Adapt. Behav. **29**, 395–415 (2020)
14. Nalepka, P., Kallen, R.W., Chemero, A., Saltzman, E., Richardson, M.J.: Herd those sheep: emergent multiagent coordination and behavioral-mode switching. Psychol. Sci. **28**(5), 630–650 (2017)
15. Raoufi, M., Turgut, A.E., Arvin, F.: Self-organized collective motion with a simulated real robot swarm. In: Althoefer, K., Konstantinova, J., Zhang, K. (eds.) TAROS 2019. LNCS (LNAI), vol. 11649, pp. 263–274. Springer, Cham (2019). https://doi.org/10.1007/978-3-030-23807-0_22
16. Schranz, M., et al.: Swarm intelligence and cyber-physical systems: concepts, challenges and future trends. Swarm Evol. Comput. **60**, 100762 (2021)
17. Son, J.H., Ahn, H.S., Cha, J.: Lennard-jones potential field-based swarm systems for aggregation and obstacle avoidance. In: 2017 17th International Conference on Control, Automation and Systems (ICCAS), pp. 1068–1072. IEEE (2017)
18. Stranieri, A., et al.: Self-organized flocking with an heterogeneous mobile robot swarm. In: ECAL, pp. 789–796 (2011)
19. Turgut, A.E., Çelikkanat, H., Gökçe, F., Şahin, E.: Self-organized flocking in mobile robot swarms. Swarm Intell. **2**(2), 97–120 (2008)
20. Vicsek, T., Czirók, A., Ben-Jacob, E., Cohen, I., Shochet, O.: Novel type of phase transition in a system of self-driven particles. Phys. Rev. Lett. **75**(6), 1226 (1995)
21. Virágh, C., et al.: Flocking algorithm for autonomous flying robots. Bioinspir. Biomimet. **9**(2), 025012 (2014)
22. Zheng, Y., Huepe, C., Han, Z.: Experimental capabilities and limitations of a position-based control algorithm for swarm robotics. Adapt. Behav. (2020)

Evaluating Feedback Modalities
in a Mobile Robot for Telecare

Noa Markfeld, Samuel Olatunji[(✉)], and Yael Edan

Department of Industrial Engineering and Management, Ben-Gurion University of
the Negev, Be'er Sheva, Israel
olatunji@post.bgu.ac.il

Abstract. Different feedback modalities while using a mobile robot in
a telecare task were compared. An experimental setup in which caregivers teleoperated a robot to perform several tasks remotely, outside the
immediate environment of a patient, while they simultaneously managed
other secondary tasks was designed. The robot provided feedback related
to status information on the robot's path and on tasks it performed.
Two feedback modalities (textual and audio) and their combination were
investigated to determine the most suitable for a remote operator in a
simulated telecare task with secondary tasks. Additionally, the influence
of the secondary task location on interaction was evaluated. Experiments
with 40 participants with a teleoperated mobile robot revealed that the
interaction was influenced mainly by the feedback modality, while the
secondary task location had less influence. The feedback modality that
combined textual and audio feedback yielded a better outcome as compared to the other single feedback modalities.

Keywords: Teleoperation · Telerobotic assistance · Assistive robots ·
Human-robot collaboration · Feedback modalities · Secondary task

1 Introduction

As the aging population increases there is increasing demand for caregivers [12].
The shortage of caregivers [11] along with the rising proportion of older people
[12] leads to an increased need to support these caregivers. A promising solution
to meet these needs is using robots that can support the caregivers and reduce the
workload by performing various assistive functions [15]. One of these functions is
the ability to remotely perform tasks such as pre-diagnosis, health monitoring,
distribution of food, medicine and laboratory specimens [15]. An upgraded role
for the assistive robots is to work alongside the caregivers to support their work
and enhance efficiency [4]. This enables the caregivers to remotely manage tasks
in places and in situations where they cannot be physically present. In many care
giving contexts, the caregiver must attend several tasks (primary and secondary
tasks) simultaneously. This usually constitutes challenges such as role overload
[13]. Teleoperated robots can be employed for some tasks and thereby reduce

© Springer Nature Switzerland AG 2021
C. Fox et al. (Eds.): TAROS 2021, LNAI 13054, pp. 136–146, 2021.
https://doi.org/10.1007/978-3-030-89177-0_14

the workload. A teleoperated robot is controlled by a human operator from a distance and performs tasks (services) as if the operator were on the spot [5].

Caregivers play a major role in providing and coordinating patient care [8]. This care, in addition to other duties, usually involves documenting information on patients, to facilitate care and to provide adequate and timely information for all health-related actions [1]. This is a time consuming task which consequently limits the time dedicated to care of the patient, affects outcomes and also influences the caregiver's work performance [8]. The work involved in documenting is also usually not entirely electronic, as some aspects are sometimes carried out on the desk, on an equipment or at the bedside of a patient. The effect of these differences in location and procedure of documentation on overall performance are not clear cut in previous evaluations [3]. Using teleoperated robots to support these type of tasks therefore requires investigation of the impact on the overall performance for the primary task of care giving and for secondary tasks such as documenting patients' information.

In this research, a hospital environment is simulated in which a caregiver (the user) delivers medication with other supplies to the patient and receives samples from the patient with a teleoperated robot. This is needed in situations where the caregiver (e.g. a nurse) cannot get near the patient for several possible reasons (e.g., task load, risk of infection). Feedback from equipment used in such care settings in general, have been found to improve patient care by providing alerts when needed [8]. The feedback from the robot can help inform the remote operator on different robotic aspects [2]: the robot's state of operation (e.g., moving towards goal or stopped due to an obstacle; details and constraints in the local environment (e.g., location of door to patient's room ahead, direction of passer-by in the corridor); and on state of the task being performed (e.g., delivery of an item at the desired destination, vital sign checks of the patient). In order to maximize the benefits of such alerts and information in the feedback from the teleoperated system, we developed suitable feedback modalities through which alerts and information can be provided by the robot. We then examined the influence of these modalities on the interaction between the caregiver and the teleoperated robot and on the performance. Additionally, we investigated if the location of the secondary task and the interaction with the feedback modalities influence performance and interaction between the robot and the operator.

2   Materials and Methods

2.1   The Experimental System

The experimental system consists of a mobile robot platform, remote user interfaces and a server-client communication architecture that used a rosbridge websocket to connect to the robot operating system (ROS) platform of the robot. Two user interfaces were developed - one runs on the robot while the other runs on the operator's computer. These interfaces (programmed using HTML, CSS, JS and PHP) run within a standard web browser making them independent of the operating system of the device or any specific software.

The Robot Platform. The robot platform is a Keylo telepresence robot[1]. Its height is approximately 1.64 m with a low center of gravity and circular footprint 52 cm of diameter. Keylo is equipped with a 24″ multi-point high FOV touchscreen. It runs Ubuntu 18.04 LTS, ROS Melodic with a standard ROS API to all its sensors and features. The navigation sensor specifications are: Hokuyo URG-04LX-UG01 lidar (5.6 m range, FOV 240°); 2 × 4 front and rear ultrasonic range sensors (5 m range); 2 × 2 IR edge detectors hard-wired to the motors controller. Cameras include two front and one rear 3D RGB-D camera Intel RealSense[TM] R200.

User Interfaces. The user interface running on the robot's browser was designed for the local user (e.g. patient directly interacting with the robot). The remote user interface through which the caregiver teleoperates the robot is displayed on a computer located remotely with the caregiver. The remote user interface was divided into three sections: a left, central and right panel (Fig. 1). The video from the camera on the robot is broadcasted on the left panel. Feedback from the robot is displayed on the central panel. This feedback includes status information about: start of the mission, arrival at the destination (e.g. patient's bed), various conditions along the way (e.g. malfunction/something unexpected on the way or information regarding attention such as code to access the patient's room).

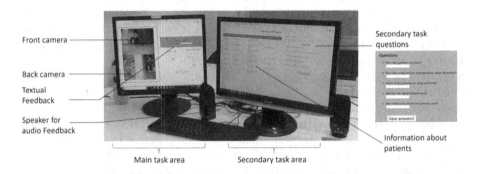

Fig. 1. Remote user interface

The right panel contains information related to the secondary task where participants are expected to answer questions related to the provided information. Two different secondary task locations were considered:

On the screen only - all information is displayed on the right panel. This includes a compilation of patients' health records and some questions on these patients.

---

[1] https://www.wyca-robotics.com/.

Combination of screen and desk - the information is divided between the screen and papers containing health records on the desk below. The right panel contains only the questions on the patients while the compilation of patients' health records is in paper format on the desk.

The feedback modalities examined were based on previous findings [10]:

Textual - Textual feedback appeared on the central panel in the form of written messages. These messages were designed to convey the information clearly and immediately.

Audio - Audio feedback was given via voice commands as the robot navigates. The content of these commands was the same as the content that appeared in the on-screen messages in the textual feedback.

Textual and audio combination - feedback was transmitted to the participant through on-screen messages and voice commands simultaneously.

2.2 Task

The tasks involved navigating the robot from a control position to the location where the patient is. The caregiver sends the robot towards the patient to accomplish the main task while s/he carries out a secondary task. Feedback is provided during the process to indicate important points along the robot's path that require user involvement.

Main Task. The main task was to deliver food and medicine (which was represented by specific objects in the actual experiment) to the patient and retrieve samples (also represented by specific objects) from the patient. The robot moves autonomously in the environment but may require user involvement at certain points (e.g., code for entering a particular room, floor number for the elevator, which were represented by an access confirmation to enter a specific care unit) before continuing with its task.

Secondary Task. The caregiver completes an electronic health record which involves answering some questions related to the patients. This starts once the robot commences the main task of delivery to the patient. The participant is expected to answer the questions according to the relevant information as best they can. Once the robot returns from the patient (main task ends), the secondary feedback section ends.

2.3 Research Hypotheses

The first two hypotheses are based on a previous study which revealed that feedback coming from more than one source increases the quality of the interaction [10], similar to work by [2]. It revealed that different feedback modalities improved effectiveness of control: the audio feedback will draw the participant's attention at the appropriate time and the textual feedback will serve as a backup in case the user is focused on the tasks and missed the voice instructions. These studies focused on evaluation with a stationary manipulator robot operated by a user who worked with the robot that was situated nearby [10] and at a distance [2] as opposed to the current work which focused on a teleoperated mobile robot. Also, the main task in these previous studies was a pick and place task with the stationary robotic manipulator. These studies also did not consider the influence of a secondary task, as well as the location of secondary task in the overall inter-action. Considering the differences between the previously studied pick and place task and the current telecare task which also involved the potential influences of the secondary task inclusion, we propose the following hypotheses:

H1: A combination of textual and audio feedback modality in a teleoperated task increases the overall performance of users (as measured by the objective variables) relative to a single feedback modality.

H2: Combination of textual and audio feedback modality in a teleoperated task will increase the overall positive user perception of the interaction (as assessed through the subjective variables) compared to a single feedback modality.

Studies in a driving scenario show that the farther the display of the sec-ondary task is from the main screen, the lower the performance [16]. This is particularly relevant when the distance is a vertical distance, the response times increase and there are more errors [7]. This inspired the third hypothesis:

H3: Executing the secondary task only on-screen will improve the performance for users compared to executing the secondary task between desk and screen.

2.4   Experimental Design

The experiment was designed as a mixed (3×2) design experiment with the feed-back modality (textual, audio and combination) and the location of secondary task (screen only and combination) defined as the independent variables. The feedback modality was the within-participants variable while the location of sec-ondary task was the between-participants variable. Each participant experienced one location of the secondary task only for each of the three trials involving the three feedback modalities provided in a random order.

2.5   Dependent Measures

Objective Measures. For each participant and trial, overall user performance was measured in terms of efficiency, effectiveness and understanding. Efficiency was evaluated as the completion time (in seconds) of the task, the time between the robot's departure and return to the control point. Effectiveness was eval-uated as user performance in the secondary tasks since the participants were expected to complete the primary task. The primary task completion time deter-mined the secondary task completion time. Completeness of secondary task is denoted as the number of subtasks in the secondary tasks completed, which was represented by the number of complete answers (completeness); the number of correct answers from total questions (global accuracy, GA) and the number of correct answers from total questions that answered (response accuracy, RA). Understanding was evaluated by the reaction time. The reaction time is the time (in seconds) that it took the participant to respond to the feedback the robot provided. Understanding was additionally evaluated by the number of clarifications the participant requested from the experimenter during the experiment after the initial explanation of the procedure at the beginning of the experiment.

Subjective Measures. The post-trial questionnaires (assessed after each trial) were used to assess usability, understanding, and satisfaction through 5-point Likert scales, with 5 representing "Strongly agree" and 1 representing "Strongly disagree".

2.6 Participants

40 third year undergraduate industrial engineering students (27 females, 13 males) at Ben-Gurion University were recruited as participants for the role of the caregiver (Mean age = 26.5 years, SD = 1.11). All of them had experience with computers and limited experience with robots. The students were compensated with a credit in an obligatory course they took, which was commensurate with their time of participation in the experiment.

2.7 Procedure

At the start of the experiment, after reading and signing the consent form, participants were asked to provide some background information regarding their age, gender and on their attitude toward robots. To assess their level of anxiety towards robots [14], we used a sub-set of the Negative Attitude toward Robots Scale (NARS). Following this, they were briefed on the scenario, tasks and procedure. Each participant performed the task three times - in each trial they experienced a different feedback modality. The order of feedbacks was randomly selected. Each trial was followed by a questionnaire enquiring about the experience with the condition (details on the measures are given below). After completion of all three trials, participants answered a final questionnaire in which they rated their overall experience with the robot and tasks. It afforded the opportunity to receive additional feedback or remarks from the participants.

2.8 Analysis

Analyses were performed using a two-tailed General Linear Mixed Model (GLMM) analysis to address non-normally distributed response variables, heteroscedasticity, and non-linear relationships between the mean of the dependent variables and the independent variables. This ensured that both fixed effects and random effects were accounted for. The fixed effects were the feedback and secondary task modes. Random effect was included to account for individual differences among participants. To ensure that analyzed variables conformed to the GLMM requirements, the variables that included time were log transformed. The cumulative logit model was used for variables with ordinal values. The tests were designed with a significance level of 0.05. Mean and median results were also compared for the objective and subjective variables respectively.

3   Results

3.1   Efficiency

The efficiency, measured as the completion time (seconds) of the task (mean = 80.27, SD = 1.81) was significantly affected by the feedback modality ($F(2, 114)$ = 13.1, p = 0.001). The completion time of those using only audio feedback was lower (mean = 70.61, SD = 2.75) than that of the participants that used both audio and textual feedback (mean = 78.42, SD = 2.75). The highest completion time was observed in trials with only textual feedback (mean = 93.40, SD = 3.64). The completion time was not significantly affected by the location of the secondary task ($F(1, 114) = 1.283$, p = 0.260). Completion time of participants was, on average, lower (mean = 78.25, SD = 2.49) for the screen-only condition compared to the screen and desk condition (mean = 82.34, SD = 2.62).

3.2   Understanding

Understanding was measured both objectively and subjectively. Most of the participants (75.8%, med = 4, SD = 0.11) indicated in the questionnaire that they understood the system well and most indicated that the robot's feedback was received clearly (78.4%, med = 4, SD = 1.05). The feedback modality significantly affected comprehension ($F(2, 113) = 10.254$, p < 0.001) and clarity ($F(2, 112) = 12.015$, p < 0.001). Participants reported higher understanding while using either audio or combined feedback (med = 5, SD = 0.5) compared to when using textual feedback (med = 3, SD = 1.32). Using only the screen resulted in higher understanding (med = 4.5, SD = 0.96) compared to when using the combination of screen and desk (med = 4, SD = 0.97).

The reaction time (seconds) of the participants in the first trial (mean = 7.45, SD = 0.52) was significantly affected by both the feedback modality ($F(2, 114) = 49.905$, p = 0.001) and the location of secondary task ($F(1, 114) = 4.94$, p = 0.028). The combination of textual and audio feedback provided the shortest reaction time (mean = 3.68, SD = 0.62) when only the screen was used.

3.3   Effectiveness

In terms of completeness, the feedback modality did not significantly affect the number of questions that were answered by the participants (mean = 3.7, SD = 0.18, $F(2, 114) = 2.17$, p = 0.12). Participants who experienced textual feedback only have higher completeness score (mean = 4.18, SD = 0.32) as compared to participants with only audio feedback (mean = 3.28, SD = 0.29) and with combined feedback (mean = 3.71, SD = 0.30). The completeness was not significantly affected by the location of secondary task (F (1, 114) = 0. 89, p = 0.35). The completeness of answers when using the screen only (mean = 3.54, SD = 0.24) was slightly lower than the completeness when using desk and screen (mean = 3.87, SD = 0.25).

The feedback modality did not significantly affect the global accuracy, GA (mean = 0.59, SD = 0.04, F(2, 114) = 2.07, p = 0.13). The GA measure was also not significantly affected by the location of secondary task (F (1, 114) = 0.455, p = 0.501). In terms of response accuracy, RA (mean = 0.71, SD = 0.06;), the influence of the feedback modality (F(2, 114) = 0.005, p = 0.95) and the location of secondary task (F(1, 14) = 0.342, p = 0.56) was not significant.

3.4 User Perception

The scores of the questionnaire responses of the participants related to satisfactory communication was significant with respect to the feedback modality (med = 3.75, SD = 1.22, F (2, 113) = 10.25, p = 0.001). Feedback that contained verbal commands in either audio feedback (med = 4, SD = 0.99) or combined feedback (med = 4, SD = 0.99) led to a higher communication score compared to when using feedback that contained only textual modality (med = 3, SD = 1.23). The feedback modality had a significant effect on fluency (F(2, 112) = 10.04, p = 0.001). 72.5% of the participants indicated that the feedback from the robot was received at the right timing. It was observed that the feedback that contained verbal commands in both audio feedback (med = 5, SD = 0.93) and combined feedback (med = 5, SD = 0.93) resulted in a very high score while textual feedback had a reduced score (med = 3, SD = 1.19). The secondary task location did not have a significant effect on fluency. Fluency score was similar for both secondary task locations (med = 4, SD = 0.94).

The feedback modality had significant influence on situation awareness (SA) (med = 4, SD = 1.13; F (2, 112) = 21.74, p < 0.001). The audio feedback yielded higher SA score (med = 4.5, SD = 0.95) compared to combined feedback (med = 4, SD = 0.86) and to textual feedback (med = 3, SD = 1.244). SA was not significantly affected by the location of secondary task (F (1, 112) = 0.872, p = 0.352).

The feedback modality was significant on comfortability (F (2, 112) = 14.93, p = 0.001). The lowest comfortability score was observed when participants used the textual feedback (med = 2.5, SD = 1.29). When participants used the audio feedback, the comfortability score was higher (med = 4.37, SD = 0.99) compared to when they used the combined feedback (med = 4.25, SD = 1.14). The comfortability score was similar at both secondary task locations (med = 4, SD = 1.21).

Regarding usability, the frequency of use (F(2, 112) = 10.51, p < 0.001) and ease of use (F(2, 112) = 4.26, p = 0.02), were significantly affected by the feedback modality but learnability was not (F(2, 112) = 0.35, p = 0.71). The usability scores were higher when using the audio feedback only (med = 4, SD = 0.10) compared to the combined feedback (med = 3.67, SD = 0.11) or the textual feedback only (med = 3, SD = 0.12). The usability scores when using the screen only (med = 3.67, SD = 0.04) was slightly higher than the usability when using screen and desk (mean = 3.33, SD = 0.14).

4 Discussion

This research examined how the feedback modality and secondary task location influence the interaction between a caregiver (for instance, a nurse) and a tele-operated robot and their effect on performance. Results showed that feedback modality had significant effect on the interaction, with a mix of audio and visual feedback yielding best results (supporting H1 and H2). The secondary task location had less influence on performance but influenced some of the performance interaction parameters (supporting H3). More details are discussed as follows:

4.1 Impact of Feedback Modality

88% of participants preferred voice feedback, of which 67% claimed that feedback that combined audio and textual was most comfortable for them (in line with H2). The difference between the combined feedback and the two other feedback modalities was most significant in the understanding. However, there were also major differences in the effectiveness and efficiency. These contributed to the overall significant values seen through the objective and subjective variables. Even though the audio feedback reduced both response times and completion times, it did not result in the highest performance in the study. This seems to point to some pitfalls of audio-only feedback which may have affected the quality of the performance. The audio feedback usually prompts a quick response, which may have caused some stress or additional workload, consequently lowering the performance quality. This is in line with previous research which showed that sound alone requires higher attentional demand [9]. When the task is simple, concentration required from the caregiver is low. In such cases, the transition between the tasks (primary and secondary) when giving a voice command is usually easier and does not often impair the performance of any of the tasks. But as the task complexity increases, more concentration is required, and the transition between tasks becomes more difficult and may take longer. In this regard, the combined feedback seems better than the voice-only feedback (in line with H1). This agrees with the conclusions reached in an HCI context [6] where it was stated that auditory information proves superior to textual-only information but that this is not always the case when both auditory and textual modalities were used.

4.2 Impact of Secondary Task Location

The secondary task location did not statistically influence most results. However, better performance scores were obtained when the secondary task was performed on the screen only and not when it was divided between the screen and desk (in line with H3). An interesting point relates to the performance in the secondary task - the participants answered more questions when the task was divided between the screen and the desk, however the RA (number of correct answers out of the total answered) was higher when the task was performed on screen only.

This seemed to imply that the transition between desk and screen may have caused more errors. This agrees with a previous study in which multiple eye movements increased user's mistakes [7].

5   Conclusions and Future Work

This experiment simulated a hospital environment in which a caregiver teleoperates a mobile robot while performing another task. In this type of scenario where the time, accuracy and understanding of the scenario are critical, we found that the feedback that combined textual and audio feedback modalities yielded better performance, compared to the single modality feedback. Note that, if the goal is to shorten the performance time, audio feedback is optimal. However, due to some of the shortcomings of the audio-only feedback discussed, combined audio and textual feedback is recommended. It is also worth noting that additional visual feedback modalities superimposed on the camera image and other feedback modalities such as haptic feedback were not tested in this experiment. It is important to note that these experiments examined specific scenarios and were not performed with real caregivers. In order to generalize these conclusions, additional experiments examining different interfaces and different tasks must be performed with real caregivers.

Acknowledgements. This research was supported by the EU funded Innovative Training Network (ITN) in the Marie Skłodowska-Curie People Programme (Horizon2020): SOCRATES (Social Cognitive Robotics in a European Society training research network), grant agreement number 721619. Partial support was provided by Ben-Gurion University of the Negev through the Helmsley Charitable Trust, the Agricultural, Biological and Cognitive Robotics Initiative, the Marcus Endowment Fund, and the W. Gunther Plaut Chair in Manufacturing Engineering.

References

1. Ash, J.S., Berg, M., Coiera, E.: Some unintended consequences of information technology in health care: the nature of patient care information system-related errors. J. Am. Med. Inform. Assoc. **11**(2), 104–112 (2004)
2. Bolarinwa, J., Eimontaite, I., Dogramadzi, S., Mitchell, T., Caleb-Solly, P.: The use of different feedback modalities and verbal collaboration in tele-robotic assistance. In: 2019 IEEE International Symposium on Robotic and Sensors Environments (ROSE), pp. 1–8. IEEE (2019)
3. Burnie, D.J.: Electronic health records documentation in nursing: nurses' perceptions, attitudes and preferences (2010)

4. Christoforou, E.G., Avgousti, S., Ramdani, N., Novales, C., Panayides, A.S.: The upcoming role for nursing and assistive robotics: opportunities and challenges ahead. Front. Digit. Health **2**, 39 (2020)
5. Eliav, A., Lavie, T., Parmet, Y., Stern, H., Edan, Y.: Advanced methods for displays and remote control of robots. Appl. Ergon. **42**(6), 820–829 (2011)
6. Kalyuga, S., Chandler, P., Sweller, J.: Managing split-attention and redundancy in multimedia instruction. Appl. Cogn. Psychol.: Off. J. Soc. Appl. Res. Mem. Cogn. **13**(4), 351–371 (1999)
7. Katsuyama, R.M., Monk, D.L., Rolek, E.P.: Effects of visual display separation upon primary and secondary task performances. In: Proceedings of the IEEE National Aerospace and Electronics Conference, pp. 758–764. IEEE (1989)
8. Kossman, S.P., Scheidenhelm, S.L.: Nurses' perceptions of the impact of electronic health records on work and patient outcomes. CIN: Comput. Info. Nurs. **26**(2), 69–77 (2008)
9. Lee, S.C., Kim, Y.W., Ji, Y.G.: Effects of visual complexity of in-vehicle information display: age-related differences in visual search task in the driving context. Appl. Ergon. **81**, 102888 (2019)
10. Markfeld, N.: Feedback design for older adults in robot assisted table setting task. Ben-Gurion University of the Negev, Beer Sheva, Israel (2019)
11. Murray, M.K.: The nursing shortage: past, present, and future. JONA: J. Nurs. Adm. **32**(2), 79–84 (2002)
12. World Health Organization, et al.: Ageing (2020)
13. Perkins, E.A., Haley, W.E.: Compound caregiving: when lifelong caregivers undertake additional caregiving roles. Rehabil. Psychol. **55**(4), 409 (2010)
14. Syrdal, D.S., Dautenhahn, K., Koay, K.L., Walters, M.L.: The negative attitudes towards robots scale and reactions to robot behaviour in a live human-robot interaction study. Adapt. Emerg. Behav. Complex Syst. (2009)
15. Vandemeulebroucke, T., Dzi, K., Gastmans, C.: Older adults' experiences with and perceptions of the use of socially assistive robots in aged care: a systematic review of quantitative evidence. Arch. Gerontol. Geriatr. **95**, 104399 (2021)
16. Wittmann, M., et al.: Effects of display position of a visual in-vehicle task on simulated driving. Appl. Ergon. **37**(2), 187–199 (2006)

Demonstrating the Differential Impact of Flock Heterogeneity on Multi-agent Herding

Chris Bennett[1(✉)], Seth Bullock[2], and Jonathan Lawry[1]

[1] Department of Engineering Mathematics, University of Bristol, Bristol, UK
christopher.bennett@bristol.ac.uk
[2] Department of Computer Science, University of Bristol, Bristol, UK

Abstract. This paper explores the differential impact of multi-agent system heterogeneity in the context of an idealised herding task. In simulation, a team of simple herders must move a flock towards a target location in a continuous 2d space. Flock heterogeneity is controlled by dividing the flock into a number of non-overlapping social groups that influence sheep movement. Results demonstrate that increasing system heterogeneity (i.e., the number of different social groups) *reduces* herding performance when social groups are self-attracting, but conversely, the same increase in system heterogeneity can *increase* herding performance when groups are other-attracting. Implications for designing heterogeneous multi-agent systems are considered.

Keywords: Heterogeneous · Multi-agent · Herding

1 Introduction

Intelligent systems comprising some combination of robots, humans and software agents promise to deliver increased flexibility and efficiency by sharing and coordinating their resources, information and capabilities. However, designing these multi-agent systems (MAS) brings considerable challenges. Their control may be decentralised to some extent, they may need to operate in noisy and uncertain environments, and finally the different agents involved may need to be designed (and to operate) without complete knowledge of the way in which other agents in the system have been designed or are operating. Consequently, the challenge of engineering these systems is strongly influenced by the extent to which the agents involved exhibit *heterogeneity* of different kinds.

A heterogeneous MAS involves agents that are different from each other, e.g., a team of human carers working alongside robot care assistants to deliver

This work was funded and delivered in partnership between the Thales Group and the University of Bristol, and with the support of the UK Engineering and Physical Sciences Research Council Grant Award EP/R004757/1 entitled 'Thales-Bristol Partnership in Hybrid Autonomous Systems Engineering (T-B PHASE)'.

© Springer Nature Switzerland AG 2021
C. Fox et al. (Eds.): TAROS 2021, LNAI 13054, pp. 147–157, 2021.
https://doi.org/10.1007/978-3-030-89177-0_15

services to patients [1], or the coordination of aerial and ground based robots to map the surface of Mars [11]. Such heterogeneity may arise for many reasons: team diversity may be required in order to satisfy multiple functional requirements; mixing sub-systems with different provenance or legacy issues may be unavoidable; agents with differing degrees of degradation or component failure may be expected to inter-operate, etc.

Achieving systems such as these will require engineers to design solutions that exploit the positives of system heterogeneity while mitigating any negatives. This will require better understanding of when and how heterogeneity impacts system performance. This paper characterises the differential impact of agent heterogeneity on system performance in a simple multi-agent setting. A team of artificial dogs, driven by simple reactive controllers, are tasked with herding a flock of sheep that exhibit a parameterisable degree of heterogeneity. The paper's key contribution is to characterise the way in which the positive and negative impact of this heterogeneity differs with aspects of the agent's social structure.

1.1 Motivation

Heterogeneity has been studied extensively in social systems. In books such as *The Difference* [16] and *The Wisdom of Crowds* [20] it is argued to be a positive, as diverse views and strategies inject useful resilience and redundancy into human systems. By contrast, heterogeneity is typically regarded as an unwanted feature of engineered systems, where uniformity and regularity are associated with predictable and reliable performance. Perhaps consequently, the value of heterogeneity for artificial autonomous systems is not clear cut.

On the one hand, the Law of Requisite Variety tells us that a more heterogeneous system requires a more complex controller [12]. This reinforces the belief that heterogeneity is strongly associated with complexity, and something engineers want to avoid in order to create reliable systems. On the other hand, the El Farol Bar problem suggests a diverse, heterogeneous system performs better [2]. It can be seen as an allegory for the view that *homo*geneous systems can be brittle; if one element has a vulnerability then all have a vulnerability.

The dual nature of heterogeneity poses a problem for the design of autonomous robotic systems. Just when is heterogeneity helpful and when is it harmful? There is a lack of prior work which investigates this specific question, particularly within a single task domain. This prevents direct comparisons which makes it difficult to understand how heterogeneity could affect a system.

1.2 Related Work

An important step to understanding MAS heterogeneity is to devise a means to measure it. In [4], concepts from taxonomy are drawn on in order to measure heterogeneity in terms of dendrograms and social entropy. Both [4] and [21] present means to measure differences between agents in terms of distance norms. Distance norms and entropy seem common ways of characterising heterogeneity but it is rare to see measures of heterogeneity linked to performance. An exception is [6]. An evolutionary framework and heterogeneity measure are developed based on agent fitness. These are then used to show that heterogeneous agents suited a travelling mailman task but homogeneous agents suited a foraging task. In similar work, [4] shows via reinforcement learning that a single policy suited foraging but agents with different policies were better at playing robot soccer.

The natural world is often used as a source of inspiration when discussing heterogeneity. The work of [14] demonstrated through simple modelling that having a mix of age and mass can improve the success of wolf pack hunting. In [23], artificial evolution was used to create teams of heterogeneous and homogeneous agents which were tested on tasks requiring different amounts of cooperation. A framework for human MAS is used in [16] to show that, provided certain conditions are met, a heterogeneous system of lesser agents performs better in problem solving than a homogeneous system of superior agents.

Perhaps the most pertinent question for a MAS designer is how to exploit heterogeneity to benefit performance. To this end, exploiting heterogeneity can be viewed as a resource allocation problem, for examples see [8,9,17]. While effective, these prior works only consider heterogeneity in the scope of functional capability. While it could be concluded that the weight of prior work views heterogeneity as positive, there are exceptions. In [5], the author comments that trials with heterogeneous agents were not successful because agents reacted differently to the same stimulus. This led to confused behaviour at the population level and poor overall performance.

Overall, the majority of prior work studies heterogeneity as a means to solve a given task. General design principles for heterogeneity are rarely, if ever, proposed. Consequently, there remain unanswered questions concerning when and how heterogeneity (or homogeneity) should be employed by a MAS designer. This paper presents a comparative analysis of heterogeneity in the context of a single multi-agent herding task, demonstrating that its effect on performance can change from negligible to significant as only a single parameter is varied, and showing that heterogeneity can be beneficial or detrimental to performance in a manner that depends on subtle changes to agent behavioural rules.

2   Model

Herding is a multi-agent task in which one or more herding agents attempts to influence a second group of herded agents towards a goal. Here we use a common formulation of the task in which a number of "dog" agents are tasked with moving a number of "sheep" agents to a target location. The task has been studied by a number of different authors. This paper uses a relatively traditional model however there are number of alternatives, for example applying the unicycle model to the dogs [18], encircling the flock with relatively many dogs and then moving them in formation towards the goal [15], or using a motion control strategy for the dogs based on goal occlusion by the flock [10].

2.1 Experimental Setup

The work by [22] is widely regarded as one of the earliest in the area. In their research, a single robot sheepdog herds a flock of geese in an enclosed pen. [19] took this a step further and their paper typifies the traditional approach: the herding strategy adopted by a dog is split into separate collecting and driving phases, and the dog uses heuristics to choose steering points from which to influence the sheep. A solution to the problem of reaching these steering points without adversely affecting the flock is provided by [13] and [7].

The work here makes a number of contributions to this traditional model. It uses Voronoi partitioning [3] to subdivide the task of gathering the flock amongst multiple dogs. Previous works, [7,13], suggests a planning based controller, here, a simple reactive behaviour is described that accomplished the same task (to our knowledge for the first time). Finally, each sheep belongs to a social group that is influenced by a target group (either itself or a different group). This influence may be a positive bias (sheep inside this target group are attractive) or a negative bias (sheep outside this target group are attractive).

This simulation is conducted as follows within a 2D space measuring 400 by 400. Thirty sheep are initially distributed over a 270 square region centred on the point (200, 220) using a uniform random distribution. Two dogs aim to move all the sheep to within a threshold distance of a goal located at (40, 30) in minimum time. The goal and starting locations of the dogs remain the same throughout the experiments. A two phase strategy first collects the sheep together into a single group and then drives the flock to the goal. A single herding episode lasts 2000 time steps and results are averaged over 50 episodes to reduce the effect of random initial conditions.

For each time step, an acceleration is calculated for each agent, based on virtual forces that are influencing it at that instant. Each agent's velocity is updated according to their new acceleration, and their new positions are calculated. A physics check tweaks the simulated positions of two agents if they occupy the same space. The dogs can always see all the sheep, and the experiment was repeated for sheep with a small (60) and large (600) visible range.

2.2 Sheep Agent Model

Each sheep experiences a weighted combination of three virtual forces (Fig. 1a) exerted by agents within their visual range: repulsion from visible dogs (F_D), very short range repulsion from any other sheep (F_S), and a longer range social attraction to other sheep (F_G).

$$F = K_D F_D + K_S F_S + K_G F_G \tag{1}$$

Here, $K_D = 20$, $K_S = 200$ and $K_G = 1$, and are parameters governing the strength of the influence of each of the three force. The forces are determined as follows:

$$F_D = \sum_k^D \frac{s_i - d_k}{\|s_i - d_k\|} e^{-\lambda_D \|s_i - d_k\|} \tag{2}$$

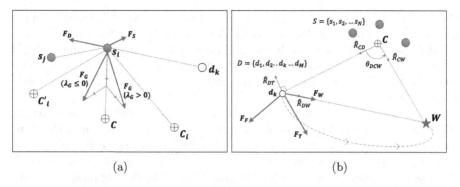

(a)   (b)

Fig. 1. The virtual forces acting on (a) a sheep, s_i, and (b) a dog, d_k, where C is the overall flock centre of mass, C_i is the centre of mass for visible sheep in s_i's preferred social group, and C_i' is the centre of mass for sheep that are outside this group, W is the dog's current steering point, $\hat{R}_{CD}$, $\hat{R}_{CW}$, $\hat{R}_{DW}$ and $\hat{R}_{DT}$ are unit vectors, and $S = \{s_1, s_2 \dots s_N\}$ is the set of visible sheep.

$$F_S = \sum_{j \neq i}^{S} \frac{s_i - s_j}{\|s_i - s_j\|} e^{-\lambda_S \|s_i - s_j\|} \tag{3}$$

$$F_G = \begin{cases} \lambda_G \frac{C_i - s_i}{\|C_i - s_i\|} + (1 - \lambda_G) \frac{C - s_i}{\|C - s_i\|} & \text{if } \lambda_G > 0 \\ |\lambda_G| \frac{C_i' - s_i}{\|C_i' - s_i\|} + (1 - |\lambda_G|) \frac{C - s_i}{\|C - s_i\|} & \text{if } \lambda_G \leq 0 \end{cases} \tag{4}$$

where D and S are the set of visible dogs and visible sheep respectively, λ_D and λ_S are set to 0.1 & 0.6 respectively and determine the length scale of the two repulsive forces. The social grouping mechanic uses three centre of mass: C, C_i and C_i'. These are the centres of mass for (i) all visible sheep, (ii) all visible sheep in i's target social group and, (iii) all visible sheep not in i's target social group, respectively. Centres of mass are always calculated as the average position of a set of sheep, given by $\sum s_j / N$, where N is the number of sheep in the set.

The influence of a sheep's target social group is governed by two parameters: the identity and location of the visible group members, and the social bias towards the group, denoted λ_G. This bias controls the degree of *heterophily* $(-1 < \lambda_G < 0)$ or *homophily* $(0 < \lambda_G < 1)$ displayed by the sheep. When $\lambda_G = 0$ sheep are influenced by group members and non group members indiscriminately.

2.3 Dog Agent Model

The strategic part of the Dog model follows that specified in [19] to identify steering points as locations for the dogs to move towards. Initially, during the *collecting* phase each dog chooses a steering point to target a peripheral sheep, i.e., the one furthest from the flock's centre of mass (CoM), and drives it towards the flock's current CoM. Once all sheep are within a threshold distance, d, of the CoM, the dogs transition from collecting to *driving*. During the driving phase, the dogs move the flock towards the goal by choosing a steering point which is colinear with the goal and the flock CoM. A dog will re-collect any sheep that strays further than $1.6d$ from the CoM during driving. The dogs have a visible range of 600.

To enable multiple dogs to coordinate their activities, the space occupied by the flock is partitioned into Voronoi cells seeded with the location of the dogs. This partitioning is performed at a global level. During the collecting phase, each dog targets a succession of the most peripheral sheep within its own cell. A single dog is then chosen to drive the flock during the driving phase while the other dogs hold a position away from the flock (unless and until a sheep strays too far from the flock).

A dog's movement between steering points in controlled by a reactive controller comprised of two behaviours: a force to interact with the sheep (F_H) and a repulsive force to avoid getting too close to other dogs (F_D). The resultant behaviour is a weighted vector of these forces:

$$F = K_H F_H + K_D F_D \tag{5}$$

where $K_H = 1$ and $K_D = 10$.

The repulsion, F_D, is designed to causes the dog (d_k) to rotate around another dog (d_j) rather than simply be repulsed. This creates a graceful way of handling deadlock situations and is modelled as:

$$F_D = F_{DD} + 0.75 F_{\perp DD} \tag{6}$$

where:

$$F_{DD} = \sum_{j \neq k}^{D} \frac{d_k - d_j}{\|d_k - d_j\|} \tag{7}$$

The herding force, F_H, is a weighted combination of 3 behaviours: Repulsion from sheep (F_F), attraction towards the current steering point (F_W), and an orbital force around the flock (F_T). These behaviours interact to cause the dog to move around the flock, towards the steering point, at a sufficient distance from the sheep to leave them undisturbed. As the dog approaches the steering point, the repulsion to the sheep rolls off and it moves closer to interact with its target sheep. The forces are combined via the equation:

$$F_H = K_F F_F + K_W F_W + K_T F_T \tag{8}$$

where $K_F = 20$, $K_W = 2$, and $K_T = 8$.

The herding behaviours in Eq. 8 are a function of the dog position d_k, the positions of the sheep $S = \{s_1...s_N\}$, and the angular error (θ_{DCW}) between the dog's desired and current approach directions (Fig. 1b). The component forces are calculated as:

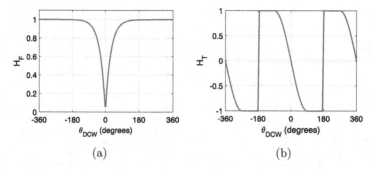

(a)   (b)

Fig. 2. a) The roll off in sheep repulsion force, $H_F = 1 - e^{-2|\theta_{DCW}|}$, as the dog approaches its steering position, b) The magnitude of the orbital force rolls off as the angle between the ideal and current approach direction decreases. The sign ensures the dog takes the shorter orbital direction around the flock.

$$F_F = H_F(\theta_{DCW}) \sum_i^S \frac{d_k - s_i}{2\|d_k - s_i\|} \tag{9}$$

$$F_W = \hat{R}_{DW} \tag{10}$$

$$F_T = H_T(\theta_{DCW})\hat{R}_{DT} \tag{11}$$

$H_F(\theta_{DCW})$ rolls off the sheep repulsion as the dog lines up with its steering point. The form of $H_F(\theta_{DCW})$ is given in Fig. 2a. The orbital force (F_T) acts tangentially to the flock circumference, and its magnitude is controlled by $H_T(\theta_{DCW})$ which, similar to the sheep repulsion, rolls off as the dog approaches its steering point. The form of $H_T(\theta_{DCW})$ is shown in Fig. 2b.

3   Results

The following results characterise the performance of the multi-agent herding system as we vary three aspects: i) the number of different sheep social groups, ii) the nature of the social group bias, and iii) whether a sheep's target social group is its own group, or a different group. System performance is measured in terms of minimising goal absement, i.e., minimising the distance between the goal location and the centre of mass of all sheep, C, integrated over time. While this doesn't capture the cohesion of the flock explicitly, it proved to be a reliable indicator of how difficult the task was to complete.

Figure 3a shows results for scenarios in which a sheep's own social group is also its target social group. When sheep are attracted towards members of this social group (*homophily*, $\lambda_G > 0$), the performance of the system degrades as heterogeneity increases. That is, the more social groups exist within the flock, the harder the flock is to herd. By contrast, when each sheep is attracted to

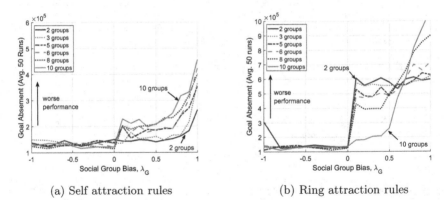

(a) Self attraction rules   (b) Ring attraction rules

Fig. 3. Herding performance under two flock social structures: a) sheep are influenced by their own social group, b) sheep are influenced by another social group. In both cases, negative social bias extinguishes the effects of heterogeneity. However, under positive social bias, increasing heterogeneity helps or hinders performance depending on the flock social structure.

flock members outside its target social group (*heterophily*, $\lambda_G < 0$), the impact of heterogeneity is extinguished. This makes flocks easy to herd regardless of the social structure within the flock. These results can be explained by noting that heterophily tends to encourage mixing of the flock's social groups resulting in global cohesion, whereas homophily tends to encourage each social group to form a sub-flock, reducing the overall global cohesion of the flock and thereby making it more difficult to herd. Increasing the number of types exacerbated this effect of homophily. In summary, when agents are attracted to their own group, heterogeneity has a negative effect on performance, but this does not hold when agents exhibit heterophilic behaviour.

Figure 3b depicts an analogous set of results for the herding system where a sheep's target social group is not its own but instead one other social group in the flock. The target social group is determined according to a ring arrangement. For n social groups, G_1, G_2, through G_n, members of group G_i are influenced by members of G_{i+1} and members of group G_n are influenced by members of G_1. The nature of the influence may be positive (each sheep is attracted towards members of its target group, $\lambda_G > 0$) or negative (each sheep is attracted towards sheep that are not members of its target group, $\lambda_G < 0$).

Under these conditions, the impact of heterogeneity changes. As before, for $\lambda_G < 0$ performance is not influenced by heterogeneity, with herding being easy regardless of the number of social groups within the flock. However, where $\lambda_G > 0$ (i.e., sheep are attracted to their target social group), increasing heterogeneity can either improve performance (when social bias is weak, $0 < \lambda_G \lesssim 0.6$), or decrease performance (when social bias is strong, $0.6 \lesssim \lambda_G < 1.0$). The interaction between positive social bias and heterogeneity can be explained by noting that strongly positive social bias means sheep are strongly attracted to

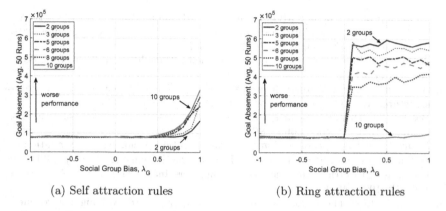

(a) Self attraction rules   (b) Ring attraction rules

Fig. 4. As Fig. 3 except sheep vision range is increased from 60 to 600.

their target group CoM, C_i. A large number of groups and the fixed population size means only a small number of sheep are in each group. This, combined with the limited visible range (60), creates circumstances where sheep in the same social group calculate different C_i's which causes the flock to fragment. This does not occur when the social bias is weekly positive due to sheep being attracted to the CoM of all visible sheep, C, which is more consistent across a group of sheep. Consequently, results for sheep with a much larger sensor range extinguish this effect (Fig. 4). Note also that while the differences in performance depicted in Fig. 3a could be attributable to a difference between the number of sheep inside and outside each social group, the contrast between Fig. 3a and Fig. 3b cannot be so attributed as the number of members within social groups is equivalent between these two sets of results, indicating that it is the nature of the flock heterogeneity that is accounting for performance differences.

4 Conclusions

By characterising how the performance of a relatively simple multi-agent system changes as system heterogeneity is varied, both in terms of its magnitude and character, we have shown that understanding whether heterogeneity will be a positive or negative influence on multi-agent systems is a subtle question. Simply knowing whether or not a system is heterogeneous, or knowing the amount of heterogeneity exhibited by a system is not enough to anticipate MAS design challenges or guide good MAS design decisions. A deeper understanding of the link between heterogeneity and multi-agent system dynamics is needed. Future work will take this a step further by investigating the effect of functional heterogeneity, such as movement speed and sight range, on the herding problem.

References

1. Ahn, H.S., Lee, M.H., Macdonald, B.A.: Healthcare robot systems for a hospital environment: CareBot and ReceptionBot. In: Proceedings - IEEE International

Workshop on Robot and Human Interactive Communication, vol. 2015-Novem, pp. 571–576. Institute of Electrical and Electronics Engineers Inc., November 2015. https://doi.org/10.1109/ROMAN.2015.7333621

2. Arthur, W.: Inductive reasoning and bounded rationality. Am. Econ. Rev. **84**(2), 406–411 (1994)

3. Aurenhammer, F.: Voronoi diagrams–a survey of a fundamental geometric data structure. ACM Comput. Surv. (CSUR) **23**(3), 345–405 (1991)

4. Balch, T.: Hierarchic social entropy: an information theoretic measure of robot group diversity. Auton. Robot. **8**(3), 209–237 (2000)

5. Baray, C.: Evolving cooperation via communication in homogeneous multi-agent systems. In: Proceedings - Intelligent Information Systems, IIS 1997, pp. 204–208. Institute of Electrical and Electronics Engineers Inc. (1997). https://doi.org/10.1109/IIS.1997.645219

6. Bongard, J.C.: The legion system: a novel approach to evolving heterogeneity for collective problem solving. In: Poli, R., Banzhaf, W., Langdon, W.B., Miller, J., Nordin, P., Fogarty, T.C. (eds.) EuroGP 2000. LNCS, vol. 1802, pp. 16–28. Springer, Heidelberg (2000). https://doi.org/10.1007/978-3-540-46239-2_2

7. Elsayed, S., et al.: Path planning for shepherding a swarm in a cluttered environment using differential evolution. In: 2020 IEEE Symposium Series on Computational Intelligence, SSCI 2020, pp. 2194–2201, December 2020. https://doi.org/10.1109/SSCI47803.2020.9308572

8. Emam, Y., Mayya, S., Notomista, G., Bohannon, A., Egerstedt, M.: Adaptive task allocation for heterogeneous multi-robot teams with evolving and unknown robot capabilities. In: Proceedings - IEEE International Conference on Robotics and Automation, pp. 7719–7725. Institute of Electrical and Electronics Engineers Inc., May 2020. https://doi.org/10.1109/ICRA40945.2020.9197283

9. Grocholsky, B., Keller, J., Kumar, V., Pappas, G.: Cooperative air and ground surveillance. IEEE Robot. Autom. Mag. **13**(3), 16–26 (2006)

10. Hu, J., Turgut, A.E., Krajnik, T., Lennox, B., Arvin, F.: Occlusion-based coordination protocol design for autonomous robotic shepherding tasks. IEEE Trans. Cogn. Dev. Syst. (2020)

11. Johnson, A., Hautaluoma, G., Agle, D.: NASA's ingenuity mars helicopter succeeds in historic first flight. https://www.nasa.gov/press-release/nasa-s-ingenuity-mars-helicopter-succeeds-in-historic-first-flight. Accessed 10 May 2021

12. Ashby, W.R.: Requisite variety and its implications for the control of complex systems. In: Klir, G.J. (ed.) Facets of Systems Science, vol. 7, pp. 405–417. Springer, Boston (1991). https://doi.org/10.1007/978-1-4899-0718-9_28

13. Lien, J.M., Bayazit, O.B., Sowell, R.T., Rodríguez, S., Amato, N.M.: Shepherding behaviors. In: Proceedings - IEEE International Conference on Robotics and Automation, vol. 2004, pp. 4159–4164 (2004). https://doi.org/10.1109/robot.2004.1308924

14. Madden, J.D., Arkin, R.C.: Modeling the effects of mass and age variation in wolves to explore the effects of heterogeneity in robot team composition. In: 2011 IEEE International Conference on Robotics and Biomimetics, ROBIO 2011, pp. 663–670 (2011). https://doi.org/10.1109/ROBIO.2011.6181362

15. Özdemir, A., Gauci, M., Gross, R.: Shepherding with robots that do not compute, pp. 332–339. MIT Press - Journals (2017). https://doi.org/10.1162/isal_a_056

16. Page, S.: The Difference. Princeton University Press, Princeton (2008)

17. Parker, L.E.: Lifelong adaptation in heterogeneous multi-robot teams: response to continual variation in individual robot performance. Auton. Robot. **8**(3), 239–267 (2000)

18. Pierson, A., Schwager, M.: Bio-inspired non-cooperative multi-robot herding. In: Proceedings - IEEE International Conference on Robotics and Automation, vol. 2015-June, pp. 1843–1849. Institute of Electrical and Electronics Engineers Inc., June 2015. https://doi.org/10.1109/ICRA.2015.7139438
19. Strömbom, D., et al.: Solving the shepherding problem: heuristics for herding autonomous, interacting agents. J. R. Soc. Interface **11**(100), 20140719 (2014)
20. Surowiecki, J.: The wisdom of crowds (2004)
21. Twu, P., Mostofi, Y., Egerstedt, M.: A measure of heterogeneity in multi-agent systems. In: Proceedings of the American Control Conference, pp. 3972–3977. Institute of Electrical and Electronics Engineers Inc. (2014). https://doi.org/10.1109/ACC.2014.6858632
22. Vaughan, R., Sumpter, N., Henderson, J., Frost, A., Cameron, S.: Experiments in automatic flock control. Robot. Auton. Syst. **31**(1), 109–117 (2000)
23. Waibel, M., Keller, L., Floreano, D.: Genetic team composition and level of selection in the evolution of cooperation. IEEE Trans. Evol. Comput. **13**(3), 648–660 (2009)

Evaluation of an OpenCV Implementation of Structure from Motion on Open Source Data

Ali Alouache[1](✉) and Qinghe Wu[2]

[1] Centre des Techniques Spatiales, Agence Spatiale Algérienne, Arzew, Algeria
[2] Automation School, Beijing Institute of Technology, Beijing, China
qinghew@bit.edu.cn

Abstract. Structure from Motion (SfM) is the technology of recovering the 3D model from multiple 2D views. It has received a great attention from computer vision community to construct large scale 3D models whose spatial resolution of comparable quality to LiDAR. Nowadays, aerial SfM is becoming even more important due to the rapid growth of low cost commercial UAV and small satellite market. This paper presents the evaluation of an OpenCV implementation of incremental SfM approach on open source data. The results of 3D construction obtained by OpenCV are compared to Visual SfM program in terms of precision, density of features and spatial resolution.

Keywords: 3D reconstruction · Structure from motion · OpenCV

1 Introduction

Light detection and ranging (LiDAR) is very useful 3D data source that is commonly adopted to construct 3D models of the world [1–4]. An increasing number of applications in the field of geography and environmental science require 3D model as input source such as remote sensing [5–7], topographic mapping [8, 9], and geographic information systems (GIS) [10, 11]. LiDAR sends out pulses of laser light and measures the exact time it takes for these pulses to return as they bounce from the ground. Then through measuring the timing and intensity of the returning pulses, it can provide readings of the terrain and of points on the ground.

The 3D map generated from LiDAR provides elevation information, which can be colorized based on either elevation or intensity to aid interpretation. The major advantages of LiDAR are the accuracy in terms of spatial resolution, and its capability of capturing 3D data in the day as well as in the night time. In addition, LiDAR performs well when it used to capture 3D data over terrains that contain power lines and dense vegetation [12, 13]. However, a visual inspection of the results shows that the 3D point cloud constructed by LiDAR in urban areas is difficult to interpret, and this may be explained due to the absence of the color in the point cloud which has a strong relevance to object recognition. Moreover, LiDAR is high cost because in addition to the laser sensor that captures 3D data, some other sensors are usually required such as high

© Springer Nature Switzerland AG 2021
C. Fox et al. (Eds.): TAROS 2021, LNAI 13054, pp. 158–167, 2021.
https://doi.org/10.1007/978-3-030-89177-0_16

precision satellite positioning system (GNSS) and inertial measurement unit (IMU) in order to determine the position of LiDAR in space.

Recently, the Structure from Motion (SfM) technology has received a great attention from the researchers of computer vision community to construct large scale 3D models whose spatial resolution of comparable quality to Lidar [14–19].

Nowadays, aerial SfM is becoming even more important due to the availability of low cost commercial UAV and small satellite market. However, the images should captured at the same height and contain at least 50% overlap in order to make SfM more suitable for 3D mapping. The output of SfM is a 3D model that contains not only elevation/height information, but also texture, shape, and color for every point on the map, which enables easier interpretation of the resulting 3D point cloud. Moreover, using low cost RGB cameras for capturing the images, then processing these images based on SfM will reduce the cost of 3D construction compared to Lidar [18].

Structure from Motion is similar to visual simultaneous localization and mapping (visual SLAM) in robotics [20]. The work [21] demonstrated that visual SLAM can be considered as a special case of SfM. However, both visual SLAM and SfM require computer vision algorithms for 3D mapping by using RGB cameras [22]. While LiDAR requires knowledge about how to exploit 3D data, and construct a surface model based on geometry post processing algorithms. Hence, the choice between LiDAR, visual SLAM or SfM depends on many factors such as the desired 3D output, the considered application, the available datasets, and the equipment to be used for 3D mapping.

There have been many different implementations of SfM pipelines in the literature. This paper searched for the most effective pipelines with publicly available source code that could allow customization of the pipeline itself. Examples of the available pipelines include the followings. Bundler [23] is a 3D reconstruction software that provides all of the executable version and source code. COLMAP [24] is a SfM and Multi-View Stereo (MVS) pipeline with a graphical and command-line interface. OpenMVG [25], is a SfM library well documented and accessible, including all the dependent libraries for simple installation. VisualSFM [26] is GUI application for 3D construction from a set of uncalibrated images based on SfM and MVS software. Theia [27] is a computer vision library aimed at providing efficient and reliable algorithms for SfM.

This paper presents the evaluation of an OpenCV implementation of incremental SfM approach [28] on open source data. Efficient algorithms are used in this implementation such as ORB with brute force for features detection and matching. The rejection of outliers based on RANSAC to obtain a robust estimation. Moreover, Google Ceres solver is embedded in this code to further optimize the 3D model by minimizing the reprojection errors given by Levenberg–Marquardt algorithm.

To the best of our knowledge this the only OpenCV implementation of incremental SfM that is available as open source code in the internet. However, it is a monocular SfM approach which considers that the images are captured by the same camera. Therefore, the contributions of this paper are two folds. First, the monocular SfM approach of [28] is extended to multi view SfM which makes it possible to construct 3D point cloud using images taken from different cameras that is more advantageous than a monocular camera. Second, a comparison is made between the characteristics of the OpenCV implementation of SfM and Visual SfM program.

The remainder of this paper is structured as follows. Section 2 describes the algorithm of incremental SfM. Section 3 presents the OpenCV implementation and the experimental results. Section 4 presents the comparison made between the OpenCV and Visual SfM program. Section 5 presents the conclusions and the future works.

2 Algorithmic Description

There are two approaches of incremental SfM. The first approach involves performing iteratively the two view SfM algorithm over multiple 2D views. After computing the intrinsic and extrinsics parameters for the first two views. The next step would be to get the 3D points of the two views using the projection matrix. Upon getting the initial estimate of the 3D points, these points have to be triangulated. Triangulation is performed iteratively over every image pair in a similar fashion. However, one of the main drawbacks of this approach is that the 3D reconstruction is up to scale. Which means that the motion obtained between the two views is going to have an arbitrary unit of measurement, that is, it is not in centimeters or inches but simply a given unit of scale. Thus, the reconstructed cameras will be one unit of scale distance apart. This has a big implications when extending the two views SfM to multiple views, as each pair of cameras will have their own units of scale, rather than a common one.

The second approach is based on using the Perspective-n-Point (PnP) algorithm [29] for multi view reconstruction. PnP takes care about the scale issue that existed in the first approach. However, it is observed in some cases that PnP algorithm don't give a reasonable projection matrix. Therefore, PnP is used in conjuction with RANSAC algorithm which is more robust. After getting the projection matrices of the first image pair, a triangulation is performed to get the initial 3D points. Now a baseline structure is computed, the projection matrix of the next view is calculated by using the 3D points that correspond to the 2D points of the new frame which is in turn used as input to PnP RANSAC module. Then, the 3D reconstruction is performed by triangulation and the process is repeated iteratively to get the projection matrix of successive views. However, this approach involves bookkeeping which means one needs to keep a track of the 3D points reconstructed using the previous two frames that correspond to the 2D points in the new frame. For each point in the 3D model, a vector denoting the 2D points is stored, then features matching is used to get a matching pair.

The incremental SfM approach presented in this paper is based on the robust PnP RANSAC module. The flowchart of Fig. 1 shows the architecture of the incremental SfM approach proposed in this paper. It mainly introduces an additional operation compared to the monocular approach of [28], that is extract EXIF data. This operation is needed only for initialization at the beginning of the 3D reconstruction, because after that all the parameters are refined based on bundle adjustment.

The flowchart of Fig. 1 cover the following four phases.

1. Extraction of EXIF data.
2. Finding 2D corresponding features points.
3. Initialization.
4. Incremental reconstruction.

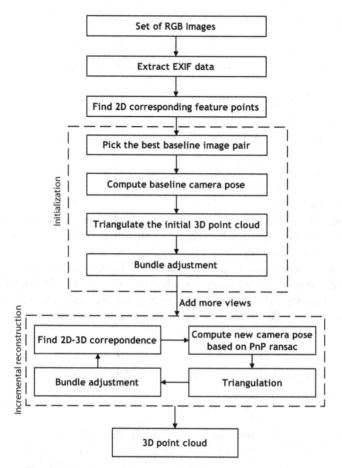

Fig. 1. Flowchart of the proposed incremental SfM approach

A. Phase 1: extraction of EXIF data

EXIF information that is stored in the header of each image is parsed to get the camera focal length information for each input ith image. Then the focal length is used to construct the internal calibration matrix that is further optimized based on bundle adjustment.

B. Phase 2: finding 2D corresponding feature points

The purpose of this phase is to detect the 2D locations of the feature points in all the images, then estimating their corresponding points in all the possible image pairs using RANSAC. The algorithm is described below.

Algorithm of finding corresponding features
Input: set of *n* RGB images
For each ith image
 1. Apply the robust features detector.
End for
For each ith and j^{th} image pair
 2. Match the features points.
 3. Compute the fundamental matrix (F_{ij}).
 4. Estimate again the 2D features based on RANSAC.
End for
Output: fundamental matrices, corresponding feature points.

C. Phase 3: initialization

In this phase it is desired to pick the best baseline image pair in order to construct an initial 3D model. Indeed, if the baseline is small it is clear that it is not possible to determine the depth of the scene.

The accuracy of the initial baseline structure will determine the quality of the 3D model. Which means if the initialization is bad then the quality of the final 3D model will be low. Otherwise, if the initialization is accurate, then the overall 3D model will have a good accuracy. The initialization algorithm is given as follows.

Initialization Algorithm
Input: corresponding 2D feature points, focal lengths, baseline=false
For the image pair (Im_i, Im_j) with large number of matching features
 1. Compute the Homography matrix H_{ij} using RANSAC
If the number of inliers is below the threshold *then* baseline=true
 2. Set the projection matrix of the first camera is $M_1 = [I \ 0]$ where *I* denotes the identity matrix.
 3. Compute the essential matrix E_{ij}.
 4. Decompose E_{ij} based on SVD to get M_2.
 5. Reconstruct the 3D points based on triangulation.
 6. Refine the reconstruction of the 3D model based on bundle adjustment.
 7. Get the colors of the 3D points.
 8. Store the 3D point cloud #1.
Else
 9. Increment *i* and *j*
 10. *Check if the number of matches is enough then baseline is true*
 11. Back to step 3
 12. Otherwise, initialization is failed
End if
 End for
Output: 3D point cloud #1, M_1, M_2.

D. Phase 4: incremental reconstruction

After getting the initial baseline structure, the following algorithm is carried out to construct the 3D model from multiple views based on the robust PnP RANSAC module.

```
Algorithm of incremental reconstruction
Input: M₁,M₂, 3D point cloud #1, 2D features points of the re-
maining images, focal lengths.
For each registered iᵗʰ image
  1. Find 2D-3D correspondence points between the 2D corre-
     sponding feature points of the iᵗʰ image and the 3D point
     cloud #1.
  2. Compute the projection matrix of the camera pose Mᵢ based
     on PnP ransac.
  3. Reconstruct the 3D points based on triangulation accord-
     ing to the initial baseline structure and the registered
     images.
  4. Refine the reconstruction of the 3D model based on bundle
     adjustment.
  5. Get the colors of the 3D points.
End For
  6. Increment i
  7. Back to step 1
Output: 3D point cloud, RGB data, camera pose.
```

3   Implementation and Experimental Results

A. Implementation based on OpenCV

OpenCV provides a range of feature detectors, descriptor extractors, and matchers. Hence ORB (Oriented Binary Robust Independent Elementary Features) is used to get the location of the feature points and their respective descriptors. ORB may be preferred over traditional 2D features such as the Speeded-Up Robust Features (SURF) or Scale Invariant Feature Transform (SIFT) because it is unencumbered with intellectual property and shown to be faster to detect, compute, and match.

After detecting feature points based on ORB, brute force binary matcher is used to get the matching, which simply matches two feature sets by comparing each feature in the first set to each feature in the second set.

Bundle adjustment is performed by Google Ceres solver [30] that is embedded in the code. Ceres Solver is an open source C++ library for modeling and solving large, complicated optimization problems. It can be used to solve Non-linear Least Squares problems with bounds constraints and general unconstrained optimization problems. It is a mature, feature rich, and performant library that has been used in production at Google since 2010.

Point cloud library (PCL) is used for real time visualization of the 3D reconstruction. After compiling the code, an executable file is generated in order to run SfM process. The point cloud that arises from the images is saved to PLY files, which can be opened in most 3D editing software.

B. Results of 3D construction

This section demonstrates the evaluation of the OpenCV implementaion of SfM compared with Visual SfM program.

Visual SfM saves on computation time by using GPU-accelerated SIFT in feature tracking to locate keypoints. In addition to its speed, Visual SfM has an excellent graphical user interface (GUI) that allows it to be operated easily. Moreover, it can be integrated with multi view stereo programs to produce dense 3D models. For more details about how to compile Visual SfM and use its GUI interface to generate sparse and dense 3D models the reader is referred to [31].

However, note that any other SfM software can be used as well for comparing the results of 3D reconstruction with Open CV.

Consider as dataset the 3 images depicted in Fig. 2(a) that are captured for façade of Merton College. The open source data is downloaded from the following link [32]. The ground truth model which includes 3D points, lines and cameras are shown in Fig. 2(b). The software that is used for visualizing the (.wrl) model is view3dscene.

The results of 3D reconstruction based on Visual SfM and OpenCV are depicted in Fig. 3. The software used for visualizing the 3D model is Meshlab.

The 3D model constructed based on Visual SfM shown in Fig. 3(a) contains 2983 points, which is very sparse and leaves many holes on the surface. Whereas the 3D model constructed based on OpenCV shown in Fig. 3(b) contains 24482 points, which is dense and most of the objects appear clearly on the surface of the model.

(a)   (b)

Fig. 2. Image dataset and the ground truth 3D model

4 Comparison

The comparison that is made between the OpenCV and Visual SfM program is summarized in Table 1. The following points are noted.

- There are some algorithms that are not available about the Visual SfM that are denoted by (n/A) in Table 1.

(a)   (b)

Fig. 3. 3D construction based on Visual SfM and OpenCV

- Extraction of feature points in the images is the most important part of SfM process, and consists the main difference between the approaches of Table 1. Based on the comparative results it is noticed that SIFT algorithm used by Visual SfM is accurate and robust but time costs even though it can be used with GPU. Whereas ORB of OpenCV that is fast and more efficient than SIFT.
- Even though Visual SfM utilizes GPU-accelerated SIFT in feature tracking and multi core bundle adjustment to save on computation time, but the constructed 3D model is very sparse. In most cases the 3D point cloud generated based on Visual SfM is refined to a finer resolution using Multi-View Stereo (MVS) programs. However, the MVS software are computationally expensive in terms of processing time and memory resources because they are based on dense matching algorithms.
- The comparative results shown in Fig. 3, it is concluded that OpenCV implementation of SfM is effective to satisfy the near real time requirements in terms of computation time, precision and spatial resolution of the 3D model.

Table 1. Comparison between Visual SfM and OpenCV

Characteristics	Visual SfM	OpenCV
Features extraction	SIFT	ORB
Features matching	Sequential preemptive	Brute force
Robust estimation	RANSAC	RANSAC
Triangulation	n/A	DLT
Image registration	n/A	PnP RANSAC
Bundle adjustment	Multicore BA	Ceres
Visualization	OpenGL	PCL

5 Conclusions

This paper presents the evaluation of an OpenCV implementation of incremental SfM approach using open source data. The comparative results with Visual SfM program demonstrate that the proposed SfM approach is capable to produce high quality 3D point clouds in terms of precision and spatial resolution.

In the future works the following tasks are suggested. Developing the proposed SfM approach for very large scale 3D reconstruction. Using parallel computing methods based on GPU processors to accelerate SfM process. Investigation of visual SLAM and 3D reconstruction by considering no prerecorded dataset.

References

1. Wang, R., Peethambaran, J., Chen, D.: LiDAR point clouds to 3-D urban models: a review. IEEE J. Sel. Top. Appl. Earth Obs. Remote Sens. **11**(2), 606–627 (2018)
2. Kühner, T., Kümmerle, J.: Large-scale volumetric scene reconstruction using LiDAR. In: Proceedings of the IEEE International Conference on Robotics and Automation (ICRA), pp. 6261–6267 (2020)
3. You, R.J., Lin, B.: A quality prediction method for building model reconstruction using LiDAR data and topographic maps. IEEE Trans. Geosci. Remote Sens. **49**(9), 3471–3480 (2011)
4. Orthuber, E., Avbelj, J.: 3D building reconstruction from LiDAR point clouds by adaptive dual contouring. In: ISPRS Annals of the Photogrammetry, Remote Sensing and Spatial Information Sciences (2015)
5. Shao, Z., Yang, N., Xiao, X., Zhang, L., Peng, Z.: A multiview dense point cloud generation algorithm based on low-altitude remote sensing images. Remote Sens. MDPI **8**(5), 381 (2016)
6. Hu, T., et al.: Development and performance evaluation of a very low-cost UAV-LiDAR system for forestry applications. Remote Sens. **13**(1), 77 (2020)
7. Obanawa, H., Shibata, H.: Applications of UAV remote sensing to topographic and vegetation surveys. In: Avtar, R., Watanabe, T. (eds.) Unmanned Aerial Vehicle: Applications in Agriculture and Environment, pp. 131–142. Springer, Cham (2020). https://doi.org/10.1007/978-3-030-27157-2_10
8. James, M.R., Robson, S., Smith, M.: 3-D uncertainty-based topographic change detection with structure-from-motion photogrammetry: precision maps for ground control and directly georeferenced surveys. Earth Surf. Proc. Land. **42**(12), 1769–1788 (2017)
9. Stott, E., Williams, R.D., Hoey, T.B.: Ground control point distribution for accurate kilometre-scale topographic mapping using an RTK-GNSS unmanned aerial vehicle and SfM photogrammetry. Drones 4–55 (2020)
10. Biljecki, F., Sindram, M.: Estimating building age with 3D GIS. In: ISPRS Annals of Photogrammetry, Remote Sensing and Spatial Information Sciences, vol. IV-4/W5 (2017)
11. Kulawiak, M., Kulawiak, M., Lubniewski, Z.: Integration, processing and dissemination of LiDAR data in a 3D web-GIS. ISPRS Int. J. Geo Inf. **8**(3), 144 (2019)
12. Ahmad, J., Malik, A.S., Xia, L., Ashikin, N.: Vegetation encroachment monitoring for transmission lines right-of-ways: a survey. Electr. Power Syst. Res. **95**, 339–352 (2013)
13. Shi, Z., Lin, Y., Li, H.: Extraction of urban power lines and potential hazard analysis from mobile laser scanning point clouds. Int. J. Remote Sens. **41**(9), 3411–3428 (2020)
14. Olsson, C., Enqvist, O.: Stable structure from motion for unordered image collections. In: Heyden, A., Kahl, F. (eds.) SCIA 2011. LNCS, vol. 6688, pp. 524–535. Springer, Heidelberg (2011). https://doi.org/10.1007/978-3-642-21227-7_49

15. Moulon, P., Monasse, P., Marlet, R.: Global fusion of relative motions for robust accurate and scalable structure from motion. In: Proceedings of the IEEE Conference on Computer Vision, pp. 3248–3255 (2013)
16. Dzenan, L., Jasmin, V., Haris, B.: Framework for automated reconstruction of 3D model from multiple 2D aerial images. In: Proceedings of the International Symposium ELMAR, pp. 173–176 (2017)
17. Al Khalil, O.: Structure from motion (SfM) photogrammetry as alternative to laser scanning for 3D modelling of historical monuments. Open Sci. J. 5(2) (2020)
18. Wallace, L., Lucieer, A., Malenovský, Z., Turner, D., Vopěnka, P.: Assessment of forest structure using two UAV techniques: a comparison of airborne laser scanning and structure from motion (SfM) point clouds. Forests 7(3), 62 (2016)
19. Alouache, A., Yao, X., Wu, Q.: Creating textured 3D models from image collections using open source software. Int. J. Comput. Appl. 163(9), 14–19 (2017)
20. Saputra, M.R.U., Markham, A., Trigoni, N.: Visual SLAM and structure from motion in dynamic environments: a survey. ACM Comput. Surv. (CSUR) 51(2), 37 (2018)
21. Özyeşil, O., Voroninski, V., Basri, R., Singer, A.: A survey of structure from motion. Acta Numer. 26, 305–364 (2017)
22. Ham, H., Wesley, J., Hendra, H.: Computer vision based 3d reconstruction: a review. Int. J. Electr. Comput. Eng. 9(4), 2394–2402 (2019)
23. Snavely, N., Seitz, S.M., Szeliski, R.: Modeling the world from internet photo collections. Int. J. Comput. Vis. 189–210 (2008)
24. Schönberger, J.L., Frahm, J.M.: Structure-from-motion revisited. In: Proceedings of the IEEE Conference on Computer Vision and Pattern Recognition (CVPR), pp. 4104–4113 (2016)
25. Moulon, P., Monasse, P., Perrot, R., Marlet, R.: OpenMVG: open multiple view geometry. In: Kerautret, B., Colom, M., Monasse, P. (eds.) RRPR 2016. LNCS, vol. 10214, pp. 60–74. Springer, Cham (2017). https://doi.org/10.1007/978-3-319-56414-2_5
26. Wu, C.: VisualSFM: A Visual Structure from Motion System (2011). http://www.cs.washington.edu/homes/ccwu/vsfm/
27. Sweeney, C.: Theia Multiview Geometry Library: Tutorial & Reference. http://theia-sfm.org
28. Baggio, D.L., Emami, S., Escriva, D., Ievgen, M.K., Saragih, J., Shilkrot, R.: Mastering OpenCV 3. Packt Publishing (2017)
29. Lepetit, V., Moreno-Noguer, F., Fua, P.: EPnP: an accurate o(n) solution to the PnP problem. Int. J. Comput. Vis. 81(2), 155–166 (2009)
30. Agarwal, S., Mierle, K.: Ceres solver (2012). http://ceres-solver.org
31. Torres, J.C., Arroyo, G., Romo, C., De Haro, J.: 3D digitization using structure from motion. In: Proceeding of the Spanish Computer Graphics Conference (2012)
32. https://www.robots.ox.ac.uk/~vgg/data/mview

Benchmark of Visual and 3D Lidar SLAM Systems in Simulation Environment for Vineyards

Ibrahim Hroob(✉), Riccardo Polvara, Sergi Molina, Grzegorz Cielniak, and Marc Hanheide

Lincoln Center for Autonomous Systems, University of Lincoln, Lincoln, UK
{ihroob,rpolvara,smolinamellado,gcielniak,mhanheide}@lincoln.ac.uk

Abstract. In this work, we present a comparative analysis of the trajectories estimated from various Simultaneous Localization and Mapping (SLAM) systems in a simulation environment for vineyards. Vineyard environment is challenging for SLAM methods, due to visual appearance changes over time, uneven terrain, and repeated visual patterns. For this reason, we created a simulation environment specifically for vineyards to help studying SLAM systems in such a challenging environment. We evaluated the following SLAM systems: LIO-SAM, StaticMapping, ORB-SLAM2, and RTAB-MAP in four different scenarios. The mobile robot used in this study equipped with 2D and 3D lidars, IMU, and RGB-D camera (Kinect v2). The results show good and encouraging performance of RTAB-MAP in such an environment.

Keywords: Agricultural robotics · Visual SLAM · 3D lidar SLAM

1 Introduction

Precision agriculture relies on collecting data from multiple sensors to help improving farm management and crop yield. Better management of the farm requires continuous monitoring of the plant health and soil condition, discovering diseases at an early stage and reducing chemical treatment. To achieve these goals, one solution would be to use a mobile robot to autonomously inspect the plants and the crops. In that context, the mobile robot must have an accurate representation of the farm to accurately localize itself and navigate to the goals. For this reason, many solutions have been proposed to overcome the localization problem in an outdoor environment. The most common solution is to use Real-Time Kinematic Global Positioning Systems (RTK-GNSS) [1], however, this solution is quite expensive and requires good coverage of base stations to guarantee accuracy. Other solutions rely on consumer-grade GNSS with fusing the output with different onboard sensors to enhance localization accuracy [2].

GNSS is not always available and the signal may not be reliable due to environmental conditions; loss of signal for the autonomous robot may lead to

© Springer Nature Switzerland AG 2021
C. Fox et al. (Eds.): TAROS 2021, LNAI 13054, pp. 168–177, 2021.
https://doi.org/10.1007/978-3-030-89177-0_17

catastrophic failures. Therefore, alternative solutions have been proposed based on the Simultaneous Localization and Mapping (SLAM) concept [3], where robot pose is estimated using sensory input, while at the same time building map of the environment. Various SLAM systems have been developed in that regard [4]. The selection of a suitable SLAM system depends on multiple factors, such as type (indoor or outdoor) and scale of the environment. Another factor is the sensors' cost, for example, some systems rely on data from relatively expensive 3D lidars whilst others use data from cheap consumer-grade monocular cameras. However, most of the developed solutions were targeting either the indoor environments or outdoor urban environments [3]. Nevertheless, SLAM in agricultural applications is still a growing field due to challenges related to harsh environmental conditions, seasonal changes in appearance, and repeated visual features in large open fields.

The main contributions of this paper are (i) Releasing to the public an open-source realistic vineyard simulator, offering uneven terrain and five different stages of plant growth[1]. (ii) Comparing and benchmarking 4 SLAM systems in an environment with repeating structure and appearance. The algorithms chosen for this study represent the sate-of-the-art visual and 3D-lidar systems including LIO-SAM [5], StaticMapping [6], ORB-SLAM2 [7], and RTAB-MAP [4].

2 Related Work

There has not been much work done in comparing various SLAM systems specifically for the vineyard environment, nevertheless, there have been many research papers dealing with analyzing and comparing SLAM methods for indoor static environments. In this section, we review the most relevant papers in this area.

The authors in [8] evaluated the trajectory generated from different ROS-based SLAM algorithms in a typical office indoor environment. The mobile robot was equipped with a 2D laser scanner, a monocular and stereo camera. The evaluation was on a specifically acquired data-set. The authors used the estimated trajectory from the best performing 2D lidar SLAM as the ground truth for visual SLAM systems. The results were good and encouraging for RTAB stereo with Root Mean Square Error (RMSE) of 0.163 m, and for ORB-SLAM monocular with RMSE of 0.166 m. A precise laser tracker was used in [9] for accurate ground truth to evaluate the accuracy of the map and the expected trajectory generated from the three most common 2D SLAM algorithms, gmapping, hector_slam, and google cartographer. The results showed that in this particular scenario, Google Cartographer is the most accurate algorithm compared to others.

Part of the work in [4] is an evaluation of the trajectory performance between different sensor configuration of RTAB-MAP (stereo and lidar), LSD-SLAM (stereo), ORB-SLAM2 (stereo) and SOFT-SLAM (stereo) in the outdoor KITTI dataset [10]. At this dataset, the authors stated both lidar and stereo configuration have followed well the ground truth. However, in some sequences with not

---

[1] github.com/LCAS/bacchus_lcas.

a complex structure, stereo setup systems outperform the lidar configuration of RTAB-MAP. Stereo RTAB with ORB feature detection has performed well in 9 out of 11 sequences, but that configuration was computationally expensive and was not able to meet real-time constraint on their hardware setup.

An Extended Information Filter (EIF) was used for mapping an agricultural environment and localizing a mobile robot [11]. The system makes use of a 2D laser scanner and monocular camera to detect olive tree stems. The tests were done in a real agricultural environment. However, the authors stated that they find some errors in identifying features and detecting loop closure. In [12] the authors evaluated visual SLAM methods, such as ORB-SLAM2 and S-PTAM, against visual-inertial SLAM system as S-MSCKF on the Rosario dataset [13]. The result showed poor accuracy and robustness compared to an indoor or urban environment, where those algorithms are designed for. Another study [14] comparing three visual SLAM algorithms in an orchard of fruit trees. The results showed that ORB-SLAM2 is the most accurate system with its loop closure ability.

Based on the above literature, there is a lack of comparison between SLAM methods in vineyards environment. Therefore, more research needs to be done in that field.

3   SLAM Algorithms

The SLAM systems used in this work can be classified into two main categories: visual SLAM and 3D lidar SLAM. This section briefly describes the four tested algorithms, RTAB-MAP and ORB-SLAM2 under visual SLAM, LIO-SAM, and StaticMapping under 3D lidar SLAM. Those systems have been chosen since they are the state-of-the-art, and the most popular algorithms by the time writing this paper. However, StaticMapping is not very popular yet. A brief list of sensors employed by each system is shown in Table 1 including the front-end back-end algorithms used by each method. The sensors that are used by each system in our setup are marked as bold text in the table.

3.1   RTAB-Map

Real-Time Appearance Based Mapping (RTAB-Map) is a graph-based SLAM approach [4] that supports input from RGB-D, Stereo, and lidar sensors. It combines two main algorithms which are *loop closure detector* and *graph optimizer*. The system uses the bag-of-words concept for loop closure detection by determining if the new image comes from a previously visited location or a new location; If the hypothesis of the new image is above a certain threshold, the new location will be added to the map as a new graph constraint. Then, in the background, the map graph is optimized to reduce the drift error in the overall map [15]. To achieve real-time performance for large scale environments, the system has a memory manager that limits and control the number of locations that are used for loop closure detection [4]. The system implements two standard

Table 1. The SLAM systems used for benchmarking together with supported sensors, front end and back end algorithms.

System	Sensors support	Front-end	Back-end
LIO-SAM	**3D lidar + IMU,** GNSS (Optional)	ICP	GTSAM
Static-Mapping	**3D lidar,** IMU (Optional), GNSS (Optional)	ICP	GTSAM
ORB-SLAM2	Monocular, **RGB-D** or Stereo cameras	ORB features extraction. PnP RANSAC for motion estimation	g2o
RTAB-MAP	**RGB-D** or Stereo camera (Mainsensors) 2D or 3D lidar (Optional to enhance map build from main input sensors)	Visual odom: GFTT/BRIEF for feature detection, NNDR for feature matching, PnP RANSAC for motion estimation lidar odom: ICP	GTSAM (default) g2o, TORO

odometry methods, Frame-To-Map (F2M) and Frame-To-Frame (F2F) using 3D visual features. In F2M, the system registers the new frame against upon local map, while the F2F registers the new frame to the last key-frame. RTAB-MAP can generate 2D and 3D occupancy grid map with dense point cloud, which is very useful for robotics applications. Furthermore, there is a full integration of this algorithm in Robot Operating System (ROS) as rtabmap_ros[2] package.

3.2   ORB-SLAM2

ORB-SLAM2 is a feature-based visual SLAM method that can create a sparse 3D map, which can be used with monocular, stereo, and RGB-D cameras to compute the camera trajectory. This algorithm has three main threads running in parallel, which enable real-time performance. The first thread is for tracking the camera pose in the new frames by finding feature matches in the local map. The second thread for local map management and optimization by applying local Bundle Adjustment (BA). The final thread is for loop closure detection and pose-graph optimization; this process is mainly for correcting the accumulated drift [7]. The system uses the bag-of-words DBoW2 concept [16] for place recognition, loop closure, and localization. However, when mapping a large-scale environment, the processing time of loop closure detection and graph optimization will increase as the map grows. This leads to a significant delay when making loop closure corrections after being detected. This system does not generate an occupancy

---

[2] wiki.ros.org/rtabmap_ros.

grid map, which makes it difficult to use directly in real robotics applications [4]. ORB-SLAM2 does not have full integration with ROS, it only subscribes to the camera topics and there are no output topics. However, it offers a visualizer for the trajectory and a sparse point cloud.

3.3   LIO-SAM

LIO-SAM is a factor graph tightly-coupled lidar inertial odometry via smoothing and mapping system [5]. The main input sensors to the system are 3D lidar and 9-axis IMU, but it can also use data from GNSS sensors for absolute measurement and map correction. LIO-SAM estimates lidar motion during the scan by using the raw IMU data. Then, for point cloud de-skewing, it assumes a nonlinear motion model. The novelty of this algorithm is that it uses the idea of keyframes and sliding windows from visual SLAM systems. In this way, the scan registration is performed at the local window scale instead of the global map improving the real-time performance significantly. On the other hand, the old scans are used for pose optimization. The IMU data is critical for this system to work properly. LIO-SAM is fully integrated into ROS. The generated output map and trajectory could be saved on a disk after finishing the scan.

3.4   StaticMapping

StaticMapping is a 3D lidar SLAM algorithm with optional IMU, odometry and GNSS inputs [6]. The back end of this algorithm uses M2DP [17] global descriptor for loop closure detection, and iSAM2 [18] for smoothing and mapping. This is an offline map-building algorithm from the recorded data.

4   Evaluation

This section describes our simulation environment, the different scenarios to test the algorithms, and the metrics we used for evaluation. Finally, we present and discuss the results.

4.1   Environment

We created a digital twin of an actual vineyard located at the University of Lincoln Riseholme campus under ROS/Gazebo as shown in Fig. 1. The virtual environment offers realistic uneven terrain, plus multiple growth stages of the vine plants and the crops. The vineyard has nine rows that are 18 m long with a 3 m distance between the rows. The mobile robot used is Thorvald produced by Saga Robotics[3] equipped with the following sensors: two 2D Hokuyo laser scanners, 3D lidar VLP-16 by Velodyne, ROS-IMU plugin and a Kinect V2 camera. A video of the environment can be seen in the link below[4].

---

[3] sagarobotics.com/.

[4] Field: youtu.be/L9ORZNyWdT0. Uneven terrain: youtu.be/L9ORZNyWdT0.

(a) Real field   (b) Simulation   (c) Growth stages

(d) Robot front camera view   (e) The final growth stage

Fig. 1. Digital twin of the vineyard environment.

4.2 Testing Scenarios

We designed four different scenarios in which we evaluated the 4 different SLAM methods we aim to compare.

- Scenario 0 (S0): Move in a straight line. That is mainly to evaluate the drift of the generated trajectory. Trajectory length is 25 m.
- Scenario 1 (S1): Send the robot to inspect a row and get back from the same row. Trajectory length is 48.6 m.
- Scenario 2 (S2): Send the robot to inspect a row and get back from the adjacent row. Trajectory length is 54.6 m.
- Scenario 3 (S3): Inspect multiple rows. That is to simulate a real-life inspection scenario with multiple loop closures. Trajectory length is 101.2 m.

4.3 SLAM Algorithms Configurations

As mentioned earlier, the tested SLAM systems have some integration with ROS, either partially like ORB-SLAM2, or fully as in LIO-SAM. The configuration file for each algorithm has been modified to work with our setup. (a) For ORB-SLAM2, we used the RGBD configuration and modify the camera parameters in the setting file based on the used camera. (b) In RTAB-MAP, the configurations are passed through the launch file. We used the `rgbd_sync` node to synchronize the RGB-D camera data before passing them to `rtabmap_ros` node. A laser scan data was passed to construct a 2D occupancy grid map. (c) StaticMapping is an offline system, it can only construct the map from recorded data. The default parameters were used and `accumulate_cloud_num` was set to 1. (d) For LIO-SAM we used the default configurations but disabled the GNSS optimization.

4.4 Metrics

The output trajectory of a SLAM system can be evaluated by finding the absolute distance between the estimated trajectory and the ground truth. The Absolute Trajectory Error (ATE) is defined as the average deviation from the ground truth trajectory [19].

$$\text{ATE}_{rmse} = \left(\frac{1}{n} \sum_{i=1}^{n} \|\text{trans}(Q_x^{-1} SP_i)\|^2 \right)^{\frac{1}{2}},$$

where i is the time sample or frame, SP_i is the spatial translation at time i, $trans$ is the translation error, and Q_x is the ground truth pose. To find the statistical metrics of ATE, we used the open-source library evo[5] to calculate the following metrics: Maximum, Mean, Median, Root Mean Square Error (RMSE), and Standard deviation (STD).

4.5 Results

The error metrics of the experiments are summarized in Table 2. Figure 2 shows the output trajectories of the four algorithms compared to the ground truth. As it can be observed from Table 2 RTAB achieves superior performance with the lowest RMSE across all scenarios compared to other systems.

Table 2. ATE statistical metrics for various SLAM systems on 4 different scenarios

	S0				S1				S2				S3			
	LIO-SAM	STATIC	ORBSLAM2	RTAB-MAP	LIO-SAM	STATIC	ORBSLAM2	RTAB-MAP	LIO-SAM	STATIC	ORBSLAM2	RTAB-MAP	LIO-SAM	STATIC	ORBSLAM2	RTAB-MAP
MAX	1.65	1.55	1.62	**0.20**	1.32	1.85	1.42	**0.08**	0.83	0.79	1.34	**0.20**	0.77	2.64	8.95	**0.12**
MEAN	1.00	0.97	0.81	**0.08**	0.53	0.77	0.86	**0.05**	0.20	0.42	0.69	**0.12**	0.36	1.23	4.35	**0.07**
MEDIAN	1.11	1.03	0.81	**0.05**	0.40	0.29	1.04	**0.05**	0.18	0.40	0.78	**0.12**	0.34	0.98	3.91	**0.06**
RMSE	1.13	1.07	0.95	**0.09**	0.68	1.04	0.96	**0.05**	0.22	0.45	0.84	**0.14**	0.40	1.51	5.22	**0.07**
STD	0.53	0.46	0.50	**0.05**	0.43	0.70	0.42	**0.01**	0.10	0.17	0.47	**0.06**	0.19	0.88	2.90	**0.03**

In the first scenario S0, all SLAM methods except RTAB-MAP reported big drift in the estimated trajectory, with a maximum value of 1.65 m from LIO-SAM, while RTAB-MAP has the minimum drift with a maximum value of 0.20 m and RMSE of 0.09 m. For scenario S1, RTAB-MAP has the minimum drift and smallest RMSE with 0.05 m, the performance of the remaining algorithms were close. There is no loop closure in this scenario even though the robot got back to the same place, which is due to the difference in the camera viewpoint. In

---

[5] github.com/MichaelGrupp/evo.

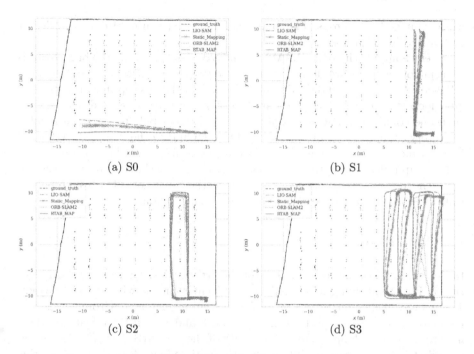

(a) S0   (b) S1

(c) S2   (d) S3

Fig. 2. Output trajectory from various SLAM systems in different test scenarios.

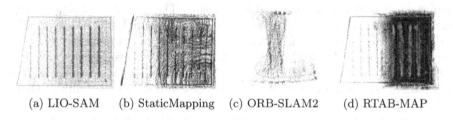

(a) LIO-SAM   (b) StaticMapping   (c) ORB-SLAM2   (d) RTAB-MAP

Fig. 3. Output maps and estimated trajectory from different SLAM system for scenarios 3

scenario S2, the second-best algorithm after RTAB-map is LIO-SAM, followed by StaticMapping, and finally ORB-SLAM2 with the largest RMSE of 0.84 m. The final scenario is the most interesting and realistic one, where the robot traverses multiple rows before going back to its starting point. This scenario with multiple loop closures represents a very interesting benchmark for the algorithms, as represented in Fig. 2. ORB-SLAM2 has failed to create a reliable map, we think that might be due to the repeated visual appearance of the environment; on the other hand, LIO-SAM and StaticMapping did not completely fail. However, the drift of the trajectory is too large to be used for robot navigation. This is because, in a vineyard, the distance between two rows is usually between 2 to 3 meters, in which if the mobile robot fails to localize itself accurately it can cause damage to the crops. The map generated for scenario 3 from the different systems is shown in Fig. 3.

Even though both ORB-SLAM2 and RTAB-MAP are using the bag-of-words concept for loop closure detection, the pose-graph optimization is different. In ORB-SLAM2, global bundle adjustment is used for the pose optimization process after loop closure. So, since there are lots of visual features shared between the keyframes due to similar appearance, this algorithm fails to estimate reliable trajectory as represented in Fig. 2d and Table 2. On the other hand, RTAB-MAP is much more robust to false loop closures, since it checks the transformation in the graph after the optimization process, if the translation variance was too large, the loop closure is rejected. The lidar methods did not suffer from repeated feature issue, due to the large field of view of the 3D lidar.

5   Conclusion

In this work, we compared four state-of-the-art visual and 3D lidar SLAM algorithms in a challenging simulated vineyard environment with uneven terrain. The main challenge for the visual SLAM system in such an environment is represented by a repeated pattern of appearance and less distinct features. This may result in false loop closures. The state of the art ORB-SLAM2 failed when the robot moved across multiple rows with multiple loop closures, we think this may be due to an identical visual appearance between vineyard rows. RTAB map is much more robust to invalid loop closure. The trajectory generated from the RTAB-MAP algorithm was the most accurate in our test scenarios. The estimated trajectories from LIO-SAM and StaticMapping suffer from big drift but the trajectories shape is acceptable, we believe in real-world tests, this drift could be fixed with the availability of GNSS signal. For future work, we will add some unique features within vineyard rows to test the reliability of ORB-SLAM2. Those unique features could be to have some variation in the plant models instead of having them identical across all the rows. In addition, we would like to test the localization ability within the generated maps from the SLAM systems. Finally, we will test those methods in a real vineyard.

Acknowledgement. This work has been supported by the European Commission as part of H2020 under grant number 871704 (BACCHUS).

References

1. Nørremark, M., Griepentrog, H., Nielsen, J., Søgaard, H.: The development and assessment of the accuracy of an autonomous GPS-based system for intra-row mechanical weed control in row crops. Biosys. Eng. **101**(4), 396–410 (2008)
2. Imperoli, M., Potena, C., Nardi, D., Grisetti, G., Pretto, A.: An effective multi-cue positioning system for agricultural robotics. IEEE Robot. Autom. Lett. **3**(4), 3685–3692 (2018)

3. Aguiar, A.S., dos Santos, F.N., Cunha, J.B., Sobreira, H., Sousa, A.J.: Localization and mapping for robots in agriculture and forestry: a survey. Robotics **9**(4), 97 (2020)

4. Labbé, M., Michaud, F.: RTAB-map as an open-source lidar and visual simultaneous localization and mapping library for large-scale and long-term online operation. J. Field Robot. **36**(2), 416–446 (2019)

5. Shan, T., Englot, B., Meyers, D., Wang, W., Ratti, C., Daniela, R.: LIO-SAM: tightly-coupled lidar inertial odometry via smoothing and mapping. In: IEEE/RSJ International Conference on Intelligent Robots and Systems (IROS), pp. 5135–5142. IEEE (2020)

6. Liu, E.: Atinfinity: Edwardliuyc/staticmapping: Release for DOI, May 2021

7. Mur-Artal, R., Tardos, J.D.: ORB-SLAM2: an open-source SLAM system for monocular, stereo, and RGB-D cameras. IEEE Trans. Rob. **33**(5), 1255–1262 (2017)

8. Filipenko, M., Afanasyev, I.: Comparison of various SLAM systems for mobile robot in an indoor environment. In: 2018 International Conference on Intelligent Systems (IS). IEEE, September 2018

9. Yagfarov, R., Ivanou, M., Afanasyev, I.: Map comparison of lidar-based 2d SLAM algorithms using precise ground truth. In: 2018 15th International Conference on Control, Automation, Robotics and Vision (ICARCV). IEEE, November 2018

10. Geiger, A., Lenz, P., Urtasun, R.: Are we ready for autonomous driving? the KITTI vision benchmark suite. In: 2012 IEEE Conference on Computer Vision and Pattern Recognition. IEEE, June 2012

11. Cheein, F.A., Steiner, G., Paina, G.P., Carelli, R.: Optimized EIF-SLAM algorithm for precision agriculture mapping based on stems detection. Comput. Electron. Agric. **78**(2), 195–207 (2011)

12. Comelli, R., Pire, T., Kofman, E.: Evaluation of visual slam algorithms on agricultural dataset, September 2019

13. Pire, T., Mujica, M., Civera, J., Kofman, E.: The Rosario dataset: multisensor data for localization and mapping in agricultural environments. Int. J. Robot. Res. **38**(6), 633–641 (2019)

14. Capua, F.R., Sansoni, S., Moreyra, M.L.: Comparative analysis of visual-SLAM algorithms applied to fruit environments. In: 2018 Argentine Conference on Automatic Control (AADECA). IEEE, November 2018

15. Altuntas, N., Uslu, E., Cakmak, F., Amasyali, M.F., Yavuz, S.: Comparison of 3-dimensional SLAM systems: RTAB-map vs. kintinuous. In: 2017 International Conference on Computer Science and Engineering (UBMK). IEEE, October 2017

16. Galvez-López, D., Tardos, J.D.: Bags of binary words for fast place recognition in image sequences. IEEE Trans. Robot. **28**(5), 1188–1197 (2012)

17. He, L., Wang, X., Zhang, H.: M2dp: a novel 3D point cloud descriptor and its application in loop closure detection. In: 2016 IEEE/RSJ International Conference on Intelligent Robots and Systems (IROS). IEEE, October 2016

18. Kaess, M., Johannsson, H., Roberts, R., Ila, V., Leonard, J., Dellaert, F.: iSAM2: incremental smoothing and mapping with fluid relinearization and incremental variable reordering. In: 2011 IEEE International Conference on Robotics and Automation. IEEE, May 2011

19. Prokhorov, D., Zhukov, D., Barinova, O., Anton, K., Vorontsova, A.: Measuring robustness of visual SLAM. In: 2019 16th International Conference on Machine Vision Applications (MVA). IEEE, May 2019

Lidar-Only Localization with 3D Pose-Feature Map

Chaokun Zhang[1,2(✉)], Taotao Shan[1], Bolin Zhou[1], and Yu Guo[1]

[1] College of Intelligence and Computing, Tianjin University, Tianjin, China
{zhangchaokun,starlight,zhoubolin,guoyu001}@tju.edu.cn
[2] China Xiong'an Group Digital City Technology Co., Ltd., Xiong'an, China

Abstract. Real-time and accuracy are the two most important indicators for unmanned vehicle localization. In this paper, we propose a novel map representation and its corresponding Lidar-only localization framework. In essence, we first extract geometric features from Lidar key-frames, and bundle these features with their observation poses (i.e., ground truth) to form a prior map named *Pose-Feature Map*. Then, the position of vehicle will be achieved by integrating Lidar-Odometry (LO) and Map-Matching (MM) with the Pose-Feature Map. In our framework, these two solutions are complementary. LO provides smooth and real-time pose estimation for MM, while MM can correct the accumulated drift of LO. During MM, we adaptively generate local maps to replace the global map for matching. Therefore, our proposed framework can further reduce the mismatch between the current frame and the map while maintaining low computational complexity. We demonstrated the framework in the KITTI dataset. The results confirm that our approach is superior to independent localization solutions in terms of real-time and accuracy.

Keywords: Localization · Lidar Odometry · Pose-Feature Map matching · Integration

1 Introduction

As one of the key technologies of unmanned vehicles, localization has a variety of mature technical solutions. However, due to the challenges posed by the environment and sensors, no localization solution can be applied to all scenarios. For example, the Global Navigation Satellite System (GNSS) is widely used in most open environments, but due to signal occlusion and canyon effects, it cannot be used in the closed or semi-enclosed environment (e.g., the garage, and the

This research is supported in part by National Key R&D Program of China under Grant 2019YFB2102400, in part by China Postdoctoral Science Foundation 2020M680906, in part by Hebei Province High-level Talent Funding project B202003027, in part by National Natural Science Foundation of China under Grant 61832013.

© Springer Nature Switzerland AG 2021
C. Fox et al. (Eds.): TAROS 2021, LNAI 13054, pp. 178–187, 2021.
https://doi.org/10.1007/978-3-030-89177-0_18

urban building block). Therefore, in order to solve the localization problem of unmanned vehicle, we need multiple solutions to achieve localization redundancy.

Our research motivation comes from the specific requirements of Lidar for vehicle self-location. In the past decade, various Lidar-only localization solutions have emerged. It can be simply divided into Simultaneous Localization And Mapping (SLAM) and Map-Matching (MM) solutions. Lidar-SLAM solutions, such as [3,7,12,14], estimate 6 Degrees of Freedom (6-DOF) of motion by comparing the continuously scanned point clouds frame by frame and registering them finely. Therefore, their localization frequency is equal to the Lidar, and their real-time performance is better. Nevertheless, all SLAM solutions have their inherent flaws. In long-distance driving, the lack of prior constraints will cause errors to accumulate, and the trajectory drift will become larger and larger, until the localization is lost. Lidar-MM solutions, such as [8,9,13], register the Lidar scans with the prior map to obtain the localization results, so that the above-mentioned error accumulation does not occur. However, a large prior map will lead to heavy computation and poor real-time localization, and its repetitive structure will lead to mismatches. This makes it unsatisfactory in practical applications.

To address these challenges above, we propose a novel map representation called **Pose-Feature Map** to reduce the computation and mismatch in MM, and a new framework that integrates MM and LO to increase the frequency of localization. During operation, the Pose-Feature Map change MM from frame-to-global-map matching into adaptive frame-to-local-map registration, thereby reducing the computation and avoiding mismatches caused by repeated environmental structures. Moreover, interpolating the SLAM localization result into MM can make it smoother and more real-time. Also MM localization results can correct the cumulative drift of SLAM. Their complementary allows us to obtain real-time and accurate localization results.

The remaining part of this paper is organized as follow. Related research work of Lidar localization solutions is presented in Sect. 2; Sect. 3 introduces the framework architecture and the background of Lidar-only odometry; Sect. 4 presents the Pose-Feature Map and the special Map-Matching base it in detail; the experiment and conclusion are located in the Sect. 5 and 6, respectively.

2   Related Work

Lidar is considered to be an indispensable sensor for future unmanned vehicles. How to apply Lidar as the only sensor to the localization system, in recent years, three methods have been mainly proposed: Lidar-SLAM, Lidar-MM, and integration scheme.

Lidar-SLAM is a branch of the SLAM system. Among the Lidar-SLAM solutions in recent years, the most popular one is LOAM [14]. It performs down-sampling through curvature features, and converts the real-time registration from point-to-point to point-to-line/surface in iterative optimization. LOAM has maintained a long-term leading position in the KITTI test. In LeGO-LOAM [12], the outlier and ground points in scans were segmented out before registration, besides loop detection was added. This make LeGO-LOAM perform better than LOAM in certain environment. However, their biggest problem is drift, which can also be clearly observed in the experiment part.

Lidar-MM will continuously corrects drift errors during localization. The registration method is a decisive factor. With the development of deep learning on 3D point clouds registration, L3-Net [9] and DeLS-3D [13] have adopted artificial neural network methods for mapping between scans and the map. However, these AI methods are not interpretable and require expensive hardware to satisfy the computation, so they are not suitable for vehicle platforms. In contrast, the traditional method, such as ICP [11] and NDT [1], are lighter and more interpretable. For example, HDL [8] exploits multi-thread NDT. However, the general method of extracting local maps based on a certain radius can easily lead to loss of localization in many cases. In PoseMap [6], it innovatively divides global-map into surfel sub-maps based on the ground truth to solve the above problems, which inspired us. However, in vehicle platform, the frequency of MM still cannot meet the driving requirements.

Integration is actually a fusion of the above two solutions. The greatest advantage is to make them complement each other and eliminate their own shortcomings. In LOL [10], a global positioning method that merged Segmap [5] and LOAM is proposed to solve the long-distance drift of LOAM. [4] also integrates information from complementary nodes such as Lidar global matching and Lidar inertial odometry to achieve accurate and smooth position estimation. However, they are all complex and non-lightweight.

Our solution is also the integration of SLAM and MM. In SLAM, we exploit the LO algorithm part in LOAM and LeGO-LOAM; and in the MM scheme, we adopt the idea of sub-map similar to PoseMap and improved it. The mapping scheme relies on the ground truth to provide a coherent initial map that is sufficiently enough for waypoint localization. We believe that by combining LO and a prior map constraints, we can complete high-frequency and accurate localization in a long period of time.

3   Framework Architecture and Background

3.1   Framework Architecture

As shown in Fig. 1, the framework requires two inputs for operation. One is real-time scans generated by Lidar. These input point cloud frames will be processed and filtered by the pre-processing nodes to generate features. Another one is a special prior map called Pose-Feature Map. It will dynamically generate local maps based on some parameters during the running of the framework.

Next, we exploit two strategies to perform localization. LO maintains high frequency motion estimation. The matching module intermittently matches the scanned features and generated local maps to obtain the discrete anchor position of the vehicle.

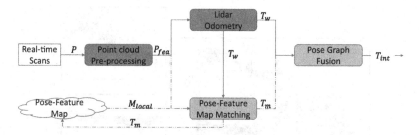

Fig. 1. Structure of Lidar-only localization framework with Pose-Feature Map. The white part is input data, the blue modules represent the LO algorithm from LOAM and LeGO-LOAM, while the green modules are our novel map matching and integration method. The localization results of LO and MM are T_w and T_m respectively. M_{local} is the local maps generated by T_m and global map. In addition, the solid line represents the high frequency, and the dashed line represents the low frequency, which are 10 Hz and 1 Hz, respectively. (Color figure online)

Then, we apply pose graph optimization to further correct the discrete mapping position. Finally we combine the lidar odometry and the optimized mapping result through interpolation, and publish it as the trajectory of the vehicle.

3.2 Lidar-Only Odometry Background

The main task of LO is to estimate high frequency self-motion based on the data flow transmitted by Lidar. Here we apply a more mature algorithm from LOAM [14] and LeGO-LOAM [12].

Point Cloud Pre-processing. Before performing the localization algorithm, the framework should extract features from real-time frames to reduce the computation in subsequent nodes. LOAM extract features P_{fea}^t in Lidar scans P^t base on the smoothness of each point. Furthermore, LeGO-LOAM noticed the interference of points generated by the ground, distant objects or plants, and designed a clustering algorithm to detect and segment them.

Lidar Odometry. The way that LO calculates the local movement T_l^t of Lidar between two consecutive scans is to register the features P_{fea}^{t-1} and P_{fea}^t. Both LOAM and LeGO-LOAM use KD-tree to find the corresponding point pairs, and then use iterative algorithms (e.g., Levenberg-Marquardt) to minimize their distance to calculate the relative motion between two frames. The whole process can be expressed as

$$\min_{T_t^l} d\left(T_t^l, X, C\right) \tag{1}$$

where X is a point in P_{fea}^t, C represent the correspond target in P_{fea}^{t-1}, and function d represent their distance.

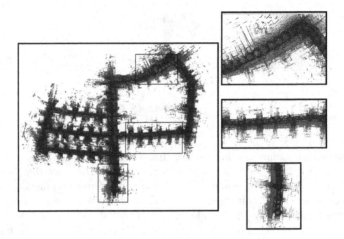

Fig. 2. Comparison of the maps generated by LeGO-LOAM and ground truth. The ground truth map (The driving time is $4'36''$ and the track length is 2200 m.) is visualized with red points, while blue is LeGO-LOAM. The larger figure on the left is a global view, and the other three on the right are enlarged partial views. (Color figure online)

By continuously multiplying all the transformation relations T_l^t, the vehicle's odometry world track estimation result T_w^t can be obtained in (2).

$$T_w^t = \prod_{i=1}^{t} T_l^i \tag{2}$$

4   Pose-Feature Map Localization

In the case of lidar-only, SLAM is unreliable. As shown in Fig. 2, in long sequence, the map and its trajectory generated by LeGO-LOAM have obvious drifts. For this reason, many researchers choose to treat ground-truth maps as prior benchmarks and use MM algorithms (e.g., NDT [1] and ICP [11]) to complete vehicle localization.

However, we found that in the real-time registration process of sans and global maps, not only the computation is heavy, but also the area in the map that does not need to be registered will seriously interfere with the result, especially when the surrounding environment changes drastically. In addition, the registration result between the local maps generated by general methods and the vehicle Lidar perception is also very poor. Based on long-term research and inspiration from PoseMap [6] we created the Pose-Feature Map. The way it generates a local map is to extract several point cloud frames near the position of the vehicle on the map. Compared with common methods, it can not only ensure the validity of local maps, but also reduce the computation of calculation.

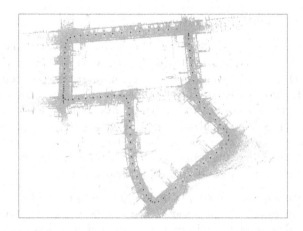

Fig. 3. Pose-Feature Map composed of key-frames (light) and their observation poses (dark).

4.1   Pose-Feature Map

The point cloud map is a layer of a high definition (HD) map used for autonomous driving. It consists of a large number of points. Their coordinate value represent the geometric information of the three-dimensional world, and provide powerful and indispensable prior 3D scene knowledge. Obviously, the construction of a normal point cloud map M generated by splicing frames f_i collected from the same or different Lidars, vehicles and even at various times. Then we set a global coordinate system, and transform these key-frames to f_i' according to their pose T_i from GNSS or Surveying and Mapping Engineering,

$$M : \left\{ f_1', f_2', \cdots, f_n' \right\}, i \in N, f_i' = f_i \cdot T_i \tag{3}$$

Our Pose-Feature Map has the normal duty of a point cloud map: represents the surrounding environment. Specially, each feature point has it's observation pose after the map is formed. This is visible in Fig. 3. Points with the same observation pose constitute a node. The general data structure is as follow,

$$M : \left\{ \left(f_1', T_1 \right), \left(f_2', T_2 \right), \cdots \left(f_n', T_n \right) \right\} \tag{4}$$

For the purpose of reducing MM computation, we adopt two methods to reduce the map size, namely key-frame extraction and down-sampling. The extraction method is mainly based on the time interval. Since the speed of the vehicle is slow when collecting road curve features, details of the corner will be strengthened, although this will cause uneven map density. In order to better match the features extracted in pre-processing step, down-sampling strategy for generating Pose-Feature Map is the same.

4.2   Adaptive Local-Map Matching

The main advantage of the Pose-Feature Map is the convenience and efficiency of fragmentation. When constructing the prior map, we also store all the key-frame poses in the KD-tree. With the vehicle localization at the last moment, we can quickly select the nearest key-frames to generate an adaptive local map M_{local}. In addition, our Pose-Feature Map matching can trade with low frequency for high accuracy. For example, multiple iterations and finer granularity can be set.

Next, we also need to consider the issue of selecting the number of frames. In our research, we found that there are two factors that affect the local map, namely driving environment and operating parameters.

Driving Environment. We simply divide them into straight or curved roads, open or closed environments. Generally, the changes between consecutive frames of a straight road or an open environment is much smaller than that in curved or closed environment. Therefore, when the vehicle is turning or driving in a closed environment, more key-frames should be selected to generate a local map, and when driving in a straight or open environment, fewer should be selected.

Operating Parameters. These parameters include vehicle speed, map matching frequency and key-frame distance, which should be adapted to the framework. Reflected in adaptive matching process, the proportion of overlap area between the vehicle perception and local map should be large enough. That is, the adaptive local map must cover the area that the vehicle may reach in the next cycle, while avoid mismatches caused by oversize.

Figure 4 nicely shows the advantages of our novel Map. Compared with the method that roughly selecting a point cloud within a certain range (e.g., 50 m), the adaptive local map we extracted overlaps well with the vehicle's perception, simultaneously the point cloud size is reduced by 70%.

Our next task is to register $P_{fea}^k (k \in t)$ with the M_{local}^k fragmented from Pose-Feature Map to obtain the anchor MM position T_m^k of the vehicle by NDT [1]. This is also the purpose of the entire matching node. Where k represents a certain moment in the time stream t. In this paper, the interval between k and $k - 1$ is 1 s, and the interval between t and $t - 1$ is 0.1 s. Their initial values are 0 s.

4.3   Integrating Localization

During the Pose-Feature Map matching process, our global localization result T_m^k is obtained through NDT registration. Here, we will further optimize the NDT results with pose graph to increase confidence. Then, we integrated the odometry to increase frequency.

Optimization. We know that the errors come from the short-time (1 s) drift of LO and the NDT algorithm. Now we define the results of MM and odometry as vertices and edges to construct a pose graph. Their errors can be expressed as,

$$r_k = \left(T_w^k\right)^{-1} \cdot T_w^{k-1} \cdot \left(T_m^{k-1}\right)^{-1} \cdot T_m^k \tag{5}$$

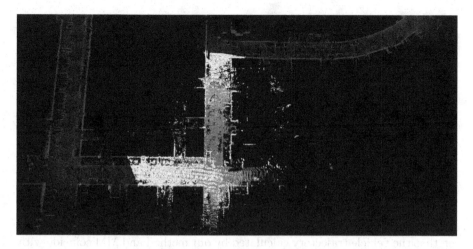

Fig. 4. Comparison of the points handed by radius search (white) and our Pose-Feature Map (green). The red points are the global map. (Color figure online)

where the residual cost in k-th cycle is r_k. The non-linear least squares optimization is solved by using the GTSAM [2] solver, and get the optimized result defined as T_o^k.

Fusion. In our proposed framework, the frequency of odometry is the same as Lidar operating frequency. The integration process is actually interpolation. We treat the T_o^k as a anchor localization, the odometry result T_w^t continuously interpolated until a new MM optimization result is obtained. The method is expressed as follow,

$$T_{int}^t = T_o^k \cdot \left(T_w^k\right)^{-1} \cdot T_w^t \tag{6}$$

where T_{int}^t is the final output of our entire framework and consistent with the map coordinate system.

5   Experiments

5.1   Hardware, Datasets and Parameter Setting

The computing platform is NVIDIA JETSON AGX XAVIER, equipped with ARMv8 Processor rev 0(v8l), 32 GB of RAM. Our framework has been tested many times on the KITTI dataset. The driving distance in data sets range from 800 m to 3700 m. Their environment is variable, and full of curves. The trajectories are also diverse, such as straight-line, closed-loop, and regional repeated driving.

5.2   Localization Performance

Figure 5 is the quantitative result of our method compared with the original LeGO-LOAM algorithm, MM with Pose-Feature Map and the ground truth in

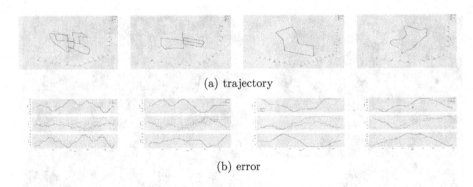

(a) trajectory

(b) error

Fig. 5. The result of KITTI Drive 00, 05, 07, 09.

certain datas. The Fig. 5a shows the trajectory comparison that can be clearly seen that the vehicle trajectory calculated by our method and MM coincide with the ground truth, which corrects the drift in LeGO-LOAM. The Fig. 5b shows the error comparison of the positioning results for each frame. In these datas, the drive distance are 3724 m, 2205 m, 695 m and 1705 m respectively. The LeGO-LOAM deviated by 23.4 m, 23.93 m, 4.19 m and 22.57 m, and our result (same as MM) are 9.57 m, 2.94 m, 0.45 m and 6.13 m. The above results can be concluded that: compared with SLAM, MM and our framework can effectively reduce drift.

Table 1 shows the results of several localization frequencies. It can be seen that the frequency of localization of our framework is consistent with LeGO-LOAM, and is almost consistent with the operating frequency of Lidar. However, the frequency of MM is only about one-tenth. It is worth mentioning that under the same NDT parameters, this computing platform can no longer increase the MM frequency. This also shows that if you completely rely on MM, the localization frequency will be greatly reduced.

Table 1. Localization frequency of each Drive sequence with different solutions.

Solution\sequence	Drive 00 (470.4 s)	Drive 05 (287.3 s)	Drive 07 (113.1 s)	Drive 09 (164.8 s)
Ground truth	9.65 Hz	9.61 Hz	9.73 Hz	9.65 Hz
LeGO-LOAM	9.65 Hz	9.61 Hz	9.72 Hz	9.64 Hz
ILM (ours)	9.65 Hz	9.61 Hz	9.72 Hz	9.64 Hz
Pose-Feature Map matching	1.00 Hz	1.00 Hz	1.00 Hz	0.99 Hz

6 Conclusion

This paper proposes a novel map representation called Pose-Feature Map for the map matching solution, which bundles key-frames with their correspond observation poses. In the registration step, the module extracts a more effective local map from it, which improves the localization accuracy and reduces the computation of calculation. At the same time, we integrated the above Pose-Feature Map-Matching and Lidar-Odometry into a new framework, enabling the two localization methods to make up for their respective shortcomings. The KITTI's data set confirms that our framework performs well in terms of accuracy and real-time.

References

1. Biber, P., Strasser, W.: The normal distributions transform: a new approach to laser scan matching. In: Proceedings 2003 IEEE/RSJ International Conference on Intelligent Robots and Systems (IROS 2003) (Cat. No. 03CH37453), vol. 3, pp. 2743–2748 (2003). https://doi.org/10.1109/IROS.2003.1249285
2. Dellaert, F.: Factor graphs and GTSAM: a hands-on introduction (2012)
3. Deschaud, J.E.: IMLS-SLAM: scan-to-model matching based on 3D data. In: 2018 IEEE International Conference on Robotics and Automation (ICRA), pp. 2480–2485 (2018)
4. Ding, W., Hou, S., Gao, H., Wan, G., Song, S.: Lidar inertial odometry aided robust Lidar localization system in changing city scenes. In: 2020 IEEE International Conference on Robotics and Automation (ICRA), pp. 4322–4328 (2020)
5. Dubé, R., Cramariuc, A., Dugas, D., Nieto, J., Siegwart, R., Cadena, C.: SegMap: 3D segment mapping using data-driven descriptors. In: Robotics: Science and Systems (RSS) (2018)
6. Egger, P., Borges, P.V.K., Catt, G., Pfrunder, A., Siegwart, R., Dubé, R.: Posemap: lifelong, multi-environment 3D Lidar localization. In: 2018 IEEE/RSJ International Conference on Intelligent Robots and Systems (IROS), pp. 3430–3437 (2018)
7. Gentil, C.L., Vidal-Calleja, T., Huang, S.: IN2LAMA: inertial Lidar localisation and mapping. In: 2019 International Conference on Robotics and Automation (ICRA), pp. 6388–6394 (2019)
8. Koide, K., Miura, J., Menegatti, E.: A portable 3D LIDAR-based system for long-term and wide-area people behavior measurement. Int. J. Adv. Rob. Syst. **16**(2), 1–13 (2019)
9. Lu, W., Zhou, Y., Wan, G., Hou, S., Song, S.: L3-Net: towards learning based LiDAR localization for autonomous driving. In: 2019 IEEE/CVF Conference on Computer Vision and Pattern Recognition (CVPR), pp. 6392–6391 (2019)
10. Rozenberszki, D., Majdik, A.L.: LOL: Lidar-only odometry and localization in 3D point cloud maps. In: 2020 IEEE International Conference on Robotics and Automation (ICRA), pp. 4379–4385 (2020)
11. Rusinkiewicz, S., Levoy, M.: Efficient variants of the ICP algorithm. In: Proceedings Third International Conference on 3-D Digital Imaging and Modeling, pp. 145–152 (2001). https://doi.org/10.1109/IM.2001.924423
12. Shan, T., Englot, B.: LEGO-LOAM: lightweight and ground-optimized Lidar odometry and mapping on variable terrain. In: 2018 IEEE/RSJ International Conference on Intelligent Robots and Systems (IROS), pp. 4758–4765 (2018)
13. Wang, P., Yang, R., Cao, B., Xu, W., Lin, Y.: DeLS-3D: deep localization and segmentation with a 3D semantic map. In: 2018 IEEE/CVF Conference on Computer Vision and Pattern Recognition (CVPR), pp. 5860–5869 (2018)
14. Zhang, J., Singh, S.: LOAM: Lidar odometry and mapping in real-time. In: Robotics: Science and Systems (RSS) (2014)

Toward Robust Visual Odometry Using Prior 2D Map Information and Multiple Hypothesis Particle Filtering

Sarah Edwards[✉], Lyudmila Mihaylova, Jonathan M. Aitken, and Sean Anderson

Department of Automatic Control and Systems Engineering, University of Sheffield, Sheffield S1 3JD, UK
sedwards4@sheffield.ac.uk

Abstract. Visual odometry can be used to estimate the pose of a robot from current and recent video frames. A problem with these methods is that they drift over time due to the accumulation of estimation errors at each time-step. In this short paper we propose and briefly demonstrate the potential benefit of using prior 2D, top-down map information combined with multiple hypothesis particle filtering to correct visual odometry estimates. The results demonstrate a substantial improvement in robustness and accuracy over the sole use of visual odometry.

Keywords: Visual odometry · Deep learning · Multiple hypothesis · Particle filter · Map prior

1 Introduction

Visual odometry (VO) is a popular method of pose estimation in mobile robots and there are many methods for this including key-frame optimisation [8] and recently deep learning [3,6]. The deep learning methods are advantageous because they avoid the need for camera calibration and online optimisation used in key-frame methods, although they tend to be less accurate than the optimisation methods.

One problem that is common to all VO methods (and indeed all odometry methods) is that the pose estimate drifts over time due to the accumulation of estimation errors. Yet, there is often additional information we can use to help reduce drift, such as prior map information. This is true in scenarios of driver-less cars (road maps), mobile robots moving along corridors in indoor environments (architectural floor-plans), and pipe inspection robots such as in the oil, gas, sewer/water and nuclear industries (where pipe network plans tend

This work is supported by the UK's Engineering and Physical Sciences Research Council (EPSRC) Programme Grant EP/S016813/1 Pervasive Sensing for Buried Pipes (Pipebots) https://pipebots.ac.uk.

© Springer Nature Switzerland AG 2021
C. Fox et al. (Eds.): TAROS 2021, LNAI 13054, pp. 188–192, 2021.
https://doi.org/10.1007/978-3-030-89177-0_19

to be readily available). In all these cases we potentially have prior information in the form of a top-down 2D view of the map, and the mobile agent is largely constrained to move along routes in this map. So, it appears attractive to make use of this information in scenarios where it is available. This idea is used in a VO system in [1], where the probability of being located in a discrete road segment is estimated using a particle filter.

The algorithm developed in this paper fuses VO with prior 2D map information using multiple hypothesis particle filtering: when a moving agent reaches a junction in the map, multiple particle filters are used to fuse the VO data with each possible route away from the junction. The most likely hypothesis is probabilistically selected using the distribution of particles for each filter, which acts as a likelihood function, similar to methods that have been used in multiple model particle filtering for fault detection [4]. The results demonstrate that simply using knowledge of the map alone with VO does not lead to successful pose estimation but instead a multiple hypothesis method must be used to ensure accuracy and robustness.

2   Methods

The proposed method of map hypothesis switching is intended for robots or vehicles operating in environments that highly constrain the agent's motion but whose exact layout is uncertain. Examples of such situations are road or pipe networks where the location of junctions and the connections between junctions are approximately known and available in the form of a 2D, top-down map.

The system performs VO via a deep network similar to those presented in [5,6] using optic flow calculated via the Horn-Shunck method. The VO outputs are filtered via a particle filter that uses accelerometer and gyroscope data as the basis for a state-space model.

The map provided to the system is represented as a set of coordinates of known junctions with connections between each junction. The system uses the straight lines between each pair of connected junctions as its prior map. Multiple models are instantiated upon reaching a junction and we make one important assumption that the system can identify when it has reached a junction via a separate system. A standard method of multiple model particle filtering, as in [4], is adapted here to switch between particle filter models that express different hypotheses, where the distribution of particles for each filter acts as a likelihood function, and this is used to probabilistically select the most likely hypothesis.

We use the KITTI data set [2] consisting of camera and GPS data from a car, to both train the visual odometry and test the multi hypothesis system. We use different sequences for training and testing, to ensure testing is independent.

3   Results

In order to evaluate our proposed algorithm we tested 1. a system that used VO only, 2. a VO system using a map with a single particle filter, and 3. a

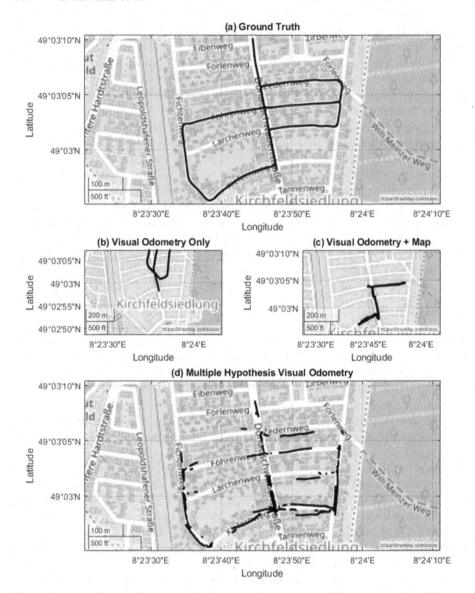

Fig. 1. Comparison of ground truth GPS vehicle data with pose estimation algorithms on independent validation data (KITTI, sequence 5). (a) Ground truth. (b) Visual odometry only (note that the pose estimate exits the area of the ground truth but we retain a comparable zoom-level to the other plots for clarity). (c) Visual odometry with map information. (d) Multiple hypothesis visual odometry.

VO system using a map with multiple hypothesis particle filtering on separate test data. Figure 1 shows the ground truth and pose estimates for each method overlaid on a street map. As can be seen, the raw VO system performs poorly and a single map hypothesis results in unrecoverable failure when the system believes itself to be in the wrong section of the map. The multiple hypothesis system is generally much more accurate. This system occasionally selects an incorrect hypothesis (corresponding to the apparent gaps in location estimates in Fig. 1d) but then automatically recovers. The principal improvement of this system over simple odometry is the ability to recover from failure, however it also demonstrates an improved pose accuracy, with VO alone resulting in a mean position and heading error of 335.2 m (343.20) and -1.65 (-2.20) radians respectively and a final positional error of 230.4 m, and the multi hypothesis system resulting in mean errors of 49.2 m (40.3) and 0.28 (0) radians and a final error of 0.85 m.

4 Conclusions

In this work we have presented a novel VO method that uses prior 2D map information and multiple hypothesis particle filtering. We demonstrated that the method was more accurate and robust than solely using VO, and that using multiple hypothesis particle filtering substantially improved on using a single particle filter with map information, particularly in it's ability to recover from errors. In future work we aim to resolve the problem of junction recognition in order to make a fully standalone algorithm and also develop a compact system that can run in real-time on mobile hardware.

Additionally we aim to address the system's main weakness, that of temporarily selecting an incorrect hypothesis, which occurs regularly after junctions. Improvements here may come from including additional information in the probability calculations, such as designed or learned features from each hypotheses parameters similar to [7], or from more complex assessments of each hypotheses probabilities compared to each other and possibly the system's states and sensor inputs.

References

1. Brubaker, M.A., Geiger, A., Urtasun, R.: Map-based probabilistic visual self-localization. IEEE Trans. Pattern Anal. Mach. Intell. **38**(4), 652–665 (2016)
2. Geiger, A., Lenz, P., Stiller, C., Urtasun, R.: Vision meets robotics: the KITTI dataset. Int. J. Robot. Res. **32**(11), 1231–1237 (2013)
3. Han, L., Lin, Y., Du, G., Lian, S.: DeepVIO: self-supervised deep learning of monocular visual inertial odometry using 3D geometric constraints. In: 2019 IEEE/RSJ International Conference on Intelligent Robots and Systems (IROS), pp. 6906–6913 (2019)
4. Kadirkamanathan, V., Li, P., Kirubarajan, T.: Sequential Monte Carlo filtering vs. the IMM estimator for fault detection and isolation in nonlinear systems. In: Willett, P.K., Kirubarajan, T. (eds.) Component and Systems Diagnostics, Prognosis, and Health Management, vol. 4389, pp. 263–274. International Society for Optics and Photonics, SPIE (2001)

5. Konda, K., Memisevic, R.: Learning visual odometry with a convolutional network. In: The 10th International Conference on Computer Vision Theory and Applications (VISAPP), pp. 486–490 (2015)
6. Muller, P., Savakis, A.: Flowdometry: an optical flow and deep learning based approach to visual odometry. In: 2017 IEEE Winter Conference on Applications of Computer Vision (WACV), pp. 624–631. IEEE (2017)
7. Ossig, D.L., Kurzenberger, K., Speidel, S.A., Henning, K.U., Sawodny, O.: Sensor fault detection using an extended Kalman filter and machine learning for a vehicle dynamics controller. In: The 46th Annual Conference of the IEEE Industrial Electronics Society, IECON 2020, pp. 361–366. IEEE (2020)
8. Scaramuzza, D., Fraundorfer, F.: Visual odometry [tutorial]. IEEE Robot. Autom. Mag. 18(4), 80–92 (2011)

Comparison of Concentrated and Distributed Compliant Elements in a 3D Printed Gripper

Jordan Cormack[1]([✉])[ID], Mohammad Fotouhi[2][ID], Guy Adams[3],
and Tony Pipe[1][ID]

[1] Bristol Robotics Laboratory, University of the West of England, Bristol, UK
jordan.cormack@uwe.ac.uk
[2] School of Engineering, University of Glasgow, Glasgow, Scotland
[3] HP Development UK Ltd., Bristol, UK

Abstract. Compliant elements overcome many of the shortfalls of using 3D printing to create mechanisms, as print artefacts such as 'stair stepping' can cause issues with conventional joints. One of the key decisions when designing a compliant mechanism is choosing to either concentrate the compliance into a small region that resembles a conventional hinge, or distribute it over a larger area. This research details the simulated deformation and stress difference between these two types of compliant elements for a 3D printed gripper. Results show that for the same gripper deformation, the distributed compliant element experiences much less stress, at the expense of stiffness in secondary loading directions.

Keywords: 3D printing · Compliant mechanism · Gripper

1 Introduction

One of the benefits to 3D printing grippers, is the ability to produce complex geometries which would be difficult to create using conventional manufacturing methods. The majority of 3D printing processes create parts which are built up of many individual layers, which causes an effect known as stair-stepping on surfaces which are not parallel or perpendicular to the print bed (Fig. 1). This effect can cause problems with parts which need to interface with each other like revolute joints, which can require calibration to perform well when 3D printed [2]. Printing curved surfaces parallel to the print bed can reduce stair stepping, but this is not always possible for every joint on a part. Although work has been done to improve the performance of 3D printed conventional joints [4,7], issues such as excess material/support removal still remain. Compliant mechanisms overcome these issues by consolidating multiple parts into a single element featuring some form of compliance. This not only reduces the number of parts, but can also reduce or remove backlash, noise and frictional losses as well

This work was supported by HP Development UK Ltd.

© Springer Nature Switzerland AG 2021
C. Fox et al. (Eds.): TAROS 2021, LNAI 13054, pp. 193–197, 2021.
https://doi.org/10.1007/978-3-030-89177-0_20

(a) Concentrated   (b) Distributed

Fig. 1. Stair stepping   **Fig. 2.** Comparison of concentrated and distributed
compliant elements

as the need for maintenance or lubrication [5,6]. Blanes *et al.* [1] showed a single
piece gripping mechanism featuring two coils to allow rotation of the digits,
using an external pneumatic cylinder for actuation. This shows that a simple
one-piece 3D printed gripper can be created to transfer a linear input motion
to an opposed gripping motion. Compliant mechanisms can be classified into
two sub-divisions. The first and most common type is concentrated or lumped
compliance [3], which is where a mostly rigid part has small regions where elastic
deformation is concentrated as a hinge. The second type is where the compliant
region is spread over a much larger area, distributing the stress concentration and
compliance [8]. Figure 2 shows two elements, one with concentrated compliance
(2a), and one with distributed compliance (2b).

2   Compliant Gripper Simulation

Figure 3 shows the deformation of two grippers. The first features rigid elements
with compliant regions concentrated as hinges. The second is the same gripper but with sections which distribute the compliance. The same 5N load is
applied to the tab of each gripper in the −Y direction (shown by black arrow).
It can be seen that the 5N load results in approximately the same deformation
of the input tab and tips for both mechanism designs. Analysing the stress in
the compliant regions showed a maximum (von-Mises) stress of 120 MPa for the
concentrated compliance element, and 24.6 MPa for the distributed element. A
significant difference, considering how similar the overall deformation is. As the
tensile strength of many common 3D printing materials such as PLA, PETG, and
Nylon is around 50 MPa, this would cause the concentrated compliant regions to
plastically deform or break completely. Figure 4 shows von-Mises stress regions
over 10 MPa for both grippers. One observed benefit to the concentrated compliance design is that as the compliant region is much smaller, the stiffness of the
element to deflections in other axes is much higher. Figure 5 shows a simulated
comparison between deformation of the concentrated and distributed compliance
gripper mechanisms after a 5N load is applied to the side of the same tab (in
the x axis, i.e., not the direction intended for operation). It can be seen that
the distributed compliance regions allow much more deflection in this axis than
the concentrated compliance regions. The colour scales have been matched to
make visual comparison easier. The simulations assume isotropic material properties, as the gripper can be 3D printed using a process which produces isotropic
mechanical properties (such as MJF), or using an FFF process with the gripper

oriented such that the deformation will act in the plane of the layers, which will act in an essentially isotropic manor.

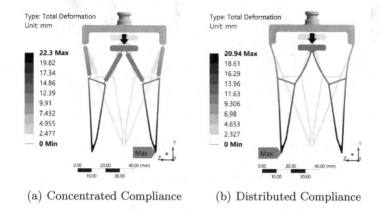

(a) Concentrated Compliance   (b) Distributed Compliance

Fig. 3. Deformation of concentrated and distributed compliance gripper

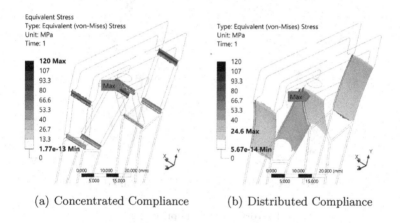

(a) Concentrated Compliance   (b) Distributed Compliance

Fig. 4. Concentrated vs distributed compliance equivalent stress capped IsoSurface

3 3D Printed Grippers

Both gripper designs were 3D printed using the Fused Filament Fabrication (FFF) process (Fig. 6). Experimental testing showed that the 3D printed compliant grippers act in the same manner as the simulated grippers, with a similar amount of deflection in the intended direction, but much less stiffness in other axes on the gripper with distributed compliance. As expected from the much higher simulated stress on the concentrated compliance gripper, plastic deformation occurs, resulting in the gripper not returning to the original position. Without limiting the deformation to prevent this, the lifespan of the gripper would likely be much lower than the one with distributed compliance.

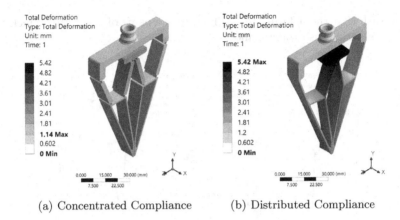

(a) Concentrated Compliance   (b) Distributed Compliance

Fig. 5. Comparison of off-axis deformation

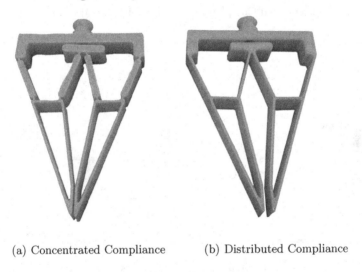

(a) Concentrated Compliance   (b) Distributed Compliance

Fig. 6. Prototype FFF 3D printed grippers

4   Conclusion

Although the concentrated compliance mechanism shows less off-axis deformation, the much higher stress causes it to plastically deform, altering the performance and likely reducing its future reliability. Distributing the compliance
across a larger region reduces the stress concentration and allows the gripper
to deform elastically without damage, but this does also make the gripper more
susceptible to deformation in other axes. Careful consideration should therefore be taken when developing one-shot 3D printed mechanisms to ensure that
the type of compliance is suitable for the desired deformation. Future simulation or experimental work into the performance of the grippers whilst interacting

with objects could show additional advantages or disadvantages between the two designs. Hybrid approaches which use a combination of concentrated and distributed compliance could also be explored, tailored based on the results found in this work.

References

1. Blanes, C., Mellado, M., Beltran, P.: Novel additive manufacturing pneumatic actuators and mechanisms for food handling grippers. Actuators **3**, 205–225 (2014)
2. Calì, J., et al.: 3D-printing of non-assembly, articulated models. ACM Trans. Graph. **31**, 1–8 (2012)
3. Chen, S., Wang, M.: Designing distributed compliant mechanisms with characteristic stiffness. In: 31st Mechanisms and Robotics Conference, Parts A and B, vol. 8 (2007)
4. Cuellar, J., Smit, G., Plettenburg, D., Zadpoor, A.: Additive manufacturing of non-assembly mechanisms. Addit. Manuf. **21**, 150–158 (2018)
5. Elgammal, A.T., Fanni, M., Mohamed, A.M.: Design and analysis of a novel 3D decoupled manipulator based on compliant pantograph for micromanipulation. J. Intell. Robot. Syst. **87**(1), 43–57 (2016). https://doi.org/10.1007/s10846-016-0452-y
6. Schotborgh, W., Kokkeler, F., Tragter, H., van Houten, F.: Dimensionless design graphs for flexure elements and a comparison between three flexure elements. Precis. Eng. **29**, 41–47 (2005)
7. Wei, X., Tian, Y., Joneja, A.: A study on revolute joints in 3D-printed non-assembly mechanisms. Rapid Prototyping J. **22**, 901–933 (2016)
8. Xu, Q.: Design and development of a novel compliant gripper with integrated position and grasping/interaction force sensing. IEEE Trans. Autom. Sci. Eng. **14**, 1415–1428 (2017)

Perception of a Humanoid Robot as an Interface for Auditory Testing

Luke Meyer[1,2(✉)] ⓘ, Gloria Araiza-Illan[1,2] ⓘ, Laura Rachman[1,2] ⓘ,
Etienne Gaudrain[1,3] ⓘ, and Deniz Başkent[1,2] ⓘ

[1] Department of Otorhinolaryngology/Head and Neck Surgery, University Medical Centre Groningen, University of Groningen, Groningen, The Netherlands
L.Meyer@rug.nl
[2] University Medical Centre Groningen, W.J. Kolff Institute for Biomedical Engineering and Materials Science, University of Groningen, Groningen, The Netherlands
[3] Lyon Neuroscience Research Centre, CNRS UMR 5292, INSERM UMRS 1028, Université Claude Bernard Lyon 1, Université de Lyon, Lyon, France

Abstract. Perception tasks that require long and frequent testing can result in a loss of attention and focus, contributing to erroneous and inconsistent data. To maintain engagement and improve reliability of data, a more interactive interface could be used. This study aims to investigate if a humanoid NAO robot could provide such an interface to improve or maintain engagement during testing. More specifically, human-robot interaction (HRI) will be explored when performing various auditory perception tasks, played in the form of games, on the NAO robot. Evaluation of the HRI will be performed using questionnaires derived from the system usability, Godspeed, and similarity-attraction scales, as well as through video analysis. Future research will extend the evaluation of the HRI to children and aim to further improve the engagement and social acceptability of the NAO robot as a game interface.

Keywords: HRI · Auditory perception · Robot perception · Task engagement

1 Introduction

Maintaining focus and engagement during perception tasks that require long or frequent repetitions can become challenging for individuals with limited attention spans, such as children [1]. More interactive interfaces, such as humanoid robots, could help, as they have been shown to be adept at retaining attention in comparison to more commonly used laptops [2]. As a preliminary investigation into engagement when using a humanoid robot, this study aims to explore the impression adults have of a NAO V5 humanoid robot as an interactive interface for games designed for auditory perception testing. The Perception of Indexical Cues in Kids and Adults (PICKA) test battery [3] is a set of auditory perception tasks, on perception of voice and speech, as an ongoing investigation into hearing loss. To obtain reliable data, these tests – played in the form of games on a laptop – are performed frequently over relatively long testing times, often resulting

© Springer Nature Switzerland AG 2021
C. Fox et al. (Eds.): TAROS 2021, LNAI 13054, pp. 198–202, 2021.
https://doi.org/10.1007/978-3-030-89177-0_21

in a loss of concentration; thus, necessitating a more engaging interface. Maintaining engagement during the PICKA games could lead to longer testing times, providing more consistent data.

2 Experimental Design

Thirty normal hearing, proficient English speaking, locally recruited adult participants, both from Dutch and international backgrounds, thus far between the ages of 19–38 (24.04 ± 5.26) years, play one of the four PICKA games on either the laptop or NAO interface, randomly determined, followed by the same game on the other interface. Due to the game duration and repetitive procedure, the study is divided into two experiments in which two of the games are paired together. Which games participants play is also randomly determined; however, counterbalancing was performed across both experiments for games and interfaces. When using the NAO, it both plays the stimuli for the game and logs responses, given through the tactile sensors, from participants. In comparison, when using the laptop, stimuli are presented from the laptop speakers and responses are given using the laptop screen and external mouse.

Each of the four PICKA games is composed of an introduction, a training phase, a testing phase, and breaks (where applicable). At the start of each game, NAO stands up, introduces the game, and familiarizes the participant with how and where to touch the tactile sensors. Following the introduction, NAO returns to a seated position for the rest of the game. In this position, the motors and fans are switched off, making NAO much quieter and the auditory stimuli easier to hear.

Prior to the experiment, participants are asked to complete the revised personality index (neo-PIR) questionnaire [4] to obtain an indication of their extroversion/introversion, as this would provide an additional parameter for analysing how one's personality influences their interaction with the robot. If a trend exists, this could potentially be used to adapt the interaction based on an individual's personality [5] to improve the level of engagement, as well as to enhance the interaction. Additionally, the Negative Attitude towards Robots Scale (NARS) [4] questionnaire is included to account for potential factors that may influence the interaction and used in covariate analyses. Video recordings of the participants are taken from two cameras of both the laptop and NAO versions of the games. One video camera is placed behind the laptop/NAO to capture the face of the participant, and another to the side of the participant to capture the participant's movements and interactions with the interfaces. After the completion of the game on both interfaces, the participant is asked to complete a new set of questionnaires to evaluate their experience with the robot and the laptop. Questionnaires include the system usability scale (SUS) [6], questions about the experiment, the Godspeed questionnaire [7], and the similarity-attraction questionnaire [8]. Evaluation of the HRI is performed using both questionnaires and video recordings.

2.1 Voice Cue Sensitivity

Three pseudowords are presented, one of which sounds different to the other two in a three-interval three-alternative-forced-choice paradigm. Participants must identify which of the three stimuli was different by touching NAO's right hand, head, or left hand (for first, second and third stimuli, respectively). The acoustic difference between the stimuli becomes progressively smaller as the participant answers correctly. If an incorrect response is given, the acoustic difference becomes greater, making it easier to discern. To obtain reliable data, this paradigm is presented four times separated by a short break, totalling 30–40 min. When NAO is used, it offers a break to the participant, to which they verbally reply. If they take the break, NAO offers them to join in a stretch routine. If not, NAO remains seated for a short time before asking them if they are ready to continue. In the laptop version of the game, progress is displayed with a progress bar, as well as a running tally of correct responses. The displaying of a progress bar is not currently implemented on NAO, and thus to accommodate for the lack of progress tracking, NAO praises participants if they provide consistent correct answers or motivates them if incorrect responses are given. NAO also provides visual feedback for each answer, nodding for a correct response or shaking its head for an incorrect response.

2.2 Gender Categorization

An English word is presented to the participant, and they must subjectively categorize the gender (male or female) of the spoken voice. After the stimulus is presented, NAO indicates which of its hands can be touched for which gender (they are randomized after each stimulus to avoid association of a gender to a specific hand). No visual feedback is presented to the participant after their responses. The eyes, however, do change colour to indicate when a response can be given, and again when the response has been stored. Since this game is much shorter (8–10 min) than the voice cue sensitivity, no breaks are offered.

2.3 Emotion Identification

This game presents the participant with a nonsensical sentence spoken with either a happy, angry, or sad voice. The participant uses NAO's hands and head to input their responses. In comparison to the gender categorization game, the hand-emotion pair is kept constant as it could confuse participants if randomized each time, or significantly increase the duration if NAO indicates the pair after each stimulus. Identifying the emotion of the voice is not subjective; thus, visual feedback is provided after an answer is given. Again, no breaks are offered to the participant as the game is relatively short (5–10 min).

2.4 Speech-on-Speech Perception

This game uses an adapted version of the coordinate response measure (CRM) [9]. A sentence containing a colour and number is presented to the participant, who uses a tablet with a coloured and numbered grid to indicate the heard colour and number. A tablet is used here as there are more combinations of colours and numbers than inputs on NAO. The stimuli also contain masker signals to simulate background speech, varying the difficulty of identifying the colour and number. Half-way through the game (total duration is 15–20 min), NAO offers an optional break to the participant, identical to that described above. Visual feedback is provided to the participant based on their responses.

2.5 Video Analysis

A combination of social cues described by Giuliani et al. [10] and Desideri et al. [11], including both verbal and non-verbal cues, are used to code videos of both the laptop and robot interfaces. Segments between one to two minutes from each part of the PICKA games are taken for each participant, which are then randomized and merged into a single video. Four reviewers are used to code the videos, which are divided such that each game from each participant is coded by at least two reviewers in a fully crossed coding design.

3 Further Work

As this study is still underway, results cannot yet be reported. However, it is expected that the perception of NAO as the interface for the PICKA games will be favoured over the laptop interface. It is also expected that the results of the questionnaires will correlate with the video analysis of the interaction; i.e., a higher useability score, similarity-attraction, and likeability of NAO will also be present as longer maintained engagement and improved enjoyment with the robot. Furthermore, it is expected that the results of the neo-PIR would give an indication toward future adaptations; i.e., how the interaction could be improved for introverted/extroverted individuals.

Further investigation will include playing the PICKA games on the NAO robot with more vulnerable populations, starting with normal hearing children followed by hard-of-hearing children. This will provide additional data on how the interaction can be further adapted to better establish and maintain engagement with them. Anticipated challenges regarding the next phase primarily concern children becoming distracted when using the robot and thus contradicting the intention of the NAO robot, or the duration of the test protocol being too long for the limited attention spans of children.

References

1. Gaudrain, E., Başkent, D.: Discrimination of voice pitch and vocal-tract length in cochlear implant users. Ear Hear. **39**(2), 226–237 (2018)
2. Looije, R., van der Zalm, A., Neerincx, M.A., Beun, R.-J.: Help, I need some body the effect of embodiment on playful learning. In: 2012 IEEE RO-MAN: The 21st IEEE International Symposium on Robot and Human Interactive Communication, Paris, France, pp. 718–724. IEEE (2012). http://ieeexplore.ieee.org/document/6343836/
3. Nagels, L., Gaudrain, E., Vickers, D., Hendriks, P., Başkent, D.: Development of voice perception is dissociated across gender cues in school-age children. Sci. Rep. **10**(1), 5074 (2020)
4. Ivaldi, S., Lefort, S., Peters, J., Chetouani, M., Provasi, J., Zibetti, E.: Towards engagement models that consider individual factors in HRI: on the relation of extroversion and negative attitude towards robots to gaze and speech during a human–robot assembly task: experiments with the iCub humanoid. Int. J. Soc. Robot. **9**(1), 63–86 (2017).
5. Bernier, E.P., Scassellati, B.: The similarity-attraction effect in human-robot interaction. In: 2010 IEEE 9th International Conference on Development and Learning, Ann Arbor, MI, USA, pp. 286–290. IEEE (2010). http://ieeexplore.ieee.org/document/5578828/

6. Brooke, J.: SUS - a quick and dirty usability scale. In: Jordan, P.W., Thomas, B., Weermeester, B.A., McClellend, A.L. (eds.) Usability Evaluation in Industry. Taylor and Francis, London (1996)

7. Bartneck, C., Kulić, D., Croft, E., Zoghbi, S.: Measurement instruments for the anthropomorphism, animacy, likeability, perceived intelligence, and perceived safety of robots. Int. J. Soc. Robot. 1(1), 71–81 (2009)

8. Lee, K.M., Peng, W., Jin, S.-A., Yan, C.: Can robots manifest personality?: an empirical test of personality recognition, social responses, and social presence in human-robot interaction. J. Commun. 56(4), 754–772 (2006)

9. Eddins, D.A., Liu, C.: Psychometric properties of the coordinate response measure corpus with various types of background interference. J. Acoust. Soc. Am. 131(2), EL177–183 (2012)

10. Giuliani, M., Mirnig, N., Stollnberger, G., Stadler, S., Buchner, R., Tscheligi, M.: Systematic analysis of video data from different human–robot interaction studies: a categorization of social signals during error situations. Front Psychol. 6, 931 (2015). http://journal.frontiersin.org/Article/10.3389/fpsyg.2015.00931/abstract

11. Desideri, L., Ottaviani, C., Malavasi, M., di Marzio, R., Bonifacci, P.: Emotional processes in human-robot interaction during brief cognitive testing. Comput. Hum. Behav. 90, 331–342 (2019)

Deep Learning Traversability Estimator for Mobile Robots in Unstructured Environments

Marco Visca[1]($\boxtimes$), Sampo Kuutti[1], Roger Powell[2], Yang Gao[3], and Saber Fallah[1]

[1] Connected and Autonomous Vehicles Lab (CAV Lab), University of Surrey, Guildford GU2 7XH, UK
m.visca@surrey.ac.uk
[2] Cybernetics Group, Remote Applications in Challenging Environments, UK Atomic Energy Authority, Culham Science Centre, Abingdon OX14 3DB, UK
[3] Space Technology for Autonomous and Robotic Laboratory (STAR LAB), Surrey Space Centre, University of Surrey, Guildford GU2 7XH, UK

Abstract. Terrain traversability analysis plays a major role in ensuring safe robotic navigation in unstructured environments. However, real-time constraints frequently limit the accuracy of online tests especially in scenarios where realistic robot-terrain interactions are complex to model. In this context, we propose a deep learning framework trained in an end-to-end fashion from elevation maps and trajectories to estimate the occurrence of failure events. The network is first trained and tested in simulation over synthetic maps generated by the OpenSimplex algorithm. The prediction performance of the Deep Learning framework is illustrated by being able to retain over 94% recall of the original simulator at 30% of the computational time. Finally, the network is transferred and tested on real elevation maps collected by the SEEKER consortium during the Martian rover test trial in the Atacama desert in Chile. We show that transferring and fine-tuning of an application-independent pre-trained model retains better performance than training uniquely on scarcely available real data.

Keywords: Deep Learning · Transfer learning · Mobile robotics

1 Introduction

Autonomous traversability analysis of unstructured terrains is a crucial task in many sectors, such as rescue robots for disaster areas, agriculture, nuclear plants,

This work has been carried out within the framework of the EUROfusion Consortium and has received funding from the Euratom research and training programme under grant agreement No. 633053. The views and opinions expressed herein do not necessarily reflect those of the European Commission. The authors are grateful to the Autonomous Systems Group of RAL SPACE for providing the SEEKER dataset.

© Springer Nature Switzerland AG 2021
C. Fox et al. (Eds.): TAROS 2021, LNAI 13054, pp. 203–213, 2021.
https://doi.org/10.1007/978-3-030-89177-0_22

and space exploration. The primary goal of traversability analysis is to ensure the safety of the robotic system and reduce its dependency on human control by autonomously assessing the surrounding terrain. Moreover, in contrast to navigation in structured environments, where a clear distinction between obstacle and non-obstacle is possible, unstructured natural terrains present continuous difficulty values which mostly depend on the specific robot mobility capabilities. This makes the definition of safe trajectories considerably more challenging as the algorithm has to take more numerous and complex metrics into account. On the other hand, real-time navigation requirements often impose stringent constraints on the overall software complexity.

In this context, several terrain analysis algorithms, which differently trade-off between accuracy and computational speed, have been proposed [13]. Among them, square-grid cost maps based on geometric analysis are often considered the most successfully deployed on real systems [3, 16]. The main reason for their success is their implementation simplicity and relatively low computational workload. However, they often make use of overly conservative assumptions which could lead to sub-optimal navigation performance [3, 16]. Other works have proposed to use accurate physics-based simulators to assess the traversability of trajectories [6]. However, in spite of their accuracy which allows to maximise the optimality of trajectory planning, their computational workload is often unbearable for on-board resources and real-time navigation.

In recent years, deep learning methods have gained an increasing popularity for their ability of extracting features from high-dimensional inputs and their efficient parallel computing [8]. In this context, deep learning has demonstrated remarkable capabilities to improve the autonomy of mobile robots [9]. Other works have proposed to exploit deep learning models to estimate mobile robot traversability metrics [1,2]. However, these methods often assess traversability over arbitrary-shaped patch of terrains (e.g. circular, or squared). Moreover, state-of-the-art deep learning methods often require substantial amounts of data to provide sensible predictions, while their availability is often limited for many robotic applications of interest.

In this paper, we propose a deep learning model to estimate traversability metrics from a simulator (Sect. 2). Our formulation has the advantage to explicitly address learning over feasible trajectories, thereby considering the robot mobility constraints and providing direct information in terms of trajectory planning. Furthermore, we propose to address the problem of data scarcity by developing a synthetic dataset based on the OpenSimplex noise algorithm (Sect. 3). We show that, despite some degradation in performance, a model trained on the synthetic dataset can retain characteristics of generic unstructured terrains and, thus, be used as the baseline model of a real use-case scenario. We show evidence of this by transferring on real data from the SEEKER Martian rover test trial in the Atacama desert in Chile and comparing the synthetic model performance with training based solely on the limited amount of available real data (Sect. 4).

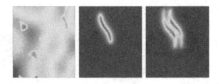

Fig. 1. The three input layers. From the left: the terrain elevation map, the trajectory centre, and the wheel trace.

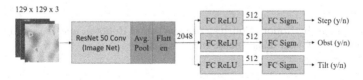

Fig. 2. The proposed CNN architecture.

2 Traversability Prediction Model

We propose to formulate the traversability prediction as an image classification problem by using a standard Convolutional Neural Network (CNN) architecture. This choice is motivated by the well-demonstrated CNNs' capabilities to process and find patterns in high-dimensional spatial inputs [4]. Moreover, we propose to assess terrain traversability directly over feasible trajectories. In this way, failure prediction can be achieved by considering the actual robot mobility constraints, thereby increasing the accuracy of prediction. The remainder of this section illustrates the proposed methodology.

2.1 Input Features

To enable the use of CNN architectures, an approach is devised which gives the terrain and trajectory input features a three-channel image-like representation. Each channel is a 129 × 129 grid, where each pixel position corresponds to an (x,y) coordinate with respect to the rover centre (between −4 and +4 m) and the robot is assumed positioned in the centre of the map and oriented in the positive direction of the vertical axis. A visual description of the three channels is illustrated in Fig. 1. The three channels from left to right are: (1) the terrain elevations, where the value of each cell is the normalized z elevation value for that (x,y) coordinate, (2) the trajectory left from the robot on the map, where the channel has its peak (value of 1) at the robot centre and exponentially decreases to 0 at the wheel track, and (3) the trace left from the wheels on the map, where each trace has its peak at the wheel centre and exponentially decreases to 0 outside the wheel; furthermore, a higher value is given to the cells where both the front and rear wheels pass.

In this way, the feature processing can be addressed on regions of the terrain of particular relevance to the failure prediction (i.e. the regions under the robot

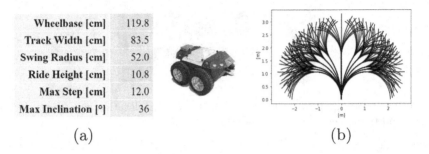

Wheelbase [cm]	119.8
Track Width [cm]	83.5
Swing Radius [cm]	52.0
Ride Height [cm]	10.8
Max Step [cm]	12.0
Max Inclination [°]	36

(a)   (b)

Fig. 3. (a) Seekur Jr. Robot (Courtesy of Generation Robots), and (b) portion of the robot action space for no initial point turn rotation.

ride and the wheels) and directly over feasible trajectories. Hence, each $129 \times 129 \times 3$ image represents one terrain-trajectory input feature that is fed to the neural network for traversability prediction.

2.2 Network Architecture

Figure 2 illustrates the proposed neural network architecture. The ResNet50 network [5] pre-trained on ImageNet [12] is chosen as the baseline of the prediction model. This choice is motivated by the remarkable performance demonstrated by Imagenet pre-trained residual networks as baseline architectures for transfer learning problem. Indeed, although our inputs are quite dissimilar from ImageNet images, exploiting pre-learned low level features (e.g. vertical or horizontal edges, which are common to all image classification problems) has proved to give faster convergence than training from scratch [15]. Conversely, the original top Fully Connected (FC) layer is removed and replaced with three randomly initialized FC layers to learn the application-dependent features (one for each failure event as described in Sect. 2.3). Each FC layer has 512 neurons and randomly initialized weights. Finally, three FC layers with sigmoid activation functions provide the failure predictions.

2.3 Robot Model and Failure Events

A simplified kinematic robot model is developed in Python to emulate the robot navigation over unstructured terrains. The dimensions and the mobility capabilities of the robot model are selected according to the 4-wheel skid-steering Seekur Jr robot [10]. Its main features are summarised in Fig. 3a. Hence, each trajectory is defined according to the mobility capability of our robot as a combination of an initial point turn rotation (18 rotations for multiple of 20° including no rotation) followed by two arcs of length 1.65 m and different radius (13 different possibilities). This leads to a total of 3042 possible trajectories 3.3 m long each. Figure 3b illustrates a portion of the action space for no initial rotation.

Three failure events are defined: *step*, *obstacle*, and *tilt*. Failure for *step* occurs when the differential elevation of the terrain underneath the robot wheels for two

Algorithm 1. Generating natural terrains with OpenSimplex

1: **for** all x,y **do**
2:    $m = noise2d(x * \alpha_m, y * \alpha_m) * \beta_m + \gamma_m$
3:    $p = (noise2d(x * \alpha_p, y * \alpha_p) * \beta_p + \gamma_p)^\delta$
4:    $w = intrp(noise2d(x * \alpha_w, y * \alpha_w) * \beta_w + \gamma_w, u, d)$
5:    $Z(x,y) = p * w + m * (1 - w)$
6: **end for**
7: **return** Z

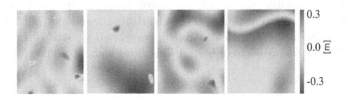

Fig. 4. Examples of $8\,\mathrm{m} \times 8\,\mathrm{m}$ maps generated using the OpenSimplex algorithm.

consecutive time steps is above the maximum traversable step of the robot. Failure for *obstacle* occurs if one or more of the terrain elevation points underneath the robot base is higher than the robot ride height. Finally, failure for *tilt* occurs if the inclination of the robot with respect to the vertical direction is above the maximum traversable inclination. To reduce the computational workload, the dynamics of the system are not taken into account. This is a reasonable assumption for robotics navigation at low speed (which could be the case in some realistic scenarios, such as planetary exploration and nuclear reactor maintenance) [7,16]. Traverse is simulated by placing the robot on sequential trajectory points (equally spaced at 6 cm intervals along each arc) and computing for each one of them the robot static pose and orientation and the elevation of the points under the rover base. Hence, the occurrence of the three failure events is recorded for each combination of terrain and trajectory.

3   Dataset Generation

3.1   OpenSimplex Synthetic Maps Generation

To reduce the data scarcity problem of mobile robot applications, synthetic maps are generated using the OpenSimplex noise algorithm, a popular approach to generate realistic unstructured environments [14]. In this work, the OpenSimplex Python API is used along with three filtering techniques to render realistic terrains. A description of the approach is illustrated in Algorithm 1. The *noise2d* function is the Python API which takes as input an (x,y) coordinate and outputs a number in $[-1,1]$ according to the OpenSimplex algorithm. Hence, additional heuristic parameters are used to filter the result of Opensimplex. Specifically, α_m, α_p, and α_w act on the noise frequency, β_m, β_p, and β_w scale the output, while γ_m, γ_p, γ_w offset the output. In this way, α_m, β_m, and γ_m are set in Line

2 to control the generation of obstacles. Line 3 controls the generation of plain regions by using a smoothing coefficient $\delta \in [0,1]$ in addition to the α_p, β_p, and γ_p parameters. Line 4 controls the interpolation between obstacles and plains, where *intrp* is a function returning 1 if the first argument is larger than u, 0 if it is lower than d, or linearly interpolates between 0 and 1 otherwise. Finally, Line 5 combines the results of the previous three operations by interpolating between obstacles and plain regions and assigning the elevation value to the elevation matrix Z. The implementation of Algorithm 1, with the parameters used in this paper, is made available at UNSTR-NAV. We remark that the process is fully automated and, by different tuning of the algorithm parameters, different terrain conditions can be achieved, such as rough, wavy, and smooth terrains, as well as mountains and depressions. Figure 4 illustrates some examples of generated maps.

3.2 Dataset Collection and Training

A total of 56840 synthetic elevation maps is generated with the method described in Sect. 3.1. Then, the robot traverses each map with 3042 trajectories and collects failure events with the method described in Sect. 2.3. The resulting dataset is composed of approximately 1.7e8 samples. The dataset is randomly divided among training (90%), validation (8%), and test (2%) datasets. Moreover, since safe trajectories are considerably more numerous than failures for each terrain (90.4% against 9.6%), a reduced and better balanced subset is extracted for training and validation to avoid excessive bias in prediction (5.7e5 and 4.9e4 samples respectively). Conversely, all maps and trajectories of the test set are retained to assess final performance (3.4e6 samples).

The network is trained by means of supervised learning and binary cross-entropy loss function [11]. The parameters used for training are: RMSprop optimizer, learning rate $1e-4$, dropout 20%, and L2 regularization 0.001. During the first epoch, only the 3 FC layers are trained, while the ResNet weights are kept frozen. Then, the whole network is unfrozen and trained for 10 epochs.

4 Results

4.1 Prediction Performance - Synthetic Dataset

The results of the trained model on the synthetic test dataset are illustrated in Table 1. An overall accuracy of 98% can be observed, with the accuracy of each failure event above 96%. However, since safe and unsafe trajectories are extremely unbalanced in the test set (roughly 1e7 vs 4e5 samples respectively), accuracy by itself can not be considered as a representative metric. For this reason, recall, precision, and F1 score are used to provide a more informed representation of the actual model performance. Specifically, an overall high recall (94.4%), and low precision (68.4%) are observed, with a consequent F1 score of 79%. This means that the network tends to be conservative, being able to correctly predict the majority of dangerous trajectories, but at a price of relatively

Table 1. Synthetic dataset model performance

(a) Confusion Matrices

Step	Pred. Safe	Pred. Fail
True Safe	3126951	113457
True Fail	13615	201689

Obstacle	Pred. Safe	Pred. Fail
True Safe	3211837	53842
True Fail	9644	180389

Tilt	Pred. Safe	Pred. Fail
True Safe	3425479	15806
True Fail	163	14264

(b) Classification Performance

	Acc.	Recall	Prec.	F1 Score
Step	0.963	0.937	0.640	0.760
Obstacle	0.982	0.950	0.770	0.850
Tilt	0.995	0.989	0.474	0.641
Overall	0.980	0.944	0.684	0.793

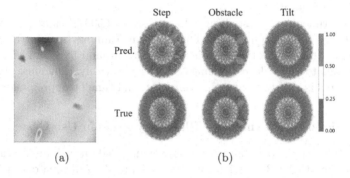

(a)   (b)

Fig. 5. Qualitative example of events prediction. (a) Synthetic elevation map, (b) prediction (top) and ground truth (bottom) of step, obstacle, and tilt probability.

high false-positive rate. A possible explanation for the low network precision could depend on the high sensitiveness of a correct prediction to small variations in the image. Indeed, even just one different pixel in the elevation map could lead the same trajectory to be safe or unsafe, making it a relatively challenging image classification problem. Therefore, while the model could have successfully learned macro-associations of elevation points and trajectories to safe or unsafe areas, it might struggle to seize much more subtle local differences. However, the tendency to conservativeness is not excessively detrimental for the specific application of robotic navigation as long as safety is ensured. For instance, an increased rate of false alarms can be tolerated if it results in reliable identification of dangerous trajectories.

A qualitative example of the failure prediction is illustrated in Fig. 5. The image on the left represents the elevation map under analysis, while each subsequent image represents the robot action space (i.e. 3042 different trajectories from the map centre) with probability of failure occurrence encoded with 3 colours (**green:** less than 0.25, **yellow:** 0.25–0.5, **red:** more than 0.5). The network accurately predicts most of the dangerous trajectories due to obstacle,

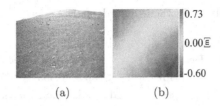

(a)   (b)

Fig. 6. (a) Image from the Atacama desert and (b) the extracted elevation map.

as wells as the absence of tilt failures. Conversely, some conservativeness can be observed for the step failure predictions. Nevertheless, trajectories laying in completely failure-free areas of the map are correctly predicted as safe which is a sign that the network has successfully learned to differentiate among macro distributions of elevation points.

The experiments are tested on a Intel Core i5 6500 Skylake and NVIDIA GeForce GTX 1050 graphic card. The resulting running time for a complete simulation of the 3042 trajectories is assessed at around 58 s and 17 s for the Python simulator and deep learning model respectively. Therefore, the deep learning model is able to reduce the computational time by approximately 70%.

4.2   Prediction Performance - Planetary Mission Use Case

In this section, the traversability estimator is analysed on real unstructured terrains from the SEEKER Martian rover test trial in the Atacama desert in Chile [17]. Figure 6a shows an example of stereo camera image from which the test site elevation maps have been generated. From the SEEKER dataset, elevation maps from 10 traverses are selected for a total of 1289 m. The real data are partitioned in 8 × 8 m elevation maps to be consistent with the dimensionality of the input data accepted by our model. An example of extracted map from the SEEKER dataset can be observed in Fig. 6b. The final dataset is composed of 645 maps, which is approximately 1.1% of the synthetic dataset size. Moreover, data augmentation is performed to help reducing the data scarcity problem (by rotating each image by 90, 180, and 270°). Hence, each sample is labelled according to the three failure events by running the traverse simulator. Finally, one of the rover traverse is randomly selected and all its samples are removed from the training set to be used as the test set.

First, the transferring performance on the SEEKER test set of our baseline model (i.e. pre-trained on the synthetic data but without further training on the real data) can be observed in Table 2. We observe that no failure for tilt is present in the real data. Therefore, we are limited in the evaluation of this event. However, the network is able to predict 99.9% of the samples correctly as tilt safe. Furthermore, also the step and obstacle classes are extremely unbalanced towards safe trajectories. Similarly to the synthetic data, the accuracy is above 99% (i.e. the model is able to classify nearly all the samples correctly as safe). Conversely, the performance for the failure prediction considerably drops both

Table 2. Real dataset transferring model performance

(a) Confusion Matrices

Step	Pred. Safe	Pred. Fail
True Safe	132880	811
True Fail	109	48
Obstacle	Pred. Safe	Pred. Fail
True Safe	132622	521
True Fail	269	436
Tilt	Pred. Safe	Pred. Fail
True Safe	133735	113
True Fail	0	0

(b) Classification Performance

	Acc.	Recall	Prec.	F1 Score
Step	0.993	0.306	0.056	0.094
Obst.	0.994	0.618	0.456	0.525
Tilt	0.999	-	-	-
Overall	0.995	0.561	0.251	0.347

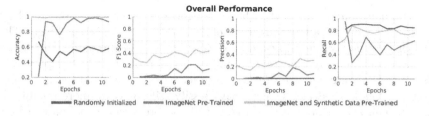

Fig. 7. Overall test performance of differently pre-trained models while training on the real data. Epoch 0 on the yellow line is the transfer learning performance (i.e. our synthetic pre-trained baseline model before training on the real data).

for the step and obstacle events. A possible explanation for this is that the synthetic data may not represent with sufficient realism many of the geometric distributions responsible for failure events in the real data. Specifically, the step event seems the most largely influenced both in terms of recall and precision (respectively 46% and 6%), while the obstacle event has been able to retain considerably better performance (recall of 62% and precision of 46%), which means that the network has learned to generalize more effectively to this type of failure in the real scenario.

Then, the performance of training on the SEEKER dataset is analysed for three differently pre-trained models: (1) a model with randomly initialized network parameters, (2) a model pre-trained on ImageNet only, and (3) our baseline model initialized with ImageNet weights and pre-trained on our synthetic dataset as described in Sects. 2 and 3. Hence, the three models are trained on the SEEKER training set for 11 epochs and the maximum F1 score on the test set is used as the convergence point of their performance. Figure 7 summarises our findings. The randomly initialized network fails to learn useful features in the dataset, resulting in poor performance. Meanwhile, the network pre-trained on ImageNet shows some initial improvement, learning useful features for its task, but overfits after 8 epochs at 21% F1 score, resulting in 54% recall and 14% precision. Conversely, the model pre-trained on our synthetic dataset improves

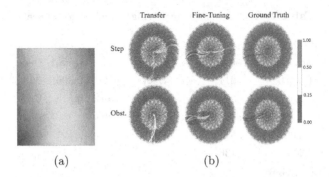

Fig. 8. (a) Elevation map from SEEKER dataset, and (b) step and obstacle predictions before and after model fine-tuning compared with the ground truth.

its performance more effectively when fine-tuning on the real dataset, resulting in a final F1 score, recall and precision of 46%, 76% and 31%, respectively. This provides evidence of the improved capability of our baseline model to transfer features of relevance to the traversability analysis problem. Most importantly, this model is able to outperform the ImageNet model in terms of recall, demonstrating it has learned how to correctly classify failure events more reliably. In Fig. 8 a qualitative example is illustrated of the prediction capabilities of our baseline model before and after fine-tuning on the real data. As with the previous results, the transferred model is initially unable to correctly identify the dangerous trajectories both for the step and obstacle events while evidently improves after the model fine-tuning.

5   Conclusion and Future Work

This paper has investigated the use of deep learning as a traversability estimator for mobile robots in unstructured terrains. We provided insights on the benefits of the proposed method to predict the occurrence of failure events over feasible trajectories and at a fraction of the time of a sequential traverse simulator. We also showed that by generating a domain-independent synthetic dataset we can learn general features for traversability analysis. Then, by fine-tuning the learned model on the domain-specific real-world data, we can transfer the knowledge to enable the deep neural network to learn traversability analysis on datasets that would be excessively small to train on. Therefore, this technique enables more efficient learning for domains where large real world datasets are not available and where deep learning might not otherwise be a feasible solution due to the scarcity of data.

We are extending this work in several directions. While binary failure metrics could be sufficient to enforce safety in navigation, they cannot provide adequate information to perform optimal path planning. Future works may consider an extension of learning to include more complex continuous metrics. Finally, we discussed how the representativeness of the synthetic data could have a crucial impact during transfer learning. In future works, this could be addressed by generating more realistic synthetic data and by using algorithms specifically devised for efficient transfer learning (e.g. meta-learning).

References

1. Blacker, P., Bridges, C.P., Hadfield, S.: Rapid prototyping of deep learning models on radiation hardened CPUs. In: 2019 NASA/ESA Conference on Adaptive Hardware and Systems (AHS), pp. 25–32, July 2019
2. Chavez-Garcia, R.O., Guzzi, J., Gambardella, L.M., Giusti, A.: Learning ground traversability from simulations. IEEE Robot. Autom. Lett. 3(3), 1695–1702 (2018). https://doi.org/10.1109/LRA.2018.2801794
3. Goldberg, S.B., Maimone, M.W., Matthies, L.: Stereo vision and rover navigation software for planetary exploration. In: Proceedings of IEEE Aerospace Conference, vol. 5, p. 5 (2002)
4. Gu, J., et al.: Recent advances in convolutional neural networks. Pattern Recogn. 77, 354–377 (2018)
5. He, K., Zhang, X., Ren, S., Sun, J.: Deep residual learning for image recognition. CoRR abs/1512.03385 (2015)
6. Helmick, D., Angelova, A., Matthies, L.: Terrain adaptive navigation for planetary rovers. J. Field Robot. 26, 391–410 (2009)
7. Iqbal, J., Tahir, A.M., ul Islam, R., Riaz-un-Nabi: Robotics for nuclear power plants – challenges and future perspectives. In: 2012 2nd International Conference on Applied Robotics for the Power Industry (CARPI), pp. 151–156, September 2012
8. LeCun, Y., Bengio, Y., Hinton, G.: Deep learning. Nature 521(7553), 436–444 (2015)
9. Ono, M., Fuchs, T.J., Steffy, A., Maimone, M., Yen, J.: Risk-aware planetary rover operation: autonomous terrain classification and path planning. In: 2015 IEEE Aerospace Conference, pp. 1–10, March 2015
10. Generation Robots: Seekur Jr mobile robot. https://www.generationrobots.com/en/402399-robot-mobile-seekur-jr.html
11. Ruby, U., Yendapalli, V.: Binary cross entropy with deep learning technique for image classification. Int. J. Adv. Trends Comput. Sci. Eng. 9(10), (2020)
12. Russakovsky, O., et al.: ImageNet large scale visual recognition challenge. CoRR abs/1409.0575 (2014)
13. Sancho-Pradel, D., Gao, Y.: A survey on terrain assessment techniques for autonomous operation of planetary robots. JBIS - J. Br. Interplanetary Soc. 63(5–6), 206–217 (2010)
14. Spencer, K.: Introducing OpenSimplex Noise. https://www.reddit.com/r/proceduralgeneration/comments/2gu3e7/like_perlins_simplex_noise_but_dont_like_the/ckmqz2y/
15. Tan, C., Sun, F., Kong, T., Zhang, W., Yang, C., Liu, C.: A survey on deep transfer learning. In: Kůrková, V., Manolopoulos, Y., Hammer, B., Iliadis, L., Maglogiannis, I. (eds.) ICANN 2018. LNCS, vol. 11141, pp. 270–279. Springer, Cham (2018). https://doi.org/10.1007/978-3-030-01424-7_27
16. Winter, M., et al.: Detailed description of the high-level autonomy functionalities developed for the ExoMars rover. In: 14th Symposium on Advanced Space Technologies in Robotics and Automation, June 2017
17. Woods, M., et al.: Seeker–autonomous long-range rover navigation for remote exploration. J. Field Robot. 31(6), 940–968 (2014)

Systems

Predicting Artist Drawing Activity via Multi-camera Inputs for Co-creative Drawing

Chipp Jansen[1]([✉])[iD] and Elizabeth Sklar[2][iD]

[1] Centre for Robotics Research, King's College London, London, UK
chipp.jansen@kcl.ac.uk
[2] Lincoln Institute for Agri-Food Technology, University of Lincoln, Lincoln, UK
esklar@lincoln.ac.uk

Abstract. This paper presents the results of computer vision experiments in the perception of an artist drawing with analog media (pen and paper), with the aim to contribute towards a human-robot co-creative drawing system. Using data gathered from user studies with artists and illustrators, two types of CNN models were designed and evaluated. Both models use multi-camera images of the drawing surface as input. One models predicts an artist's activity (e.g. are they drawing or not?). The other model predicts the position of the pen on the canvas. Results of different combination of input sources are presented. The overall mean accuracy is 95% (std: 7%) for predicting when the artist is present and 68% (std: 15%) for predicting when the artist is drawing. The model predicts the pen's position on the drawing canvas with a mean squared error (in normalised units) of 0.0034 (std: 0.0099). These results contribute towards the development of an autonomous robotic system which is aware of an artist at work via camera based input. In addition, this benefits the artist with a more fluid physical to digital workflow for creative content creation.

Keywords: Human-robot collaboration · Co-creative drawing · Computer vision · Deep learning · Convolutional neural networks · Sketch-based computing

1 Introduction

Visual artists enjoy a large economy of creative digital tools to produce their work. In our recent study into co-creative artistic workflows [10], we found artists often use physical analog media (e.g. pen and ink on paper) for initial idea exploration and desire for a more fluid transition from analog to digital media. In addition, when considering collaboration with an Artificial Intelligence (AI),

This research is supported through an EPSRC (UK) DTP Studentship "Collaborative Drawing Systems", Grant Reference EP/N509498/1.

© Springer Nature Switzerland AG 2021
C. Fox et al. (Eds.): TAROS 2021, LNAI 13054, pp. 217–227, 2021.
https://doi.org/10.1007/978-3-030-89177-0_23

we found that artists preferred an inspirational or co-creative AI role to that of a didactic one.

In this paper, we investigate vision-based methods to build models of artists' **activity** (e.g. are they currently *drawing*—pen touching the page—or *not*—pen hovering above the page while the artist is thinking about what to draw next) and **output** (e.g. predicting the pen position on the page to understand what is being drawn on the canvas) while drawing.

Understanding the pen movements would then allow for a vision-based system to digitally recreate a drawing without being tethered to a drawing tablet or to rely on a scanner set-up. A camera-based system would allow an artist freer physical range in the studio, as well as a more diverse set of mediums to draw upon—an important point of feedback gathered previously [10].

Ultimately, we see these vision-based methods as models that would be components of a co-creative drawing system enhanced with visual-based awareness of the artist. Since the drawing process is a 3-D activity, despite having 2-D outputs, we evaluate which image inputs (e.g. camera positions for observing the artist) are most useful for these models through the experiments presented in this paper. We believe the results of these experiments would not only be useful for the creative computing community, but also the greater human-robotic interaction community, as they describe predicting fine human motor control (e.g. drawing) at a personal robot scale.

2   Background

Artist's drawing behaviour with physical media has been studied in psychology, from manual annotation of video frames of an artist's hand motion [18] to using techniques such as *saliency analysis*, or analysing the movement of an individual's eye fixation to understand where the their attention lies [16,17]. Sensor fusion has also been used to study the painting process through combining axis-aligned cameras and acoustic sensors attached to a canvas to record the contact of a paint brush onto the canvas surface [6]. Within the computer graphics and human-computer interaction literature, there is a rich tradition of sketch-based computing and interaction via digital interfaces such as drawing tablets [12,15].

Co-creative drawing systems aim to be a drawing partner, such as the *Drawing Apprentice* [4], where an improvising drawing agent analyzes the user's input and responds with its own artistic contributions upon a shared digital canvas. Neural network approaches to sketching, such as the *sketch-rnn* model [7] (and the availability of large-scale drawn datasets, e.g. *QuickDraw!* [11]) have inspired a class of deep learning driven co-creative drawing systems [5,13,14]. In all of these systems, the medium is digital drawing, which is immediate for the creative agent to observe the state of the artist, where they are drawing and for the agent to interact with the canvas. However, there are a few recent examples of physical co-creative work with robotic systems, such as *D.O.U.G* [2], which involves an industrial robot to mimic what the artist is drawing and in turn the artist can respond; and the *ArtTherapyRobot* [3] which uses a Baxter[1] robot to conduct research into socially assisted robotics for art therapy. Instead of a robot, projected interfaces serve as a platform to physical co-creative drawing as well, such as the *DialogCanvasMachine* [1].

Most of these physical co-creative drawing examples feature a bespoke system created to facilitate the co-creation with a specific individual artist or artist-group, as opposed to being research into more general physical co-creative drawing. In addition, while some of the examples capture the artist's drawing process for reflective post-processing [1,6], none of these systems build a real-time model of what the artist is currently drawing or their behaviour. In addition, artists and illustrators still use physical media as part of their workflow and desire a more fluid way of capturing their drawings [8], a feature which is currently lacking in contemporary sketch-based computing research.

3   Research Set-Up

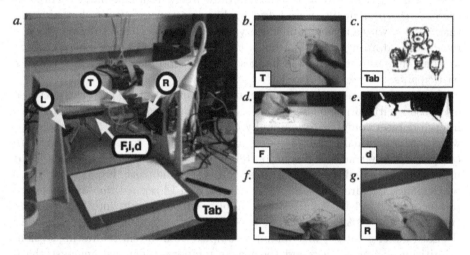

Fig. 1. *(a)* Prototype hardware setup with components: top, right and left cameras **T**, **R** and **L**; front camera **F** with infrared **i** depth **d** components; and drawing tablet **Tab**. *(b–g)* input from the components: top camera, drawing tablet, front camera rgb, front camera depth, left camera and right camera respectively (front infrared camera component is not shown).

We have developed a co-creative drawing system research prototype [9], shown in Fig. 1, comprising multiple cameras that observe an artist's drawing surface. There are 3 RGB cameras[2] (an overhead top down camera (**T**), and side oblique

---

[1] https://robots.ieee.org/robots/baxter/.

[2] Raspberry PI Camera Module V2 https://www.raspberrypi.org/products/camera-module-v2/.

right (**R**) and left (**L**) cameras). There is also a front facing depth camera[3] (with separate RGB (**F**) and infrared sensors (**i**) integrating into a depth image (**d**)). All of the cameras record at 25 frames per second to produce images at 1280 × 960 resolution (for **T, R, L**) and 640 × 480 resolution (for **F, d, i**). In addition, the artist draws on paper on top of a drawing tablet (**Tab**), which records the position (x and y coordinates) and pressure of the drawing pen at 200 vector points per second at a discrete 0.01mm resolution. This set-up allows us to gather drawing data that correlates camera images with a drawn vector representation from the tablet.

4   Drawing Data Gathering Study

In early 2020, we conducted a drawing data gathering study ($n = 13$) involving full-time drawing practitioners (professionals and students) to test our prototype system and to collect the drawing dataset used in the models presented in this paper. Participants were instructed to undertake two separate drawing exercises: draw from *observation* of a still-life, and draw freely from *imagination*. For each exercise, the participants were asked to draw for at least 10 min, but no more than 30 min (with a time reminder every 10 min). In total, our research prototype recorded 26 drawing exercises. However, due to technical issues, our prototype was only able to record from all input sources for both drawing exercises from 7 participants.

In this paper, we utilised data from these 7 participants to produce two types of datasets with corresponding models: *activity* and *pen_position*. The examples in each dataset comprise 6 temporally correlated input images (**T, R, L, d, i**), which are individually resized (using nearest-neighbor) to a smaller and more computationally tractable resolution (80 × 60 pixels). Each example is labelled using the corresponding drawing tablet data as ground truth. From each of the 7 participants' two drawing sessions, 14 *activity* and 14 *pen_position* datasets were produced. Every dataset had 3500 examples, which we split into 80% training ($n = 2800$) and 20% testing sets ($n = 700$).

Each *activity* dataset was randomly sampled from the entire drawing session, prioritising examples that had the lowest temporal difference amongst the 6 image frames. Categorising artist's "activity" while drawing is a multi-faceted and deeply complex phenomenon. For the purposes of these experiments, we take advantage of the drawing tablet, which senses the proximity of the pen once it is within 2–3 cm. The pen senses a pressure level as an integer value ($[0, 2047]$), which is a relative measure of the pressure of the pen's tip upon the drawing surface. A pressure level of 0 indicates that the pen is "hovering" above the page. A pressure level >0 indicates the pen is "drawing". Otherwise, when no points are being recorded, the pen (and thus the artist) is "away". We use these pen states to label the *activity* dataset examples with a 3-class *pen_state* variable ("drawing", "hovering", "away"). While these are a natural classification

---

[3] Intel Depth Camera SR305 https://www.intelrealsense.com/depth-camera-sr305/.

Table 1. Distribution of *pen_state* classes for each participant exercises dataset. Rows are labelled by the participant id (**1** to **7**) and the drawing exercise: observation (**obs**) and imagination (**img**).

		Training				Test			
		Total	Drawing	Hovering	Away	Total	Drawing	Hovering	Away
1	img	2800	1985 (71%)	593 (21%)	222 (8%)	700	468 (67%)	181 (26%)	51 (7%)
	obs	2800	1654 (59%)	721 (26%)	425 (15%)	700	427 (61%)	164 (23%)	109 (16%)
2	img	2800	1071 (38%)	1181 (42%)	548 (20%)	700	261 (37%)	317 (45%)	122 (17%)
	obs	2800	1389 (50%)	1277 (46%)	134 (5%)	700	380 (54%)	281 (40%)	39 (6%)
3	img	2800	873 (31%)	1372 (49%)	555 (20%)	700	220 (31%)	357 (51%)	123 (18%)
	obs	2800	596 (21%)	957 (34%)	1247 (45%)	700	142 (20%)	232 (33%)	326 (47%)
4	img	2800	921 (33%)	1236 (44%)	643 (23%)	700	227 (32%)	314 (45%)	159 (23%)
	obs	2800	1295 (46%)	1342 (48%)	163 (6%)	700	328 (47%)	329 (47%)	43 (6%)
5	img	2800	2001 (71%)	473 (17%)	326 (12%)	700	501 (72%)	108 (15%)	91 (13%)
	obs	2800	2113 (75%)	594 (21%)	93 (3%)	700	552 (79%)	133 (19%)	15 (2%)
6	img	2800	1443 (52%)	1201 (43%)	156 (6%)	700	363 (52%)	294 (42%)	43 (6%)
	obs	2800	1009 (36%)	1419 (51%)	372 (13%)	700	253 (36%)	330 (47%)	117 (17%)
7	img	2800	1388 (50%)	1263 (45%)	149 (5%)	700	342 (49%)	315 (45%)	43 (6%)
	obs	2800	1532 (55%)	1136 (41%)	132 (5%)	700	393 (56%)	279 (40%)	28 (4%)

from the pen; however, from the perspective of developing a controller for a co-creative system, it is useful for the AI to be able to discern two things: first, is the artist present; and second, is the artist drawing. We derive two further binary classes: *is_drawing* (*activity* == *drawing*) and *is_present* (*activity* == *drawing* ∨ *activity* == *hovering*) based on the pen state.

Table 1 shows the distribution of examples for each of the three *pen_state* classes. Due to the random sampling regime, the distribution for each participant-drawing exercise *activity* dataset varied. For the experiments presented here, the balance of examples across classes was not adjusted; future work will consider re-balancing (e.g. boosting) some classes to improve prediction accuracy.

Finally, each *pen_position* dataset was randomly sampled *only when the artist was drawing* and are labeled with the normalised pen position: $(x, y) = ([0, 1], [0, 1])$.

5   Visual Based Models

We produced two types of models, based on the previously described datasets: *activity* and *pen_position*. Each model takes the 6 camera images as input (from individual sources or in combination of multiple sources). Each image is fed independently through a sequence of *Convolutional Neural Network (CNN)* layers, to be concatenated in a single layer that is fully connected to output variables.

The concatenation layer is then connected via a single hidden layer to the output. There are three different variations of the *activity* model, each based on the multi-class output variables: *pen_state* (3 classes), *is_present* (2 classes) and *is_drawing* (2 classes). There is a single *pen_position* model, which produces pen positions (x and y), normalised to the width and height of the drawing tablet.

Models were built and trained using *Tensorflow*[4], with a split of 80:20 on the training to the test data subsets, using an ADAM optimiser with a learning rate of 0.01, for 30 epochs each. The *activity* models were trained to optimise a cross-entropy loss for multi-class variables (Boolean variables were treated as multi-class to maintain consistency in the experimental methods) with an accuracy metric evaluated on the test dataset. The *pen_position* models were trained to minimise the combined *Mean Squared Error (MSE)* loss for the normalised x and y output variables.

6   Experiments and Results

We experimented with 22 different combinations of input images (6 single individual image input, 15 pairs of images and the set of all images) on the three flavours of *activity* models and the *pen_position* model. Each model was trained and evaluated independently with a corresponding user-session dataset to explore 308 variations per model type.

Figure 2 shows the accuracy results for the three *activity* models: *pen_state*, *is_drawing*, *is_present* for specific image combinations. Each bar is a summary of the 14 participant-exercises datasets.

Overall (all sessions and combinations together), the accuracy for the *is_present* binary model was higher (mean 95.7%, std 6.7%, n = 308) than the *is_drawing* (mean 68.3%, std 15.1%, n = 308) model. Accuracy for the 3-class *pen_state* (mean 68.5%, std 16.0%, n = 308) model had a wide variation amongst the different input combinations, with the Front camera (**F**) having the best performance. The Right camera (**R**) had noticeably worse performance, as shown by the spread in the *is_present* model. All of the participants in the selected datasets were right-handed and their hand often occludes the pen tip in the Right camera view, which may explain this variation. The Front infrared (**i**) camera also performed poorly within the *is_present* model, although the RGB component of the same camera (**F**) produced a high mean accuracy for the *pen_state* model.

Figure 3 shows the MSE of the x and y components, and the combined x *and* y training metric for the *pen_position* model for specific image combinations. The MSE is in terms of normalised x, y positions of the pen with respect to the width (29.7 cm) and height (21.6 cm) of the drawing tablet.

Overall, the MSE for x (mean 0.001298, std 0.004564, n = 308) was lower than y (mean 0.002054, std 0.005789, n = 308). The combined (x *and* y) MSE (mean 0.003352, std 0.009936, n = 308) was highest. For the *pen_position* model, there seems to be little difference amongst the individual RGB cameras (**T, L, R,**

---

[4] https://www.tensorflow.org/.

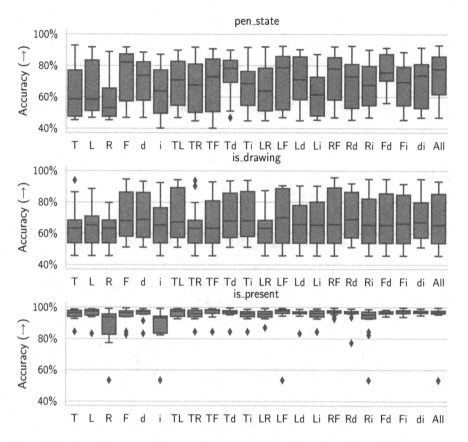

Fig. 2. Accuracy of predicting the activity of the artist: (*top to bottom*): *pen_state*, *is_drawing*, *is_present*. Accuracy values fall between 40–100%, higher is better (↑).

F), while the individual depth (**d**) performs worse, and the individual infrared (**i**) has an out-sized comparative variance. In addition, the pair-wise images also seem to have little difference amongst themselves. However, models that use all the input images (**All**) yielded a far better result than the individual image sources, and had the best mean MSE overall.

7   Discussion and Limitations

Sensing when the artist is present visually, using the *is_present* model, is by far the most successful model from our experimentation aside from relying solely on the same-handed oblique side camera (i.e. Right camera (**R**) for a right-handed artist). Sensing when artist is drawing, using the *is_drawing* model, proves to be more difficult. This may be due to the slight visual differences between the pen touching the canvas and that of the pen hovering just above the canvas, especially at the lower image resolution of 80 × 60. In addition, the wide variation in the

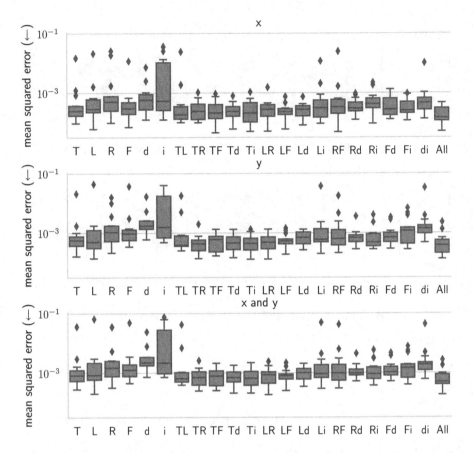

Fig. 3. Mean Squared Error (MSE) (log scale) of the pen attribute predictions for the *pen_position* models (*top to bottom*): x, y and combined x and y. Each error bar summaries the 14 drawing sessions for the specific images combination, lower is better ($\downarrow$).

balance for the different *pen_state* classes as shown in Table 1 may be a reason for the results for the *activity* models having a wide variation.

Basing the artist's activity on the pen state also has limitations. For example, an artist who draws with grand arm motions will, at moments, lift their pen beyond the 2–3 cm bounds of pen proximity for the drawing tablet, thus recording "hover" as "away" activity. Or, when the artist sets their pen down upon the tablet to take a break, this will be recorded as a continuous stream of "hover" points, but the artist is in fact "away". These limitations reinforce the advantage of having a vision based system which adds additional context to recording an artist's activity. These labels could be further refined, through manual annotation of the artist's states from the camera images.

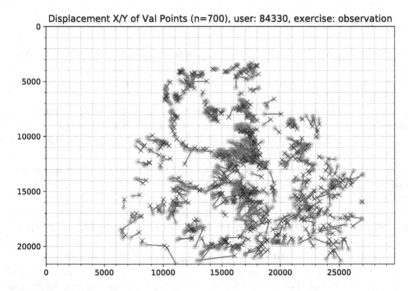

Fig. 4. Example rendering using the *pen_position* model using test points ($n = 700$) from an observational drawing session. Actual points (light grey dots) are connected to predicted points (black X's).

Predicting the pen's position had a clearer result with the combined image inputs model (**All**) having the lowest error. While the MSE for the *pen_position* model is low, initial attempts to use a model with visual-driven drawing did not produce coherent results (Fig. 4). This might be due the variation in predicted points being too high at the camera frame rate (i.e. 25 frames per second as opposed to the 200 point per second produced by the drawing tablet).

8   Summary and Future Work

We have demonstrated that using vision-based input from a multi-camera system with a trained CNN can predict the activity and output of an artist drawing with physical media—being able to predict that an artist is present and drawing within a relatively localised area on the canvas.

While these models were trained and evaluated on individual drawing session datasets, possible future work in *transfer learning* is possible to evaluate one artist's model on another artist's drawing data. Our current rationale for training only on an individual session is to work towards a system which is bespoke and custom to a particular artist's drawing style. However, another avenue of work would be to train a more general purpose model that later adapts to a specific artist's style.

Next steps in our research is to integrate these models into a framework for co-creative drawing, and to evaluate this framework with various co-creative drawing agents in an artist's studio setting.

References

1. Cabannes, V., Kerdreux, T., Thiry, L., Campana, T., Ferrandes, C.: Dialog on a canvas with a machine. arXiv:1910.04386 [cs], October 2019
2. Chung, S.: Drawing Operations (DOUG) (2015). https://sougwen.com/project/drawing-operations
3. Cooney, M., Berck, P.: Designing a robot which paints with a human: visual metaphors to convey contingency and artistry. In: ICRA-X Robots Art Program at IEEE International Conference on Robotics and Automation (ICRA), Montreal QC, Canada, p. 2, May 2019
4. Davis, N., Hsiao, C.P., Singh, K.Y., Magerko, B.: Co-creative drawing agent with object recognition. In: Artificial Intelligence in Interactive Digital Entertainment, Burlingame, California, USA, p. 8 (2016)
5. Fan, J.E., Dinculescu, M., Ha, D.: Collabdraw: an environment for collaborative sketching with an artificial agent. In: Proceedings of the 2019 on Creativity and Cognition, C&C 2019, pp. 556–561. Association for Computing Machinery, San Diego, CA, USA, June 2019. https://doi.org/10.1145/3325480.3326578
6. Fernando, P., Weiler, J., Kuznetsov, S., Turaga, P.: Tracking, animating, and 3D printing elements of the fine arts freehand drawing process. In: Proceedings of the Twelfth International Conference on Tangible, Embedded, and Embodied Interaction - TEI 2018, Stockholm, Sweden, pp. 555–561. ACM Press (2018). https://doi.org/10.1145/3173225.3173307
7. Ha, D., Eck, D.: A neural representation of sketch drawings. arXiv:1704.03477 [cs, stat], May 2017
8. Jansen, C., Sklar, E.: Co-creative physical drawing systems. In: ICRA-X Robots Art Program at IEEE International Conference on Robotics and Automation (ICRA), Montreal, QC, Canada, p. 2, May 2019
9. Jansen, C., Sklar, E.: Towards a HRI system for co-creative drawing. In: ACM/IEEE International Conference on Human-Robot Interaction (HRI), Workshop on on Exploring Creative Content in Social Robotics (2020)
10. Jansen, C., Sklar, E.: Exploring co-creative drawing workflows. Front. Robot. AI 8, 92 (2021)
11. Jongejan, J., Rowley, H., Kawashima, T., Kim, J., Fox-Gieg, N.: The Quick, Draw! - A.I. Experiment (2016). https://quickdraw.withgoogle.com/
12. Jorge, J., Samavati, F.: Sketch-Based Interfaces and Modeling. Springer, London (2010). https://doi.org/10.1007/978-1-84882-812-4
13. Karimi, P., Maher, M.L., Davis, N., Grace, K.: Deep learning in a computational model for conceptual shifts in a co-creative design system. arXiv:1906.10188 [cs, stat], June 2019
14. Oh, C., Song, J., Choi, J., Kim, S., Lee, S., Suh, B.: I lead, you help but only with enough details: understanding user experience of co-creation with artificial intelligence. In: Proceedings of the 2018 CHI Conference on Human Factors in Computing Systems, CHI 2018, Montreal QC, Canada, pp. 1–13. Association for Computing Machinery, April 2018. https://doi.org/10.1145/3173574.3174223
15. Olsen, L., Samavati, F.F., Sousa, M.C., Jorge, J.A.: Sketch-based modeling: a survey. Comput. Graph. 33(1), 85–103 (2009). https://doi.org/10.1016/j.cag.2008.09.013
16. Sarvadevabhatla, R.K., Suresh, S., Babu, R.V.: Object category understanding via eye fixations on freehand sketches. IEEE Trans. Image Process. 26(5), 2508–2518 (2017). https://doi.org/10.1109/TIP.2017.2675539

17. Tchalenko, J., Nam, S.H., Ladanga, M., Miall, R.C.: The gaze-shift strategy in drawing. Psychol. Aesthet. Creat. Arts **8**(3), 330–339 (2014). https://doi.org/10.1037/a0036132

18. Van Sommers, P.: Drawing and Cognition: Descriptive and Experimental Studies of Graphic Production Processes. Cambridge University Press, Cambridge (1984)

3D Printed Mechanically Modular Two-Degree-Of-Freedom Robotic Segment Utilizing Variable-Stiffness Actuators

Alfred Wilmot[1,2(✉)] and Ian S. Howard[2(✉)]

[1] University of Sheffield, Sheffield S1 3JD, UK
aiawilmot1@sheffield.ac.uk
[2] SECAM, University of Plymouth, Plymouth PL4 8AA, UK
ian.howard@plymouth.ac.uk

Abstract. Here we describe the initial development of a 3D printed modular robotic segment that is driven by *variable stiffness actuators* (VSAs). The novelty of the presented work is the combination of cost-effective antagonist VSAs with mechanical modularity: this enables multiple segments to be used either as a stand-alone serpentine robot or as compliant joints that can easily be integrated into other robotic systems. The VSAs are comprised of antagonist DC motor pairs that separately actuate two orthogonal revolute joints via a viscoelastic tendon-based transmission system. The simplistic nature of the design also aims to minimize the effects of joint coupling. Joint-level control is performed on a microcontroller which transmits motor current and joint position information over USB to a computer. ROS packages, including those needed for *Gazebo* and *MoveIt!* were created to enable physics simulations and motion-planning of either a single isolated segment, multiple chained segments, or some combination of segments and other robotic devices. We present results of a preliminary physical prototype of one such robotic segment whose joint positions and co-contractions were manually controlled using a gamepad and subsequently visualized using the developed ROS packages. The dynamics of the VSA were analyzed and the joint-torque equations were derived as functions of tendon parameters, joint angles, and motor electrical characteristics.

Keywords: 3D-printing · Variable-stiffness · Passive-compliance · ROS

1 Introduction

In recent years, there has been a growing research interest in the development of variable stiffness actuators, known as VSAs, that enable impedance control [1]. One of the major driving factors for developing such actuators is to address safety concerns regarding physical human-robot interaction (HRI). According to [2], there is a strong indication that VSAs enable safer and faster payload handling compared to purely rigid actuators. In this work, a prototype two-degree-of-freedom (2-DoF) mechanically modular VSA segment was developed to meet the HRI safety and performance criteria in a

© Springer Nature Switzerland AG 2021
C. Fox et al. (Eds.): TAROS 2021, LNAI 13054, pp. 228–237, 2021.
https://doi.org/10.1007/978-3-030-89177-0_24

cost-effective manner by 3D-printing most components. Currently, the segment consists of embedded joint encoders and off-board current-sensing circuits for inferring motor load to control tendon stiffness. The sensor read-outs of a single segment were inspected using rqt-plot and were also used to control simulations in ROS. Although many compliant tendon-driven robots designs exist, few have a modular construction. One exception is the VSA-CubeBot, which makes use of low-cost servo units, and whose performance characteristics were very thoroughly investigated and characterized [3]. Unlike the VSA-CubeBot, the design of the system we present here consists of internal wiring cavities that ensure cabling is routed away from pinching points, secondary tendon channels to address the risk of overloading segments at the base of multi-segment assemblies, and integration with ROS. The latter is key for further researching the controllability of multi-segment implementations in a timely manner as the ever-expanding ecosystem of ROS packages is rich with state-of-the-art open-source trajectory-planning libraries, along with other useful software stacks. Furthermore, the mechanical coupling implementation of the design we present here is inherently very mechanically stable, only requires a single bolt to chain two segments together, and is almost fully 3D printed. These and additional features which are important for both the practical and cost-effective application of such a system will be elaborated upon in the following sections.

2 Design Considerations

Serpentine robots are effectively a compromise between continuum-style and conventional rigid robots, as they are characterized by many discrete joints connected via small rigid links. Given that the joints of serpentine robots can be clearly defined by a kinematic chain, modelling using Denavit-Hartenberg (DH) parameters is possible. This avoids the control challenges associated with continuum-style robotics, and the high degree of joint redundancy of multi-segment chains facilitates many inverse-kinematic solutions for a particular motion-plan, which is useful for obstacle avoidance in unstructured environments. However, as the number of segments increases so too does the torque experienced at the bottom-most segment. Hence, this latest prototype is most appropriate for use in neutrally buoyant environments, mounted overhead to a gantry, or as a robotic wrist. Improving the load-bearing capacity of multi-segment manipulators will be the subject of later studies as this will greatly broaden the potential applications of this system, such as for use as a cost-effective robotic arm mounted on a wheelchair. In order for a user to teleoperate the manipulator's end-effector to perform pick-place tasks, a closed-loop control model was required. This allowed a motion-planner to accept goal end-effector pose data from a gamepad or 6-DOF joystick, generate a set of actuator commands to achieve the planned trajectory, receive sensor feedback to determine whether the manipulator is following the planned trajectory, and finally either confirm that the goal position is reached or indicate a failure to execute the planned motion.

3 Segment Design

As is illustrated in Fig. 2A, the segment design adopted here consists of male & female mechanical coupling elements sandwiching two offset/orthogonal revolute joints and an actuator block above the female connector at the base of the segment. Figure 1 demonstrates how the mechanical-modularity facilitated by these coupling elements enables the combination of multiple chain segments and the ease with which other periph-eral elements such as end-effectors can be incorporated. Each joint can be deflected from the centered upright position by 45 degrees in either direction, yielding a total *range-of-motion* (ROM) of 90 degrees per joint. Embedded into each joint is an I2C-capable Hall-effect rotary magnetic encoder that is oriented opposite a radially magnetized mag-net. The top and bottom joint sections rotate relative to one-another, and given that the encoder is static relative to the bottom section while the magnet is static relative to the top, the magnet rotates in front of the encoder IC as the joint actuates. Vis-coelastic tendons, originally developed for the GummiArm [4], were used to connect the actuators to their respective joints to impart both variable-stiffness and passive com-pliance characteristics onto the segment, thereby facilitating safe HRI capabilities on the hardware level. These tendons exhibit an approximately linear response for low co-contractions and a quadratic response for higher co-contractions. An antagonist pair is required as each motor can only pull the joint in a single direction and not push in the other. The benefit of this setup is that joint stiffness can be controlled by varying the ten-don co-contraction. Given the reciprocal nature of stiffness and compliance, the joint can also be made more passively compliant by relaxing the antagonist pair. To modulate the stiffness in this manner, the viscoelastic element must behave like a non-linear spring, otherwise the stiffness is independent of tendon length. If the response is quadratic, then the joint stiffness is linearly dependent on co-contraction [5, 6].

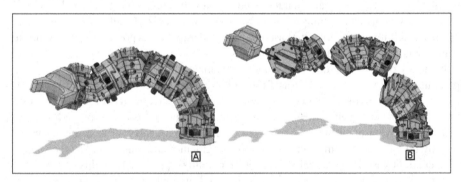

Fig. 1. Illustration of the segment's mechanical modularity. **A** Three segments are assembled together with a dummy end-effector at the distal-most end. **B** Illustrates how segments are fastened to each other using the mechanical coupling element.

4   Control Electronics

The I2C communications protocol was chosen for an initial implementation due to its ease of use and extensive documentation. As can be seen in Fig. 2G, each joint is braced at two coupling points to mitigate axial torsion. Each coupling point consists of three bearing mount elements that are sandwiched together with an M3 bolt which is secured with a nut inserted into the head of the inside bearing mount. The M3 bolt straddles a steel axial bearing installed into the head of the central bearing mount. The magnet is placed into the head of the larger bearing mount facing the encoder. These bearing mounts are embedded into the joint plates and secured with M2 nuts and bolts. The joint plates holding the bearing mounts are partially hollowed to internally accommodate cabling for the I2C BUS, thereby protecting electronics from direct impact with the environment or from being pinched between moving parts. The joints are symmetric, so they can be combined such that their axes of rotation are either parallel or orthogonal. The latter configuration was chosen since this results in a 3D workspace. As the system is tendon-driven from the base, the distal joint tendon length can be indirectly varied as the proximal joint moves through its range of motion. To mitigate the effects of joint coupling, the tendon-channel that intersects a joint's axis of rotation is brought as close to that axis as possible; this and all other design features are illustrated in Fig. 2.

5 Mechanical Construction

Fused deposition modelling (FDM) is a 3D printing technique based on the layer-wise deposition of a thermoplastic filament from a heated nozzle. PLA was selected as the build material due to its affordability and ease of use. There is an inherent delamination strength associated with printed parts that is dependent on the material properties of the filament used and the surface area between printed layers. The orientation of the printed layers of a part relative to the forces that the part will experience when used had to be considered. The bearing mount elements were designed and printed in such a way as to maximize the joint's resistance to torque when under load and minimize the risk of delaminating printed layers. Furthermore, all printed parts were designed in such a way that few-to-no support structures were needed during manufacture, thereby reducing the post-processing overhead. The actuator block shown in Fig. 2C consists of an array of four DC motors where the tip of each motor shaft is braced by a bearing installed into the housing of an adjacent motor, thereby mitigating any moment experienced at the gearbox-shaft interface when the shaft is under load.

6 Position Sensing and Torque Estimation

Joint angle and motor current-draw were monitored using PCBs fabricated by the authors. This enabled the variation of joint stiffness through controlling the tension applied to the tendons by the motors. Tendon tension is related to the torque exerted by the shaft of the motor, which in turn is related to the amount of current drawn.

Monitoring the current drawn by motors also means that safety-measures can be implemented to prevent them from being damaged. Modulating the applied voltage to control shaft velocity, thereby preventing overloading of the motor, will enhance the longevity of the system and enable joint torque control via tendon tension modulation. This also makes the system safer to use around people as the segment will be able to control the amount of force exerted as well as enforce low tendon tensions to ensure collisions result in minimal damage.

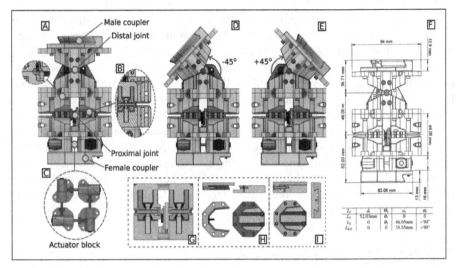

Fig. 2. Illustrations of segment design. **A** Internal channels in joint plates for routing electronics. **B** Proximal joint bearing mounts can be seen to the left. Of the two tendon channels towards the right, only the inner channel is used for connecting tendons to the actuator block associated with that segment. The outer channel is intended for a second set of tendons connected to powerful motors at the base of the segment-chain which pass through all segments and coupling to the distal-most segment. The viability of controlling a chain of segments in this manner is the subject of future work. **C** Layout of two antagonist pairs of brushed-DC motors forming the actuator block. **D, E** Illustrations of the 90-degree range of motion of the distal joint and mechanical hard-stops. **F** Table of DH parameters (bottom) and a schematic with the measurements that were used to calculate them (top). **G** Cross-sectional view of a rotary joint shows the position of the captive radially magnetized magnet (part of left axle) relative to the rotary magnetic encoder (located at the center of the joint). **H, I** Illustrations showing how the mechanical coupling element achieves a secure connection due to the tapered design using a single screw and captive nut.

7   Characterizing VSA Dynamics

By considering the electrical characteristics of the DC motors used for the VSA, illustrated in Fig. 3A, the generated torques can be derived as functions of *armature current* (i_a) its differential (i_a'), and shaft *angular velocity* (ω_m). This is shown in Eq. (1).

$$\tau_m = \frac{i_a}{\omega_m} \cdot (v_s - R \cdot i_a - L \cdot i_a') \tag{1}$$

The joint openings α_r and α_l, referred to generally as α, relate to the *joint angle* (θ_j) according to Eq. (2).

$$\theta_j = \frac{\pi}{4} - \alpha_r = \alpha_l - \frac{\pi}{4} \tag{2}$$

The tendons exhibit a characteristic restorative force which we describe using the standard quadratic equation for simplicity, though in practice there is typically an initial region of linearity that is observed when the tendon is below a critical extension length, beyond which the response becomes quadratic. The constants of the quadratic equation shown in Eq. (3) are unique to each tendon and need to be determined through experimentation. Although the forces exerted on an individual tendon by either *joint torque* (τ_j) or *motor torque* (τ_m) are acting in opposite directions, the net *tendon displacement* (x) is positive. Hence, these forces can be considered as acting on a fixed tendon in the same direction, resulting in the expression shown in Eq. (3), where the torque lever arms are the joint-side lengths (a) and shaft radii (b), respectively.

$$\phi(x) = Ax^2 + Bx + C = \frac{\tau_m}{b} + \frac{\tau_j}{a}\sin\left(\frac{\alpha}{2}\right) \tag{3}$$

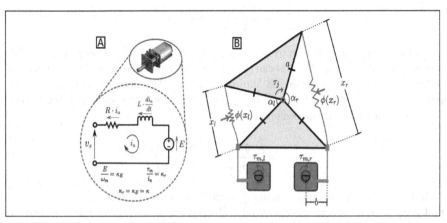

Fig. 3. Diagrams used to characterize the system dynamics. **A** Shows an equivalent electrical circuit of the DC motor used to drive the VSA. Definitions of the electrical constant (κ_E) and torque constant (κ_τ) are shown, and these are equivalent in the case of DC motors. This information is used to relate motor torque with its electrical characteristics. **B** Illustration of the geometric layout of a single VSA joint driven by an antagonist motor pair. Both tendons are assumed to exhibit identical responses for the same amount of deflection, governed by quadratic force functions ($\phi(x_l)$, $\phi(x_r)$), and as having lengths (x_l, x_r) that are functions of motor torque ($\tau_{m,l}$, $\tau_{m,r}$) and joint angle (θ_j). The effective shaft-radius (b) and joint side-lengths (a) affect the displacement characteristics for a particular motor shaft angle.

When the joint is static, the motor torque can be expressed purely in terms of the *tendon force function* ($\phi(x)$) of the tendon coupled to its shaft, as shown in Eq. (4).

$$\tau_m = \phi(x) \cdot b \tag{4}$$

Equation (5) shows that the displacement of an individual tendon is a function of both the joint angle and motor shaft position. This becomes apparent when we consider a co-contraction event: wherein the joint angle does not change, but the tendons are being elongated by their respective motors. The displacement due to the *joint position* (x_j) can be derived via the law of cosines, and that due to *movement of the motor shaft* (x_m) is the arc-length swept by the shaft as it rotates.

$$x = x_j + x_m = \left(a \cdot \sqrt{2} \cdot \sqrt{1 - \cos\left(\frac{\alpha}{2}\right)}\right) + (b \cdot \theta_m) \tag{5}$$

Given that we are treating the joint as being static when its stiffness is being modulated, the tendon displacement associated with this value can be treated as a constant, and so the derivative of the tendon displacement is purely that induced by the motor torque, resulting in Eq. (6).

$$x' = x'_m = b \cdot \omega_m \tag{6}$$

Therefore, when we combine Eqs. (1), (3), (4), and (6), the result is the differential Eq. (7) that relates the tendon displacement due to the motor with the tendon parameters and the electrical characteristics of the motor.

$$x' = \frac{i_a \cdot (v_s - R \cdot i_a - L \cdot i'_a)}{Ax^2 + Bx + C} \tag{7}$$

In the case of a joint driven by an antagonist motor pair, as is illustrated in Fig. 3B, the torque experienced at the joint can be described as a function of the forces generated by these two opposing tendons, as shown in Eq. (8). The derivative of Eq. (8) with respect to *tendon displacements* (x_l, x_r) results in the joint stiffness, which needs to be controlled to achieve impedance control.

$$\tau_j = a \left(\frac{\phi(x_r)}{sin\left(\frac{\alpha_r}{2}\right)} - \frac{\phi(x_l)}{sin\left(\frac{\alpha_l}{2}\right)} \right) \tag{8}$$

In future work, these equations that govern the system dynamics will be used for the implementation for a state space controller. However, in this work, a facile implementation was set-up to manually demonstrate the impedance-controllable nature of the VSA using a gamepad.

8   Control and Simulation Using ROS

Various IK solving algorithms are available via the *MoveIt!* open-source motion-planning framework, which is a plugin for the *rviz* 3D visualization package available through the *Robot Operating System* (ROS). Motion-planning, preliminary qualitative simulations, and controlling the segment test-rig with a gamepad, were all performed using the ROS peer-to-peer nodal network of publishers and subscribers. To utilize ROS motion-planning packages, a *Universal Robotic Description File* (URDF) is needed. A URDF is essentially an xml-type file that describes how a robot's links and joints are arranged to form the resultant kinematic chain. URDFs treat a link's inertial, visual, and collision frames as separate entities. A Fusion360 plugin was used as a starting point for generating the URDF package from an assembly of the CAD model. Once finished, a ROS package is generated containing STLs representing each link, a URDF that references these STLs, and a launch-file that can be executed to visually debug the URDF in the *rviz* ROS package. When using *rviz*, a 3D representation of the system described by the URDF is shown in a GUI which includes track-bars for controlling what each virtual joint publishes to the *joint states* topic. Figure 4D shows the corresponding system node-graph. Chapter 18 of Morgan Quigley's book, Programming Robots with ROS,

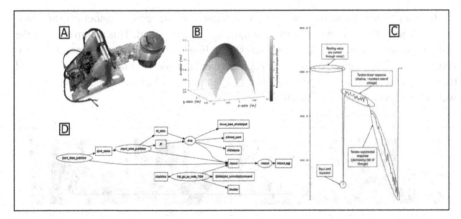

Fig. 4. Diagrams illustrating various aspects of the robot. **A** Testing platform for evaluating the performance characteristics of the developed segments. **B** Heat-map wherein each point indicates the reachable workspace of a single two-degree-of-freedom segment, and the color-coding indicates the corresponding theoretical torque experienced at the proximal joint of a single segment while a 10 kg payload is connected to the distal joint at each point in the reachable workspace. **C** Annotated experimental current-measurements of a motor during a contraction event. There is a transient spike, an initial region of linearity as the tendon is being tensioned, then the quadratic response can be observed. **D** rqt node-graph showing how the GUI (the/joint_state_publisher node) controls the model in the rviz simulation (the /rviz node).

was used as a guideline for setting up a ROS package that could utilize *MoveIt!* For motion planning, and simulations using the *Gazebo* physics engine.

To perform experiments for evaluating the performance characteristics of the segment in a timely manner, a testing rig shown in Fig. 4A was constructed. Given that the tension of a particular tendon is inferred from the current drawn by its associated motor, the motor must be actively driving the joint for the tension to be modulated. For initial testing, tendon-tension modulation was controlled directly by the operator via a gamepad in order to experiment with various levels of co-contraction by manually modulating joint stiffness using the *rqt_plot* data-visualizer as a means of visually inferring the real-time joint stiffness and observe the system stability at different co-contraction levels.

9   MATLAB Simulations and Demo

To evaluate the effective workspace of the serpentine-segment, the kinematic chain was derived using conventional DH parameters, and the relevant measurements used to derive them are shown in Fig. 2F. To estimate the expected torque that a single segment would experience at its proximal joint when the end-effector is carrying a 10 kg load, the inverse Jacobians of each possible joint configuration of the two joint setups were evaluated and multiplied with the force vector resulting from the 10 kg load. The Forward-Kinematics of the segment for the joint-angle pair was evaluated in order to determine the (x, y, z) coordinates of the end-effector in the work-space. The end-effector coordinates were plotted on a 3D plot and the proximal joint torque associated with each end-effector position was encoded as a value for the heat-map shown in Fig. 4B.

In order to investigate the response characteristics of the segment under various loading conditions, the testing platform shown in Fig. 5 was devised. This set-up enables the study of joint deflection angles under various loading conditions at particular tendon co-contractions. The degree to which the segment can be made to reliably follow a planned trajectory and recover from path deviations when perturbed can also be investigated, as well as the controllability of multi-segment systems.

Fig. 5. Demonstration of the 2-DOF VSA prototype. **A** The mechanically modular nature of the design can be demonstrated by placing an end-effector on a segment that is itself mounted to a testing platform. **B** The graphs in the background represent the joint angles (top) and the current-draw (bottom) of each motor. The resulting current-draw profile corresponds to the force generated by the segment as it attempts to maintain a particular joint configuration when deflected by an external force. This enables the system to exert either a known amount of force or comply (relax the tendons) as needed. **C, D** Actuation of the segment while an end-effector is mounted with either a stable mass (C), or an unstable mass (D). Link to video of demo

10   Discussion

A modular 2-DOF actuator was developed, and some preliminary evaluations were made using a testing platform. A simple closed-loop controller demo with teleoperation was devised, ROS packages were created for motion-planning and physics simulations, and further analysis was also performed using MATLAB. Overall, this project involved the design and development of mechanical, electronic, and software components. Future developments will explore the scalability of the system and investigate embedding all the electronics used to control the segment into the segment body itself, such that the mechanical coupling of multiple segments places them on a common communications bus. The joint-torque equations presented were derived as functions of motor current and joint positions and are the first steps towards realizing simultaneous closed-loop control of the segment's joint positions and exerted torques (impedance control).

Acknowledgments. The authors would like to thank the University of Plymouth for supporting this work, *Access Robotics Ltd* for funding this research with a grant from the *European Regional Development Fund* (ERDF), and Dr. Federico Belmonte Klein for developing the Fusion360 URDF-generator plugin while also providing guidance in its use.

References

1. Grioli, G., et al.: Variable stiffness actuators: the user's point of view. Int. J. Robot. Res. **34**(6), 727–743 (2015). https://doi.org/10.1177/0278364914566515

2. Bicchi, A., Tonietti, G.: Fast and "soft-arm" tactics [robot arm design]. IEEE Robot. Autom. Mag. **11**(2), 22–33 (2004)
3. Catalano, M.G., et al.: VSA-CubeBot: a modular variable stiffness platform for multiple degrees of freedom robots. In: 2011 IEEE International Conference on Robotics and Automation, pp. 5090–5095. IEEE (2011)
4. Stoelen, M., Bonsignorio, F., Cangelosi, A.: Co-exploring actuator antagonism and bio-inspired control in a printable robot arm. In: Tuci, Elio, Giagkos, Alexandros, Wilson, Myra, Hallam, John (eds.) SAB 2016. LNCS (LNAI), vol. 9825, pp. 244–255. Springer, Cham (2016). https://doi.org/10.1007/978-3-319-43488-9_22
5. Ham, R., Sugar, T., Vanderborght, B., Hollander, K., Lefeber, D.: Compliant actuator designs. IEEE Robot. Autom. Mag. **3**(16), 81–94 (2009)
6. Migliore, S.A., Brown, E.A., DeWeerth, S.P.: Biologically inspired joint stiffness control. In: Proceedings of the 2005 IEEE International Conference on Robotics and Automation, pp. 4508–4513. IEEE (2005)

Design of a Multimaterial 3D-Printed Soft Actuator with Bi-directional Variable Stiffness

Oliver Shorthose(✉), Liang He(✉), Alessandro Albini(✉), and Perla Maiolino(✉)

Oxford Robotics Institute, University of Oxford, Oxford OX1 2JD, UK
{ollies,liang,ale,perla}@robots.ox.ac.uk
https://ori.ox.ac.uk/

Abstract. A multi-material 3D printed soft actuator is presented that uses symmetrical, parallel chambers to achieve bi-directional variable stiffness. Many recent soft robotic solutions involve multi-stage fabrication, provide variable stiffness in only one direction or lack a means of reliably controlling the actuator stiffness. The use of multi-material 3D printing means complex monolithic designs can be produced without the need for further fabrication steps. We demonstrate that this allows for a high degree of repeatability between actuators and the ability to introduce different control behaviours into a single body. By independently varying the pressure in two parallel chambers, two control modes are proposed: complementary and antagonistic. We show that the actuator is able to tune its force output. The differential control significantly increases force output with controllable stiffness enabled within a safe, low-pressure range (≤ 20 kPa). Experimental characterisations in angular range, repeatability between printed models, hysteresis, absolute maximum force, and beam stiffness are presented. The proposed design demonstrated a maximum bending angle of $102.6°$, maximum output force 2.17N, and maximum beam stiffness 0.96mN m^2.

Keywords: Soft robot · 3D printing · Variable stiffness actuator

1 Introduction

Soft and compliant materials have been increasingly implemented into robotics research in the last decade. These soft robots have shown benefits over their rigid counterparts with regards to higher levels of safety and the ability to adapt to unknown environments or tasks [1,2]. However, the compliance of the materials and non-linear behaviour limit precise position control and the force that can be applied to the environment [1,3].

Various research works have proposed solutions to solve the above issues. In particular, to increase the force that can be applied, variable stiffness actuators

We gratefully acknowledge support by EPSRC Programme Grant 'From Sensing to Collaboration' (EP/V000748/1).

ⓒ Springer Nature Switzerland AG 2021
C. Fox et al. (Eds.): TAROS 2021, LNAI 13054, pp. 238–248, 2021.
https://doi.org/10.1007/978-3-030-89177-0_25

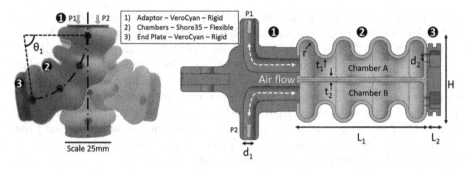

Fig. 1. Left: The multi-material actuator bent in both directions and at the neutral position. P1 and P2 are the independently applied driving pressures. θ_1 is the output angle. Right: Section view of the actuator showing the two chambers and the different regions utilising multi-material fabrication. Geometric properties are presented in mm: $r_i = 2.75$; $t_1 = 1.2$; $t_2 = 1.5$; $d_1 = 4.5$; $d_2 = 3$; $L_1 = 48$; $L_2 = 5$; $H = 31$.

have been proposed based on several methods [4,5]. These solutions, based on composite materials, introduce challenges in the actuator fabrication and control because they require the integration of extra systems into the soft actuators. In contrast, antagonistic pneumatic actuators, composed of parallel chambers, achieve variable stiffness behaviour whilst avoiding the need for extra internal parts [6–8]. Many of these designs excel in one-directional bending stiffening to improve force output but are limited in having a one-sided active region [8,9]. Bi-directional variable stiffness actuators have successfully improved the bending performance with a larger workspace [6]. However, fabricating multiple chambers in the actuator is challenging with moulding and casting methods, where multiple stages of assembly or lost-wax casting are typically needed [6,10].

Recent advances in soft material 3D printing have provided an effective solution to quickly fabricate soft actuators precisely with high repeatability [11–13]. Compared to conventional silicone moulding methods, actuators fabricated via 3D printing can also have higher design freedom. Complex internal geometries that can optimise the bending motions can be introduced into the design [14,15]. Furthermore, recent advances in additive manufacturing have provided the ability to use multi-material printing. By introducing a variety of materials into a fully-integrated monolithic actuator, designs can be extended to exploit complex material behaviours [9,16].

In this work, we present the design of a multi-material 3D printed soft monolithic actuator which incorporates parallel symmetrical chambers to achieve bi-directional variable stiffness. The actuator is experimentally characterised to demonstrate its performance improvements compared to the state of the art. Figure 1 shows the printed actuator in both neutral and bent poses. The two parallel chambers can be actuated independently with two modes: complementary and antagonistic. Complementary control is the method of applying positive pressure to one chamber whilst exerting negative pressure in the other, and antagonistic control applies the same pressure in both chambers. Currently available 3D printed soft materials are still limited in the range of elongation at break compared to conventional silicone polymers. For instance, Ecoflex 00– 30 (Smooth-on [17]) has elongation at failure of 900% compared to Agilus 30 (Stratasys [18]), which exhibits a range of 220–270%. This limitation implies that 3D printed bending actuators are more prone to failure when only driven with positive pressures. To address this issue, we have proposed the two control modes, which increase the actuator workspace and force output while maintaining the capability of tunable stiffness. Crinkles are also integrated into the design to mitigate the limited material elongation where structual compliance is explored predominantly instead of material compliance.

2   Design and Fabrication of the Actuator

The actuator consists of two parallel bellow-shaped flexible chambers connected by a common midlayer. By regulating the pressure variation between the two chambers, bidirectional bending motions with tunable stiffness can be achieved. The design utilises novel 3D printing technology to maximize the ease and precision of fabrication and significantly reduces the time between design-fabrication cycles. Figure 1 shows the schematics of the actuator with design specifications in the chambers, end plate, and base attachment.

The design consists of two expanding chambers bonded to an inextensible central layer. The compliant region expands to enforce a bending motion about the central layer with the increase of driving pressure. A bellows shape design has been incorporated to reduce the chamber's strain during expansion and facilitate easy extension/contraction of the chambers [19]. The Shore 35 Agilus/VeroCyan blend was used in the fabrication of the actuator to ensure maximum compliance. The bellow structure design further reduces the stress concentration on the material during the inflation, where a smaller principal strain is required for the material during bending. When the bellows expand, there is little tensile stress induced in the material compared to a design without bellows [13].

The parallel chambers enable variable stiffness control of the actuator without requiring the addition of granules or extra internal layers through antagonistic behaviour. Furthermore, a higher force output than a single-sided chamber (with the same driving pressure) can be achieved through complementary control behaviour. The end plate is designed to be rigid (VeroCyan) to prevent ballooning at the end which wouldn't contribute to the curvature of the body and would increase local bending strains. The surface area between the end plate and chambers was maximised to reduce warping or delamination at multimaterial interfaces. Similarly to the end plate, the base is designed to be rigid to prevent unfavourable displacements when pressurised.

The relationship between bending angle, stiffness and pressure cannot simply be presented in analytical form and so optimum parameters have to be determined through simulation. A parametric analysis was run in CAD to determine the optimum geometry for the chambers. The thickness of the chamber and the inner radius of the crinkle were identified as critical parameters governing the bending behaviour of the actuator and were applied to a grid search optimisation algorithm. The body's principal stresses and tip displacement were allocated as the key metrics. An internal pressure of 10 kPa was applied to the model whilst the thickness of the material was varied between 1 mm and 3 mm, and the inner radius of the crinkle pattern was varied between 1.5 mm and 2.75 mm. These ranges were chosen to satisfy printing constraints for minimum feature size, and to ensure the overall length of the actuator was less than 50 mm.

The optimised design parameters are illustrated in Fig. 1. The normalised simulated results of the displacement and stress were weighted towards prioritising the maximisation of the displacement over minimising the stress at a weighting ratio 5:4. The difference of the weighted values was minimised to find the optimal combination of thickness and inner radius, which was found when the chamber thickness was 1.2 mm and the inner radius was 2.75 mm. The overall length of the chambers is 48 mm, the height is 31 mm, and the weight is 35 g. The central layer was empirically set to be 1.5 mm.

Polyjet technology (Stratasys J735 printer) was used for multi-material printing of the actuator (VeroCyan and Agilus30). VeroCyan is a rigid plastic that has a quoted tensile strength of 50-65MPa and Shore hardness 83-86D. Agilus30 is a compliant and rubber-like material, which has a quoted tensile strength of 2.1–2.6 MPa and a Shore hardness of 30A.

3   Control Setup

The actuator was controlled by an Arduino. The pneumatic setup used one Delaman air pump, four Yosoo1210 solenoid valves, and one Panasonic ADP5101 pressure sensor per chamber. The pressures were sampled at 50 Hz. A 30 Hz HD Webcam was used to acquire a video stream for angle detection. The setup

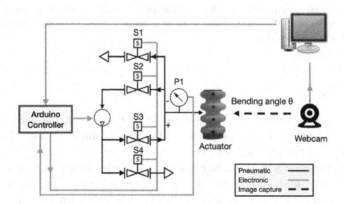

Fig. 2. Control architecture for one chamber of the soft actuator. The Arduino controls the pumps and valves, responding to real-time pressure values from the pressure sensor. The data from the Arduino and webcam is stored and post-processed to plot.

is shown in Figs. 2 and 3. For the actuator characterisation, closed-loop PI (proportional-integral) control was used to compare the internal pressure value against a target value. The output of the PI control governed a pulse-width modulated (PWM) pump input, and the inflate and deflate valves. The angle of the actuator was acquired by identifying black markers down the centre of the actuator (shown in Fig. 1) and fitting them to a circular profile using a constant curvature approximation.

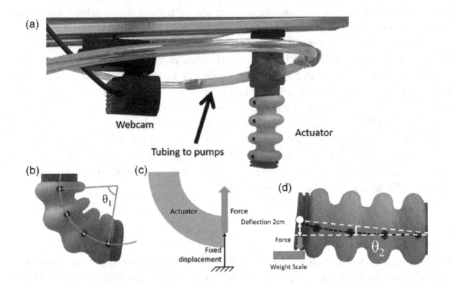

Fig. 3. (a) Experimental setup: the webcam is used for angle acquisition. (b) A circular profile is fitted to identify markers from the webcam stream to determine the angle, θ_1. (c) Complementary force test: the actuator is attached to a weight and inflated/deflated to change the force output. (d) Antagonistic stiffness test: the deflection was set at 2 mm as the chambers were inflated and the force was recorded. θ_2 indicates the angle used in the small angle approximation.

4   Testing

In this section, the performance of the proposed actuator was physically tested as the bending angle versus driving pressure, hysteresis, and the effect of increased force output and tunable stiffness via complementary and antagonistic control. To evaluate differences in the printed actuators' performance, a total of 3 actuators were tested under identical experimental conditions. The actuators were tested 5 times for each test category with time between each test of more than 5 min to allow any residual strain energy to fully dissipate. Chambers A and B are indicated in Fig. 1 and used interchangeably between tests to validate the bi-directionality.

Pressure Versus Angle. This test is used to evaluate the repeatability of the actuators' performance. Using PI control, Chamber A was inflated at a continuous rate of 0.5 kPa/sec to a maximum target pressure of 16 kPa with Chamber B maintained at atmospheric pressure. Although the chamber was empirically found to withstand pressures up to 22.3 kPa, the targeted range was chosen to be 0–16 kPa. This is to examine mid-range performance without risking breaking the actuator. Figure 4 shows the results for a single chamber being actuated. Across all 15 tests for the 3 actuators, the single chamber actuation test shows that, at the target pressure of 16 kPa, the mean angle is 44.8°, with a standard deviation of 1.3°. This translates to only a 2.9% variation compared to the full range of the test, which validates the repeatability of the fabrication method. It is also worth noting that the actuator requires lower pressures than other comparable designs [7,9,13].

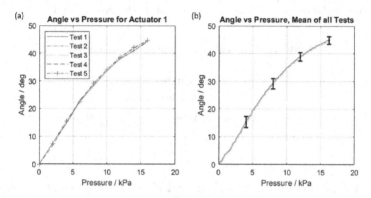

Fig. 4. Result of the single chamber pressure versus angle test. (a) 5 tests on one actuator. (b) average of 15 tests across 3 actuators.

Hysteresis. The amount of hysteresis in a design can complicate the control of the system by adding a reliance on the historic behaviour of the actuator. The tests were undertaken by increasing the pressure in Chamber A by 0.5 kPa/sec with PI control up to 16 kPa target, holding the pressure steady for 2 s, and then decreasing the pressure by the same rate until the actuator returned to the neutral pose. Figure 5 is shown with the lower curve indicating the inflation sequence and the higher curve indicating the deflation sequence. The amount of hysteresis is presented as the percentage difference between the area under the curves for the increasing and decreasing pressure cycles. This value was calculated to be 24.7%.

Complementary/Antagonistic Control. Using two parallel chambers, the force output and beam stiffness of the actuator can be tuned. The force output was tested for both complementary and antagonistic control.

The actuator's performance (Complementary control) with respect to stiffness variation was tested in terms of the actuator's maximum force. In this

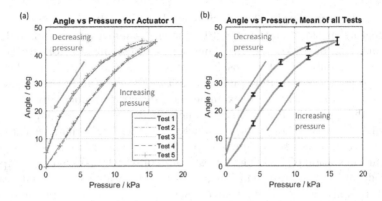

Fig. 5. Hysteresis test results. The pressure was increased/decreased at 0.5 kPa/s for the inflation and deflation phases. 16 kPa was the maximum targeted pressure in Chamber A before deflation. (a) 5 tests on one actuator. (b) average of 15 tests across 3 actuators.

Table 1. Complementary/Antagonistic control

		Chamber A	
		Positive pressure	Negative pressure
Chamber B	Positive pressure	Antagonistic	Complementary
	Negative pressure	Complementary	Antagonistic

regard, a thread was wound around the end plate of the actuator and attached to digital weight with displacement constrained. By measuring the change in weight on a set of scales, the exerted force was deduced (Fig. 3c). For each change in pressure, the pressure was held constant for 5 s to ensure a static force was recorded. Chamber A was inflated to a maximum pressure of 20 kPa to achieve a bent position and provide a reference force before Chamber B was depressurised to increase the force output. The depressurisation was done in 5 decrements between 0 and –22.5 kPa.

The actuators' resistance to deflection (Antagonistic control) was tested by enforcing a tip deflection, pressurising the chambers, and measuring the imposed lateral force as shown in Fig. 3d. The tip was deflected by 2 mm to ensure that the force being applied is normal to the end of the actuator under a small angle approximation ($\sin \theta \approx \theta$). The chambers were equally pressurised in 2 kPa increments up to 20 kPa with 5 s wait to ensure static force acquisition. Classical beam theory was applied to calculate the beam stiffness of the actuator at each pressure increment. The actuator was approximated to be a cantilever, fixed at one end, with stiffness $k = 3EI/L^3$. By applying this to Hooke's law, the beam stiffness (EI) was deduced.

To acquire a maximum force output for the actuator that can be used for benchmarking the actuator within the literature, Chamber A was pressurised to

20 kPa and Chamber B was completely evacuated before the force measurement was made.

When only one chamber was actuated, the force output was 0.56N. The complementary variable force plot (Fig. 6b) shows that the design is able to increase the output force linearly by 1.56N by reducing the pressure in Chamber B. This behaviour provides an overall maximum force output of 2.17N. The antagonistic variable force plot (Fig. 6a) demonstrates that the beam stiffness of the actuator can be increased by 0.64mN m^2, which corresponds to more than a 300% increase. Whilst this is a low absolute stiffness output, it is comparable to similar work at a considerably lower pressure and validates the use of the control modes to improve the force and output of the actuator [6].

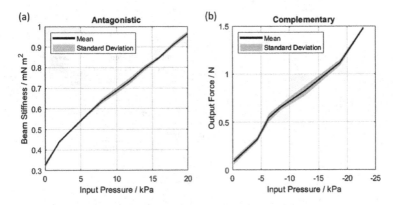

Fig. 6. (a) Result of the antagonistic actuator force test. Both chambers were inflated simultaneously from 0–20 kPa in 2 kPa increments. (b) Result of the complementary control force test. Chamber A was pressurised to 20 kPa before starting this test and the presented data is the difference in force recorded as Chamber B was depressurised from 0 to –22.5 kPa in 5 kPa increments.

Effect of Stiffness Variation on Angle. The effect of independently varying the pressure in the parallel chambers leads to a change in the output angle. To enact precise position control, it is important to understand the extent of this effect for the complementary control mode. Chamber A was inflated to a single target pressure, the valves were closed, and then Chamber B was deflated. The target pressure in Chamber A was set at 13 kPa and the target pressure in Chamber B was set at –10 kPa. Both target pressures were, again, chosen to demonstrate the mid-range performance. The test was then used to determine a value for the maximum angle of the actuators, which can be used for easily benchmarking the design within the literature, by inflating Chamber A to 22.5 kPa and deflating Chamber B to –20 kPa.

The results are presented in Fig. 7 with a common x-axis to indicate the timing for the test. The test presents the effect of the change of stiffness on the actuator's angle. By actuating the second chamber, the angle is increased from 33.1° to 85.7° over the pressure change of −10 kPa. This indicates that the stiffness variation has a significant effect on the output angle. This variation can be accounted for by mapping the pressure in each chamber to the output angle. The mean maximum angle across 15 samples is 85.5°, with a standard deviation of 2.9°. This corresponds to a 3.4% variation compared to the full range of the test, which further demonstrates the repeatability of the fabrication process.

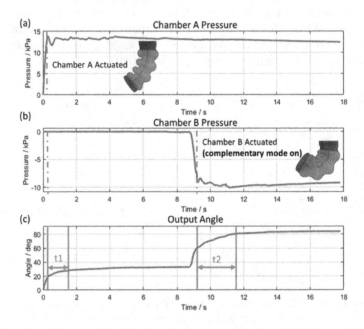

Fig. 7. Results of the two chamber pressure versus angle test. (a) Pressure in Chamber A. (b) Pressure in Chamber B. The rise times are calculated as: t1: 1.5 s, t2: 1.9 s. The pressure in Chamber A continues to drop over time as the volume is affected by the contraction in Chamber B. (c) Angle subtended by the actuator.

The maximum values of the actuators' input pressure, force, and angle are −25 to 22.3 kPa, 2.17 N, and 102.6°, respectively. The maximum pressure value was acquired by applying pressure until the actuator failed; the minimum pressure was determined by completely evacuating the actuator; the force and angle measurements were taken at slightly lower pressure values than the extremes (−24.5 kPa and 22 kPa) and measured in accordance with Fig. 3b and c.

5   Conclusion

This paper presents a multi-material 3D printed soft monolithic actuator that incorporates parallel symmetrical bellow chambers to implement bi-directional variable stiffness. Complementary and antagonistic control modes were proposed and implemented in the design while the two chambers can work collaboratively with either positive pressure or negative pressure. For pneumatic actuators that operate in the low-pressure region (<20 kPa), output force and bending angle performance is always a challenge. Compared to actuators that can only be actuated in a single mode with either positive or negative pressure, the presented design achieves higher output force, larger bending angle, or tunable stiffness without the need to increase the driving pressure.

3D printing rather than silicone moulding introduces quicker prototyping, better reproducibility, and stronger interfacial bonds to the actuator. The test results confirm the high level of reproducibility with low deviation between test results. The actuator was fully physically characterised under two-chamber PI control. The results show that the proposed complementary and antagonistic control method is promising for future work in bi-directional bending actuators. The key metrics to take from the studies are: maximum angle of curvature 102.6°; maximum output force 2.17N; controlled force variability 1.56N; and maximum beam stiffness 0.96mN m^2. With the proposed complementary/antagonistic control modes, this design achieves a higher output force and comparable bending angles to the similar designs [6,13] at a fraction of the driving pressure.

Future work plans to further explore the potential of this actuator design and investigate the possible applications in grasping and in-hand manipulation. The authors will investigate variations on this preliminary design: increasing the stiffness to improve force output; adding modularity; scaling down the size of the actuator; and adding tactile sensing as a means of feedback.

Supplementary video: https://youtu.be/F-ANfUwE0XY

References

1. Kim, S., Laschi, C., Trimmer, B.: Soft robotics: a bioinspired evolution in robotics (May 2013)
2. Abondance, S., Teeple, C.B., Wood, R.J.: A dexterous soft robotic hand for delicate in-hand manipulation. IEEE Robot. Autom. Lett. **5**(4), 5502–5509 (2020)
3. Iida, F., Laschi, C.: Soft robotics: challenges and perspectives. In: Procedia Computer Science. vol. 7, pp. 99–102. Elsevier B.V. (January 2011)
4. Manti, M., Cacucciolo, V., Cianchetti, M.: Stiffening in soft robotics: a review of the state of the art. IEEE Robot. Autom. Mag. **23**(3), 93–106 (2016)
5. He, L., Leong, F., Dulantha Lalitharatne, T., de Lusignan, S., Nanayakkara, T.: A haptic mouse design with stiffening muscle layer for simulating guarding in abdominal palpation training. In: 2021 IEEE International Conference on Robotics and Automation (ICRA). IEEE (2021)
6. Babu, S.P.M., Sadeghi, A., Mondini, A., Mazzolai, B.: Antagonistic pneumatic actuators with variable stiffness for soft robotic applications. In: 2019 2nd IEEE International Conference on Soft Robotics (RoboSoft), pp. 283–288 (2019)
7. Suzumori, K., Wakimoto, S., Miyoshi, K., Iwata, K.: Long bending rubber mechanism combined contracting and extending fluidic actuators. In: IEEE International Conference on Intelligent Robots and Systems, pp. 4454–4459 (2013)
8. Chen, Y., Chung, H., Chen, B., Sun, Y.: A lobster-inspired bending module for compliant robotic applications. Bioinspir. Biomimet. **15**(5), 56009 (2020)

9. Zhu, M., Mori, Y., Wakayama, T., Wada, A., Kawamura, S.: A Fully Multi-Material Three-Dimensional Printed Soft Gripper with Variable Stiffness for Robust Grasping, vol. 6, pp. 507–519 (2019)
10. Yirmibesoglu, O., Morrow, J., Walker, S.: Direct 3D printing of silicone elastomer soft robots and their performance comparison with molded counterparts. In: 2018 IEEE International Conference on Soft Robotics, RoboSoft 2018, pp. 295–302. Institute of Electrical and Electronics Engineers Inc. (July 2018)
11. Sachyani Keneth, E., Kamyshny, A., Totaro, M., Beccai, L., Magdassi, S.: 3D Printing Materials for Soft Robotics. Advanced Materials (2020)
12. Yap, H.K., Ng, H.Y., Yeow, C.H.: High-force soft printable pneumatics for soft robotic applications. Soft Robot. 3(3), 144–158 (2016)
13. Peele, B.N., Wallin, T.J., Zhao, H., Shepherd, R.F.: 3D printing antagonistic systems of artificial muscle using projection stereolithography. Bioinspir. Biomimet. 10(5), 055003 (2015)
14. He, L., Tan, X., Suzumori, K., Nanayakkara, T.: A method to 3d print a programmable continuum actuator with single material using internal constraint. Sens. Actuators A Phys. 324, 112674 (2021)
15. Gul, J.Z., et al.: 3D printing for soft robotics-a review (December 2018)
16. Zolfagharian, A., Mahmud, M.A., Gharaie, S., Bodaghi, M., Kouzani, A.Z., Kaynak, A.: 3D/4D-printed bending-type soft pneumatic actuators: fabrication, modelling, and control. Virtual Phys. Prototyp. 15(4), 373–402 (2020)
17. Smooth-On: Ecoflex 00–30 product information. https://www.smooth-on.com/products/ecoflex-00-30/
18. Stratasys: Agilus 30. https://www.stratasys.com/materials/search/agilus30
19. Dammer, G., Gablenz, S., Hildebrandt, A., Major, Z.: Design and shape optimization of PolyJet bellows actuators. In: 2018 IEEE International Conference on Soft Robotics (RoboSoft), pp. 282–287. IEEE (April 2018)

Designing a Multi-locomotion Modular Snake Robot

Jack M. Frampton, Sara Djoudi, Angelina Murphy, Thomas Scammell,
Toby Wright, and Ze Ji$^{(\boxtimes)}$ⓘ

School of Engineering, Cardiff University, Cardiff CF24 3AA, UK
jiz1@cardiff.ac.uk

Abstract. Snakes possess multi-locomotion abilities to best suit different environments. This work explores the design of a robot to replicate three types of snake motions: rectilinear, serpentine and sidewinding. The design featured identical modular housing units containing all the components for movement, a biomimetic skin to replicate the anisotropic friction created by the scales of the snakeskin and smart servos motors that produce adjacent housing rotation to imitate the body motion of a snake. Two prototypes are manufactured using rapid prototyping. Prototype 1 is designed to replicate rectilinear motion produced by the biomimetic snakeskin and collinear movement of each housing. Prototype 2 is powered by the smart servos and the rotation of adjacent housings to produce serpentine and sidewinding motions. From initial tests, prototype 1 is shown to be able to replicate rectilinear motion at low speeds, and prototype 2 is shown to be able to undertake 6 different movement options utilising both sidewinding and serpentine motions.

Keywords: Snake robot · Biomimetic · Kirigami · Chain configuration

1 Introduction

Snake-like robots have numerous applications in an industrial context. Such examples include travelling over, or through, hazardous terrain for rescue missions [9], the development of medical equipment for stereotactic surgery due to enhanced flexion and dexterity [8] or even a role in facilitating complex tasks required by space rovers exploring extra-terrestrial environments [5]. The first snake-like robot, ACM-R5 [10], was invented in 1972. The ACM-R5 propelled forwards by twisting and turning. This robot had one degree of freedom (DoF) joints, resulting in its movement being constrained to a sine wave configuration on a flat surface simulating serpentine motion. The robot is able to travel in both water and on the ground. To allow for movement in water, paddle blades were attached around the side of the body. To aid movement on the ground, small wheels were attached to the paddle blades.

J. M. Frampton, S. Djoudi, A. Murphy, T. Scammel and T. Wright—Contributed equally.

© Springer Nature Switzerland AG 2021
C. Fox et al. (Eds.): TAROS 2021, LNAI 13054, pp. 249–259, 2021.
https://doi.org/10.1007/978-3-030-89177-0_26

Various designs have been actively explored on robot joint configuration in recent years [5]. For example, researchers focused on developing robots with a greater number of DoFs [2], enabling 3-DoF motions. The mechanism includes a moving platform and three mechanical joints: one universal joint and two composite spherical joints. Two symmetrical prismatic legs are connected to the sphere joints to replicate the snake's intercostal muscles. These joints eliminate torque, which is normal to the moving platform to protect the universal joint. To keep the original length of snake segments, the parallel joint is designed to prevent simultaneous yaw and pitch movement. The rotating axis is the cross axis of the universal joint, which entails two rotating directions perpendicular to each other.

Rectilinear motion is produced with a different principle. The scales of the skin help propel the snake forward. To replicate the behaviour of the scales, anisotropic frictional behaviour is to be simulated based on the theory in [7]. One study achieved this with nibs designed to allow for smooth and swift motion in one direction, but high friction in the opposite direction [6]. However, while a particular scale orientation would facilitate rectilinear motion perfectly, the concern is over how this might interfere with the other motion sequences our robot is intending to achieve. Another design [4] uses the art of kirigami to create a sheet of scales that buckle and pop out when the sheet is extended. During material extension, the scales pop out and contact the ground. With the scales protruded, a higher coefficient of friction with the ground in the direction opposite to the desired motion would be created. Upon retraction, this enables the elastomer to push forwards off the ground. The system is optimised to function with a pneumatic elastomer actuator.

This work aims to develop a prototype with multi-locomotion capabilities to be adaptable to its environment, allowing for effective travel across numerous terrains. We explore three main topics: modular robotics, chain robots commonly referred to as snake robots and biomimetic snakeskin. All three areas are brought together to design and manufacture a snake-like robot prototype consisting of individual identical modules connected in a chain formation capable of three types of snake motion: rectilinear, serpentine and sidewinding. A novel biomimetic snakeskin is designed and manufactured to propel the robot forwards during rectilinear motion. The modular design of the snake consists of identical housing all components necessary to produce the movement of a singular model such that they can be operated individually or linked together with inter-modular communication to form systems of varying numbers of modules. Ultimately, this would allow for greater flexibility of module configuration in the future in addition to the chain formation the current prototypes are based on.

2   Proposed Design

2.1   Locomotion

Below is a summary of the three snake locomotion models to be implemented in this work. Rectilinear motion is useful for a snake travelling through tight spaces, entailing the snake moving in a straight line through contracting muscles to control the movement of the scales. The scales are alternatively lifted from the ground, and then pulled downward and backwards. The friction between the scales and the ground will pull the body forwards. When the scales are lifted forwards, they are stretched out creating a rougher surface in contact with the ground. This inspired us for our design. To replicate rectilinear motion, the biomimetic silicone snakeskin is developed with cuts to mimic the movement of scales using the Kirigami method. The movement of the contracting muscles to lift the scales are simulated using micro linear actuators to extend and retract the housing units. With the scales lifted, a higher coefficient of friction is created in one direction, propelling the snake forwards upon housing retraction.

Serpentine motion consists of waves of lateral bending being propagated along the body from head to tail using objects on the ground to propel itself forwards. To simulate this slithering-like motion, smart servo motors are used to insti-gate 180° rotation between adjacent housing units orthogonal to the direction of travel of the robot. When the surface is slippery, such as sand, the most com-mon locomotion used is sidewinding, where two parts of the body are solely in contact with the ground with the remainder being held above it. The body is propelled laterally from these anchor points creating new anchor points a fixed distance away. Like serpentine motion, this movement will be replicated using servo motors to rotate the housing units. Sidewinding can be simplified by adding a vertical wave to the lateral existing wave of serpentine motion.

2.2   Housing

The focus for the housing design is to enable collinear and rotational movement of the housing modules and contain all components required to produce the robots motion in a compact package. Thus a 3-part module was developed, consisting of external and internal housings and an internal mounting tray.

The housing components of the module facilitated all modes of locomotion by enabling 2 modes of actuation, both within each module and between adjacent modules. The first mode of actuation is extension and retraction of the unit caused by the external housing of each module sliding over the internal housing of the same module on a fixed path (Fig. 1(a)). This enables the rectilinear motion of the modular system when combined with the biomimetic snakeskin. The second mode of actuation is rotation of two adjacent modules facilitated by the rotation of the external housing and internal mounting tray of adjacent modules about a fixed axis with a set of brackets, (Fig. 1(b)), to which the rotational actuator mounts.

Each of the housing parts has further functions to enable system mobility. The external module has one main purpose, ensuring that the biomimetic skin can function effectively; the smooth external surface does this by ensuring that the scales are only able to protrude in the correct direction when under extension, this was a functional priority over potential weight savings of removing material from this part (Fig. 1(a)). The internal module facilitates the movement of the system with its slatted covering for the rotational actuator and bracket, this both protects the actuator from impact during function and gives the system a smoother surface, preventing it from catching on obstacles during function (Fig. 1(b)). The internal mounting tray enables the assembly of the control systems for each module to be carried out externally of the module itself, sliding and locking into place when assembled. This facilitated easy assembly and component replacement, ensuring easy maintenance during lab testing and real-world function (Fig. 1(c)). Figure 2 shows a final module additively manufactured by Selective laser sintering (SLS) in Nylon and the final assembled prototype.

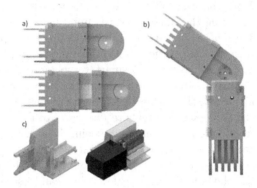

Fig. 1. CAD design of modules (a) external and internal housing in extension and retraction, (b) rotational bracket between adjacent modules, (c) internal mounting tray with and without components)

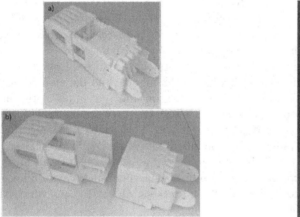

Fig. 2. Final module printed with SLS in extension and exploded views, and the assembled prototype

2.3   Smart Servos

To mimic the serpentine and sidewinding movements, servo motors are chosen due to their precise control of angular position, velocity, and acceleration. Additionally, compared to other motor types, servos have a high power-output to size and weight ratio, which is ideal for a modular-based robot. The DYNAMIXEL "smart" servos are used due to their ability to be connected in series in a daisy-chain-like formation, simplifying the electric wiring, and in-turn make the housing design more accommodating.

The motors within the body of the snake followed a coordinated sequence of movements to mimic not just the type of movement of serpentine and sidewinding, but also the direction of movement. To achieve these simulated movements, the motors followed a triangular waveform, formulated by Eq. 1:

$$\theta(n,t) = \pm \begin{cases} V_n(t - \delta_t), & \delta_t \leq t \leq \frac{T}{4} + \delta_t \\ -V_n(t - \delta_t) + \frac{\pi}{2}, & \frac{T}{4} + \delta_t \leq t \leq \frac{3T}{4} + \delta_t \\ V_n(t - \delta_t) - \pi, & \frac{3T}{4} + \delta_t \leq t \leq T + \delta_t \end{cases} \tag{1}$$

where θ is the angle of motor n at time t, v_n is the joint speed of motor n, t is the elapsed time, δ_t is the time delay between motors, T is the waveform period.

2.4   Biomimetic Snakeskin

The primary purpose of the skin design is to facilitate rectilinear motion through friction as demonstrated by snakeskin scales in nature [1,3]. Below is the summary of our design principle:

1. Simulating muscle propulsion to propel robot forward by the electrical actuator system
2. Creating anisotropic frictional interaction with robot's surface of travel by the skin kirigami mechanism
3. Integration of skin layer with robot body housing through strong adhesion of the skin attachment to the housing.

To simulate contracting muscles that control the movement of scales, linear actuation is used. This would extend and retract the housing, which would stretch the skin layer from its normal state. At the normal state, the housing is retracted, the skin relaxed and the scales lying flat, upon extension the skin stretches, and the scales protrude out. With the scales protruding, a higher coefficient of friction would be created in one direction, propelling the snake forwards upon retraction. In this project, electromechanical actuators are chosen as they do not require the extra external equipment or sealing of hydraulic and pneumatic actuators, which is difficult for the small scale of our modules.

Actuonix PQ12 Linear Actuators are chosen to be the most desirable for this project. They have a weight of 15 g and are capable of smooth and consistent linear stroke length of up to 20 mm with a load up to 50 N. They also have an internal potentiometer, which can provide positional feedback.

Several materials were investigated and compared based on their properties. The skin material selected is silicone due to its high stiffness, good flexibility and anti-adhesive properties, so that it would minimise the coefficient of friction with the ground when flat (in the direction of motion) and not interfere with the other robotic motions.

Tension testing was conducted to establish the kirigami pattern that would yield the best performance. Several samples underwent extension under a load of 20 N at 8 mm/s (as these are the peak efficiency settings of the actuator) until complete failure. Sample 1 represented the dimensions proportional to the derived equations found in the kirigami research undertaken in [4]. As for the subsequent samples, factors that were varied included adjusting the cut size, the hinge size, the angle of the cut with respect to the horizontal plane and the number of scales per row (Fig. 3). The snakeskin width and height are kept the same to accommodate for the housing dimensions, so there are limitations in varying some of these factors e.g. the cut size can only be reduced compared to the original design as any substantial increase would exceed the skin width.

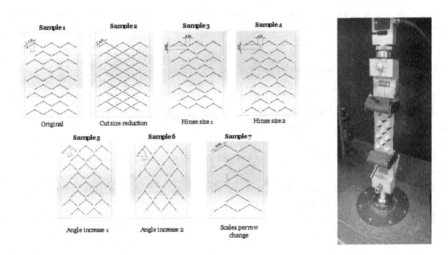

Fig. 3. Snakeskin samples designed at approximately height = 70 mm and width = 48 mm and the tension testing

Briefly, the following conclusions are derived from the performance results: 1) Cut size has minimal influence on the stiffness, 2) There is a positive correlation between hinge size and the stiffness, and 3) As the angle size increase, so does the stiffness. Ideally, the cut sizes need to be large enough to effectively protrude under the robot body weight, but not too large so as to deform and flatten against the ground surface [7]. Additionally, it is desirable for the skin to be as flexible as possible so that the layer may be extended easily by the actuator, but the skin also needs to be as stiff as possible to allow for the hinges to trigger the protrusion of the scales, without any failure propagation through the skin.

From the results, sample 3 in Fig. 3 is found to be the stiffest sample that did not hinder actuator extension, and is thus selected for the robot design.

3 Experiments and Discussion

3.1 Prototype 1 - Snakeskin Testing

Three tests were performed to assess the performance of the skin mechanism to extend and retract the housing and its effect on the skin layer. The areas that are examined include actuator retraction-extension motion, housing retraction-extension motion and function of the scales when the skin is in tension.

Actuator with Housing. The actuators were initially tested by implementing a continuous sweeping motion, causing the actuator to go from fully retracted to fully extended. Parameters of this motion were then adjusted until the actuator functioned in a smooth cyclic motion to establish the optimal values for these parameters. This code was then adjusted such that future connection of sensors to the Arduino would not be detrimental to the performance of the actuators. The actuator took 3 s to fully extend the housing to a 20 mm distance and another 3 s to fully retract the housing. It would have been desired for this duration to be faster. This would not cause any issues with performing rectilinear motion except it is just slower. The actuators could be swapped out for quicker ones in the future if desired.

Actuator in Housing with Skin Attachment. This test for the skin mechanism is to test the housing extension with the skin attached to the module, in order prove whether the attachment can withstand the tension force indirectly produced by the actuator, and how the scales behave during the motion.

This was executed by the actuator performing a sweep motion continuously from full extension to full retraction (Fig. 4). Under full extension, the scales simultaneously protruded outwards (Fig. 4(a)). The cuts within the skin layer created a higher coefficient of friction with the ground in the direction opposite to the desired motion. Therefore, on module retraction, the robot was able to push forwards off the ground. At full retraction, the scales flatten allowing for ease of motion (Fig. 4(b)).

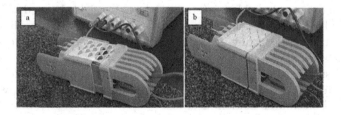

Fig. 4. Skin behaviours (a) housing extension with scales protruding, (b) housing retraction with scales flattened

Based upon the testing conducted with one housing unit, it has given a strong indication that the same mechanism could work with multiple units joined together. With more segments, the robot would have had a higher pushing force during rectilinear motion, and thus may have moved a greater distance under each cycle of the actuator extension-retraction motion. Due to time constraints, a full quantitative analysis of this prototype could not be undertaken and should be considered if the project is carried forward in future.

Frictional Testing. The snakeskin layer function is heavily reliant on its interaction with the surface it is travelling on. Therefore, it was imperative that frictional testing was conducted in order to quantify these interactions through obtaining the static (μs) and kinetic (μk) coefficients of friction between the silicone layer and various substrates.

Data was recorded for the performance of both a flat silicone sample and a scaled silicone sample to compare their interactions with various substrate surfaces. The set-up shown in Fig. 5 is employed to conduct the testing.

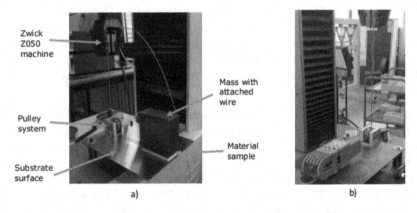

Fig. 5. Frictional testing rig (a) Set-up for the flat silicone sample (b) Set-up for the scaled silicone sample

The flat silicone sample is attached under a 3.5 kg mass block, which is not the case with the scaled sample. It is expected that the scales would have been crushed due to not being able to sustain the block's weight. Instead, this sample was attached to a module housing prototype weighing 171.91 g. The difference in weight is not an issue, as any mass difference is accounted for when calculating coefficients of friction.

The flat silicone sample was tested along four substrate surfaces (steel, carpet, acetate, laminate). The skin layer was tested across steel and carpet, with both forwards and backwards motion recorded.

Flat Silicone Results. From Fig. 6, it appears that the frictional resistances across carpet, acetate and laminate are relatively similar. This suggests that,

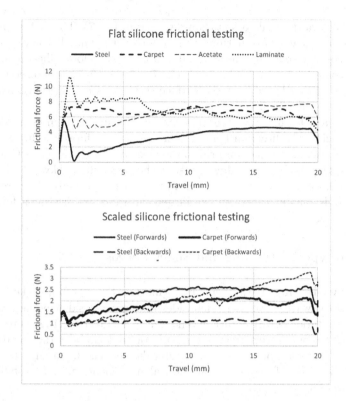

Fig. 6. Frictional testing results for flat silicone and scaled silicone samples across various substrates

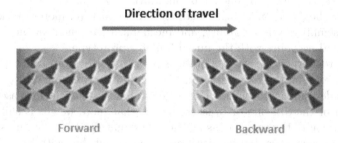

Fig. 7. Scale orientation in the 'forwards' and 'backwards' directions.

when the scales are flat against the module housing, they will not hinder the robot's serpentine and sidewinding motion. However, it should be noted that the steel and acetate tests did not produce a stabilised force range during travel.

Scaled Silicone Results. Although three of the four tested cases did not display a consistent magnitude of frictional force during motion, there are meaningful findings with regards to the impact of the scale direction on motion. For the steel surface, there is more resistance to the scales in the forwards direction than backwards (scale orientation depicted in Fig. 7). This is because, on a flat surface, the scales have nothing to interlock with. They become compliant, increasing contact area with the steel substrate and therefore adhesion-mediated friction becomes the dominant interaction [7]. In the backwards direction, only the points of the scales contact the surface so there is less frictional resistance due to adhesion in this direction.

For the carpet substrate, the opposite relationship is demonstrated, with μk in the backwards direction being larger than in the forwards direction. The scales in the forwards direction grip more effectively with the carpet, with the stiff points propelling the module housing ahead. In the backwards direction, the scale orientation and carpet roughness interlock opposingly, thus preventing smooth travel. This may explain the jagged nature of the frictional force data recorded in Fig. 6.

3.2   Prototype 2 - Housing and Smart Servos

Smart Servo Testing. We implemented 6 motions for the robot snake: forwards serpentine, backwards serpentine, left sidewinding, right sidewinding, clockwise rotation, and anticlockwise rotation. The aim of this testing stage is to observe these different motions performed by the robotic snake in both the standard and custom SLS brackets and identify associated issues. The hierarchy of potential issues includes ease of assembly, mechanical movement, motion stability, and bracket durability.

The housing enables the full function of the robot without restriction, enabling the full rotation of servo motors at each bracket whilst providing the rigidity necessary for controlled motion. Initially a 5-motor snake robot was used to test the 6 motions using the standard manufacturer motor brackets. The bracket assembly, motion stability, and mechanical movement of the 6 motions demonstrated no issues with the initial 5-motor prototype.

Backwards serpentine is considerably slower than forwards serpentine, as this movement relies on the tail contacting the ground and pushing off from it. Left and right sidewinding movements have some stability issues, the increased weight and length of the SLS motor brackets means that more weight is shifted onto the mid-section of the snake, causing the robot snake to turn onto its side. It is still able to achieve the desired direction of movement, but with less efficiency.

Initial testing, performed upon the assembly of the prototype, showed that target joint angles greater than 45° produce smoother forwards and backwards serpentine motions. An angle of 45° was originally chosen as it was observed to cause certain sections to not be in contact with the ground to assist the different motions. Angles of 55° and 60° showed smoother movements; these greater angles allowed the "tail" end of the snake to contact the ground and push off. It is also noted that angles lower than 45° give the sidewinding movements more stability. This has the effect of evening out the weight distribution. Due to time constraints, a test to give a quantitative characterisation of each locomotion could not be undertaken. Further testing would be required to identify the exact causes within the movement issues identified, and to identify optimum angles and joint speeds for the different motions by assessing their speed and stability.

4 Conclusion

This project endeavoured to construct a snake-inspired robot based on the principles of a modular robotic system. Using modular robotics as a base, identical housing units were developed and interlinked to produce a housing chain with alternating degrees of freedom producing rotational and collinear movement. Software was created to incorporate servo motor control and produce serpentine and sidewinding motion. A segregated system was packed into the housing to control the linear actuators to facilitate rectilinear motion. An extendible elastomer skin layer was also manufactured with retractable scales to exclusively facilitate the rectilinear motion of the robot. Two prototypes were assembled, including 1) prototype 1, used to test the snakeskin, demonstrating a single actuator's ability to extend and contract a module housing with a scaled skin layer fixed on, shifting the module housing forwards and 2) prototype 2, used to test the smart servos, demonstrating the motors' ability to allow a housing chain of 5 modules to perform the serpentine and sidewinding motions.

References

1. Abdel-Aal, H.A.: Surface structure and tribology of legless squamate reptiles. J. Mech. Behav. Biomed. Mater. **79**, 354–398 (2018)
2. Li, M., Cao, Z., Zhang, D., Fu, Y.: 3-DOF bionic parallel mechanism design and analysis for a snake-like robot. In: 2016 IEEE International Conference on Robotics and Biomimetics (ROBIO), pp. 25–30 (2016)
3. Lissmann, H.W.: Rectilinear locomotion in a snake (Boa Occidentalis). J. Exp. Biol. **26**(4), 368–379 (1950)
4. Rafsanjani, A., Zhang, Y., Liu, B., Rubinstein, S.M., Bertoldi, K.: Kirigami skins make a simple soft actuator crawl. Sci. Robot. **3**(15) (2018)
5. Siciliano, B., Khatib, O. (eds.): Springer Handbook of Robotics. Springer Handbooks, 2nd edn. Springer, Berlin (2016). https://doi.org/10.1007/978-3-319-32552-1
6. Ta, T.D., Umedachi, T., Kawahara, Y.: Design of frictional 2D-anisotropy surface for wriggle locomotion of printable soft-bodied robots. In: 2018 IEEE International Conference on Robotics and Automation (ICRA), pp. 6779–6785 (2018)
7. Tramsen, H.T., Gorb, S., Zhang, H., Manoonpong, P., Dai, Z., Heepe, L.: Inversion of friction anisotropy in a bio-inspired asymmetrically structured surface. J. R. Soc. Interface **15**, 20170629 (2018)
8. da Veiga, T., et al.: Challenges of continuum robots in clinical context: a review. Progr. Biomed. Eng. **2**(3), 032003 (2020)
9. Whitman, J., Zevallos, N., Travers, M., Choset, H.: Snake robot urban search after the 2017 Mexico City earthquake. In: 2018 IEEE International Symposium on Safety, Security, and Rescue Robotics (SSRR), pp. 1–6 (2018)
10. Yamada, H., Hirose, S.: Study on the 3D shape of active cord mechanism. In: 2006 Proceedings 2006 IEEE International Conference on Robotics and Automation, ICRA 2006, pp. 2890–2895 (2006)

Deep Robot Path Planning from Demonstrations for Breast Cancer Examination

Marta Crivellari[1], Oluwatoyin Sanni[2], Andrea Zanchettin[1],
and Amir Ghalamzan Esfahani[2]([envelope])

[1] Politecnico di Milano, Milan, Italy
[2] University of Lincoln, Lincoln, UK
aghalamzanesfahani@lincoln.ac.uk

Abstract. In 2020, breast cancer affected around two million people worldwide. Early cancer detection is, therefore, needed to save many lives and reduce treatment costs. Nowadays, mammography and self- palpation are the most popular monitoring methods. The high number of cases and the difficulty of correct self-diagnosis has prompted this research work to design a fully autonomous robot to perform breast palpation. Specifically, this study focuses on learning the path for a successful breast examination of a silicone model. Learning from demonstrations proved to be the most suitable approach to reproduce the desired path. We implemented a teleoperation control between two Franka Emika Panda robots with tactile and force feedback to perform palpation on both simple and complex shapes. Moreover, we created a dataset of simple palpation strategy. Finally, we developed and tested different sequential neural networks such as Recurrent Neural Network (RNN), Long short-term memory (LSTM), Gated recurrent unit (GRU) and Temporal Convolutional Network (TCN) to learn the stochastic behaviour of the acquired palpation trajectories. The results showed that TCN is capable of reproducing the desired behaviour with more accuracy and stability than the other models.

Keywords: Robotic palpation · Learning from demonstration · Teleoperation · Force and tactile feedback · Sequential neural networks

1 Introduction

Breast cancer affects many people in the world every year. According to the *GLOBOCAN Cancer Today* database from the International Agency for Research on Cancer, 2.261.419 new cases were identified in 2020 [4]. Early cancer detection is of utmost importance as it can allow faster, simpler and more

This work was partially supported by Cancer Research UK C24524/A30038 in ARTEMIS project.

© Springer Nature Switzerland AG 2021
C. Fox et al. (Eds.): TAROS 2021, LNAI 13054, pp. 260–272, 2021.
https://doi.org/10.1007/978-3-030-89177-0_27

effective treatment; hence saving many lives. Breast self-examination, expert palpation and Mammography are currently the means of detecting breast cancer. Expert and Self-examination are composed of a visual inspection of the breasts and palpation of the breasts and lymph nodes. Nonetheless, these are subjective approaches and may result in many false negative [15]. On the other hand, in mammography, the body is exposed to radiation. Hence, early breast cancer detection is not well practised illustrating a technology gap. Robot palpation is a solution to fill this gap. For example, during robotic minimally invasive surgery [19,22,24], palpation is essential to identify anomalies [6]. Nowadays, the palpation action for breast cancer detection is performed by the patient, consequently of the subjects, the diagnosis is not always reliable, or by expert which is not convenient for many subjects, revealing an autonomous robot for palpation an interesting solution.

Advanced Robotic breasT ExaMination Intelligent System (ARTEMIS) project funded by Cancer Research UK aims to develop a completely autonomous robot that substitutes the palpation action in order to obtain higher accuracy in the diagnosis. There are studies focused on the estimation of mechanical characterisation [5,16,17,19]; but, to the best of our knowledge, this is the first work in literature that study data collection and palpation path planning for autonomous palpation to be used for breast cancer examination. Robotic palpation is complex because combined haptic feedback and visual information determine the interaction between the robotic end-effector and breast tissue, which is complex geometry and has varying mechanical properties across different breasts. Here we consider two phases of path/trajectory planning: (1) palpation path/trajectory planning based only on visual information provided by RGB-D sensor/s and (2) trajectory adaptation based on the tactile information – i.e. according to change of stiffness in the examined tissue by the tactile sensor the robot generates exploration trajectory for that part to gain more information necessary for later cancer detection classifier. The complexity of path planning comes from the alternation between contact and no-contact actions and the correlation between the path and RGB-D sensory information representing different geometry, i.e. the path has to change in accordance to the patient's breast.

Palpation of a breast is an intuitive test technique in which the pads of the three middle fingers are used to identify and locate diseased tissue. It is very important to examine the entire surface, hence, the doctors suggest following a predefined path that can be circles, wedges and/or lines during the palpation [1–3]. Recent research highlights the potential of Learning from demonstration (LfD) in path planning [20]. Recent LfD approaches are reviewed in [23]. Elliot et al. [8] presented LfD to extract the tool application pattern for cleaning task. However, they use many hard-coding and preprocessing operations which is not feasible in breast palpation case due to high geometrical variability across subjects at different palpation tasks. In this work, we aim to develop a data-set and deep model learning the palpation trajectory from human demonstrations without human interference. Palpation trajectory is complicated and stochastic due to human factors. Thus, it is difficult to capture a correct path using traditional machine learning methods. Deep models instead seem to be an appropriate solution correlating visual information to proper palpation trajectory.

[11] used a deep model to learn the robot control action for inserting a needle into a soft tissue. Zhang et al. [25] used a Temporal Convolutional Network (TCN) to predict the long-term lane-changing behaviour trajectory. The results showed that the model could successfully predict the trajectory behaviour with higher performance than RNN and CNN. The contribution of this paper is threefold: (1) a data collection setup for tele-operating palpation actions, (2) a palpation data-set, (3) a series of deep recurrent models generating palpation trajectories based on visual information. These models can capture the behaviour of the palpation trajectory by sequential architectures Recurrent Neural Network (RNN), Long Short Term Memory (LSTM) [10], Gated Recurrent Units (GRU) [9] and TCN. This study demonstrates deep time series are suitable tools for learning palpation trajectory for a phantom at different position and orientation. We created a palpation data set publicly available and baseline deep time series model. This is a proof of concept study. Future works include the big data set more suitable for deep time series model, considering forceful interactions in our experimentation and the use of a breast phantom.

2   Methodology

Learning from the demonstration method achieved good where a human demonstration is not expensive while programming the robot can be time consuming and expensive. The main concept is to record demonstrations of palpation action and extrapolate from them the main features to predict a successful path. It is important to understand what to learn and how to learn before going through the details of the methodology. As such, we made demonstrations using a simple silicon phantom and moving the follower arm end-effector from right to left with a contact motion and from left to right with a no-contact motion, as shown in Fig. 1c), and repeat the motion until all the surface is examined. Then, a deep model will be trained on the data acquired. In the following, we describe the experimental setup, data-set acquisition and deep-model implementation.

2.1   Data-Set Acquisition

Set-Up: We use two Franka Emika Panda robots where the right one (called follower-arm) mirrors the left one (called leader-arm). I.e. the left arm follows the movement of the right arm in Fig. 1a. A real-sense RGB-D camera is mounted on the wrist of The follower and a 4 by 6 Xela sensor is attached to the left finger of Panda arm as shown in Fig. 1b. Each sensing cell of the Xela sensor measures a normal force and two tangent forces during palpation actions. The leader is compliant controlled so that it feels zero mass while a human is moving the follower far from the phantom. If the follower is close to the surface of the phantom the leader will guide the user to keep the leader be normal to the phantom surface and does not allow too much penetration in the phantom (see the Control

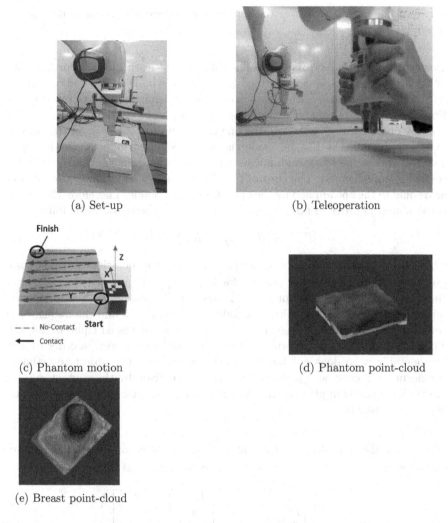

(a) Set-up

(b) Teleoperation

(c) Phantom motion

(d) Phantom point-cloud

(e) Breast point-cloud

Fig. 1. The experimental setup to perform teleoperated palpation actions consisting of 2 Panda arm manufactured by Franka Emika Gmbh (a) and (b); the palpation are applied on a phantom with rectangle cross section made of silicon. The movements pattern during palpation (c); the depth map of the silicon phantom (d) and the breast phantom (e).

for data acquisition section!). We have two phantoms (1) breast phantom which is a model of a real breast, (2) a simple flat surface silicon phantom. In our first implementation in this paper, we use the silicone piece (2A Shore scale) to develop necessary control, learning and experimental setups, shown in Fig. 1c. We fabricated two silicone layers of 15 × 15 × 2 cm dimension and stacked one on the other where two harder objects were embedded as simulation of lumps betweeen the layers. We cover the top silicone surface with a paper to help the sensor sliding.

Control for Data Acquisition. The robot has to learn a behaviour from one or several demonstrations performed by a human who is considered an expert. A teleoperation control with force feedback is implemented to give input to the Franka arm. For terminologies, robots are going to be called 'leader', the one used by operator, and 'follower', the one that computes the task on the silicone phantom. Looking at Fig. 1a, leader is on the left and follower on the right. The two robots have to communicate with each other. For that purpose, a PD control is implemented. The control's goal is to impose a motion to the follower arm equal to the one applied by the operator on leader side. Therefore, the torque is calculated in order to apply same in the follower's actuator T_f as follows:

$$T_f = K_p(\theta_l - \theta_f) + K_d(\dot{\theta}_l - \dot{\theta}_f) \tag{1}$$

where K_p and K_d are the proportional and derivative coefficient, θ is the joint position and $\dot{\theta}$ is the angular velocity for leader (l) and follower (f) side. Notice that the control works only for small $\Delta\theta$ and $\Delta\dot{\theta}$. To satisfy this hypothesis, the initial positions of the leader and the follower are set equal, and the frequency of the control loop has to be higher than a limit value estimated equal to 200 Hz. The palpation action is performed in a perpendicular direction. In order to help the operator, who does not have a direct contact with the object to estimate the normal direction and to fill the reaction force given by the contact, a force feedback control is implemented. The torque on the leader side is modelled and was set T_l equal to:

$$T_l = J^T \cdot F_f^{EE} \tag{2}$$

where J is the Jacobian matrix and F_f^{EE} is the force apply on the follower end-effector. F_f^{EE} is a 6×1 dimensional vector defined as follow:

$$F_f^{EE} = \begin{bmatrix} F_x^{EE} \\ F_y^{EE} \\ F_z^{EE} \\ T_\alpha^{EE} \\ T_\beta^{EE} \\ T_\gamma^{EE} \end{bmatrix} = K \cdot f \left(\begin{bmatrix} x^{EE} \\ y^{EE} \\ z^{EE} \\ \alpha^{EE} \\ \beta^{EE} \\ \gamma^{EE} \end{bmatrix} - \begin{bmatrix} x^{ref} \\ y^{ref} \\ z^{ref} \\ \alpha^{ref} \\ \beta^{ref} \\ \gamma^{ref} \end{bmatrix} \right) \tag{3}$$

Where ref are the variable related to the frame attached to each point of the object's surface with the z axis equal to the normal vector in that point to the surface, while EE refers to the frame attached to the follower's end-effector. The force in x and y direction are considered null, instead the one along z is estimated as:

$$\begin{cases} F_z^{EE} = 0, & z > z_{ref} \\ F_z^{EE} = k_1 \cdot |z - z_{ref}|, & z_{ref} > z > z_{ref} - \delta z \\ F_z^{EE} = k_1 \cdot |\delta z| + k_2(e^{|z-(z_{ref}-\delta z)|} - 1), & z < z_{ref} - \delta z \end{cases} \tag{4}$$

k_1 and k_2 are coefficient chosen experimentally and δz is the area within the object is easily deformed. The three torques T^{EE} are calculated as a coefficient times the difference between the Euler angles of the end-effector frame and reference surface frame. During the demonstrations, the object's point closer to the end-effector is used as reference. The point cloud of the object was used for the estimation of the reference frame in each points of the object (Fig. 1e and 1d). During the teleoperation, the distance between the end-effector and all the points is calculated. If the minimum value of the distance is lower than 2 cm, then the force feedback control is activated.

The z^{ref} is estimated on-line taking the average value of z of the closest 1000 points with respect to the end-effector position. On the other hand, the reference of the orientation, the rotational matrix which corresponds to the closest point is considered. The control was tested on both the simple phantom as well as the real breast with excellent results.

2.2   Deep-Model

The extraction of palpation path from the raw demonstration is a crucial task for robot motion planning. Therefore, the goal is to capture the common features of an entire execution and estimating a global pattern to follow.

Data-Set. 31 demonstrations were collected with the phantom fixed to the table and only one subject as operator. The data-set is composed by X, Y and Z Cartesian's coordinates of the follower's end-effector. The first and the last contact between the end-effector and the object are the initial and last point acquired. The trajectory is described in a relative frame fixed to the object in such a way that the x coordinates corresponds to the repetition direction, y to the task direction and z to the contact direction (Fig. 1c). One trial lasts about 2.5–3 min. In the phase of modelling our trajectories, shallow methods like Hidden Markov models or Bayesian inverse reinforcement learning lack the capacity to model data that has the long-term dependencies property, this is why RNN was chosen for the implementation of our model. They have demonstrated strength in modeling variable length sequence. Hao Wu et al. adopted RNN to predict trajectories on a real world taxi GPS trajectory datasets. Similarly, the behaviour of our trajectories coordinates are periodical, and this makes it sufficient for the network to learn the behaviour of a time series. They can learn the time-dependent mechanisms underlying the expert palpation on the breast phantom. In this work, RNN and its variants like LSTM, GRU and TCN are designed to work with sequential data, they have all been tested to observe which performs best.

Model Architecture. The experiments have been tested on RNN, LSTM, GRU and TCN since each of them have a unique distinction to their structure. RNN is not enough because they cannot solve the vanishing gradient problem, a common problem encountered when training artificial neural networks with

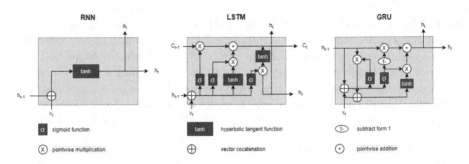

Fig. 2. Schematic comparisons of RNN, LSTM and GRU

gradient-based learning methods and backpropagation. During training, the gradient becomes very small in a vanishing fashion and prevents the weights of the model from changing its value. LSTM's and GRU's were created as the solution to the vanishing gradient problem, they both use a gate system that controls the memorization process. LSTM composes of a cell, an input gate, an output gate and a forget gate. The cell remembers values over arbitrary time intervals and the three gates regulate the flow of information into and out of the cell, it learns to bridge minimal time lags in discrete time steps by enforcing constant error flow through the cell. GRU on the other hand, composes of two gates, a reset gate and update gate. The network has fewer tensor operations since it has a simpler network than the LSTM, and this makes it computationally faster than LSTM.

Conversely, TCN is a recent network different from previous models described. Lea et al. [14] introduced it as a modification of Convolutional Neural Networks for sequence modelling tasks, by combining RNN and CNN architectures. It's a combination of two different network with dissimilar architectures. The first network is a CNN that functions as a feature extractor by encoding spatial-temporal information, while the second network, usually a RNN, takes the low-level dimensional features output of the CNN and acts as a classifier by capturing a high-level temporal information from these features. The CNN is a Casual convolution, a type of network which ensures the model cannot violate the ordering in which we model the data. This means prediction emitted by the model at timestep t cannot depend on any of the future t+1 timesteps. This work focus is not to much focus on how the sequential models shown in Fig. 2, however, we invite readers to get more information about these architectures from the original authors, RNN [21], LSTM [13], GRU [7] and TCN [14].

Defining a sequence modelling as $f : X^{T+1} \rightarrow Y^{T+1}$ with the mapping: $\hat{y}_0, ..., \hat{y}_T = f(x_0, ..., x_T)$ where $(x_0, ..., x_T)$ is the input sequence that predict the output $y_0, ..., y_T$. In our case, T is set as 50, i.e. 50 time steps in past are considered to predict 50 time steps in the future. Even if 50 time steps in the future are predicted, the input temporal window is shifted only by one time step for the next iteration with respect to the previous one, i.e. if the first input is from t_0 to t_{49}, the second input will be from t_1 to t_{50} and so on. 50-time

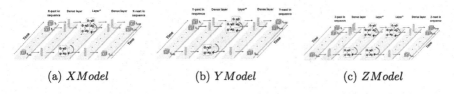

(a) *X Model*   (b) *Y Model*   (c) *Z Model*

Fig. 3. Deep-model

steps in the past are considered to predict 50-time steps in the future. For this research, 67% of the data-set are considered for training and validation while the remaining 33% were used in test phase (Fig. 3).

The four sequential models described above were trained to predict each coordinate i.e. X, Y, Z separately. The structures of the models for the 3 coordinates are very similar: they start and finish with one or more Time Distributed Dense (TDD) layers and in the middle, there are one or more sequence layers (*layer**).

The X and Y model consists of: *InputLayer - TimeDistributedLayer₁ - NNLayer - TimeDistributedLayer₂*.

The Z model consists of: *InputLayer - TimeDistributedLayer₁ - TimeDistributedLayer₂ - NNLayer₁ - NNLayer₂ - TimeDistributedLayer₃* where NNLayer is replaced with either RNN, LSTM, GRU or TCN layer.

The Time Distributed layer serves as a wrapper by applying a Dense layer to every temporal slice of the input. The addition of the extra NNLayer and TimeDistributedLayer in the Z model was done to optimize the prediction of the trajectory efficiently because it's a different type of trajectory in comparison to X and Y. The optimizer chosen is Adam and the loss function used is Mean Absolute Error between the trajectory predictions and ground truth for each coordinate. The number of epochs in accordance with the validation losses is set to 15 for all the models. The performance of models are discussed in the next section. We have used Adam optimiser, the Learning rate is 0.001, 15 epochs, and the loss function used was Mean Absolutes Error.

3   Results

The implemented models show interesting results in both test phase and real-time prediction. In test phase, the inputs sequences given to the model are taken directly from the acquisitions; in real-time instead, the sequences used as inputs are taken from the previous prediction, obviously an exception is made for the first one. The interest is not in replicating the single demonstration but only the correct trend of each coordinate. As a matter of fact, the performance of a network is compared on the capability of estimating the common trend of each demonstrations.

Figure 4(a) represents the X prediction for all the possible networks. The trends of the curves are very similar to each other and there are not relevant differences. For the Y prediction (Fig. 4(b)), it is evident that the peaks of

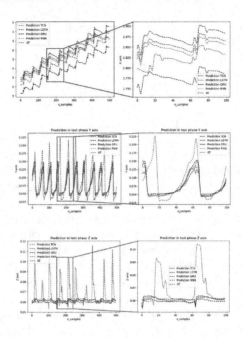

Fig. 4. Test results: (a) Prediction test results of behaviour for X; (b) Prediction test results of behaviour for Y; (c) Prediction test results of behaviour for Z.

the ground-truth do not correspond to the predicted one. This should not be surprising since the periodicity is related to each execution. On the contrary, this fact is interpreted as a strength because the model can learn a medium time period to complete the task. It is significant that all the models identify the same periodicity. Another strength is that the amplitudes of the data acquired have variations in repetitions, instead the predicted trajectory replicates a constant behaviour in accordance with the fixed shape of the phantom. The peaks have a smoother shape along the positive slope and steeper shape along the negative one; the trend reflects perfectly what happens during the execution. In the ascent phase, the sensor is in contact with the surface and the velocity is slower, while in the descent phase, the end-effector is no more in contact and it can reach higher velocity.

Looking at the prediction, one can conclude that Y best estimation is given by GRU, thanks to the smoother shape. Finally, some considerations about Z are needed. It is very difficult to correctly estimate the amplitude of the peaks (no-contact motion) due to the low number of samples with respect to the contact phase since the velocity of the robot is very high. Moreover, most of the samples have same value because the phantom has a constant surface, this is why the model tends to predict a constant output. Nevertheless, a behaviour similar to the ground-truth is achieved by the TCN (Fig. 5). To conclude, unseen inputs were tested on the trained models, and they exhibited the ability to predict a path with a correct trend. Out of all four, GRU had the best performances for Y prediction while TCN performed best for Z.

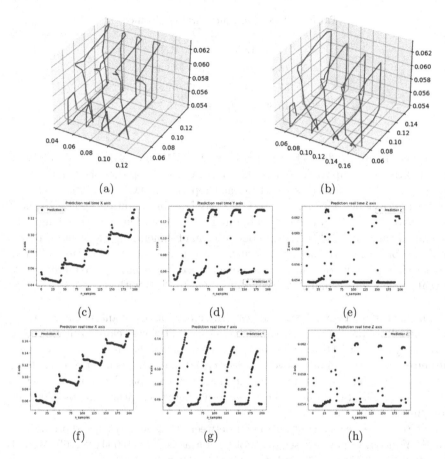

Fig. 5. Predicted 3D trajectory by TCN (a) and GRU in real-time (b); TCN predicted values for (f) x, (g) y, (h) z and GRU predicted values for (i) x, (j) y, (k) z.

In both train and test phase, the sequences given as inputs to the network are taken from the ground-truth. In the following results, only the first sequence is considered as known and the others inputs are taken directly from the prediction. The goal is to find a unique path (Γ) for a correct palpation on the specific phantom. The first 50 points of Γ was given in advance to predict the whole curve. The function is initialised with 50 points and it uses the first element of the output vector as the first element of the input for the next iteration.

TCN and GRU result to be the best models from the testing phase, for the real-time only they are implemented. Figure 5 and 5 summarise the results of TCN and GRU model respectively. The x axis is designed to be equal to repeated direction thus an ideal shape for the X coordinates will look like an ascendant step function since the repetitions should be parallel to x axis. The X prediction in TCN is closer to this ideal trend with respect to the GRU (Table 1).

Table 1. Dynamic time warping distance

	TCN	LSTM	GRU	RNN
X	16.39	39.71	14.5	14.46
Y	57.93	27.40	41.37	57.80
Z	15.89	17.50	16.94	15.75

Y coordinate prediction is unstable in the GRU model (decrease in time), but in TCN, the amplitude remains constant. Considering that the length of the phantom to be examined is equal in each repetition, TCN prediction achieves better performance with respect to GRU. Similar consideration applies to the Z coordinate, the TCN was more stable in Z prediction. On the other hand, the predicted value of X is like the real one in term of dimension. The contact points of Z are comparable to the ground-truth, but the no-contact points are only 1cm higher than the phantom surface, therefore these values have to be increased for a real application. Finally, Y predictions were 0.5 less with respect to the real value.

In conclusion, TCN reflects the best trajectory for the phantom examination. The model can predict a whole trend trajectory that is very close to the expected using only the first 50 time steps, but the dimensions of the final trajectory do not fit perfectly the real values. Nevertheless, the obtained results must be considered a fundamental basis for future works in this research topic. The implementation of the Neural Networks have been made available on github: https://github.com/imanlab/artemis_dpd.

The cumulative mean absolute error between the ground truth and predictions for X, Y and Z in our test set (33% of the data) is $X = 0.03412817658471579$, $Y = 0.03194648418311379$, and $Z = 0.006836229386848896$.

4   Conclusion

Mammography and self-examination are the only tools known for detecting breast cancer in the early stage. The increasing number of new cases all over the years and the importance of correct diagnosis motivated the development of a completely autonomous robot for breast cancer examination. One of the key elements of such a system is learning how to palpate different breasts from expert palpation. This work built the basis of learning from demonstration for breast cancer examination. The highly complex geometry of breasts and different palpation practice, makes it challenging to hard code the palpation actions; hence, we built the palpation trajectory directly from human demonstrations.

We implemented a teleoperation control with force and tactile feedback for data acquisition where this setup enables us to perform palpation on different environments. We collected data of a series of palpation actions on a silicon phantom. Finally, we studied the implementation and results of different deep models for trajectory planning from demonstrations including LSTM, GRU, TCN and

GRU. These baseline implementations revealed the pros and cons of each deep model. Although TCN is among the best model, considerable improvements on the trajectory generation is still needed before making autonomous palpation in future developments.

We identified the limitations of optimisation based approaches, e.g. [18], and conventional learning from demonstration approaches, e.g. DMP [12] can only generalise to new start and goal points whereas in our application the entire palpation path should be adapted to a new breast geometry. Hence, we explored the use of deep model as the mean to generalise the palpation action across different breast geometry.

References

1. Breast self-examination (it can save your life) (2017). https://www.youtube.com/watch?v=LrfE6JUwIms&t=142s&ab_channel=RafflesHospital
2. The breast exam - stanford medicine 25 (2018). https://www.youtube.com/watch?v=pJ55UtP0_nA&t=410s&ab_channel=StanfordMedicine25
3. Examination of female breasts (2018). https://www.youtube.com/watch?v=LrfE6JUwIms&t=142s&ab_channel=RafflesHospital
4. Cancer today (2021). https://gco.iarc.fr/today/home
5. Ahn, B., Kim, Y., Oh, C.K., Kim, J.: Robotic palpation and mechanical property characterization for abnormal tissue localization. Med. Biol. Eng. Comput. **50**(9), 961–971 (2012)
6. Ayvali, E., Ansari, A., Wang, L., Simaan, N., Choset, H.: Utility-guided palpation for locating tissue abnormalities. IEEE Rob. Autom. Lett. **2**(2), 864–871 (2017)
7. Cho, K., Van Merriënboer, B., Bahdanau, D., Bengio, Y.: On the properties of neural machine translation: encoder-decoder approaches. arXiv preprint arXiv:1409.1259 (2014)
8. Elliott, S., Xu, Z., Cakmak, M.: Learning generalizable surface cleaning actions from demonstration. In: 2017 26th IEEE International Symposium on Robot and Human Interactive Communication (RO-MAN), pp. 993–999. IEEE (2017)
9. Fu, R., Zhang, Z., Li, L.: Using LSTM and GRU neural network methods for traffic flow prediction. In: 2016 31st Youth Academic Annual Conference of Chinese Association of Automation (YAC), pp. 324–328. IEEE (2016)
10. Gers, F.A., Schmidhuber, J., Cummins, F.: Learning to forget: continual prediction with LSTM. Neural Comput. **12**(10), 2451–2471 (2000)
11. Ghalamzan, A., Nazari, K., Hashempour, H., Zhong, F.: Deep-LfD: deep robot learning from demonstrations. Softw. Impacts **9**, 100087 (2021)
12. Ghalamzan Esfahani, A., Ragaglia, M.: Robot learning from demonstrations: emulation learning in environments with moving obstacles. Rob. Auton. Syst. **101**, 45–56 (2018)
13. Hochreiter, S., Schmidhuber, J.: Long short-term memory. Neural Comput. **9**(8), 1735–1780 (1997)
14. Lea, C., Flynn, M.D., Vidal, R., Reiter, A., Hager, G.D.: Temporal convolutional networks for action segmentation and detection. In: proceedings of the IEEE Conference on Computer Vision and Pattern Recognition, pp. 156–165 (2017)
15. McDonald, S., Saslow, D., Alciati, M.H.: Performance and reporting of clinical breast examination: a review of the literature. CA: Cancer J. Clin. **54**(6), 345–361 (2004)

16. Nichols, K.A., Okamura, A.M.: Autonomous robotic palpation: machine learning techniques to identify hard inclusions in soft tissues. In: 2013 IEEE International Conference on Robotics and Automation, pp. 4384–4389. IEEE (2013)

17. Nichols, K.A., Okamura, A.M.: Methods to segment hard inclusions in soft tissue during autonomous robotic palpation. IEEE Trans. Rob. **31**(2), 344–354 (2015)

18. Pardi, T., Ortenzi, V., Fairbairn, C., Pipe, T., Ghalamzan Esfahani, A., Stolkin, R.: Planning maximum-manipulability cutting paths. IEEE Rob. Autom. Lett. **5**(2), 1999–2006 (2020)

19. Pastor, F., Gandarias, J.M., García-Cerezo, A.J., Gómez-de Gabriel, J.M.: Using 3D convolutional neural networks for tactile object recognition with robotic palpation. Sensors **19**(24), 5356 (2019)

20. Pérez-Higueras, N., Caballero, F., Merino, L.: Learning human-aware path planning with fully convolutional networks. In: 2018 IEEE International Conference on Robotics and Automation (ICRA), pp. 5897–5902. IEEE (2018)

21. Rumelhart, D.E., Hinton, G.E., Williams, R.J.: Learning internal representations by error propagation. Technical report, California Univ San Diego La Jolla Inst for Cognitive Science (1985)

22. Xiao, B., et al.: Depth estimation of hard inclusions in soft tissue by autonomous robotic palpation using deep recurrent neural network. IEEE Trans. Autom. Sci. Eng. **17**(4), 1791–1799 (2020)

23. Xie, Z., Zhang, Q., Jiang, Z., Liu, H.: Robot learning from demonstration for path planning: a review. Sci. China Technol. Sci. 1–10 (2020)

24. Yan, Y., Pan, J.: Fast localization and segmentation of tissue abnormalities by autonomous robotic palpation. IEEE Rob. Autom. Lett. **6**(2), 1707–1714 (2021)

25. Zhang, Y., Zou, Y., Tang, J., Liang, J.: A lane-changing prediction method based on temporal convolution network. arXiv preprint arXiv:2011.01224 (2020)

Priors Inspired by Speed-Accuracy Trade-Offs for Incremental Learning of Probabilistic Movement Primitives

Daniel Schäle$^{(\boxtimes)}$ ⓘ, Martin F. Stoelen ⓘ, and Erik Kyrkjebø ⓘ

Department of Computer Science, Electrical Engineering and Mathematical Sciences,
Western Norway University of Applied Sciences, Førde, Norway
dasc@hvl.no

Abstract. Probabilistic Movement Primitives (ProMPs) model robot motor skills by capturing the mean and variance of a set of demonstrations provided by a human teacher. Such a probabilistic representation of motor skills is beneficial in physical human-robot cooperation (pHRC) where robots have to respond to the inherent variance in human motion. However, learning ProMPs incrementally and from scratch, as it is desirable in pHRC, is difficult due to the large number of parameters required to model the distribution of a motor skill compared to the few demonstrations available at the beginning of training. In this paper we propose to predict the variance structure of a motor skill based on the speed found in the individual demonstrations and to incorporate this prediction into the prior parameter distribution of the ProMP. Our basic approach is taking inspiration from the speed-accuracy trade-off found in human motion. Experimental evaluation suggests that with the proposed prior parameter distributions, the true distribution is approached faster in incremental learning of a motor skill than with the priors previously proposed for batch learning.

Keywords: Speed-accuracy trade-off · Movement primitives · Learning by demonstration

1 Introduction

In physical human-robot cooperation (pHRC) robots are placed in unstructured environments where they have to deal with changing surroundings and, since human and robot are in continuous physical contact over longer periods, the variance inherent in the motions of their human partners. Some of the variations in the environment and human motion can be captured by probabilistic representations of motor skills, as for example probabilistic movement primitives (ProMPs) [5]. ProMPs represent probability distributions over trajectories, summarizing motor skills in terms of a mean trajectory and corresponding variance.

This work was funded by the Research Council of Norway through grant Nr. 280771.

ⓒ Springer Nature Switzerland AG 2021
C. Fox et al. (Eds.): TAROS 2021, LNAI 13054, pp. 273–283, 2021.
https://doi.org/10.1007/978-3-030-89177-0_28

ProMPs can be learned from human demonstrations which is a common app-roach in robotics, enabling humans to teach robots new motor skills fast and without writing code. In learning by demonstration (LbD) a human demon-strates multiple instances of a movement to a robot by moving the robot's end effector around either directly or through a jointly gripped object. The robot then learns a ProMP by computing e.g. maximum likelihood estimates (MLE) of the ProMP parameters based on the provided examples.

This learning process can either happen incrementally or in batch. Learning in batch means that a set of demonstrations is recorded at the beginning of training. Thereafter, a learning algorithm computes the ProMP parameters on basis of all demonstrations in the set. Since the robot remains passive during the demonstration phase, any cooperation between human and robot is delayed and the human experiences no support in providing the demonstrations in coop-erative tasks such as the joint manipulation of objects. A possibility to achieve human-robot cooperation with batch learning is to first train a ProMP covering all expected variations in a task and then use conditioning to adapt the ProMP to the preferences and circumstances at the time. However, this approach requires external sensor systems to detect changes in the environment, aggravating its use in practice. Furthermore, lay users have a limited understanding of how a robot learns motor skills and how it reacts to new demonstration inputs, making it dif-ficult to deliver just the right demonstrations to the robot without any preview of the resulting motor skill. The training in batch mode has the advantage that a larger data set is available, making the estimation of the ProMP parameters easier, but is however unintuitive in cooperative tasks, where humans expect an incremental training progress of their partner. Batch learning is thus better suited for tasks outside the pHRC domain, where human and robot are not con-tributing actively and simultaneously to the same task, and where tasks can be broken down intuitively into a training and an execution phase.

In incremental learning, the ProMP parameters are updated sequentially – each time a new demonstration arrives [6]. With that, incremental learning is well suited to pHRC, where human and robot solve tasks together and a new demonstration naturally arrives with each execution of a task. After each execution, the motor skill can be slightly adjusted to the most recent preferences of how to execute the task. Incremental learning has the advantage that the human can observe the robot's training progress while they learn a new task together. Cooperation can emerge after the first demonstration and the human can focus on corrections and adaptations – compared to batch learning, the time in which the human has to take on the full leader role is minimized. Shaping motor skills over time with corrective demonstrations can be further facilitated by a forgetting factor which gives more weight to recent demonstrations over what was learned earlier [6]. Incremental learning using a forgetting factor is a step towards life long learning of motor skills.

A challenge in incremental learning is the low number of demonstrations available at the beginning of training. When learning a motor skill from scratch, the ProMP distribution initially has to be estimated on basis of a single demonstration, leading to a degenerate distribution with zero covariance. Also the subsequent estimates, as long as the number of demonstrations is small compared to the dimension of the covariance matrix, suffer from numerical instability caused by rank deficient (singular) covariance matrices. Poor estimates of the covariance matrix are especially severe when the robot's compliance along the trajectory is adjusted according to the variance of the ProMP.

The problem of poor parameter estimates in face of a small sample of demonstrations can be countered with regularization in the form of prior parameter distributions, and hence the computation of maximum a posteriori estimates (MAP) of the parameters, which has been shown to improve the robustness of parameter estimates in batch [3] and incremental [6] learning of ProMPs. The authors in [3] propose to use an uninformative prior for the mean of the ProMP and an informative, data-dependent prior for its covariance matrix, where they use the (scaled) block-diagonal maximum likelihood estimate of the covariance matrix as an initial guess for the parameter. With this setting, the MAP of the mean is equal to its MLE. The block-diagonal prior for the covariance matrix favours the off-diagonal elements representing the correlations between the robot's joints to be zero in presence of a small number of demonstrations, yielding numerically more robust estimates while holding the variances of each joint close to their MLEs. Even though this prior has a positive effect on the robustness of the covariance estimates, it does not actually input prior knowledge into the system but instead utilizes information from all available demonstrations. Hence, it does not cope with the lack of information about the movement/task itself encountered when learning new motor skills incrementally.

It is of course difficult to make general prior assumptions about all arbitrary movements that could possibly be learnt, but it may be possible to make assumptions about the distribution of a specific motor skill based on individual demonstrations. Considering that the demonstrations come from a human manipulating the robot's end effector, characteristics/features of human motion can potentially serve as a source for such prior assumptions. One such feature is the speed accuracy trade-off found in human motion, implying that movement accuracy decreases as speed increases. The most renowned model of this trade-off may be Fitts' law [2]. Fitts' law, originally proposed for translational movements, states that the movement time in a pointing task is a function of the distance to the target and the target width. The smaller the target width, the greater the elapsed time to reach the target. Experiments show that also one-dimensional rotational movements and combined translational and rotational movements can be modelled well with a Fitts' law equivalent [7]. Fitts' law was later generalized to trajectory-based movements, resulting in the steering law [1]. The steering law proposes a linear relationship between the steering time and the "tunnel" width which imposes a spatial accuracy constraint on the movement. Further research has been devoted to the steering law, investigating the effects of combinations of spatial and temporal constraints [11], the effects of narrowing or widening tunnels on the steering time [9] and steering through sequential linear path segments [10]. The aforementioned research is rooted in the field of human

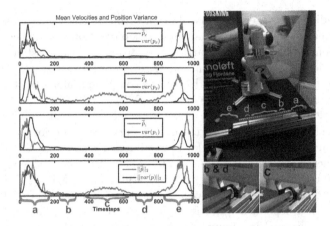

Fig. 1. Example data supporting our assumption of a speed-accuracy trade-off in kinesthetic teaching. The data are computed from 51 kinesthetic demonstrations recorded in the setup on the top-right. The plot shows in **light grey** the absolute mean task-space velocities in X, Y, Z as well as the 2-norm of the mean velocity vector. The sample variance of the mean task-space positions in X, Y, Z and the 2-norm of the mean position vector are shown in **black**. When the task-space velocity is high the variance of the task space position is high as well. The variance and thus the velocity is low at sections **b** and **d** and **c** where the movement is physically constraint by the environment. Note that the velocity peak in section **c** has no corresponding peak in the variance since we aligned the data with dynamic time warping (DTW). Without DTW the speed-accuracy relationship is even more distinct.

computer interaction and the derived models are only verified for simple 1 or 2 dimensional movements in absence of force interactions with the environment. Only recently, motivated by the growth of virtual and mixed reality technology, the development of higher dimensional speed-accuracy models suited to describe 3D object interactions has gotten into focus [8].

Even though we did not find specific studies proving the speed-accuracy trade-off to be present while a human is manipulating a robot's end effector in 3D space by kinesthetic teaching, we suggest to exploit the basic idea of Fitts' law to make prior assumptions about the variance of a ProMP/motor skill based on individual demonstrations. We assume that while delivering demonstrations, the human is subject to a speed-accuracy trade-off limiting the human to guide the robot in a slower pace in directions in which the spatial constraints of the movement are stringent. Figure 1 shows observations we found in kinesthetic demonstration data from a setup that imposes a spatial constraint on the robot's end effector that support this assumption. We propose, that by examining the task-space velocity along the path, we are able to make an estimate of the variance that can be expected in one section relative to other sections of the movement. These estimated variances can be incorporated into the prior of the covariance matrix, enhancing the ProMP with context about the task in early stages of training.

2 Probabilistic Movement Primitives

A ProMP represents a distribution over trajectories [5]. A trajectory $\boldsymbol{\tau} = \{\boldsymbol{y}_t\}_{t=1}^T$ is a time-series of vector-valued robot states $\boldsymbol{y}_t \in \mathcal{S}$ in a state space $\mathcal{S} \subseteq \mathbb{R}^D$, where D is the dimension of the state space. In this paper we encode trajectories in task space by recording the robot's end effector position in 3D Euclidean space. Trajectories are concisely represented as weight vectors $\boldsymbol{w} \in \mathbb{R}^{KD}$ in the basis function model $\boldsymbol{y}_t = \boldsymbol{\Phi}_t \boldsymbol{w} + \boldsymbol{\epsilon}_y$, where $\boldsymbol{\Phi}_t \in \mathbb{R}^{D \times KD}$ is a time dependent, block diagonal basis function matrix containing on its diagonal a row vector $\boldsymbol{\phi}_{d,t}^\mathsf{T} \in \mathbb{R}^K$ for each degree of freedom, which again contains the values of K normalized, evenly spaced, Gaussian basis functions $\phi_k(t)$ evaluated at time t. The last term $\boldsymbol{\epsilon}_y \in \mathbb{R}^D$ is a vector containing the observation noise which is assumed to be independent and identically distributed according to the normal distribution $\mathcal{N}(\boldsymbol{0}, \boldsymbol{\Sigma}_y)$. Given a weight vector $\boldsymbol{w}$, it follows that a trajectory $\boldsymbol{\tau}$ consisting of T time steps is distributed according to

$$p(\boldsymbol{\tau}|\boldsymbol{w}) = \prod_{t=1}^T \mathcal{N}(\boldsymbol{y}_t|\boldsymbol{\Phi}_t \boldsymbol{w}, \boldsymbol{\Sigma}_y). \tag{1}$$

Multiple demonstrations of the same movement are expected to differ slightly. This implies that different weight vectors $\boldsymbol{w}_n$ are needed to represent the n different instances of a movement. The underlying mechanism generating the weight vector samples is assumed to be a Gaussian distribution

$$p(\boldsymbol{w}|\boldsymbol{\theta}_w) = \mathcal{N}(\boldsymbol{w}|\boldsymbol{\mu}_w, \boldsymbol{\Sigma}_w), \tag{2}$$

where $\boldsymbol{\theta}_w = \{\boldsymbol{\mu}_w, \boldsymbol{\Sigma}_w\}$ are the distribution parameters. The mean vector $\boldsymbol{\mu}_w \in \mathbb{R}^{KD}$ summarizes the mean of the demonstrations in each degree of freedom. The covariance matrix $\boldsymbol{\Sigma}_w \in \mathbb{R}^{KD \times KD}$ represents the variances and covariances of the demonstrations in respectively between each degree of freedom.

Learning a ProMP from demonstration can be done by maximizing the likelihood of the N observed trajectories $\boldsymbol{Y} = \{\boldsymbol{\tau}_n\}_{n=1}^N$ with respect to the ProMP parameters i.e. computing the maximum likelihood estimate (MLE) $\boldsymbol{\theta}_w^{MLE} = \arg\max_{\boldsymbol{\theta}_w} p(\boldsymbol{Y}|\boldsymbol{\theta}_w)$, where the marginal likelihood is given by

$$p(\boldsymbol{Y}|\boldsymbol{\theta}_w) = \prod_{n=1}^N \int p(\boldsymbol{w}_n|\boldsymbol{\mu}_w, \boldsymbol{\Sigma}_w) \prod_{t=1}^T p(\boldsymbol{y}_{nt}|\boldsymbol{w}_n) d\boldsymbol{w}_n. \tag{3}$$

For regularization of the MLE, a prior distribution $p(\boldsymbol{\theta}_w)$ over the ProMP parameters can be incorporated into the maximization problem which becomes $\boldsymbol{\theta}_w^{MAP} = \arg\max_{\boldsymbol{\theta}_w} p(\boldsymbol{Y}|\boldsymbol{\theta}_w)p(\boldsymbol{\theta}_w)$. Where $\boldsymbol{\theta}_w^{MAP}$ is the mode of the posterior distribution $p(\boldsymbol{\theta}_w|\boldsymbol{Y})$ known as the maximum a posteriori estimate (MAP). This maximization can be accomplished by means of the expectation-maximization (EM) algorithm in batch [3] and incremental [6] learning settings. Details about the learning algorithms can be found in the respective publications. Since the distribution in Eq. 1 is assumed to be a multivariate normal with unknown mean and variance its conjugate prior is a normal-inverse Wishart distribution [4]. Using the conjugate prior has the advantage that the computations in the EM can be solved in closed form. The normal-inverse Wishart prior has the form

$$p(\boldsymbol{\theta}_w) = \text{NIW}(\boldsymbol{\mu}_w, \boldsymbol{\Sigma}_w | \boldsymbol{m}_0, k_0, \boldsymbol{S}_0, v_0)$$
$$= \mathcal{N}(\boldsymbol{\mu}_w | \boldsymbol{m}_0, \tfrac{1}{k_0}\boldsymbol{\Sigma}_w)\text{IW}(\boldsymbol{\Sigma}_w | \boldsymbol{S}_0, v_0), \tag{4}$$

where $\mathcal{N}(\boldsymbol{\mu}_w | \boldsymbol{m}_0, \frac{1}{k_0}\boldsymbol{\Sigma}_w)$ is a normal distribution representing our prior belief about the ProMP mean with $\boldsymbol{m}_0$ being the prior mean and k_0 controlling the prior strength, and $\text{IW}(\boldsymbol{\Sigma}_w | \boldsymbol{S}_0, v_0)$ is an inverse Wishart distribution representing our prior belief about the covariance matrix of the ProMP with $\boldsymbol{S}_0$ being (proportional to) the prior mean and v_0 controlling the prior strength [4].

3 Prior Parameters Inspired by Speed-Accuracy Trade-Off

Inspired by the speed-accuracy trade-off described in studies on human motor control, we investigate the design of the scale matrix $\boldsymbol{S}_0$ specifying our initial guess of the ProMP variance based on the velocities in the demonstrations. For our initial investigation of this idea in this paper we choose a straight-forward approach. We consider learning a new motor skill incrementally and from scratch, using the incremental learning algorithm for ProMPs presented in [6]. The computation steps are shown in Fig. 2. The training process begins with the human providing the first demonstration to the robot via kinesthetic teaching. During the teaching, we record the Cartesian coordinates of the robot's end effector $\boldsymbol{\tau} = \{\boldsymbol{y}_t\}_{t=1}^T = \left\{ \left(p_x^t \; p_y^t \; p_z^t \right) \right\}_{t=1}^T$. Each time a new demonstration is available, the learning algorithm is executed to incorporate the new demonstration into the ProMP. Between the M-step for the mean $\boldsymbol{\mu}_w$ and the M-step for the covariance matrix $\boldsymbol{\Sigma}_w$ we compute the prior parameter $\boldsymbol{S}_0$ as follows:

$$\dot{\boldsymbol{q}} = \dot{\boldsymbol{\Psi}}\boldsymbol{\mu}_w \tag{5}$$

$$\dot{\boldsymbol{Q}}^{abs} = diag(abs_\circ(\dot{\boldsymbol{q}})) \tag{6}$$

$$\boldsymbol{S}_0^* = v_{min}\boldsymbol{I} + \frac{v_{max}-v_{min}}{max(\dot{\boldsymbol{Q}}_{ii}^{abs}\forall i) - min(\dot{\boldsymbol{Q}}_{ii}^{abs}\forall i)}(\dot{\boldsymbol{Q}}^{abs} - min(\dot{\boldsymbol{Q}}_{ii}^{abs}\forall i)\boldsymbol{I}) \tag{7}$$

$$\boldsymbol{S}_0 = (v_0 + KD + 1)\boldsymbol{\Psi}^{-1}\boldsymbol{S}_0^*\boldsymbol{\Psi}^{-\intercal} \tag{8}$$

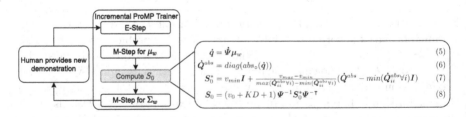

Fig. 2. Computation steps during incremental learning with the speed-accuracy trade-off (SAT) prior proposed in this paper. The SAT prior is computed in the grey block between the M-step of the mean $\boldsymbol{\mu}_w$ and the M-step of the covariance matrix $\boldsymbol{\Sigma}_w$.

where $\boldsymbol{\Psi}, \dot{\boldsymbol{\Psi}} \in \mathbb{R}^{HD \times KD}$ are a block diagonal basis function matrices with each block containing K normalized Gaussian basis functions respectively the derivatives of K normalized Gaussian basis functions evaluated at $H = K$ evenly spaced time steps. $\dot{q}$ is the concatenation of the velocity profiles in x, y, z. By setting $H = K$ the velocity profiles will be coarse and consist only of as many time steps as there are basis functions. In Eq. 6 the operator $abs_o(\cdot)$ computes the element wise absolute values of the velocity vector. The $diag(\cdot)$ operator forms a diagonal matrix from a given vector. In Eq. 7 the absolute velocities are rescaled to the range between the minimum and maximum desired variance $[v_{min}, v_{max}]$, where $0 < v_{min} \leq v_{max}$. The resulting diagonal matrix $\boldsymbol{S}_0^*$ contains the rescaled absolute velocities on its diagonal, thus when interpreted as a covariance matrix $\boldsymbol{S}_0^*$ has higher variance at sections of the movement where the velocity was high – representing a speed-accuracy trade-off. Multiplying $\boldsymbol{S}_0^*$ by the inverse of the basis function matrices has the effect that v_{min} and v_{max} correspond to actual minimum and maximum variance of the ProMP in task space, making it more intuitive to set the scaling parameters. So can we set them in task space units in terms of the smallest and biggest standard deviation we expect for the task. The scaling still has to be set manually but is at least limited to the maximum precision and maximum reach of the robot and can be estimated from the dimensions of the real world set up of the task.

Similar to [3], we multiply $\boldsymbol{S}_0^*$ by $(v_0 + KD + 1)$ such that the MAP estimate $\boldsymbol{\Sigma}_w$ becomes a convex combination of $\boldsymbol{S}_0$ and $\boldsymbol{\Sigma}_w^{MLE}$ with a coefficient dependent on the number of demonstrations N. We set the parameter $v_0 = KD + 2$ to ensure that the expected value of the inverse Wishart distribution equals $\boldsymbol{S}_0$.

Instead of using the scaling matrix computed in Eq. 5–7 alone, we can also blend it with the block diagonal MLE of the covariance matrix, yielding

$$\boldsymbol{S}_0 = (v_0 + KD + 1)\left((1 - \lambda)\boldsymbol{\Psi}^{-1}\boldsymbol{S}_0^*\boldsymbol{\Psi}^{-\mathsf{T}} + \lambda\,\text{blockdiag}(\boldsymbol{\Sigma}_w^*)\right) \tag{9}$$

$$\lambda = \begin{cases} \frac{n-1}{\eta} & 1 \leq n \leq \eta \\ 1 & \text{otherwise} \end{cases}, \tag{10}$$

where n is the current number of demonstrations and η is the desired number of demonstrations in which the influence of $\boldsymbol{S}_0^*$ on $\boldsymbol{S}_0$ diminishes to zero. By setting $\eta \approx 15$, the prior assumption based on the speed-accuracy trade-off helps to bridge the initial phase of training where only a few demonstrations are available. As more and more demonstrations are accumulated the influence of the MLE on the prior can be increased.

4   Experimental Evaluation: Comparison of Prior Parameters in Incremental Learning

For a brief experimental evaluation of our proposed approach, we compare the effects of different prior parameters for the covariance matrix on a data set generated from demonstrations recorded on a Franka Emika Panda manipulator.

The experimental setup is shown in Fig. 1. The goal of the task was to hand-guide the robot's end effector from the round mark on the right to the round mark on the left, while following along the tube with the circular gripper fingers without touching it. The tube poses a physical constraint in task space that could correspond to sliding/insertion movements or tasks like glueing, cutting or welding in industrial settings. During the tube section, the human has to be precise (diameter of the tube 10mm, diameter of the gripper 40mm), hence we argue that he/she is guiding the robot slowly. Our prior computed as described in Sect. 3 incorporates this assumption and suggests a lower variance during the tube section than during the sections before and after the tube.

We recorded 51 demonstrations on the physical setup. Dynamic time warping (DTW) was used for temporal alignment of the demonstrations to rule out that our proposed prior predicts variance stemming from temporal misalignment of the data and not from the speed-accuracy trade-off of the human. Since DTW removes the variance tangential to the path, we removed the tangential variance from our prior by transforming S_0^* to the Frenet-Serret frames of the path represented by the mean vector $\boldsymbol{\mu}_w$, setting the tangential component to zero, and transforming it back to task space coordinates. From the aligned demonstrations, we compute MLE estimates of the parameters of a ProMP with the batch EM algorithm from [3]. We use this ProMP as a reference to compare the parameter estimates during the incremental training under the different priors. We compare following four priors with different prior parameter S_0: MLE, SAT, blended and const. tube. MLE is computed from the block diagonal MLE estimate of Σ_w as proposed by [3]. SAT is computed as proposed in this paper in Eq. 5-8. Blended is computed as a blending of SAT and blkdiag MLE as proposed in Eq. 9-10 with $\eta = 15$. Const. tube is computed as in Eq. 8 with $S_0^* = \frac{v_{min}+v_{max}}{2}I$ which yields a constant tube with a radius equal to the mean of the minimum and maximum radius of the SAT prior. The const. tube prior serves as a benchmark to get an impression how much information is conveyed in the scaling of the SAT prior alone and whether the information about the variance structure based on the speed-accuracy trade-off is beneficial. All other prior parameters are set to same values: $\boldsymbol{m}_0 = \boldsymbol{0}$, $k_0 = 0$ and $v_0 = KD + 2 = 62$. To check the sensitivity of the performance of our proposed prior to the scaling parameters v_{min} and v_{max}, we tested and compared three different parameter settings. As training data for the incremental training, we sampled 500 demonstrations from the reference ProMP. These 500 demonstrations where split into 10 blocks of $N = 50$ demonstrations. The results presented in Fig. 3 are averaged results of the 10 blocks. All ProMPs in the experiment have $K = 20$ basis functions. We compare the effect of the different priors on the incremental training performance by means of the Kullback-Leibler divergence (KLD) between the reference ProMP and the ProMPs under test. In addition, and to emphasize the effect of the variances, we compute the KLD where we set all off-diagonal elements of the covariance matrices Σ_w of reference and ProMPs under test to zero. To monitor the numeric stability of the covariance estimates, we compute the matrix condition number of Σ_w during the course of training.

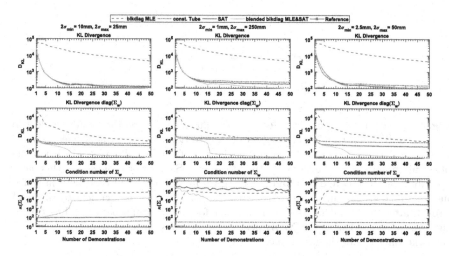

Fig. 3. Results of the experimental evaluation. Each column shows the results of a different scaling setting of the SAT prior and the const. tube. The first row shows the Kullback-Leibler divergence (KLD) of the ProMPs with different priors to the reference ProMP. The second row shows the KLD where only the diagonal elements of the covariance matrix Σ_w are considered. The last row shows the matrix condition number of Σ_w. All y-axes are in logarithmic scale.

The KLD of the *MLE* prior from [3] is greater throughout the entire training than those of the other priors in all three scaling settings. The other three priors perform relatively similar during the first 15 demonstrations, towards the end of training the *SAT* and *blended* perform slightly better than the *const. tube*. The performance of all priors is better when we only consider the diagonalized covariance matrices. The *MLE* and hence also the *blended* show the biggest performance increase. The *blended* prior achieves the lowest final KLD in all experiments, followed by the *SAT* prior which has the second lowest final KLD except for the second scaling setting where the upper scaling bound is very large. For a qualitative comparison of the effects of the different priors on the initial training phase we show the ProMPs after training on only the first demonstration in Fig. 4. The ProMP trained with the *SAT* (*blended* and *SAT* are identical after one demonstration) resembles the reference best and already gives hints about the task constraints after just one demonstration.

5   Discussion and Conclusion

The experimental results in this paper show that the *MLE* prior from [3] is not the best choice for incremental learning settings. The three other priors tested approach the true distribution faster within 50 demonstrations of training. Measured in terms of the KLD, the difference between the *const. tube* and the *SAT* and *blended* is not large, but slightly more distinct when considering the diagonalized covariance matrices. We conclude that the proposed prior inspired by the

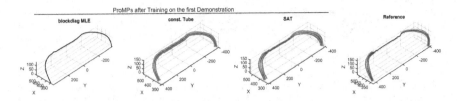

Fig. 4. Qualitative comparison: effects of the different priors on the variance structure of the ProMPs after training on the first demonstration only. The **black** lines show the mean and the grey **tubes** two standard deviations of the ProMPs, plotted without the observation noise Σ_y. The ProMP trained with the **SAT** prior proposed in this paper resembles the **Reference** best and already gives hints about the task constraints after just one demonstration. The ProMP with the *blended* prior is identical to the **SAT** ProMP after the first demonstration and therefore not shown separately. The tube of the ProMP trained with the **MLE** prior appears black since its diameter is smaller than the thickness of the mean line.

speed-accuracy trade-off provides additional beneficial information compared to a constant variance structure along the movement. How much this additional information helps in practice, e.g. in the cooperative learning of a new task, has to be determined in real world experiments. Based on the qualitative comparison of the ProMPs which shows that our *SAT* prior reveals more information about the spatial constraints of the task than the others after the first demonstration, we speculate that our prior can have a noticeable effect in incremental, cooperative learning settings where the physical interaction between human and robot is controlled according to the variance of the ProMP. We speculate that when using the proposed prior, the robot would take over the leader role in precise sections of a task early, relieving the human from the tedious precise control in these sections. Since we only predict variance of the human in interaction with the environment but not variations in the environment itself, our approach fails in tasks that have precise sections (e.g. via points) that change position. In such cases either separate primitives for the via point positions have to be learnt, or the position of the via point has to be captured and encoded as a context variable of the primitive. More work has to be devoted to the proposed method for computing priors before it can be used in practice. At this stage, it is rather a tool to demonstrate the principle idea to estimate task constraints from movement speed. We have only tested our approach on a limited set of tasks and there are still some open parameters that have to be guessed when computing the prior, e.g. the scaling of minimal and maximal desired variance of the prior. Even though the experiments did not show a strong sensitivity towards the scaling, the influence of the parameters on the performance has to be studied in further experiments.

Regardless of the applicability and possible benefits of our prior, it is interesting that it is possible to predict, to some extent, the variance structure of a motor skill by means of the speed-accuracy trade-off. This paper did not aim to provide conclusive proof of a relationship between movement speed and spatial accuracy in kinesthetic teaching, but we think it shows that further investigation of the underlying idea of this paper with regard to incremental learning of movement primitives may be worthwhile.

6   Future Work

To develop the idea of priors inspired by the speed-accuracy trade-off further and to establish them for use in practice, we need to test them on a wider range of tasks. We also need to investigate how to include orientations in addition to translations and how to determine the overall scaling of the variance structure automatically by some algorithm. Furthermore, it is interesting to explore whether there are differences in predicting the variance of point-to-point and trajectory based movements and if priors resembling Fitts' law or the steering law work better in either of them.

References

1. Accot, J., Zhai, S.: Beyond Fitts' law. In: Pemberton, S. (ed.) Human Factors in Computing Systems, pp. 295–302. ACM Press, Addison-Wesley (1997)
2. Fitts, P.M.: The information capacity of the human motor system in controlling the amplitude of movement. J. Exp. Psychol. **47**(6), 381–391 (1954)
3. Gomez-Gonzalez, S., Neumann, G., Scholkopf, B., Peters, J.: Adaptation and robust learning of probabilistic movement primitives. IEEE Trans. Rob. **36**(2), 366–379 (2020)
4. Murphy, K.P.: Machine Learning: A Probabilistic Perspective. Adaptive Computation and Machine Learning Series. MIT Press, Cambridge and London (2012)
5. Paraschos, A., Daniel, C., Peters, J.R., Neumann, G.: Probabilistic movement primitives. In: Burges, C.J.C., Bottou, L., Welling, M., Ghahramani, Z., Weinberger, K.Q. (eds.) Advances in Neural Information Processing Systems, vol. 26, pp. 2616–2624. Curran Ass., Inc. (2013)
6. Schäle, D., Stoelen, M.F., Kyrkjebø E.: Incremental learning of probabilistic movement primitives (ProMPs) for human-robot cooperation (2021, preprint available on arXiv). https://arxiv.org/abs/2105.13775
7. Stoelen, M.F., Akin, D.L.: Assessment of Fitts' law for quantifying combined rotational and translational movements. Hum. Factors **52**(1), 63–77 (2010)
8. Triantafyllidis, E., Li, Z.: The challenges in modeling human performance in 3D space with Fitts' law (2021)
9. Yamanaka, S., Miyashita, H.: Modeling the steering time difference between narrowing and widening tunnels. In: Kaye, J., Druin, A., Lampe, C., Morris, D., Hourcade, J.P. (eds.) CHI 2016, pp. 1846–1856. The Association for Computing Machinery, New York (2016)
10. Yamanaka, S., Stuerzlinger, W., Miyashita, H., et al.: Steering through sequential linear path segments. In: Mark, G. (ed.) Proceedings of the 2017 CHI Conference on Human Factors in Computing Systems, pp. 232–243. ACM, New York (2017)
11. Zhou, X., Cao, X., Ren, X.: Speed-accuracy tradeoff in trajectory-based tasks with temporal constraint. In: Gross, T., et al. (eds.) INTERACT 2009. LNCS, vol. 5726, pp. 906–919. Springer, Heidelberg (2009). https://doi.org/10.1007/978-3-642-03655-2_99

Tactile Dynamic Behaviour Prediction Based on Robot Action

Kiyanoush Nazari[✉], Willow Mandill, Marc Hanheide,
and Amir Ghalamzan Esfahani

School of Computer Science, University of Lincoln, Lincoln, UK
{KNazariSasikolomi,wimandil,mhanheide,aghalamzanesfahani}@lincoln.ac.uk

Abstract. Tactile sensing provides essential information about the state of the world for the robotic system to perform a successful and robust manipulation task. Integrating and exploiting tactile sensation enables the robotic systems to perform wider variety of manipulation tasks in unstructured environments relative to pure vision based systems. While slip detection and grip force control have been the focus of many research works, investigation of tactile dynamic behaviour based on robot actions is not yet sufficiently explored. This analysis can provide a tactile plant which can be used for both control methods and slip prediction using tactile signals. In this letter, we present a data driven approach to find an efficient tactile dynamic model with different tactile data representations. Having evaluated the performance of the trained models, it is shown that the tactile action conditional behaviour can be predicted in a sufficiently long time horizon in future for doing robot motion control.

Keywords: Tactile sensing · Robotic manipulation · Data dimensionality reduction

1 Introduction and Related Works

Tactile sensation is an essential tool for intelligent interactions with a surrounding environment. In manipulation tasks in particular, we use tactile sensing to help inform and reinforce our understanding of an objects dynamics and physical properties beyond outputs from visual assessments. Grasping an object whose weight was different than visual assessment suggested, or an object's centre of mass was in an unexpected location are examples where visual information must be reinforced with tactile data to produce reliable manipulation of an object. Visual assessment alone typically falls short due to being physically remote and occlusion by the end effector at the points of contact [1].

As manipulation tasks push from structured environments into more realistic real world states, the ability to utilise tactile information for manipulation control tasks becomes a more critical challenge and still remains an open problem.

Supported Cancer Research UK.

© Springer Nature Switzerland AG 2021

C. Fox et al. (Eds.): TAROS 2021, LNAI 13054, pp. 284–293, 2021.
https://doi.org/10.1007/978-3-030-89177-0_29

Humans rely heavily on the use of tactile sensing for grasping and manipulation, and the difficulty (and complete failure) of manipulation without tactile feedback was excellently shown in Johansson et al. [2] who anaesthetised peoples fingertips and had them attempt to perform a match striking task. Its importance within the robotics community has also been stated in [1, 3–5].

Romeo et al. [4] state "control algorithms for force regulation or minimisation and grasp stabilisation" as a key open problems for tactile feedback. However, solving these problems has remained a fiendish problem to solve for the key reasons outlined in [1], (i) tactile sensing technology and fabrication is limited to visual information of soft materials or sparse point-wise force measurements, well behind the resolution of a human skin. (ii) modelling contact forces between objects and fingertip are difficult to create. (iii) specifying a desired tactile signal for use in controlled manipulation is also complex to define.

In this paper, a multi-step tactile predictive model is developed to predict future tactile state vector for a pick and move manipulation task with in hand objects using tactile sensors with point-wise force measurements. The contributions of this paper are as follows: We train a variety of deep neural networks and show that a multi-modal recurrent neural network can accurately predict the future fingertip tactile readings of a robot grasping a slippery object while moving through a non-linear trajectory. We show that this prediction model can be trained with entirely unlabelled data. We exploit data compression methods on tactile data to remove the redundancy in tactile sensory information and reduce the computational complexity of tactile dynamic behaviour prediction. Finally, we prove that accurate predictions can be made with 3D, unconfined trajectories of a 7DOF robotic manipulator with variance in pose, velocity and acceleration with a real object.

We demonstrate and evaluate these contributions with a data set of pseudo random trajectories generated by human kinesthetic motions of a Franka Emika robot arm. This arm has two Xela uSkin sensors attached to a two finger parallel type gripper. The force of the gripper is insufficient to keep the object in a stable location and so the motion of the robot creates slipping and eventually the object falls out of the robots grasp. The purpose of this data set is to produce a rich set of sequences where the motion of the robot has direct effect on the sensation felt at the fingertips.

Research in the field of tactile sensor use for control is in the reactive application of slip detection, surveyed in depth in [4]. However, fewer research works can be found in slip prediction. [1] proved that with accurate tactile predictions of a GelSight tactile sensor by a video prediction model introduced in [6], model predictive control could be used to reach the target tactile reading, in this case rolling a ball on the end of a CNC machine to a desired location on a table. While for doing a manipulation task in our case, specifying the goal tactile signal (or image) is not feasible beforehand.

[7] converted the xela uSkin tactile sensor readings to a visual representation; However, there are significant issues with the proposed representation including reduced resolution of the tactile readings, and taxel objects cross over produces

an impossible problem for the prediction model to interpret. The model presented, uses a simplified convolutional LSTM chain structure presented in [6].

Model-based approaches are also applied for tactile data exploitation from the large variety of tactile sensors available [8]. Spike trains analysis [9], threshold on derivatives of normal and shear tactile forces for slip detection [10], applying PCA and Hidden Markov Models for slip prediction [11], using friction cone for slip detection by estimating friction coefficient [12,13] are among these model-based approaches. Model-based approaches usually suffer from being limited to the type of the sensor and gripper and the known object characteristics are required in advance.

Deep neural networks (DNNs) have also been extensively used on processing tactile information; Such as fusing tactile data with other sensory information for texture recognition [14,15], grasp stability estimation [16], train RL policy in a peg-in-hole task [17]. [18] classifies the direction of slip into seven categories by using ConvLSTM cells on the constructed tactile images from BioTac sensor. Having AEs for dimensionality reduction [19] uses multi-dimensional scaling for tactile servoing. [12] divides each manipulation task to four types of manipulation primitives and friction cone slip detection is used to regenerate robot trajectory.

Overall, while tactile signals are exploited for slip detection, grasp stability estimation, stable grasp policy learning, data fusion, grip force control, and robot motion control, only a few [1,18] items try to learn a predictive model to capture the dynamic of a tactile system to predict its behaviour in a sufficiently long time horizon for robot control. We propose an approach in which a model combines recent tactile readings and robot states and based on the future planned robot action, the tactile readings will be predicted in the planned time horizon. The pipeline can be used for different types of tactile data including vision and non-vision tactile sensors and also the trained forward model which learnt the dynamic behaviour of the tactile readings, can be used in different control architectures including tactile Reinforcement Learning controllers.

2   Methodology

2.1   Problem Statement

Let's assume $\vec{S}(t) \in \mathbb{R}^n$ and $\vec{O}(t) \in \mathbb{R}^d$ denote the tactile state and observation space vectors at time t respectively. The external input vector to the system is robot state $\vec{r}(t)$ which effects the tactile interaction with the world. With the curse of dimensionality for $\vec{O}(t)$, there is a highly ambiguous non-linear mapping between the observation to state space. As such, it is desired to map $\vec{O}(t)$ to an abstract lower dimension feature space $\vec{Z}(t)$ which can give us a closer representation to the state space. For the tactile system, $\vec{Z}(t)$ is achieved by applying dimensionality reduction methods on the raw tactile data. The problem of latent tactile state prediction in a time horizon of length τ, can be denoted as follows:

$$\vec{Z}(t+1 : t+\tau) = \vec{f}(\vec{Z}(t-\tau : t), \vec{r}(t-\tau : t+\tau)) \tag{1}$$

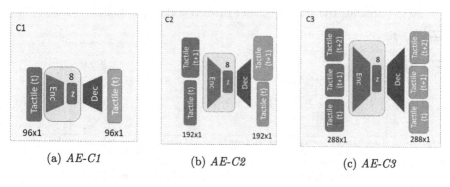

(a) *AE-C1*   (b) *AE-C2*   (c) *AE-C3*

Fig. 1. AE structures for tactile data dimensionality reduction

Where $\vec{f}$ is the vector function mapping recent tactile state and robot trajectory to future tactile vector; which is trained by the deep recurrent network. Therefore, the pipeline that we apply for tactile dynamic modelling is to map observation space to lower dimension abstract feature space and then investigate the correlation of tactile features with robot state using the RNN cells.

2.2 Tactile Data Dimensionality Reduction

As the main objective of tactile state signal prediction is for slip prediction, the 96 values of the 32 taxels are having redundant readings which could be more compact by dimensionality reduction methods. In this regard, we use two main approaches for tactile data reduction while trying to avoid any major information loss. First, is the Principal Component Analysis (PCA) which finds orthogonal vectors consisting of linear combination of the original data while preserving as much as variability as possible [20]. In tactile data dimensionality reduction with PCA, keeping at least 80% variance of the data is considered as the threshold value. This means fewer number of principle components which could not preserve the minimum value of the variability are ignored. 20 PCs was the minimum number of PCs which resulted larger than 80% variance.

The second approach is utilising a deep Auto-encoder (AE) [21] for data dimensionality reduction. AEs are self-supervised DNNs which consist of two main components, the encoder which compresses the input data into smaller dimensions, and the decoder which tries to reconstruct the same input data in the output. To include a temporal dependency in encoding the tactile data three types of input data are used for the AEs, I. 96 dimensional tactile vector at each time step t, II. 192 dimensional tactile vector including the readings at time t-1 and t stacked row-wise together, and III. 188 dimensional tactile vector including readings at t-2, t-1, and t. We call the three classes of AEs, *AE-C1*, *AE-C2*, and *AE-C3* respectively for easier referencing. Figure 1 presents the structure of the input data for tactile AEs. The depth and hyper-parameters for each AE network are optimised independently.

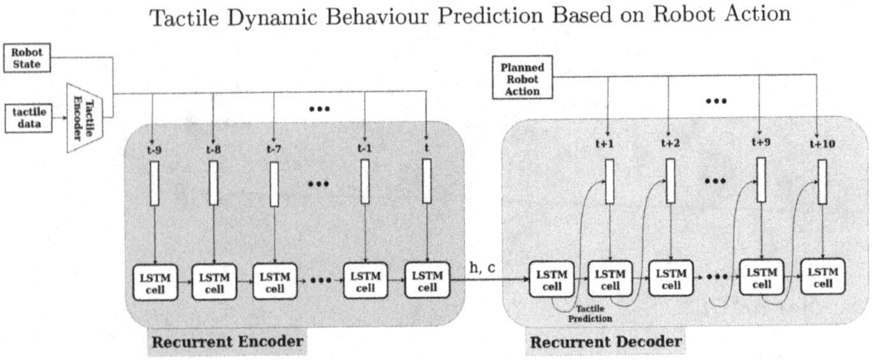

Tactile Dynamic Behaviour Prediction Based on Robot Action

Fig. 2. Recurrent forward model

After training, the latent vector $\vec{Z}$ inholds the compact representation of the input data. The dimension of the latent vector is a hyper parameter which is chosen based on a trade-off between how compact the latent vector is and the reconstruction loss. For tactile data compression, the latent vector is a 8 dimensional vector. The size is chosen based on trying various sizes and comparing the loss values.

2.3   Deep Recurrent Model for Prediction

The problem of predicting a system's behaviour in a time horizon with having its recent past data can be categorised in the type of sequence to sequence modelling in the context of deep learning. In the input we are having sequences of tactile readings, robot state, and robot planned action; and in the output future tactile readings are predicted. To process the sequential data we use LSTM cells which are preserving two main components, C_t and h_t which are called cell and hidden state respectively. The update rule for each time step will be defined with the elements called gate values. The *forget, input,* and *output* gates are defined by applying sigmoid function over the independent weight matrices multiplied by the input vectors to the cell, scaling them between zero and one to tell the cell how much of the previous state and current data it should forget, take as input or send as output. C_t and h_t can be initialised with either zero or random values after processing each batch of training data.

In tactile prediction model, the hidden state of the LSTM cell should represent the dynamic behaviour of the tactile signals and the correlation between tactile and robot state. Figure 2 shows the architecture of the recurrent model. As Fig. 2 shows, the Recurrent Encoder block encodes the tactile and robot state correlation for the past 10 time steps until present time t into h and c. These RNN state vectors are then used as initial state for Recurrent Decoder. From time t onward, at each time step cell's prediction is concatenated with planned robot action at that time step, and then fed back as an input to the next cell. The difference between the input tactile data for Encoder and Decoder blocks is that

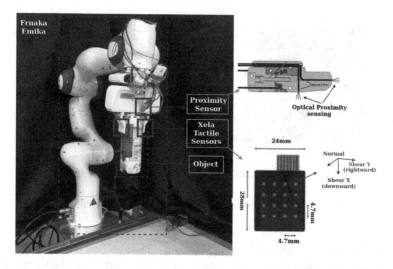

Fig. 3. Experimental setup for in hand manipulation including xela tactile sensors and proximity sensor [22].

while in the Encoder ground truth tactile data are combined with past robot states as final input, in the Decoder block, tactile prediction at each time step is combined with future robot action as the final input. This helps the Recurrent Forward Model to efficiently use past tactile and robot state and future planned action to deduce future tactile state as Eq. 1 denotes.

3   Experiments

In order to define a manipulation task as a train/test case for tactile state prediction, Franka arm does a pick and move motion consisting of two linear motion trajectory in Z and X directions. The velocity/acceleration profile varies among different pick and move trials. We use a commercially available magnetic based tactile sensor from XELA robotics which is shown in Fig. 3. The sensor works with average 50 Hz frequency and has one kg normal force threshold. There are tri-axial readings for each taxel and by having 16 taxels on each sensor the overall 48 readings are available including 16 for normal, shear x and y directions. We have mounted two of the XELA sensors on designed interfaces to connect to Panda Franka normal grippers. Figure 3 shows the sensors mounted on the Panda EE.

In order to have labelled data for slip detection we use a proximity sensor attached to the robot wrist which looks directly to the top surface of the object. After grasping the object, as long as the distance measured by the proximity sensor is constant there is no relative motion between the object and the fingers hence no slippage. However, changes in the proximity readings larger than a small specified threshold is indicative of slippage. These proximity readings are

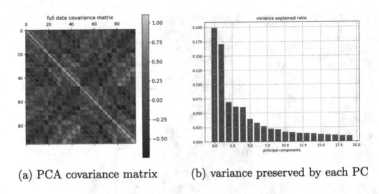

(a) PCA covariance matrix   (b) variance preserved by each PC

Fig. 4. PCA results with 20 principle components

then binarized and saved with the data for slip classification labelling purposes. For the object we use a bottle with plastic structure and the weight can change between 5 categories based on the objects inside the bottle. In data acquisition robot, proximity, and tactile data are publishing with 1000, 400, and 50 Hz respectively. All data readings are synchronised in ROS subscriber to have the same frequency for all of the data (50 Hz).

For data collection for a manipulative task we have applied two approaches to achieve rich enough data for training our tactile prediction recurrent model. The first approach was to do a linear motion pick and place task for the bottle and send Cartesian velocity profiles with trapezoidal shapes and different acceleration/deceleration values to the robot. This is designed to have structure for robot motion for doing control in the next steps of the project once the forward model is learned. As such, for an object with constant weight, while with lower acceleration the task was completed successfully, by increasing the acceleration in the profile the object was dropped in the middle of the task. Therefore, robot motion profile was the only parameter causing the slippage and hence the changes in tactile readings. The second strategy was data collection with robot kinaesthetic teaching. In this mode a human operator does various manipulation motions until the object is dropped. The benefit of this mode is that the zero impedance robot motion lets the user to execute motions with large variety of velocity and acceleration ranges; which might not be possible with robot motion controller in the previous mode. This will provide richer tactile data for training the model.

4   Results

In order to achieve the most precise tactile behaviour prediction we have utilised data dimensionality reduction methods to further remove the redundancy of the tactile readings and reduce the computational complexity of the prediction problem. As such, the performance of the recurrent model will be evaluated by three types of tactile inputs: 1. Original raw data, 2. principle components (PCs)

Table 1. Evaluation of recurrent forward models

Tactile input	Validation loss[†]	Test loss[†]
Raw data	0.0484	0.0552
AE-C1	0.0330	0.0403
AE-C2	0.0351	0.0453
AE-C3	0.0405	0.0510
PCA	0.0298	0.0363

[†] *MSE* Loss

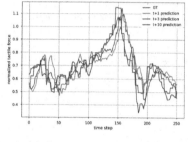
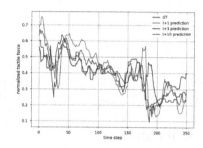

(a) first principle component   (b) second principle component

Fig. 5. Two main PCA principle components and prediction with recurrent model

resulted from PCA, and 3. latent vectors of three classes of AEs namely *AE-C1*, *AE-C2*, and *AE-C3*. For the implementation, PCA function from python's sklearn library is used. Figure 4 shows the result of applying PCA on the raw tactile data. Figure 4a presents the covariance matrix between the PCs and Fig. 4b illustrates the variance contained in each of the 20 PCs. Overall, 82% of the variance are preserved by all of the PCs.

Having the tactile data analysed by dimensionality reduction methods, we can now evaluate the performance of the recurrent model on the compressed tactile data. As Fig. 2 shows we combine tactile data with the robot state as the input for the Recurrent Encoder block; and the predicted tactile vector at each time step and the robot action as the input to the Recurrent Decoder block. As Table 1 shows the PCA and *AE-C1* tactile input resulted in the best prediction results. Figure 5 shows the ground truth signal and the model prediction for the first two major PCs of the dimensionality reduction resulted from PCA. For visualising model prediction, the ground truth tactile feature vector is plotted alongside the prediction for three different time steps in prediction horizon. The graphs for $t+3$, $t+5$, and $t+10$ are plotted without the shift in time axis, since these data are available at time step t and are compared with the ground truth data available at that time. Figure 6 presents the predictions for two components of the C1 AE latent vector. It can be observed that $t+10$ prediction signal captures the change in ground truth signal before it happens. This is a desired feature to enable the model to be used for slip prediction. Although the loss value

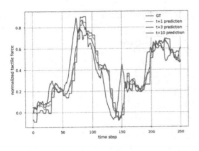

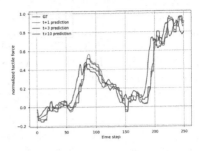

(a) 2nd latent vector components   (b) 4th latent vector components

Fig. 6. Recurrent model prediction for sample latent vector components

for PCA input is smaller than the corresponding value for AE-C1 (table1), the AE-C1 model has the advantage to predict the sudden rise of the latent tactile feature before it happens in the ground truth.

5   Conclusion

We have applied a data driven approach on exploring action conditional tactile dynamic behaviour with deep recurrent neural networks. Data compression could improve the tactile prediction accuracy and diminish the computational complexity of the problem. Having been trained on the collected data from the real robotic setup, the model can predict the tactile behaviour for slippage case in advance of time which is the desired purpose of the model for slip prediction in the next step. With this learnt tactile dynamic, the models can now be used for a closed loop control for object slippage avoidance.

References

1. Tian, S., et al.: Manipulation by feel: touch-based control with deep predictive models. In: 2019 International Conference on Robotics and Automation (ICRA), pp. 818–824. IEEE (2019)
2. Johansson, R.S., Flanagan, J.R.: Coding and use of tactile signals from the fingertips in object manipulation tasks. Nat. Rev. Neurosci. **10**(5), 345–359 (2009)
3. Yousef, H., Boukallel, M., Althoefer, K.: Tactile sensing for dexterous in-hand manipulation in robotics—a review. Sens. Actuat. A: Phys. **167**(2), 171–187 (2011)
4. Romeo, R.A., Zollo, L.: Methods and sensors for slip detection in robotics: a survey. IEEE Access **8**, 73027–73050 (2020)
5. Dahiya, R.S., Metta, G., Valle, M., Sandini, G.: Tactile sensing—from humans to humanoids. IEEE Trans. Rob. **26**(1), 1–20 (2009)
6. Finn, C., Goodfellow, I., Levine, S.: Unsupervised learning for physical interaction through video prediction. arXiv preprint arXiv:1605.07157 (2016)
7. Zhou, X., Zhang, Z., Zhu, X., Liu, H., Liang, B.: Learning to predict friction and classify contact states by tactile sensor. In: 2020 IEEE 16th International Conference on Automation Science and Engineering (CASE), pp. 1243–1248. IEEE (2020)

8. Yamaguchi, A., Atkeson, C.G.: Recent progress in tactile sensing and sensors for robotic manipulation: can we turn tactile sensing into vision? Adv. Robot. **33**(14), 661–673 (2019)
9. Yi, Z., Zhang, Y., Peters, J.: Biomimetic tactile sensors and signal processing with spike trains: a review. Sens. Actuat. A: Phys. **269**, 41–52 (2018)
10. Saen, M., Ito, K., Osada, K.: Action-intention-based grasp control with fine finger-force adjustment using combined optical-mechanical tactile sensor. IEEE Sens. J. **14**(11), 4026–4033 (2014)
11. Jamali, N., Sammut, C.: Slip prediction using hidden markov models: Multidimensional sensor data to symbolic temporal pattern learning. In: 2012 IEEE International Conference on Robotics and Automation, pp. 215–222. IEEE (2012)
12. Hogan, F.R., Ballester, J., Dong, S., Rodriguez, A.: Tactile dexterity: manipulation primitives with tactile feedback. In: 2020 IEEE International Conference on Robotics and Automation (ICRA), pp. 8863–8869. IEEE (2020)
13. Chen, W., Khamis, H., Birznieks, I., Lepora, N.F., Redmond, S.J.: Tactile sensors for friction estimation and incipient slip detection—toward dexterous robotic manipulation: a review. IEEE Sens. J. **18**(22), 9049–9064 (2018)
14. Takahashi, K., Tan, J.: Deep visuo-tactile learning: estimation of tactile properties from images. In: 2019 International Conference on Robotics and Automation (ICRA), pp. 8951–8957. IEEE (2019)
15. Luo, S., Yuan, W., Adelson, E., Cohn, A.G., Fuentes, R.: ViTac: feature sharing between vision and tactile sensing for cloth texture recognition. In: 2018 IEEE International Conference on Robotics and Automation (ICRA), pp. 2722–2727. IEEE (2018)
16. Murali, A., Li, Y., Gandhi, D., Gupta, A.: Learning to grasp without seeing. In: Xiao, J., Kröger, T., Khatib, O. (eds.) ISER 2018. SPAR, vol. 11, pp. 375–386. Springer, Cham (2020). https://doi.org/10.1007/978-3-030-33950-0_33
17. Lee, M.A., et al.: Making sense of vision and touch: self-supervised learning of multimodal representations for contact-rich tasks. In: 2019 International Conference on Robotics and Automation (ICRA), pp. 8943–8950. IEEE (2019) . IEEE (2019)
18. Zapata-Impata, B.S., Gil, P., Torres, F.: Learning spatio temporal tactile features with a ConvLSTM for the direction of slip detection. Sensors **19**(3), 523 (2019)
19. Sutanto, G., et al.: Learning latent space dynamics for tactile servoing. In: 2019 International Conference on Robotics and Automation (ICRA), pp. 3622–3628. IEEE (2019)
20. Jolliffe, I.T., Cadima, J.: Principal component analysis: a review and recent developments. Philos. Trans. R. Soc. A: Math. Phys. Eng. Sci. **374**(2065), 20150202 (2016)
21. Ng, A., et al.: Sparse autoencoder. CS294A Lect. Notes **72**(2011), 1–19 (2011)
22. Konstantinova, J., Cotugno, G., Stilli, A., Noh, Y., Althoefer, K.: Object classification using hybrid fiber optical force, proximity sensor. In: 2017 IEEE SENSORS, pp. 1–3. IEEE (2017)

State Space Analysis of Variable-Stiffness Tendon Drive with Non-back-Drivable Worm-Gear Motor Actuation

Ian S. Howard[1]([✉]) and Martin F. Stoelen[2,3]

[1] SECAM, University of Plymouth, Plymouth 4 8AA, UK
ian.howard@plymouth.ac.uk
[2] Western Norway University of Applied Science, Førde, Norway
Martin.Fodstad.Stolen@hvl.no
[3] Fieldwork Robotics Ltd, Cambridge CB24 9AD, UK

Abstract. Here we investigate variable-stiffness tendon drive for a robot arm. The novel aspect of our design is that it makes use of non-back-drivable worm-gear motor actuation, so static arm configurations can be maintained at a desired stiffness level without requiring motor power. We first analyze a link that is driven via uni-directional agonistic-antagonistic non-linear elastic tendons and construct the state space model of the system. We then design an observer-based state feedback controller. This ensures the output link can track a reference input vector consisting of a desired joint angle as well as tendon extension realized by tendon co-contraction. We simulated the controller and plant in MATLAB and show examples of typical movement trajectories for angular control of the link.

Keywords: Agonistic-antagonistic tendons · Worm drive · State space control

1 Introduction

There is much interest in the development of actuators that exhibit compliance [1, 2], and there are many potential applications areas for compliant robotic arms. They are well suited for operation in unstructured environments where occasional collisions are possible and are potentially safe around people. High compliance is not always desirable and variable compliance assists payloads manipulation [3], and high stiffness assists operation with unstable loads, as it does in human manipulation and movement [4]. Various methods have been proposed to implement compliance and modulate stiffness [2]. We extend the approach taken in the Gummiarm, which achieves variable stiffness by means of non-linear elastic tendon co-contraction [5]. We use a uni-directional agonist-antagonist tendon setup, but bi-directional designs are also possible [6]. Here we use low-cost worm-gear motor actuation, which is not back drivable, to ensure static joint configuration at a fixed tendon tension and consequently fixed joint stiffness, can be maintained without requiring drive to the motors. This makes the overall design power-efficient and well suited to mobile applications. An example could a mobile autonomous berry picking system, where compliance increases robustness to collisions and power

© Springer Nature Switzerland AG 2021
C. Fox et al. (Eds.): TAROS 2021, LNAI 13054, pp. 294–303, 2021.
https://doi.org/10.1007/978-3-030-89177-0_30

consumption must be minimized to extend operating time between recharging of the platform's batteries.

2   Tendon Drive System

Much previous work has been done on tendon driven mechanisms [7]. Here we analyse the motor-tendon system illustrated in Fig. 1A and develop a state space description. A feedback controller is used to drive the motors that operate the left and right pulleys, ensuring the output angle follows the reference input angle. Similarly, the controller maintains co-contraction to achieve a target tendon extension. Turning both input pulleys in opposite directions increases tension in both tendons, but results in no net torque on the output pulley and it remains stationary. Rotating them in the same direction results in a net torque, which causes the output pulley to rotate. A rod representing a robot link is attached to the output pulley, as shown in Fig. 1B. This resists the applied torque due to viscous friction from the bearing and air, and due to the moment of inertia of the rotating components. Brushed worm-drive DC motors rotate the pulleys.

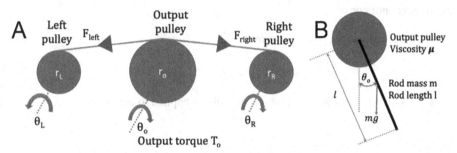

Fig. 1.   Panel A: Schematic of agonist-antagonist two-tendon drive. The tendons wrap-around and are firmly attached to the pulleys and do not just rely of friction to transfer force. Panel B: Simple robot link connected to the output pulley.

3   State Space Analysis of DC Motor

Many researchers have investigated the analysis and control of DC motors, e.g. [8, 9], including those that make the use of worm gear drives [10, 11]. Here we run DC motors under voltage control. Consider the equivalent circuit of a single DC motor as shown in Fig. 2. Motor torque Tm generated by current passing through the motor coils is given by the product of armature current and the motor torque constant kt.

$$T_m = k_t i \tag{1}$$

Motor torque T_m is resisted by the motor's inertia J, as well as its viscous friction b

$$T_m = b\frac{d\theta_t}{dt} + J\frac{d^2\theta_t}{dt^2} \tag{2}$$

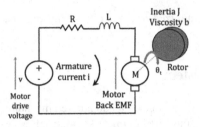

Fig. 2. Equivalent electrical circuit of a DC motor, including armature mechanical properties.

Equating the two terms gives

$$k_t i = b\frac{d\theta_t}{dt} + J\frac{d^2\theta_t}{dt^2} \qquad (3)$$

$$\Rightarrow \frac{d}{dt}(\dot{\theta}_t) = -\frac{b}{J}\dot{\theta}_t + \frac{k_t}{J}i \qquad (4)$$

Summing voltages around the circuit leads to a voltage equation, where v represents the motor control input voltage, L is motor inductance, R motor resistance, and K_e is motor generator constant

$$v = iR + L\frac{di}{dt} + k_e\frac{d\theta_t}{dt} \qquad (5)$$

$$\Rightarrow \frac{d}{dt}(i) = -\frac{k_e}{L}\dot{\theta}_t - \frac{R}{L}i + \frac{1}{L}v \qquad (6)$$

Choosing the states and the input as the voltage applied to the motor

$$x_1 = \dot{\theta}_t \qquad (7)$$

$$x_2 = i \qquad (8)$$

$$\Rightarrow \frac{d}{dt}(x_1) = -\frac{b}{J}x_1 + \frac{k_t}{J}x_2 \qquad (9)$$

$$\Rightarrow \frac{d}{dt}(x_2) = -\frac{k_e}{L}x_1 - \frac{R}{L}x_2 + \frac{1}{L}v \qquad (10)$$

Angular position output can be computed by integrating motor angular velocity, so

$$\frac{d}{dt}(x_3) = x_1 \qquad (11)$$

This leads to the state space matrix equation for a motor

$$\Rightarrow \frac{d}{dt}\begin{bmatrix} x_1 \\ x_2 \\ x_3 \end{bmatrix} = \begin{bmatrix} -\frac{b}{J} & \frac{k_t}{J} & 0 \\ -\frac{k_e}{L} & -\frac{R}{L} & 0 \\ 1 & 0 & 0 \end{bmatrix}\begin{bmatrix} x_1 \\ x_2 \\ x_3 \end{bmatrix} + \begin{bmatrix} 0 \\ \frac{1}{L} \\ 0 \end{bmatrix}v \qquad (12)$$

We represent the worm gear motor gearing ratio by G_e which increases the mechanical advantage and scales the overall motor output position by a factor $\frac{1}{G_e}$. We note in practice that $K_t = K_e$ but choose to keep them separate here for clarity.

4   Analysis of Two-Tendon Rotary Series Elastic Actuator

4.1   Modeling Tendon Extension

In an agonistic-antagonist arrangement, if tendon extension force is a quadratic function of extension, then stiffness is a linearly function of extension [12, 13]. However, for small displacement around their extension point, we can consider the tendons as locally linear springs with spring constant k, so local force is proportional to local extension. Thus, the local linear constant k is dependent on tension, which can be modulated by co-contraction. We assume that both tendon springs are always operating under pre-tension, so neither ever goes slack. With drive and output angles in radians, output torque is given by the differences in torques exerted by the right and left tendons

$$T_o = k(\theta_R\, r_R - \theta_o\, r_o\,)r_o - k(\theta_o\, r_o + \theta_L\, r_L)r_o \sum \tag{13}$$

Where $+$ ve directions are shown on Fig. 1. If both drive pulleys have same radius r_{in}

$$T_o = kr_o((\theta_R - \theta_L)r_{in} - 2\theta_o\, r_o) \tag{14}$$

We can re-write the expression in terms of a new spring constant $K_r = kr_o^2$

$$T_o = K_r\left(\tfrac{r_{in}}{r_o}(\theta_R - \theta_L) - 2\theta_o\right) \tag{15}$$

4.2   Modeling to 2-tendon Actuator Dynamics

When the link (modelled as a rod) moves in a vertical plane, the torque exerted on the output pulley by the tendons is resisted by mechanism's inertia I, a torque term arising from the gravity and viscous friction μ.

$$T_o = I\ddot{\theta}_o + \mu\dot{\theta}_o + \tfrac{mgl}{2}\sin(\theta_o) \tag{16}$$

Equating the two expressions

$$K_r\left(\tfrac{r_{in}}{r_o}(\theta_R - \theta_L) - 2\theta_o\right) = I\,\ddot{\theta}_o + \mu\dot{\theta}_o + \tfrac{mgl}{2}\sin(\theta_o) \tag{17}$$

Rearranging with only the highest order differential on the LHS

$$\ddot{\theta}_o = -\tfrac{\mu}{I}\dot{\theta}_o - \tfrac{mgl}{2I}\sin(\theta_o) - \tfrac{2K_r}{I}\theta_o + \tfrac{K_r}{I}\tfrac{r_{in}}{r_o}(\theta_R - \theta_L) \tag{18}$$

We note the gravity term will be small in comparison to the restoring force due to tendon stiffness. It is also zero when the link moves horizontally. More generally, when the link is hanging down vertically, linearizing for small angles gives

$$\ddot{\theta}_o = -\tfrac{\mu}{I}\dot{\theta}_o - \left(\tfrac{mgl}{2I} + \tfrac{2K_r}{I}\right)\theta_o + \tfrac{K_r}{I}\tfrac{r_{in}}{r_o}(\theta_R - \theta_L) \tag{19}$$

4.3   State Space Model of 2-tendon Drive Dynamics

To build a state space model of this 2-tendon system we choose states x_1 and x_2

$$x_1 = \dot{\theta}_o \tag{20}$$

$$x_2 = \theta_o \Rightarrow \dot{x}_2 = \dot{\theta}_o = x_1 \tag{21}$$

This leads to two 1st order equations

$$\dot{x}_1 = -\frac{\mu}{I}x_1 - \left(\frac{mgl}{2I} + \frac{2K_r}{I}\right)x_2 + \frac{K_r}{I}\frac{r_{in}}{r_o}\theta_R - \frac{K_r}{I}\frac{r_{in}}{r_o}\theta_L \tag{22}$$

$$\dot{x}_2 = \dot{\theta}_o = x_1 \tag{23}$$

Writing in matrix form gives the state space equations

$$\Rightarrow \frac{d}{dt}\begin{bmatrix} x_1 \\ x_2 \end{bmatrix} = \begin{bmatrix} -\frac{\mu}{I} & -\left(\frac{mgl}{2I} + \frac{2K_r}{I}\right) \\ 1 & 0 \end{bmatrix}\begin{bmatrix} x_1 \\ x_2 \end{bmatrix} + \begin{bmatrix} \frac{K_r}{I}\frac{r_{in}}{r_o} & -\frac{K_r}{I}\frac{r_{in}}{r_o} \\ 0 & 0 \end{bmatrix}\begin{bmatrix} \theta_R \\ \theta_L \end{bmatrix} \tag{24}$$

4.4   Tendon Extension and Output Actuation

When the link is in equilibrium position hanging downwards or is horizontal, and exerting no load on the tendons, tension stretching is only due to the co-contraction extension from the control pulleys (again note rotation directions on Fig. 1)

$$\theta_{stretch} = (\theta_R + \theta_L) \tag{25}$$

$$\Rightarrow \theta_R = \theta_{stretch} - \theta_L \tag{26}$$

$$\Rightarrow \theta_L = \theta_{stretch} - \theta_R \tag{27}$$

Output angle will be midway between the two control angles

$$\theta_{target} = \frac{(\theta_R - \theta_L)}{2} \tag{28}$$

Substituting for θ_R from Eq. (26)

$$\Rightarrow \theta_{target} = \frac{(\theta_{stretch} - \theta_L - \theta_L)}{2} \tag{29}$$

$$\Rightarrow \theta_L = \frac{\theta_{stretch}}{2} - \theta_{target} \tag{30}$$

Substituting for θ_L from Eq. (27)

$$\Rightarrow \theta_{target} = \frac{(\theta_R - \theta_{stretch} + \theta_R)}{2} \tag{31}$$

$$\Rightarrow \theta_R = \theta_{target} + \frac{\theta_{stretch}}{2} \tag{32}$$

5 State Space Model for Motor Driven 2-tendon Drive

We now build as single state space model for two DC worm-drive motors and the tendon dynamics for the unloaded arm. Since we use a worm drive gear that is not back-drivable and the load on the motors due to arm is very low, we assume the output position of the worm gear motors are unaffected by the link mechanism. However, we could easily add an additional effective inertial term to the motor to account for the link's inertial resistance. Given our simplifying assumptions, the tendons are only influenced by motor output actuator angles. We can thus combine the state space models for motor actuation and tendon drive into single matrix as follows:

$$\frac{d}{dt}\begin{bmatrix} x_1 \\ x_2 \\ x_3 \\ x_4 \\ x_5 \\ x_6 \\ x_7 \\ x_8 \end{bmatrix} = A \begin{bmatrix} x_1 \\ x_2 \\ x_3 \\ x_4 \\ x_5 \\ x_6 \\ x_7 \\ x_8 \end{bmatrix} + B \begin{bmatrix} \theta_{target} \\ \theta_{stretch} \end{bmatrix} \tag{33}$$

Where the A and B matrices are given by Eqs. (34) and (35). It can be seen that the 3×3 regions in the A matrix denoted by the black rectangles represent the state space matrix contributions from the two motors and follow the A matrix in Eq. (12). We drive these two motors with target angle and co-contraction stretch extension inputs in the input vector $\begin{bmatrix} \theta_{target} & \theta_{stretch} \end{bmatrix}^T$, where θ_{target} is the joint output target angle and $\theta_{stretch}$ is co-contraction. These inputs are mapped onto the control inputs for the left and right motors by Eqs. (30) and (32), as implemented in the combined input matrix B given in (35); note the transpose. A full list of parameters is given in Table 1.

$$A = \begin{bmatrix} -\dfrac{b}{J} & \dfrac{Kt}{J} & 0 & 0 & 0 & 0 & 0 & 0 \\[2mm] -\dfrac{Ke}{L} & -\dfrac{R}{L} & 0 & 0 & 0 & 0 & 0 & 0 \\[2mm] 1 & 0 & 0 & 0 & 0 & 0 & 0 & 0 \\[2mm] 0 & 0 & 0 & -\dfrac{b}{J} & \dfrac{Kt}{J} & 0 & 0 & 0 \\[2mm] 0 & 0 & 0 & -\dfrac{Ke}{L} & -\dfrac{R}{L} & 0 & 0 & 0 \\[2mm] 0 & 0 & 0 & 1 & 0 & 0 & 0 & 0 \\[2mm] 0 & 0 & \dfrac{Kr\, r_{in}}{G_e I\, r_o} & 0 & 0 & -\dfrac{Kr\, r_{in}}{G_e I\, r_o} & -\dfrac{\mu}{I} & -\left(\dfrac{mgl}{2I} + \dfrac{2Kr}{I}\right) \\[2mm] 0 & 0 & 0 & 0 & 0 & 0 & 1 & 0 \end{bmatrix} \tag{34}$$

$$B = \begin{bmatrix} 0 & -\frac{1}{L} & 0 & 0 & \frac{1}{L} & 0 & 0 & 0 \\[1mm] 0 & \frac{1}{2L} & 0 & 0 & \frac{1}{2L} & 0 & 0 & 0 \end{bmatrix}^T \tag{35}$$

The states x_3 and x_6 represent motor drive angles prior to reduction by the worm gears. These values are scaled by the reciprocal of the gearing ratio and drive the input to the left and right tendon pulley system. The latter is represented by the lower dashed rectangle, which follows the A matrix for the tendon dynamics captured in Eq. (24). This leads to a system with 8 states in total. To implement state feedback control we need to estimate the full system state. We use a Luenberger observer for this purpose. Figure 3. shows the structure of the controller. Since motor and link angular velocities are be hard to measure directly in a mechanical implementation, they are estimated. However angular position from the motors, motor currents, and output link angle are often available and can be used to correct the state estimate. The C matrix shown in Eq. (36) thus selects motor current, position and link position from the full state vector:

Table 1. List of all parameters for agonist-antagonist compliant drive system

	Link and tendon		Worm-drive motor
I	Link mechanism's inertia	L	Motor inductance
mg	Link gravity force term	R	Motor resistance
μ	Link viscous friction coefficient	J	Motor inertia
K_r	Effective tendon spring constant	b	Motor viscous friction
r_{in}	Drive pulley radius	G_e	Worm gearing ratio
r_o	Output pulley radius	K_e	Motor generator constant
l	Link length	K_t	Motor torque constant

6   Observer-Based State Feedback Control of Link Angle

To find a linear quadratic regulator gain K to implement full state feedback control of the system, diagonal terms in the Q and R matrices were specified, to penalized the system states and controls.

$$
\begin{bmatrix} y_1 \\ y_2 \\ y_3 \\ y_4 \\ y_5 \end{bmatrix} = \begin{bmatrix} 0\,1\,0\,0\,0\,0\,0\,0 \\ 0\,0\,1\,0\,0\,0\,0\,0 \\ 0\,0\,0\,0\,1\,0\,0\,0 \\ 0\,0\,0\,0\,0\,1\,0\,0 \\ 0\,0\,0\,0\,0\,0\,0\,1 \end{bmatrix} \begin{bmatrix} x_1 \\ x_2 \\ x_3 \\ x_4 \\ x_5 \\ x_6 \\ x_7 \\ x_8 \end{bmatrix} \tag{36}
$$

They consisted of costs for the motor states $Cost_{mv} = 0.01$, $Cost_{ml} = 0.01$ and $Cost_{ma} = 10$ for the motor velocity, current and angle respectively. In addition, costs were specified for the tendon system consisting of $Cost_{lv} = 0.01$ and $Cost_{la} = 10$ for the link velocity and angle states. The values used were found by experimentation. The cost matrix Q was composed of these elements:

$$Q = \begin{bmatrix} Cost_{mv} & 0 & 0 & 0 & 0 & 0 & 0 & 0 \\ 0 & Cost_{mi} & 0 & 0 & 0 & 0 & 0 & 0 \\ 0 & 0 & Cost_{ma} & 0 & 0 & 0 & 0 & 0 \\ 0 & 0 & 0 & Cost_{mv} & 0 & 0 & 0 & 0 \\ 0 & 0 & 0 & 0 & Cost_{mi} & 0 & 0 & 0 \\ 0 & 0 & 0 & 0 & 0 & Cost_{ma} & 0 & 0 \\ 0 & 0 & 0 & 0 & 0 & 0 & Cost_{lv} & 0 \\ 0 & 0 & 0 & 0 & 0 & 0 & 0 & Cost_{la} \end{bmatrix} \tag{37}$$

Similarly, the control voltages to the motors were penalized by $Cost_{cv}$ terms along the diagonal of the R matrix:

$$R = \begin{bmatrix} Cost_{cv} & 0 \\ 0 & Cost_{cv} \end{bmatrix}$$

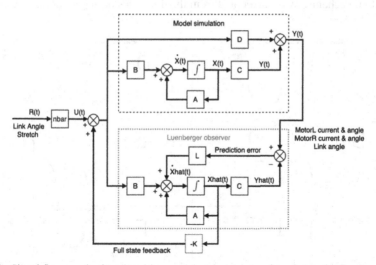

Fig. 3. Signal flow graph of tendon drive model under observer-based state feedback control.

For weak control penalization we set $Cost_{cv} = 5$ and for strong control penalization $Cost_{cv} = 50$. Pre-compensation was implemented to track the reference link angle target by computing nbar, so that the corresponding angular position DC gain of the system was unity. The Luenberger observer state estimator uses the state space a model of the plant as captured by the matrices A and B, given in Eqs. (34, 35), and a correction term arising from the difference between actual and predicted output. The Luenberger gain L was again calculated using the MATLAB lqr command. The state space controller was implemented in MATLAB and the trapezoid method was used to implement integration, which is also suitable for a real-time implementation [14].

7 Results and Conclusions

Simulation results are shown in Fig. 4. Panels A-C show results when low control voltage penalization of 5 was used and no limits were placed on the drive voltage to the motors. We use a point to point angular movement task, which is representative of typical operation. The target joint angle follows a sequence of 2-s-long values held at [0, 1, 0, –1, 0] Rad. It can be seen that the link follows the target angle specified with a rise time of about 200 ms. To demonstrate that extending the tendons due to co-contraction does not affect output angle, the extension angle simultaneous follows the sequence of [0, 0.5, 0, –0,5, 0]. Panels B and C show the link velocity and motor voltages rises to high values. Panels D-E show results when control voltage penalization of 50 was used, with limits placed on the motors of 48v (to simulate the effects of using a real controller with the motors). Results in panel D shows that more cost for the voltage drive to the motors and clipping the maximum values slows down the rise time to about 700 ms, although this system still reaches the target link angle. The limitation on motor voltages makes the latter scenario suitable for a real-time hardware implementation.

To summarize, we analysed a variable-stiffness tendon drive system using worm gear actuation. The non-back drivability of the drive lead to a simplifying assumption that the tendon mechanism was uncoupled from the dynamics of the motor and vice-versa.

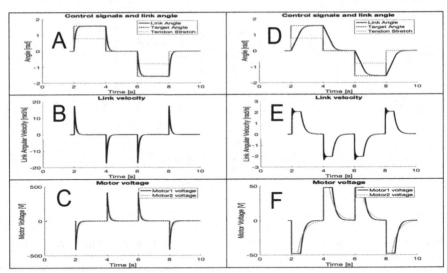

Fig. 4. Simulation in MATLAB. Panels A-C for case when no limit was placed on the voltage control and its cost was small. Panels A The square wave envelope (black line) shows a positive and negative rectangular target angle applied to the controller. The response (solid line that quickly reaches the target) shows the link output link angle. Note that co-contraction results in tendon extension (dotted line) but had no effect on the output angle. Panel B shows the corresponding link velocity. Panel C shows the two motor control voltages. Panels D-E show the corresponding results when motor voltage magnitude is limited to 48v and voltage control cost was set a factor 5 higher than before. It can be seen penalized and limiting the drive voltage, necessary in a hardware implementation, affects behavior, but not catastrophically.

Simulation showed observer-based state feedback control can realise angle position control of a single link. Results from an EtherCAT implementation on a mechanical motor-driven tendon system are described in a companion manuscript [14].

Acknowledgments. We thank Simon Bates and Innovate UK project No: 104622 SoSehRaH, and the University of Plymouth for support, and Fieldwork Robotics Ltd for helpful discussion and access to their technology.

References

1. Grioli, G., et al.: Variable stiffness actuators: the user's point of view. Int. J. Robot. Res. **34**(6), 727–743 (2015)
2. Vanderborght, B., et al: Variable impedance actuators: a review. Robot. Auton. Syst. **61**(12) 1601–1614 (2013). and Control (ICAC3) (pp. 1–5). IEEE
3. Bicchi, A., Tonietti, G.: Fast and soft-arm tactics [robot arm design]. IEEE Robot. Autom. Mag. **11**(2), 22–33 (2004)
4. Burdet, E., Osu, R., Franklin, D.W., Milner, T.E., Kawato, M.: The central nervous system stabilizes unstable dynamics by learning optimal impedance. Nature **414**(6862), 446–449 (2001)
5. Stoelen, M.F., Bonsignorio, F., Cangelosi, A.: Co-exploring actuator antagonism and bio-inspired control in a printable robot arm. In: Tuci, E., Giagkos, A., Wilson, M., Hallam, J. (eds.) From Animals to Animats 14. SAB 2016. Lecture Notes in Computer Science, vol. 9825, pp. 244–255. Springer, Cham (2016). https://doi.org/10.1007/978-3-319-43488-9_22
6. Petit, F., Friedl, W., Höppner, H., Grebenstein, M.: Analysis and synthesis of the bidirectional antagonistic variable stiffness mechanism. IEEE/ASME Trans. Mechatron. **20**(2), 684–695 (2015)
7. Ozawa, R., Kobayashi, H., Hashirii, K.: Analysis, classification, and design of tendon-driven mechanisms. IEEE Trans. Rob. **30**(2), 396–410 (2013)
8. Chotai, J., Narwekar, K.: Modelling and position control of brushed DC motor. In: 2017 International Conference on Advances in Computing, Communication (2017)
9. Ruderman, M., Krettek, J., Hoffmann, F., Bertram, T.: Optimal state space control of DC motor. IFAC Proc. Vol. **41**(2), 5796–5801 (2008)
10. Pinto, V.H., Gonçalves, J., Costa, P.: Model of a DC motor with worm gearbox. In: Gonçalves, J.A., Braz-César, M., Coelho, J.P. (eds.) CONTROLO 2020. CONTROLO 2020. Lecture Notes in Electrical Engineering, vol. 695, pp. 638–647. Springer, Cham (2021). https://doi.org/10.1007/978-3-030-58653-9_61
11. May, D.C., Jayasuriya, S., Mooring, B.W.: Modeling and control of a manipulator joint driven through a worm gear transmission. J. Vib. Control **6**(1), 85–111 (2000)
12. Ham, R.V., Sugar, T., Vanderborght, B., Hollander, K., Lefeber, D.: Compliant actuator designs. IEEE Robot. Autom. Mag. **3**(16), 81–94 (2009)
13. Migliore, S.A., Brown, E.A., De Weerth, S.P.: Biologically inspired joint stiffness control. In: Proceedings of the 2005 IEEE International Conference on Robotics and Automation, pp. 4508–4513. IEEE (2005)
14. Howard, I.S., Stoelen, M.F.: EtherCAT implementation of a variable-stiffness tendon drive with non-back-drivable worm-gear motor actuation, TAROS 2021, University of Lincoln (2021)

Development of a ROS Driver and Support Stack for the KMR iiwa Mobile Manipulator

Hatem Fakhruldeen$^{(\boxtimes)}$, David Marquez-Gamez, and Andrew I. Cooper

Leverhulme Research Centre for Functional Materials Design,
University of Liverpool, Liverpool, UK
{h.fakhruldeen,dmarquez,aicooper}@liverpool.ac.uk

Abstract. Mobile manipulators are expected to revolutionise robotics applications because they combine mobility and dexterity. Robotics middlewares such as ROS (Robot Operating System) is a key component to develop the capability of these platforms and to research their novel applications. In this paper, we present a complete ROS stack for the KMR iiwa mobile manipulator. This stack comprises of a ROS driver, with a novel architecture, running natively on the platform controller and the essential support packages that allow motion planning, navigation, visualisation and simulation using ROS standard tools and frameworks. To our knowledge, this work is the first *ROS 1* (For the purpose of this work the term ROS will refer to *ROS 1*) package for the KMR iiwa. To demonstrate the capabilities of our work, we present example applications both in simulation and using the real robot. Finally, the proposed stack is used in a heterogeneous multi-robot system in the context of an autonomous chemistry laboratory.

1 Introduction

Mobile manipulators are becoming more common and are expected to revolutionise various sectors using robotics [12]. A mobile manipulator comprises of a robotic manipulator mounted on a mobile base, which provides both mobility and dexterity. In the coming years, it is expected for these platforms will be widely employed in different indoor and outdoor applications such as providing assistance in manufacturing [9], transporting goods in warehouses [3], performing chemistry workflows [2] and picking fruits in farms [7], among others.

The expansion in the use and development of these platforms in recent years has been accelerated by the growth of e-commerce and its aim to have fully automated warehouses run by robots [1]. This trend is reflected in the increasing number of commercially available mobile manipulators such as KUKA KMR iiwa, MiR ER-FLEX, OMRON MoMa, to name but a few. Furthermore, these

---

We acknowledge the Leverhulme Trust via the Leverhulme Research Centre for Functional Materials Design for funding.

© Springer Nature Switzerland AG 2021
C. Fox et al. (Eds.): TAROS 2021, LNAI 13054, pp. 304–314, 2021.
https://doi.org/10.1007/978-3-030-89177-0_31

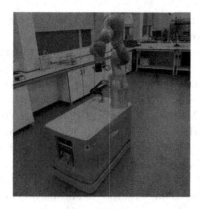

Fig. 1. KMR iiwa mobile manipulator.

platforms are still widely studied in academic research labs as their potential application domains and full capabilities are still being investigated.

The Robot Operating System (ROS) is an open source robotics middleware framework that allows to connect various hardware and software components together [11]. This allows for the easy addition and integration of new peripherals with robots such as sensors and grippers. Also, it provides a number of tools and frameworks for robot's control, motion planning, navigation and simulation, that also allow to develop new algorithms and test them on real and simulated robots. For these reasons, ROS has become a very popular and widely used as middleware in robotics research.

ROS support is crucial to advance research with mobile manipulators and to develop novel applications. Specifically, this includes having a ROS-based driver for the platform and supporting ROS packages that utilise that driver for planning and controlling the robot. Some mobile manipulators have ROS compatibility features out of the box by virtue of having ROS-based support for their individual components, *i.e.*, the mobile base and mounted manipulator. In that case, additional development and integration work is needed to fully use these robots with ROS. On the other hand, some mobile manipulators lack of ROS support because one or both of their components (the robotic manipulator or the mobile base) do not have developed drivers and supporting packages.

The KMR iiwa mobile manipulator is one such platform that lacks ROS support and compatibility. It was developed by the German company KUKA (Keller und Knappich Augsburg) as a collaborative robot (Cobot) for the purpose of meeting the requirements of Industry 4.0. It is a highly flexible and mobile platform that is intended for handling manufacturing automation tasks. This mobile manipulator is shown in Fig. 1. It comprises of the KMP200 omni-Move mobile base and a LBR iiwa14 R820 robotic arm. The robot is programmed using KUKA's proprietary Sunrise.OS that utilises the Java programming language. Currently, there is no official KUKA support to provide ROS packages for the KMR iiwa mobile manipulator, the work presented in [3] was one of the first attempts to produce a ROS compatible software to control the first generation of the KUKA mobile platform, however that was explored to a limited extent and the produced source code was not made public.

The installed manipulator, LBR iiwa14, has a ROS-based driver and accompanying support packages that allow to control and interact with the arm [5]. The KMP200 mobile base does not have any public ROS-based driver at the moment. On the other hand, there exists a *ROS 2* (the second generation of ROS)[1] driver for the KMR iiwa platform that allows to control the mobile base and receive its sensors' data [4]. However, *ROS 2* nodes and topics are not compatible with *ROS 1*. There exists a special *ROS 1 - ROS 2* bridge[2] that can facilitate their interaction but is of limited use because it only offers restricted functionality and is cumbersome to set up and use. Furthermore, *ROS 1* is predominately used in research and few robots and peripherals currently offer *ROS 2* support, which limits the applicability of the driver in [4] in the context of heterogeneous robotic applications and use with other peripherals.

In this paper, we present a novel complete ROS stack for the KMR iiwa mobile manipulator that allows the control of its arm and mobile base, and the gathering of sensory data. This stack is composed of a ROS driver running natively on the robot controller and accompanying support packages that collectively allow to perform motion planning, navigation, visualisation and simulation using ROS standard tools. To the best of our knowledge this is the first public ROS package for the KMR iiwa mobile manipulator that provides an interface and complete integration between the platform, and the Robot Operating System (ROS). Furthermore, this paper details our contribution of the novel design of the driver architecture and describes the various tests performed to validate the stack operation with the robot. This will allow other robotic researchers to utilise this platform with ROS in their research and development endeavours. Our aim is to use this ROS-based mobile manipulator in the context of an autonomous chemistry laboratory and develop hardware and software architectures for chemist robots (robots that research chemistry); but, we envisage that there will be other real-world applications that would also benefit from this architecture.

This paper is structured as follows. A description of the KMR iiwa platform is presented in Sect. 2. Section 3 describes the developed software stack and its components. In Sect. 4, the results and tests performed to validate the software architecture are detailed. Finally, Sect. 5 summarises the key conclusions.

2   KMR iiwa Robot

2.1   Platform Description

The KMR iiwa mobile manipulator (see Fig. 1) comprises of a LBR iiwa14 R820 robotic manipulator, a KMP200 omniMove mobile base and two SICK S300 safety laser scanners. The LBR iiwa14 arm is a 7-DOF (Degrees Of Freedom) robotic manipulator with 14 Kg payload. It is designed to be used in human robot collaboration settings.

---

[1] https://docs.ros.org/en/galactic/index.html.
[2] https://github.com/ros2/ros1_bridge.

The KMP200 is an omnidirectional mobile base that has four mecanum wheels. This base is equipped with two SICK S300 safety laser scanners mounted diagonally opposite to each other. These scanners emit laser beams at a height of 15 cm above the floor. Each scanner covers an area spanning 270° and thus covers one long and one short side of the base. The platform controller, named The Sunrise cabinet, along with the drive battery, are located inside the KMP200 base.

2.2 Operation and Safety

KUKA Sunrise.OS is the current operating system software for the KMR iiwa mobile manipulator. It is used by all KUKA robots that are controlled by the Sunrise cabinet. It provides tools for the development, deployment and configuration of robotic applications. Moreover, these applications are developed in the Sunrise Workbench programming environment using Java programming language and Sunrise.OS software packages. These collectively represent Sunrise.OS API (Application Programming Interface) that allows to interact and control the robot's components. This API allows to command and access the robot resources locally via the Sunrise cabinet or the platform's teach pendant, named Smart-PAD. Consequently, in contrary to using a middleware such as ROS, this makes the system harder to integrate in heterogeneous robotic experiments and interface with other systems.

The platform has three operating modes: T1 mode, in which the platform is manually operated in reduced speed mode for the purposes of testing and debugging the developed application, T2 mode that is the same as T1 without the speed reduction and AUT mode where the platform executes its program autonomously.

The operation safety of this mobile platform is monitored by means of the SICK S300 laser scanners. Each scanner monitors a predefined area around the mobile base, which is divided into warning and protective fields. The size of these fields depends on the vehicle's velocity, where higher velocities translates to larger fields. Any violation of the protective fields result in an emergency stop in all modes except for T1 and T2 modes when the velocity is less than 0.13 m/s. Violations of the warning fields depends on the mode but mostly result in maximum speed reduction. Moreover, the installed robotic arm, by virtue of it being a Cobot, has built-in force/torque sensors in the joints that ensure safe and compliant robotic manipulation.

2.3 Interfacing with ROS

To interface the Sunrise.OS with ROS middleware and consequently make the mobile platform compatible with it, two approaches in the literature were discussed. One approach to achieve that, suggested by [5], was to run ROS nodes natively on the Sunrise cabinet as part of the robotic application. This was achieved by using ROSJava[3] libraries, which provided a complete native Java

---

[3] https://wiki.ros.org/rosjava.

implementation of the ROS framework. This allowed these nodes to directly access the robot's data and commands on the controller, and at the same time to interact with the outside "ROS ecosystem" without restrictions. This approach required the installation of third-party libraries on the robot controller to run RosJava nodes.

Another approach suggested by [10] and [4], which did not require any external libraries, was to have a *daemon thread* running on the Sunrise cabinet that allowed access to the robot data and commands over TCP/IP or UDP sockets. This thread would be exchanging string messages with an external ROS node that would parse inbound and outbound messages and exchange them accordingly with the ROS ecosystem. However, this approach, when compared to the first one, is less versatile and robust because: i) raw string messages are prone to parsing errors and difficult to handle when transmitting complicated data, ii) programming with low level sockets instead of established frameworks leads to reliability issues and corner-case errors and iii) having the ROS node running on a separate machine increases the delay of interaction with the robot and adds an extra point of failure to the system. For these reasons, we have opted to utilise the first approach when developing our proposed ROS driver and use it as a starting point for our architecture.

3   KMR iiwa ROS Stack

Robotic applications developed with ROS are usually composed of multiple nodes that are running on different machines/robots communicating and interacting with each other in order to execute their tasks. This is only possible because ROS provides the communication middleware. As a result, in this framework, everything is a node that exposes certain interfaces and expects other nodes' interface in return in order to operate.

We utilised this philosophy in our work when designing the ROS driver for the KMR iiwa robot. As a result, the developed stack is composed of: i) a robot driver that creates a ROS node running natively on the robot controller, which exposes various standard ROS interfaces, and ii) a number of accompanying support ROS packages that utilise these interfaces to control the robot and get its sensors data, such as MoveIt[4], Navigation stack[5], RViz[6], Gazebo[7]. The following subsections describe the software design, the developed support ROS packages of the stack and their relationship with the robot safety system.

The source code of the work presented in this paper, the ROS driver and the related support packages for the KMR iiwa mobile platform are available in the following links:

- KMR iiwa ROS driver: https://github.com/stoic-roboticist/kmriiwa_ros_java
- Support packages: https://github.com/stoic-roboticist/kmriiwa_ros_stack.

---

[4] https://moveit.ros.org.
[5] https://wiki.ros.org/navigation.
[6] https://wiki.ros.org/rviz.
[7] http://gazebosim.org.

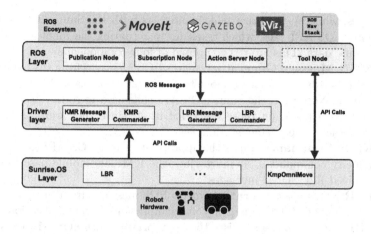

Fig. 2. KMR iiwa ROS driver architecture.

3.1 KMR isiwa Driver Design

Architecture: In order to interact with the robot and its controller, the KUKA's Sunrise.OS API need to be wrapped using the Java programming language. Moreover, to fully leverage ROS middleware capabilities and not develop custom communication solutions like in [4,10], the software need to run ROS libraries natively on the controller as described in [5]. For these reasons, the driver was developed as a robotic application running on Sunrise.OS that utilised RosJava libraries. The developed software architecture and interactions is illustrated in Fig. 2. The driver is composed of three principal layers:

– **ROS Layer:** Is an abstract layer that represents the driver's interface with the outside ROS ecosystem, which includes ROS core and all the other nodes. This layer is composed of three main nodes and one optional node:
   • **Publication Node:** that allows the driver to publish messages to different ROS topics.
   • **Subscription Node:** that allows the driver to receive messages from different ROS topics.
   • **Action Server Node:** that provides the driver with an action server that can interact with external action clients.
   • **Tool Node:** is an optional node that is provided such that it can be utilised to interact with any tools attached to the robot, such as grippers, that expose their functionality via Sunrise.OS API. In order to utilise this node, the user needs to provide the implementation of this node's methods. Table 1 lists the different topics exposed by this layer's components.
– **Driver Layer:** Is a communication layer that represents the core layer of the driver that transforms inbound ROS messages to robot's actions and at the same time transforms robot's sensors readings to outbound ROS messages. This layer interacts with the ROS layer via generated and received ROS

messages; while on the other end, it interacts with the Sunrise.OS layer via
its Sunrise.OS API calls, which translate to actuating the robot and reading
its sensors' data. This layer is composed of four components:

- **KMR Message Generator:** creates ROS messages from the readings of
  the base's laser scanners, odometry, emergency status and battery information. Note that, the Sunrise.OS API calls used to retrieve the sensors'
  data were based on those described in [4] since they were not readily
  available in the documentation.
- **KMR Commander:** uses the appropriate Sunrise.OS API calls to issue
  velocity commands that moves/jogs the KMP200 mobile base from the
  received ROS *Twist* messages.
- **LBR Message Generator:** creates ROS messages from the LBR iiwa14
  arm's joints' states, emergency and calibration status information.
- **LBR Commander:** utilises the appropriate Sunrise.OS API calls from
  the received ROS messages to issue joint position commands to actuate
  the LBR iiwa14 arm. It also creates motion trajectory commands for the
  arm to follow from the received *follow joint trajectory* action goals.

- **Sunrise.OS Layer:** Is a physical layer that represents all the native Sun-
  rise.OS classes such as *LBR* for the robot arm and *KmpOmniMove* for the
  base that are utilised to call its API and consequently interact with the robot
  system.

Table 1. The different topics exposed by the ROS layer components.

Topic name	Message type	Description
Publication node topics		
arm/joint_states	sensor_msgs.JointState	LBR iiwa14 joint states
arm/state/RobotStatus	kmriiwa_msgs.LBRStatus	LBR iiwa14 general status
base/state/LaserB1Scan	sensor_msgs.LaserScan	Front SICK S300 laser readings
base/state/LaserB4Scan	sensor_msgs.LaserScan	Back SICK S300 laser readings
base/state/odom	nav_msgs.Odometry	KMP200 odometry readings
Subscription node topics		
/arm/command/JointPosition	kmriiwa_msgs.JointPosition	LBR iiwa14 joint position motion target
/base/command/cmd_vel	geometry_msgs.Twist	KMP200 velocity twist jog target
Action server node actions		
/arm/manipulator_controller	control_msgs.FollowJointTrajectoryAction	LBR iiwa14 joint trajectory controller

Operation: The driver is running on the controller as a native Sunrise.OS
robotic application. This application is composed of two running threads. A
main thread that synchronously polls the *Subscription Node* and *Action Server
Node* for any newly received ROS messages or action goals and subsequently
execute them using the appropriate driver layer commander. The second thread
is a publication thread, that utilises the ROS messages generated from the driver
layer and publish them using *Publication Node* at a constant rate.

3.2 Support ROS Packages

The ROS ecosystem provides a standard set of tools/frameworks for robot motion planning, navigation, visualisation and simulation. These respectively include Moveit, ROS navigation stack, Rviz and Gazebo. The developed stack provides fully configured and ready to use packages to run these tools with the KMR iiwa mobile manipulator. These packages utilise the developed driver and its exposed interfaces to interact with the robot. All these packages are name-spaced by default, which make them readily usable in multi-robot applications. A short description of these packages follows:

- **KMR iiwa Description Package:** contains the robot's description and its URDF models.
- **KMR iiwa MoveIt Package:** allows Moveit to control the robot's arm by utilising the *FollowJointTrajectory* action server running on the robot to execute the planned trajectories. This is achieved by using the interfaces provided by *LBR Commander* and *Action Server Node*. In the current implementation, ros_control, which is a generic controller interface package, is not supported because we do not currently have access to the official KUKA software packages that allow low level control of the arm.
- **KMR iiwa Navigation Package:** allows to control the robot's base and navigate it in a known or unknown environments using SLAM [6], localisation and path planning algorithms. To do so, it relies on the interfaces provided by *KMR Commander* and *KMR Message Generator*.
- **KMR iiwa Visualisation Package:** contain different Rviz configurations to visualise the robot in different contexts.
- **KMR iiwa Gazebo Package:** allows to simulate the robot in Gazebo. It exposes the same interfaces as the robot driver and allows to control both the robot's base and the arm.

3.3 Robot Safety

The KMR iiwa safety system is managed by a PLC (Programmable Logic Controller) that monitors safety signals received from the robot's various devices, *i.e.*, laser scanners, mobile base and arm, and based on their values and its programmed logic determines the safety state of robot operation. These signals and their combinations can be configured using a special safety configuration file, which is part of every Sunrise.OS project running on the robot controller. Consequently, every application running on the controller will be subjected to these settings and would stop executing if any safety rules are violated.

The developed driver, being a native Sunrise.OS application, is also subject to these safety rules and would stop executing if they are violated. As a result, using our developed stack does not violate the robot safety rules and rely on them for safe operation. Furthermore, all the stack components were tested with the default safety settings of the robot with no modifications.

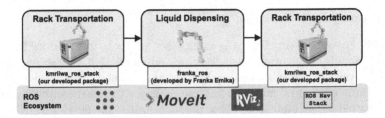

Fig. 3. The demonstrated sample preparation workflow. Note that ROS is used as a communication and execution layer for the robots.

4   System Testing and Applications

The proposed ROS-based driver is used in two example applications. This is not intended to be a particular challenging application or example, it is simply used to take the reader through the functionalities and capabilities of the developed software presented in this paper.

4.1   Manipulation, Navigation and Simulation with ROS

A series of demonstrations was carried out to illustrate the stack's individual components' readiness for operation and showcase their utility. These demonstrations included: i) controlling the LBR iiwa14 arm using MoveIt, ii) controlling the KMP200 base using ROS navigation stack and iii) simulating and controlling the platform in Gazebo simulation environment. The demonstrations for MoveIt and navigation stack, which involved the real robot, were carried out by running the developed driver alongside the relevant individual package; where the user commanded the platform via RViz to different target poses. For the Gazebo demonstration, two KMR iiwa robots were simulated and then commanded using a script that utilised their available interfaces. A result video of these demonstrations can be viewed on the following link: https://youtu.be/ODOPMoMAK-o.

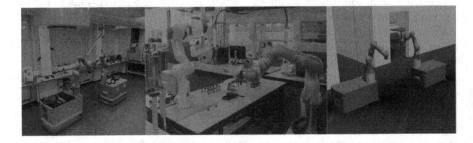

Fig. 4. (Left): Two KMR iiwa robots interacting with each other. (Centre): KMR iiwa placing the rack of vials in order for the Frank Emika robot to dispense liquid. (Right): two KMR iiwa robots interacting in Gazebo simulation environment.

4.2 Example Robotic Application in a Chemistry Laboratory

An example robotic application in the context of an autonomous chemistry laboratory was implemented. Specifically, a sample preparation workflow, this task is very common in manual and automated chemistry workflows [2]. This example application, besides illustrating the stack's navigation and manipulation capabilities, also demonstrates an heterogeneous system where our package is able to interact with other robots and interfacing with external sensors operating in the ROS ecosystem.

The sample preparation workflow example can be described as follow: (1) the KMR iiwa navigates autonomously to a rack station. In the rack station, the robot use the information provided by a camera (Intel® Realsense™ D435) positioned on the mobile base to align the robot with the station and arrive at the correct manipulation position. The visual information use an AprilTag fiducial marker [8] to calculate the pose correction, compensate the navigation and localisation errors and correct the final position based on the sensor reading at the target rack-station-position. (2) the robot picks the rack of vials from the station and place it on top of its base. (3) the platform navigates to the liquid dispensing station, as in the first step, the robot use the camera to align the mobile base before placing the rack on the liquid station table. (4) a Franka Emika Panda robot dispenses liquids by operating a pipette. (5) after finishing the liquid dispensing process, the KMR iiwa robot picks the rack of vials and transports it back to the rack station thus completing the task. Figure 3 shows the described example and the interaction between the components of the system with our developed ROS-based package. In this task, all the manipulation and navigation operations were handled by Moveit and the ROS navigation stack, respectively. Moreover, ROS topics were used to coordinate the KMR iiwa and the Franka Emika Panda robot work as well as to publish the attached camera pose correction information. The task was repeated eight times. In all of the runs, the developed stack performed reliably with no performance issues. There were two failed runs due to the camera failing to detect the AprilTag and the robot navigating too close to an obstacle due to the path planner choosing a sub-optimal path that triggered an emergency stop. Figure 4 shows screenshots of the example applications presented in this section and the package running in simulation and real robots as described in the previous section. A video result of the robotic application in a chemistry laboratory example can be viewed in the following link: https://youtu.be/psyFOOgRlyE.

5 Conclusion

Mobile manipulators and their application are becoming more common, new platforms are being released and novel application domains are being explored. Providing ROS compatibility to these platforms will allow research and development of novel applications. In this paper, we presented a fully developed ROS stack for the KMR iiwa mobile manipulator. This stack is composed of a ROS driver running natively on the controller and a number of essential accompanying ROS packages. The driver has a novel architecture with three layers that interact with each other to allow robot control and compatibility with ROS. The stack was tested in an real-world robotic application in the context of an autonomous chemistry laboratory where the use of heterogeneous hardware platforms: robotics arms, mobile manipulators and standard lab equipment (*e.g.*, pipette) was presented. Future work includes the integration of the Sunrise.OS safety configuration into ROS planning frameworks as constraints.

References

1. Bogue, R.: Growth in e-commerce boosts innovation in the warehouse robot market. Ind. Rob.: Int. J. **43**, 583–587 (2016)
2. Burger, B., et al.: A mobile robotic chemist. Nature **583**(7815), 237–241 (2020)
3. Dömel, A., Kriegel, S., Kaßecker, M., Brucker, M., Bodenmüller, T., Suppa, M.: Toward fully autonomous mobile manipulation for industrial environments. Int. J. Adv. Robot. Syst. **14**(4) (2017)
4. Heggem, C., Wahl, N.M., Tingelstad, L.: Configuration and control of KMR iiwa mobile robots using ROS2. In: 2020 3rd International Symposium on Small-scale Intelligent Manufacturing Systems (SIMS), pp. 1–6, June 2020
5. Hennersperger, C., et al.: Towards MRI-based autonomous robotic US acquisitions: a first feasibility study. IEEE Trans. Med. Imaging **36**(2), 538–548 (2017)
6. Jaulin, L.: Range-only slam with occupancy maps: a set-membership approach. IEEE Trans. Rob. **27**(5), 1004–1010 (2011)
7. Johan From, P., Grimstad, L., Hanheide, M., Pearson, S., Cielniak, G.: RASberry - robotic and autonomous systems for berry production. Mech. Eng. **140**(06), S14–S18 (2018)
8. Krogius, M., Haggenmiller, A., Olson, E.: Flexible layouts for fiducial tags. In: International Conference on Intelligent Robots and Systems, October 2019
9. Meng, J., et al.: Iterative-learning error compensation for autonomous parking of mobile manipulator in harsh industrial environment. Rob. Comput.-Integr. Manuf. **68**, 102077 (2021)
10. Mokaram, S., et al.: A ROS-integrated API for the KUKA LBR iiwa collaborative robot. IFAC-PapersOnLine **50**(1), 15859–15864 (2017)
11. Quigley, M., et al.: ROS: an open-source robot operating system. In: ICRA Workshop on Open Source Software, Kobe, Japan, vol. 3, p. 5 (2009)
12. Štibinger, P., et al.: Mobile manipulator for autonomous localization, grasping and precise placement of construction material in a semi-structured environment. Rob. Autom. Lett. **6**, 2595–2602 (2021)

Collision Avoidance with Optimal Path Replanning for Mobile Robots

Vibhakar Mohta[1]([✉])(iD), Sagar Dimri[2](iD), Hariharan Ravichandran[2](iD), and Sikha Hota[2](iD)

[1] Department of Mechanical Engineering, Indian Institute of Technology, Kharagpur, Kharagpur, India
vib2810@iitkgp.ac.in
[2] Department of Aerospace Engineering, Indian Institute of Technology, Kharagpur, Kharagpur, India

Abstract. This paper generates a collision-free trajectory for wheeled mobile robots in presence of dynamic obstacles. The existing literature solves the collision avoidance problem by changing the velocity vector instantaneously, which is not feasible due to the non-holonomic constraints of robots. So in this work, a smooth change in the velocity vector along with constraints in turn radius has been considered for any required maneuvers. This work also re-plans the path evading re-collision to reach the goal ensuring minimum deviation from the initial path, which was also not addressed in the literature. The low computational requirement of the proposed algorithm allows for online applications on wheeled mobile robots with limited computational resources. The approach is validated through simulations on multiple randomized configurations.

Keywords: Collision avoidance · Optimal path · Dynamic obstacles

1 Introduction

Mobile robots play an integral role in shaping mankind's lifestyle but have many challenges associated to address. Reaching a specified goal while avoiding unwanted obstacles in a cluttered environment is one of the important requirements for automation. Collision-free navigation depends upon the vehicle model, sensor arrangement and optimality. [11] and [19] reviewed different avoidance systems for collision-free navigation.

Motion-planning algorithms like vector-field histograms and the bug algorithm [22] can provide a feasible path to the goal but they are not optimal. Such algorithms use occupancy-grid methods to model the environment. A^* [15], RRT [16] and Delaunay triangulation [25] can provide a near-optimal path in finite time. But, these algorithms are fraught with the problem of large computational

We would like to thank ECR grant, SERB and GOI for their support.

© Springer Nature Switzerland AG 2021
C. Fox et al. (Eds.): TAROS 2021, LNAI 13054, pp. 315–325, 2021.
https://doi.org/10.1007/978-3-030-89177-0_32

costs. Geometry-based algorithms, which have significantly lower computational costs, have recently been used for collision avoidance. They are extensively used for optimal path planning in various missions both in two-dimensional (2D) plane ([3] and [14]) as well as in three-dimensional (3D) space ([10] and [9]). Finding the shortest path to converge to a circular path [3] and reaching a target via circular boundaries for vehicles with bounded curvature [14] are a few planning algorithms based on Dubins curves [5].

Dynamic-Window Approach (DWA) ([7] and [24]) discusses two-dimensional space-search algorithms for translational and rotational speeds to provide the permissible trajectories for short-intervals of time. Constraints over the velocities are taken into account while creating the dynamic window. Hybrid DWA [20] utilises a 3D search space for collision avoidance. Potential field-based methods [4] and [29] create a field-based upon forces of attraction towards goals and repulsion from obstacles. These methods are mainly used with velocity obstacle methods [27] and can be implemented on manipulators, Autonomous Underwater Vehicles [6] and quadrotors [12]. Potential field methods have a limitation of getting stuck in local minima, but extensions like simulated annealing [30] and modified Artificial Potential Field [23] have the potential overcome them.

A powerful collision cone approach was proposed in [2], which was utilised in reactive-collision avoidance maneuvers [21], velocity obstacle methods [13] and conflict detection and resolution techniques in aircraft [8] and [1]. [28] uses the dynamics of an omnidirectional robot to solve the avoidance problem in a cluttered environment. Analytical solutions for the optimal path can be obtained by integrating vehicle dynamics with obstacle geometry. [17] and [18] proposed a velocity obstacle technique for collision avoidance with spherical and cylindrical safety bubbles for multiple aircraft. But, it requires an instantaneous change in velocity directions, which is not feasible for the dynamical constraint of vehicles.

The novelty of this work is to ensure smooth changes of the velocity vectors for all the maneuvers required for collision avoidance and re-planning the path making it implementable in nonholonomic robotic platforms. This work also finds a solution to evade re-collision while re-planning the path to the goal ensuring minimum deviation from its initial trajectory, which was also not explored in the literature. The low computational requirement of the proposed algorithm makes it online implementable on wheeled mobile robots.

2   Problem Formulation

Let us consider a ground robot initially at A_0, with the position vector $\overrightarrow{r_u}$, and the velocity $\overrightarrow{u}$ directed towards its goal (G) $\overrightarrow{r_g}$. The state of the robot is $X : [x, y, \theta]$ and the minimum turn radius is ρ. It detects a dynamic obstacle, B_0 at $\overrightarrow{r_v}$ headed on a collision course towards it with a velocity $\overrightarrow{v}$. The objective is to re-plan the path for the robot such that it avoids the obstacle B_0 with a safety radius $d_{\min}$, and reach the goal, G with state $X_g : [x_g, y_g, \theta_g]$. The kinematic equations of motion are:

$$\dot{x} = |\overrightarrow{u}|\cos\theta \qquad \dot{y} = |\overrightarrow{u}|\sin\theta \qquad \dot{\theta} = \omega \qquad (1)$$

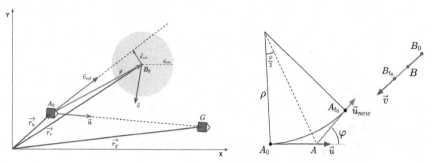

(a) Position vectors of the mobile robot A_0, obstacle B_0 and goal G

(b) Turning maneuver of robot in a circular path

Fig. 1. Problem formulation and collision avoidance maneuver

where, ω is the angular rate at any given instant. It is assumed that the robot moves with a constant speed $|\vec{u}|$ and the velocity of the obstacle remains constant. All vectors are measured in an x-y inertial frame as shown in Fig. 1a.

3   Collision Detection and Avoidance

The avoidance maneuver is executed only after collision with the obstacle is predicted. In Fig. 1a, the *minimum separation* in vector between the robot and the obstacle is given by $\overrightarrow{d_{rel}} = (\overrightarrow{r} \cdot \hat{v}_{rel})\hat{v}_{rel} - \overrightarrow{r}$, where, $\overrightarrow{r}$ is the relative position of the obstacle with respect to the robot and $\hat{v}_{rel}$ is the unit vector along $\overrightarrow{v_{rel}}$. Let, d_{min} be the *radius of the obstacle avoidance sphere*. Collision is possible if the following conditions are satisfied:

$$|\overrightarrow{d_{rel}}| \le d_{min} \text{ and } \dot{r} < 0 \qquad (2)$$

In addition to the above conditions, collision is certain if time to reach the goal t_g is greater than the time of collision t_c,

$$t_g = |\overrightarrow{u}|^{-1}|\overrightarrow{r_G} - \overrightarrow{r_u}| \qquad t_c = |\overrightarrow{v_{rel}}|^{-1}\left[\sqrt{|\overrightarrow{r}|^2 - |\overrightarrow{d_{rel}}|^2} - \sqrt{d_{min}^2 - |\overrightarrow{d_{rel}}|^2}\right] \qquad (3)$$

A geometry-based collision avoidance algorithm that avoids the detected dynamic obstacle is proposed. It is assumed that the speed of the robot remains constant throughout the avoidance maneuver. Let us consider that the robot takes a turn with *minimum turn radius*, ρ for time t_0 with a constant speed $|\overrightarrow{u}|$ and avoids the incoming obstacle. The relation between the angle subtended at the centre φ, minimum turn radius ρ and t_0 is:

$$\varphi = \frac{|\overrightarrow{u}|t_0}{\rho} \qquad (4)$$

Let A_{t_0}, B_{t_0} be the respective positions of the robot and the obstacle respectively, after time t_0. As shown in Fig. 1b the backward extension of $\overrightarrow{u_{new}}$ intersects the

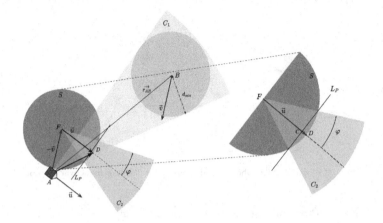

Fig. 2. Collision avoidance formulation

original trajectory at A. If the robot kept moving with the same velocity, and had it travelled to A, then the time taken to reach A would have been,

$$t = \frac{AA_{t_0}}{|\vec{u}|} = \frac{\rho \tan(\varphi/2)}{|\vec{u}|} \tag{5}$$

Hence position vectors of virtual positions $\vec{r_A}$ and $\vec{r_B}$ are dependant on t, which in-turn is a function of φ and can be calculated as

$$\vec{r_A} = \vec{r_u} + \vec{u}.t = \vec{r_u} + \rho \vec{u} \left[\frac{\tan(\varphi/2)}{|\vec{u}|} \right] \tag{6}$$

$$\vec{r_B} = \vec{r_v} + \vec{v}.(t_0 - t) = \vec{r_v} + \rho \vec{v} \left[\frac{\varphi - \tan(\varphi/2)}{|\vec{u}|} \right] \tag{7}$$

Hence the problem statement can be restated as follows: *"Given that the robot and the obstacle are at virtual positions, A and B, with velocities $\vec{u}$ and $\vec{v}$, respectively, find the instantaneous change in the velocity vector $\vec{u}$ to $\overrightarrow{u_{new}}$ required to avoid the collision"*

In Fig. 2, points A and B are the virtual position of the robot ($\vec{r_A}$) and obstacle ($\vec{r_B}$), respectively. $\overrightarrow{AF}$ is such that its direction is opposite to $\vec{v}$ and magnitude is the same as $\vec{v}$. Similarly, we have $\overrightarrow{FD}$ whose magnitude is $|\vec{u}|$ and the direction is the same as $\vec{u}$. The resultant of the vectors $\overrightarrow{AF}$ and $\overrightarrow{FD}$, i.e. $\overrightarrow{AD}$, gives the sense of the relative velocity between the robot and the obstacle. Hence, the position vectors of the points, D and F, can be given as

$$\vec{r_D} = \vec{r_A} + \overrightarrow{AD} \quad \text{and} \quad \vec{r_F} = \vec{r_A} + \overrightarrow{AF} \tag{8}$$

C_1 is the collision cone and any solution that moves the relative velocity vector outside the cone will avoid the collision. However, optimal conflict resolution is provided if the new relative velocity vector is tangential to the collision cone $C1$ [8]. A circle, S centered at F is defined with the radius equalling to the magnitude of $\overrightarrow{u}$. The vector joining A to any point on the circle, S, represents a possible configuration of the relative velocity vector with constant robot speed. The cone, C_2 is constructed such that the new velocity vector, $\overrightarrow{u_{new}}$, makes an angle, φ, with $\overrightarrow{u}$. Since the vertex of the cone lies at the center of the circle, the intersection is a straight line, say L_P. The slope of L_P is perpendicular to $\overrightarrow{u}$ and it passes through a point, $\overrightarrow{r_C}$ given as

$$\overrightarrow{r_C} = \overrightarrow{r_F} + (1 - cos\varphi)\overrightarrow{FD} \tag{9}$$

Equations of the different curves shown in Fig. 2 are,

$$L_P : u_x(x - x_C) + u_y(y - y_C) = 0 \tag{10}$$
$$S : (x - x_F)^2 + (y - y_F)^2 - |\overrightarrow{u}|^2 = 0 \tag{11}$$
$$C_1 : (|\overrightarrow{r_{AB}}|^2 - d_{min}^2)[(x')^2 + (y')^2] - [x_{AB}(x') + y_{AB}(y')]^2 = 0 \tag{12}$$

where, $x' = x - x_A$, $y' = y - y_A$, $\overrightarrow{r_{AB}} = \overrightarrow{r_B} - \overrightarrow{r_A}$, x_{AB} and y_{AB} are the x and y components of $\overrightarrow{AB}$, and u_x, u_y are the x and y components of $\overrightarrow{u}$. $\overrightarrow{r_F}$ and $\overrightarrow{r_C}$ can be computed using (8) and (9). It is now required to find out the point $Q(x, y)$ which satisfies constraints (10), (11) and (12) and minimizes the change in $\overrightarrow{u}$, i.e. the point is nearest to D. Hence this can be formulated as a multi-variable optimization problem as follows:

$$\min_{x,y,\varphi} f = \sqrt{(x - x_D)^2 + (y - y_D)^2} \quad \text{s.t. } S = 0, C_1 = 0, L_P = 0, \varphi > 0 \tag{13}$$

where (x_D, y_D) is the position of point D. Using x and y components obtained from the above optimization problem, we can find $\overrightarrow{u_{new}} = (x - x_F, y - y_F)$, where (x_F, y_F) is the position of point F. The duration for which turning takes place can be obtained using (4), where φ is calculated from (13).

4   Path Re-planning

The collision avoidance maneuver is complete when the robot passes the point of the closest approach with the obstacle. Let this point be P. It now has to re-plan its path back to the final goal. If the re-planning maneuver starts as soon as it finishes its collision avoidance phase, there is a possibility that the re-planned trajectory may intersect with the obstacle, leading to a re-collision. Hence, to minimize the probability of this event, a design parameter has been proposed which is the ratio of the *safe re-planning distance* (the safety distance between the obstacle and the robot after which the re-planning maneuver begins), d_{safe} and the *radius of the obstacle avoidance sphere*, d_{min}: $r_{safe} = \frac{d_{safe}}{d_{min}}$.

After reaching a distance d_{safe} away from the obstacle at the point, P', the robot then plans a Dubins-like path [5] back to the goal point as illustrated in Fig. 3a. The Dubins path provides the shortest path between any two poses of a robot with a bounded turn radius. The procedure for generating Dubins paths

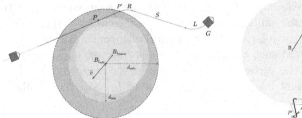 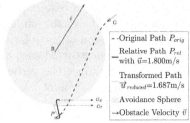

(a) Illustration of the safe re-planning maneuver with $r_{safe} = 1.4$. Re-planning begins after reaching a distance d_{safe} away from the obstacle at point P' and time t_{safe}.

(b) Illustration of the re-planning algorithm in case of re-collision with $|u| = 1.8$m/s. G_R and G_T are the transformed goal poses with $|\overrightarrow{u}_{in}| = 1.8$m/s and 1.687m/s ($a_{rp} = 3m/s^2$)

Fig. 3. Re-planning Maneuver

has been described in [26] and [15]. The optimal Dubins path, P_{orig} is generated maintaining a constant speed to reach the goal $X_g : [x_g, y_g, \theta_g]$.

In an unlikely event of the re-planned path coming on the way of the obstacle, a strategy which involves lowering the speed of the robot until the collision is re-avoided is proposed. The approach of re-planning a longer path to the goal is avoided due to the increased actuation cost. Re-collision with the obstacle is checked by projecting the original Dubins path P_{orig} to the obstacle frame. To carry out this projection, we sample points P_{orig_i} (an array of sampled points) on the path. During sampling, the path corresponding to motion primitive S (straight line) can be sampled by just at its start and end points. For L (Left turn with the minimum turn radius) and R (Right turn with the minimum turn radius) motion primitives, a hyper parameter (sample density, s_D) which represents samples per unit length of the curved path, is used to uniformly sample the points on the curve. We assume the robot velocity decreases from $\overrightarrow{|u|}$ to $\overrightarrow{|u|}_{in}$ with a deceleration, a_{rp}. Hence we define $\overrightarrow{|u|}_i$ as

$$\overrightarrow{|u|}_i = \begin{cases} \sqrt{\overrightarrow{|u|}^2 + \frac{2a_{rp}i}{s_D}} & i \le \left[\frac{s_D(\overrightarrow{|u|}_{in}^2 - \overrightarrow{|u|}^2)}{2a_{rp}} \right] \\ \overrightarrow{|u|}_{in} & \text{otherwise} \end{cases} \tag{14}$$

Then the relative path, P_{rel}, in the obstacle fixed frame can be obtained:

$$\overrightarrow{P_{rel_i}} = \overrightarrow{P_{orig_i}} - \overrightarrow{v} \left[\frac{PathDist(\overrightarrow{P_{orig_i}})}{\overrightarrow{|u|}_i} \right] \tag{15}$$

Obstacle velocity $\overrightarrow{v}$, final robot speed $\overrightarrow{|u|}_{in}$ and the original sampled path points P_{orig_i} are the inputs to this equation. $PathDist(\overrightarrow{P_{orig_i}})$ gives the distance between the initial and ith point along the path. It can be seen that for larger $\overrightarrow{|u|}_{in}$ values, the relative path will almost be the same as the original path, and

---

Algorithm 1: Path Re-planning

$P_{\text{orig}} \leftarrow$ Plan Dubins path between P' and G;
$P_{\text{rel}} \leftarrow TransformPath(P_{\text{orig}_i}, |\overrightarrow{u}|_{\text{in}} = |\overrightarrow{u}|)$;
if *CheckCollision(P_{rel})=true* **then**
| Binary search in $(0, |\overrightarrow{u}|)$ to obtain $|\overrightarrow{u}|_{\text{reduced}}$ for a fixed a_{rp};
| Decrease speed to $|\overrightarrow{u}|_{\text{reduced}}$ by decelerating with a_{rp} while following P_{orig};
else
| Follow P_{orig} with speed $|\overrightarrow{u}|$;
end

---

for a smaller $|\overrightarrow{u}|_{\text{in}}$ value, points further away in the path will deviate by a large amount along $\overrightarrow{v}$. The strategy for finding an optimal lower speed $|\overrightarrow{u}|_{\text{reduced}}$ is elaborated in Algorithm 1. Figure 3b illustrates this procedure.

5   Simulation and Analysis

5.1   Implementation and Trajectory Visualization

The optimization problem described in (13) can be solved using an Interior Point Algorithm. During the analysis, it is found that a randomized initial condition fails to converge to the optimal point in many cases. Hence we run multiple instances of the solver parallely, and report back the most optimum solution. This addition greatly improves the accuracy of the algorithm while keeping the

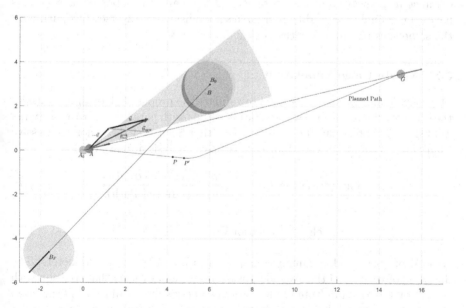

Fig. 4. Trajectory visualization with parameters as mentioned in Table 1

Table 1. Parameters for trajectory visualization

Goal State X_g	$[15 \text{ m}, 3.5 \text{ m}, 13.124°]$
Robot initial state X_0	$[0, 0, 13.124°]$
Robot initial velocity $\vec{u_0}$	$[1.85, 0.431] \text{ m/s}$
Minimum turn radius ρ	1.8 m
Obstacle avoidance distance $d_{\min}$	1.2 m
Obstacle initial position B_0	$[6, 3] \text{ m}$
Obstacle velocity $\vec{v}$	$[-0.92, -0.92] \text{ m/s}$
Re-planning safe distance ratio r_{safe}	1.25
Path sample density s_D	100 pts/m

computation time the same due to parallel implementation. An i7-7700HQ 8GB RAM machine is used to carry out all simulations.

For visualizing the planned path of the robot, a random simulation with the parameters shown in Table 1 is performed. Figure 4 illustrates the various aspects of this simulation. B_0 is the position of the obstacle when it is initially detected. The optimizer outputs a turning time $t_0 = 0.301$s with a $\vec{u_{\text{new}}} = [1.893, -0.168]$ m/s. The corresponding instantaneous change virtual positions are marked as A and B, and the collision cone with various vectors at this position is shown in the figure. The robot performs a smooth turn for t_0 seconds to change its velocity from $\vec{u}$ to $\vec{u_{\text{new}}}$. It continues with the same velocity till it reaches its point of the closest approach at P. The re-planning maneuver begins after reaching a safe distance d_{safe} away from the obstacle at P'. Finally the robot plans a Dubins path to the final goal, and as there is no re-collision, it traverses this path with the same speed and reaches the goal at $t = 8.266$ s.

5.2   Monte Carlo Simulation

Monte carlo analysis has been used to validate the proposed algorithm. Consider the setup shown in Fig. 5. Two simulation setups with parameters are as shown in Table 2. Parameters have been chosen such that Set 1 is slightly more aggressive than Set 2. Two metrics used for comparative analysis are given below:

$$\text{Path deviation } P_D = \frac{PathDist(\text{PlannedPath})}{PathDist(\text{Initial Path})} \tag{16}$$

$$\text{Velocity deviation} V_D = \frac{|\vec{u_{\text{new}}} - \vec{u}|}{|\vec{u}|} \tag{17}$$

A total of 7000 random simulations were run on each set of parameters. The direction of velocity of the obstacle was chosen randomly such that collision with the robot was certain. Table 2 also presents the results obtained. Optimization failures represent conditions where the turn radius of the robot was not sufficient

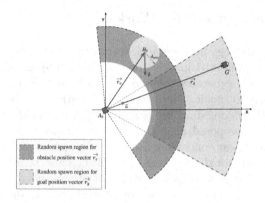

Fig. 5. Setup for randomized simulation

Table 2. Parameter variation with simulation results for randomized simulation

Parameter		Set 1	Set 2
Goal State	$X_g = \begin{bmatrix} r_{X_g} \\ \theta_{X_g} \end{bmatrix}$	$\begin{bmatrix} U(20, 40) \text{ m} \\ U(-70, 70)° \end{bmatrix}$	$\begin{bmatrix} U(60, 100) \text{ m} \\ U(-80, 80)° \end{bmatrix}$
Robot			
Robot initial state	$X_0 = \begin{bmatrix} X_{x_0} \\ X_{y_0} \\ X_{\theta_0} \end{bmatrix}$	$\begin{bmatrix} 0 \\ 0 \\ \theta_{X_g} \end{bmatrix}$	$\begin{bmatrix} 0 \\ 0 \\ \theta_{X_g} \end{bmatrix}$
Robot initial velocity	$\vec{u_0} = \begin{bmatrix} \lvert\vec{u_0}\rvert \\ \angle\vec{u_0} \end{bmatrix}$	$\begin{bmatrix} U(1.0, 2.5) \text{ m/s} \\ \theta_{X_g} \end{bmatrix}$	$\begin{bmatrix} U(1.2, 3.5) \text{ m/s} \\ \theta_{X_g} \end{bmatrix}$
Minimum turn radius	ρ	$U(0.8, 1.2)$ m	$U(1.2, 1.5)$ m
Obstacle			
Avoidance distance	$d_{\min}$	$U(1.2, 3)$ m	$U(1.8, 3.5)$ m
Initial position	$B_0 = \begin{bmatrix} r_{B_0} \\ \theta_{B_0} \end{bmatrix}$	$\begin{bmatrix} U(15, 50) \text{ m} \\ \theta_{X_g} + U(-60, 60)° \end{bmatrix}$	$\begin{bmatrix} U(35, 70) \text{ m} \\ \theta_{X_g} + U(-70, 70)° \end{bmatrix}$
Obstacle Velocity	$\vec{v} = \begin{bmatrix} \lvert\vec{v}\rvert \\ \angle\vec{v} \end{bmatrix}$	$\begin{bmatrix} U(1.5, 3.5) \text{ m/s} \\ U(-180, 180)° \end{bmatrix}$	$\begin{bmatrix} U(2.2, 4) \text{ m/s} \\ U(-180, 180)° \end{bmatrix}$
Safe re-planning ratio	r_{safe}	1.25	1.25
Path sample density	s_D	100 pts/m	100 pts/m
Simulation Results			
Success / Number of Simulations		6901 / 7000	6944 / 7000
Collisions / Optimization failures		5 / 94	11 / 45
Velocity deviation ($V_{D\max}, V_{D\text{avg}}$)		(0.6775,0.1378)	(0.6117, 0.0986)
Path deviation ($P_{D\max}, P_{D\text{avg}}$)		(1.4121,1.0174)	(1.0942,1.0038)
Accuracy		**98.58%**	**99.20%**

to avoid collision going with constant speed. It is observed an accuracy of over 98.5% in set 1 and over 99% in set 2. (It was found only 2 of the total 14000 simulation run required the speed lowering re-planning maneuver, hence 99.986% of the initial re-planned paths are collision free).

6   Conclusion and Future Work

A geometry-based strategy for generating a smooth trajectory avoiding dynamic obstacles has been presented in this paper. A novel re-planning approach has been proposed which generates the shortest path to the goal while avoiding re-collision with the obstacle. The proposed algorithm has been validated by conducting 14,000 random simulations and an average accuracy of 98.89% has been obtained. The proposed algorithm can be extended to consider vehicles dynamics, and non-linear controllers like back-stepping or sliding mode control can be developed to track the generated path. It can also be extended to irregularly shaped obstacles. A strategy to avoid multiple collisions can be devised by introducing avoidance hierarchies based on obstacle speeds and collision times.

References

1. Carbone, C., Ciniglio, U., Corraro, F., Luongo, S.: A novel 3D geometric algorithm for aircraft autonomous collision avoidance. In: Proceedings of the 45th IEEE Conference on Decision and Control, pp. 1580–1585. IEEE (2006)
2. Chakravarthy, A., Ghose, D.: Obstacle avoidance in a dynamic environment: a collision cone approach. IEEE Trans. Syst. Man Cybern.-Part A: Syst. Hum. **28**(5), 562–574 (1998)
3. Chen, Z.: On dubins paths to a circle. Automatica **117**, 108996 (2020)
4. Deng, M., Inoue, A., Sekiguchi, K.: Lyapunov function-based obstacle avoidance scheme for a two-wheeled mobile robot. J. Control Theory Appl. **6**(4), 399–404 (2008)
5. Dubins, L.E.: On curves of minimal length with a constraint on average curvature, and with prescribed initial and terminal positions and tangents. Am. J. Math. **79**(3), 497–516 (1957)
6. Fan, X., Guo, Y., Liu, H., Wei, B., Lyu, W.: Improved artificial potential field method applied for AUV path planning. Math. Probl. Eng. **2020** (2020)
7. Fox, D., Burgard, W., Thrun, S.: The dynamic window approach to collision avoidance. IEEE Robot. Autom. Mag. **4**(1), 23–33 (1997)
8. Goss, J., Rajvanshi, R., Subbarao, K.: Aircraft conflict detection and resolution using mixed geometric and collision cone approaches. In: AIAA Guidance, Navigation, and Control Conference and Exhibit, p. 4879 (2004)
9. Hota, S., Ghose, D.: Optimal geometrical path in 3D with curvature constraint. In: 2010 IEEE/RSJ International Conference on Intelligent Robots and Systems, pp. 113–118. IEEE (2010)
10. Hota, S., Ghose, D.: Optimal path planning for an aerial vehicle in 3D space. In: 49th IEEE Conference on Decision and Control (CDC), pp. 4902–4907. IEEE (2010)
11. Hoy, M., Matveev, A.S., Savkin, A.V.: Algorithms for collision-free navigation of mobile robots in complex cluttered environments: a survey. Robotica **33**(3), 463–497 (2015)
12. Iswanto, A.M., Wahyunggoro, O., Cahyadi, A.I.: Artificial potential field algorithm implementation for quadrotor path planning. Int. J. Adv. Comput. Sci. Appl. **10**(8), 575–585 (2019)

13. Jenie, Y.I., van Kampen, E.J., de Visser, C.C., Ellerbroek, J., Hoekstra, J.M.: Three-dimensional velocity obstacle method for uncoordinated avoidance maneuvers of unmanned aerial vehicles. J. Guid. Control Dyn. **39**(10), 2312–2323 (2016)
14. Jha, B., Chen, Z., Shima, T.: On shortest Dubins path via a circular boundary. Automatica **121**, 109192 (2020)
15. LaValle, S.M.: Planning Algorithms. Cambridge University Press, Cambridge (2006)
16. LaValle, S.M., et al.: Rapidly-exploring random trees: a new tool for path planning (1998)
17. Luongo, S., Carbone, C., Corraro, F., Ciniglio, U.: An optimal 3D analytical solution for collision avoidance between aircraft. In: 2009 IEEE Aerospace Conference, pp. 1–9. IEEE (2009)
18. Luongo, S., Corraro, F., Ciniglio, U., Di Vito, V., Moccia, A.: A novel 3d analytical algorithm for autonomous collision avoidance considering cylindrical safety bubble. In: IEEE Aerospace Conference. pp. 1–13. IEEE (2010)
19. Mahjri, I., Dhraief, A., Belghith, A.: A review on collision avoidance systems for unmanned aerial vehicles. In: Kassab, M., Berbineau, M., Vinel, A., Jonsson, M., Garcia, F., Soler, J. (eds.) Nets4Cars/Nets4Trains/Nets4Aircraft 2015. LNCS, vol. 9066, pp. 203–214. Springer, Cham (2015). https://doi.org/10.1007/978-3-319-17765-6_18
20. Moon, J., Lee, B.Y., Tahk, M.J.: A hybrid dynamic window approach for collision avoidance of VTOL UAVs. Int. J. Aeronaut. Space Sci. **19**(4), 889–903 (2018). https://doi.org/10.1007/s42405-018-0061-z
21. Mujumdar, A., Padhi, R.: Nonlinear geometric and differential geometric guidance of UAVs for reactive collision avoidance. Technical report, Indian Inst of Science Bangalore (India) (2009)
22. Rajko, S., LaValle, S.: A pursuit-evasion bug algorithm. In: Proceedings 2001 ICRA. IEEE International Conference on Robotics and Automation (2001)
23. Rostami, S.M.H., Sangaiah, A.K., Wang, J., Liu, X.: Obstacle avoidance of mobile robots using modified artificial potential field algorithm. EURASIP J. Wirel. Commun. Netw. **2019**(1), 1–19 (2019). https://doi.org/10.1186/s13638-019-1396-2
24. Seder, M., Petrovic, I.: Dynamic window based approach to mobile robot motion control in the presence of moving obstacles. In: Proceedings 2007 IEEE International Conference on Robotics and Automation, pp. 1986–1991. IEEE (2007)
25. Shanmugavel, M., Tsourdos, A., White, B.A.: Collision avoidance and path planning of multiple UAVs using flyable paths in 3D. In: 2010 15th International Conference on Methods and Models in Automation and Robotics, pp. 218–222. IEEE (2010)
26. Shkel, A., Lumelsky, V.: Classification of the Dubins set. Robot. Auton. Syst. **34**, 179–202 (2001)
27. Tan, C.Y., Huang, S., Tan, K.K., Teo, R.S.H.: Three dimensional collision avoidance for multi unmanned aerial vehicles using velocity obstacle. J. Intell. Robot. Syst. **97**(1), 227–248 (2020). https://doi.org/10.1007/s10846-019-01055-5
28. Williams, R.L., Wu, J.: Dynamic obstacle avoidance for an omnidirectional mobile robot. J. Robot. **2010** (2010)
29. Yang, H., Fan, X., Shi, P., Hua, C.: Nonlinear control for tracking and obstacle avoidance of a wheeled mobile robot with nonholonomic constraint. IEEE Trans. Control Syst. Technol. **24**(2), 741–746 (2015)
30. Zhu, Q., Yan, Y., Xing, Z.: Robot path planning based on artificial potential field approach with simulated annealing. In: Sixth International Conference on Intelligent Systems Design and Applications, vol. 2, pp. 622–627. IEEE (2006)

An Autonomous Mapping Approach
for Confined Spaces Using Flying Robots

Ahmad Alsayed[1,2(✉)], Mostafa R. A. Nabawy[1,3], Akilu Yunusa-Kaltungo[1],
Mark K. Quinn[1], and Farshad Arvin[4]

[1] Department of Mechanical, Aerospace and Civil Engineering, The University
of Manchester, Manchester M1 3BB, UK
ahmad.alsayed@manchester.ac.uk
[2] Department of Mechanical Engineering, Umm Al-Qura University,
Al Abdeyah, Makkah 5555, Saudi Arabia
[3] Aerospace Engineering Department, Faculty of Engineering, Cairo University,
Giza 12613, Egypt
[4] Department of Electrical and Electronic Engineering, The University
of Manchester, Manchester M1 3BB, UK

Abstract. Mapping a confined space with a drone-based system
becomes challenging when vision sensors cannot be used due to environmental constraints. This paper presents a novel scan-matching approach
based on an Iterative Closest Point algorithm that uses low-rate and low-
dense scans from a LiDAR. The proposed technique only employs the
horizontal layer from a 3D LiDAR to estimate the transformation matrices in a computationally efficient fashion, which is then used to generate
the 3D map of the scanned environment in real-time. This is, then, com-
plemented with a fit-for-purpose indoor navigation path-planning strategy. The method was successfully tested by mapping a confined space
within a cement plant simulated environment and estimating a stockpile
volume stored in that space. The volume of the reconstructed stockpile
was estimated with an error as low as 3%, which matches the accuracy
levels recommended by relevant regulations.

Keywords: Flying robots · Mapping · Confined spaces · Autonomous

1 Introduction

A confined space is an area that is substantially enclosed and where dangerous material or hazards inside the space or nearby may cause serious injury.
One of the most challenging confined spaces for robotic inspection are cement
manufacturing process storage spaces. This is due to robots having to operate
under poor lighting and visibility conditions, lack of global positioning, uneven
and slippery terrains, and sensor interference [1]. Drones have significant advantages over other mobile robotics. Hence, drones were used for inspecting confined
spaces within many real-world applications such as sewer inspection [2], search

ⓒ Springer Nature Switzerland AG 2021
C. Fox et al. (Eds.): TAROS 2021, LNAI 13054, pp. 326–336, 2021.
https://doi.org/10.1007/978-3-030-89177-0_33

and rescue (SAR) [3], and underground mines inspection and mapping [4], all of which required an indoor localisation approach to deal with the limitations imposed by operation in confined spaces. However, the aforementioned examples are not suitable to export to the missions within cement plants storage because either they cannot perform within the exceptionally harsh environmental conditions or they are commercialised solutions that do not allow flexible adjustments to the system to fit new mission requirements.

One of the essential tasks conducted frequently in cement plants is to estimate the volume of different stockpiles within storage facilities. Estimating stockpile volumes in outdoor environments typically uses photogrammetry as it is cheaper and faster when compared to other methods like surveying [5]. Many studies, such as in [6], demonstrated real applications of using drones for stockpile volume estimation. Nevertheless, these studies have only focused on applying drones within outdoor environments. In fact, dust, limited illumination, and lack of GPS signals in confined spaces are some of the severe challenges that have rarely been considered in previous studies tackling aerial stockpile volume estimation.

Simultaneous Localisation and Mapping (SLAM) is one of the popular methods for drone navigation in GPS-denied environments. SLAM is the process of using cameras, Light Detection and Ranging (LiDAR), or both to estimate the robot's navigation states and the surrounding map simultaneously [7]. In dusty, low illuminated, and large confined spaces (such as in cement plants), LiDAR is the best class of sensors for such application [8]. Here, a scan-matching technique is usually employed to compute the current state transformation of the robot and compare it to last states [9]. Iterative Closest Point (ICP) algorithm is one of the most widely applied techniques for LiDAR scan-matching in the robotic community [10]. Since the introduction of ICP by Chen and Medioni [11] and Besl and McKay [12], many variants have been introduced to enable improvements such as reduction in overall computational cost, smaller mean square error, faster convergence speed, and optimal selection of points for overall algorithm efficiency. For more details on the different ICP variants, the reader is referred to Mora et al. [13] for a comprehensive review.

In this paper, we implemented a modified ICP algorithm for real-time scan-matching to localise a drone and simultaneously generate a 3D map of a confined space. The proposed method can be deployed in indoor, dark, and dusty facilities such as the storage spaces within cement plants. Matching high dense 3D scans provides detailed set of results that are needed for applications such as 3D reconstruction of power lines [14]. However, this is very costly to implement in real-time. Given that our intended application is to map a large stockpile that has no fine geometric details, we have the luxury/excuse to sacrifice some of the collected data without reducing the accuracy of the reconstructed map. As such, to reduce computational cost taken in matching scans and to reduce memory requirements, we reduced the gathered data rate from the 3D LiDAR through using the below horizon layers only, and applying the scan-matching at rates as low as every 6 s. Therefore, our proposed method obtained the 3D transformation matrix based only on the point clouds from the 2D horizontal layer. To increase the accuracy and speed of the matching, we assigned lower weights to point clouds with greater distances from the LiDAR source because points at greater distances have more noise in dusty environments, as illustrated by Phillips et al. [8]. Whilst the model precisely simulates stockpiles in cement plants, it can be reconfigured to other applications such as agri-robotics, etc.

2   Method

2.1   Drone Localisation and 3D Map Generation

In a fully confined storage, the drone's position $(x_v, y_v, z_v, \phi, \theta, \psi)$ and the reconstructed 3D map ($\mathcal{M}$) of the scanned area are obtained by estimating the transformation matrices (rotation $\boldsymbol{R}_{3\times3}$ and translation $\boldsymbol{t}_{3\times1}$) between two LiDAR scans recorded at different locations using scan-matching based on point-to-point ICP algorithm. By maintaining flight at a constant height, h, we can simplify the problem and assume that $z_v = h$, $\phi = 0$ and $\theta = 0$. Therefore, the scan-matching process can be solved as a 2D problem by only employing the point cloud in the horizontal layer of the LiDAR scans to estimate the transformation matrices.

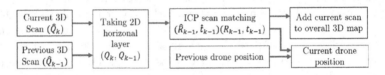

Fig. 1. Data flow diagram for 3D map reconstruction and drone's position estimating.

Figure 1 shows the data flow diagram for drone localisation and total map generation. Let $\hat{Q}$ be a scan of size $3 \times n$ received from a 3D LiDAR that contains point clouds, i.e. each column (n) in $\hat{Q}$ is a point cloud that is defined in the three-dimensional space by its coordinates (x, y, z). Moreover, let $\boldsymbol{Q}$ (size $2 \times n$) be the selected points by taking the horizontal layer from $\hat{Q}$, so that each point cloud in $\boldsymbol{Q}$ is defined within the two-dimensional space by its coordinates (x, y). The applied ICP algorithm is shown in Algorithm 1. The required 2D rotation $\boldsymbol{R}$ and translation $\boldsymbol{t}$ can be estimated by minimising the sum of the squared error in:

$$E(\boldsymbol{R}, \boldsymbol{t}) = \sum_{i=1}^{N} w_i \left\| q_i - (\boldsymbol{R}p_i - \boldsymbol{t}) \right\|^2, \tag{1}$$

where q_i and p_i are the corresponding pair points from the current scan $\boldsymbol{Q}_k$ and the previous scan $\boldsymbol{Q}_{k-1}$, respectively. The subscript k and $k-1$ are the scan index, $\|.\|$ is the norm, N is the overall number of the matched point pairs, and w_i is a weighting factor for the ith pair. For every point q in $\boldsymbol{Q}_{k-1}$, a search is conducted for the corresponding point p in $\boldsymbol{Q}_k$ which has the closest distance. The weighting factor, w_i, is set to be linear from 1 to 0, where 1 is for

---

Algorithm 1: Compute the 2D transformations (R_{k-1}, t_{k-1}) between two 3D LiDAR scans.

Input: Current 3D scan ($\hat{Q}_k$) and previous 3D scan ($\hat{Q}_{k-1}$)
Result: R_{k-1}, t_{k-1}
Initialisation: $Q = f(\hat{Q}) \leftarrow$ Take the 2D horizontal layer;
$\qquad\qquad E = \infty$;
$\qquad\qquad R = [1\ 0; 0\ 1],\ \ t = [0\ 0]^T$;
while $E >$ threshold, & iteration < maximum number of iteration **do**
$\quad\big|\quad Q_k = R\,Q_k - t \leftarrow$ Update Q_k;
$\quad\big|\quad$ Determine and weighting corresponding points q and p;
$\quad\big|\quad$ Determine the mean of the corresponding, $u_{Q'_i}$ and $u_{Q'_{i-1}}$;
$\quad\big|\quad$ Compute the cross-covarance matrix, K;
$\quad\big|\quad$ SVD(K) $\leftarrow U, V$;
$\quad\big|\quad R_{new} = U\,V^T \leftarrow$ New R;
$\quad\big|\quad R = R_{new}\,R \leftarrow$ Update R;
$\quad\big|\quad t_{new} = u_{Q_{k-1}} - R\,u_{Q_k} \leftarrow$ New t;
$\quad\big|\quad t = t_{new} + t \leftarrow$ Update t;
$\quad\big|\quad E(R, t) = \sum_{i=1}^{N} w_i \|q_i - (Rp_i - t)\|^2$;
end

---

points at minimum range of the LiDAR and 0 is for those at its maximum range. Algorithm 1 is executed for a specific number of iterations (maximum number of iteration), or until $E \leq$ threshold. After finding the transformation matrices, the drone current position can be obtained as:

$$\begin{bmatrix} x_v \\ y_v \end{bmatrix}_k = R_{k-1} \begin{bmatrix} x_v \\ y_v \end{bmatrix}_{k-1} + t_{k-1}\,, \tag{2}$$

where $\begin{bmatrix} x_v\ y_v \end{bmatrix}^T_{k-1}$ is the drone's previous position, and R_{k-1} and t_{k-1} are the obtained rotation and translation (transformation) matrices from Algorithm 1 that match the scan Q_k and Q_{k-1}.

The overall 3D map, $\mathcal{M}$, of the total scanned area is generated by appending the current 3D scan $\hat{Q}_k$ to the initial scan $\hat{Q}_1$ after applying the obtained transformation matrices. Since the transformation matrices ($R_{2 \times 2}$ and $t_{2 \times 1}$) are cast in 2D space, we applied a homogeneous transformation to allow 3D space transformation matrices ($\hat{R}_{3 \times 3},\ \hat{t}_{3 \times 1}$). The overall 3D map, $\mathcal{M}$, can, thus, be obtained as:

$$\mathcal{M}_{3 \times n} = \begin{bmatrix} [\hat{Q}_1]^T \\ [\hat{R}_1\hat{Q}_2 + \hat{t}_1]^T \\ [\hat{R}_2(\hat{R}_2\hat{Q}_3 + \hat{t}_2) + \hat{t}_1]^T \\ \vdots \\ [\hat{R}_1(\hat{R}_2(...(\hat{R}_{k-1}\hat{Q}_k + \hat{t}_{k-1}) + ...) + \hat{t}_2) + \hat{t}_1]^T \end{bmatrix}^T = \begin{bmatrix} x \\ y \\ z \end{bmatrix}_{3 \times n}\,, \tag{3}$$

where n is the total number of the registered point clouds and $\hat{Q}_1$ is the initial 3D scan at scan index, $k = 1$.

2.2   Indoor Navigation

Navigating a drone within a dusty confined space is challenging due to the need to fly the drone beyond line of sight and the inability to use cameras [15]. To address the issue, a simple algorithm is implemented for autonomous navigation that always keeps the drone at a certain distance from the walls. The point clouds from the LiDAR horizontal layer are used to obtain the normal distance from the drone to the front (d_f) and right (d_r) obstacles, as illustrated in Fig. 2. Let $\mathcal{R}_s$ be the ranges in the current scan Q_k, where s is a positive integer that donates the range index. The distances d_f and d_r can be obtained from Eq. (4) and (5) as follow:

$$d_f = \mathcal{R}_s, \quad \text{when } s = \lceil r\pi/(2\pi) \rceil = \lceil r/2 \rceil, \tag{4}$$

$$d_r = \mathcal{R}_s, \quad \text{when } s = \lceil r(\pi/2)/(2\pi) \rceil = \lceil r/4 \rceil, \tag{5}$$

where r is the total number of the ranges in $\mathcal{R}_s$ and $\lceil . \rceil$ denotes the standard rounding function that rounds to the closest integer number.

The navigation algorithm starts when the drone reaches the desired altitude, then the drone starts to fly forward whilst keeping $d_r = D$ by changing the heading direction using a proportional–derivative (PD) controller. Note that, D is the desired normal distance between the walls and the trajectory path. Then, when $d_f \leq D$, the drone starts turning. This way, the drone is always capable of keeping the distance, D, with the surrounding walls. Figure 2 shows an overall description of the trajectory planning and navigation parameters. Clearly, this is a very simple trajectory planning approach; however, it is sufficient for our storage mapping application.

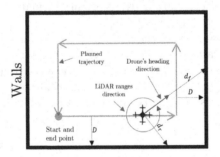

Fig. 2. The planned trajectory where d_f is the distance from the drone to the front obstacle and d_r is the distance to the right obstacle.

2.3 Surface Generation and Volume Estimation

At the end of the mapping process, the volume of the stockpile is estimated by calculating the volume of the overall 3D map, $\mathcal{M}$. The meshgrid function in Matlab is used to generate a uniform 2D grid across the inspected space $\mathcal{R}$. The heights, z, from $\mathcal{M}$ are interpolated on top of the uniform grid $\mathcal{R}$ using a linear approach (achieved using the griddata function in Matlab). Therefore, the surface of the stockpile $Z_{surface}$ can be generated from these returned values. To estimate the volume of the stockpile, $V_{stockpile}$, double integration of the surface over the inspection space is, then, performed as follow:

$$V_{stockpile} = \iint_{\mathcal{R}} Z_{surface}\left(x, y\right) dx\, dy . \tag{6}$$

3 Simulation Setup

3.1 Simulation Environment

We created a model for the environment as well as the robotic system in Webots (2021a), an open-source virtual mobile robotics simulation platform that allows users to model, programme, and simulate mobile robots in a virtual prototyping environment. In Webots, a fully confined storage was implemented along with a stockpile as a fair representation of a real cement or clinker storage within a cement plant. The stockpile is a 3D CAD model of a generic stockpile designed in SolidWorks 2019 CAD software. Hence, the CAD software provides the actual volume of the stockpile that can be compared with the estimated volume. Figure 3 shows a screenshot of the modelled environment, including the implemented stockpile.

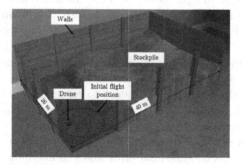

Fig. 3. A screenshot showing the developed model in Webots simulator demonstrating a stockpile in a fully confined storage. The ceiling and two walls are transparent to show the stockpile inside.

3.2 Robotic Platform

A quadcopter drone from the in-built robot libraries of Webots was inserted into the environment. To collect the 3D scans $\hat{Q}$ of the environment, the drone was equipped with a rotary 3D LiDAR that has a 45°vertical field of view below the horizon. The LiDAR was set in the simulation with five layers. Each layer has 512 point clouds (i.e. low-dense scan). Moreover, a Gaussian noise with 0.12 standard deviation was added to the LiDAR data by the simulator. The drone was programmed and controlled using Matlab codes. Furthermore, the ICP scan-matching algorithm and the navigation approach were implemented in Matlab.

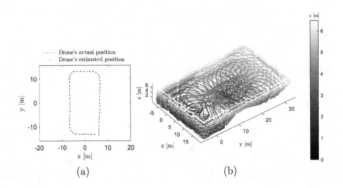

Fig. 4. Example simulation with $v_f = 0.43$ m/s and $s_r = 0.21$ Hz. (a) Estimated drone's positions superimposed on actual positions. (b) The overall 3D map ($\mathcal{M}$) of the total scanned area.

3.3 Simulations

To investigate the system's performance, we defined two parameters: drone forward speed, v_f, and scan rate, s_r. In Webots, a *pitch disturbance* value is typically used to move the drone forward. In this work, we tested three values of *pitch disturbance* $\in \{0.50, 0.75, 1.0\}$ which resulted in $v_f \in \{0.31, 0.43, 0.55\}$ m/s. Moreover, we recorded scans and applied the proposed scan-matching method described in Sect. 2 at four low-rate values by skipping $\{50, 100, 150, 200\}$ scans in the simulation loop which are equivalent to recording a scan every $\{1.6, 3.2, 4.8, 6.4\}$ seconds or $\{0.63, 0.31, 0.21, 0.16\}$ Hz. Each simulation was repeated five times with different initial positions. The doted circle in Fig. 3 indicates the area where drone is randomly placed at the start of each test. Thus, in total, 60 tests were conducted. The threshold error and the maximum number of iteration were set in Algorithm 1 to 2 and 50, respectively. Lastly, the desired normal distance D between the walls and the trajectory path was set to 6 m.

In order to measure the performance of the system, three metrics were defined: i) computing cost, c_c, ii) error of the estimated positions, e_p, and iii) error of the estimated volume, e_v. The metric c_c is defined as the sum of total iterations in the ICP algorithm throughout each test. The metric e_p is defined as

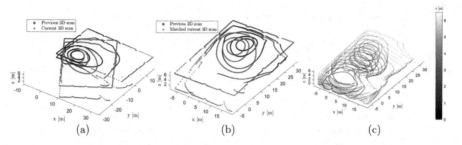

Fig. 5. An example of matching a current scan (Q_k) with a previous scan (Q_{k-1}) and adding the corrected current scan to the total map, $\mathcal{M}$. (a) Two scans before matching, (b) after matching, and (c) adding to $\mathcal{M}$. Colour in (c) encodes height from the ground.

the root mean square error between the drone's actual and estimated positions. Finally, the metric e_v is defined as the percentage error between the actual and estimated stockpile volumes.

4   Results

Using the case with $v_f = 0.43$ m/s and $s_r = 0.21$ Hz as an example, Fig. 4-a shows the drone's estimated positions superimposed on the actual ones, whereas Fig. 4-b shows the generated overall 3D map, $\mathcal{M}$. Evidently, the developed navigation strategy in Sect. 2.2 has successfully navigated the drone within the confined space by following the walls of the storage and successfully returning to the initial position. Moreover, Fig. 5 illustrates an example of matching a current scan (Q_k) with a previous scan (Q_{k-1}) and adding the corrected current scan to $\mathcal{M}$ in real-time. This matching would have not been achieved in real-time if all point clouds from both scans were used in the scan-matching. Therefore, our method and assumptions for matching 3D scans are very useful when scanning at a low-rate and whilst having low-dense scans.

The defined performance metrics of the system as well as the total recorded scans during simulation are assessed for the different flight speeds, v_f, and scan rates, s_r, Fig. 6. It is evident that higher s_r and lower v_f increase all metrics c_c, e_p, and e_v. This is because as more scans are recorded (as seen in Fig. 6-d) more scans have to be matched. Noting that the error E from Eq. (1) at the end of each scan-matching has an influence on the next scan-matching due to the corrected current scan (with the error E) being a reference scan in the next scan-matching. Hence, more recorded scans will decrease the accuracy of the drone's position estimation and the reconstructed 3D map.

It should be noted that higher flight speeds (than the three speeds simulated) were not attempted to recognise safety considerations, as it is not safe to fly at high speeds within a confined space. On the other hand, lower scanning rate can lead to blind spots (un-scanned area) or failure of the scan-matching technique. As such, these considerations defined our maximum s_r value. It is evident from

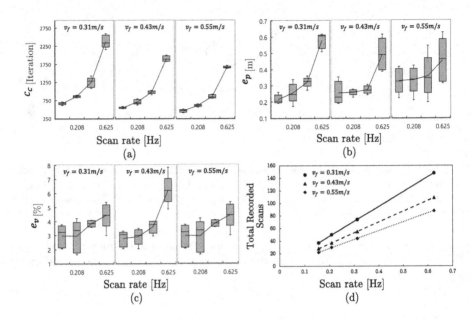

Fig. 6. Variations of the performance metrics of the system against drone forward speed, v_f, and scan rate, s_r. (a) Computing cost, c_c, (b) root mean square error of the estimated positions, e_p, (c) percentage error in volume estimation, e_v, and (d) the total recorded scans during the simulation. Each boxplot represents five repeated runs of each condition with different initial positions.

the shown results that the estimated volume is always more than the actual volume, mainly because of the walls and the ground that need to be excluded from $\mathcal{M}$. Nevertheless, the values of e_v are reasonable. In fact, according to [5], regulations regarding mine engineering often state that estimated volumes should present $\pm3\%$ accuracy of the whole amount. hence, the proposed method for mapping succeeded to estimate the stockpile volume with the recommended accuracy.

5 Conclusion and Future Work

This work demonstrated the implementation of a modified ICP algorithm for real-time scan-matching based on low-dense and low-rate scanning suitable for low computational requirements. The approach has localised a drone and simultaneously generated a 3D map of a confined space. A navigation strategy was developed to navigate the drone within the area autonomously. Using the reconstructed map of the confined space, the volume of the stored stockpile in the confined space was estimated.

The approach was tested using simulations for mapping a confined space within a cement plant. Results were demonstrated for different flight speeds and scan rates, demonstrating successful scan-matching. Moreover, the volume of the mapped stockpile was estimated with an error as low as 3%, which matches the accuracy levels recommended by relevant regulations.

In future work, we intend to develop the approach further by introducing a process to correctly remove outliers from the generated 3D map to enhance the accuracy of the results. Since the current method does not have a loop closure, our future work will, also, involve developing a strategy for accurate larger space mapping by closing the loop. We, then, intend to test the system in real-world scenarios.

References

1. Alsayed, A., Nabawy, M.R., Yunusa-Kaltungo, A., Arvin, F., Quinn, M.K.: Towards developing an aerial mapping system for stockpile volume estimation in cement plants. In: AIAA Scitech 2021 Forum, Reston, Virginia (2021)
2. Tan, C.H., et al.: A smart unmanned aerial vehicle (UAV) based imaging system for inspection of deep hazardous tunnels. Water Pract. Technol. **13**(4), 991–1000 (2018)
3. Chatziparaschis, D., Lagoudakis, M.G., Partsinevelos, P.: Aerial and ground robot collaboration for autonomous mapping in search and rescue missions. Drones **4**(4), 1–24 (2020)
4. Turner, R.M., MacLaughlin, M.M., Iverson, S.R.: Identifying and mapping potentially adverse discontinuities in underground excavations using thermal and multispectral UAV imagery. Eng. Geol. **266**, 105470 (2020)
5. Raeva, P.L., Filipova, S.L., Filipov, D.G.: Volume computation of a stockpile—a study case comparing GPS and UAV measurements in an open PIT quarry. ISPRS Int. Arch. Photogramm. Remote Sens. Spat. Inf. Sci. **41**, 999–1004 (2016)
6. Arango, C., Morales, C.A.: Comparison between multicopter UAV and total station for estimating stockpile volumes. Int. Arch. Photogramm. Remote Sens. Spat. Inf. Sci. **XL-1/W4**(1W4), 131–135 (2015)
7. Dissanayake, M., Newman, P., Clark, S., Durrant-Whyte, H., Csorba, M.: A solution to the simultaneous localization and map building (SLAM) problem. IEEE Trans. Robot. Autom. **17**(3), 229–241 (2001)
8. Phillips, T.G., Guenther, N., McAree, P.R.: When the dust settles: the four behaviors of lidar in the presence of fine airborne particulates. J. Field Robot. **34**(5), 985–1009 (2017)
9. Shu, L., Xu, H., Huang, M.: High-speed and accurate laser scan matching using classified features. In: IEEE International Symposium on Robotic and Sensors Environments (ROSE), pp. 61–66 (2013)
10. Li, X., Du, S., Li, G., Li, H.: Integrate point-cloud segmentation with 3D LiDAR scan-matching for mobile robot localization and mapping. Sensors **20**(1), 237 (2020)
11. Chen, Y., Medioni, G.: Object modelling by registration of multiple range images. Image Vis. Comput. **10**(3), 145–155 (1992)
12. Besl, P.J., McKay, N.D.: Method for registration of 3-D shapes. In: Sensor fusion IV: Control Paradigms and Data Structures, vol. 1611, pp. 586–606 (1992)
13. Mora, H., Mora-Pascual, J.M., García-García, A., Martínez-González, P.: Computational analysis of distance operators for the iterative closest point algorithm. PLoS One **11**(10), 1–19 (2016)

14. Zhang, R., Yang, B., Xiao, W., Liang, F., Liu, Y., Wang, Z.: Automatic extraction of high-voltage power transmission objects from UAV lidar point clouds. Remote Sens. **11**(22), 2600 (2019)
15. Petrlík, M., Báča, T., Heřt, D., Vrba, M., Krajník, T., Saska, M.: A robust UAV system for operations in a constrained environment. IEEE Robot. Autom. Lett. **5**(2), 2169–2176 (2020)

Maximising Availability of Transportation Robots Through Intelligent Allocation of Parking Spaces

Roopika Ravikanna$^{(\boxtimes)}$, Marc Hanheide, Gautham Das, and Zuyuan Zhu

University of Lincoln, Lincoln, England

Abstract. Autonomous agricultural robots increasingly have an important role in tasks such as transportation, crop monitoring, weed detection etc. These tasks require the robots to travel to different locations in the field. Reducing time for this travel can greatly reduce the global task completion time and improve the availability of the robot to perform more number of tasks. Looking at in-field logistics robots for supporting human fruit pickers as a relevant scenario, this research deals with the design of various algorithms for automated allocation of parking spaces for the on-field robots, so as to make them most accessible to preferred areas of the field. These parking space allocation algorithms are tested for their performance by varying initial parameters like the size of the field, number of farm workers in the field, position of the farm workers etc. Various experiments are conducted for this purpose on a simulated environment. Their results are studied and discussed for better understanding about the contribution of intelligent parking space allocation towards improving the overall time efficiency of task completion.

Keywords: Robotic farming · Agricultural robots · Autonomous parking · Robotic fleets · Swarm robotics

1 Introduction

Autonomous mobile robots have been extensively used to perform specific tasks in various application domains such as care homes, warehouses, and precision agriculture. In many of these environments, the tasks are dynamic, meaning they can appear at any time at any part of the environment, and the robots allocated to do these tasks should travel to one or more locations in the environment to execute the tasks. Most of these environments are structured, hence the path of the robot should be planned carefully in advance to reduce travelling time to these task locations. This work specifically addresses this challenge by dynamically allocating the parking spaces of robots closer to the area where demand is high. In particular, the deployment of a fleet of agricultural robots for in-field logistics operations to support human fruit pickers in a strawberry production poly-tunnel environment is considered here.

Funded by the EPSRC Centre for Doctoral Training - AgriFoRwArdS, and Saga Robotics.

© Springer Nature Switzerland AG 2021
C. Fox et al. (Eds.): TAROS 2021, LNAI 13054, pp. 337–348, 2021.
https://doi.org/10.1007/978-3-030-89177-0_34

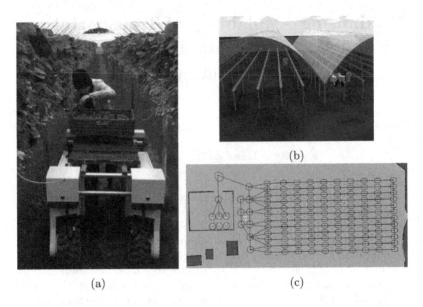

Fig. 1. (a) A representative image of a picker loading fruits into the robot; (b) Graphical representation of pickers in the rows of a poly-tunnel environment; and (c) Graphical representation of the field's Topological map.

The work we are presenting here is build upon our previous works in fleet coordination [3] and tracking of human in the field [7], with the aim of developing a robotic fleet that supports fruit pickers in soft-fruit production by automating transportation tasks, allowing the human pickers to focus on their job of picking. The overall system is readily deployed in various farm environments comprising autonomous Thorvald robotics platforms, coordinated by a central controller. A photograph of a picker performing loading of fruits is shown in Fig. 1a. The feasibility study reported in [3] has shown that although the overall task completion time and hence the picking efficiency can be improved up to 20% by deploying a fleet of robots for fruit transportation, the pickers still have to wait for the robots after they request for one. This wait time increases when the robots have to travel longer distances to reach the picker. While in our previous work, the parking positions for robots (where they will wait for new transportation tasks to be allocated) in the farm environment was randomly fixed, in this work we focus on reducing the time pickers have to wait for a robot to serve them by proposing and evaluating novel approaches to dynamically reallocate these parking spaces. Hence, the contributions in this work are i) Novel approaches to dynamically reallocate robot waiting spaces to reduce the task start delay and overall task completion time and ii) Comprehensive experimental evaluations of the proposed approaches in discrete-event simulations (DES).

2   Background and Related Work

Agricultural robotics have been widely researched and deployed at different stages of food supply chain from fully autonomous precision field operations such as seeding, weeding and harvesting [4] to human-robot interactive applications such as in-field logistics [3]. With the background research maturing, many agri-robotic platforms targeting specific crops and applications are made commercially available [2]. Deploying a fleet of such robots is beneficial to distribute the tasks among the robots [5] and to improve the task completion. Specifically looking at in-field logistics operations, positioning the fleet of robots closer to the area of high demand can reduce the robots' travel time to the task locations as well improve the overall task completion metrics. This work explores this approach to dynamically allocate parking spaces for the robots.

The researchers in [6] claim that multi-robot task allocation can be reduced to an instance of the Optimal Assignment Problem. They perform a comparative study amongst popular task allocation strategies such as ALLIANCE, BLE amd M+ to study differences in their computational complexity and impact on efficiency of task completion, which iterates the importance of strategies in task allocation towards maximising overall efficiency. The authors of [1] discuss in detail about a system of Unmanned Robotic Service Units in Agricultural tasks. Here, they point out that the three major problem areas in unmanned agricultural robots are their interaction with field workers, maneuvering and prioritisation of tasks. The problem of parking space allocation to robots can be considered vital towards enhancing the quickness of approach by the robots to farm workers, which in turn partly contributes to the improvement of the first mentioned problem area in robotised farming.

3   Methodology

For the purpose of our research, we discretise the spatial representation of the farm environment into a topological graph of nodes and edges. We assume human pickers travelling from node to node while picking, until they have exceeded the capacity of their picking crate and require a robot to take the picked fruits away and provide a new empty crate to continue picking into. Likewise, robots navigate along the topological graph, and we model their travel time along the edges, based on real-world parameters. Such a discretised representation of the problem, allows us to use the formalism of discrete event simulation (DES) to study the problem at hand [3].

DES models the operation of a multi-agent system as a discrete sequence of events in time and the basic unit agents, here, the human picker and the field robot, as *entities* [9]. The entities in the DES model compete among themselves for resources which are limited (e.g. in our case a node can only ever be occupied by single robot or picker, modelling the spatial constraints). Consequently when all robot are allocated to support pickers, any picker making a new request will have to wait in a queue to be allocated a robot. We use DES in our analysis as it allows to run simulations very fast, as any time between events (such as the waiting and travel times) discrete steps that do not occur in reality, allowing the efficient study of the proposed parking space allocation algorithms comprehensively.

As described in our previous work [3], a gang of human pickers are assumed to pick berries in a strawberry production poly-tunnel environment with plants on raised tables in this work. Typically, the farm layout looks like a fork with a head lane along one open end of the tunnel and navigation rows between the tables inside the poly-tunnel, as shown in Fig. 1b. Following our approach, a discrete topological map representation of the environment can easily capture the layout in which robots and pickers operate. A representation of the topological map of the poly-tunnel field is shown in Fig. 1c. It is assumed that there is sufficient space along the header lanes to park multiple robots as well for other robots to pass through. Different approaches to dynamically assigning parking spaces along the header lane are proposed in the following.

3.1 Parking Space Allocation Algorithms

This paper suggests five different algorithms that help with the allocation of parking spots for robots in an agricultural setup. These are designed keeping in mind their need to be adaptable to different field sizes, number of pickers and the average time each picker takes for performing the picking action at each node before moving on to the next. The parking spot algorithms vary in their complexity of decision from random allocation to speed based cumulative ranking that takes into account factors including number of pickers, their position in the field, the average time they take up while picking etc. This is to observe if the allocation of parking spaces is indeed important to conserve resources and the global task completion time, and also if the performance improvement is consistent with the increasing complexity and intuitive intelligence of the parking allocation algorithms.

Random Ranking. This is the simplest in design of all the suggested parking space allocation designs suggested. Of all of parking spaces spread across all row headers of the field, one is allocated at random to the robot irrespective of the size of the field, position of the pickers or their speed of picking. This algorithm is vital in providing a comparison of performance to all other parking space allocation algorithms. This is to firstly understand if there is in fact any positive consequence to providing intelligence to the task of parking space allocation. Figure 2c shows a demonstrative case of having implemented the Random Ranking technique. The figure shows 10 rows of crops and pickers located in rows 3, 5, 9, 10. Since Random Ranking is independent of any initial parameters of the field and pickers, it randomly generates row 2 to be the assigned parking space.

Middle Row Ranking. Middle Row Ranking is built on the logic that a robot placed at a parking space near the center of the field would enable it to fairly access picker calls from any part of the field. In case of n robots, the robots shall be recommended to be parked sequentially in parking spaces at every 1/nth of the field. This is the second most simple design for parking space allocation suggested in this paper. Figure 2d shows a demonstrative case of having implemented the Middle Row Ranking technique. The figure shows 10 rows of crops and Pickers located in rows 3, 5, 9, 10. Middle Row Ranking entirely bases its decision upon the width of the field, i.e. the number of rows in the field. Therefore, the row 5, one of the centre rows is assigned as the parking space.

Distance Based Raking. Distance Based Ranking looks at the distance in between each of the pickers in the field. The robot is allocated a parking space that lies in the approximate centre of the rows that indicate the largest gap between the pickers. The logic behind this algorithm is to tackle cases in which the concentration of pickers is to one side of the field rather than them being spread evenly across the field, which is the intuitive assumption made in the previously suggested Middle Row Ranking. Figure 2e shows a demonstrative case of having implemented the Distance Based Ranking technique. The figure shows 10 rows of crops and Pickers located in rows 3, 5, 9, 10. This technique bases its decision upon the comparative distance in between the pickers. So despite the exact same initial conditions as discussed in the previous ranking technique Middle Row, the result through Distance Based Ranking varies choosing row 7 as the assigned parking space, which lies in the centre of the largest gap $d2$, indicating the maximum distance between any two pickers in the given case.

Cumulative Ranking. Cumulative Ranking makes a parking space allocation decision by aggregating the individual parking spot preferences given out by each of the pickers based on their position in the field. Figure 2a shows a demonstrative case of having implemented the Cumulative Ranking technique. It is seen in the figure that there are four Pickers A, B, C and D located in rows 3,5,9,10. The individual preferences assigned to rows by each of the pickers can be observed in the figure. Picker A gives out its preference of parking space allocation where, the space near its own row, row 3 is given the first priority with rank 1 and the rows that are subsequently adjacent are given with incrementally increasing ranks indicating a decreased preference to rows that are farther from the row of that particular picker. Pickers B, C and D do the same to all the rows of the field. The ranks given by each of the pickers for each of the rows are added up. The aggregated ranks of rows are now observed to find the least objected row, i.e. the row with the least rank number. The parking space near the header of this row is considered to be the most suitable one. In case of multiple rows holding the minimum rank, the median of that sequence of rows is taken as the winner. As a result of this, in this example row 7 which is the most mutually agreeable row amongst the pickers is assigned as the parking space.

Preferential Cumulative Ranking. This is an extension from the Cumulative Ranking Technique but with inclusion of consideration given to the time taken

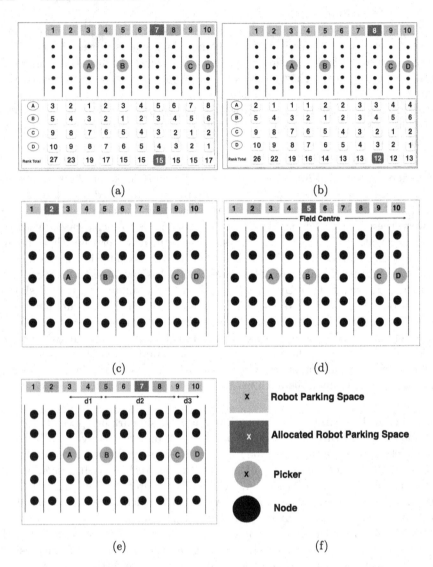

Fig. 2. Demonstrative Diagrams of (a) Cumulative Ranking, (b) Speed Based Cumulative Ranking, (c) Random Ranking, (d) Middle Row Ranking, (e) Distance Based Ranking are presented along with their reference legend in (f)

by the individual pickers to move from one node to another i.e. to perform the picking action. In simple terms, rankings given by the faster pickers are prioritised over that of the slower pickers. To enable this, the mean value of the set of times taken by each of the pickers to go from one node to another is calculated. Faster pickers are classified as those who take time less than or equal to the calculated mean value, those remaining are bracketed as the slower pickers.

After this classification, the same procedure explained in Cumulative Ranking is carried out. The only difference is that, the slower pickers change their ranking preference for every two consecutive rows instead of one as in case of faster pickers. This is done in an attempt to mathematically reduce the implication of preference given by the slower pickers. Figure 2b shows a demonstrative case of having implemented the Preferential Cumulative Ranking technique. Here, Picker A which is a picker whose picking time is assumed to fall under the average picking time of all the pickers in the field is given a lesser preference that can be noticed through the change in the ranking priority it provides for the same case as in the Cumulative Ranking Technique. Therefore, while aggregating the preferences this time, row 8 is found to be the most agreeable row, it can be noted that row 8 is further away from the slow picker, Picker A than row 7 which was the calculated result without the preferential treatment in ranking.

4 Experimental Evaluation and Results

The performance of the parking space allocation algorithms mentioned in the methodology section are put through experimentation on a simple simulated environment. In order to keep the parametric values of the simulation as realistic as possible, the values defining the spacing of nodes in the farm, speed of the pickers while picking at each node, their capacity to hold on to yield before calling for a robot are derived through an approximation of the corresponding values used in [3] that has a similar experimental setup. This paper by itself uses verified empirical data obtained from real farms.

4.1 Experimental Setup

In the simulated experimental setup the test environment is assumed to be a forked rectangular field with numerous parallel rows which have equally spaced nodes or way points that the pickers pass through in the course of their picking action. Based on data from [3], the length of each row is assumed to be 120 m, the node to node distance in the field is assumed as 5 m, thus creating 24 nodes in each row. There is a variable called 'picker time' that is used to indicate the time taken by a picker to go from one node to another, i.e. the time he spends picking at each node. This value is set at 2450 s. The robot is assumed to move at a speed of 1 m/s. This would imply that the robot takes 5 s to move from one node to another. As per the experiment the picker calls for the robot after having observed his collecting tray to be full. The rate at which he calls for the robot would differ based on how the yield of the crop/fruit is at every node. Based on the results and data observed in the experiments of [3], it is calculated that the picker approximately calls for the robot once every 7.7 nodes. So for this experiment, it is assumed that every picker calls for the robot once for every 8 nodes he traverses. All of the experimental results discussed below were aggregated over 20 randomised trials.

Comparison of Ranking Techniques by Varying the Number of Rows.
The first experiment conducted is that of varying the width of the field by
changing the number of rows (from 5 to 50) and holding the number of pickers
on the field as constant (number of pickers = 3). The performance of the different
ranking strategies are shown in comparison to one another through the graphs in
Fig. 3. The two evaluation metrics observed are Global Task Completion Time,
which is the total time taken for the task to complete. This is an indicator or the
task completion efficiency. Another is the Robot Travel Time which is the Total
Time for which the Robot has been in motion, this is an indicator of resource
conservation.

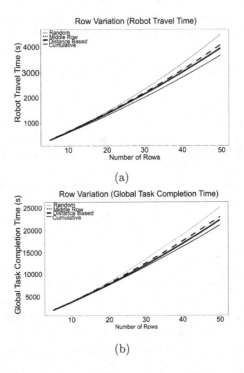

Fig. 3. Comparison of Performance of different ranking techniques by varying the number of rows from 5 to 50 and observing changes in (a) Robot Travel Time and (b) Global
Task Completion Time

**Comparison of Ranking Techniques by Varying the Number of Pick-
ers.** The next experiment conducted is that of varying the number of pickers
(from 3 to 15) with a constant number of rows (number of rows = 100) and the
same picking speed as before. The performance of different ranking strategies
for picker count variation are shown in comparison to one another through the
graphs in Fig. 4.

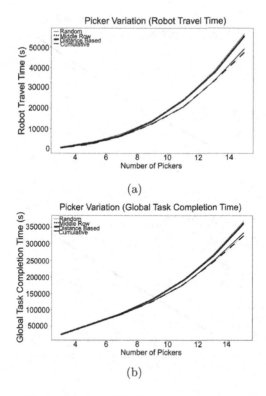

Fig. 4. Comparison of Performance of different ranking techniques by varying the number of pickers from 3 to 15 and observing changes in (a) Robot Travel Time and (b) Global Task Completion Time

Impact of Differences in Picking Time Amongst Pickers. The impact of differences in Picking Time amongst the Pickers is studied through this experiment. While assuming the number of Pickers to be 3 and varying the number of rows in the field, the performance of Cumulative Ranking is compared with that of Preferential Cumulative Ranking. It is thought that by giving a bias to faster pickers efficiency can be improved. Figure 5 represents results from the experiment studying effects of change in speed of picking amongst pickers.

5   Discussions and Conclusion

It can be observed from Fig. 3, that in the experiment of comparing the ranking techniques through varying the number of rows, that the performance of the different ranking methods are proportional with respect to the two evaluation metrics. As expected, all remaining ranking strategies out perform Random Ranking, confirming the positive impact caused by intelligent planing of parking spaces. The best performer here is Cumulative Ranking, followed by Distance based Ranking and then Middle Row Ranking.

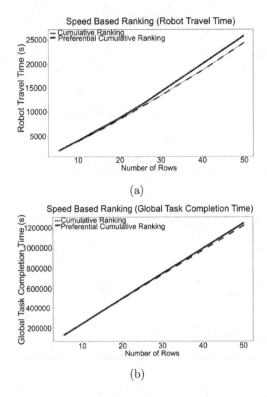

Fig. 5. Comparison of Performance of Cumulative and Preferential Cumulative Ranking techniques by varying the speed of picking amongst pickers and observing changes in (a) Robot Travel Time and (b) Global Task Completion Time

In Fig. 4, showing the results of comparison of ranking techniques through varying the number of pickers, similar to the previous case the performance of the different ranking methods are proportional with respect to the two evaluation metrics. Here, it can be seen that with increase in the number of pickers for a fixed field size, Distance Based Ranking encounters a deterioration in performance only managing to be narrowly better than Random Ranking. This is because with the rise in number of pickers, the chances of a population skew of pickers over to one side of the field decreases, which was one of the main areas combated by the Distance Ranking methods. It can also be seen that Cumulative Ranking too begins to deteriorate with increase in the number of pickers, since the almost even distributions of the picker population might marginally favour one row over the other in case of multiple equally desired row priorities. This is why Middle Row Ranking works best with a High Pickers to Rows ratio, since there would most likely be equal demand for the robot from all areas of the field that would be best tackled by Middle Row Ranking.

In Fig. 5 that represents results from the experiment studying effects of change in speed of picking amongst pickers, the results are different from what was hypothesised. The unbiased Cumulative Ranking out performs the speed based Preferential Cumulative ranking. This has been observed to be due to the following reason: though the robot might initially access the faster pickers quicker, when the demand for robot arises in the slower picker, the robot might have to for travel longer to reach this slow picker, this in turn increases the subsequent wait time of the faster pickers, slowing down the task. The results might however be different if in addition to the slowness, there is a reduction in demand from the slower pickers for access to the robots. Though this theoretically makes sense, it is highly unlikely that the changes in abilities and robot requirements of pickers working in the same field in a standard operation such as picking would produce such a case. Mathematically, it can be said that the constant of variation [8] in the picking speed and robot requirements of the pickers would not be high enough to trigger an impact due to them. Figure 5 shows the results from these experiments.

From the results obtained, it is noteworthy to observe that there is approximately a **20% decrease in the Global Task Completion time and a 30% decrease in robot usage** when switching from a Randomised parking space allocation technique to adapting the Cumulative Ranking strategy. This proves the improvement to efficiency given by intelligent parking space allocation.

The results from the experiments performed on the inclusion of intelligence in parking space allocation for the waiting period of an autonomous agricultural robot show a positive impact on mechanical conservation in the use of robot due to reduced operational time and also a reduction in the global task completion time due to lower waiting periods by the pickers. Though all of the experiments shown in this paper demonstrate the case of a single robot, the methodologies can be easily extended to a system of multiple robots. There also lies interesting possibilities for the extension of these ideas to suit various field setups and farm shapes. These aspects of this research shall be addressed through continued work in the future.

References

1. Auat Cheein, F.A., Carelli, R.: Agricultural robotics: unmanned robotic service units in agricultural tasks. IEEE Ind. Electron. Mag. **7**(3), 48–58 (2013). https://doi.org/10.1109/MIE.2013.2252957
2. Bogue, R.: Fruit picking robots: has their time come? Ind. Robot **47**, 141–145 (2020)
3. Das, G.P., Cielniak, G., From, P.J., Hanheide, M.: Discrete event simulations for scalability analysis of robotic in-field logistics in agriculture - a case study. In: ICRA 2018 Workshop on Robotic Vision and Action in Agriculture, Brisbane (2018)
4. Duckett, T., et al.: Agricultural robotics: the future of robotic agriculture. arXiv Prepr. arXiv1806.06762 (2018)
5. From, P.J., Grimstad, L., Hanheide, M., Pearson, S., Cielniak, G.: Rasberry-robotic and autonomous systems for berry production. Mech. Eng. **140**(06), S14–S18 (2018)
6. Gerkey, B.P., Mataric, M.J.: Multi-robot task allocation: analyzing the complexity and optimality of key architectures. In: 2003 IEEE International Conference on Robotics and Automation (Cat. No.03CH37422), vol. 3, pp. 3862–3868 (2003). https://doi.org/10.1109/ROBOT.2003.1242189

7. Khan, M.W., Das, G.P., Hanheide, M., Cielniak, G.: Incorporating spatial constraints into a Bayesian tracking framework for improved localisation in agricultural environments. In: IEEE International Conference on Intelligent Robots and Systems, pp. 2440–2445 (2020). https://doi.org/10.1109/IROS45743.2020.9341013
8. Pélabon, C., Hilde, C.H., Einum, S., Gamelon, M.: On the use of the coefficient of variation to quantify and compare trait variation. Evol. Lett. **4**(3), 180–188 (2020)
9. Schriber, T.J., Brunner, D.T., Smith, J.S.: Inside discrete-event simulation software: how it works and why it matters. In: 2014 Proceedings of the Winter Simulations Conference 2014, pp. 132–146 (2014). https://doi.org/10.1109/WSC.2014.7019884

A Minimalist Solution to the Multi-robot Barrier Coverage Problem

Thomas Green[(✉)], Kevin Kamel, Siyuan Li, Christopher Shinn,
Paolo Toscano, Xintong Wang, Yuchen Ye, and Roderich Groß[(✉)]

Department of Automatic Control and Systems Engineering, The University
of Sheffield, Sheffield, UK
{tdggreen1,kkgkamel1,sli101,cshinn1,ptoscano1,
xwang309,yye30,r.gross}@sheffield.ac.uk

Abstract. This paper addresses the multi-robot barrier coverage problem. It presents a group of memory-less robots that encircle a group of herd agents, by moving along a polygonal barrier. The results, produced from simulations in CoppeliaSim, demonstrate high retention of herd agents, and robust performance across a range of simulated scenarios.

Keywords: Coverage · Multi-robot system · Swarm robotics

1 Introduction

This study addresses multi-robot barrier coverage, an extensively studied problem [5–8] with a variety of potential applications in defence, and beyond, such as developing robots as alternatives to sheepdogs [7,8], mine sweeping [5], as well as in understanding swarming behaviours in sheep and other organisms [7]. For large-scale applications, such as oil spill clean-ups [9], solutions with low hardware requirements could improve feasibility. Here, the computation-free swarming paradigm [1] is used in controlling a group of barrier coverage robots.

2 Methods

A herd of n simulated terrestrial agents is to be contained within a 2-D polygonal region, delineated by p vertices, represented by non-collidable green discs on the ground. A minimalist solution is realised using m simple, memory-less, identical barrier coverage robots (BCRs) whose aim is to minimise the number of herd agents (HAs) crossing the boundary. Simulations are carried out in CoppeliaSim Edu 4.1.0. The default setup comprises a regular polygon where $p = 20$ and side length is $1\,\mathrm{m}$, $n = 10$ homogeneous HAs, and $m = 4$ BCRs. The HAs [BCRs] start from random positions and orientations within the polygonal region, less [more] than $1\,\mathrm{m}$ away from its centre. The robot controllers are updated at 2 Hz.

Barrier Coverage Robot Design: BCRs are simulated using the Pioneer P3-DX (see Fig. 1(a)), a differential wheeled robot weighing ~ 9 kg. In this

© Springer Nature Switzerland AG 2021
C. Fox et al. (Eds.): TAROS 2021, LNAI 13054, pp. 349–353, 2021.
https://doi.org/10.1007/978-3-030-89177-0_35

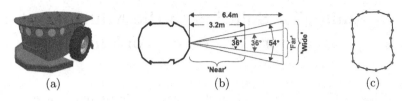

Fig. 1. (a) The barrier coverage robot (BCR), a Pioneer P3-DX. (b) BCR sensors (not to scale). The range of 'far' and 'wide' equals d, the distance between opposing boundary vertices. Range of 'near' is $d/2$. (c) Irregular polygonal barrier used in SC3.

study, the motor velocities can take continuous values in a range equivalent to $[-0.80, 0.80]$ m/s. Each BCR has three discrete-state, pyramidal sensors mounted in the forward-facing direction, detecting objects that are near, far, or in a wide range, respectively (see Fig. 1(b)). They take values $S_{near} \in \{0, G, BC, H\}$, $S_{far} \in \{0, G\}$, and $S_{wide} \in \{0, BC\}$, where $0, G, BC$, and H, respectively represent no object, green disc, other BCR, and HA detection. The BCR has hence $4 \cdot 2 \cdot 2 = 16$ sensing states. Let $\bar{v}_l, \bar{v}_r \in [-1, 1]$ represent the normalised left and right BCR wheel velocities, respectively, where a wheel velocity value of -1 [1] corresponds to the wheel turning backwards [forwards] at maximum velocity. The controller maps the sensor readings $S_{near}, S_{far}, S_{wide}$ onto the wheel velocities $\bar{v}_l, \bar{v}_r$: $\{0, 1, 2, 3\} \times \{0, 1\} \times \{0, 1\} \rightarrow [-1, 1]^{32}$. It outputs a tuple, $\boldsymbol{x} = (\bar{v}_{l0}, \bar{v}_{r0}, ..., \bar{v}_{l31}, \bar{v}_{r31}) \in [-1, 1]^{32}$, where $\bar{v}_{l_i}$ and $\bar{v}_{r_i}$ are respectively the left and right wheel velocities for the ith sensing state. The output represents one of four actions (see Table 1): spin clockwise (CW), move forward, turn left while moving forward, and turn left while very slowly moving forward. This allows the BCRs to establish a distributed formation in which they traverse the boundary counter-clockwise, while avoiding collisions.

Herd Agent Design: HAs are simulated using e-pucks [2], which are miniature, differential wheeled robots of mass ~ 150 g. For HA i, potential fields [4] are

Table 1. BCR controller lookup ('*' = 'whichever state that sensor takes')

S_{near}	S_{far}	S_{wide}	$\bar{v}_l, \bar{v}_r$	Belief of Situation and Intended Behaviour
H	*	*	0.2, −0.2	Spins CW to avoid collision with HA in path
BC	*	*	0.2, −0.2	Spins CW to avoid collision with other BCR in path
G	*	BC	0.2, −0.2	Spins CW to avoid potential collision with BCR in wide range
G	*	0	1,1	Detects green disc and no obstacles in wide range, moves forward at max speed
0	G	*	0.2, −0.2	Inside the boundary but not facing a short exit path, spins CW to find a closer green disc
0	0	BC	0.05,1	While orbiting detects BCR in wide range, turns left while very slowly moving forward until other BCR moves out of detection range
0	0	0	0.5,1	Outside the boundary, turns left & forward until a green disc is detected

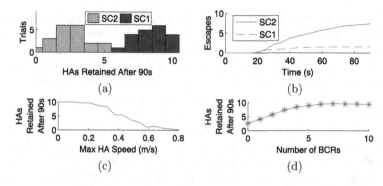

Fig. 2. (a) Histogram of HAs remaining after 90 s in SC1 and SC2, (b) Average escapes over time in SC1 and SC2 (20 trials each). Effect of maximum HA speed (2c, SC4) and number of BCRs (2d, SC5) on total HAs remaining after 90 s (10 trials per setting).

generated by other HAs within 1 m radius, BCRs within 3 m radius, and a random attraction point, unique per HA, and sampled every 15 s from a 20 m× 20 m region in the centre. Let x_{h_j} be the position vector of HA j, x_{bc_k} be the position vector of BCR k, and x_{rand} be the position vector of the random point, and thus for HA i, define $r_{h_j} = x_{h_j} - x_{h_i}$, $r_{bc_k} = x_{bc_k} - x_{h_i}$, and $r_{rand} = x_{rand} - x_{h_i}$. Thus, for HA i, defining distances $r_{h_j} = |r_{h_j}|, r_{bc_k} = |r_{bc_k}|$, and $r_{rand} = |r_{rand}|$, the field due to repulsion from other HAs is $U_h = k_h \sum_{j \neq i} \frac{1}{r_{h_j}}$, the field due to repulsion from BCRs is $U_{bc} = k_{bc} \sum_k \frac{1}{r_{bc_k}}$, and the field due to the random point of attraction is $U_{rand} = k_{rand} r_{rand}$, where k_h, k_{bc}, and k_{rand} are the weights for HA repulsion, BCR repulsion, and random motion, set to 1.5, 3, and 1.5, respectively in the default scenario. HA i is thus subject to force F equal to the negative gradient w.r.t. x_{h_i} of the total potential field (adapted from [4]):

$$F = -\nabla(U_h + U_{bc} + U_{rand}) = -\left(k_h \sum_{j \neq i} \frac{r_{h_j}}{r_{h_j}^3} + k_{bc} \sum_k \frac{r_{bc_k}}{r_{bc_k}^3} - k_{rand} \frac{r_{rand}}{r_{rand}} \right)$$

The velocity at time step t, v_t, is computed as $v_t = \frac{F - \nu v_{t-1}}{m} \Delta t + v_{t-1}$, where $\nu = 0.01$ is viscous friction, v_{t-1} is the previous velocity, initialised to $[0\ 0]^T$, m is the e-puck mass, and Δt is the simulation time step. The velocity of each HA is clipped to $[-M, M]$, where M is the maximum speed in m/s.

3   Results and Discussions

Five scenarios are considered, referred to as SC1 to SC5, respectively (for a representative selection of video clips, see [3]).

SC1 analyses HA retention under the default setup with $M \approx 0.27$ m/s. SC2 differs from SC1 only in that no BCRs are present. This comparison provides a baseline for the efficacy of the design. Figure 2(a) shows a marked separation in the distributions. An average of 2.55 ($\sigma = 1.32$) HAs are retained after 90 s in SC2 versus 8.40 ($\sigma = 1.19$) retained in SC1. Figure 2(b) shows the impact of the BCRs on the rate of HA escapes: no escapes occur before ~ 20 s in either scenario (the approximate time for HAs to reach the boundary), and a distinct plateau after ~ 25 s for SC1 (presumably, at that moment the BCRs achieved formation).

SC3 tests the robustness with respect to irregular barrier polygons. The selected polygon (Fig. 1(c)) has the most complex shape for which the design proved effective given the local nature of the sensing strategy. The area of the polygon is kept approximately equal to that of SC1 (i.e. 31.57 m^2). A mean of 7.50 ($\sigma = 1.70$) HAs are retained over 20 trials. This is similar to the performance seen in SC1, with an expected slight decrease in retained HAs possibly due to the increased initial proximity of HAs to some sections of the barrier.

In SC4, the maximum HA speed is varied through $M \in [0, 0.80]$ m/s in 18 discrete steps, under otherwise the default setup. Figure 2(c) shows that once a speed of $M \approx 0.31$ m/s is surpassed, HA retention falls below the 8.40 of SC1. Furthermore, at $M \approx 0.48$ m/s, more than 70% of the HAs escape, linearly increasing to $\sim 100\%$ at $M \approx 0.80$ m/s, rendering the design ineffective. The performance could be improved by increasing BCR speed, thus more promptly establishing a barrier, however this could result in erratic behaviour as BCR reaction time becomes a restricting factor.

In SC5, the number of BCRs, m, is varied from 0 to 10. As shown in Fig. 2(d), increasing m from 0 to 7 yields improved performance, but with diminishing returns: significant improvements occur for $m = 1 \to 4$ ($\nabla > 1$ HA/BCR), with only marginal improvements ($\nabla < 1$ HA/BCR) for $m = 5 \to 7$. The proposed design ($m = 4$) therefore offers a good trade-off between cost and performance. Beyond $m = 7$, HA retention decreases, as long chains of slowly moving, closely packed BCRs temporarily result in large gaps in barrier coverage.

This paper proposed a simple solution to multi-robot barrier coverage, which does not require the barrier coverage robots to communicate, or store information during run-time. The solution was shown to perform robustly in a range of simulation scenarios. Future work will test more realistic conditions including environments with obstacles and porting the solutions to real robots.

References

1. Gauci, M., Chen, J., Li, W., Dodd, T.J., Groß, R.: Self-organized aggregation without computation. Int. J. Robot. Res. **33**(8), 1145–1161 (2014)
2. Gonçalves, et al.: The e-puck, a robot designed for education in engineering. In: 9th Conference on Autonomous Robot Systems and Competitions, vol. 1, pp. 59–65 (2009)
3. Green, T., et al.: A minimalist solution to the multi-robot barrier coverage problem (supplementary video material) (2021). https://doi.org/10.15131/shef.data. 15082653

4. Howard, A., Matarić, M.J., Sukhatme, G.S.: Mobile sensor network deployment using potential fields: a distributed, scalable solution to the area coverage problem. In: Asama, H., Arai, T., Fukuda, T., Hasegawa, T. (eds.) Distributed Autonomous Robotic Systems 5, pp. 299–308. Springer, Tokyo (2002). https://doi.org/10.1007/978-4-431-65941-9_30
5. Lien, J.M., Bayazit, O.B., Sowell, R.T., Rodriguez, S., Amato, N.M.: Shepherding behaviors. In: 2004 Proceedings of the IEEE International Conference on Robotics and Automation. ICRA 2004, vol. 4, pp. 4159–4164. IEEE (2004)
6. Nguyen, T.M., Li, X., Xie, L.: Barrier coverage by heterogeneous sensor network with input saturation. In: 11th Asian Control Conference, pp. 1719–1724 (2017)
7. Strömbom, D., et al.: Solving the shepherding problem: heuristics for herding autonomous, interacting agents. J. R. Soc. Interface 11(100), 20140719 (2014)
8. Vaughan, R., Sumpter, N., Henderson, J., Frost, A., Cameron, S.: Experiments in automatic flock control. Robot. Auton. Syst. 31(1–2), 109–117 (2000)
9. Zahugi, E.M.H., Shanta, M.M., Prasad, T.: Design of multi-robot system for cleaning up marine oil spill. Int. J. Adv. Inf. Technol. 2(4), 33–43 (2012)

Scheduling Multi-robot Missions with Joint Tasks and Heterogeneous Robot Teams

Gricel Vázquez[✉], Radu Calinescu, and Javier Cámara

Department of Computer Science, University of York, York, UK
gnvf500@york.ac.uk

Abstract. We present a work-in-progress approach to scheduling multi-robot missions comprising tasks that need to be performed by multiple robots. Our approach (1) supports the scheduling of such missions for heterogeneous robots, (2) can take into account dependability, performance and other nonfunctional requirements, and (3) guarantees compliance with mission requirements by using a combination of formal techniques to allocate the mission tasks to individual robots, and to plan the order in which each robot will execute its allocated tasks. We show the effectiveness of our approach by applying it to the scheduling of a multi-robot mission in a hospital-support application.

Keywords: Multi-robot systems · Task allocation and planning · Constraint solving · Probabilistic model checking

1 Introduction

Multi-robots systems (MRS) have the potential to perform missions that humans find too dangerous, tedious or costly. Examples of such missions include search and rescue [10], hospital and care-home support [1,3], and inspection of critical infrastructure [13]. However, scheduling MRS missions is very challenging due to the complexity of their constraints and requirements. These missions must achieve strict dependability, performance and other nonfunctional requirements, and may need to be carried out by teams of heterogeneous robots. No existing MRS-mission scheduling solution [11] can support them together. The use of probabilistic model checkers as planners is specially useful to provide behavioural, performance and safety guarantees [4,8,14]; as well as capturing, for example: the probability of succeeding with a task [9], spatial distribution of the tasks [2], multiple decompositions of tasks [12], and partial knowledge of the environment [5]. Most studies simultaneously solve the allocation of tasks and planning problems. However, they do not consider complex task dependencies that we capture (via separating these two problems), such as tasks that require more than one robot to be completed, ordered and consecutive tasks.

Our paper introduces a work-in-progress approach for the scheduling of heterogeneous-robot MRS missions comprising ordered and joint tasks, where these

© Springer Nature Switzerland AG 2021
C. Fox et al. (Eds.): TAROS 2021, LNAI 13054, pp. 354–359, 2021.
https://doi.org/10.1007/978-3-030-89177-0_36

missions need to satisfy nonfunctional requirements such as cost minimisation. Our approach supports the *high-level scheduling* of MRS missions, i.e., we assume that the robots can navigate through their environment, avoid obstacles, etc., and we use (a) constraint solving to allocate tasks (e.g., 'R1 cleans hospital room A' and 'R3 disinfects room C') to individual robots; and (b) probabilistic model checking to decide the execution order for these tasks (e.g., 'robot R1 cleans room A, then rearranges the furniture in room D together with robot R5').

2 MRS Mission Scheduling Approach

As shown in Fig. 1, our MRS mission scheduling approach takes four inputs. First, domain experts provide a *task specification* that defines the *types of tasks* for the application domain/organisation using the MRS. This includes *atomic tasks* with their properties (mean execution time, number of robots needed, etc.), and *compound tasks*, i.e., lists of atomic and/or other compound (sub)tasks that may need to be executed in order and/or consecutively. Next, an "MRS team" of engineers provides: (i) a *world model* defining the physical layout of the environment where the MRS missions will be performed, and (ii) a *robot specification* describing the *capabilities*, initial location and other characteristics of every available robot. Each capability of a robot indicates a type of task which that robot can execute, and provides details about the performance, reliability, energy use, etc. with which the robot would execute the task. Finally, the MRS users provide a *mission specification* defining the combination of tasks that need to be performed by the available robots, at specific locations and with given timing/cost/etc. constraints and optimisation objectives.

Given these inputs, we use a two-stage approach to generate individual robot plans whose execution ensures the correct completion of the specified mission. Stage 1 of the approach uses a *constraint solver* such as the Alloy analyzer [6] to distribute the tasks of the mission among the available robots, such that all the constraints from the task specification *and* the mission specification are satisfied. This involves using a *constraint problem generator* to encode these constraints in a format that the constraint solver can use to generate feasible task allocations.

Stage 2 of the approach optimises the order in which each robot will execute its tasks. Optimal robot plans are produced for each feasible task allocation from Stage 1, and the best combination of plans across all task allocations is adopted. To generate the optimal robot plans, we use a *Markov decision process (MDP) generator* to encode the task-order optimisation as an MDP policy synthesis problem that we then solve using a probabilistic model checker such as PRISM [7]. For increased efficiency, a separate, small MDP is generated for each subset of robots that were allocated interdependent tasks, e.g., joint tasks, or tasks of a compound task with an order or sequence (https://git.io/JGLRZ).

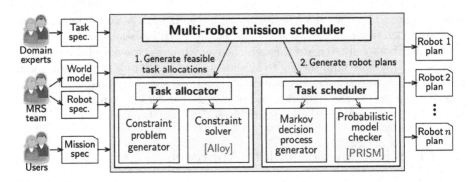

Fig. 1. Two-stage MRS mission scheduling approach

3   Implementation and Case Study Summary

We developed a first version of our MRS mission scheduler using the Alloy analyser [6] for the task allocation, and the model checker PRISM [7] for the robot plan generation. Figure 2 shows the use of our solution to schedule an MRS mission in a hospital scenario. The mission is carried out in an area comprising four rooms (A to D), and consists of four tasks (t1 to t4): cleaning empty rooms A and B (t1 and t2); moving medical equipment within room D (t3); and cleaning patient room C (t4). Room cleaning is a compound task (ct2) requiring patient permission (at4) (unless the room is empty – ct1), floor cleaning (at1), and sanitizing (at2). To move medical equipment (at3), two robots are needed. Four robots are available, two cleaner robots (r1, r2) and two pick-and-place robots (r3, r4). This information is encoded in XML (Fig. 2a) and supplied to our task allocator, which uses the Alloy Analyser as a constraint solver to create 672 feasible task allocation models. These allocation models (Fig. 2b) fulfil a set of constrains, called *facts* in Alloy language. For example: a) every atomic task is linked to a specific capability, and b) every atomic task states how many (different) robots needs to be completed.

Each of the allocations are passed to the Task Scheduler which applies *transitive closure* to divide each allocation into independent robot groups (groups of robots that do not have tasks in common and do not share constrained tasks), and generates their corresponding MDP encodings (Fig. 2c). Finally, correct-by-construction robot plans are obtained through optimal MDP policy synthesis (Fig. 2d). The optimisation objective used in our hospital case study (specified as a PRISM reward property at the bottom of Fig. 2c) is the minimisation of the overall robot travelling cost. We provide a detailed description of the case study, and the specifications, models, intermediate results and robot plans from Fig. 2 in our project's GitHub repository https://git.io/Js1Yj.

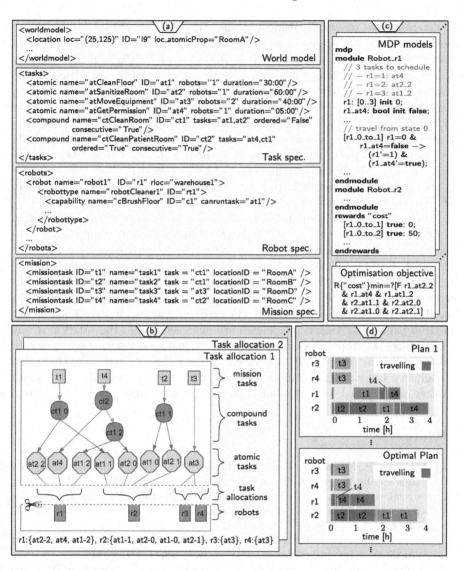

Fig. 2. Application of our MRS mission scheduling approach to a hospital case study, showing: (a) the problem specification (world model, tasks, robots and mission); (b) the Alloy-generated task allocations (the robots are shown in red at the bottom and the mission tasks in grey at the top); (c) the MDP models for each subset of robots allocated interdependent tasks; and (d) the robot plans obtained through MDP policy synthesis

4   Conclusions and Discussion

We introduced a new approach for the scheduling of multi-robot missions comprising joint, ordered and consecutive tasks that need to be executed by teams of heterogeneous robots. By using a combination of constraint solving and MDP policy synthesis, our approach generates correct-by-construction robot plans. In future work, we will leverage the capabilities of probabilistic model checkers to expand the range of optimisation objectives supported by our MRS mission scheduling so that they include minimising mission cost and robot-team size, maximising mission reliability, etc. Additionally, we will improve the scalability of the Alloy task allocation by (a) adding constraints that preclude the generation of permutations of the same task allocation, (b) combining it with AI techniques for a faster identification of optimal or nearly optimal task allocations, and (c) optimising the allocation of tasks considering, for instance, the spatial distance between tasks (e.g., group the tasks by capabilities in a certain area and assign them to a single robot, similar to [2]).

Understanding the computational complexity of our approach is another area of future work for the project. Analysing the complexity of the approach is nontrivial, as it depends on the configuration of the Alloy Analyser's SAT solver (MiniSat, SAT4J, ZChaff, etc.), and of the PRISM engine (MTBDD, sparse, hybrid, explicit). The time to find an optimal solution depends on these configurations, and on the size of the MDP model; which in turn depends on the number of robots, number of tasks and task dependencies. As mentioned on our GitHub page, most task dependencies are modelled within the MDP in a way that reduces the state space. In addition, the evaluation comparing the system to related solutions (e.g., [2,12]) is planned for the full-paper version of this work. Finally, we will extend our approach to support adaptation of the robot plans as they are executed, so that robot failures, mission changes, etc. are supported.

References

1. Benavidez, P., Kumar, M., Agaian, S., Jamshidi, M.: Design of a home multi-robot system for the elderly and disabled. In: SoSE 2015, pp. 392–397 (2015)
2. Carreno, Y., Pairet, È., Petillot, Y., Petrick, R.P.: Task allocation strategy for heterogeneous robot teams in offshore missions. In: AAMAS 2019, pp. 222–230 (2020)
3. Das, G.P., McGinnity, T.M., et al.: A distributed task allocation algorithm for a multi-robot system in healthcare facilities. JINT **80**(1), 33–58 (2015)
4. Gavran, I., Majumdar, R., Saha, I.: Antlab: a multi-robot task server. ACM Trans. Embed. Comput. Syst. (TECS) **16**(5s), 1–19 (2017)
5. Guo, M., Dimarogonas, D.V.: Multi-agent plan reconfiguration under local LTL specifications. Int. J. Robot. Res. **34**(2), 218–235 (2015)
6. Jackson, D.: Alloy: a lightweight object modelling notation. ACM Trans. Softw. Eng. Methodol. (TOSEM) **11**(2), 256–290 (2002)
7. Kwiatkowska, M., Norman, G., Parker, D.: PRISM 4.0: verification of probabilistic real-time systems. In: Gopalakrishnan, G., Qadeer, S. (eds.) CAV 2011. LNCS, vol. 6806, pp. 585–591. Springer, Heidelberg (2011). https://doi.org/10.1007/978-3-642-22110-1_47
8. Lacerda, B., Faruq, F., Parker, D., Hawes, N.: Probabilistic planning with formal performance guarantees for mobile service robots. IJRR **38**(9), 1098–1123 (2019)

9. Lacerda, B., Parker, D., Hawes, N.: Optimal policy generation for partially satis-fiable co-safe LTL specifications. In: IJCA'24 (2015)

10. Pujol-Gonzalez, M., Cerquides, J., Meseguer, P., Rodríguez-Aguilar, J.A.: Efficient inter-team task allocation in RoboCup rescue. In: AAMAS, pp. 413–421 (2015)

11. Rizk, Y., Awad, M., Tunstel, E.W.: Cooperative heterogeneous multi-robot sys-tems: a survey. ACM Comput. Surv. (CSUR) **52**(2), 1–31 (2019)

12. Schillinger, P., et al.: Simultaneous task allocation and planning for temporal logic goals in heterogeneous multi-robot systems. IJRR **37**, 818–838 (2018)

13. Sukkar, F., Best, G., Yoo, C., Fitch, R.: Multi-robot region-of-interest reconstruc-tion with Dec-MCTS. In: ICRA, pp. 9101–9107 (2019)

14. Yu, P., Dimarogonas, D.V.: Distributed motion coordination for multi-robot sys-tems under LTL specifications. arXiv preprint arXiv:2103.09111 (2021)

Area Coverage in Two-Dimensional Grid Worlds Using Computation-Free Agents

Arjan Dhesi[(⊠)] and Roderich Groß

Department of Automatic Control and Systems Engineering, The University of Sheffield, Sheffield, UK
{adhesi1,rgross}@sheffield.ac.uk

Abstract. This work proposes a novel solution to the problem of covering a bounded grid world using a swarm of robotic agents. The controller requires no run-time memory and only few, discrete sensory inputs. Two variants of the solution to the problem are studied, one effectively modulating the sensing range based on the agent's context. It is found that during the dispersion, the controller with sensing range modulation outperforms the default controller in terms of speed and evenness of the dispersion. Due to its simplicity, the solution could be realised on swarms of agents with ultra-low power and computational requirements, making it potentially relevant for large-scale swarm applications.

Keywords: Area coverage · Multi-robot system · Swarm robotics

1 Introduction

The problem of area coverage concerns a group of robots, or mobile sensing units, that operate in a bounded environment, seeking to maximise the area that their sensors collectively monitor at any given time. Assuming simple, range-limited sensors and that all parts of the area to be monitored are of equal importance, one strategy for the group is to spread as uniformly as possible. In general, the types of sensors and computational resources can affect both the cost and performance of multi-robot coverage solutions. In some practical applications (e.g. search & rescue or monitoring pollution), cost-effective solutions for covering vast areas in limited time are desirable, prompting related research in the field of swarm robotics. Numerous distributed controller solutions have been proposed to the area coverage problem, which are relevant for swarms of robots. One of these employs the potential field method [3], which requires each robot to estimate the relative positions of other robots in its neighbourhood. A similar approach [4] requires each robot to move away from its k closest neighbours. Ramaithitima et al. [7] propose an approach that requires the robots to obtain only contact and bearing estimates. Recently, Özdemir [6] proposed a coverage controller that, when tested on a swarm of e-puck robots, outperformed a random walk controller. The approach was based on the "computation-free" control paradigm introduced in [2]. This paradigm assumes no run-time memory. The

© Springer Nature Switzerland AG 2021
C. Fox et al. (Eds.): TAROS 2021, LNAI 13054, pp. 360–364, 2021.
https://doi.org/10.1007/978-3-030-89177-0_37

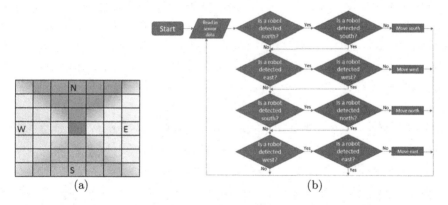

Fig. 1. Distributed area coverage solution: (a) The agent (in centre) has four contact sensors (not shown) and four optical sensors, with the respective field of view indicated (bi-coloured cells are within the range of multiple sensors). Here the range of the optical sensors is of length three. (b) Flowchart for the memoryless coverage controller.

robots simply map a discrete sensory input to the output, which was used to set the continuous velocities of the e-puck robot's wheels.

The present work considers the problem of covering a bounded, 2-D grid world using a swarm of robotic agents. It presents a computation-free controller which to the best of the authors knowledge is currently the only memoryless solution to the multi-robot area coverage problem in grid environments.

2   Design

The environment is a bounded 2-D grid world comprised of square cells. Time is discrete, and one robot is updated at a time. The robots are updated in the same order during the run, but this order is randomised between runs.

The robots are modelled as squares the size of a cell in the grid, and are based off the MIT modular re-configurable robot M-Blocks [8]. Each time step, a robot either moves to an empty neighbouring cell in its von Neumann neighbourhood, or remains in place. Each robot is assumed to have activated an LED light that can be seen from all directions. On each face, it has an optical (light) sensor and a contact sensor. The light sensor detects any other robot within its respective range (see Fig. 1(a)). The environment boundary cannot be detected, but restricts movement. The overall setup is similar to the setup in [5].

All robots execute an identical controller (see Fig. 1(b)). The basic idea is that the robot moves into a direction where no robot is currently detected (i.e. no direct neighbour and no light) and that is opposite to a direction in which a robot is currently detected (i.e. direct neighbour or light). If no such direction exists, the robot remains in its current cell. As an alternative solution, a mechanism for sensing range modulation is explored. In this case, the robot first checks whether it is in contact with another robot on any face. If this is the case, it

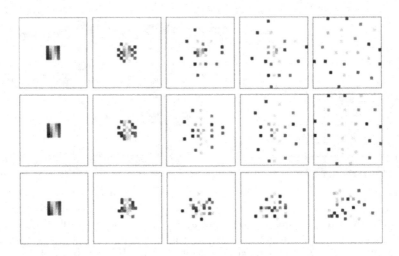

Fig. 2. Swarm dispersion after 0, 1, 6, 10 and 30 cycles with sensing range modulation off (first row) vs on (second row) vs random walk (third row). Each coloured square represents a robot.

does not probe its optical sensors. This modulates the sensing range between the full optical range (when the robot has no contact neighbours) and the contact range.

3   Results

Each robot is said to cover all of the cells within its sensing range, as well as the cell it resides in. Area coverage is defined as the number of cells covered by all the robots collectively at a given time.

A square environment of 25×25 cells is considered. It contains 25 robots, each with a sensing range of 4. Figure 2 (first and second rows) shows two typical runs, one with the default controller, the other with sensing range modulation activated. For the swarm without sensing range modulation, it can be seen that the outermost robots in the swarm disperse relatively evenly, but the inner robots in the swarm do not disperse well. The initial square configuration of the robots achieved a coverage of 27.0%. The mean amount of coverage in the 10th time-step over 10 runs of this simulation was 82.8%. For the swarm with sensing range modulation, it can be seen that the robots disperse more evenly. The mean amount of coverage in the 10th time-step over 10 runs of this simulation was 89.9%. Comparatively, in the same situation a uniform random walk achieved a mean of 52.5% coverage over 10 runs. Figure 2 (third row) shows a typical run using this random walk.

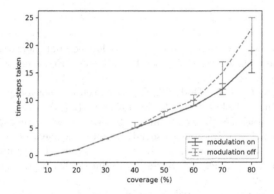

Fig. 3. Comparison of the time taken for different levels of coverage to be achieved with sensing range modulation on vs off. Runs for different levels of coverage are independent. Error bars indicate the range.

Using 25 robots with a sensor range of 5 in a 35 × 35 cells environment, the swarm without sensing range modulation takes longer to disperse than the swarm with sensing range modulation (see Fig. 3). However, when the desired level of coverage is low, both swarms perform equally well, presumably as at the start of the run they spread out at the same rate. After initial dispersion, the swarm with sensing range modulation spreads out at a faster rate. At the start, when the robots are still in contact, the different behaviour as a result of the sensing range modulation may put the swarm in a better configuration to spread out faster later. When increasing the environment size further, without increasing either the number of robots or their sensing range, the robots disperse until out of range of one another, possibly resulting in uneven distributions [1].

4   Conclusions

This work proposed a novel solution to the problem of covering a bounded grid world using a swarm of robotic agents. To the best of our knowledge, it is the simplest solution to this problem so far. The controller requires no run-time memory and only few, discrete sensory inputs. The agents lack global information, and do not communicate. Two variants of the solution were studied, one effectively modulating the sensing range based on the context. It was found that during the dispersion, the controller with sensing range modulation outperformed the default controller. In particular, the sensing range modulation increases the speed and evenness of the dispersion. Due to its simplicity, the coverage solution could be realised on swarms of agents with ultra-low power and computational requirements, making it potentially relevant for large-scale swarm applications. In the future, the solution could be implemented on a physical platform such as the M-Blocks robots [8], and tested in more realistic scenarios.

References

1. Dhesi, A.: Covering an area with a swarm of low computation robots. Bachelor's thesis, Department of Automatic Control and Systems Engineering, The University of Sheffield, UK (2021)
2. Gauci, M., Chen, J., Li, W., Dodd, T., Groß, R.: Self-organized aggregation without computation. Int. J. Robot. Res. **33**(8), 1145–1161 (2014)
3. Howard, A., Matarić, M.J., Sukhatme, G.S.: Mobile sensor network deployment using potential fields: a distributed, scalable solution to the area coverage problem. In: Asama, H., Arai, T., Fukuda, T., Hasegawa, T. (eds.) Distributed Autonomous Robotic Systems 5, pp. 299–308. Springer, Berlin (2002). https://doi.org/10.1007/978-4-431-65941-9_30
4. McLurkin, J., Smith, J.: Distributed algorithms for dispersion in indoor environments using a swarm of autonomous mobile robots. In: Alami, R., Chatila, R., Asama, H. (eds.) Distributed Autonomous Robotic Systems 6, pp. 399–408. Springer, Tokyo (2007). https://doi.org/10.1007/978-4-431-35873-2_39
5. Özdemir, A., Romanishin, J.W., Groß, R., Rus, D.: Decentralized gathering of stochastic, oblivious agents on a grid: a case study with 3D m-blocks. In: International Symposium on Multi-Robot and Multi-Agent Systems, MRS 2019, pp. 245–251 (2019)
6. Özdemir, A., Gauci, M., Kolling, A., Hall, M.D., Groß, R.: Spatial coverage without computation. In: 2019 IEEE International Conference on Robotics and Automation (ICRA), pp. 9674–9680. IEEE (2019)
7. Ramaithitima, R., Whitzer, M., Bhattacharya, S., Kumar, V.: Sensor coverage robot swarms using local sensing without metric information. In: 2015 IEEE International Conference on Robotics and Automation (ICRA 2015), pp. 3408–3415. IEEE (2015)
8. Romanishin, J.W., Gilpin, K., Claici, S., Rus, D.: 3D M-Blocks: self-reconfiguring robots capable of locomotion via pivoting in three dimensions. In: 2015 IEEE International Conference on Robotics and Automation, pp. 1925–1932 (2015)

Online Scene Visibility Estimation as a Complement to SLAM in UAVs

Rory Haggart[(⊠)] and Jonathan M. Aitken[(⊠)]

Department of Automatic Control and Systems Engineering, University of Sheffield,
Sheffield, UK
{rdehaggart1,jonathan.aitken}@sheffield.ac.uk

Abstract. Simultaneous localisation and mapping (SLAM) relies on low-cost on-board sensors such as cameras and inertial measurement units. It is crucial that the surroundings are visible to the cameras to maximise the accuracy of the system. An estimation strategy is proposed to augment ORB-SLAM2 that considers feature extraction capability, distribution of the extracted features in the image frame, and the ability of the algorithm to track features over time. The method is tested on challenging datasets, and the output is evaluated against different visibility conditions. The proposed method is shown to react appropriately and consistently to 'less visible' conditions such as fog, sunlight, and rapid motion in real time, with minimal computational load.

Keywords: Simultaneous localisation and mapping · Visibility

1 Introduction

In the field of robotic navigation, simultaneous localisation and mapping (SLAM) uses low-cost, on-board sensors to build up a three-dimensional representation of the local surroundings and localise the robot relative to points in this map.

Semi- and fully-autonomous systems are on the rise. Between 2011 and 2017 the number of patents relating to automated driving that were filed at the European Patent Office rose by 330% [2]. In vehicles employing these systems, the role of action and reaction is assumed by on-board sensors and actuators interfacing with decision making systems to control the vehicle. If a system using SLAM with visible-light cameras can 'understand' how visible the scene is to those cameras, it could adapt - re-orienting the cameras, or adjusting how many features should be extracted from the incoming image stream.

Supported by the Department of Aerospace Engineering and the Department of Automatic Control and Systems Engineering at the University of Sheffield. Also this work is supported by the UK's Engineering and Physical Sciences Research Council (EPSRC) Programme Grant EP/S016813/1.

© Springer Nature Switzerland AG 2021
C. Fox et al. (Eds.): TAROS 2021, LNAI 13054, pp. 365–369, 2021.
https://doi.org/10.1007/978-3-030-89177-0_38

2   Related Work

2.1   SLAM

ORB-SLAM2 [5] is an indirect visual SLAM technique, meaning features are extracted from preprocessed images and tracked between frames. The features are described using binary descriptors and used to perform global bundle adjustments and loop closures that allows for a consistent position estimation.

VINS-Mono [8] is a popular and sophisticated visual-inertial algorithm that has consistent and accurate tracking of sensor pose. The authors note that whilst their technique may operate in poor visibility, improvements to investigate observability properties of the online camera data would be beneficial.

2.2   Scene Visibility Estimation

The authors of [6] present a model that accounts for the multiple scattering of light in the atmosphere due to conditions such as fog and rain. This is based on the glow surrounding light sources in inclement weather. It is one of several attempts to estimate dynamic visibility distance based on the presence of fog.

In [7], the authors develop a technique that uses the observed contrast of road markings. The system is tested for a variety of conditions - e.g. when sunrise causes glare in the image, which interestingly resulted in a lower visibility estimate than the more frequently studied case of fog. The method is shown to be robust to a range of conditions, but relies on the presence of known features.

3   Methodology

The ORB-SLAM2 code was modified to use information about extracted features in each frame to calculate the visibility estimation metric components (see Table 1). Additional processes, such as ones to save the outputs, were also added.

(a)   (b)   (c)

Fig. 1. Example frames of (left to right) partially occluded, foggy, and featureless scenes from the Midair [3] and InteriorNet [4] datasets

Table 1. Three ORB-SLAM2 SVE calculated components.

	Equation	Description
a	$S_a = \frac{N_F}{N_{F,max}}$	S_a is defined as the ratio of the number of extracted features (N_F) to the target, defined by the user ($N_{F,max}$). This is how well the camera can 'see' the scene
b	$S_b = 1 - \frac{\chi^2}{\chi_w^2}$ $\chi^2 =$ $\sum_{i=0}^{N_B} \frac{(O_{b_i} - E_{b_i})^2}{E_{b_i}}$ $E_{b_i} = \frac{N_F}{N_B}$	Each frame is divided into N_B 'bins', each containing some number (O_{b_i}) of the extracted features. A chi-square value (χ^2) of this binned distribution is calculated, where E_{b_i} is the 'expected' number of features in each bin b_i if the distribution of features was homogeneous. S_b is defined as the complement to the chi-squared value when normalised against a 'worst-case' value (χ_w^2), representing the condition of all extracted features being positioned exclusively in $1/8^{th}$ of the frame. This evaluates the homogeneity of the distribution
c	$S_c = \frac{N_T}{N_{L_v}}$	S_c is defined as the number of features that are tracked (N_T) as a fraction of the number of features that are theoretically located within the frustum of the camera (N_{L_v}). For more dynamic visibility, features may be lost even whilst they remain within the cameras line of sight

4   Results and Discussion

Table 2. The mean values of S ($S = 0.2S_a + 0.4S_b + 0.4S_c$) and of the percentage of the trajectory that was successfully tracked by ORB-SLAM2 over 15 tests of three conditions in a trajectory from the MidAir dataset.

Trajectory	Condition	Mean S	Mean % tracked
VO_test 0	Sunny	0.737	96.92%
	Sunset	0.723	94.76%
	Foggy	−0.324	2.59%

With ORB-SLAM2 augmented to become ORB-SLAM2 SVE (ORB-SLAM2 with Scene Visibility Estimation), tests were performed using the MidAir [3], InteriorNet [4], and Malaga [1] datasets. The set of visibility impairments that could be tested were fog (Fig. 1b), partial lens soiling (Fig. 1a), direct sunlight (Fig. 2c), rapid motion, featureless scenery (Fig. 3c), and planar scenery. Tracking sustainability and visibility for some of the MidAir data are shown in Table 2 with a sample visibility output from ORB-SLAM2 SVE in Fig. 2a.

An assessment of the execution time using a tool developed by the authors of ORB-SLAM3 revealed that the additional components had minimal impact on the computational load, and that the implementation was efficient allowing the algorithm to perform a high accuracy estimation.

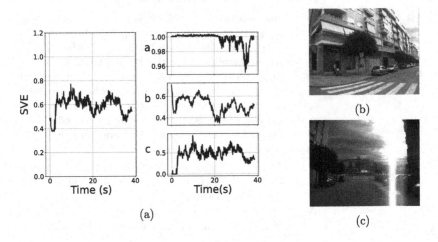

Fig. 2. (a) shows the visibility outputs from ORB-SLAM2 SVE for trajectory 15 of the Malaga dataset (b) shows the image frame with the highest associated S_b ($t \approx 0.4$ s) (c) shows the frame with the lowest associated S_b ($t \approx 22.3$ s)

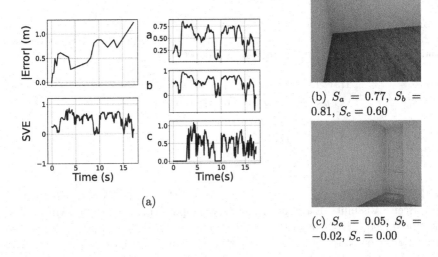

Fig. 3. (a) shows the visibility outputs from ORB-SLAM2 SVE for trajectory 'original_3_3' in the '3FO4K7I2Q0PG' subset of the InteriorNet dataset. (b) shows the image frame with the highest associated visibility ($t \approx 4$ s) (c) shows the frame with the lowest associated visibility ($t \approx 9, 19$ s)

5   Conclusions

Refinement is still required. Across all tests, the strategy responded appropriately in real time to qualitatively less visible frames as a result of factors including fog, direct sunlight, and featureless scenery, improving on existing methods that account for single factors. S_b proved the most intuitive metric, but no direct correlation between S_b and tracking accuracy was observed. However, using the ORB-SLAM2 visualiser, it was recognised that a poor distribution of tracked features - rather than extracted features - in the frame led to a worsened pose estimate. A detailed assessment was not completed. Additionally, S_b did not always show adequate sensitivity in conditions such as partial lens soiling (see Fig. 1a), and this could indicate the need for tuneable parameters.

S_c should have been useful - as the number of tracked features decreases, tracking accuracy should worsen. The expectation was that before tracking is lost, S_c should start decreasing, though this was not always observed. The value was also highly variable between frames, and trends were hard to decipher - applying this calculation to keyframes rather than all frames may be a solution.

After these problems have been addressed, the visibility information could be fed to the system to adapt performance or re-orient the hardware, as discussed in Sect. 1.

References

1. Blanco, J.L., Moreno, F.A., Gonzalez-Jimenez, J.: The málaga urban dataset: high-rate stereo and lidars in a realistic urban scenario. Int. J. Robot. Res. **33**(2), 207–214 (2014)
2. European Patent Office: Patents and self-driving vehicles. Technical report, European Patent Office (2018)
3. Fonder, M., Droogenbroeck, M.V.: Mid-air: a multi-modal dataset for extremely low altitude drone flights. In: Conference on Computer Vision and Pattern Recognition Workshop (CVPRW) (2019)
4. Li, W., et al.: InteriorNet: mega-scale multi-sensor photo-realistic indoor scenes dataset. In: British Machine Vision Conference (BMVC) (2018)
5. Mur-Artal, R., Tardós, J.: ORB-SLAM2: an open-source slam system for monocular, stereo, and RGB-D cameras. IEEE Trans. Rob. **33**(5), 1255–1262 (2017)
6. Narasimhan, S.G., Nayar, S.K.: Shedding light on the weather. In: 2003 Proceedings of IEEE Computer Society Conference on Computer Vision and Pattern Recognition, vol. 1, p. I (2003)
7. Pomerleau, D.: Visibility estimation from a moving vehicle using the RALPH vision system. In: Proceedings of Conference on Intelligent Transportation Systems, pp. 906–911 (1997)
8. Qin, T., Li, P., Shen, S.: VINS-Mono: a robust and versatile monocular visual-inertial state estimator. IEEE Trans. Rob. **34**(4), 1004–1020 (2018)

Statics Optimization of a Hexapedal Robot Modelled as a Stewart Platform

Enrico Donato[1]([⊠])⬤, Giacomo Picardi[1]⬤, and Marcello Calisti[2]⬤

[1] The Biorobotics Institute, Sant'Anna School of Advanced Studies, Pisa, Italy
enrico.donato@santannapisa.it
[2] Lincoln Institute for Agri-food Technology, University of Lincoln, Lincoln, UK

Abstract. SILVER2 is an underwater legged robot designed with the aim of collecting litter on the seabed and sample the sediment to assess the presence of micro-plastics. Besides the original application, SILVER2 can also be a valuable tool for all underwater operations which require to interact with objects directly on the seabed. The advancement presented in this paper is to model SILVER2 as a Gough-Stewart platform, and therefore to enhance its ability to interact with the environment. Since the robot is equipped with six segmented legs with three actuated joints, it is able to make arbitrary movements in the six degrees of freedom. The robot's performance has been analysed from both kinematics and statics points of view. The goal of this work is providing a strategy to harness the redundancy of SILVER2 by finding the optimal posture to maximize forces/torques that it can resist along/around constrained directions. Simulation results have been reported to show the advantages of the proposed method.

Keywords: Legged robot · Parallel robot · Statics · Manipulability

1 Introduction

Mobile robots, with their ability of moving in space, represent the possibility of extending the work-space of robotics and opened the way to explorations and interventions in areas which are normally inaccessible to humans [1]. Besides the more established categories such as wheeled robots [2], aerial drones [3], underwater vehicles [4], several mobile bio-inspired robots have been recently presented [5] with the promise of augmented exploration capabilities. Legged robotics is probably the most studied category of bio-inspired mobile robots due to their potential of adapting to irregular terrains, negotiate obstacles and interact gently with surroundings [6].

When a mobile robot is equipped with a manipulator we speak of mobile manipulation. This allows to harness the locomotion ability of mobile robots to extend the work-space of the manipulator and perform manipulation tasks in previously inaccessible locations. Depending on the category of mobile robot on which the manipulator is mounted on, different challenges arise [7]. On ground-based mobile manipulation, either implemented on wheeled/tracked [8] or legged

© Springer Nature Switzerland AG 2021
C. Fox et al. (Eds.): TAROS 2021, LNAI 13054, pp. 370–380, 2021.
https://doi.org/10.1007/978-3-030-89177-0_39

vehicle [9,10], the mobile robot is capable of providing sufficient reaction force at the base of the manipulator while holding its position. Moreover, the redundancy provided by multiple articulated legs allows to implement different strategies for manipulation: on one hand the same linkage can be used for both locomotion and manipulation, as presented in [11], and on the other when the robot is in a fixed position, legs can be used to change the position and orientation of the base of the manipulator as proposed in [12,13].

In the underwater environment, robots are used for a wide set of manipulation tasks which range from opening and closing valves to collecting biological samples. Despite its inherent complexity, the field of floating manipulation has made remarkable progresses and the development of propeller-driven autonomous intervention robots (Intervention AUV, or I-AUV) is currently among the most interesting research topics in robotics [14]. However, some intrinsic limitations still exists such as raising debris with the perturbation introduced by the thrusters, introducing significant acoustic noise, and counteracting high forces at the manipulator without the reaction force provided by the ground. For this reason, the novel category of underwater legged robots, of which SILVER2 [14] is one representative, may be an effective solution to manipulation tasks when operations are carried out directly on the seabed. In a previous work [15] SILVER2 demonstrated the ability to collect different objects using a soft manipulator and its maximum lifting force was experimentally assessed.

To improve adaptability to different tasks and environments, Reconfigurable Parallel Platform (RPP) [16,17] are gaining more attention, such as Free-Hex [18]. SILVER2 is an hexapedal robot with 3-dofs legs, and could be considered a RPP since it has not a base anchored to the ground, but movable. The articulated legs improve the workspace with respect to its linear counterpart [19].

In this work, we modelled SILVER2 as a Gough-Stewart (GS) platform, a classic parallel robot consisting of a platform actuated by six linear pistons. This allowed us to solve the inverse kinematic problem and compute the joint angles to set a desired position and attitude of SILVER2 body. The performance obtained in [20] could be further improved by distributing the forces more efficiently and adapting the positioning of the legs to specific manipulation task. On top of this, following the results presented in [21], we derived the manipulability ellipsoids of SILVER2 and set up an optimization problem to find the legs configuration which maximizes the forces/torques that the robot can resist along a preferred direction. Since the derivations presented in this work pertain to the statics of the robots, hydrodynamic contributions do not hold and the results obtained are valid also for terrestrial hexapedal robots.

2 Materials and Methods

SILVER2 is modeled as a parallel manipulator and its Inverse Kinematics (IK) and Differential Kinematics (DK) are presented. Force ellipsoids are introduced to compute its Statics, and an optimization algorithm is set to find the legs configuration which maximizes forces and torques along/around arbitrary axes.

Table 1. Summary of most common used symbols. Subscripts omitted when considered wrt world reference frame.

Symbol	Format	Description
t	$\Re^{3\times1}$	Translation of the body from the ground
R_{xy}	$\Re^{3\times3}$	Rotation matrix of $\{y\}$ wrt $\{x\}$
ω_x	$\Re^{3\times1}$	Angular velocities of the body in $\{x\}$
l_x	$\Re^{3\times1}$	Feet position wrt $\{x\}$
q_i	$\Re^{3\times1}$	i-th leg joints angles
$J_l(q_i)$	$\Re^{3\times3}$	i-th leg Jacobian matrix
J_{P_T}, J_{R_T}	$\Re^{18\times3}$	Linear/Angular SILVER2 Jacobian matrix
v_i	$\Re^{3\times1}$	i-th ellipsoid's axis vector
λ_i	$\Re$	i-th ellipsoid's semi-axis length

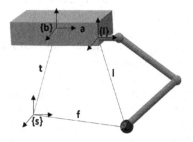

Fig. 1. Inverse Kinematics of the Stewart platform adapted to SILVER2

2.1 Kinematics of the GS Platform

To solve the IK of the platform, we take into account the world $\{s\}$, the robot's body $\{b\}$ and the legs base $\{l\}$ reference frames. We choose $R_{sb} = R_{sl}$. By taking as a reference Fig. 1, the feet position in the leg reference frames is:

$$l_l = R_{bs}(f - t) - a_b \tag{1}$$

The length of the leg is the vector norm of Eq. (1): $\|l_l\| = \sqrt{l_l^T l_l}$.

In the case of the Gough-Stewart platform, the DK has already been analysed [22], and it accounts just for six linear actuators. By extension to our case, both members of Eq. (1) can be multiplied by R_{sb}. For the i-th leg:

$$R_{sb}l_{l,i} = f_i - t - R_{sb}a_b \tag{2}$$

By differentiation with respect to time:

$$[\omega]R_{sb}l_{l,i} + R_{sb}\dot{l}_{l,i} = \dot{f}_i - \dot{t} - [\omega]R_{sb}a_b - R_{sb}\dot{a}_b \tag{3}$$

where $[\omega]$ is the skew-symmetric matrix of of the angular velocity ω, and the notation $\dot{x}$ is the time derivative of x. The linear velocity of the feet on $\{s\}$ is null $\dot{f}_i = 0$, since they are supposed to be fixed. Moreover, the distance of the leg anchor point to the center of geometry of the body will not change, since the body is rigid, thus $\dot{a}_b = 0$. Consequently, the Eq. (3) can be simplified to

$$\dot{l}_{l,i} = -(R_{bs}\dot{t} + R_{bs}[\omega]R_{sb}(a_b + l_{l,i})) = -(\dot{t}_b + [\omega_b](a_b + l_{l,i})) \tag{4}$$

Eq. (4) strictly relates the moving platform to the leg in the velocity space: both linear and angular speed of the body are affected by the leg change-over.

2.2 Kinematics Adapted to SILVER2

SILVER2 has six segmented legs instead of linear actuators: to inherit the IK solution of the GS platform [23], the length vectors of the linear legs of the GS platform are used as input to the IK of the SILVER2's segmented legs. When SILVER2 contacts the ground with all legs, it creates 5 closed chains (by pairing two consecutive legs together); then, they generate $5 \times 6 = 30$ constraints. The tip of the leg is able to omnidirectionally rotate on the ground, thus we consider it as a passive spherical joint. Each leg has 6 DoFs (three of them come from the actuated joints, while the others from the spherical joint), with a total of $6 \times 6 = 36$ DoFs. Consequently, there will be $36 - 30 = 6$ independent DoFs, that coincide with position and orientation of the robot's body.

The velocity of the feet with respect to the leg anchor point comes from the discussion of its DK; indeed, it is a function of the joint angular velocities, that can be substituted in Eq.(4).

$$J_l(q_i)\dot{q}_i = -(\dot{t}_b + [\omega_b](a_b + l_{l,i})) \tag{5}$$

where $J_l(q_i)$ is the analytical Jacobian of the i-th leg and q_i is the respective joint angles vector. $J_l(q_i)$ is assumed to be invertible, and it happens whenever the legs are not in a singular configuration (the IK of the leg always admits only one solution because of mechanical constraints [24]). Moreover, the cross-product property of the skew-symmetric matrix is exploited.

$$\dot{q}_i = -J_l^{-1}(q_i)\dot{t}_b - J_l^{-1}(q_i)[\omega_b](a_b + l_{l,i}) \tag{6}$$

Considering a generic matrix $A \in \Re^{3\times3}$ and two vectors $b, c \in \Re^{3\times1}$, it holds that $A(b \times c) = -(A^T \times c)^T b$. The cross product between A and c is a matrix whose columns are the cross product between the respective column of A and c. Therefore, Eq. (6) can be simplified to

$$\dot{q}_i = -J_l^{-1}(q_i)\dot{t}_b + (J_l^{-T}(q_i) \times (a_b + l_{l,i}))^T\omega_b = J_{P_i}^{-1}\begin{bmatrix} \dot{t}_b \\ \omega_b \end{bmatrix} \tag{7}$$
$$J_{P_i}^{-1} = [-J_l^{-1}(q_i), (J_l^{-T}(q_i) \times (a_b + l_{l,i}))^T]$$

Starting from the inverse kinematics of the Stewart Platform, the inverse Jacobian $J_{P_i}^{-1} \in \Re^{3\times6}$ has been computed. $J_{P_i}^{-1}$ is the contribute of the i-th leg to the parallel robot's inverse Jacobian. In the case that only linear velocities are considered ($\omega = 0$), the forward Jacobian can be obtained via the Jacobian matrix pseudo-inverse:

$$
\begin{bmatrix} \dot{q}_1 \\ \vdots \\ \dot{q}_6 \end{bmatrix} = \begin{bmatrix} -J_L^{-1}(q_1) \\ \vdots \\ -J_L^{-1}(q_6) \end{bmatrix} \dot{t} \quad \rightarrow \quad \dot{Q} = J_{P_T}^{-1}(Q)\dot{t} \tag{8}
$$

$$
J_{P_T}(Q)\dot{Q} = \dot{t}, \quad J_{P_T}(Q) = (J_{P_T}^{-T}(Q)J_{P_T}^{-1}(Q))^{-1}J_{P_T}^{-T}(Q) \tag{9}
$$

The same procedure can be applied in the case $\dot{t} = 0$, when only angular velocities are considered.

$$
J_{P_R}(Q)\dot{Q} = \omega \tag{10}
$$

The kinematic features of the hexapod are necessary to assess its statics. In particular, the manipulability of SILVER2 will be exploited in the next sections.

2.3 Manipulability of Parallel Manipulators

At a kinematic singularity, a robot's end-effector loses the ability to translate or rotate in one or more directions. The manipulability ellipsoid $E_M = (JJ^T)^{-1}$ allows one to geometrically visualize the directions in which the end-effector moves with least or greatest effort. It corresponds to the end-effector velocities for joint rates $\dot{q}$ satisfying $||\dot{q}|| = 1$. Like for manipulability ellipsoids, the force ellipsoid $E_F = JJ^T$ can be found for joint torques τ satisfying $||\tau|| = 1$. It holds that $E_F E_M = I$, so the two ellipsoids are orthogonal and their product is a unit sphere in the three-dimensional space.

The equivalent to manipulability and force ellipsoids can be constructed even with respect to angular velocities and torques, by taking as a reference the Jacobian matrix of the parallel robot related to angular motions expressed in Eq. (10).

If the ellipsoid is not rotated with respect to the frame axes, it is represented by the quadratic curve

$$
\frac{x^2}{\rho_1^2} + \frac{y^2}{\rho_2^2} + \frac{z^2}{\rho_3^2} = 1 \tag{11}
$$

where ρ_i is the length of the i-th semi-axis. An ellipsoid is uniquely defined by its axes of symmetry v_i and the length of respective semi-axes ρ_i, which correspond to the eigenvectors and eigenvalues of the matrix $E \in \Re^{3\times3}$. A custom ellipsoid is computed via the Eq. (12), where $v_i \cdot v_j = 0, i \neq j$.

$$
E = \begin{bmatrix} | & | & | \\ v_1 & v_2 & v_3 \\ | & | & | \end{bmatrix} \begin{bmatrix} ||\lambda_1|| & 0 & 0 \\ 0 & ||\lambda_2|| & 0 \\ 0 & 0 & ||\lambda_3|| \end{bmatrix} \begin{bmatrix} | & | & | \\ v_1 & v_2 & v_3 \\ | & | & | \end{bmatrix}^{-1} \tag{12}
$$

From Eqs. (11)–(12) it holds that the length of the manipulability ellipsoid's i-th semi-axis is $\rho_i = 1/\sqrt{||\lambda_i||}$, where λ_i is the i-th eigenvalue. The greater ρ_i is, the more easily the end-effector can move in the v_i direction. The force ellipsoid is obtained from the manipulability ellipsoid simply by stretching it along v_i by a factor $1/\|\lambda_i\|$.

In order to define how close the robot is to a singular configuration, we resorted to condition number μ [25], defined as the ratio between the highest and the lowest eigenvalues of E. If $\mu = 1$, the ellipsoid is spherical and the end-effector is able to move towards any direction with the same ability; when the robot approaches a singularity, then $\mu \to +\infty$.

$$\mu = \frac{\lambda_{\max}}{\lambda_{\min}} \geq 1 \tag{13}$$

Another common measure is the *manipulability index* [26], that is proportional to the volume of the ellipsoid. If the structure tends to a singularity, then $MI \to 0$.

$$MI = \sqrt{\|\det JJ^T\|} = \sqrt{\|\lambda_1\lambda_2\lambda_3\|} \geq 0 \tag{14}$$

2.4   Statics Optimization

Manipulation tasks with SILVER2 may require high forces along certain axes. Exploiting force ellipsoids, the longest semi-axis should be parallel to the direction in which the highest force needs to be exerted. The same concept can be applied to the rotational case: the axis of symmetry should be parallel to the direction around which the highest torque has to be applied. By keeping the body in a fixed pose, the goal is to identify a new admissible legs configuration that achieves the aforementioned objectives.

A non-linear optimization problem is constructed. The optimization variables $q_i, i = 1, \cdots, 18$ coincide with the leg joint angles. The position of feet and knees with respect to the anchorage points of the legs are identified via their forward kinematics. In addition, the force ellipsoid of the parallel robot can be constructed as previously discussed.

The objective function exploits the largest projection of the force ellipsoid's axes along a given direction $\bar{G} \in \Re^{3 \times 1}$. Consequently, the optimal solution coincides with the legs configuration which maximize the projection of the force ellipsoid along $\bar{G}$.

$$\max_q \max_i \left[\frac{v_i}{\sqrt{\lambda_i}} \cdot \bar{G} \right], i = 1, 2, 3 \tag{15}$$

The admissibility of a solution is assessed by satisfying the following constraints $[i \in \{1, 2, 3\}, j \in \{1, \cdots, 6\}]$.

(a) *Joints* can rotate in limited ranges.

$$q_{\min,i} \leq q_i \leq q_{\max,i} \tag{16}$$

(b) *Feet* have to lie at zero height and the central legs has to be positioned among the lateral ones in the y-direction.

$$l_{z,j} = 0 \quad l_{y,3} \leq l_{y,2} \leq l_{y,1} \quad l_{y,6} \leq l_{y,5} \leq l_{y,4} \tag{17}$$

Moreover, central legs' feet will never be under the body for stability reasons.

$$l_{x,2} \geq \text{body\_width}/2 \qquad l_{x,5} \leq -\text{body\_width}/2 \qquad (18)$$

(c) Constraints on *knees* are similar to those on feet. The height of the knee must always be greater than zero, since the legs cannot penetrate the ground.

$$k_{z,j} \geq 0 \quad k_{y,3} \leq k_{y,2} \leq k_{y,1} \quad k_{y,6} \leq k_{y,5} \leq k_{y,4} \qquad (19)$$

The algorithm needs an initial guess to find the optimal solution: since the initial pose of the body is fixed and known, the IK of the hexapod is computed and used as starting solution. The optimal solution is an admissible configuration of SILVER2, and its force ellipsoid has the highest projection along the given direction with respect to other admissible configurations. In any case, the robot will tend to take on a configuration closer and closer to one of its singularities.

3   Results

Results come from simulations, which find and show the optimal solutions to the respective problems. The optimizer is based on the *fmincon* function with the *sqp* algorithm, from the Matlab Optimization Toolbox; it looks for the minimum of a constrained nonlinear multivariable function. Bounds to variables and non-linear inequalities have been considered.

The optimization strategy of the SILVER2 Statics is tested against chosen directions, which coincide with the standard basis of the three-dimensional space.

$$\bar{G}_x = [1,0,0]^T \quad \bar{G}_y = [0,1,0]^T \quad \bar{G}_z = [0,0,1]^T \qquad (20)$$

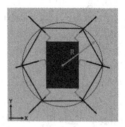

Fig. 2. Leg tips are placed on the vertexes of the regular hexagon. The choice of r affects the initial guess of the problem.

The initial guess of the optimization problem is chosen by arbitrarily setting the side length r of the regular hexagon on whose vertexes the feet are placed, and the quote of the body. The body and the ground are considered to be coplanar in the following simulations. The optimization problem has been solved six times: Figs. 3a–3b–3c are referred to linear forces along the axes in Eq. (20), while Figs. 3d–3e–3f concern torques.

Table 2. Numerical results of reported cases.

	MI	μ	ρ_x	ρ_y	ρ_z
(a)	6.92e-5	9.95e4	154.17	**172.00**	0.55
(b)	1.15e-4	2.74e5	154.17	**172.00**	0.33
(c)	8.02e-6	14.03	25.35	51.78	**94.95**
(d)	0.03	1.41e6	**0.27**	8.93e-5	0.03
(e)	4.14e-10	1.13e15	6.61	**1.11e8**	3.29
(f)	181.13	5.50	0.16	0.12	**0.28**

(a) All the legs reach their own kinematic singularities. The ellipsoid converges to an ellipse almost in the X-Y plane: it means that the structure is much more able to reject forces along those directions with respect to vertical.
(b) The current SILVER2 configuration is very similar to case (a) since it prevents movements in the X-Y plane.
(c) The pose of the robot permits to maximize the length of the ellipsoid along the Z-axis. Consequently, the hexapod can sustain larger forces on the vertical direction than on others.
(d) SILVER2 assumes this configuration to prevent rotations around the X-axis; this is the reason why the torque ellipsoid is maximised along the X direction.
(e) The current configuration can be explained as the case (d), but along the Y-axis. The ellipse collapses on a straight line, consequently the parallel structure is near to a singular configuration.
(f) Rotations around the vertical axis are limited, but admitted. The current legs configuration limits the twist of the body around Z.

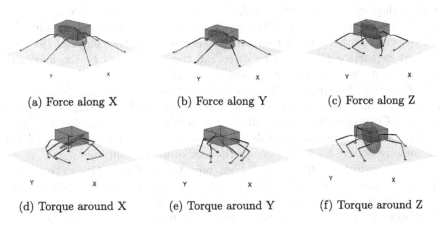

(a) Force along X   (b) Force along Y   (c) Force along Z

(d) Torque around X   (e) Torque around Y   (f) Torque around Z

Fig. 3. Optimal solutions to the SILVER2 Statics. The ellipsoids have been normalised with respect to the longest semi-axis.

In a previous work [15], a soft continuum arm was installed on the hexapod. Among other tests, the amount of force exerted by the action of the legs alone was measured, being 44 N on the vertical direction. By simulating the same experimental conditions, the ellipsoid semi-axis along the Z direction is 47.36, which increases to 50 following the proposed optimization procedure. Even if this experimental condition was already close to the maximum value, in other directions (see Fig. 3) the stance will be not trivial and may significantly diverge from initial guesses.

4   Discussion

The hexapod robot SILVER2 has been modeled as a Stewart platform. The main difference among the two robots consists in the fact that the serial actuators of the parallel manipulator have a fixed position on the ground, whereas SILVER2 is capable of independently positioning its feet within the work-space of its 3 DOFs segmented legs. This difference leads to two major consequences, on one hand, when SILVER2 stands with all its feet on the ground it presents a wider work-space with respect to its counterpart. On the other hand, the feet of SILVER2 may slip on the seabed, with the consequent lost of the static configuration. In addition to that, when operating SILVER2 underwater, external disturbances such as currents may occur. In this work feet slipping and currents have been neglected. The former assumption is justified by the possibility of developing high friction feet, for example through the use of micro-spines [27], or operating on high friction surfaces. The latter assumption is justified by the possibility of operating SILVER2 in low current environment, as commonly done for other underwater vehicles or by exploiting poses which result in low hydrodynamic disturbances (e.g. low stance).

In particular in this work, force/moment ellipsoids have been introduced as a tool to characterize the statics of the hexapod. They are helpful to understand how much force/moment the robot can resist along/around a certain direction with respect to others: the longer the distance between the center of the ellipsoid and its surface along a given direction, the greater will be the maximum force/moment that the robot can resist along/around it.

This way of thinking may be very helpful in case of manipulation tasks. It may happen that the robot is not able to resist enough force along the required direction. Consequently, moving the legs in order to obtain the force ellipsoid with the largest projection towards the desired direction may solve the problem. The same reasoning could be done in the case of torque ellipsoids.

Several optimal solutions have been reported in Fig. 3. Once the pose of the body is chosen, the best configuration of the legs is computed via an optimization procedure. We have reported the results relative to forces and torques along/around the three axes of the world frame, however any arbitrary direction can be chosen by the user according to the task to fulfill.

The reason why the optimizer gives the reported solution as output can be better explained via the manipulability ellipsoid. Indeed, since manipulability and force ellipsoid are inversely proportional, a higher manipulability along the shortest force ellipsoid's axes is observed; it means that along those axes, the robot is able to move much more easily. For instance, Fig. 3a represents the configuration which optimizes the forces exerted along the X-axis; in this case, the robot is much more able to move on the Z-axis direction instead of the X- and Y-axes because of the straight legs. A similar reasoning can be done in the case of rotations and moments as shown in Fig. 3d. The configuration prevents rotations with respect to the X-axis, but allows movements around Y- and Z-axes.

The mathematical tool proposed in this work may be helpful to optimize the static configuration of legged robots, while interacting with the external environment. The pose of the body could be chosen accordingly to the task to be completed, and further developments could involve the increase of the degrees of freedom during the optimization process (e.g. the position of the body in the case of required rotation, or vice versa). Moreover, the presented optimization procedure can be generalized to include, along with static loads, dynamic ones. Further developments may include the realization of a physical simulator and an actual experimental setup, to support simulation results and validate the model.

References

1. Francisco, R., Valero, F., Llopis-Albert, C.: A review of mobile robots: concepts, methods, theoretical framework, and applications. Int. J. Adv. Robot. Syst. **16**(2) (2019)
2. Ortigoza, R.S., et al.: Wheeled mobile robots: a review. IEEE Latin Am. Trans. **10**(6) (2012)
3. Hassanalian, M., Abdessattar, A.: Classifications, applications, and design challenges of drones: a review. Prog. Aerosp. Sci. **91**, 99–131 (2017)
4. Bogue, R.: Underwater robots: a review of technologies and applications. Ind. Robot. **42**(3), 186–191 (2015)
5. Calisti, M., Picardi, G., Laschi, C.: Fundamentals of soft robot locomotion. J. R. Soc. Interface **14**(130) (2017)
6. Silva, M.F., Machado, T.: A literature review on the optimization of legged robots. J. Vib. Control **18**(12), 1753–1767 (2012)
7. Khatib, O.: Mobile manipulation: the robotic assistant. Robot. Auton. Syst. **26**(2), 175–183 (1999)
8. Bayle, B., Fourquet, J.-Y., Renaud, M.: Manipulability of wheeled mobile manipulators: application to motion generation. Int. J. Robot. Res. **22**(7), 565–581 (2003)
9. Rehman, B.U., et al.: Towards a multi-legged mobile manipulator. ICRA (2016)
10. Galvez, J.A., Estremera, J., De Santos, Gonzalez, P.: A new legged-robot configuration for research in force distribution. Mechatronics **13**(8), 907–932 (2003)
11. Ding, X., Yang, F.: Study on hexapod robot manipulation using legs. Robotica **34**, 468–481 (2014)
12. Katz, D., et al.: The umass mobile manipulator uman: An experimental platform for autonomous mobile manipulation (2006)
13. Youakim, D., et al.: Moveit!: autonomous underwater free-floating manipulation. IEEE Robot. Autom. Mag. **24**(3), 41–51 (2017)
14. Conti, R., et al.: A free floating manipulation strategy for autonomous underwater vehicles. Robot. Auton. Syst. **87**, 133–146 (2017)

15. Liu, J., et al.: Underwater mobile manipulation: a soft arm on a benthic legged robot. IEEE Robot. Autom. Mag. **27**(4), 12–26 (2020)
16. Dash, A.K., Chen, I.M., Yeo, S.H., Yang, G.: Task-oriented configuration design for reconfigurable parallel manipulator systems. Int. J. Comput. Integr. Manuf. **18**(7), 615–634 (2005)
17. Camacho-Arreguin, J., Wang, M., Dong, X., Axinte, D.: A novel class of reconfigurable parallel kinematic manipulators: concepts and fourier-based singularity analysis. Mech. Mach. Theory **153** (2020)
18. Russo, M., Dong, X.: A calibration procedure for reconfigurable gough-stewart manipulators. Mach. Mach. Theory **152** (2020)
19. Picardi, G., Laschi, C., Calisti, C.: Model-based open loop control of a multigait legged underwater robot. Mechatronics **55**, 162–170 (2018)
20. Stewart, D.: A platform with six degrees of freedom. Proc. Inst. Mech. Eng. **180**(1), 371–386 (1965)
21. Mendes Lopes, A., Gomes de Almeida, F.: Manipulability optimization of a parallel structure robotic manipulator. Multibody Sys. Dyn. **9**(1), 1–23 (2003)
22. Gewald, D.: Dynamics and control of hexapod systems
23. Ropponen, T., Arai, T.: Accuracy analysis of a modified Stewart platform manipulator. 1995 IEEE ICRA (1995)
24. Picardi, G., et al.: Bioinspired underwater legged robot for seabed exploration with low environmental disturbance. Sci. Robot. **5**(42) (2020)
25. Lynch, K.M., Park, F.C.: Modern Robotics: Mechanics, Planning, and Control, 1st edn. Cambridge University Press, Cambridge (2017)
26. Yoshikawa, T.: Manipulability of robotic mechanisms. Int. J. Robot. Res. **4**(3) (1985)
27. Wang, S., Jiang, H., Cutkosky., M.R.: A palm for a rock climbing robot based on dense arrays of micro-spines. 2016 IEEE IROS (2016)

EtherCAT Implementation
of a Variable-Stiffness Tendon Drive
with Non-back-Drivable Worm-Gear Motor
Actuation

Ian S. Howard[1]([⊠]) and Martin F. Stoelen[2,3]

[1] SECAM, University of Plymouth, Plymouth 4 8AA, UK
ian.howard@plymouth.ac.uk
[2] Western Norway University of Applied Science, Førde, Norway
Martin.Fodstad.Stolen@hvl.no
[3] Fieldwork Robotics Ltd., Cambridge CB24 9AD, UK

Abstract. Here we present the design for a compliant actuator than makes use of agonistic-antagonistic tendons. Its novelty lies in its use of worm-gear motor drive and industrial EtherCAT control. We first describe a test rig to investigate variable-stiffness tendon drive for a single link and the construction of a corresponding EtherCAT controller. The tendon drive was based on the shoulder joint in the GummiArm and made use of tendons that exhibit a non-linear extension characteristic, so co-contraction increases joint stiffness. To ensures power was only needed when the arm is moving, low-cost worm-drive DC motors were used. An LQR observed-based controller was designed to realize angular position control of the link. The link controller was implemented using the custom-build EtherCAT panel. We present preliminary results of moving the joint link between angular target positions.

Keywords: Tendons · Worm drive · Variable stiffness · Real-time EtherCAT

1 Introduction

Fruit harvesting for the agriculture industry will soon become a major application area for robotic technology. It is desirable for robot actuation to be compliant, to avoid damage arising from collisions that may occur in the working environment, and also to maximize the safety of human co-workers operating in close proximity to robotic platforms. The development of suitable actuators that exhibit compliance is an active field of research [1, 2]. Tendon driven mechanisms provide one approach to build such actuators [3] and the use of agonistic-antagonist elastic tendons with a non-linear extension characteristic enables compliance to be modulated using co-contraction [4, 5].

© Springer Nature Switzerland AG 2021
C. Fox et al. (Eds.): TAROS 2021, LNAI 13054, pp. 381–390, 2021.
https://doi.org/10.1007/978-3-030-89177-0_40

2 Motors

One major component of robotic arms are their actuators, which often make use of electric motors. Several motor types are currently available. Stepper motors are low cost, robust and can directly generate high output torques without the need for gearing. However, they are relatively heavy for their torque output compared to geared DC motors and require continuous drive current to maintain stationary position. High torque DC brushless motors are becoming increasingly popular in robotics applications, due to their high performance stemming from the availability of powerful magnets, and out-runner designs are capable of directly generating very large torques. However, they also require drive current to maintain a stationary position under load. DC brushed motors are also popular and are straightforward to model [6] and to control [7].

Brushed worm-drive DC motors are another good choice for constructing powerful servo drive system, since they are a mass-produced low-cost item and deliver high-torque [8]. Their non-back-drivability is advantageous in our application since maintenance of static posture then requires no power. In a variable-stiffness design, such an arm can also maintain postures at a fixed level of passive compliance. In mobile applications this is highly advantageous, since it would reduce the drain on limited battery power resources, whilst compliance enables the arm to absorb unforeseen impacts due to its own movement, or that of other agents. Therefore, we consider actuator design that makes use of worm-gear motors.

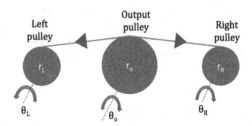

Fig. 1. Schematic of the two-tendon drive based on the design of the GummiArm.

3 Passive Compliance

Active compliance in a robot arm can be achieved by means of force sensing and feedback. However, this cannot protect against the shock arising from hard impacts, like a hammer blow, since the bandwidth limitations of a typical controller makes it unable to react fast enough to compensate such impulsive disturbances. In contrast, passive compliance achieved using a series elastic element in the mechanical drive, can protect the arm and actuator mechanism against impacts, since the load is transferred to the actuator via a physical spring. However, high compliance is not always desirable and stiff operation can be advantageous when dealing with unstable loads. Also, in machining operations, stiff industrial robots are ideal. Various methods have been proposed to modulate stiffness [9, 10], which allows the effective spring constant to change to better fit a given task. Here, we follow the approach taken in the GummiArm, which is a soft robotic arm that makes use of the co-contraction of non-linear tendon drive to achieve variable stiffness [11]. We match the dimensions of the drive and link pulleys used in the GummiArm shoulder. In the original design, research-grade Dynamixels were used for actuation. Here we extend the design using low-cost worm-gear motors to drive the tendons. A schematic of the tendons, drive and output pulley mechanisms used here is shown in Fig. 1. The tendons wrap-around the pulleys and are firmly attached and therefore do not just rely of friction to transfer force.

4 Motor Test Rig

A Motor test rig was developed to provide a testbed for experimental investigations of compliant actuation and corresponding control algorithms. In order to support position control of the robotic link driven by compliant tendons, it was necessary to compensate for tendon deformation. The necessitated the measurements of drive and output angles pulleys. This was achieved using incremental encoders mounted on the pulleys. We used GummiArm tendons supplied by Fieldwork Robotics Ltd. which exhibited a non-linear spring constant that increased with extension.

Fig. 2. Test rig and controller. Panel A: Tendon worm-drive link test rig on stand. Panel B: DIN rail Beckhoff EtherCAT panel.

The rig was comprised of several 3D printed parts, mounted on 20mm aluminum profile that forms its structural support. The custom components were designed using AutoCAD Fusion 360. Subsequently STL format files were generated and the mechanical parts were manufactured in PLA using a LutzBot TAZ6 3D printer. All parts were attached to the aluminum profile sections with T-nuts, so they could be easily adjusted. The motor tendon-drive test rig is shown in Fig. 2A. The test rig could be mounted in two orientations due to its square cross-section. When the link was orientated in a horizontal orientation. gravity has no effect on its motion. This provides a means to investigate control when movement was only resisted by link moment of inertia and viscous friction. When re-orientated by 90°, the effect gravity on the link could be investigated.

5 Beckhoff EtherCAT Control Panel

To control the 2-tendon link, we designed and built a DIN panel based on the industrial Beckhoff EtherCAT platform (Beckhoff Automation GmbH, Verl, Germany). This is widely used for production line automation and ideally suited to the task. Many Beckhoff EtherCAT system components are available, streamlining the implementation of automation and control systems. We implemented the EtherCAT framework using an embedded PC running the real-time Beckhoff TwinCAT3 software which is integrated into the Microsoft Visual Studio development environment. This supports the development of controllers, and interfaces with all the necessary signal I/O and motor drivers. I/O modules consist of electronic terminal block 'slices', which can be slid into the FieldBus system to add functionality in an elegant fashion with no messy wiring. The platform realizes a precise frame rate (typically 1kHz) for signal acquisition and control. In our panel we made use of the following Beckhoff components, although other slices were installed on the FieldBus:

- CX5130 Embedded PC with Intel Atom® processor
- EL5152 Incremental encoder interface (24 V HTL, 100 kHz)
- EL7342 2-channel DC motor terminal (48 V DC, 3.5 A without fan)

The hardware was built into a Rittal GmbH (Herborn, Germany) AE1076.500 Compact AE enclosure (600 × 760 × 210 mm). We used industrial DIN rail assembly technology, so Beckhoff components could be quickly and securely attached, providing an elegant and tidy means of panel construction. The DIN standard supports a wide range of off-the-shelf components, including AD/DC switching power supplies. Panel wiring was routed in cable ducts to maintain a neat layout and connection wires were all terminated appropriately using ferrules. The control panel could be programmed and operated via a single Ethernet cable connection. The panel (Fig. 2B) was mounted on a custom-built stand that also supports the tendon test rig on its rear side. The panel could can easily be expanded to control a multi-joint robotic arm by adding additional I/O slice.

6 Transfer Function and Response of Tendon Mechanism

A full analysis of the worm gear motor actuated tendon system and derivation of the state space model and controller are described in [12]. Here we first note the state space equations for the linearized tendon drive (without motor) is given by the equation:

$$\frac{d}{dt}\begin{bmatrix} \dot{\theta}_o \\ \theta_o \end{bmatrix} = \begin{bmatrix} -\frac{\mu}{I} & -\left(\frac{mgl}{2I} + \frac{2K_r}{I}\right) \\ 1 & 0 \end{bmatrix} \begin{bmatrix} \dot{\theta}_o \\ \theta_o \end{bmatrix} + \begin{bmatrix} \frac{2K_r}{I}\frac{r_{in}}{r_o} & -\frac{K_r}{I}\frac{r_{in}}{r_o} \\ 0 & 0 \end{bmatrix} \begin{bmatrix} \theta_{target} \\ \theta_{stretch} \end{bmatrix} \tag{1}$$

Where θ_o is the output pulley angle. Although component and model parameters (see Table 1) are sometimes available from datasheets and component measurements, it is also useful to have a means to validate, or even estimate them, though simple observations of system behavior such as the open-loop system step response. To analytically compute the step response of the tendon-link system, we first derive the transfer function for the system for θ_{target} given a constant extension $\theta_{stretch}$ value. Setting the latter to zero, leads to the expression

$$\ddot{\theta}_o = -\frac{\mu}{I}\dot{\theta}_o - \left(\frac{mgl}{2I} + \frac{2K_r}{I}\right)\theta_o + \frac{K_r}{I}\frac{r_{in}}{r_o}2\theta_{target} \tag{2}$$

Taking Laplace transforms with zero initial conditions

$$s^2\Phi_o(s) = -\frac{\mu}{I}s\Phi_o(s) - \left(\frac{mgl}{2I} + \frac{2K_r}{I}\right)\Phi_o(s) + \frac{2K_r}{I}\frac{r_{in}}{r_o}\Phi_{target}(s) \tag{3}$$

The transfer function of output to input angle is then given by

$$\frac{\Phi_o(s)}{\Phi_{target}(s)} = \frac{\frac{2K_r}{I}\frac{r_{in}}{r_o}gl}{\left(s^2 + \frac{\mu}{I}s + \left(\frac{mgl}{2I} + \frac{2K_r}{I}\right)\right)} \tag{4}$$

Equating the transfer function to canonical form

$$\frac{\frac{2K_r}{I}\frac{r_{in}}{r_o}gl}{\left(s^2 + \frac{\mu}{I}s + \left(\frac{mgl}{2I} + \frac{2K_r}{I}\right)\right)} \Leftrightarrow \frac{K}{(s^2 + 2\xi\omega_n s + \omega_n^2)} \tag{5}$$

Comparing terms yields the natural frequency ω_n and damping ratio ξ of the system

$$\omega_n^2 \Leftrightarrow \left(\frac{mgl}{2I} + \frac{2K_r}{I}\right) \Rightarrow \omega_n = \sqrt{\left(\frac{mgl}{2I} + \frac{2K_r}{I}\right)} \tag{6}$$

$$2\xi\omega_n \Leftrightarrow \frac{\mu}{I} \Rightarrow \xi = \frac{\mu}{2I\omega_n} \tag{7}$$

We note that Eqs. (6) and (7) provides a simple way to estimate system parameters from measurements of natural frequency ω_n and the damping ratio ξ. The latter can be estimated by pulling the link away from equilibrizing, suddenly releasing it, and quantifying the response. This of course changes as a function of tendon co-contraction.

7 State Space Model of System

The A and B matrices of the motor-tendon system, after [12], are given by:

$$A = \begin{bmatrix} -\frac{b}{J} & \frac{Kt}{J} & 0 & 0 & 0 & 0 & 0 & 0 \\ -\frac{Ke}{L} & -\frac{R}{L} & 0 & 0 & 0 & 0 & 0 & 0 \\ 1 & 0 & 0 & 0 & 0 & 0 & 0 & 0 \\ 0 & 0 & 0 & -\frac{b}{J} & \frac{Kt}{J} & 0 & 0 & 0 \\ 0 & 0 & 0 & -\frac{Ke}{L} & -\frac{R}{L} & 0 & 0 & 0 \\ 0 & 0 & 0 & 1 & 0 & 0 & 0 & 0 \\ 0 & 0 & \frac{Kr}{G_e I}\frac{r_{in}}{r_o} & 0 & 0 & -\frac{Kr}{G_e I}\frac{r_{in}}{r_o} & -\frac{\mu}{I} & -\left(\frac{mgl}{2I} + \frac{2Kr}{I}\right) \\ 0 & 0 & 0 & 0 & 0 & 0 & 1 & 0 \end{bmatrix} \tag{8}$$

$$B = \begin{bmatrix} 0 & -\frac{1}{L} & 0 & 0 & \frac{1}{L} & 0 & 0 & 0 \\ 0 & \frac{1}{2L} & 0 & 0 & \frac{1}{2L} & 0 & 0 & 0 \end{bmatrix}^T \tag{9}$$

Table 1. List of all parameters for agonist-antagonist compliant drive system

	Link and tendon		Worm-drive motor
I	Link mechanism's inertia	L	Motor inductance
mg	Link gravity force	R	Motor resistance
μ	Link viscous friction coefficient	J	Motor inertia
K_r	Effective tendon spring constant	b	Motor viscous friction
r_{in}	Drive pulley radius	G_e	Worm gearing ratio
r_o	Output pulley radius	K_e	Motor generator constant
l	Link length	K_t	Motor torque constant

The C matrix is used by the Luenberger observer. It extracts system output that can be measured from the full state (here only the joint angles) and is used to correct the state estimate.

$$C = \begin{bmatrix} 0 & 0 & 1 & 0 & 0 & 0 & 0 & 0 \\ 0 & 0 & 0 & 0 & 0 & 1 & 0 & 0 \\ 0 & 0 & 0 & 0 & 0 & 0 & 0 & 1 \end{bmatrix} \tag{10}$$

8 Pseudocode and EtherCAT Implementation

The signal flow graph for the controller is illustrated in Fig. 3. The A, B and C matrices (Eqs. 8, 9, 10) were evaluated in MATLAB. The controller gain vector K and observer gain vector L were designed using the MATLAB lqr command following the derivation described in [12]. Pre-scaling factor nbar was computed in MATLAB as

$$nbar = -inv[Cinv(A - BK)B]$$ (11)

The observed-based state feedback controller design was tested using a Simulink implementation, as illustrated in Fig. 4 and using sub-systems shown in Fig. 5. The target angle and link output from the simulation are shown in Fig. 6. The output followed the input target angle without overshoot or ringing.

We note the mixing matrix M, shown in Eq. (12), is needed in a physical implementation, since the control inputs need to be transformed from target and stretch angles to the corresponding left and right motor inputs:

$$M = \begin{bmatrix} -1 & 0.5 \\ 1 & 0.5 \end{bmatrix}$$ (12)

We implemented open-loop control, P-control (where error is just the scaled difference between target and output) and an observer-based real-time controller on the Beckhoff EtherCAT platform using structured text. To do so, we first linked variables to the hardware slices, providing access to input sensors and connecting output variable to the motor controllers. This framework provided an update function called repetitively at the selected system frame rate of 1 kHz. Within the update frame, we implemented the control of the motors as follows:

- We accessed the encoder slice variables to read the angular orientation of the two drive and output pulleys.
- In the case of open-loop and P-control, the motor drive voltage controls were either set directly or as the proportional error respectively.
- In the case of state feedback control, we estimated the full state of the motor-tendon system using a Luenberger observer. The state estimate was corrected by the prediction error between measured and predicted pulley angles. We calculate the state feedback control signal using the full estimated state and the reference input angle vector scaled by nbar. We used trapezoid integration to update the estimated system state, since it is more robust than Euler integration.
- The output control signals, (drive voltages to the two worm drive motors) were written to the motor slices, which drove the motors appropriately.

9 Results

We tested the tendons at a single level of co-contraction. A video of open loop operation of the EtherCAT controller driving the 2-tendon arm is shown in this link: https://youtu.be/1L07mjgcbNI. Part1 shows driving the link between target angles as desired, part2 shows tensioning single tendons at a time (which affect joint angle) and part3 shows tensioning followed by moving between targets. A plot of another set of point-to-point angular movements is shown in Fig. 7. It can be seen that despite open-loop operation, there is only a slight overshoot of the link after reaching the target angle.

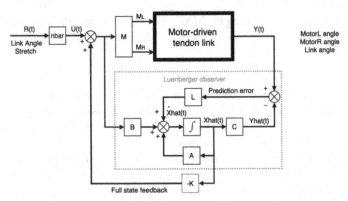

Fig. 3. State feedback control of motor driven tendon link hardware. The reference input is first weighted by a feedforward compensation gain nbar to achieve unity system DC gain. The input error is linearly transformed by matrix M to generate left and right motor drive. A Luenberger observer is used to estimate the full state of the motor driven tendon link and multiplied with gain K to generate feedback.

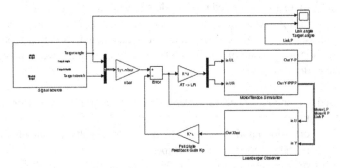

Fig. 4. Simulink simulation top level schematic. nt. Bus creator and selector blocks are used to appropriately combine and separate signals. Sub-systems, shown in Fig. 5, are used to implement a model of the plant and the Luenberger observer.

10   Discussion

We constructed a test rig to examine the operation of variable-stiffness tendon drive with non-back-drivable worm-gear motor actuation. We suggested a simple method of system identification, using step response. We simulated observer-based state feedback control with Simulink and showed our controller design was capably of controlling the link using only measurements of motor and output angles. To control a real link, we built an EtherCAT controller panel. We presented preliminary results of the panel driving the test link making point-to-point movements. Clearly extensive testing of the system is now required, including a rigorous comparison between open-loop. P-control and observer-based state feedback control, which was unfortunately outside the scope of the current work. Finally, we note that from a hardware perspective, our EtherCAT panel design

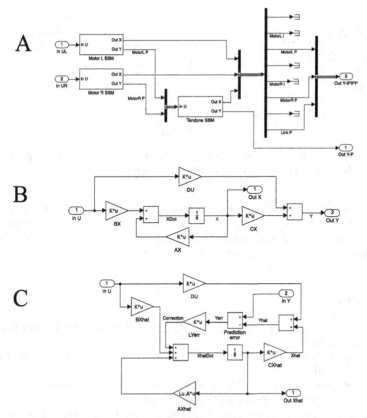

Fig. 5. Simulink sub-systems. Panel A: Motor-tendons controller schematic. State space models for the motors and tendon are shown as sub-systems. Panel B: State space model sub-system schematic. Panel C: Luenberger observer sub-system schematic.

is fully expandable and will support the testing of others joint configurations and full robotic arms, including those which are biologically inspired.

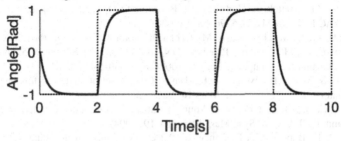

Fig. 6. Simulink simulation of the responses of the motor-tendon system under observer-based state feedback control. Dotted line is square-wave input target angle and solid line is output link angle. Note the link follows the target angle and reaches it without overshoot.

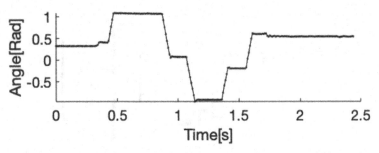

Fig. 7. Open-loop response of the real physical motor-tendon system during point-to-point movements. Note the slight overshoot of the link after reaching the target angle.

Acknowledgments. We thank Simon Bates and Innovate UK project No: 104622 SoSehRaH and David Mozley at the University of Plymouth for EtherCAT Controller Proof of Concept support, Beckhoff (UK) for technical assistance and Fieldwork Robotics Ltd for supplying the GummiArm tendons, helpful discussion and access to their technology.

References

1. Grioli, G., et al.: Variable stiffness actuators: the user's point of view. Int. J. Robot. Res. **34**(6), 727–743 (2015)
2. Vanderborght, B., et al.: Variable impedance actuators: a review. Robot. Auton. Syst. **61**(12), 1601–1614 (2013)
3. Ozawa, R., Kobayashi, H., Hashirii, K.: Analysis, classification, and design of tendon-driven mechanisms. IEEE Trans. Robot. **30**(2), 396–410 (2013)
4. Ham, R.V., Sugar, T., Vanderborght, B., Hollander, K., Lefeber, D.: Compliant actuator designs. IEEE Robot. Autom. Mag. **3**(16), 81–94 (2009)
5. Migliore, S.A., Brown, E.A., DeWeerth, S.P.: Biologically inspired joint stiffness control. In: Proceedings of the 2005 IEEE International Conference on Robotics and Automation, pp. 4508–4513. IEEE (2005)
6. Chotai, J., Narwekar, K.: Modelling and position control of brushed DC motor. In: 2017 International Conference on Advances in Computing, Communication and Control (ICAC3), pp. 1–5. IEEE (2017)
7. Ruderman, M., Krettek, J., Hoffmann, F., Bertram, T.: Optimal state space control of DC motor. IFAC Proc. Vol. **41**(2), 5796–5801 (2008)
8. Pinto, V.H., Gonçalves, J., Costa, P.: Model of a DC motor with worm gearbox. In: Gonçalves, J.A., Braz-César, M., Coelho, J.P. (eds.) CONTROLO 2020. LNEE, vol. 695, pp. 638–647. Springer, Cham (2021). https://doi.org/10.1007/978-3-030-58653-9_61
9. Jacobsen, S.C., Ko, H., Iversen, E.K., Davis, C.C.: Control strategies for tendon-driven manipulators. IEEE Control Syst. Mag. **10**(2), 23–28 (1990)
10. Lee, Y.T., Choi, H.R., Chung, W.K., Youm, Y.: Stiffness control of a coupled tendon-driven robot hand. IEEE Control Syst. Mag. **14**(5), 10–19 (1994)
11. Stoelen, M.F., Bonsignorio, F., Cangelosi, A.: Co-exploring actuator antagonism and bio-inspired control in a printable robot arm. In: Tuci, E., Giagkos, A., Wilson, M., Hallam, J. (eds.) SAB 2016. LNCS (LNAI), vol. 9825, pp. 244–255. Springer, Cham (2016). https://doi.org/10.1007/978-3-319-43488-9_22
12. Howard I.S., Stoelen, M.F.: State space analysis of variable-stiffness tendon drive with non-back-drivable worm-gear motor actuation. TAROS 2021, University of Lincoln (2021)

Growing Robotic Endoscope for Early Breast Cancer Detection: Robot Motion Control

Carmen Larrea[1]([⊠]), Pierre Berthet-Rayne[2], S. M. Hadi Sadati[2], Daniel Richard Leff[3], Christos Bergeles[2], and Ioannis Georgilas[1]

[1] Department of Mechanical Engineering, University of Bath, Bath, UK
i.georgilas@bath.ac.uk
[2] Robotics and Vision in Medicine Lab, School of Biomedical Engineering and Imaging Sciences, King's College London, London, UK
[3] Hamlyn Centre for Robotic Surgery and Imperial College Healthcare NHS Trust, London, UK

Abstract. The direct relationship between early-stage breast cancer detection and survival rates has created the need for a simple, fast and cheap method to detect breast cancer at its earliest stages. Endoscopic evaluation of the mammary ducts known as ductoscopy has great potential to detect early breast cancers. Unfortunately, there are technical limitations, most notably lack of steerability and high tissue damage, limiting its practicality. A promising alternative to rigid endoscopy tools is the use of soft robots.

This paper presents the computational multidomain model for the MAM-MOBOT soft growing prototype. The prototype is using pressurised saline solution to achieve elongation in the breast's ductal tree, a tendon driven catheter for steering, and an active channel for soft material storage. The derivation of the model is based on plant cell expansion, and physical modelling of the actuation and hydraulic systems.

The model is validated in 1 D using experimental data from the MAMMOBOT prototype. All unknown model variables were identified during a parameter investigation using Latin Hypercube Sampling. The developed hydraulic model predicted the measured elongation with a 1.7 mm RMSE error, 3.5% of the total robot length, while the combined actuation and hydraulic models predicted the elongation with 2.5 mm RMSE, 5% of total length.

The results presented here is the first attempt to implement the growing robot concepts in small scales and demonstrate their accuracy. The developed model will be used to improve the closed loop control of the growing robot, improving steerability and positional accuracy, enhancing the cancer detection process.

Keywords: Soft robotics · Hydraulic actuation · Robot control

1 Introduction

Breast cancer is the most common type of cancer in the UK with more than 55 thousand cases diagnosed every year [1] and with a 5-year mortality rate of 15%. For years, doctors and investigators have searched for ways of decreasing mortality through early

© Springer Nature Switzerland AG 2021
C. Fox et al. (Eds.): TAROS 2021, LNAI 13054, pp. 391–401, 2021.
https://doi.org/10.1007/978-3-030-89177-0_41

detection. When diagnosed in its early stages 98% of people will survive breast cancer for 5 years or more against a 26% survival rate with a late-stage diagnosis [1]. These statistics highlight the importance of a procedure that will diagnose breast cancer in its earliest stages.

In its earliest form (stage 0) cancer is known as Ductal Carcinoma in Situ (DCIS). The detection of DCIS could increase the chances of survival of the patient and could even avoid the need for chemotherapy or surgical intervention. Current methods have numerous limitations such as being expensive, time-consuming or have reduced sensitivity and specificity [2]. For example, mammography screening is relatively inefficient in detecting DCIS as it only detects those tumours associated with calcifications which are less than 50% of all DCIS cases [3]. Considering 80–90% of breast cancers start developing as DCIS, a high number of cases go undetected or present as invasive cancers downstream.

Ductoscopy facilitates early diagnosis through the use of an endoscope which accesses the mammary ducts via the nipple in order to have a visual of the tumour [4]. Rigid endoscopes, however, are difficult to manipulate and cause significant strain on the surrounding tissue. This inflexibility means that the ductoscopy procedure is not yet widely used. Most MI tools currently have steerable tips but their length stops them from achieving optimal dexterity and stability when they reach the surgical site [5]. A good solution to overcome these challenges is the use of soft robotics as endoscopic tools since they can exploit their high flexibility to reach the target [6].

Robotic surgery has been a reality in the medical field for some time, but it is only relatively recently that soft robots have been adopted for use in surgical procedures. In 1997 Frazer [7] patented a worm-like robot to be used as a colonoscopy tool. Since then, many doctors and surgeons have realised the advantages that come with the use of a precise, manoeuvrable, and flexible tool in MI procedures. A technique that has shown great potential for catheter use is that of concentric tube robots [8]. This technology overcomes the difficulty in steering by the use of concentric pre-curved super elastic tubes which can form complex 3D shapes.

Another promising soft robotic technology that has shown potential is that of growing robots [9]. Their use has been investigated in many applications such as search and rescue, exploration of coral reefs [10] or archaeological sites [11], as well as medical procedures [12]. These robots are inspired by plant growth and elongate through eversion using air pressure inside a thin membrane. The MAMMOBOT project [13] explores using a growing robot as a ductoscopy tool, with the key novelty being the significant reduction of size allowing it to flexibly navigate the mammary duct system.

One of the common complexities for this class of robots is the modelling description of their behaviour to ensure safe and reliable control. The preferred methods of modelling come from nature given the similarities between robots and plants. One proposed approach is to use plant growth-inspired models for motion generation [14] while another is to draw inspiration from biological models of apical extension and mechanical models of compliant Bowden cable actuation [15].

The work presented here is building on existing apical models, extending them to match the structure and characteristics of the MAMMOBOT robot. The proposed model incorporates the unique features of the robot and offers modelling of the actuation system and the impact on robot growth and control. The final result is a step towards accurate operation of miniature growing robots.

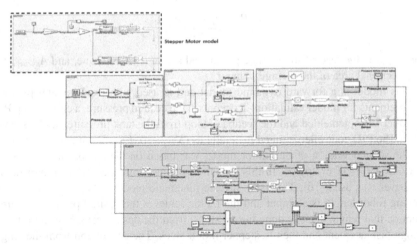

Fig. 1. Simulink multidomain model of MAMMOBOT. Green is the (generic) torque source model (dashed insert: stepper motor), yellow is the mechanical model of the syringe pump, blue is the hydraulic elements of the pressure tank, and purple is the growing element model. (Color figure online)

2 Methods

There are three key methodical aspects in this study, firstly the development of the proposed model consisting of the actuation system, the hydraulic system and the growing robot element. Secondly, the data analysis metric for comparison of experimental and compuational results, and thirdly the parameter investigation for the unknown model parameters.

2.1 Actuation and Hydraulics Model

The actuation and hydraulics model is following the physical MAMMOBOT prototype developed by Berthet-Rayne et al. [13] and presented in green, yellow and blue in Fig. 1. It consists of a syringe pump (mechanical domain model) powered by a motor (electrical domain model) and a custom pressurized tank (hydraulic domain model) that supplies pressure to the growing robot. To simplify the actuation model the physical implementation of the catheter and the active channel were not included in this work.

Motor Model. Two different models for the motor were created to allow investigation of different model aspects. In the first instance the motor is modelled as an ideal torque source ensuring a direct control of the applied pressure. This model allows for the evaluation of different motors and relies on pressure sensing. This model is presented with green in Fig. 1 and is connected to the rest of the model. The demanded pressure (P_d) is provided as an input and the equivalent torque is calculated by the characteristics of the pressure source, the syringe in this case:

$$T_d = \frac{P_d \times l_{lead} \times A_{syringe}}{2\pi} \tag{1}$$

where l_{lead} is the lead of the syringe pump lead screw, T_d the torque, and $A_{syringe}$ the cross-sectional area of the syringe plunger.

This model is a forward dynamic model and is used with experimental pressure measurements for model validation. To maintain the desired pressure, a closed loop PID controller is implemented and the feedback loop from the tank pressure can be seen in Fig. 1. The PID controller is tuned manually as ($K_P = 80$, $K_I = 25$ and $K_D = 0.5$).

The second version of the motor model was based on the stepper motor used in the MAMMOBOT prototype. In this case the existing Simscape stepper motor model and driver was used [16]. This is an inverse kinematic model with which the desired growing robot length is an input and the motor achieves the desired pressure required to obtain that length. This is done in two steps, from the desired length of the robot to syringe displacement and then to stepper motor steps. The conversion from the length of the robot to syringe displacement assumes there are no fluid losses and the fluid is incompressible thus the relationship between syringe and robot pressures and volumes:

$$\frac{L_{syringe}}{L_{robot}} = \frac{A_{syringe}}{A_{robot}} \tag{2}$$

where, $L_{syringe}$ is the displacement of the syringe pump plunger, L_{robot} is the desired length of the robot and A_{robot} is the cross-section area. For the conversion from the length to the steps for the motor the dimensions of the lead screw for the plunger are used.

Syringe Pump Model. The pump subsystem is formed by available Simscape elements that can be seen in yellow in Fig. 1. The motors are driving lead screws which are coupled via a carrier platform with the syringe plungers The syringes were modelled using single acting cylinder blocks as they have the same functions and underlying equations. The function of this subsystem is to generate fluidic pressure which will be transmitted to the pressurized tank.

Pressurized Tank Model. The pressurization tank used in the MAMMOBOT prototype is custom made and an approximation has to be made as seen with blue in Fig. 1. A hydraulic pipeline with a non-circular cross-section was used. The tank has two top nozzles, one for pressure sensing and another for hydraulic pressurisation connected to the syringe pump. Hydraulic pressure is applied from the syringes to the tank through flexible hydraulic pipelines and an orifice. The flexible hydraulic pipelines in the model represent the silicone tubes that connect the syringe and the tank. The flexible property will cause some pressure absorption. The tank ends in a nozzle to which one end of the growing robot membrane is attached; this was modelled through the use of a gradual area change block. The nozzle outputs fluid into the growing robot with a pressure sensor measuring at this point.

The hydraulic fluid used in the MAMMOBOT robot is 0.9%NaCl saline water, which is the most common solution in medical applications. The differences in the mechanical properties of saline solution and water are negligible and therefore the system was modelled using pure water.

The detailed Simscape model and image of the experimental setup can be found at Robot model github page.

2.2 Growing Robot Model

The growing robot modelling is based on the apical model described by Blumenschein et al. [15] and gives the pressure force (PA) of the robot as:

$$PA = \left[YA + \left(\frac{1}{\phi}v\right)^{\frac{1}{n}} A \right] + \left[\mu_s \omega L + C_e^{\frac{\mu_c L_i}{R_i}} \right] \tag{3}$$

where, Y is the yield pressure below which no growth happens, $\left(\frac{1}{\phi}v\right)^{\frac{1}{n}} A$ is a velocity term due to the material's resistance to elongation, $\mu_s \omega L$ is a friction term from outside contacts of the robot and $C_e^{\frac{\mu_c L_i}{R_i}}$ is a term due to the curvature of the robot. The first two terms are path independent and the latter two are path dependent and relate to the environment.

Equation 3 must be adapted for the MAMMOBOT robot. The introduction of a catheter tool through the centre of the growing robot will cause a friction force. The friction term in (3) can be substituted by the friction between the catheter and the growing robot. Assuming that the catheter moves forward relative to the growing robot this will result in a forward friction force (F_{fr}) in the growing robot which will accelerate its growth:

$$F_{fr} = PA \times 2\pi \times r_i \times L_c \times \mu_{rc} \tag{4}$$

where r_i is the radius of the catheter, L_c is the length of the catheter in contact with the robot and μ_{rc} is the coefficient of friction between the catheter and the robot. The dependence on length makes the force a path-dependent term.

The MAMMOBOT design introduces the use of an active channel that has the ability to exert a force (F_{AC}) on the growing robot in order to better control the elongation behaviour and is thus path-independent. As a result of this and (4), (3) becomes:

$$PA = \left[YA + \left(\frac{1}{\phi}v\right)^{\frac{1}{n}} A + F_{AC} \right] + \left[-F_{fr} + C_e^{\frac{\mu_c L_i}{R_i}} \right] \tag{5}$$

It must be noted that no friction term has been added for the interaction of the growing robot with the walls of the ducts (lumen). As explained above, one of the main advantages of the growing robot technique is its ability to elongate without relative movement between the body and its environment. The friction between the growing robot and the lumen can therefore be neglected.

Since (5) is written in terms of forces it was concluded that an ideal single-acting cylinder could be used to model the robot in the Simulink environment. The underlying equations which govern the single-acting cylinder are:

$$F_{cyl} = A_{pis}P_{in} \text{ and } q = A_{pis}v \tag{6}$$

where F_{cyl} is the force developed by the cylinder, A_{pis} is the piston area and P_{in} is the pressure at the cylinder inlet. The term q represents flow rate and v represents velocity.

The forces from (5) can be substituted into (6) to calculate the force into the single-acting cylinder. In this study, the growing robot is analysed in straight paths only, while the velocity can be substituted from (6). The resulting force equation is:

$$F_{cyl} = \left[YA + \left(\frac{q}{\phi A} \right)^{\frac{1}{n}} A + F_{AC} \right] + \left[-F_{fr} \right] \tag{7}$$

This force is modelled in Simulink as an ideal force source to the single-acting cylinder, acting against elongation as it is a resistive force. The length data for the friction force from (4) is obtained from experimental catheter displacement data as the model created has not simulated catheter behaviour. The force from the active channel will remain zero for this work as it was not used to apply force during the experiment.

In order to ensure safety a pressure limit is introduced to prevent yield failure of the growing robot membrane. To make a stress analysis of the robot, the growing robot element is considered as a thin pressure vessel. Due to the low ratio of thickness to radius, an approximation can be made to assume that the membrane experiences negligible radial stress when pressurized and only experience longitudinal (σ_L) and circumferential (σ_θ) stress will be considered.. Failure due to yielding in the robot membrane will be caused when the circumferential stress reaches the yield stress (σ_y) [17]. The maximum permitted pressure is therefore described by:

$$P_{max} = \frac{2t\sigma_y}{r_o} \tag{8}$$

The membrane material in this case is LDPE with a yield stress value of 40 MPa. The growing element has a thickness (t) of 35 μm with an outer radius (r_o) of 1.5 mm and an inner radius of (r_i) of 0.45 mm. With a safety factor of 5 the maximum pressure was calculated to be 373.3 kPa. This limit was added as a simulation stop limit in the model.

The initial resistance of the growing robot to elongation due to the Yield Pressure was modelled hydraulicly as a check valve after the pressure tank and before the growing element. This approach is useful for setting a pressure limit below which no flow occurs and acts as a static pressure resistance. Because this approach will prevent unidirectional flow, a three-way directional valve is used to override the check valve when the flow changes direction. The valve is controlled based on the flow direction as detected through the use of a flow rate sensor. After the initial pressure is overcome the Yield Pressure term is added via the single-acting cylinder and (7).

2.3 Data Analysis

The evaluation of the model was performed by comparing model predicted results for robot elongation, flow and pressure with experimental observations as collected via the work by Berthet-Rayne et al. [13]. The comparison was performed using the Root Mean Square Error (RMSE).

2.4 Parameter Investigation

Equation 7 has three main unknown parameters that have to be found empirically: yield pressure, extensibility and n term. The values were found using the computational model and the experimental data available, through a parameter investigation. This was done by determining the set of values that will give a model response most closely approximates the experimental data. Through the use of Latin Hypercube Sampling (LHS) a distribution of 500 parameter sets were obtained. The different combinations of values are then inputted into the system and the RMSE value is calculated to identify which parameter combination gives a result that simulates the behaviour of the experimental data most closely. The ideal torque source version of the model was used to perform this analysis.

3   Results and Discussion

The model developed above was validated with the single run data from the work by Berthet-Rayne et al. [13] to evaluate accuracy but more repeats are needed for evaluating repeatability. Both versions of the motor model were tested, i.e. the model using the ideal torque source to drive the leadscrew and the model using the stepper motor. Prior to validation tests the parameter investigation was done to identify the unknown parameters of the system and based on those validate the models.

3.1 Parameter Investigation

Figure 2 presents the results from the parameter investigation for the three parameters identified in (7). The 3D graph shows all 500 points generated using LHS. The ranges for the random generation were selected following an initial manual sampling investigation of the wider parameter space and observing the range that would most affect RMSE. Parameter n is a scaling power term close to unity and therefore a range of 0.9 to 1.1 was selected. A Yield Pressure, i.e. before growth can commence, range of 5 kPa–15 kPa was selected while an extensibility, i.e. the ability of the robot to extent, range of 4000–10000 Pa^{-n}m/s was selected. The table in Fig. 2 gives the values achieving the minimum RMSE which will be used for the validation tests.

The parameter with the most significant effect on RMSE is yield pressure since the RMSE value greatly changes along that axis. It can be observed that the optimal yield pressure value is around 8 kPa. This is expected as a change in the resistive force acting against elongation would affect the rate of growth of the robot. On the other hand, for extensibility and n $term$ it can be observed that there is no clear correlation between either of them and the RMSE value. Considering that extensibility and *n term* are part of the velocity term in (7), a high value in the extensibility term will greatly reduce the effect of this force on the growing robot which will also mean that the *n term* effect will be reduced as well.

3.2   Model Validation

For the validation two assumptions are made, first, the model takes into account the movement of the robot in 1D only i.e., extension, ignoring curvature. Therefore, only experimental data of extension are being used. The second assumption has to do with the application of the pressure experimentally. As explained in [13], no pressure control was performed but a "duty cycle controller" was used of no pressure-pressure.

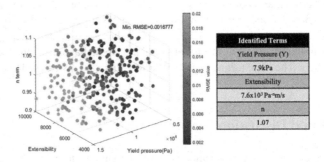

Fig. 2. Parameter Investigation Results. The 500 points generated with the LHS are presented, with the color scale being the RMSE value. On the right the identified values are given.

Growing Robot Validation. In the validation of the growing robot model with the ideal torque model, the duty cycle pressure demand for the *Growing Cycle*, thus a pulse pressure signal of 0 to 150 kPa, is the demand to the model and the elongation of the robot was observed and compared to the experimental results as shown in Fig. 3. The pressure was controlled via the closed-loop PID controller.

In this experiment it can be observed that the robot length is shown to follow the same behaviour as the experimental length data, Fig. 3. The overall rate of growth for both is similar, reaching a length of 50mm in 10 s. An RMSE value of 1.7 mm corresponds to a total error of 3.4% of the final length of the growing robot. This is a promising result, for surgical robotic applications aim for a 1–2 mm accuracy [18]. Analysing both elongation signals, it can be observed that the experimental data has bigger peaks than the model data. The biggest variation occurs in the positive gradient of the peak sections, the experimental data has a higher rate of growth. Contrastingly the retracting section of the peak is larger and less steep than in the model. The lower negative gradient could be attributed to a pulling force from the active channel that is not included in the model currently. It must also be noted that there is no experimental pressure data available to confirm the actual pressure applied to the robot. This uncertainty surrounding the experimental pressure could mean the input pressure was representative, causing the differences in gradients. The catheter movement (not modelled) could also have had an unexpected effect on the growing robot behaviour causing some material to fold or buckle.

Actuation System Validation. The validation of the actuation system was done by using as stepper motor demand the desired growing robot length using Eq. (2) and the length-to-stepper motor steps conversion. The pressure generated was recorded as well as the model predicted vs the desired growing robot length, Fig. 4.

The actuation system model is overall less accurate. However, the length response can still be seen to follow a similar pattern to the experimental observations. The pressure response to the length inputs has a faster triangular frequency which can be attributed to the stepper motor as it actuates the syringe pump. Nonetheless, the predicted robot length produced from this pressure is smoother than the observed length and the error is still low, and the overall rate of growth is similar reaching a length of 50 mm in 10 s.

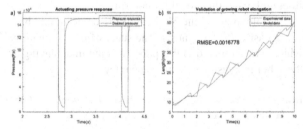

Fig. 3. Growing robot model validation. a) Demand and response of the actuating pressure b) Growing robot length data model predicted and experimental.

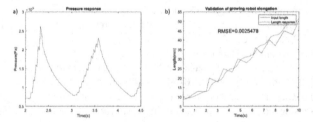

Fig. 4. Actuation model validation a) Pressure response to the demanded length. b) Growing robot length response compared to the desired length.

An RMSE of 2.5 mm means that there is a 5% error compared to the final length of the robot. It must be noted that there is no pressure feedback loop to correct for losses and variations caused by the system. It can still be observed that there are advancements and retraction by the robot at approximately the same rate as the observed behaviour. There is a time lag in between demand and response which can be associated with viscous frictional losses across the actuation system.

4 Conclusion

This work introduces a computational model for the MAMMOBOT robot, a novel grow-ing robot for early breast cancer detection which aims to serve as an endoscopy tool entering the ductal network via the nipple. The multidomain model was created and validated using experimental observations and the results showed that the prediction of growth behaviour was accurate for both an ideal torque actuator and the stepper motor used in the experiments. The former resulted in an RMSE error of 1.7 mm while the latter of 2.5 mm, at 3.5% and 5% of the total length of the robot.

In this work the basis for an accurate analytical model to describe the behaviour of the MAMMOBOT device was created, however, more repeatability assessment of the result is needed. More investigation is needed on the effect of curvature in the robot when expanding the model from 1D to 2D and 3D. Moreover, in its current form the model ignores the active channel and the guiding catheter but from initial observations a detailed analysis of their impact needs to be conducted. Finally, investigations should also look into how the addition of sensing instrumentation such as multiple pressure and flow sensors will complement the model for control.

The successful development of the MAMMOBOT device could be incredibly valu-able in the field of breast cancer diagnosis. The successful computational model of the first prototype which was presented in this paper will aid in achieving a precise motion and control of the robot increasing detection accuracy.

Acknowledgments. This work is being supported by Cancer Research UK (CRUK) via the MAMMOBOT – A flexible robot for early breast cancer diagnosis grant.

References

1. Cancer Research UK. Breast cancer statistics
2. Mokbel, K., Cutuli, B.: Heterogeneity of ductal carcinoma in situ and its effects on management. Lancet Oncol. **7**, 756–765 (2006)
3. Breast cancer in women - Diagnosis - NHS
4. Mokbel, K., Escobar, P.F., Matsunaga, T.: Mammary ductoscopy: current status and future prospects (2005). https://doi.org/10.1016/j.ejso.2004.10.004
5. Polygerinos, P., et al.: Soft robotics: review of fluid-driven intrinsically soft devices; manu-facturing, sensing, control, and applications in human-robot interaction. Adv. Eng. Mater. **19**, 1700016 (2017)
6. Cianchetti, M., Menciassi, A.: Soft robots in surgery. Biosyst. Biorobot. **17**, 75–85 (2017)
7. Frazer, R.E.: Apparatus for endoscopic examination united states patent. Patent Number: 4,176,662 (1979)
8. Bergeles, C., et al.: Concentric tube robot design and optimization based on task and anatomical constraints. IEEE Trans. Robot. **31**, 67–84 (2015)
9. Hawkes, E.W., et al.: A soft robot that navigates its environment through growth. Sci. Robot. **2**, 1–8 (2017)
10. Luong, J., et al.: Eversion and retraction of a soft robot towards the exploration of coral reefs. In: 2nd IEEE International Conference on Soft Robotics (RobSoft), pp. 801–807 (2019)
11. Coad, M.M., et al.: Vine robots: design, teleoperation, and deployment for navigation and exploration. IEEE Robot. Autom. Mag. **27**, 120–132 (2020)

12. Slade, P., et al.: Design of a soft catheter for low-force and constrained surgery. In: IEEE International Conference on Intelligent Robots and Systems, vol. 2017-Septe, pp. 174–180 (2017)
13. Berthet-Rayne, P., et al.: MAMMOBOT: a miniature steerable soft growing robot for early breast cancer detection. IEEE Robot. Autom. Lett. 1–8 (2021)
14. Wooten, M., et al.: Exploration and inspection with vine-inspired continuum robots. In: Proceedings - IEEE International Conference on Robotics and Automation (ICRA), pp. 5526–5533 (2018)
15. Blumenschein, L.H., Okamura, A.M., Hawkes, E.W.: Modeling of bioinspired apical extension in a soft robot. In: Mangan, M., Cutkosky, M., Mura, A., Verschure, P.F.M.J., Prescott, T., Lepora, N. (eds.) Living Machines 2017. LNCS (LNAI), vol. 10384, pp. 522–531. Springer, Cham (2017). https://doi.org/10.1007/978-3-319-63537-8_45
16. Lyshevski, S.E.: Electromechanical Systems, Electric Machines, and Applied Mechatronics. CRC Press (2018)
17. Godaba, H., Putzu, F., Abrar, T., Konstantinova, J., Althoefer, K.: Payload capabilities and operational limits of eversion robots. In: Althoefer, K., Konstantinova, J., Zhang, K. (eds.) TAROS 2019. LNCS (LNAI), vol. 11650, pp. 383–394. Springer, Cham (2019). https://doi.org/10.1007/978-3-030-25332-5_33
18. Haidegger, T., et al.: Spatial accuracy of surgical robots. In: Proceedings - 2009 5th International Symposium on Applied Computational Intelligence and Informatics, SACI 2009, pp. 133–138 (2009)

Design and Characterisation of a Variable Stiffness Soft Actuator Based on Tendon Twisting

William King[1,2], Luke Pooley[1,2], Philip Johnson[1,2], and Khaled Elgeneidy[1,2(✉)] (iD)

[1] School of Engineering, University of Lincoln, Lincoln, UK
kelgeneidy@lincoln.ac.uk
[2] Lincoln Centre for Autonomous Systems, University of Lincoln, Lincoln, UK

Abstract. This short paper presents a preliminary investigation into the implementation of a controllable variable stiffening mechanism, which is achieved through the twisting of tendons around the central axis of a soft actuator. The gradual stiffening effect is realised through the increase in friction between the tendons as those are twisted against each other. This enables an easy to control variable stiffness actuator which is driven through the rotation of a DC motor driving the tendon twisting. The proposed mechanism was integrated within the core of a soft pneumatic actuator based on the STIFF-FLOP design, in order to characterise the increase in stiffness per twist angle for three different tendon materials. The initial experimental results presented here demonstrated that a controllable stiffening effect can be achieved using this technique, which shows dependency on the choice of tendon material. The results also highlighted the impact of braiding the softer tendons to potentially enhance stiffening, although further experimentation is necessary to characterise this behaviour in more detail.

Keywords: Soft robotics · Soft actuators · Variable stiffness

1 Introduction

The field of soft robotics aims to address the challenges faced by traditional rigid robots in less structured and dynamic environments which require more adaptive interactions. Taking inspiration from biological organisms' such as octopus tentacles and elephant trunks, soft robots commonly use elastic materials and novel actuation methods to mimic the continuous deformation of their mostly soft bodies [1]. Flexible Fluid Actuators (FFAs) are one approach to soft robotic actuation that makes use of elastomeric chambers patterned specifically to induce asymmetries when a fluid is forced (or removed) through them [2]. While conventional robotic manipulators, such as those used in the DaVinci surgical robot, offer high precision for minimally invasive surgeries, the capability of soft manipulators to provide a greater degree of flexibility and inherently safe interactions shows great promise that motivates further study. Nevertheless, introducing softness consequently opens new challenges in achieving accurate positional control, stability and sufficient force generation to meet application requirements.

© Springer Nature Switzerland AG 2021
C. Fox et al. (Eds.): TAROS 2021, LNAI 13054, pp. 402–407, 2021.
https://doi.org/10.1007/978-3-030-89177-0_42

One of the approaches in addressing those challenges can be achieved through varying the stiffness of a soft actuator when more stability or higher force output is required [3, 4]. A common approach is achieved through granular material jamming, which can be simply demonstrated by placing fine granules into a malleable chamber and applying a negative pressure to increase the friction effect between particles causing a "phase change" [5]. The STIFF-FLOP successfully demonstrated the benefits of variable stiffening in the context of minimally invasive surgery by combining material jamming with flexible fluid actuation (FFA) techniques to produce a highly flexible soft arm inspired by the variable stiffness achieved by octopus tentacles [6].

Effective scaling down of soft manipulators utilising granular jamming is often challenging as the granular jamming encounters issues at tighter channel volumes due to material packing, which blocks the vacuum being applied to the rest of the channel. Additionally, as the stiffening channel diameter is reduced, the stiffness effect becomes much weaker due to a reduction in overall surface friction between the fewer particles present. This has motivated the investigation of other jamming techniques such as layer jamming approaches [7, 8], or jamming through interlocking structures [5]. In this paper, the feasibility of a controlled stiffening mechanism based on tendon-twisting is investigated, which draws inspiration from textile applications in which the modelling of structure and mechanical parameters of ropes used in yarns is of interest [9]. Recent work has also demonstrated the potential of twisting individual tendons along their axis to achieve a controlled stiffening effect [10]. The proposed tendon-twisting approach is an alternative stiffening mechanism for soft actuators that can be potentially scaled up or down as needed based on the number and diameter of tendons, material properties, and the arrangements, while offering simple means of controlling a gradual increase in stiffening during operation.

2 Design and Fabrication

The design of the soft fluidic actuator used in this work was based on the STIFF-FLOP surgical manipulator [6]. The actuator retains the three pneumatic chambers of the STIFF-FLOP module, while replacing the granular jamming in the middle core with 4 flexible tendons of equal width (Fig. 1-a), which are secured in place with a plate at the actuator tip (Fig. 1-b) and connected to a Nema 17 stepper motor (rated at 3.7 Nm of holding torque) at its base (Fig. 1-c). This motor is responsible for driving the rotation of the tendons at the base end of the actuator causing the tendons to twist against each other, which creates the desired stiffening effect due to friction between the tendons. The stiffening is hence a function of the degree of rotation, so can be changed gradually to achieve desired stiffness, unlike other stiffening methods that switch between stiff or relaxed states.

A custom enclosing mould was designed and 3D printed to facilitate moulding the proposed tendon-twisting soft actuator from Ecoflex-50 and following the dimensions on the Soft Robotics Toolkit[1]. Three off-the-shelf tendons of varying degree of flexibility were compared here which are: Ninjaflex, polypropene rope, and steel wire. The

---

[1] More information can be found at www.softroboticstoolkit.com.

Silicone Body (EcoFlex)

Tendons

Fig. 1. Actuator construction from left to right: (a) Actuator design showing internal core, (b) braided polypropylene rope with end cap, (c) stepper motor twisting the tendons in the core.

choice was made based on the ease of availability and to cover a wide range of material flexibility to assess the feasibility of achieving the desired stiffening effect through twisting. Furthermore, the tendons were tested in two arrangements; straight and braided (Fig. 1-b) - to evaluate the impact of braiding the tendons on the stiffening range.

3   Experimental Characterisation of Stiffening

The experimental setup shown in Fig. 2 was used to assess the range of stiffness achieved when testing the tendon-twisting soft actuator using each of the three tendon materials at both braided and straight cases. An Arduino Uno board controls two stepper motors through a motor driver circuit to control the z-axis displacement of the actuator on the test rig and the twisting angle of the tendons inside the actuator core. For each experiment, the actuator is gradually driven downwards along the z-axis against a 3D printed rectangular object mounted on top of a sensitive force-torque sensor (ATI mini45), then reset to the initial location. This is repeated automatically four times for each test. Tendons are twisted by rotating the torsion control motor clockwise by 2/5 of a full rotation between iterations until the fixed end starts slipping or the actuators becomes too stiff to twist any further. A Matlab Simulink model simultaneously records time-series force data from the force-torque sensor and image feeds from a camera to monitor the actuator deformation during testing.

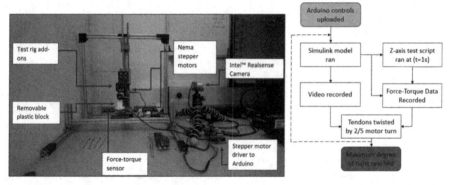

Fig. 2. From left to right: (a) components of the experimental setup, with the z-axis acting vertically, (b) simplified model of experiment procedure.

4   Results

The preliminary results of the experiment are summarised in Fig. 3 which compares the three tendon materials used for each of the braided and unbraided cases. Overall, the results in both graphs show a proportional increase in stiffness as the tendon twisting is increased, although the response is not always linear as it is the case for the Ninjaflex tendons. This is likely due to the non-linear material behavior and slippage between tendons particularly when braided. Additionally, the results indicate that when using straight (unbraided) tendons (Fig. 3-a), the stiffer tendons exhibit a higher percentage increase in force, reaching a maximum of around 268% for the steel wire within the tested twisting range. The percentage change in force was calculated along the z-axis direction (Fz) by comparing the first value recorded without tendon twisting (relaxed state) and the final Fz value achieved at maximum possible degree of rotation (stiff state). However, using very soft and flexible tendons, like the polypropylene rope, causes a negligible change in Fz. On the other hand, when tendons are braided (as in Fig. 3-b) the stiffening effect is potentially enhanced for the flexible tendons, with Ninjaflex tendons achieving a maximum overall increase in Fz of nearly 332%. At the same time, the percentage increase in Fz for the steel rod actually reduces upon braiding due to a significant increase in the actuator's initial stiffness, which results in double the initial forces recorded before any twisting (relaxed state), while the final achieved force at maximum twisting remained nearly the same. This has also limited the maximum possible twisting angle as the motor reached its torque limit.

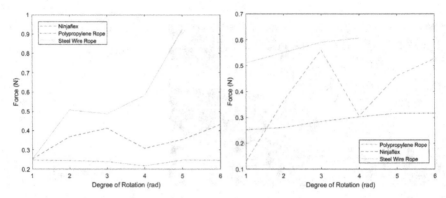

Fig. 3. Z-axis force-torque data plotted until second peak from left to right: (a) unbraided tendon configuration, (b) braided tendon configuration.

5 Conclusions and Future Work

The results of this feasibility study highlighted the potential of achieving controlled variable stiffness in a soft cylindrical actuator based on the proposed idea of flexible tendon twisting. The method offers an easy to control stiffening method using stepper motor rotation, which can be scaled up or down based on the number and diameter of the tendons used. The results generally suggest that the choice of materials plays a critical role, although would require further study to characterise and model the impact of specific material properties such as elasticity and surface roughness in more details. Among the tested three materials, there was a correlation between material flexibility and an increase in stiffness upon twisting. If the tendon is too soft and flexible (such as the case of polypropylene rope) it does not generate a noticeable increase in stiffness, while a significant increase in stiffness can be achieved using the stiffer steel wires. Furthermore, preliminary tests showed that braiding the tendons rather than inserting those as straight can potentially enhance the stiffening effect for those flexible filaments, yet decreased the stiffening for stainless-steel wire. This is due to the increase of the initial stiffness of the actuator before any twisting, so the range of generated forces becomes narrower and hence reduces the desired variable stiffening behaviour. Further work will investigate the effect of specific material properties on enhancing the stiffening effect via modelling and further experimental validation to identify the optimum choice of materials properties to maximise the stiffening range. This would be desired in various applications where a soft touch as well as forceful interactions could be simultaneously required, as it is the case with non-invasive surgeries. Furthermore, varying the number of tendons and types of braiding patterns using thinner tendons will be further investigated as a way to enhance the range of force generation while retaining the compactness and desired initial softness of the actuator before stiffening.

References

1. Coyle, S., Majidi, C., LeDuc, P., Hsia, K.J.: Bio-inspired soft robotics: material selection, actuation, and design. Extreme Mech. Lett. **22**, 51–59 (2018)

2. Marachese, A.D., Katzschmann, R.K., Rus, D.: A recipe for soft fluidic elastomer robots. Soft Robot. **2**(1), 7–25 (2015)
3. Manti, M., Cacucciolo, V., Cianchetti, M.: Stiffening in soft robotics: a review of the state of the art. IEEE Robot. Autom. Mag. **23**(3), 93–106 (2016)
4. Fitzgerald, S.G., Delaney, G.W., Howard, D.: A review of jamming actuation in soft robotics. MDPI, Brisbane (2020)
5. Goti, K., Katz, S., Baharlou, E., Vasey, L., Menges, A.: Jamming Formations - Intuitive design and fabrication process through human-computer interaction. Interact. – Hum.-Comput. **1**, 669 (2020)
6. Cianchetti, M., Ranzani, T., Gerboni, G., De Falco, I., Laschi, C., Menciassi, A.: STIFF-FLOP surgical manipulator: mechanical design and experimental characterization of the single module. In: International Conference on Intelligent Robots and Systems, Tokyo (2013)
7. Kim, Y.J., Cheng, S., Kim, S., Iagnemma, K.D.: Design of a tubular snakelike manipulator with stiffening capability by layer jamming. In: Proceedings of IEEE/RSJ International Conference on Intelligent Robots and Systems, pp. 4251–4256 (2012)
8. Kim, Y.J., Cheng, S., Kim, S., Iagnemma, K.: A novel layer jamming mechanism with tunable stiffness capability for minimally invasive surgery. IEEE Trans. Rob. **29**(4), 1031–1042 (2013)
9. Grabowska, K., Ciesielska, I.: Micro-CT supporting structural analysis and modelling of ropes made of natural fibers. Text. Res. J. (2015)
10. Helps, T., Taghavi, M., Wang, S., Rossiter, J.: Twisted rubber variable-stiffness artificial muscles. Soft Rob. **7**(3), 386 (2020)
11. Li, S., Vogt, D.M., Rus, D., Wood, R.J.: Fluid-driven origami-inspired artificial muscles. In: Proceedings of the National Academy of Sciences of the United States of America (2017)

WhiskEye: A Biomimetic Model of Multisensory Spatial Memory Based on Sensory Reconstruction

Thomas C. Knowles$^{(\boxtimes)}$ (ID), Rachael Stentiford, and Martin J. Pearson (ID)

Bristol Robotics Laboratory, University of the West of England, Bristol, UK
tom.knowles@brl.ac.uk
https://www.bristolroboticslab.com/

Abstract. We present WhiskEye, a visual tactile robot supporting a neurorobotic investigation of spatial memory as a multisensory reconstructive process. This article outlines the motivation for building WhiskEye; the technical details of the physical robot, and the publicly available simulated platform via the NeuroRobotics Platform (NRP) from the Human Brain Project; and the biomimetic control architecture. The multisensory reconstruction model of place recognition based on deep predictive coding network is presented and datasets collected from the NRP are used to train and test the network. We demonstrate that the joint latent representations inferred by this system are positively correlated to displacements in pose space suggesting it is an advantageous sensory processing front-end for our neuro-plausible model of spatial memory.

Keywords: Neurorobotics · Neural networks · Multisensory inference

1 Introduction

As we move through the world we see, touch, smell, taste and hear the environment around us. We use this sensory information to navigate safely and to plan routes to previously visited locations. How this multisensory information is represented, stored and recalled by the brain to aid in navigation is not fully understood. In the 19th century Heinrich von Helmholtz proposed that the brain was not a passive observer of the environment through the senses, rather it was actively engaged in predicting how the world behaves [8]. This conceptual shift in understanding has become increasingly popular in contemporary neuroscience research with many works advocating and demonstrating the role of prediction in describing physiology and behaviour [2,6,18]. Models for how the neocortex may implement this learning have also been proposed [19] which in turn has resulted in neural network models that can be constructed and implemented using the readily available machine learning toolboxes [3]. Deep predictive coding neural networks differ from conventional deep learning neural networks in that the error correction step applied to the weight array is computed locally in each training

© Springer Nature Switzerland AG 2021
C. Fox et al. (Eds.): TAROS 2021, LNAI 13054, pp. 408–418, 2021.
https://doi.org/10.1007/978-3-030-89177-0_43

epoch in parallel across the network, i.e., the global derivative and back propagation of error is not required. Instead each layer in the network attempts to predict the output of the previous layer, refining its predictions by comparing them to the actual output. In other words, higher layers are trained to reconstruct the activity of lower layers but using an increasingly smaller dimensional representation space to do so. This enables a hierarchical learning of representations but with the benefit of priors that can anticipate familiar sensory inputs by generating predictions that are tested against incoming evidence.

In this paper we describe how such a network has been integrated into the processing architecture of a biomimetic multisensory robot called WhiskEye. WhiskEye has an array of active tactile whiskers and cameras for eyes that explores its environment in an ethologically plausible way. Using a model of tactile attention, it gathers visual and tactile impressions from its environment which are used to train a multimodal predictive coding implementation called MultiPredNet. The representations generated by this network show a strong correlation to pose space, and thus are useful for place recognition.

The main contributions of this paper are:

1. Overview of a novel multisensory biomimetic robot platform
2. Introduction of a publicly available simulation platform of the WhiskEye
3. A neuroplausible multimodal deep predictive coding network model that can combine vision and tactile sensory information
4. A demonstration that the network model can generate representations that are beneficial to place recognition.

2   Related Work

The brain is renowned for its ability to combine different modalities to solve problems, in artificial systems we refer to this ability as sensor fusion [10]. Model free approaches to sensor fusion include Variational AutoEncoders (VAEs) which have proven successful by being able to create joint latent spaces that encode the regularities between multiple modalities [11]. Predictive coding systems take this a step further by using bio-plausible learning rules and generating representations at each layer, whilst also showing the ability to extract disentangled latent variables [13]. To the best of our knowledge this approach has not been applied specifically to place recognition.

RatSLAM [14] is a successful Simultaneous Localisation and Mapping (SLAM) approach inspired, like WhiskEye, by rat behaviour. Unlike RatSLAM, this paper does not purport to solve the full SLAM problem, instead focusing on representation learning for place recognition. This is equivalent to the sensory front-end of RatSLAM, processing raw sensor data into a form suitable for a future downstream mapping system. The use of whisker-based touch has been successfully incorporated into a SLAM system before [5] and is promising in terms of the redundancy and robustness it offers. WhiskEye builds on prior works using whisker based tactile sensing for mobile robots [16,17] by introducing the head-mounted cameras to coarsely approximate rat vision and allowing us to capture rich multisensory datasets during mobile exploration.

3   Materials and Methods

3.1   WhiskEye Platform

(a) Physical WhiskEye in the BRL test arena

(b) Simulated WhiskEye in an NRP virtual arena

Fig. 1. Both incarnations of WhiskEye. Note the differences in whisker shape and simplified structure of the simulated model, with extraneous detail like wires and the onboard display omitted.

Hardware. The main physical components of WhiskEye are the head, neck and body. The body is a Robotino™ chassis from Festo Didactic, with an onboard Intel computer running the robot control software, including ROS. This computer communicates to a head mounted master SPI bus that controls much of the robot's behaviour. Within the Robotino™ is an ARM microcomputer that itself runs ROS, interacting as a ROS device with the onboard computer. Logs and data are sent via wi-fi to a remote desktop. Three omni-wheels allow for arbitrary motion in x, y and θ (Fig. 1).

The neck is custom-built, attaching to the front of the Robotino chassis with a USB connection to the onboard computer. This USB is set up as a ROS device, allowing for data to be read from sensors and commands to be sent to neck and head actuators.

The head is also custom-built, mounting the aforementioned head SPI master. This controls the 6 whisker arrays and neck via 7 slave SPIs. Each whisker array consists of 4 whisker complexes, each with its own motor, ARM processor, a 2-axis Hall Effect sensor and the whisker proper; a flexible, tapering plastic rod that mimics small mammal whiskers. Each ARM processor coordinates its whiskers to generate 'whisks' of synchronised movement across the array, but allows each to respond individually to impingement for whisker-specific retraction.

Neurorobotics Platform. The NeuroRobotics Platform (NRP) [4] is a web based robotics and neuroscience research tool for neuroscience based robotics experiments, particularly through time sensitive coupling between Gazebo and spiking neural network simulators such as NEST. For very large network models it also provides an API to deploy on the SpiNNaker neuromorphic supercomputer [7]. A CAD model of WhiskEye has been instantiated into the NRP with a Gazebo-ROS plugin deployed to mirror the interface of the physical platform described above. To accommodate the flexible whiskers within Gazebo's rigid body physics, whisker collisions were disabled; instead, surface penetration depth was used to calculate the corresponding force experienced at the base of each whisker in the 2 orthogonal planes (x_{whisk}, y_{whisk}). Crucially, the NRP hosts the same ROS control architectures as the physical robot, ensuring parity between simulated and physical behaviour.

Control Architecture. WhiskEye's movements are initiated and coordinated through a model of whisker based tactile attention derived from prior work [15]. It is composed of an interconnected network of functional models of mid brain structures of the rat that have been modelled using Python and compatible with ROS. Each module encapsulates a specific set of functions necessary for control, with many modules implementing neuro-plausible functional models.

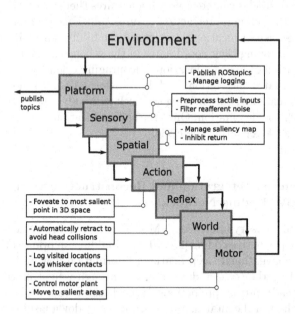

Fig. 2. Cascading view of control functions. Each function is called sequentially and contributes to the final, salience-guided foveation, sampling the environment in an ethologically plausible way. ROStopics of cameras and whiskers are published, permitting collection of datasets for MultiPredNet training (Sect. 3.2)

Figure 2 shows WhiskEye's cascade of controller functions that each contribute to the final behaviour of the robot:-

– Platform - creates publishers for all relevant ROStopics that can be subscribed to both internally (such as whisker inputs for tactile attention) and externally (for monitoring and data collection).
– Sensory - preprocesses incoming sensory data, reshaping and removing reafferent noise with a high-pass filter, preserving deflections caused by impingement; loosely analogous to a proposed cerebellar role for re-afferent sensory prediction [1].
– Spatial - manages a Superior Colliculus-inspired salience map fed by tactile data. This determines where the robot will orient to. Local space is mapped as head-centric (x_h, y_h, z_h) and the most salient location identified. If its salience exceeds a threshold, the coordinates pass to the Action module. If not, structured noise is applied that raises salience around the fovea until a candidate location is found.
– Action - inspired by the Basal Ganglia - deciding how to act, and how much - the desired position in head space is transformed into world space (x_w, y_w, z_w). The difference between the current and desired position forms the movement vector describing the orient required.
– Reflex - responds via callbacks to any potential collisions that a movement can cause; since obstacles can be interesting features themselves, this is a common occurrence. Proportional retraction ensures collisions are minimised.
– World - logs visited locations, implementing Inhibition of Return (IoR) by temporarily masking their coordinates in the salience map. This avoids incessant exploration of a single location, encouraging orienting to novel areas.
– Motor - translates the Action module transformations to motor commands. Orienting is head-led, only moving the neck and body if head movement alone cannot reach the destination. Once the salient location is reached, a whisking bout is induced, repeating the cycle.

3.2   Multisensory Integration and Reconstruction Using Multimodal Predictive Coding Network

To generate multisensory inferences, a MultiPredNet architecture is used[1]. Based on principles of predictive coding [2,6,19] and building on prior work [3], this network flips the conventional Deep Learning information flow on its head. Rather than being led by the sensory data filtering through weight matrices, the MultiPredNet instead leads by predictions. Hypothesised 'causes', high-level predictions of what the world contains, are passed in a top-down fashion and compared with the sensory input at each level. The remainder of the signal - that not predicted by the causes - will continue to propagate upwards.

---

[1] Code and data can be found at:
https://github.com/TomKnowles1994/MultiPredNet/releases/tag/1.3.2.

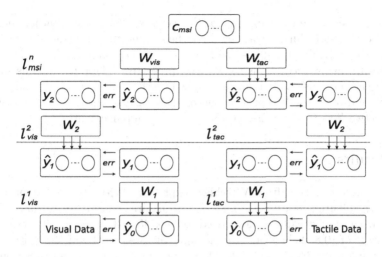

Fig. 3. The MultiPredNet architecture. Each layer contains a filter of learned weights (W_x) and receives top-down, hypothesised causes (c_x) of the input at the preceding ($l - 1$) layer. Causes pass through these weights, generating predictions of lower layer cause values. Discrepancy between predictions and causes propagate to higher layers as error gradients. The topmost layer integrates both modalities, learning a single set of causes that, filtered through modality-specific weights, reconstruct each unimodal data input.

The MultiPredNet begins with randomly initialised weights and arbitrary cause values (0.1 by default). Each layer of causes ($\mathbf{y}^{(l)}$) is updated in parallel with a Hebbian-like learning rule:

$$\Delta\mathbf{y}^{(l)} = \eta_y \left(\mathbf{W}^{l(l-1)}\phi'(\hat{\mathbf{y}}^{(l-1)}) \left(\left(\mathbf{y}^{(l-1)} - \hat{\mathbf{y}}^{(l-1)}\right) + \left(\mathbf{y}^{(l)} - \hat{\mathbf{y}}^{(l)}\right) \right) \right) \quad (1)$$

where η_y is the learning rate and ϕ' is the derivative of the activation function. Error component ($\mathbf{y}^{(l-1)} - \hat{\mathbf{y}}^{(l-1)}$) is the bottom-up error, comparing the prediction derived from the upper cause to the actual value of the causes. This penalises causes that cause poor predictions of lower layer causes. Error component ($\mathbf{y}^{(l)} - \hat{\mathbf{y}}^{(l)}$) is the top-down error, comparing the current value of the cause to what it was predicted to be by $\mathbf{y}^{(l+1)}$. This penalises causes that are difficult to predict by higher layers. Note that $\mathbf{y}^{(l+1)}$ is not a component of this learning rule, as its own value is not required to update $\mathbf{y}^{(l)}$, only its prediction ($\hat{\mathbf{y}}^{(l)}$). Note that for the uppermost layer, there is no higher layer to predict causes, and thus top-down error is treated as 0.

Each layer has a threshold defines the margin of error (10^{-3} to 10^{-4}) between a cause (or data item) and its prediction. Once all layers are within their error criteria (or after a maximum number of iterations), inference stops and the final causes values compared to the predictions. Further discrepancy between final causes and predictions leads to a weight update as per:

$$\Delta\mathbf{W}_{l(l-1)} = \eta_w \mathbf{y}^{(l)}\phi'(\hat{\mathbf{y}}^{(l-1)}) \left(\mathbf{y}^{(l-1)} - \hat{\mathbf{y}}^{(l-1)} \right)^T \quad (2)$$

with η_w being the learning rate for the weights. This iterative adjustment of causes occurs both during training and when generating inferences. Inferences do not invoke weight updates - the filters are 'fixed' - and rely on adjustment of causes to match predictions to the data presented. These predictions should therefore not be considered a direct window into the latent representations of the network, nor a decoded reconstruction of such, instead being a live hypothesis of the network as to the causes of the l_x^0 sensory impingement.

4 Results

Datasets were collected from WhiskEye exploring a virtual ovoid arena populated with coloured cubes and cylinders. Visual data consisted of 3-channel RGB images from the left camera, downsized to $80 \times 45 \times 3$ pixels and flattened into a 1-D array of 10,800 elements. Tactile data consisted of 24 whisker protractions (θ_{whisk}) and 24×2 values of deflection data (x_{whisk} and y_{whisk}) concatenated into a 1-D, 72 element array. Sampling was driven by the rat-inspired whisking behaviour described in Sect. 3.1, with 'views' in both modalities captured at the moment of whisker peak protraction; whether the whiskers reached their desired theta angle or not (due to obstacles and/or IOR).

Note the relationship between visual and tactile data (Fig. 4); a visual scene displaying largely wall implies proximity to the wall (f), and thus many whiskers colliding with the surface. The tactile data reflects this, with greater and more numerous deflections (d) in comparison to a clear visual scene (c, e). Relationships like these can be learned by MultiPredNet's multisensory layer, inferring that denser tactile input implies a more occluded visual scene and vice-versa.

The MultiPredNet was initialised with random filter weights and causes set to 0.1; two visual layers of 1000 (L_{vis}^1) and 300 (L_{vis}^2) neurons; two tactile layers of 50 (L_{tac}^1) and 20 (L_{tac}^2) neurons; and a single L_{msi} layer of 100. Causes were allowed to infer for 50 cause epochs before weight updates took place. 1900 samples of training data were divided into minibatches of 10 and the network trained for 200 training epochs. During some inferences, modalities were masked to test robustness to sensory dropout.

Figure 5 shows sample inferences generated from testsets 1 and 4 as per Sect. 3.2. Representational Similarity Analysis [12] was used to compare the distances between samples within each space. Assuming the robot can only rotate its head around the z-axis and is bound to a flat plane, its position and orientation is represented completely by a pose vector (x_{pose}, y_{pose}, θ_{pose}); a high quality reference representation useful for localisation. Therefore, if dissimilarity within pose space correlates well with that of MultiPredNet inference space, the inference will be of good quality proportional to that correlation. Results from all test sets under all conditions show a mean correlation well above significance, thus the representations generated are useful for localisation.

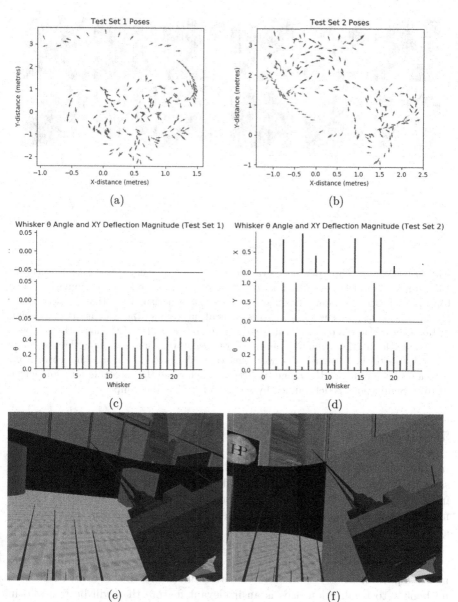

Fig. 4. A sample of MultiPredNet data from testsets 1 and 4. *a* and *b*: Quiver plot of poses $(x_{whisk}, y_{whisk}, \theta_{whisk})$ *c* and *d*: Sample instances of whisker θ_{whisk} angle alongside the resulting magnitude of whisker deflection in x_{whisk} and y_{whisk} axes. *e* and *f*: Sample instances of camera visual input.

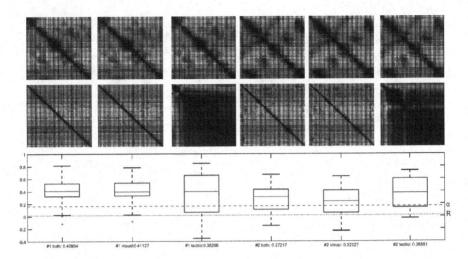

Fig. 5. RDM plots and Spearman's rank correlation coefficient scores for inferences on 100 samples from test sets 1 and 2 with visual, tactile, or both inputs unmasked. The top row of heatmaps show Euclidean distance between visited locations in pose space (x_{pose}, y_{pose}, θ_{pose}). The bottom rows of heatmaps show the 1-Pearson correlation distance between samples in MultiPredNet inference space; [12] shows this to be a more suitable metric for high-dimensional representation spaces. Below the heatmaps are boxplots of the correlation between spaces, with dotted line R marking correlation with a uniform random RDM, and dashed line α showing the threshold for significance (0.167). Significance is determined by $p < 0.05$ for $N = 100$ samples.

5   Discussion

In this paper we have described a novel multisensory robot which investigates salient environmental features in an ethological manner. The datasets from these investigations have then been used to train a multisensory predictive coding network that can generate inferences useful for place recognition. Furthermore, generated inferences remain useful even when modalities are obscured, a trait useful for real-world situations where vision is poor or whiskers are damaged.

Though fit for purpose, the datasets gathered have several areas of improvement. A prominent feature in every camera frame is the whisker array itself; with no benefit to localisation, this is an irrelevant feature that will be removed in future work to allow the network to learn more about the external environment, rather than itself. The unused right camera feed (with its own whisker array portion removed) can be used to make up the difference without altering the input shape of the network; important both for comparing results and re-using trained weights.

The results show a clear correlation between inference space and pose space, showing that *something* useful for place recognition is captured by the network, and the correlation with pose specifically suggests that the MultiPredNet's is able to extract latent features relating to the observer; namely position and orientation. However, unlike in some other generative models such as β-VAEs [9], these latent features are highly entangled and not human-legible; there are no explicit 'x_{pose}', 'y_{pose}' or 'θ_{pose}' variables in the representation, and to the extent these are represented, it is as a high-dimensional mix of other variables. In a similar vein, MultiPredNet current stores representations as single, discrete numbers, rather than as a distribution (as VAEs in general do); as VAE disentanglement factors e.g. Kullbach-Leiber Divergence require distributed representations, this makes disentangling MultiPredNet's representations by these methods intractable in their current form.

To address both these issues, future work will look towards creating a 'Variational MultiPredNet' to learn disentangled representations at each layer. We will then use this as the sensory front end of a full localisation system, using the multimodal inferences produced by the MultiPredNet as a prediction of the current pose. This inferred pose will then be used to correct for inherent drift in internal representations of self motion modelled as spiking neural networks inspired by mammalian spatial cells, a task made easier by the NRP's integration with both SpiNNaker and NEST.

Acknowledgments. This research has received funding from the European Union's Horizon 2020 Framework Programme for Research and Innovation under the Specific Grant Agreement No. 945539 (Human Brain Project SGA3).

References

1. Anderson, S.R., Porrill, J., Pearson, M.J., Pipe, A.G., Prescott, T.J., Dean, P.: An internal model architecture for novelty detection: implications for cerebellar and collicular roles in sensory processing. PLOS ONE **7**(9), 1–17 (2012)
2. Clark, A.: A nice surprise? Predictive processing and the active pursuit of novelty. Phenomenol. Cogn. Sci. **17**(3), 1572–8676 (2018)
3. Dora, S., Pennartz, C., Bohte, S.: A deep predictive coding network for inferring hierarchical causes underlying sensory inputs. In: Kůrková, V., Manolopoulos, Y., Hammer, B., Iliadis, L., Maglogiannis, I. (eds.) ICANN 2018. LNCS, vol. 11141, pp. 457–467. Springer, Cham (2018). https://doi.org/10.1007/978-3-030-01424-7_45
4. Falotico, E., et al.: Connecting artificial brains to robots in a comprehensive simulation framework: the neurorobotics platform. Front. Neurorobot. **11**, 2 (2017)
5. Fox, C., Evans, M., Pearson, M., Prescott, T.: Tactile slam with a biomimetic whiskered robot. In: 2012 IEEE International Conference on Robotics and Automation, pp. 4925–4930 (2012)
6. Friston, K.: The free-energy principle: a unified brain theory? Nat. Rev. Neurosci. **11**, 127–138 (2010)
7. Furber, S., Bogdan, P.: SpiNNaker: A Spiking Neural Network Architecture. Now publishers, Boston-Delft (2020)
8. von Helmholtz, H.: Treatise on Physiological Optics, vol. III. Dover Publications (1867)
9. Higgins, I., et al.: beta-VAE: learning basic visual concepts with a constrained variational framework. In: ICLR 2017 (2016)
10. Khaleghi, B., Khamis, A., Karray, F.O., Razavi, S.N.: Multisensor data fusion: a review of the state-of-the-art. Inf. Fusion **14**(1), 28–44 (2013)

11. Korthals, T., Hesse, M., Leitner, J., Melnik, A., Rückert, U.: Jointly trained variational autoencoder for multi-modal sensor fusion. In: 2019 22th International Conference on Information Fusion (FUSION), pp. 1–8 (2019)

12. Kriegeskorte, N., Mur, M., Bandettini, P.: Representational similarity analysis - connecting the branches of systems neuroscience. Front. Syst. Neurosci. **2**, 4 (2008)

13. Lotter, W., Kreiman, G., Cox, D.: Deep predictive coding networks for video prediction and unsupervised learning. ArXiv abs/1605.08104 (2017)

14. Milford, M., Wyeth, G., Prasser, D.: RatSLAM: a hippocampal model for simultaneous localization and mapping. In: 2004 Proceedings of IEEE International Conference on Robotics and Automation, ICRA 2004, vol. 1, pp. 403–408 (2004)

15. Mitchinson, B., Prescott, T.J.: Whisker movements reveal spatial attention: a unified computational model of active sensing control in the rat. PLOS Comput. Biol. **9**(9), 1–16 (2013)

16. Pearson, M.J., Fox, C., Sullivan, J.C., Prescott, T.J., Pipe, T., Mitchinson, B.: Simultaneous localisation and mapping on a multi-degree of freedom biomimetic whiskered robot. In: 2013 IEEE International Conference on Robotics and Automation, pp. 586–592 (2013)

17. Pearson, M.J., Pipe, A.G., Melhuish, C., Mitchinson, B., Prescott, T.J.: Whiskerbot: a robotic active touch system modeled on the rat whisker sensory system. Adapt. Behav. **15**(3), 223–240 (2007)

18. Pennartz, C.M.: The Brain's Representational Power: On Consciousness and the Integration of Modalities. The MIT Press, Cambridge (2015)

19. Rao, R., Ballard, D.: Predictive coding in the visual cortex: a functional interpretation of some extra-classical receptive-field effects. Nat. Neurosci. **2**, 79–87 (1999)

Equipment Detection Based Inspection Robot for Industrial Plants

Mohamed Heshmat[1,2](✉) ⬤ and Yang Gao[3]

[1] University of the West of England, UWE Bristol, Bristol, UK
mohamed.abdelwahab@uwe.ac.uk
[2] Faculty of Science, Sohag University, Sohag, Egypt
[3] Surrey Space Centre, University of Surrey, Guildford, UK
yang.gao@surrey.ac.uk

Abstract. Industries move toward the replacement of labours engaged in dangerous tasks with fully automated systems. The sixth sense technology aims at achieving that by integrating different technologies in such a way that enables monitoring of industrial plants and predicting any faults that could happen. One important module of the sixth sense technology is inspection robots. This paper aims at providing the inspection robots with equipment-detection capability, resembling the human inspectors performing the customised inspection for a variety of equipment. The types of equipment, used in this study, are reactor, boiler, pump, isolated pipes, meter gauge, and valves. Given the complexity of the industrial environment, we propose a real-time deep-learning-based equipment detection model. The results show that the mean average precision is above 90%, which ensure the significant performance of the proposed solution. This work validates the practicality of our equipment-detection model and shows its potential to be employed on our inspection robot.

Keywords: Industrial inspection · Inspection robot · Equipment detection

1 Introduction

Industry 4.0 is transforming industrial processes into complex, smart cyber-physical systems that require intelligent methods to support safer operations. Under these conditions, it is extremely difficult to manage all available information, infer the desired conditions of the plant and take timely decisions to handle abnormal operations [1]. Thus, a technology that could help in preventing human error and stop chain reactions that can transform small incidents into catastrophic failure is required. The sixth sense, 6S technology aims to achieve that need by analysing the present data and generating a vision of the future.

Inspection is the practice of examining the condition of equipment to find out if it operates as intended. The implementation of routine inspection is an essential measure to ensure a safe and efficient production process. For the inspection tasks, checkpoints which mainly include key equipment, pipelines, key valves, gauges, and control points

© Springer Nature Switzerland AG 2021
C. Fox et al. (Eds.): TAROS 2021, LNAI 13054, pp. 419–429, 2021.
https://doi.org/10.1007/978-3-030-89177-0_44

are defined for the inspector. A leak of gas or liquid is searched by sight and smell. Valves and gauges are examined to understand the operating status of the equipment. For equipment such as pumps, human inspectors need to listen to the sound of their operation or use specific instruments to detect vibration anomalies.

Although these tasks are repetitive and time-consuming, and some of these environments may be hazardous, humans are still relied on for doing these tasks. Long-time close exposure to such environment may cause diseases or even kill in anomalies such as toxic gas leaks and explosions which are not infrequent. Therefore, there is a strong motivation to replace manual inspectors with robots and free them up to perform more complex tasks. On the other hand, manual inspection or operation can be error-prone since human errors are key causes of accidents [2].

Inspector robots can be considered the logical human replacement for doing these tasks. The current robots' capabilities enable these tasks to be carried out efficiently. Examples of these capabilities are autonomous navigation, exploring dangerous or inaccessible sites, a variety of sensors that can be equipped on the robot, quick analysis of sensors data, and relatively lower cost and less time for executing tasks. As the modern plants become larger and more complex, qualified professional's capabilities are required more creative tasks than routine inspections.

In inspecting any site human inspectors are familiar with the equipment and tools that are available on this site, in addition to, equipment history. The 6S framework could provide robots with the required information and history of available equipment. For the inspection tasks, robots need a very basic skill for human inspectors which is detection and identification of available equipment in the environment. The main contribution of this paper can be described as follows: a deep-learning-based equipment-detection method for inspection robots in industrial sites within the vision of industry 4.0 and the 6S technology.

The rest of this paper is structured as follows. Section 2 reviews the previous works in robotic inspection systems. Section 3 explains the 6S technology and the robot inspection strategy. Section 4 shows the deep-learning-based equipment-detection method development and evaluation. Section 5 presents conclusions and future works of this work.

2   Robotic Inspection Literature

In the last decade, there was a growing interest in employing robots for inspection tasks in process plants, due to the compatibility of robots for these tasks. The potential of applying robots for these tasks has been proven [3]. Some projects were funded in this direction such as RoboGasInspector [4], MAINBOT [5], and PETROBOT [6]. The main target for these projects was to develop robotic inspection systems for different industrial environments. In the recent past, Total company organized the ARGOS challenge of creating the first autonomous robot for oil and gas sites [7]. This competition was organized in three rounds. Through these rounds, the robot is required to work autonomously for surveillance tasks. During these rounds, the robot should inspect various visual checkpoints like pressure gauges and valves, and monitor the plant for thermal hot spots, gas leaks and sound signals.

In [8], the authors developed an inspection system to inspect substation equipment. They used a four-wheel robot equipped with a magnetic sensor, RFID reader, pan-tilt camera, lidar sensor, Infrared thermal camera, and directional microphone. The robot follows magnetic markers as checkpoints for the inspection tasks. For this system, checkpoints are needed to be defined for the robot to execute the inspection tasks using the right sensors. We aim at advancing our inspector with a higher perception advantage which is the equipment identification. The importance of that has been demonstrated in [9]. As a result, the inspector robot will not need checkpoints to be defined. The human inspectors can identify equipment types and based on that decide inspection tasks for this type of equipment. For instance, upon detecting a boiler, the inspector ensures that there is no leakage and checks the upper valve state. If a pipe is detected, he checks the pipe visually, especially, the connections and uses the thermal camera to detect the temperature of this pipe. The 6S technology framework keeps track of the history of available equipment and will provide the inspector robots with such information to facilitate inspection tasks. Likewise, the inspector robot will send routine equipment inspection information to the main system, and if a new piece of equipment is detected.

3   System Overview

3.1   The Industrial 6S

The 6S technology is an intelligent monitoring and control framework for industrial processes, which takes advantage of technological advances such as wireless sensor networks, 5G communication, cooperative control, intelligent decision-making framework, and robotics to ensure stable process operation. The general framework of 6S technology is shown in Fig. 1. Six main modules constitute the structure of this framework. These modules are the holistic system models and cooperative control, massive connectivity resilient network communication, machine learning fault detection and prediction, intelligent adaptive decision-making, virtual reality system, and autonomous inspector robots.

The 6S architecture divides into physical and cyber layers. The physical layer where the industrial process itself, wireless sensors and actuators, physical controllers, and inspector robots are available. In the cyber layer, the wireless communication network, data and models centre, fault detection and prediction algorithms, and decision-making framework are located.

The architecture is designed as a modular architecture. Within the 6S technology, the decision-making framework should make recommendations about the process state to the human operator. Also, it defines the tasks for the inspector robots, normal inspection tasks or other more specific tasks based on the current situation. The main task for the inspector robot is to patrol around the plant to detect abnormal situations (routine inspection) within the vision of 6S technology. The application of the proposed architecture is investigated on a pilot plant that is available at University of Surrey, United Kingdom. Photos of this pilot plant are shown in Fig. 2. These photos show the complex tanged environment where the robots work.

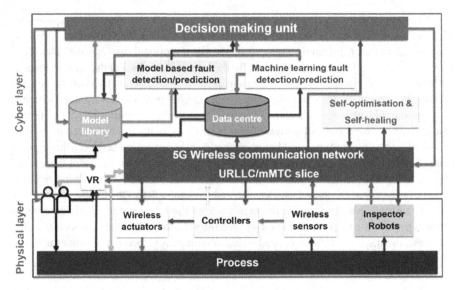

Fig. 1. The 6S technology framework

Fig. 2. The pilot plant photos on the left and the inspector robot for industrial sites on the right.

3.2 The Inspection Strategy

Our inspector robot is a small four-wheel Pioneer 3-AT mobile robot equipped with an RGBD camera, 2D laser range finder, infrared camera, acoustic & gas sensors board as shown in (Fig. 2). These sensors were selected based on their suitability for inspection tasks in this environment. The robot size is chosen to be suitable for the inspection application in small and medium industrial processes, as the robot may need to maneuver around equipment and pipes which are, usually, available in this environment.

In the current state of periodic inspection tasks of industrial sites, the human inspectors could perform these tasks with a degree of efficiency, but these tasks are repetitive, the environment itself could be hazardous, and in the end, errors still could happen. Therefore, the need for inspector robots became clear. The current robots' systems able to fill human inspector duties efficiently.

In inspecting any site, human inspectors are familiar with the equipment and tools available on this site in addition to the history behind each piece of equipment. The 6S framework could do this role and provide the robots with information and history about available equipment. One skill still the robots need to be equipped with to be able to do inspection tasks is the identification of the available equipment in the environment.

As a general system is targeted, solely defining the equipment positions is not sufficient for the robot to do the inspection tasks. Also, these sites are, usually, dynamic environments and a lot of equipment could be added or removed from the site. Thus, the inspector robots need to be equipped with this capability to execute these tasks efficiently. Moreover, the inspector robots may need to interact and integrate with other human inspectors if they are available. Consequently, they need to have the same philosophy of doing the inspection tasks which make the interaction much easier.

For our inspection strategy hierarchy, the first task is the detection of equipment type. Six types of equipment are investigated in this study and these pieces of equipment are available in our pilot plant environment where our robot will be tested. Based on the equipment type, the robot decides the required inspection task list to be carried out. Each type of equipment requires different sensors to be used and different inspection checklists to be executed. These types of equipment are reactor, boiler, pump, isolated pipes, meter gauge, and valves.

Table 1 summarizes the inspection checklist for each equipment type. Inspired by the human inspector, the robot will begin any inspection task by collecting information history of this piece of equipment from the 6S main system. The 6S framework supplies the robot with information about the equipment previous status, maintenance history, and normal working condition. This information will differ from one to another and will support the robots in proceeding with their tasks and detecting anomalous conditions. Later, the robots will forward their inspection data to the main 6S framework for records.

4   Equipment Detection

4.1   Development

For an equipment-detection based robotic inspection system, a real-time solution is needed to fulfil task necessity. The object detection process includes the classification and localization of objects in the image. Single-shot object detectors which take one shot to detect objects that are presented in the image are considered appropriate in the context. These algorithms are fast and high-accurate object detection algorithms. From these algorithms, we selected the You Only Look Once, YOLO algorithm [10].

YOLO is considered the state of art object detection, single-shot algorithm. It is a real-time object detection that is developed for object detection of camera images. It consists of a single convolutional network that simultaneously predicts multiple objects with class probabilities for those objects. YOLO trains on full images and, directly optimises

Table 1. Equipment inspection checklist.

Equipment	Checklist
Reactor	- Get history information from the 6S main system - Check the pipes and the pump that are usually attached - Check the body with the IR camera
Boiler	- Get history information from the 6S main system - Check the pipes and the valve that are usually attached - Check the body with the IR camera
Isolated pipe	- Get history information from the 6S main system - Check the pipe with IR camera especially the connections
Pump	- Get history information from the 6S main system - Check the body with the IR camera - Check the sound with the acoustic sensor
Meter gauge	- Get history information from the 6S main system - Read the gauge measurement value
Valve	- Get history information from the 6S main system - Detect the valve state (Open or Closed)

detection performance. The YOLO algorithm detects, classifies, and identifies objects in the image frame and draw a rectangular bounding box around it. Through this work, the darknet YOLO v3 framework has been used. The darknet is an open-source neural network framework written in C and CUDA [11].

The development work was conducted in three stages, dataset collection, training, and validation. The dataset collection has two purposes: a collection and annotation of the equipment image dataset at University of Surrey pilot plant. After human visual inspection of images and confirmation of their correctness and quality, these images were annotated manually. The dataset was split into training and validation datasets. The whole dataset was 1267 images, the training dataset was 80% of the original dataset, and the validation dataset was the remaining 20%. Visual inspection of the resulting datasets reveals multiple challenges associated such as blurring, scale variation, occlusion, and background clutter.

To accelerate the training process, we used partial pre-trained weights as the initial training model [12]. The training process was carried out using GPU (GeForce GTX 1050) and Intel Core i7 2.8 GHz CPU. During the training process, loss function was monitored all the time. YOLO uses the sum-squared error between predictions and ground truth to calculate the loss value. The loss function composes of classification loss, localization loss (errors between predicted boundary box and ground truth), and confidence loss. The final loss value is the sum of these values.

The validation process takes place, using the validation dataset, periodically during the training process. The trained model should achieve an appropriate accuracy for the intended task, and so the PASCAL VOC evaluation metrics are used, to evaluate the classification and localization performance of the equipment detection model [13]. The first of these metrics is detection precision, which is calculated as the ratio between the number of positive samples correctly classified to the total number of samples classified as positive (either correctly or incorrectly). The precision measures the model's accuracy in classifying a sample as positive. Second, the detection recall, which is calculated as the ratio between the number of positive samples correctly classified as positive to the total number of positive samples. The recall measures the model's ability to detect positive samples. Third, the intersection-over-union (IoU), which represents the intersection over the union of objects and detections for a certain detection confidence threshold.

Average precision (AP) is another popular evaluation metric in measuring the accuracy of object detectors. AP can be defined as the average of maximum precision at different recalls. Mean average precision (mAP), which is used to evaluate the validation process, is defined as the average of APs over all classes. Another evaluation metric that is investigated in this work $F1_{score}$. The $F1_{score}$ is another measure of model accuracy, it considers both precision and recall of the model to compute the score. It represents the harmonic mean of the precision and recall, where an $F1_{score}$ reaches its best value at 1 (perfect precision and recall) and worst at 0.

$$F1_{score} = \frac{(Precision * Recall)}{(Precision + Recall)} \tag{1}$$

4.2 Evaluation

To validate and monitor detector performance, mAP was periodically calculated using the validation dataset during the training process. This helps ensure that the detector maintains global performance during training without overfitting or underfitting problems. Overfitting is where a model learns the training dataset too well, performing well on the training dataset but does not perform well on a holdout sample. On the opposite, underfitting is where a model fails to sufficiently learn the problem and performs poorly even on a training dataset.

The threshold of object bounding boxes confidence is an important parameter to tune for better object detection. The confidence threshold is defined as IoU between the predicted box and the ground truth. a confidence threshold of 50% means that we will accept proposals that believe their bounding boxes have more than 50% overlap with a real object. The increased confidence threshold leads to fewer bounding box proposals for each image. The decrease in the confidence threshold results in more bounding boxes.

Figure 3 shows the training loss value and validation mAP percentage over 12000 iterations. The validation mAP was computed over periods of training iterations. The minimal variation in loss during training as well as steady convergence to a small number (0.0875) shows that the optimiser was able to find the global minimum of the loss function. The validation of this model shows accurate detection with (91.6%) mAP. Also, from Fig. 3, we can observe that the use of a partial pre-trained initial model helped the neural network to converge very quickly.

Table 2 summarizes the evaluation details for each class and the whole model in general. The general model evaluations have been done on Confidence = 0.50. The evaluation results show 0.96 precision which shows the recognisable consistency of our model. The 0.86 recall result shows that our model can mostly return the relevant results.

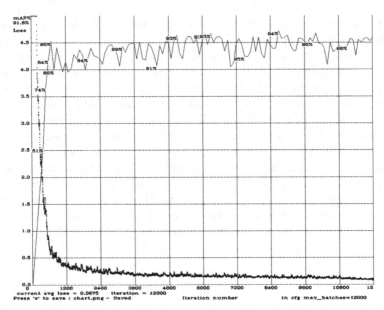

Fig. 3. The training loss and validation mAP of the equipment detection model.

The F1score combines the precision and recall of the model. The result F1score = 0.91 reflects the robustness of the detector overall performance. The predicted bounding boxes overlapping with the ground truth is shown with IoU = 78.09%, which means that that the predicted and ground truth bounding boxes almost overlap. The evaluation metrics show the accuracy of our model for detecting equipment in the industrial environment.

Table 2. Equipment detection evaluations.

Equipment	AP	True positive	False positive
Reactor	81.08%	27	3
Boiler	93.48%	62	3
Isolated pipe	86.35%	170	11
Pump	99.43%	119	2
Meter gauge	99.74%	121	2
Valve	89.53%	230	8
General model evaluation (confidence = 0.50)			
Precision = 0.96	Recall = 0.86	F1$_{score}$ = 0.91	IoU = 78.09%

The resulting evaluation of the model shows a promising accuracy in detecting different types of equipment in this difficult environment. The relatively low performance in the reactor and isolated pipes cases is due to the following reasons. The reactor case

Fig. 4. Qualitative results of the equipment detection for robotic industrial inspection

had the least amount of training data, so it needs more training data under various conditions. On the other side, although the case of the isolated pipes has the second-highest training data, it represents a very complex model to be learned as the isolated pipes can have different sizes and shapes. Also, various other objects, which are usually available in the industrial environment, could easily be misclassified as isolated pipes.

Figure 4 Shows the model qualitative results. These results show the accuracy and generalization of our model. Despite the equipment having different sizes, scales, and tangled together, our model could correctly detect the equipment available in the input images. We have tested the model for real-time equipment detection operation at the pilot plant. The recorded video shows the equipment detection capability of the model, and it could achieve more than 10 frames per second. Videos of the Industrial Robotic Inspector and the real-time equipment detection model testing is available[1].

5 Conclusions

A deep-learning-based solution for real-time equipment-detection-based inspection robotic system has been proposed for industrial plants within the vision of industry 4.0. The robotic inspection module is part of the sixth sense technology framework, which aims at monitoring the industrial plants to ensure their safety.

The development phase of the proposed solution has involved dataset collection and annotation and then training, validation, and testing of the model. This study has proposed an equipment-detection model based on the Darknet YOLO framework. The model has been carefully developed to consider the accuracy and real-time operational requirements. The trained model has evaluated, and its capabilities have been shown. The quantitative and qualitative results of the model evaluation have shown the accuracy of the equipment-detection model.

In the future, more types of equipment will be incorporated into our model using transfer learning techniques. Also, the sub-inspection tasks include valve state detection (video of visual valve state detection is available[2]), meter gauge reading, acoustic sensing, gas sensing, and thermal sensing are going to be accomplished subsequently. Eventually, we can test our inspection robot for undertaking the routine inspection at our pilot plant.

References

1. Natarajan, S., Srinivasan, R.: Implementation of multi-agents based system for process supervision. Comput. Chem. Eng. **60**, 182–196 (2014)
2. Ramos, M.A., Droguett, E.L., Mosleh, A., das Chagas Moura, M., Martins, M.R.: Revisiting past refinery accidents from a human reliability analysis perspective: the BP Texas City and the Chevron Richmond accidents. Can. J. Chem. Eng. **95**, 2293–2305 (2017)

---

[1] https://www.youtube.com/watch?v=-w1_LDqRJfk. https://www.youtube.com/watch?v=UDe lE65qZzs.

[2] https://www.youtube.com/watch?v=9URzc8RUnyo.

3. Bengel, M., Pfeiffer, K., Graf, B., Bubeck, A., Verl, A.: Mobile robots for offshore inspection and manipulation. In: IEEE/RSJ International Conference on Intelligent Robots and Systems (2009)

4. Soldan, S., Bonow, G., Kroll, A.: RoboGasInspector - a mobile robotic system for remote leak sensing and localization in large industrial environments: overview and first results. IFAC Proc. Vol. **45**(8), 33–38 (2012)

5. Maurtua, I., et al.: MAINBOT – mobile robots for inspection and maintenance in extensive industrial plants. Energy Proc. **49**, 1810–1819 (2014)

6. Van den Bos, B., et al.: Robotic inspection solutions for petrochemical pressure vessels, developed and tested in the PETROBOT project. In: World Conference on Non-Destructive Testing (2016)

7. ARGOS Robotics Competition Website. https://www.total.com/dossiers/argos-challenge-bui lding-tomorrows-oil-and-gas-robot. Accessed 01 May 2021

8. Zhang, H., Su, B., Meng, H.: Development and implementation of a robotic inspection system for power substations. Ind. Robot. **44**(3), 333–342 (2017)

9. Shaukat, A., Gao, Y., Kuo, J.A., Bowen, B.A., Mort, P.E.: Visual classification of waste material for nuclear decommissioning. Robot. Auton. Syst. **75**, 365–378 (2016)

10. Redmon, J., Farhadi, A.: YOLOv3: an incremental improvement. arXiv (2018)

11. Redmon, J.: Darknet: open source neural networks in C. http://pjreddie.com/darknet/. Accessed 01 May 2021

12. Wang, C.-Y., Liao, H.-Y.M., Yeh, I.-H., Wu, Y.-H., Chen, P.-Y., Hsieh, J.-W.: CSPNet: a new backbone that can enhance learning capability of CNN. arXiv (2019)

13. Everingham, M., Van Gool, L., Williams, C.K.I., Winn, J., Zisserman, A.: The PASCAL visual object classes (VOC) challenge. Int. J. Comput. Vis. **88**, 303–338 (2010)

Inference of Mechanical Properties of Dynamic Objects Through Active Perception

Nikolaus Wagner[⊠][iD] and Grzegorz Cielniak[iD]

University of Lincoln, Brayford Pool, Lincoln LN6 7TS, UK
{nwagner,gcielniak}@lincoln.ac.uk

Abstract. Current robotic systems often lack a deeper understanding of their surroundings, even if they are equipped with visual sensors like RGB-D cameras. Knowledge of the mechanical properties of the objects in their immediate surroundings, however, could bring huge benefits to applications such as path planning, obstacle avoidance & removal or estimating object compliance.

In this paper, we present a novel approach to inferring mechanical properties of dynamic objects with the help of active perception and frequency analysis of objects' stimulus responses. We perform FFT on a buffer of image flow maps to identify the spectral signature of objects and from that their eigenfrequency. Combining this with 3D depth information allows us to infer an object's mass without having to weigh it.

We perform experiments on a demonstrator with variable mass and stiffness to test our approach and provide an analysis on the influence of individual properties on the result. By simply applying a controlled amount of force to a system, we were able to infer mechanical properties of systems with an eigenfrequency of around 4.5 Hz in about 2 s. This lab-based feasibility study opens new exciting robotic applications targeting realistic, non-rigid objects such as plants, crops or fabric.

Keywords: Active perception · Image flow · Frequency analysis

1 Introduction

When exploring unknown scenes, current state-of-the-art (SOTA) robots typically use RGB & depth (RGB-D) or RGB-only cameras to record, analyse and possibly reconstruct a model of their surroundings. This, however, provides only shape and geometry information but no internal mechanical properties. Human explorers on the other hand would either rely on previous experience or when encountering unknown objects would interact with them, observe the reactions haptically and visually and infer mechanical properties of objects therefrom.

This way of interactively exploring scenes is commonly referred to as "active perception". While it offers a lot of benefits for scene understanding, it also poses many, potentially yet unsolved, challenges, which is why most robots currently do

© Springer Nature Switzerland AG 2021
C. Fox et al. (Eds.): TAROS 2021, LNAI 13054, pp. 430–439, 2021.
https://doi.org/10.1007/978-3-030-89177-0_45

not employ it. However, like humans, robots benefit from a deeper understanding of mechanical properties of objects. This knowledge can be incorporated when performing path planning, when interacting with soft materials such as cloth or flexible objects like plants, or generally in order to understand the compliance of nearby objects. In industrial settings, a lot of time and money could be saved by being able to infer the mass of fruits and crops or the stiffness of sheet materials without having to conventionally measure any of those properties.

Active perception has already been a prominent area of research in the past, however contributions are typically very application specific [1,10]. In this paper we present an easy and widely applicable way to infer mechanical properties of objects with help of an RGB-D camera through simple, direct interaction like controlled pushing. The contributions we present include:

- a novel vision-based approach for inferring mechanical properties of dynamic objects through direct interaction;
- an algorithm for 3D-vision-based motion segmentation;
- a feasibility study based on an adjustable spring-mass demonstrator which confirms the applicability of our approach in real world scenarios.

2   Previous Work

Prior to the ascent of machine learning algorithms, active perception was being investigated to improve object detection and recognition results [10], but interest in it faded again once neural networks significantly improved performance in these areas. The approach was also studied in relation to the reconstruction of 3D models [1], but in recent years mostly pure learning-based algorithms have dominated this area of interest as well. Nevertheless, as highlighted by recent advancements in object throwing robots [14], the combination of analytical and learning-based approaches, as in learning to estimate a "delta" correcting systematic errors, similar to residual networks [7], can bring significant improvements. A machine vision solution with the capabilities to not only control perception but also action could similarly learn to remove systematic errors.

As highlighted more recently, advances in object detection, object recognition and 3D-reconstruction depend on the capabilities of the robot to control its perception. Bajcsy et al. state that "an agent is an active perceiver if it knows why it wishes to sense, and then chooses what to perceive, and determines how, when and where to achieve that perception" [2]. This implies a situational awareness as well as physical capabilities of interacting with the scene. In the past, this has typically been achieved by changing the viewpoint and actively adjusting the pose of the camera. Novel approaches rather aim for interaction with objects themselves through pushing, for example [12]. Similarly, our algorithm entails applying a controlled amount of force to an object and observing the reaction.

In robotic applications active perception is enabled by kinematic elements of the robot interacting with objects of interest and monitoring the reactions with the vision system. Mavrakis et al. [12] explore this by inferring mechanical properties from pushing objects on a flat surface, however they rely on surface friction for their calculations, restricting applicability of their approach.

Nevertheless, using those properties a novel representation of the world can be created using a voxel map similar to the one presented by Macenski et al. [11]. This representation may contain long- as well as short-term dynamic and material specific properties like eigenfrequency [3], maximum displacement under a certain stimulus or the degree of damping present for movable objects. From this, secondary properties can be obtained, like overall compliance of objects in the scene, which is highly beneficial for trajectory planning and scene understanding.

All this could be used to improve path-planning by aiming for obstacle-separation or -removal instead of -avoidance like in [13]. Furthermore, reconstruction of static parts of a scene with a separate reconstruction of movable objects as in [9] could benefit from this approach as it enables a robot to identify movable objects more easily and thus to remove them from static reconstruction.

Overall, the ideas proposed in this paper open up possibilities to obtain deeper insights into mechanical properties of objects without having to rely on conventional measurement methods.

3   Methods

This section provides an overview of our algorithm and uses images of the demonstrator we created for our experiments. A more detailed setup explanation with images follows in Sect. 4.1.

We aim to use a minimal amount of hardware additional to the typical equipment of a robot for interacting with and monitoring the behaviour of objects. We assume a way to apply a controlled amount of external force, like a robotic manipulator, and an RGB-D camera as a baseline for our system. Using this, we try to infer the eigenfrequency as well as secondary properties of objects, such as mass or stiffness, by exciting them and monitoring their frequency response.

Basic workflow of our algorithm, illustrated in Fig. 1, starts with excitation of the oscillating object of interest using a controlled amount of force. We record the reaction with an RGB-D camera and calculate image flow for every new image, storing results in a buffer. Once full, we perform pixelwise fast Fourier transform (FFT) on the buffer and extract the dominant frequency for each pixel. Finally, we cluster pixels by similarity in frequency response to achieve segmentation. A detailed explanation of the individual steps is provided hereinafter.

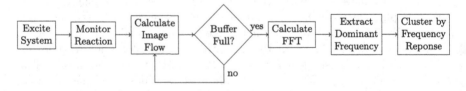

Fig. 1. Flowchart illustrating the basic workflow of our algorithm.

3.1 Eigenfrequency

The eigenfrequency ω is the frequency at which an excited system capable of oscillation moves around its idle point if no external forces are acting upon it. For a simple, undamped spring-mass model the eigenfrequency ω is given as

$$\omega = \sqrt{\frac{k}{m}}, \tag{1}$$

where k represents the spring constant of the system and m its mass.

If the system is excited by an external force F, we can monitor the maximum displacement x from the system's idle position to deduce the spring constant according to Hooke's law given in Eq. 2.

$$k = \frac{F}{x} \tag{2}$$

We assume a known force of excitation F, since we typically control the robot exciting the system. Using the RGB-D camera we track objects of interest and determine the maximum deflection x. These two parameters allow us to calculate a system's spring constant k. By furthermore monitoring the system's frequency response we obtain its eigenfrequency ω as described in more detail hereinafter. Knowing ω and k allows us to infer the mass of objects of interest.

3.2 Image Flow

In order to monitor the system's frequency response after excitation, we calculate the image flow for each new image obtained by the camera relative to the last one, using the Farnebäck optical flow method [5]. This method uses polynomial expansion to estimate the motion of objects between two subsequent images, providing an estimate for motion direction as well as magnitude of interest points in the images. An image illustrating this concept, depicting the magnitude of image flow at each individual pixel as a gray scale value, is given in Fig. 2b.

Subsequently, we store each new image flow map in a circular buffer of a predefined size N. Once that buffer is full, we extract $w \cdot h$, i. e. the dimensions of the input images, vectors of length N from the buffer, thus one vector containing change in magnitude of image flow over time for each pixel location. We use these vectors for inferring dynamic properties of objects, as explained in Sect. 3.3.

3.3 Inferring Dynamic Properties of Objects

By exciting an oscillator system such as described in Sect. 3.1 using a known force, we cause the mass to oscillate at the system's eigenfrequency, allowing us to monitor the process with an RGB-D camera. We use the methods described in Sect. 3.2 to obtain $w \cdot h$ vectors of length N containing the variation in image flow magnitude over time. Next, we perform FFT using FFTW3 [6] on each of these vectors to obtain the spectral signature for each pixel location. We disregard the

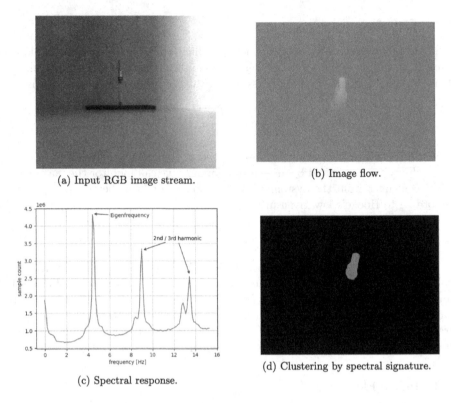

(a) Input RGB image stream.

(b) Image flow.

(c) Spectral response.

(d) Clustering by spectral signature.

Fig. 2. Process flow of our algorithm to cluster objects by their spectral response. We use a stream of RGB images (a), calculate the image flow for each new image relative to the previous one (b), store the image flow maps in a buffer and perform pixelwise FFT on it. We then analyse the spectral response for each pixel (c) and cluster pixels by similarity in their spectral signature (d).

phase information obtained from FFT since it is insignificant to our analysis. The resulting vectors containing the signatures thus have the length $\frac{N}{2} - 1$ with the buffer size N as before. By multiplying the indices of the vector with $\frac{FPS}{N}$, wherein the numerator is the frames per second (FPS) of the RGB camera, we receive the frequency in $\frac{1}{s}$, with the value at a certain index corresponding to the number of samples matching each specific frequency. By summing up the individual spectral signatures we receive the spectral signature for the entire image. This could look like the example provided in Fig. 2c.

In this image we see three peaks with the highest peak at roughly 4.5 Hz being the eigenfrequency of the monitored system and two subsequent peaks 9 Hz and 13.5 Hz, being the 2nd and 3rd harmonic. By extracting the index of maximum value present in the result of the sum of FFTs, we obtain the eigenfrequency at 4.5 Hz by calculating it from the index as described above. The presence of the harmonics as additional peaks can have various reasons, one of them being the non-linearity of the spring-mass-system [4], but deeper investigation is required.

Using the buffer once more, we can extract the maximum value of image flow V_{max} at the center of each cluster. Interpreting this value as object speed allows us to calculate an estimate of the maximum object displacement x_{max}:

$$x_{max} \approx \frac{V_{max}}{4 \cdot \hat{\omega}} \qquad (3)$$

In this equation, we use $\hat{\omega}$ for the previously calculated value of the eigenfrequency, furthermore we divide by 4 since maximum deflection happens at a quarter of one full oscillation. This approach, chosen for its simplicity, yields only an estimation, e.g. because only the 2D components of movement parallel to the image plane are used.

Knowing the excitation force F and having obtained the maximum displacement x_{max} as well as the eigenfrequency ω, we deduce the spring constant k of the oscillator system as per Eq. 2 and from this the mass m using Eq. 1. This allows us to deduce the mass of objects without actually weighing them.

We can then furthermore use the vectors containing the results of the FFT for each individual pixel to extract the maximum frequency present for each pixel and segment the image by frequency values thus obtained. An example of a segmentation map showing the clusters obtained for a video of our demonstrator, using only pixels with the single dominant (eigen-)frequency, is given in Fig. 2d.

4   Results and Analysis

In this section, we describe and evaluate the experiments performed, as well as the results obtained and the influence of system parameters on the outcome.

4.1   Experiment Scenario

We evaluate our approach and the system parameters on a demonstrator consisting of an exchangeable spring and a variable mass (see Fig. 3).

4.2   Mass Estimation

We experiment with a varying amount of weights and springs, comparing the measured eigenfrequency with the mass of the oscillator. Using these parameters to calculate a value for the spring constant $k = \omega^2 \cdot m$ according to Eq. 1 and comparing them allows us to conclude how well our estimation of the eigenfrequency actually performed. This is inverse to the intended mode of use in practice, but it allows us to evaluate performance in a lab setting. We use a buffer size N of 256, requiring about 8 s of measurement at 30 FPS and excite the system manually. Since we know the weights of the system a priori, knowledge of excitation force is not necessary in this case. The results are shown in Table 1.

We can see the calculated value of the spring constant has a maximum deviation from the mean of about $\pm 12\%$ and $\pm 15\%$ respectively. We can therefore assume the estimation of the eigenfrequency worked reasonably well, given that

Fig. 3. Demonstrator consisting of a 3D-printed frame, an exchangeable steel spring and a variable amount of hex nuts for varying the mass.

Table 1. Eigenfrequencies obtained for varying masses and springs using the demonstrator from Fig. 3.

Spring #	Mass m [g]	Eigenfrequency ω [Hz]	Spring constant k [N/m]	Mean k [N/m]	Deviation from mean k [%]
1	2.12	4.5	0.043	0.041	4.9
	3.13	3.8	0.045		9.8
	4.04	3.0	0.036		12.2
2	2.12	10.0	0.212	0.189	12.2
	3.13	7.9	0.195		3.2
	4.04	6.3	0.160		15.3

it is a very rudimentary setup with many possible error sources. Furthermore, an error of 15% in the calculated spring constant corresponds to an error of only $\sqrt{15\%}$, i. e. roughly 3.9%, in the deduced eigenfrequency, since $\omega = \sqrt{\frac{k}{m}}$.

4.3   Parameter Analysis

The default buffer size used in our experiments was chosen as $N = 256$, which limits the applicability of our approach since at a frame rate of 30 FPS, as provided by many industrial cameras, we would need to record roughly 8.5 s long samples to perform a single analysis. We therefore explore the influence a varying buffer size has on the quality of the results. This is illustrated in Fig. 4.

We can see the quality of the results directly correlates with buffer size, i. e. smaller buffer size leads to poorer results. For the sample we investigated with an eigenfrequency of about 4.5 Hz a minimum of 64 samples is necessary to achieve usable results. However, a lower buffer size also leads to a larger granularity of the frequency results causing more inaccurate results as well. This, as well as the largest and smallest frequency of interest, needs to be taken into consideration when choosing a buffer size. Furthermore, as mentioned above, a larger buffer

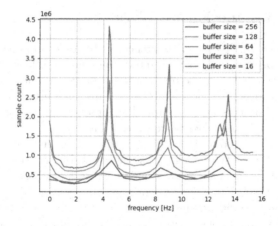

Fig. 4. Influence of the buffer size on the results of the FFT.

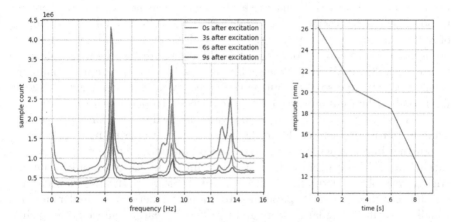

Fig. 5. Spectral signature and maximum amplitude of oscillation in relation to the time passed since initial excitation of the system.

size corresponds to a longer period of recording necessary for each sample. This means that, at a frame rate of 30 FPS and assuming the smallest buffer size $N = 64$, the time required to collect sufficient data for a single analysis is still roughly 2 s.

Next, we analyse the change in spectral signature during a period of ringdown after initial excitation. We collect samples for 3 s, 6 s and 9 s after excitation and compare the results to samples collected directly after excitation. This is shown in Fig. 5.

We can see a correlation between the absolute height of the peaks and time passed since excitation, i. e. the maximum amplitude of oscillation which decreases over time. However, further research is needed to establish the exact relationship between amplitude and results of the FFT.

5   Conclusions and Future Work

As we have shown in this paper, inference of dynamic properties from active perception and spectral analysis is an interesting and feasible approach, offering many benefits like allowing us to obtain the weight of an object without having to weigh it. We can obtain the spectral signature of objects, cluster images by eigenfrequency of objects and monitor the ring-down of an oscillator system. Nevertheless, many improvements are conceivable.

Using only RGB-based optical flow algorithms, an issue is shadows of objects being clustered in the same category as the actual object, since they move at the same frequency. This can be overcome by using depth based 3D optical flow as described in [8] and [15]. Furthermore, we have presented the spectral signature containing the eigenfrequency as well as the 2nd and 3rd harmonic in Fig. 2c, however we only consider the eigenfrequency itself for clustering, sometimes leading to poorer results since a lot of valid pixels are filtered out. By incorporating pixels with harmonics as dominant frequency, which are likely due to non-linearities present in the system, we could account for the 2D-mapping of a 3D-oscillator system. Currently, we consider only 2D-oscillator systems, so our approach could fail for objects not oscillating parallel to the image plane. In future work, 3D-oscillations should also be considered, for example by mapping them to a 2D-plane so they can be estimated by a 2D-system. An additional limitation is the minimum recording time needed to perform a single analysis which is limited by buffer size and frame rate provided by the camera. A possible solution to this problem could be the use of a camera offering more FPS.

Further improvements to the system could include a different mode of excitation, e.g. by exciting objects with a stream of air to avoid direct contact. An analysis of the damping coefficient, deductible from the ring-down analyses shown in Fig. 5, can be performed to obtain further system understanding. Finally, creating a similarity score and transferring learned information to similar objects in the scene would allow for obtaining the properties of many objects by interacting with only one. This could subsequently be used to create a full 3D-compliance map of the scene incorporating all dynamic properties obtained.

Concluding, we have demonstrated in this paper the feasibility of using active perception to infer mechanical properties of dynamic objects. This requires minimal contact with the object and yields promising initial results. We have shown the possibility of inferring eigenfrequency, spring constant and mass of a system using nothing but a known force for excitation of the system and an RGB-D camera. Using these parameters, we were able to segment image pixels by similar mechanic properties. Many approaches for future work have been suggested, and there is large potential for further developments in this area.

References

1. Aleotti, J., Lodi Rizzini, D., Caselli, S.: Perception and grasping of object parts from active robot exploration. J. Intell. Robot. Syst. **76**, 401–425 (2014). https://doi.org/10.1007/s10846-014-0045-6

2. Bajcsy, R., Aloimonos, Y., Tsotsos, J.K.: Revisiting active perception. Auton. Robot. **42**(2), 177–196 (2017). https://doi.org/10.1007/s10514-017-9615-3
3. Chen, J.G., Wadhwa, N., Cha, Y.J., Durand, F., Freeman, W.T., Buyukozturk, O.: Modal identification of simple structures with high-speed video using motion magnification. J. Sound Vibr. **345**, 58–71 (2015). https://doi.org/10.1016/j.jsv.2015.01.024. https://www.sciencedirect.com/science/article/pii/S0022460X1500070X
4. Chillara, V.K., Lissenden, C.: Towards a micro-mechanics based understanding of ultrasonic higher harmonic generation. In: Proceedings of SPIE - The International Society for Optical Engineering, vol. 9438, March 2015. https://doi.org/10.1117/12.2179894
5. Farnebäck, G.: Two-frame motion estimation based on polynomial expansion. In: Bigun, J., Gustavsson, T. (eds.) SCIA 2003. LNCS, vol. 2749, pp. 363–370. Springer, Heidelberg (2003). https://doi.org/10.1007/3-540-45103-X_50
6. Frigo, M., Johnson, S.: The design and implementation of FFTW3. Proc. IEEE **93**(2), 216–231 (2005). https://doi.org/10.1109/JPROC.2004.840301
7. He, K., Zhang, X., Ren, S., Sun, J.: Deep residual learning for image recognition (2015)
8. Hornáček, M., Fitzgibbon, A., Rother, C.: SphereFlow: 6 DoF scene flow from RGB-D pairs. In: 2014 IEEE Conference on Computer Vision and Pattern Recognition, pp. 3526–3533 (2014). https://doi.org/10.1109/CVPR.2014.451
9. Jiang, C., Paudel, D., Fougerolle, Y., Fofi, D., Demonceaux, C.: Static-map and dynamic object reconstruction in outdoor scenes using 3-D motion segmentation. IEEE Robot. Autom. Lett. **1**, 1 (2016). https://doi.org/10.1109/LRA.2016.2517207
10. Le, Q.V., Saxena, A., Ng, A.Y.: Active perception: interactive manipulation for improving object detection (2010)
11. Macenski, S., Tsai, D., Feinberg, M.: Spatio-temporal voxel layer: a view on robot perception for the dynamic world. Int. J. Adv. Robot. Syst. **17**, 172988142091053 (2020). https://doi.org/10.1177/1729881420910530
12. Mavrakis, N., Ghalamzan E., A.M., Stolkin, R.: Estimating an object's inertial parameters by robotic pushing: a data-driven approach. In: 2020 IEEE/RSJ International Conference on Intelligent Robots and Systems (IROS), pp. 9537–9544 (2020). https://doi.org/10.1109/IROS45743.2020.9341112
13. Xiong, Y., Ge, Y., From, P.J.: Push and drag: an active obstacle separation method for fruit harvesting robots (2020)
14. Zeng, A., Song, S., Lee, J., Rodriguez, A., Funkhouser, T.: TossingBot: learning to throw arbitrary objects with residual physics (2020)
15. Zhang, T., Zhang, H., Li, Y., Nakamura, Y., Zhang, L.: FlowFusion: dynamic dense RGB-D slam based on optical flow (2020)

Author Index

Printed in the United States
by Baker & Taylor Publisher Services

Printed in the United States
by Baker & Taylor Publisher Services